THE CRISIS OF
THE TWELFTH CENTURY

❋ ❋ ❋

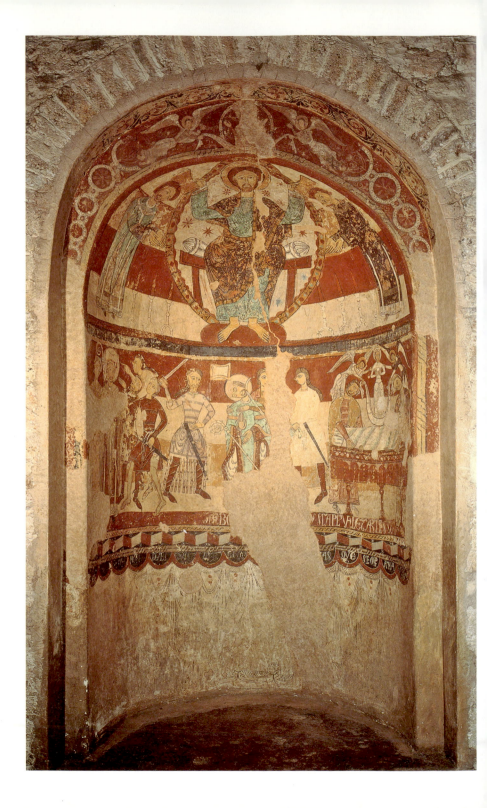

THE CRISIS OF
THE TWELFTH CENTURY

❈ ❈ ❈

Power, Lordship, and the Origins
of European Government

Thomas N. Bisson

PRINCETON UNIVERSITY PRESS · PRINCETON AND OXFORD

Copyright © 2009 by Princeton University Press

Published by Princeton University Press, 41 William Street, Princeton, New Jersey 08540

In the United Kingdom: Princeton University Press, 3 Market Place, Woodstock, Oxfordshire OX20 1SY

Library of Congress Cataloging-in-Publication Data

Bisson, Thomas N.

The crisis of the twelfth century : power, lordship, and the origins of European government / Thomas N. Bisson.

p. cm.

Includes bibliographical references and index.

ISBN 978-0-691-13708-7 (cloth : alk. paper)   1. Europe—Politics and government— 476–1492.   2. Power (Social sciences)   I. Title.

D201.8.B57 2009

940.1'8—dc22   2008007535

British Library Cataloging-in-Publication Data is available

This book has been composed in Bembo Typeface

Printed on acid-free paper. ∞

press.princeton.edu

Printed in the United States of America

3   5   7   9   10   8   6   4   2

Frontispiece: Martyrdom of Thomas Becket (29 December 1170, canonized 1173), fresco painting of the later twelfth century in the apse of Santa Maria of Terrassa. Above, Christ with Becket's advocates; below, the detention, the murder, and the ascent of the saint's soul to heaven. (Museu de Terrassa, Conjunt monumental de les Esglésies de Sant Pere de Terrassa, reproduced by permission.)

To the students and teachers in Historical Studies B-17
my colleagues all
and
in memory of Carroll

· P R E F A C E ·

THE TITLE of this book will appear to many to contain a flagrant contradiction. A' crisis 'in the twelfth century!' Is not this great epoch, with its flowerings and fulfillments in so many domains of human endeavour, with its Renaissance of learning and faith, a time of maturation and progress? Was this not very specially so of government? If in the famous book I have presumed to echo, Charles Homer Haskins chose not to insist on government as such, he nonetheless showed throughout how revivals of letters, law, and history were bound up with institutional and political progress, of which his earlier work on Normandy afforded a classic demonstration.[1] Subsequent historians were even more insistent on government among the associated revivals of the twelfth century. Heinrich Mitteis thought of the 'feudal state' as a progressive structure. R. W. Southern wrote of 'the emergence of stable political institutions and the elaboration of a new system of law.' Joseph. R. Strayer spoke of 'political revival' and, in an essay of elegant economy, of a process of 'state-building' in the high Middle Ages. Even one so insistent on a sociology of lordship as Karl Bosl could refer to a 'personal state.'[2]

It is not necessary to reject these hardy views, which figured in works of abiding value, to notice their limitations. They rested on

---

[1] C. H. Haskins, *The renaissance of the twelfth century* (Cambridge, M., 1928); *Norman institutions* (Cambridge, M., 1918).

[2] Heinrich Mitteis, *Der Staat des hohen Mittelalters. Grundlinien einer vergleichenden Verfassungsgeschichte des Lehnszeitalters*, 9th ed. (Weimar 1974 [1940]); R. W. Southern, *The making of the Middle Ages* (London 1953) 88; J. R. Strayer, *On the medieval origins of the modern state* (Princeton 1970); Karl Bosl, 'Die alte deutsche Freiheit. Geschichtliche Grundlagen des modernen deutschen Staates,' and other essays, in *Frühformen der Gesellschaft im mittelalterlichen Europa. Ausgewählte Beiträge zu einer Strukturanalyse der mittelalterlichen Welt* (Munich 1964).

evolutionary and teleological conceptions of institutional history that made it difficult to see what happened in the twelfth century in terms other than our own. Historians spoke of 'government' in Norman England without qualification and continue to do so; they were impatient with the evidence of resistance to authority to the point of overlooking some deeply symptomatic events; and they clung assuredly to political formulations of historical process even as their students (and mine) deserted us for social and cultural history. Perhaps it was not surprising that proponents of new histories neglected government. They were reacting against the preoccupations with elites, a disabling disregard for women, and sometimes against institutions identified with establishments. But views so influenced are partial in their own ways, and it is curious to realize how long it has taken for methods devised to bring past societies and cultures to life to be applied to the historical study of power.

The author of this book was among the reluctant. Working on consultation and fiscal administration, I was repeatedly brought to reflect that, whatever the broadly conceptual limitations of traditional institutional history, its practitioners often persuaded me better than the 'new historians.' They wrote better (I thought), or at least more cogently. They seemed to draw strength from knowing something of what is undoubtedly universal in political nature; not content to mine one or another special seam, they were familiar with medieval records in their generality. Above all, they had the advantage of working on what most interested medieval people themselves, as it most interests most people: namely, power. It came to seem worth asking how people experienced and exercised power in those generations when, as Southern and Strayer well showed, something collectively new and potentially transforming had its origins. And when the question was put in this way, the twelfth century appeared to me in a new light: as a time of strain and crisis.

This book is an attempt to reconsider an old subject in this light. What I found in the sources was not the 'feudalism' of my teachers: was not so much what power looked like as what it felt

like in an age of castles. What turned up, moreover, neither felt
nor looked like government. When simply defined as the exercise
of power for social purpose, government became the (wobbly) end
of a story that, in the twelfth century, begins and persists with the
powers and liabilities of lordship; with violence, suffering, and aspirations to nobility only belatedly overtaken by routines of justice, administration, and political persuasion. What I have written
is not a systematic treatise, still less a textbook, but an essay on the
history of human power during the long century when medieval
lordship—the domination of people by one or a few, in extremely
variable forms—came to maturity. In the nature of my conception, the book may also be read as a reflection on the social and
cultural origins of European government.[3] While open in this
facet to the objection that attaches to all studies of origins, this
work aims at a fresh understanding of the very concept of origina-
tion, holding to a descriptive mode of historical analysis as close to
contemporary usage and as free of tendency, of anachronistic assumptions, as I can make it. Its argument is exemplified widely yet
far from exhaustively. The societies that succeeded to Charlemagne's west-Frankish dominions lie at its center, with León-
Castile, England, Lombardy, Bavaria, Saxony, and Poland on its
wings; but even for these lands the story of principalities and lordships is told selectively and, undoubtedly, impressionistically.
Should it seem to some readers that Catalonia has a bigger place
than it warrants, I can only plead that I have felt obliged to question that appearance. On several points exemplified in later chapters, that society is virtually a unique witness in this European
history. It must further be admitted that the sources are by nature
such as to respond less conclusively to some of my queries than to
those of constitutionalist historians. The late Timothy Reuter saw
this clearly in his critique of my article on 'the "feudal revolution"' (*Past & Present* no. 155, 1997), calling for a better chronology
and geography of exploitative lordship and violence that it is one

---

[3] The concepts of lordship and government are further introduced in chapter I.

purpose of this book to provide. All I can hope is that my better-supported conclusions will lend plausibility to the more speculative ones, which might then be tested in further research.

The gist of this book was first offered as a course in Harvard's Core Curriculum in 1988. I am grateful to the students in that course and in its successors of 1990, 1993, 2001, and 2003 and to the Teaching Fellows, not only for their patience with a professor who seemed at times to share their bewilderment, but also for their sympathetic engagement with my new model of an old subject and for their helpful criticism. It is no mere whimsy that I think of them all as colleagues. Some of the material in chapter II was first published in *Past & Present* in 1994 (no. 142) and in *Speculum* (1996); it is here reworked in response to debate that ensued in the former journal in 1996 and 1997 (nos. 152, 155). I wish further to record my obligation to other scholars bringing new questions to the records of medieval power: to Philippe Buc and Geoffrey Koziol working on ideas and ritual; to Amy Remensnyder for helping me to understand twelfth-century ideology; to Stephen D. White for his severe yet helpful critique of my treatment of violence; and to several others working on nobility, law, justice, property, and vengeance: Dominique Barthélemy, Paul Hyams, Chris Wickham, and the late Patrick Wormald. If I have not much insisted on theoretical approaches and contexts, other than my imagined yet by no means untutored sociology of lordship, it is from no lack of appreciation for new ways of making sense of our sources. Nor have I intended to substitute 'crisis' for 'Renaissance': the twelfth century, with its luxuriant legacy of records and artifacts, is far too vast to be comprehended in a single perspective, as has been well shown by Giles Constable.[4]

I owe warm thanks to the Andrew W. Mellon and Rockefeller Foundations. A residency in the (Rockefeller) Study Center at Bellagio (Italy) enabled me to resume writing in a time of personal difficulty; and the final stages of research and writing were supported by a Mellon Emeritus Faculty Fellowship. I wish also to

[4] *The reformation of the twelfth century* (Cambridge 1996).

thank the Dean and Students of Christ Church, Oxford, where I worked on chapter V as Fowler Hamilton Research Fellow during Hilary and Trinity Terms 2004. Many other foundations, institutes, and the departments of history at Berkeley and Harvard (as acknowledged in previous publications) together with friends and colleagues have helped me in studies begun half a century ago.

Professor Wickham gave me the benefit of a searching critical reading. He above all, yet like the others, bears no responsibility for my failings. Michael and Magda McCormick have outdone themselves in supportive friendship and collegiality. Three persons dear to me died in 2005. Pierre Bonnassie, a humane teacher as well as a scholar of power and vision, was an inspiration. Professor Sir Rees Davies read and commented on a draft-prospectus of this book during his final illness. And my wife of forty-three years, Margaretta Carroll Webb Bisson, urged me at the end to finish what she had so patiently encouraged. Without her this work could not have been started, let alone finished. Our daughters and their husbands have valiantly borne with me in our bereavement; my loved ones, yet they too my nurturing colleagues. They have my deepest thanks.

T.N.B.

·CONTENTS·

·ILLUSTRATIONS·

Frontispiece

Martyrdom of Thomas Becket. Fresco in Santa Maria of Terrassa, late twelfth century.

Plates

between pages 288 and 289

Illustration

Maps

·USAGE AND CONVENTIONS·

THIS BOOK is documented as compactly as possible. Full citations are found only in the Bibliography or Abbreviations, not in both. First citations in footnotes are full enough to inform, subsequent ones abbreviated, and many works are cited only as abbreviated. Books and chapters in medieval texts are cited (as on p. 26 note 10): iii.24, vii.50, with page references (if any) in parentheses: e.g., iii.24 (128). Volume numbers are in small capitals, often followed by a comma and Arabic numerals for pages. The abbreviation p. (or pp.) is avoided, figuring, as a rule, only for cross-references within this book, or where required for clarity.

In a book dealing with many lands, no attempt has been made to standardize nomenclature. Proper names and toponyms are anglicised in accordance with familiar (Anglo-American) usage: Gregory, Henry, Philip (–Augustus), Peter (the Venerable); Castile; but also figure in Polish or Castilian or Catalan or Italian, as is conventional, or in other modern forms: Kazimierz, Alfonso, Alfons, Pietro; León. Lesser personages seem (to me) more comfortably clad in modern vernacular forms: Arnau, Geoffroi; while others require no dressing at all: Berno, Guibert; a very few are left embalmed in Latin. 'Peace' and 'truce' are capitalized, or not, depending on contexts. Pedigrees are not provided, for they would vastly add to length, but regnal years for major figures appear in the index, and often in the text.

·ABBREVIATIONS·

AC   Arxiu Capitular

ACF   *Actes des comtes de Flandre, 1071–1128*, ed. Fernand Vercauteren. Commission royale d'Histoire (Brussels 1938)

ACP   *Recueil des actes des comtes de Provence appartenant à la maison de Barcelone. Alphonse II et Raimond Bérenger V (1196–1245)*, ed. Fernand Benoît, 2 vols. Collection de Textes pour servir à l'Histoire de Provence . . . (Monaco 1925)

AD   Archives départementales

AHDE   *Anuario de Historia del Derecho español*

AHN   Archivo historico nacional (Madrid)

AHR   *American Historical Review*

AN   Archives nationales (Paris)

Annales: E.S.C   *Annales: Economies-sociétés-civilisations*

ASC   [Anglo-Saxon chronicle] *Two of the Saxon chronicles parallel, with supplementary extracts from the others*, ed. John Earle, rev. ed. Charles Plummer, 2 vols. (Oxford 1892–99). See also *Peterborough chronicle* (Bibliography)

'Barnwell annals'   London, College of Arms, MS Arundel 10. Cited by folio and by derivative printed text in *Mem.*, an abbreviation listed below

BEC   *Bibliothèque de l'Ecole des Chartes*

BEFAR   Bibliothèque de l'Ecole française [des Ecoles françaises] d'Athènes et de Rome

BEHE   Bibliothèque de l'Ecole des Hautes Etudes

BL   British Library (London)

BnF   Bibliothèque nationale de France (Paris)

BRABLB   *Boletín de la Real Academia de Buenas Letras de Barcelona*

BRAH   *Boletín de la Real Academia de Historia*

Briefe   See *MGH*

BrPD   *Die Briefe des Petrus Damiani*, ed. Kurt Reindel, 4 vols. *MGH, Briefe* 4 (Munich 1983–93)

CAP   *Constitutiones et acta publica* . . . See *MGH*

CAS   First (primera) chronicle in 'Las crónicas anónimas de Sahagún,' ed. Julio Puyol (y Alonso) *BRAH* LXXVI (1920) 7–26,
111–22, 242–57, 339–56, 395–419, 512–19; LXXVII (1921) 51–59,
151–61. Parenthetical citations are to *Crónicas anónimas de Sahagún*, ed. Antonio Ubieto Arteta. TM 75 (Zaragoza 1987)

CC   Thomas N. Bisson, *Conservation of coinage: monetary exploitation
and its restraint in France, Catalonia, and Aragon (c. A.D. 1000–c.
1225)* (Oxford 1979)

CCCM   *Corpus Christianorum: continuatio mediaevalis*

CCr   *Le carte cremonesi dei secoli VIII–XII: documenti dei fondi cremonesi*,
ed. Ettore Falcøni, 4 vols. Ministero per i Beni Culturali i
Ambientali. Biblioteca Statale di Cremona. Fonti e Sussedi 1
(Cremona 1979)

CDF1   *Colección diplomática de Fernando I (1037–1065)*, ed. Pilar Blanco
Lozano (León 1987)

CDHF   Chartes et Diplômes relatifs à l'Histoire de France publiés par
les soins de l'Académie des Inscriptions et Belles-Lettres

CDIHF   Collection de Documents inédits sur l'Histoire de France
(Section d'Histoire médiévale et de Philologie)

CDL   *Colección documental del archivo de la catedral de León (775–1854)*,
ed. Emilio Sáez et al., 19 vols. Fuentes y Estudios de
Historia leonesa (León 1987–)

CDLaud   *Codice diplomatico laudense*, ed. Cesare Vignati, 3 vols. Bibliotheca historica italica cura et studio Societatis longobardicae
historiae studiis promovendis 2–4 (Milan 1879–85)

CDPol   *Codice diplomatico polironiano (961–1125)*, ed. Rossella Rinaldi,
Carla Villani, Paolo Golinelli. Il Mondo medievale. Studi di
Storia e Storiografia. Storia di S. Benedetto Polirone. Sezione
medievale (Bologna 1993)

CDS   *Colección diplomática del monasterio de Sahagún (857–1230)*, ed.
Marta de la Fuente, 5 vols. Fuentes y Estudios de Historia leonesa 17, 36–39 (León 1976–99)

CFMA   Les Classiques français du Moyen Age

CHFMA   Les Classiques de l'Histoire de France au Moyen Age

CILAS   Cambridge Iberian and Latin American Studies

CMV   *Cartulaire de Marmoutier pour le Vendômois*, ed. Charles Auguste
de Trémault. Société archéologique du Vendômois (Paris 1893)

CNA — Cartulaire noir de la cathédrale d'Angers, ed. Ch. Urseau. Documents historiques sur l'Anjou 5 (Paris-Angers 1908)

CNRS — Centre national de la Recherche scientifique

COD — Conciliorum oecumenicorum decreta, ed. Joseph Alberigo et al., 3d ed. (Bologna 1973)

CPA — Cartas de población del reino de Aragón de los siglos medievales, ed. María Luisa Ledesma Rubio. Fuentes históricas aragonesas 18 (Zaragoza 1991)

CPC — Cartas de población y franquicia de Cataluña, ed. J. M. Font Rius, 3 vols. in two parts. CSIC (Madrid-Barcelona 1969–83)

CPT — Les constitucions de pau i treva de Catalunya (segles XI–XIII), ed. Gener Gonzalvo i Bou. Textos jurídics Catalans. Lleis i Costums II/3 (Barcelona 1994)

CRAIBL — Comptes-rendus à l'Académie des Inscriptions & Belles-Lettres

C&S — Councils & synods with other documents relating to the English church. I. A.D. 871–1204, 2 parts, ed. Dorothy Whitelock, Martin Brett, C. N. L. Brooke (Oxford 1981)

CSAA — Cartulaire de l'abbaye de Saint-Aubin d'Angers, ed. Bertrand de Broussillon, 3 vols. Documents historiques sur l'Anjou 1–3 (Paris 1896–1903)

CSIC — Consejo superior de Investigaciones científicas (Madrid-Barcelona)

CSMLT — Cambridge Studies in Medieval Life and Thought

CSPCh — Cartulaire de l'abbaye de Saint-Père de Chartres, ed. Benjamin Guérard, 2 vols. CDIHF. Histoire politique. Collection de Cartulaires de France 1–2 (Paris 1840)

CTEEH — Collection de Textes pour servir à l'Etude et à l'Enseignement de l'Histoire

CTV — Cartulaire de l'abbaye cardinale de la Trinité de Vendôme, ed. Ch. Métais, 5 vols. (Paris 1893–1904)

DB — Domesday Book . . . , ed. Abraham Farley, 4 vols. Record Commission (London 1783–1816)

DD — MGH Diplomata
DDH2 — Heinrici II. et Arduini diplomata, ed. Harry Bresslau et al. (Berlin 1900–1903)
DDC2 — Conradi II. diplomata, ed. Harry Bresslau et al. (Berlin 1909)

DDH3   Heinrici III. diplomata, ed. Harry Bresslau, Paul Kehr (Berlin 1926–31)

DDH4   Heinrici IV. diplomata, ed. Dietrich von Gladiss, Alfred Gawlik, 3 parts (Berlin, Weimar, Hanover 1941–78)

DDFr1   Friderici I. diplomata, ed. Heinrich Appelt et al., 5 parts (Hanover 1975–90)

DDCo   Constantiae imperatricis diplomata, ed. Theo Kölzer (Hanover 1990)

DDFr2   Friderici II. diplomata, ed. Walter Koch et al., part 1 (Hanover 2002)

DI   Colección de documentos inéditos del Archivo general de la Corona de Aragón, ed. Próspero de Bofarull y Mascaró et al., 42 vols. (Barcelona 1847–1973)

EFHU   Elenchus fontium historiae urbanae

EHD   English historical documents, ed. David C. Douglas, 12 vols. to date (London 1953–). Vol. 2 is cited in 2d ed., 1981: EHD ii²

EHR   English Historical Review

EPHE   Ecole pratique des Hautes Etudes

ES   Flórez, Henrique et al., España sagrada. Teatro geográfico-histórico de la iglesia de España, 52 vols. (Madrid 1747–1918)

FAC   Fiscal accounts of Catalonia under the early count-kings (1151–1213), ed. Thomas N. Bisson, 2 vols. (Berkeley-London 1984)

FSI   Fonti per la Storia d'Italia pubblicate dell'Istituto storico italiano per il Medio Evo

GcB   Gesta comitum Barcinonensium, ed. Louis Barrau Dihigo, Jaume Massó Torrents. Cròniques Catalanes 2. Institut d'Estudis Catalans (Barcelona 1925; new ed. 2007)

GpP   Gesta principum Polonorum. The deeds of the princes of the Poles, Latin text and tr. Paul W. Knoll, Frank Schaer. Central European Medieval Texts 3 (Budapest 2003)

GrH   Gesta regis Henrici secundi Benedicti abbatis . . . , ed. William Stubbs, 2 vols. RS 49 (London 1867)

GS   Gesta Stephani, ed. and tr. K. R. Potter, with new introduction and notes by R. H. C. Davis. OMT (Oxford 1976 [1955])

GXa   Gallia christiana . . . , 16 vols. (Paris 1715–1865)

HC   Historia Compostellana, ed. Emma Falque Rey. CCCM 70 (Turnhout 1988)

HF   *Recueil des historiens des Gaules et de la France*, ed. Martin Bou-
quet *et al.*, 24 vols. (Paris 1738–1904)

HH   Henry, archdeacon of Huntingdon, *Historia Anglorum*, ed. and
tr. Diana Greenway. OMT (Oxford 1996)

HL   Claude Devic, J.-J. Vaissete, *Histoire générale de Languedoc avec
des notes et les pièces justificatives*, new ed., 16 vols. (Toulouse:
Privat, 1872–1904)

HN   William of Malmesbury, *Historia novella*, ed. Edmund King, tr.
K. R. Potter. OMT (Oxford 1998)

IRHT   Institut de Recherche et d'Histoire des Textes

JL   *Regesta pontificum Romanorum ab condita ecclesia ad annum post
Christum natum MCXCVIII*, ed. Philippus Jaffé, 2d ed.
Guilielmus Wattenbach, S. Loewenfeld, F. Kaltenbrunner,
P. Ewald, 2 vols. (Leipzig 1885–88)

JW   *The chronicle of John of Worcester*, ed. and tr. P. McGurk, 2 vols.
(of 3 projected). OMT (Oxford 1995–98)

LC   *Le Liber censuum de l'église romaine*, ed. Paul Fabre, Louis Duchesne, 3 vols. BEFAR 2d series 6 (Paris 1910 [1889]–1952)

LFM   *Liber feudorum maior. Cartulario real que se conserva en el Archivo de
la Corona de Aragón*, ed. Francisco Miquel Rosell, 2 vols. CSIC
(Barcelona 1945)

Ldl   *MGH* (q.v. below), *Libelli de lite*

LPV   *The letters of Peter the Venerable*, ed. Giles Constable, 2 vols.
Harvard Historical Studies 78 (Cambridge, M., 1967)

LTC   *Layettes du Trésor des Chartes*, ed. Alexandre Teulet *et al.*, 5 vols.
Archives (de l'Empire) nationales, Inventaires et Documents
(Paris 1863–1909)

Mansi   *Sacrorum conciliorum nova et amplissima collectio*, ed. Giovanni
Domenico Mansi, 31 vols. (Florence, Venice 1759–98)

Materials   *Materials for the history of Thomas Becket, archbishop of Canterbury (canonized by Pope Alexander III, A.D. 1173)*, ed. James
Craigie Robertson, 7 vols. RS 67 (London 1875–85)

Mem.   *Memoriale fratris Walteri de Coventria. The historical collections of
Walter of Coventry*, ed. William Stubbs, 2 vols. RS 58 (London
1872–73) II

MFrPN   Thomas N. Bisson, *Medieval France and her Pyrenean neighbours*.
SPICHRPI 70 (London: Hambledon, 1989)

MGH   *Monumenta Germaniae historica*
      Briefe   *Die Briefe der deutschen Kaiserzeit* (1949–)
      CAP   *Constitutiones et acta publica imperatorum et regum* I–II,
             ed. Ludewicus Weiland. Legum Sectio IV (Hanover
             1893–96)
      DD   *Diplomata regum et imperatorum Germaniae* (1879–). See
             DD for editions by reigns.
      LDU   *Laienfürsten- und Dynasten-Urkunden der Kaiserzeit*
             (1941–49–)
      Ldl   *Libelli de lite imperatorum et pontificum saeculis XI. et XII.
             conscripti,* ed. Ernst Dümmler *et al.,* 3 vols. (Hanover
             1891–97)
      SS   *Scriptores* (1826–)
      SSRG   *Scriptores rerum Germanicarum in usum scholarum separa
             tim editi* (1871–)
MIC   Monumenta Iuris Canonici
MSB   *Les miracles de Saint Benoît écrits par Adrevald, Aimoin, André,
      Raoul Tortaire et Hugues de Sainte Marie, moines de Fleury,* ed.
      Eugène de Certain. SHF 96 (Paris 1858)
MV   *Monumenta Vizeliacensia. Textes relatifs à l'histoire de l'abbaye de
      Vézelay,* ed. R. B. C. Huygens. *CCCM* 42 (Turnhout 1976)
NCMH *The new Cambridge medieval history,* ed. Paul Fouracre, David
      Luscombe, Jonathan Riley-Smith *et al.,* 7 vols. (Cambridge
      1995–2006)
NRHDFE   *Nouvelle Revue historique de Droit français et étranger*
OHM   Oxford Historical Monographs
OMT   Oxford Medieval Texts
OV   *The ecclesiastical history [Historia ecclesiastica] of Orderic Vitalis,* ed.
      and tr. Marjorie Chibnall, 6 vols. OMT (Oxford 1968–80)
PBA   *Proceedings of the British Academy*
PIMS Pontifical Institute of Medieval Studies (Toronto)
PL   *Patrologiae cursus completus . . . Series latina,* ed. Jacques-Paul
      Migne, 221 vols. (Paris 1844–64)
P&M   Frederick Pollock and Frederick William Maitland, *The history
      of English law before the time of Edward I,* 2d ed., 2 vols. (Cam-
      bridge 1898 [1895])
PRS   The Pipe Roll Society

PSVV Le pergamene della basilica di S. Vittore di Varese (899–1202), ed. Luisa Zagni. Pergamene milanesi dei secoli XII–XIII, 9 (Milan 1992)

PUE Papsturkunden in England, ed. Walther Holtzmann, 3 vols. Abhandlungen der Gesellschaft der Wissenschaften zu Göttingen. Philologisch-historische Klasse Neue folge 25, Dritte F. 14, 15, 33 (Berlin 1930–31; Göttingen 1952)

PUT-LeM Publications de l'Université de Toulouse–Le Mirail

QEBG Quellen und Erörterungen zur bayerischen Geschichte. Neue Folge

RAH2 Recueil des actes de Henri II roi d'Angleterre et duc de Normandie concernant les provinces françaises et les affaires de France, ed. Léopold Delisle, Elie Berger, 3 vols. CDHF (Paris 1916–27)

RAL6 Recueil des actes de Louis VI roi de France (1108–1137), ed. Jean Dufour, 4 vols. CDHF (Paris 1992–94)

RAPh1 Recueil des actes de Philippe Iᵉʳ, roi de France (1059–1108), ed. Maurice Prou. CDHF (Paris 1908)

RAPh2 Recueil des actes de Philippe Auguste roi de France, ed. H.-Fr. Delaborde, Michel Nortier et al., 6 vols. CDHF (Paris 1916–2005)

R.B. Ramon Berenguer

RBPH Revue belge de Philologie et d'Histoire

RIS Rerum italicarum scriptores ab anno aerae christianae quingentesimo ad millesimum quingentesimum . . . , ed. Ludovicus Antonius Muratorius, 25 vols. (Milan 1723–51)

RIS² New edition of the same (1900–)

RRAN Regesta regum Anglo-normannorum, ed. H. W. C. Davis et al., 4 vols. (Oxford 1913–69)

RS Chronicles and Memorials of Great Britain and Ireland during the Middle Ages ('Rolls Series')

SC Select charters and other illustrations of English constitutional history from the earliest times to the reign of Edward the First, ed. William Stubbs, 9th ed. rev. H. W. C. Davis (Oxford 1913 [1870])

SHF Société de l'Histoire de France

SPICHRPI Studies presented to the International Commission for the History of Representative and Parliamentary Institutions

TM Textos Medievales (Zaragoza)

TrFr   *Die Traditionen des Hochstifts Freising*, ed. Theodor Bitterauf, 2 vols. QEBG 4, 5 (Munich 1905–09)

TRHS   *Transactions of the Royal Historical Society*

TrP   *Die Traditionen des Hochstifts Passau*, ed. Max Heuweiser. QEBG 6 (Munich 1930)

TrSEm *Die Traditionen des Hochstifts Regensburg und des Klosters S. Emmeram*, ed. Josef Widemann. QEBG 8 (Munich 1943)

TrT   *Die Traditionen des Klosters Tegernsee, 1003–1242*, ed. Peter Acht. QEBG 9:1 (Munich 1952)

TSMA   Typologie des Sources du Moyen Age occidental

TV   Thomas N. Bisson, *Tormented voices: power, crisis, and humanity in rural Catalonia, 1140–1200* (Cambridge, M., 1998)

UrkMat *Die Urkunden und Briefe der Markgräfin Mathilde von Tuscien*, ed. Elke Goez, Werner Goez. MGH, LDU 2 (Hanover 1998)

WP   *The* Gesta Guillelmi *of William of Poitiers*, ed. and tr. R. H. C. Davis, Marjorie Chibnall. OMT (Oxford 1998)

ZRG Germ. (Kan., Rom.) Abt.   *Zeitschrift der Savigny-Stiftung für Rechtsgeschichte, germanische (kanonistische, romanistische) Abteilung*

an.   *anno(-is)*, in the year(s)

c. (cc.) *capitulum(-a)*, chapter(s)

ca.   circa

col.   column

d.   *denarii, deniers*, pennies

ed.   edited by, edition

ep(p) *epistola(e)*, letter(s)

et al.   *et alii*, and others

£   *libra(-e), livres*, pounds

l. (ll.) line(s)

MS   manuscript (*manuscrit*)

p.j.   *pièces justificatives*

rev.   revised by

s.   *solidus(-i), sou*(s), shilling(s); *seculo* (in century _)

s. melg. s(hillings) of Melgueil (southern France)

s.v.   *sub verbo*, under the word

t., tt.   *testis(-es)*, witness(es)

tr.   translated by

THE CRISIS OF
THE TWELFTH CENTURY

❖ ❖ ❖

• I •

Introduction

MEDIEVAL civilization came of age, so to speak, in a series of thunderous events on the eve of the twelfth century: the Norman Conquest of England (1066 and after); the Investiture Conflict (1075–85) with its settlements in France (1107), England (1108), and the empire (1122); and the First Crusade (1095–99) with its sequel of expeditions to the East. It would not be difficult to extend such a list—so as to include, say, the Christians' capture of Toledo (1085), the killing of King William Rufus (1100), or the murder of Count Charles the Good (1127)—for these, too, were events widely noticed by clerks and monks keeping records of faith. Our own perceptions are derived through these sources from the interests of contemporaries in the greater world about them, a world they could see daring new enterprises, expanding, outgrowing. And it is safe to say that what most interested people who lived through these conspicuous events was their witness to the experience of power.

There was something portentous about them. Normans and English alike knew why the 'long-haired star' had appeared in April 1066:[1] it presaged the most successful dynastic enterprise of the age. Starkly scandalous was the spectacle, a decade later, of the king of Germany prostrate before an inexorable pope, for was not the king the Lord's anointed?[2] Something of their zeal had to

---

[1] 'Worcester Chronicle' (D), *ASC* I, 195; *The Bayeux Tapestry*, ed. Lucien Musset, tr. Richard Rex (Woodbridge 2005) scenes 31–33 (176–79).

[2] *Das Register Gregors VII.* iv.12, ed. Erich Caspar, 2 vols. (Berlin 1920–23) I, 311–14 (tr. Brian Tierney, *The crisis of church & state, 1050–1300* [Englewood Cliffs 1964] 62–63).

be spent before cooler heads could devise the compromises in
which lay and spiritual powers came to be distinguished with
new conceptual precision. And it was the palpably momentous
phenomenon of fighting men in successive waves taking up their
crosses in Christ-imitating self-denial that inspired a flock of
chroniclers to write of the First Crusade: a 'strong movement
[*motio valida*],' remembered one of the knights, 'through all the
Frankish regions.'[3] These were events capable of striking people
with wonder, with fear. Many felt vaguely that their collective
· destinies were affected. Moreover, these events projected great
men to admire. Countess Adèle of Chartres had a tapestry depicting the Norman Conquest, her father's immortal exploit, hanging over her bed; she who would have to urge her husband Count
Stephen to return to the crusading expedition he had ignomini-
ously abandoned.[4] Valour, however problematic in mortals, created power, became the celebration of power in the exploits of
those who won battles or kingdoms. One wrote of them, of their
'deeds' (*gesta*); sang of them: of William the Conqueror, of the
Angevin counts, of Boleslaw 'Wrymouth' of Poland, of the Cid,
of Prince Louis of France;—of Charlemagne. One took little interest in their means to power other than military exploits. Power
tended to be conceived personally, charismatically. Indeed, it attached mysteriously to those who had it, who embodied it; to
those who might themselves be 'powers' (*potestates*); to others,
more numerous, who shared or aspired to it. Heroism was for
these 'powers' to exemplify, for the masses to admire.

It was not necessary to be a hero to rule in this world. A more
concrete form of power, something more like 'force' (French:
puissance) had come to be the qualitative test of nobility: the
power to command and punish, to coerce. This was, theoretically
and historically, the power of kings, and remained so towards
1100. It was, accordingly, official power, an attribute of the royal

---

[3] *Gesta Francorum*, ed. Rosalind Hill (Oxford 1972) 1.
[4] R. H. C. Davis, *King Stephen 1135–1154*, 3d ed. (London 1990) 1–4.

function objectively defined. Kings (and emperors) topped the hierarchy of powers in Christendom. But dukes and counts were also 'powers (*potestates*)'; so were marquises and (in most regions) viscounts: all those, in short, whose attributes and (as a rule) blood perpetuated the administrative and social elites of pre-millennial times. In some highly problematic way the powers exercised by the old aristocracy were official and public as well as patrimonial; and we shall need to consider where in the conceptual spectrum their more specifically feudal action falls, for that was an issue for them as well as for us. But power was felt more than it was ana- lyzed. While it may be of moment that some sense of public order persisted, even in heavily feudalized zones,[5] we may also imagine that peasant-tenants and vassals experienced a great noble's will or disposition in variable ways having little to do with status, and that patrimonial circumstances—hereditary right and the eco- nomic viability of estates and matrimonial and parental fortunes— could be hardly less important qualitative determinants of his power. Of a great lord's power. For it goes without saying that powers judicial, fiscal, coercive, and paternal were, above all, powers of lordship.

'Lordship' in this book refers diversely to personal commands over dependent people who might be peasants in quasi-servile status or knights or vassals having or seeking elite standing; the word also denotes the value or extent of such dependencies (pat- rimony, *dominium*). The lordship held by nobles accounted for much of the exercise of licit power around 1100.[6] It is tempting to include in this category the temporal dominations of prelates: bishops, abbots, priors, and the like. These were often the broth- ers or nephews of the old elite, nobles themselves; and even those of lesser blood, ever more numerous in time, must have been

---

[5] See below, ch. III.

[6] Elite power is quite differently treated by David Crouch, *The birth of nobil- ity. Constructing aristocracy in England and France 900–1300* (Harlow 2005). As with much other terminology, my references to 'nobles' ('nobility') accord with the sources in a normally untechnical sense of 'elite' or 'aristocracy.'

influenced by models of clerical office. But the complication here
is that, as a rule, prelacies of this age were electoral and thereby
exempt from one of the temptations to exploitative lordship. The
question will arise how far clerical principles of associative action
and decision-making affected prevailing structures of lordship in
the twelfth century; but it will be safe to begin by recognizing
that deference and obligations amongst the clergy were profoundly influenced by the recognition of qualitative differences
between men. Power attached to persons, to repeat, and this was
so even when, as conspicuously with the clergy, self-proclaimed
unworthies held offices by God's grace. Offices, however real in
theory, were animated by lords (kings, bishops, counts, etc.)
whose power was effluent in expression, affective in impact. As
for human collectivities, it does not appear that they were yet
normally powerful as such.[7] Associations and communities could
be found everywhere in the age of the First Crusade. They had
legal or even administrative functions notably in the uplands and
peripheries, cultural functions (as in drinking gilds) perhaps
more widely but more silently. But in the great European heartlands, communities were more or less suspect to those with (licit)
power. Only clerical congregations living according to rules were
fully acceptable: that is, associations subject to lord-prelates or
themselves exercising lordship, attaining collectively at best to
some recognition of rights as distinct from powers. Yet for all this
the empowerment of communities becomes part of the story before us.

Seen in this way, the ordering of powers was marked by systemic stability. People knew their place in the hierarchies of
church and principality, secure in the assurance that 'there is no
power but from God' (Romans xiii.1). The religious and secular
orders remained mutually reinforcing even as they became juris-
dictionally distinct following the Gregorian reform. While many
thought spiritual power intrinsically superior to secular, everyone

---

[7] See generally to the contrary Susan Reynolds, *Kingdoms and communities in
western Europe, 900–1300* (Oxford 1984).

could see that the church depended on the support and protection of lay men for its survival. Nor could anyone doubt—least of all following an apparently radical proposal in 1111 to divest imperial churches of their regalian possessions[8]—that the church was an aggregate of landlords. Like the temporal world. A tendentious reflection had it that society was formed of three orders of people—those who fight, those who pray, and those who work. Peasants, the many who worked, could hardly have arrived at such a view.[9]

But they could understand it. Power was order. People celebrated order in processions, assemblies, councils. Still in the twelfth century, as in the ancient church, bishops vied with one another for visible precedence.[10] These were not political disputes; they were concerned with status, not process. Much the same might be said of the attitude of great lords, lay and spiritual, towards their domains: God-given wealth to be used, described, retained. Domesday Book was more than a *descriptio* (and was surely a stupendous achievement), but how much more? What could one do with it? Could the order it projected be suffered to change? And a further question, even more pertinent, arises here: were there people with power but without status? Any who wished to change existing order? One fact should be underscored: the concept of the three orders, so far as we presently know, lost ideological force towards 1100. It seemed descriptive, not polemical; it was not challenged as such.[11] There was something ideal about the order of elite powers that flourished in the twelfth century. The empire recovered, the monarchies grew richer and stronger and fostered more sophisticated theories and means of power. Or so it seems. Was it really so? Let us rather ask whether

[8] Colin Morris, *The papal monarchy. The western church from 1050 to 1250* (Oxford 1989) 159.

[9] Georges Duby, *Les trois ordres ou l'imaginaire du féodalisme* (Paris 1978; tr. Arthur Goldhammer, *The three orders . . .* [Chicago 1980]).

[10] e.g., Hugh the Chanter, *The history of the church of York, 1066–1127*, ed. Charles Johnson, rev. Martin Brett *et al.* (Oxford 1990) 22.

[11] Duby, *Trois ordres* (*Three orders*), Eclipse.

contemporaries thought it was so. Was this elite order exempt from the spectre of disorder?

❋

FEW CAN have thought so. The epigraphic events we started with were not only expressions of power but also, diversely, tests of, threats to, or violations of social order. They were, indeed, manifestations of violence, although this would have been less obvious to contemporaries than it is to us. All societies think of disruption when recalling salient events; with us, too, assassinations of the great vie with wars for notoriety. What Hannah Arendt spoke of as the 'arbitrariness' of violence was even more commonplace in the eleventh century than today; and the commonplace was easy to overlook by those exempt from the suffering it caused, by the few with power, and by us.[12] Power was exercised violently in the societies that concern us, so that if the cruelties incident to conquests and crusades seem epiphenomenal, they were nonetheless expressive of a preponderant reality of human experience. Allusions to violence are so deafeningly frequent in records of the eleventh and twelfth centuries that historians have been tempted to tune them out as self-serving clerical exaggerations; it has been proposed that *violentia* may not always mean what it seems in the sources.[13] But it is safe to say that those astride horses and bearing weapons routinely injured or intimidated people in the eleventh and twelfth centuries.

Not always without purpose. Violence was a means of attaining as well as exercising power. The horsemen of Old Catalonia threatened and seized from peasants to create lordships and win knightly respectability. The Erembald clan in Flanders, having achieved power without respectability, murdered the count they feared might undo them. The social crisis that ensued may be likened not only to the virulent collapse of royal protectorates in Galicia (1112–17) and in

[12] Hannah Arendt, *Crises of the republic* . . . (NY 1972) 110.
[13] See Stephen D. White, 'The "feudal revolution": Comment 2,' *Past & Present* no. 152 (1996) 209–14.

England (1139–50) but also to a series of symptomatic urban uprisings: Cambrai (1076), Le Mans (1077), Laon (1112), and Santiago de Compostela (1117). It is usual, and hardly unjustified, to interpret these latter as anti-seigneurial revolts; but it looks as if the rebels merely thought the wrong lords were in power.[14] So we pass from violence to social stress, to normal situations of less or more repressive order vulnerable to assaults from the castle above or occasionally, if seldom, from the people below.

What most profoundly threatened the existing structure of power was the dynamics of social and economic change: increasing population and wealth and the multiplication of people with the means and will to coerce others. In the old passing world nobles had ruled, and nobles were few. In the burgeoning new world of the First Crusade more and more castellans and knights were pretending to noble powers and, inevitably, status. Characteristically, their ambitions exceeded their resources, thus predisposing them to the use of coercive force not only against their own peasants so as to secure a sufficient patrimony for the militant ease they craved, but also against the lands and peasants of others so as to entice fighting men to the rewards of their service and fidelity. Men fought for lordship, or for shares in it, and they learned to despise the peasants they felt compelled to exploit. Incipient nobility could be pitiless—and precarious. Were lord-princes to resist such vicious men?—or co-opt them?

In the event, they did both, appointing them to vicariates, shrievalties, or even curial functions against promises of fidelity, while seeking, almost everywhere in vain, to control the building of castles. The militant 'new men' were arguably more critical to the making of medieval government than the clerical ones made famous by Orderic Vitalis and his modern interpreters, for the former had to be taught the difference between fidelity and competence.[15] And this lesson courtiers of whatever station found

[14] Below, ch. IV.
[15] OV xi.2 (VI, 16). Generally Ralph V. Turner, *Men raised from the dust. Administrative service and upward mobility in Angevin England* (Philadelphia 1988).

hard to teach, and often, it seems, hard to learn. They were used to thinking in terms of largesse, generosity, and the custom of fixed patrimonies; were quite unused to the concept of 'increase [*incrementum*]' and its economic implications. The men who supplied the lord-count's table or who provisioned his entourage must often have been as tempted to overlook the failings of a customary system from which they themselves profited as to recommend a new way of reckoning that would enable their master to profit from patrimonial growth.

And there was a deeper level of tectonic stress. New notions of militant lordship had taken root in societies more nearly converted to Christianity than ever before. This produced a contradiction that distressed principled clergymen, who questioned not only a seemingly worldly trade in altars but also the deportment of prelate-lords with tenants, vassals, and pretensions. When their reform movement was carried to the extreme of attacking the king's customary control of episcopal appointments, the conflicting ideals of opposed conceptions of power were speedily deployed in conflict. The Investiture Conflict was the first and most celebrated incident of a prolonged crisis of power. Marking a newly self-conscious maturity in European affairs, it had many facets, as historians have well seen; two of these have notable bearing on the theme of this book. First, the conflict was destructively violent, undermining royal authority in Germany while subjecting the people of Rome to merciless pillage by the pope's Norman allies. Second, writers drawn to justify actions or claims gave expression to ideas about authority, office, election, and competence (or suitability) that were to win renewed currency in the twelfth-century church and must be supposed to have influenced those, themselves often clerics, at work in kingdoms and lay principalities as they were fitted out with institutions.[16] Out of this 'crisis of church and state,' to employ the usual but problematic

---

[16] Gerd Tellenbach, *Church, state and Christian society at the time of the Investiture Contest*, tr. R. F. Bennett (Oxford 1940); Morris, *Papal monarchy*, chs. 4, 5, 7–9.

term, came the organizing of ecclesiastical government. Might not a crisis, in considerable measure the same crisis, have played its part in the beginnings of lay governments?

❋

VIOLENCE, DISORDER, stress: the problems of traditional powers in western medieval lands arose chiefly from societal growth and change. They might indeed be called 'growing pains' were it not for the inadequacy of the developmental metaphor. There was a confused old head on this young body, addled with conflicting venerable views of world order that had been incompletely reconciled in the compromise over investitures. The bellowing anger of a lord-king could provoke the murder of an archbishop as late as 1170—and two other archbishops would suffer Becket's fate in the next quarter-century. Here again *libertas ecclesiae* rang forth, the old issue of the two powers; but what really links the aftershocks in England and Catalonia is a new distress about fidelity, oppression, and remedies for violence. And if, as has been plausibly argued, John of Salisbury wrote about tyranny with the young Henry II's fiscal exploitation of the English church in mind, then his *Policraticus* merits a conspicuous place in a flood of complaints against wilful violence, to say nothing of its well-known contribution to the new genre of courtly satire. John's equivocations about tyrannicide may be said to betray a learned clerk cowering before the lord-king he would correct.[17] But if the *Policraticus* is thus an ideological witness to the excesses of lord-rulership, it also helps us to understand why disorders and tensions of this age other than that of the two powers have not much interested historians. In John's philosophical exposition, ideas seem disengaged by comparison with the polemics of the Investiture Conflict and of Becket's exile. This appearance may not be entirely justified, but it

[17] Jan Van Laarhoven, 'Thou shalt *not* slay a tyrant! The so-called theory of John of Salisbury,' *The world of John of Salisbury*, ed. Michael Wilks (Oxford 1984) 319–41.

is true of so much else written about power in the twelfth century as to suggest one considerable heuristic difficulty of this inquiry: a certain discrepancy between the structural integrity of lordship as represented in theory and the perceptibly problematic character of lordship as we know it in practise.

Those who reflected on power drew on a cluster of familiar ideas, a field of moral discourses derived from the biblical-patristic inheritance, from common talk and the literary expression of militant lay values, and from a new infusion of classicising theory. It was held as axiomatic that all power was from God, that it was justly wielded on earth to remedy sin and wickedness and to protect the church, and that good and valiant deeds merited fidelity and honour. Kingship and prelacy were ministries or offices of God; good offices, that is, because tyranny was a perversion of the *deitas* a prince was held to have. Law, likewise subject to perversion, figures typically as a classical restraint on the ruler, and was, for John of Salisbury, a 'gift of God.'[18] What is common to all such platitudinous allusions—as in early *chansons de geste*, letters and *arengae* of educated clerks, and the *Policraticus*, for example[19]— was a virtual equating of power with *dominatio*, or lordship; of human power with the only form of power God was conceived to possess. But this is conceptually sophisticated lordship: an expression of public power, official and utilitarian, with no implied antithesis between arbitrary will and social purpose. John of Salisbury defines tyranny as 'violent lordship,' by which he means wilful or lawless rule.[20] Moreover, this whole administrative conception of lordship evokes a deeper strain of scriptural and patris-

---

[18] *Policraticus* iv.1–2, ed. C. C. J. Webb, 2 vols. (Oxford 1909) I, 235–37.

[19] e.g., *Le couronnement de Louis* . . . , laisses 1–10, ed. Ernest Langlois, 2d ed. (Paris 1966) 1–6; *LPV* I, no. 97; John of Salisbury, *Policr.* iii.10 (I, 205); iv.1,4,6 (I, 235–37, 244, 250–57); v.7 (I, 307–15); vi.1 (II, 2–8). John, however, seldom uses the words *dominatio, dominus*, which have for him the resonance of wilful power such as he can safely attribute only to God.

[20] *Policraticus* viii.17 (II, 345–46): 'Est ergo tirannus, ut eum philosophi depinxerunt, qui uiolenta dominatione populum premit, sicut qui legibus regit princeps est.'

tic admonitions: Christ's differentiation between domination and service, with the implied paradox that lords should serve; or Saint Benedict's comparably paradoxical prescription of the abbot who must take counsel but may then act as he wills; or Saint Gregory's psychological exposition of the pastoral office.[21] Also scriptural was the inherited doctrine of accountability, which likewise projected a norm of administrative lordship.[22]

It would be difficult to exaggerate the tenacity of these ideas in a self-renewing religious culture. Yet much in them seems out of touch with secular realities. As will become clear, this is what we should expect. John of Salisbury, sublimely wedded to his Cicero, Ambrose, and (he claimed) Plutarch, tells us he drew his tyrant from the 'philosophers,' although his depiction might well fit the bad castellan of his day. The studied conception of lordship had preserved principles of early medieval public order; Carolingian notions of rulership and administration. In the absence of any willing or premeditated assault on those principles, they had survived intact. They can be read verbatim in Galbert of Bruges' lament for the life and programme of Count Charles the Good—and Galbert was a notary engaged in the most down-to-earth life of Flanders.[23] Yet the reality beneath the platitudes must have been different. Flanders was burning. . . .

THE REALITY was not simply that power, stress, and violence were *experienced* personally, palpably, physically. They were

---

[21] Matthew xxiii.10–11; John xv.15; *The Rule of Saint Benedict*, ed. and tr. Justin McCann (London 1952) cc. 3, 63 (25, 143); Gregory the Great, *Regula pastoralis*, parts 1 and 2, *PL* LXXVII, 13–50.

[22] Matthew xviii.23, xxv.19; Luke xvi.2.

[23] Galbert of Bruges, *De multro, traditione, et occisione gloriosi Karoli comitis Flandriarum* cc. 1–12, ed. Henri Pirenne, *Histoire du meurtre de Charles le Bon, comte de Flandre (1127–28) par Galbert de Bruges* . . . (Paris 1891) 1–22; also Jeff Rider (Turnhout 1994) 2–33; (tr. James Bruce Ross, *The murder of Charles the Good*, rev. ed. [NY 1967] 81–114).

thought likewise in the doing of things. Power meant lordship and nobility, the precedence of one or (very exceptionally) a few, in the twelfth century. It was realized in submission, alliance, paternity, friendship, and ceremony; in petition, oath, or witness; in one's lord's presence, in his castles, his districts (our very word evokes the *distringere* of seigneurial constraint). It was felt mysteriously in the priested rituals of promise, bonding, festivity, consecration, ordeal, and rejection. It was felt as violence: seizure, rape, intimidation, extortion, arson, murder; felt painfully, that is, in the prevailing weakness of protection and justice. Power was *not* felt, nor was it habitually imagined, as government.

No lesson of medieval history has been so victimized by conceptual anachronism as this one. Generations of scholars, including those writing of the eleventh and twelfth centuries, have spoken of medieval 'government' or the 'state' without hesitation or explanation. Excellent scholars, to be sure. Much of what is presently known about the history of power in the twelfth century was discovered by the likes of Achille Luchaire, L. L. Borrelli de Serres, W. A. Morris, C. H. Haskins, Heinrich Brunner, Heinrich Mitteis, H. G. Richardson and G. O. Sayles. They gathered evidence for the origins and semblances of offices, institutions, legislation, and policy. We learned from them how power was exerted in shire-courts, in the production of coinages, in the levy of danegeld. But they wrote of such things not only as public services, which in some sense they surely were, but also as political institutions. More cautious than some, Joseph R. Strayer synthesized this work as 'the medieval origins of the *modern* state' (my stress) and thought of state-building as only beginning towards 1100; yet he also believed that feudalism was a form of government.[24] Most historians of institutions spoke (and speak still) of government as if all societies have it and *we* know what it is. There seemed no need to define the thing, an omission per-

---

[24] *Medieval origins of the modern state*; see also Strayer's *Feudalism* (Princeton 1965) 13.

haps encouraged by familiarity with sources in which words (and their derivatives) like *administrare, gubernare, regere, regimen, res publica,* and *status* occur frequently. One moved easily to the appropriation of concepts from the vocabulary of the modern state: administration, political power, party, 'machinery of government,' etc.

None of these concepts is warranted by what we know of Europe before 1150. Not even the classicising clerics who spoke of *administratio* or *res publica* tried to abstract a definition of government from their summations of the attributes of good rulership. Nor should very much be made of their secularising of social purpose: 'rule yourself by laws,' exhorted Archbishop Hildebert to the count of Anjou about 1123, 'and your subjects by love'; and John of Salisbury insisted on the delegacy of the material sword by the church.[25] What these prelates saw clearly—and here they were fully *au courant*—was that if the prince's will (*voluntas*), by which he was potentially a tyrant, could be limited by law, then his power could be redefined as service to subjects: specifically (in Hildebert's formulation) justice, the equitable securing of rights, and help for the afflicted. In effect, they proposed to put traditional kingship back into princely lordship, to essay a civil (or even 'political') ideal of justice in place of a personal-proprietary one. This was progressive thinking, as Sir Richard Southern well saw; scholars familiar with Cicero and Seneca 'were opening up a new vein of political theory, based on human rights and needs, and the innate dignity of the secular order of society.'[26] Their public–legal usage is very suggestive in this regard. Abbot Peter the Venerable of Cluny thanked Bishop Henry of Winchester for 'having put aside so many entanglements of your commonwealth [*res publica*, i.e., in England]' in order to visit Burgundy around 1134.[27] It looks as if Peter thought of lord-princes and their ministers as functioning in a public order, of ruling people territorially.

---

[25] *Ven. Hildeberti epistolae, PL* CLXXI, 182; John of Salisbury, *Policraticus* iv.3 (I, 239).

[26] *Making of the Middle Ages* 95. [27] *LPV* I, no. 59.

Archbishop Hildebert put the matter more concretely, recommending that Count Geoffrey take satisfaction in 'administration' and service in the *res publica*.[28] That in some sense a public order persisted in Europe cannot be doubted.[29] But how were such images related to the reality of power? Was a cowed shire-court an institution of state? Was the lord-king who dispensed favour exercising justice politically?

The trouble with assuming that power was experienced publicly and institutionally is that it closes our eyes to inconvenient evidence. Consider a more specific example. Messrs. Richardson and Sayles, who severely castigated William Stubbs for his failings, were at pains to show, no doubt correctly, that the appointment of Roger of Salisbury to supervise justice represented a resourceful innovation by King Henry I. Yet when they added, gratuitously, that Henry 'creat[ed] the office of justiciar' and 'conferred . . . the title of chief justiciar' on Roger, they themselves went beyond the evidence, victims of preconception.[30] What the records show is simply that a competent clerk of the lord-king's entourage was entrusted with an important new function. Is this so small a point? As our authorities themselves say, 'Roger of Salisbury is an outstanding, a mighty, figure in English history.'[31] Yet we know nothing directly of his function, let alone 'office'; only something of (a very few of) his acts. Silence can play tricks on us, but we must not forget to listen to it. People in the shires knew that Bishop Roger was powerful, that he wielded the king's lordship; neither he in his writs nor they seem to have insisted on any appellation other than that of 'bishop'—and that *was* an official title. It is an engaging complication of this inquiry that power

---

[28] *PL* CLXXI, 181–83 (partly quoted by Southern, 95).

[29] This is a main theme of Alan Harding, *Medieval law and the foundations of the state* (Oxford 2002).

[30] H. G. Richardson and G. O. Sayles, *The governance of mediaeval England from the Conquest to Magna Carta* (Edinburgh 1963) 157; see also 157–68; and compare Judith Green, *The government of England under Henry I* (Cambridge 1986) ch. 3.

[31] Richardson and Sayles, *Governance* 165.

could be conceived—or at any rate, envisaged—diversely in given situations.

By holding to the concept of power, we may have better hope of knowing an office when we find one. Indeed, the main objection to the study of medieval government as such is that it underrates the extent and significance of institutional change. If the behaviour of insubordinate Catalan barons in the 1190s seems sociologically different from that of their ancestors in the 1050s, was that behaviour political in both cases? If government and politics are (indeed) constants in human affairs, then (of course) they changed historically; but in such a scenario historians may be overly tempted to suppose continuity and incremental growth while discrediting evidence of disruption or transformation. Current thinking about the anarchy under King Stephen seems to betray this temptation—as well as uneasiness about it.[32] Contemporaries may have been oblivious to procedural novelties, and tiresome about wickedness, but when they speak of violence in unexpected contexts we should pay heed. The famous letter of Archbishop Hildebert cited above contains an extended coda on the old theme of the good prince ill served by bad ministers. This passage is as remarkable for what it leaves out as for what it says. It says the prince will be held accountable in God's judgment for his failure to 'repress the rapacity and exactions of your [ministers]'—(the stark *tuorum* is eloquent)—without so much as hinting that terrestrial accountability would be a convenient remedy.[33] What matters is not that the 'government' here exhorted is rudimentary, for that is manifest; but rather that power in this *res publica*, even in its ministries, is conceived as personal lordship.

If polities fitting the proto-humanist prescriptions could be found in or alongside the lordships of this turbulent world, they were few and far between. The most nearly permanent one before

---

[32] See *The anarchy of King Stephen's reign*, ed. Edmund King (Oxford 1994); and *King Stephen's reign (1135–1154)*, ed. Paul Dalton, Graeme White (Woodbridge 2008).

[33] *PL* CLXXI, 183.

1150 was the papacy, with its increasingly bureaucratic resort to law and legates, and its routinizing response to petitions and pleas. But the Roman church was an elective monarchy founded on ancient precepts and tradition; it was in this sense a survival from the pre-Gregorian public order, although quite arguably it took the de-worldifying crisis of the eleventh century to stimulate the administrative innovations that came after. In any case, we know the papacy of this age from its own records, progressively collegial in impulse, standard in form. In Germany and Italy imperial justice and patronage had never wholly lost their official natures. It was otherwise in dynastic-feudal lay societies, in which privileges were typically drafted by beneficiaries, courts were recorded as occasions, and where it may well have required the demise or absence of lord-princes to contrive something like government as a temporary expedient. Orderic Vitalis tells us that while their count was imprisoned in 1098, the barons of Maine held daily counsel wherein the *status* of the *res publica* was discussed and provided for.[34] Yet here again classicising verbiage (not to mention a long lapse of time) may have distorted the reality. It was one thing to devise a vice-gerental function in an expanding realm, as in the case of the English justiciarship; quite another to institute a collective lay lordship, let alone acephalous baronial republics. The inter-regnal troubles of 1127–28 in Flanders, in which precocious efforts to distill a general interest from partial ones were made, may be more indicative than the less surely attested occasion in 1098. Communal independence was notoriously ephemeral in northern France, all but unheard of elsewhere north of the Alps.

So it was in lordships, and notably those of princes and kings, that principles and mechanisms resembling those of public administration first became perceptible. Exceptions to this assertion must not be overrated. Some early communal governments in Italy were characteristically precarious, to the point of needing rescuers. One looked elsewhere for educated courtiers; and by

[34] OV x.8 (v, 240).

1200 their political assumptions would have seemed increasingly realistic to those who had property to lose in Catalonia and in the lands dominated by Philip Augustus, as well as in England. Statutory judicial procedures were taking hold in England. New functions, fiscal accountability, and something like lawmaking become visible in all these lands. But there was nothing inevitable about this, not even in an organic sense. What *was* inevitable was the radical survival, not to say triumph, of personal lordship, the only conceivable implement of nobility, then more prestigious than ever. The well born prevailed affectively[35] as well as functionally; no wonder servants emulated them. It cannot have been easy, given economic and patrimonial constraints and ambitions, to redefine fidelity in impersonal ways to public ends. That is why accountability was fundamental to the crisis of the twelfth century—the 'critical' issue, very precisely speaking. For on this point the disparity between moral imperative and arbitrary actuality was most acute, the biblical precepts least effectual for seeming beyond hope of realization. And it was on this point that the experience of violence converged with that of power, for the tolerance of violence prevailing in lordships of the twelfth century helps to explain the equally characteristic tolerance of imprecision in the performance of service to the powerful.

THE PROBLEM to be addressed in this book is how and why the experience of power became that of government in medieval Europe. The objective validity of this problem in no way depends on a distinction between lordship and government. Medieval government arose, with some exceptions, or revived, within lordships. The ways of this transformation were not always violent, yet they were strewn with conflicts arising from what may reasonably be regarded as a crisis of unlike mentalities. The antagonism

[35] That is, by dint of personal-emotional engagement or influence. See Glossary for this concept.

was never explicitly defined, nor even perhaps clearly grasped, save as a conflict between good and evil; and while it is unfashionable today to attend overmuch to the moralities of power, it would be cruelly misleading to ignore them in this book. If as a rule the free laity aspired to militant valour and domination—to *noblesse*, that is—, they were ever ready to taste of peace in fear for their souls. We hear of good lords in the twelfth century, yet sometimes having, like Ansold of Maule, to define their power in contrast to that of tyrants.[36] If as a rule the clergy espoused the values of competence, office, and peace, they were too engaged with the world, as the reformers found to their sorrow, to be fully redeemed. Archbishop Manasses I of Reims was the object of repeated charges of lordly exploitation and violence against the abbot and monks of Saint-Remi.[37] Popes like kings were lords (*domini*), none more so than Gregory VII, who could be likened in hostile hyperbole to a brutal master of helpless serfs.[38] But people were not accustomed to abstracting principles from immediate aims; and when in one of the rare instances where *we* can discern something like an ideological confrontation in practise, in late twelfth-century Catalonia, the outcome of the struggle was bizarrely pragmatic: a victory of barons addicted to violent lordship over legislators on the high ground of peace. In that land the crisis was prolonged.

The crisis of the twelfth century was one of conflicting aspirations in disparate multiplied populations: aspirations for lordship and nobility, and for justice. Government and the state were to be, in some senses, its resolution. The recognition of societal needs and of judicial remedy, persuasion to tenets of collective utility and management in place of exploitation: such things arose with the uneasy survival of lordship. Yet the origins of govern-

---

[36] OV v.19 (III, 194), discussed below, p. 65.

[37] C. Stephen Jaeger, 'Courtliness and social change,' in *Cultures of power. Lordship, status, and process in twelfth-century Europe*, ed. T. N. Bisson (Philadelphia 1995) 297–99.

[38] Text cited in further context below, p. 207.

ment can only incidentally be our subject. Since contemporaries appear to have lacked an empirical understanding of government (or the state) as distinct from lordship, it seems equally useless to define the phenomenon or to insist on it. No one knew when (s)he had it. What matters here was, and is, the becoming, the transformation: the history of violation, complaint, and response; of pacification, remedy, and legislation; of an unsteady adjustment between function and office; of a flickering recognition of the difference between fidelity and competence in ministerial service. What was normally lacking in the twelfth century was self-conscious action, including lawmaking, in the interest of subjects; the recognition of offices as impersonal and accountable; and the understanding of competing interests as legitimate and negotiable. None of these elements was incompatible with lordship. Some or all would develop within lordships as also in communities. All of them were implied by classical and patristic theories of power revived after 1050, familiar to many, yet perhaps more persistently ethereal than we have realized. Max Weber's differentiation between patrimonial and bureaucratic dominations remains conceptually useful, not least for suggesting how these observed types of power are not necessarily opposed absolutely, nor necessarily historically sequential. Yet his insistence on 'political' behaviour and on office in all types of domination seems to miss an historical reality very characteristic of the twelfth century.[39] For the same reason it has seemed inadvisable to follow recent social scientists and their adherents in referring to all relations of power as 'political,' a usage not merely negligent of the classical etymology but also, as already suggested, oblivious to one of the salient shifts in the social experience of medieval power.[40]

---

[39] *Economy and society: an outline of interpretive sociology*, ed. Guenther Roth, Claus Wittich, 2 vols. (Berkeley 1978) I, 215, 221, 237, 241, 252; and II, ch. 9.

[40] e.g., William Ian Miller, *Humiliation and other essays on honor, social discomfort, and violence* (Ithaca, NY, 1993); Stephen D. White, 'The discourse of inheritance in twelfth-century France: alternative models of the fief in "Raoul

An historical study of power will nonetheless inevitably seem
beholden to modernism. The very concept is social scientific
even if the medieval word *potestas* lends itself to unmediated historical interpretations. Even the historical reflections on power by
anti-modernist Michel Foucault betray their sociological genesis.[41] Modern notions of class, culture, ritual, liminality, literacy,
identity formation, strategic action, and process are only a few of
the pertinent aspects of the historical situations here in question.
But with the partial exceptions of culture and literacy, theoretical
constructs per se are less useful to the present inquiry than 'thick
descriptions' and their implications such as may be found diversely in James C. Scott's work on southeast Asian peasants or in
Alexander Murray's study of reason and society in medieval Europe.[42] Norms were changing—were 'becoming'—in the heavily
lorded societies of the eleventh and twelfth centuries. At least one
new one—the mind-set of castellans and knights in some
areas—does not easily conform to the model of feud constructed
by legal anthropologists,[43] compelling me to hold to the problematic evidence without forcing it. What it suggests is that vengeance, however constant even if seldom obvious in nonliterary
sources, cannot alone explain an abrasive experience of power.
One result of this will be to complicate the map of cultural chronology (which may, after all, be the historian's task).

---

de Cambrai"',' *Law and government in medieval England and Normandy . . .* , ed.
George Garnett, John Hudson (Cambridge 1994) ch. 6; Thomas Ertman, *Birth
of the Leviathan: building states and regimes in medieval and early modern Europe*
(Cambridge 1997); and Esther Pascua Echegaray, *Guerra y pacto en el siglo XII.
La consolidación de un sistema de reinos en Europa Occidental* (Madrid 1996). These
works, together with Harding, *Medieval law and the state* (2002), make valuable
contributions to the study of power in perspectives different from mine.

[41] See for this purpose (Michel Foucault) *Power*, ed. James D. Faubion, tr.
Robert Hurley *et al.* (London 1994) 1–89 ('Truth and juridical forms' [1973]).

[42] James C. Scott, *The moral economy of the peasant. Rebellion and subsistence in
Southeast Asia* (New Haven 1976); Alexander Murray, *Reason and society in the
Middle Ages* (Oxford 1978).

[43] Max Gluckman, 'The peace in the feud,' *Past & Present* no. 8 (1955) 1–14,
followed by much other work; see also Barthélemy as cited in next note.

So there can be nothing categorical in my approach to a subject problematic at once in its nature and its transformation. Is it a matter of 'norm' or 'construct' that human suffering seems related to power in Europe's twelfth century? The evidence of distress, like that of violence, no longer seems so easy to read as it once did,[44] yet without it too much is missing. Even in this distant age, the powerless are not quite voiceless. Their perspectives become part of the challenge of imagining how power worked in societies unlike our own. From these societies survive traces—something of their words and artifacts—for whatever we can make of them, in records to be explained, not explained away. In this survival we may hope to discern how people experienced power in the twelfth century. And perhaps even how that experience changed.

[44] As appears from the influential works of S. D. White and D. Barthélemy, of which the following are but the merest sample: Stephen D. White, 'Repenser la violence: de 2000 à 1000,' *Médiévales* xxxvii (1999) 99–113; Dominique Barthélemy, *Chevaliers et miracles. La violence et le sacré dans la société féodale* (Paris 2004).

·II·

The Age of Lordship (875–1150)

Suppose, for example, that someone is organizing cities,
provinces, kingdoms. What has he thereby arranged but a
license to possess and dominate? Or in a lesser sense, that
someone secures a horse: what . . . is that but a license to
possess, ride, and do with it whatever he wishes?
—*Cardinal Humbert (1058)*[1]

WHEN the radical religious reformers of the eleventh century
questioned the legitimacy of secular power, they were closer
to contemporary action than to prevailing thought. Few people
can then have doubted that emperors, kings, and lesser princes existed to protect and do justice; they were disposed to ignore the
psychology of actual power; and they found comforting unscholas-
tic logic in old ways of order and command. But the critique was
insistent. When Pope Paschal II proposed to renounce the clerical
entitlement to regalian rights in 1111, he observed that bishops and
abbots in some parts of Germany 'are so preoccupied by secular
cares that they are compelled assiduously to frequent the court and
to perform military service, which things indeed are scarcely or
not at all carried on without plunder, sacrilege, arson.'[2] The ex-
travagance of this denunciation should not be permitted to obscure
the insinuation that the normal exercise of public power was attended by violence. This was, to be sure, an extreme view when it
was put forward. But it was not far-fetched. It was justified not

---

[1] *Humberti cardinalis libri III adversus simoniacos* iii.2, ed. Frederick Thaner,
MGH,Ldl, 3 vols. (Berlin 1891–97) I, 199.
[2] JL 6289; *CAP* I, no. 90.

only by harsh realities, such as the Norman conquests of Kent and Yorkshire or the wars over the Vexin, but also, and more remarkably, by habits of thought hardly new in the eleventh century.

What this means is that the very conception of secular order had become problematic. It is well known that the early reformers saw *dis*order in the precedence of lay powers in ecclesiastical elections, but that was a blatantly polemical position. Episcopal elections, however conducted, were public events in a universe of offices. Those offices might be abused, might even suffer violence from mitred lords; but the real problem was that lay power proved vulnerable to tenaciously self-serving or injurious impulses. Hincmar of Reims had seen this as early as the 880s with a clarity seldom matched thereafter, and his view would long remain normative. Those who 'should rule the people under the king,' he wrote, 'that is, dukes and counts . . . understand that they are appointed for this: that they should preserve and rule the populace, not that they should dominate and afflict [it]; nor should they think of God's people as their own or to be subjected to themselves to their glory, for that pertains to tyranny and wicked power.'[3] Here the moral imperative of administration is defined by contrast, by negation; surely a concession to pessimism born of the whole weary history of Frankish kingship. It lived on, this pessimism, ever more pertinent.

There had long been reason for pessimism. Since the later ninth century people had been learning to live with danger (and without Charlemagne). Everywhere, even in lands never subject to the Franks, such as Asturias, the lands of Poles and Bohemians, and England, the pressures of hostile neighbors were real and constant; not even the heartlands of the Carolingian protectorate were exempt from alien depredations or the anxieties they caused. The monks of Saint-Philibert, having been driven with their relics by Viking attacks from one refuge to another, found their 'place of tranquillity' at Tournus on the Saône in 875.[4]

---

[3] Hincmar, *Ad episcopos regni admonitio altera*, PL CXXV, 1015.
[4] *Miracles de Saint-Philibert* c. 1; *Chronique de Tournus* cc. 16–25; both ed. René Poupardin, *Monuments de l'histoire des abbayes de Saint-Philibert* . . . (Paris 1905)

Was "tranquillity" then a normal expectation when our story—or its prelude—begins? Or was this an illusion fostered by the improbable and fragile successes of a great king in a fast receding past? These are disputed questions amongst historians. Not all today would agree with Marc Bloch that the renewed invasions of the ninth century induced a novel and transforming fixation on protection.[5] It looks as if security of life and property had never been assured in post-Roman societies, and famous examples of the weak commending themselves to the strong are to be found in the eighth century. Yet it seems likely that Bloch was right about a new regime of power commencing in the ninth century; and on one critical point the written sources bear out the great historian of 'feudal society' absolutely. They show that people almost everywhere in Christian Europe, from the later ninth century, were seeking or submitting to lords. How and by what rhythms this happened is an unsolved problem of history. What seems clear is that while protection and command were chiefly royal prerogatives in the ninth century, they remained so thereafter less in practise than in theory, as effectual power devolved to lesser mortals through usurpation and default.

What followed was an age, or ages, of lordship that, considered as an expression of focal power, lasted for some three centuries. Historians have lately been reluctant to recognize this period as such, for several reasons. First, they are habituated in the belief that lordship was a constant in *all* the Middle Ages, being an institution of biblical antiquity. Moreover, they cannot help but notice that the period 875–1200 is precisely the period when feudalism prevailed, according to the discredited view of older historians, and there is a noticeable tendency to allow this inconvenience the force of fact. Yet a third objection might be that European societies surely changed too much

---

23–25, 81–87; *Recueil des actes de Charles II le Chauve, roi de France . . .* , ed. Georges Tessier, 3 vols. (Paris 1943–55) II, no. 378.

[5] See generally *La société féodale*, 2 vols. (Paris 1939–40; tr. L. A. Manyon, *Feudal society* [Chicago 1961]) I, i part I.

during three centuries to be well characterized as one age.
Only the third of these objections has merit. Lengths of human
experience vary. Lordship came to have political meaning after
the ninth century such as it had never had before. Lordship and
feudalism[6] are altogether different things, a point that may have
eluded some radical critics of feudalism. And the societal
changes that surely marked the age of lordship are of its very
essence, as we shall see.

Old Order

What changed least, being a survival from the early Middle Ages,
was a sturdy consensus about power and its just norms. Counts,
kings, even bishops might be murdered, catastrophic defeats
might overturn dynastic and cultural traditions, but the structures of prelacy, kingship, and princely lordship persisted. Generation after generation we read of the public doings of the
powerful, of their consultations, judgments, and conflicts. In England the royal diplomas from King Alfred's time to Edgar's
(871–975) were commonly passed on ceremonial occasions attended by prelates, magnates, and thegns, whose solemn signs and
often explicitly recorded consent evoked the quasi-'statist' polity
of Old England.[7] In León the ceremonial guise of exalted Visigothic monarchy persisted in the tenth century, when Sampiro's
chronicle recorded regnal armies (not always victorious) and great
courts. There, as also in the incipient principalities of the Pyrenees, prevailed Roman principles of office, service, contract, and
liability. In all these Hispanic regions property retained the protections of Visigothic law; in all of them kings and their deputies

---

[6] For these terms, see p. 12 above; and Glossary, p. 584.

[7] *Cartularium saxonicum . . .* , ed. Walter de Gray Birch, 3 vols. (London
1885–93) II, III; F. M. Stenton, *The Latin charters of the Anglo-Saxon period* (Oxford 1955) 53–54, and ch. 3; James Campbell, *The Anglo-Saxon state* (London
2000) ch. 1.

bestowed justice on their people, even to the point of hearing peasants in their courts.[8]

Such regimes are harder to discern elsewhere, although something very comparable could be found in Italy. The nascent polities of Bohemia and Poland, where the collectivities owed nothing to Roman precedent, cannot have been so different. In these newly converted Slavic lands Christian prelates naturally allied with protector princes who mobilised subject populations in public obligations.[9] Yet the manifestations of old public order in north Frankish lands, both east and west, are in some ways even more striking, for in these regions traditions of royalist commemorative writing preserved the records of dynastic events and regulations often celebrated in solemn councils and assemblies devoted to territorial security. Most visibly in Germany and early Capetian France the collaboration of kings and bishops and the preoccupation with ecclesiastical integrity made for a theocracy founded on imperial authority and synodal tradition.[10] Moreover, these were regimes of official order. Roman rules governing accountable public service were never abrogated, while the precepts of Gregory the Great concerning competence in clerical offices were widely diffused in Benedictine monastic culture. Powers were seen to attach to office, although it must always have been difficult to compensate services impartially.

The monarchies of eleventh-century Europe were hardly 'stateless' societies. Imposed norms of justice were not lacking in

[8] *Sampiro. Su cronica y la monarquia leonesa en el siglo X*, ed. Justo Perez de Urbel (Madrid 1952) 289–305, 322ff.; Pierre Bonnassie, *La Catalogne du milieu du Xe à la fin du XIe siècle . . .*, 2 vols. (Toulouse 1975–76) I, ch. 2; Juan José Larrea, *La Navarre du IVe au XIIe siècle . . .* (Paris 1998) chs. I, 4–9.

[9] *Die Chronik der Böhmen des Cosmas von Prag*, ed. Berthold Bretholz (Berlin 1923) i–ii (1–159); *GpP* i (2–108).

[10] Richer, *Histoire de France (888–995)* iii.2,90,91, iv.5–8,10,11,51; ed. Robert Latouche, 2 vols. (Paris 1930) II, 8–10, 114–16, 150–54, 158–62, 230–34; Mansi XVIII, 263–66; *Die Chronik des Bischofs Thietmar von Merseburg*, ed. Robert Holtzmann (Berlin 1935) iii.24, vii.50,54 (128, 460, 466; tr. David A. Warner, *Ottonian Germany . . .* [2001] 146, 242, 346).

them. Everywhere people looked to kings and laws; clerks in Poland and Italy contemplated the absence of *rex* and *lex* with horror.[11] There was reason for such anxiety. But we should not confuse the failings of kings with those of laws and order, nor did kings fail everywhere. In England new legislation devised to secure life and property was fundamental to a public sphere of consensus that lasted until 1066, and in some respects, for the Norman conquerors claimed to redirect it, much longer.[12] In old Frankish lands the higher clergy joined with magnates to restore disrupted protections: in Aquitaine from the end of the tenth century in a peace movement that spread widely, in Germany from the turbulent times of Henry IV after 1080.[13] In Mediterranean regions judges and advocates spoke for laws rather than rulers, possessing authority rather than power; somewhat the same may be said of *scabini* in Flanders or moneyers in England. No such regimes of normative function achieved effective mastery of internal order after the tenth century, let alone a monopoly of it. But the imperfections of old societal order in no way detracted from its conceptual tenacity. Nor was this a purely clerical idea. Everyone, including peasants and the bereft, knew that kings and their companions had the authority to decree and coerce.

Royal order was seldom centralized order. Widely characteristic was the associative life of villages and valleys, natural communities of interest that must often have functioned autonomously to determine agrarian customs and collective rights in forests and pastoral slopes. They are all but invisible to us, figuring in writing as a rule only when activated by the pressures of kings and other powers.[14]

---

[11] Thietmar vi.9 (284; *Ottonian Germany* 243–44); *Landulphi Senioris Mediolanensis historiae libri quatuor*, ed. Alessandro Cutolo (Bologna 1942) ii.22 (58); *GpP* ii.42 (194).

[12] Patrick Wormald, *The making of English law: King Alfred to the twelfth century* I (Oxford 1999) chs. 3–10.

[13] Hartmut Hoffmann, *Gottesfriede und Treuga Dei* (Stuttgart 1964); *The Peace of God . . .* , ed. Thomas Head, Richard Landes (Ithaca, NY, 1992).

[14] See, e.g., Roland Viader, *L'Andorre du IXe au XIVe siècle. Montagne, féodalité et communautés* (Toulouse 2003) ch. 3.

That happened often in the Christian Hispanic realms, and there alone the *concejo* found a place in the diplomatic of litigation. For example, the *concilium* of Nájera (Rioja), having witnessed as such a land transaction in 1048, two years later sold communal land to a monk of Leire. In the latter case, 'we neighbours' sold and wrote and (again) invoked the witness of the 'whole *concejo*.'[15] The affective life and self-regulating power of such communities were not normally written, nor does it appear that urban communities had other than oral identity. The 'municipal deeds' (*gesta municipalia*) of late Antiquity had disappeared, although there may be some survival of public associative procedures in the impersonal styling of written judgments in Italy, the Spanish March, and León. Communities of interest in agrarian-pastoral affairs were less artificial than those created by early medieval kings, notably in England, in respect to security and to judicial and fiscal obligations.[16] Yet here, too, the power of decision-making took habitually unwritten forms, the impact of which may easily be underestimated. Such powers silently transformed rural habitats in the very decades—in Occitania from about 1030[17]—when coercive forces were subverting the inherited adjustment of social order.

In its expressive action the local community was virtually an assembly, as can be seen in words like *concejo* (council), *vista*, and hundred. Yet the conceptual identity must always have been fragile, for wherever the sources permit we see the precedence of persons or wealth taking hold, the working of influence; collective power overtaken by domination. This is why an idealised egalitarianism of communal life sounded few echoes in the insti-

---

[15] *Documentación medieval de Leire (siglos IX a XII)*, ed. Angel J. Martín Duque (Pamplona 1983) nos. 43, 46.

[16] C. J. Wickham, *Community and clientele in twelfth-century Tuscany* . . . (Oxford 1998); Larrea, *Navarre*, ch. 4; Pascual Martínez Sopena, *La Tierra de Campos occidental: poblamiento, poder y comunidad del siglo X al XIII* (Valladolid 1985) 109–18, 505–8; *Die Gesetze der Angelsachsen*, ed. Felix Liebermann, 3 vols. (Halle 1903–16) I, 150–95.

[17] Monique Bourin-Derrau, *Villages médiévaux en bas-Languedoc: genèse d'une sociabilité (X^e–XIVe siècle)*, 2 vols. (Paris 1987) I.

tutionalized assemblies of the later Middle Ages. Not even the 'parliaments' in Italian communes did much more than sound the same. It is safe to believe that peasants and shepherds harboured elemental notions of rightful powers; and it has been argued that, given the exceptional circumstance of a kingless regional interest, as in eighth-century Saxony, a representation of villages was possible.[18] What becomes visible in twelfth-century Pyrenean valleys may well be continuous with unrecorded collective action.[19] The known assemblies of the old order, while affording occasional glimpses of judicial speech, tell us more about public than political order.

Old order was public order. One need not imagine this as juridically distinguished from a private sphere (although conceptually the distinction between public and private, in those very words, was never lost in the Middle Ages). Yet in the formulaic usage of Mediterranean boundary clauses, 'public road' (*via publica*) was habitually differentiated from proprietary roads and parcels, and the same was doubtless true wherever 'public roads' were recorded. Those enticed by modernist theory should not forget that Jürgen Habermas, who opined that 'publicness' has no autonomous meaning in 'feudal society,' had never read medieval charters. The truth is that what he calls 'feudal society' is problematic precisely because it is pervaded by, indeed occupies, the 'public sphere.'[20] Flemish scribes wrote 'publicly' to record the lawful openness of transactions; Mediterranean notarial functions were sanctioned in written laws; and the survival of formulaic procedures everywhere marked a vestigial culture of public responsibility. 'The public thing,' as Karl Ferdinand Werner has rightly insisted, 'never disappeared.' Educated writers in

---

[18] See below, pp. 562, 568; Allen Bass, 'Early Germanic experience and the origins of representation,' *Parliaments, Estates and Representation* xv (1995) 1–11.

[19] See below, pp. 561–63.

[20] Although not, of course, in the modernising sense argued by Habermas, *The structural transformation of the public sphere* . . . , tr. Thomas Burger (Cambridge, M., 1991). For the opinion cited, pp. 6–7.

the eleventh and twelfth centuries continued to speak of *res publica*.[21]

The precipitating test was whether rulers could protect their peoples and keep the peace. For in reality little else mattered. Justice became abstract, a live attribute (for a time) chiefly in cases of dispossession and violence; an appurtenance of defence and peace. The old order, a passive zone of consecrated authority, was neither constitutional nor (in the modern sense) political; it could neither promote nor prevent the sort of factional bonding of magnates for patronage or dynastic advantage such as must now and then have rested on principled persuasion. Of utilitarian services (other than military) only the coinage remained in most lands, generally public in form but, save probably in England, chiefly fiscal in practise. By the eleventh century imperial and royal coinages mingled with the issues of princes and prelates to whom the profits of *moneta* had been commended.[22] But the only matters on which rulers shared the preoccupations of society were bound up with defence and the peace.

Indeed, it can be argued that the external menace of Vikings, Magyars, and Muslims worked to preserve public order, such as it was. Territorial England was forged in tenth-century counterattacks on the Viking Danelaw, a process that led to something resembling public taxation and one that ensured that conquests, from within or without, could only be total. Something similar was happening in León and Navarre, where the cohesion of kings, barons, and churches survived in proximity to the dangerous frontiers with Islam. What is striking, however, is how little, almost everywhere, the subsidence of external pressures seems to have encouraged or confirmed the old order of public powers. In west Frankland free peasants and other proprietors would have found it harder than ever to secure justice in county courts in the later tenth and eleventh centu-

---

[21] *Histoire de France. Les origines* . . . (Paris 1984) 498.

[22] Peter Spufford, 'Coinage and currency,' *The Cambridge economic history of Europe* III, ed. M. M. Postan *et al.* (Cambridge 1965) 579–86.

ries.[23] Defence gave way to internal peacekeeping, which proved hardly more successful.

In this age the concept of order became illusory. It ceased to correspond to the real experience of power. But it persisted as a norm, was never renounced as an aspiration, and would one day be substantially restored. Its conceptual persistence as a literate culture may be traced in monastic and cathedral communities possessed of the Latin classics and the decrees of Christian councils; for writers like Burchard of Worms, Ivo of Chartres, Gratian, Lampert of Hersfeld, Suger of Saint-Denis, and John of Salisbury, the public responsibilities of kings, princes, bishops, and abbots were axiomatic. When King Alfonso VII of León convoked his prelates, 'counts and princes and powers over lands' to a council at Palencia in 1129 to ratify a programme of security against violence, he was literally mobilising the 'estate of Holy Church and of the whole kingdom.'[24] Such manifestations of public order, which are widely attested in that age, were conduits of a traditional concept of government and harbingers of a new concept of state. No one can have supposed that public order as such had to be rescued in the twelfth century. Yet it badly needed defending.

The Quest for Lordship and Nobility

By that time the meaning of public order as well as the realities of power had been deeply transformed. The old way of saying this was to assert that feudalism destroyed the state. If we knew what 'feudalism' was, this might be acceptable, but the real problem with this discredited formulation is that the very institutions associated with the concept in the writings of distinguished

---

[23] J.-Fr. Lemarignier, 'La dislocation du "pagus" et le problème des "consuetudines" (Xᵉ–XIᵉ siècles),' *Mélanges d'histoire du moyen âge dédiés à la mémoire de Louis Halphen* (Paris 1951) 401–10.

[24] *HC* iii.7.1,3 (428, 430).

scholars—lordship, vassalage, and the fief—were originally elements *of*, and supports *for*, the regime they are held to have subverted.[25] Of course, such things may have changed in time. This is a case where one can have it both ways. King Athelstan thought that justice was better served when men took lords; and it was hardly subversive for kings and bishops to maintain knights, as at Reims towards 935 and in Lombard cities a generation later.[26] In the Spanish March as well as in imperial Italy conditional tenures of land often termed 'fiefs' were and long remained fiscal in nature; that is, endowments for public administrative service. Viscounties and 'honours' could be described in early eleventh-century Aquitaine as if they were conditional tenures.[27] Relations of lordship and dependence silently modified the old regime of publicly secured property, perhaps more deeply in northern lands, but progressively everywhere.[28]

If we could learn why this happened, we could say more exactly when it happened. The difficulty is that our sources are out of phase with the realities to which they (imperfectly) point. When Burchard of Worms came to define the legal status of the laity around 1020, he spoke of 'those who preside, such as emperors, kings, princes,' and of 'those who are subject to their

[25] F. L. Ganshof, *Feudalism*, tr. Philip Grierson, 3d English ed. (NY 1964 [1944]), where the old standard literature is listed; see also Strayer, *Medieval origins* 14–15.

[26] *Les annales de Flodoard*, ed. Philippe Lauer (Paris 1905) 61; Ordinance of Grately, ed. Liebermann, *Gesetze* I, 150; Hagen Keller, *Adelsherrschaft und städtische Gesellschaft in Oberitalien 9. bis 12. Jahrhundert* (Tübingen 1979) ch. 6.

[27] Elisabeth Magnou-Nortier, 'Note sur le sens du mot *fevum* en Septimanie et dans la Marche d'Espagne à la fin du Xe et au début du XIe siècle,' *Annales du Midi* LXXVI (1964) 141–52; Bonnassie, *Catalogne* I, 209–11; *Ademari Cabannensis chronicon* iii.34,35,41,57; ed. Pascale Bourgain *et al.* (Turnhout 1999) 155–58, 161–63, 178–79; François Menant, *Campagnes lombardes du moyen âge* . . . (Rome 1993) ch. 7.

[28] Cf. Petrus de Marca, *Marca hispanica* . . . (Paris 1688) col. 919: the consecration-assembly of Ripoll in 977 determined 'ut nullus Comes, Pontifex, judex publicus, vel aliqua dominatio in praedictis rebus habeat potestatem causas distringendi . . .'; cf. col. 1297.

imperium.'[29] It was a perfect description of old public order and of official power. Yet it looks as if the offices of such principalities were by this time more nearly ceremonial than administrative. Vestiges of official documentation survive from councils and courts in the tenth century, not even vestiges of delegated routine action.[30] It is little better than conjecture that stewards and managers in fiscal or domain lands were obliged to account for their service to kings, counts, bishops, or monks;[31] and unlikely that higher functions tending to become hereditary—those of seneschals or chamberlains, for example—remained accountable. These people were sharing in patrimonial power and constantly tempted to appropriate it.

Assuredly this behaviour was not new in the tenth century. We know that Carolingian counts were inclined to overlook the distinction between official and proprietary revenues, an understandable tendency in agrarian societies short of coined money. Moreover, public rights were already—indeed, since the late Roman Empire—identified with royal patrimony. But ninth-century records enable us to see that the difference between royal-fiscal and proprietary entitlements was well understood, the former often defended against encroachment by the latter. This differentiation fades from sight thereafter. Later Carolingian kings fought a losing battle to preserve it. In 877 Charles the Bald secured support for his final expedition by permitting the sons of counts and of royal vassals alike to succeed to their fathers' tenures, a regulation that effectually confused fiscal (or public) and proprietary tenures. And when his son Louis the Stammerer then attempted to act on the old right to dispose of benefices, he was forced to desist by an uprising of magnates.[32] In the generations that followed,

[29] *Decreta* xv, *PL* cxl, 895.

[30] e.g., from synod of Ingelheim (948), *CAP* i, nos. 5–7.

[31] See Philippe Dollinger, *L'évolution des classes rurales en Bavière* . . . (Paris 1949) 245.

[32] *Capitularia regum Francorum*, ed. Alfred Boretius, Victor Krause, 2 vols. (Hanover 1883–97) ii, no. 281; see also no. 273; *Annales de Saint-Bertin*, ed. Félix Grat *et al.* (Paris 1964) 218.

the inheritance of counties and honours became normal in many regions, though not everywhere: it was resisted in Germany, Aragon, and Navarre until the late eleventh century, and in León and England even later than that. But even in those lands what determined were the imperatives of royal lordship, not of government. No one renounced the glitter of high office, but power now attached to tenurial status and quasi-proprietary possession. Without ceasing to be a sphere of public order, the kingdom had become a fabric of lordships sharing patrimonial wealth.

The quest for patrimonial wealth was a dynamic force in the post-Carolingian centuries. It is easy to think of it in economic terms, which is why historians have often interpreted feudalizing as a competitive, if not quite a mercantile, phenomenon—an effort to accumulate fiefs; and why one recent scholar chose to stress the proprietary aspect of conditional tenures.[33] What has commonly been overlooked is that tenures of all kinds, including those of fiscal rights, were not only shares in higher lordships; they were invariably lordships themselves. And it is lordship that brings us closest to the lived experience of power in the post-Carolingian centuries. This is so not because all lordships were impositions of personal coercive force; much landlordship, as in all ages, was undoubtedly proprietary in impersonal ways. But there is good reason to believe that most of the new lordships that multiplied in the growing populations of the tenth and eleventh centuries aimed at creating power over people as well as mobilising wealth, whether by exploitation of beneficial tenures, or by the imposition of protective or judicial customs, and (in whatever case) by pretence to enhanced social status through command and constraint.

Lordship matters because the human realities of power—command, allegiance, accountability, coercion, and violence—were bound up with it. Few can have envied people without lords in these times. If the shepherds and small holders in Pyrenean valleys

---

[33] Susan Reynolds, *Fiefs and vassals. The medieval evidence reinterpreted* (Oxford 1994).

knew little of power, having none themselves, they like most other peasants were vulnerable to devastating thrusts by armed forces that could wipe them out. By the tenth century, lordship seemed as natural as it was venerable. It drew on a theology of inequality rooted in an ancient culture of paterfamilial mastership, subservience, and slavery. That it could be thought of in affectively personal terms was clear already in the Psalms, those songs of submissive prayer to the Lord–God; and it was equally clear, as in John's Gospel xv.15, that a familial lordship over 'friends' was preferable to mastership of the slave who 'knows not what his lord may do.' Already in Antiquity lordship, like God's abode, had many mansions, ranging from the political, as in God's territorial-national domination (Psalms cii.22), to the arbitrary and afflictive subjection of slaves recorded in the Gospels and Roman law.

What counted in the Middle Ages was that the protective (familial) and arbitrary modes of lordship tended to be confused. This was so even though, very early, lordship was assimilated to office. From the fourth century, the imperial intitulature was 'personalized and openly linked to a dynasty': one spoke of 'our Lord Flavius,' so that 'all people were placed in a state of inferiority before the lord [*dominus*], a word referring to the chief of the household and of slaves.' By the sixth century Saint Benedict could speak of the abbot as 'called lord and abbot, because he is believed to act in Christ's place.'[34] These representations of lordship promoted humility as a collective virtue in submission, a virtue that was famously underscored when Pope Gregory the Great assumed the title 'servant of the servants of God.' Yet another tradition of affective power had formed in the experience of tribal war bands. Here the dynamic lay in a followership imbued with ambition and greed while conducive to the associative virtues of largesse and loyalty. This sort of solidarity, which proved conspicuous and abhorrent in the ravages of Vikings after about 850, also gave rise to ideas of honour and fidelity such as found expression in the 'songs' of Maldon and Roland.

[34] Werner, *Origines* 234; *Rule of Saint Benedict*, ed. McCann, c. 2 (17).

So by the ninth century lordship was widely as well as diversely experienced. Historians rightly distinguish between ecclesiastical fatherhood, patrimonial exploitation (*seigneurie*, often
considered to have no equivalent in English), feudal-vassalic
lordship, etc. It is not hard to understand why lords with patrimony to spare might welcome the service of those in quest of
support for their prowess and ambition. What is less well understood, and perhaps even misunderstood, is that lordship was becoming more and more conspicuous, and that it was progressing
at the expense of obligations to regalian courts and armies. To a
Flemish hagiographer around 900 it seemed that most men of
standing (his word is 'nobility') had taken lords whom they were
obliged to follow— 'dear lords,' moreover, which hints at the
affective character of such bondings—, leaving but few who had
sufficient patrimony to avoid commendation while remaining
subject only to 'public sanctions.'[35] At about the same time, according to Saint Odo of Cluny writing a generation later, princes
were taking advantage of a disturbed 'state of the republic' to
impose their lordship on 'royal vassals'; one of the latter was
Count Gerald of Aurillac, who seems to have resisted the pressure.[36] So in west Frankish lands a twofold dynamic becomes
visible, with lesser men commending themselves for the rewards
of service even as magnates strove to remodel territorial power
by imposing fidelity on a lesser elite. Although the evidence for
these processes beyond the scope of jurisdictional order is very
inadequate, it seems reasonably clear that lordships at all levels
were multiplying. Bishop Raterio of Verona (d. 974) deplored a
new insistence on the appellation *senior*, which seemed to justify
a grasping for human precedence contrary to patristic assertions
of equality before God. God meant for people to dominate animals, not one another; yet things had got so that people now
supposed that God himself dominated the way men did: jealous

---

[35] Quoted by Ganshof, *Feudalism* 23.
[36] Odo of Cluny, *Vita Geraldi comitis Auriliacensis* c. 32, PL CXXXIII, 660–61
(tr. G. Sitwell, *St Odo of Cluny* [London 1958] 121).

of the other's advantage, avid for power and possession, swollen with greed and ambition.[37]

That Bishop Raterio viewed lay lordship with moralising severity should not surprise us. In his day lesser lords and castellans in Italy, Lotharingia, and west Frankland were increasingly addicted to self-promotion and violence. Raterio also castigated an insidious striving for lordships among the canons of Verona.[38] But he by no means rejected the God-given reality of lordship. He admonished lords to discipline servants in patience not anger, and servants to be faithfully submissive. His letters show him interacting with lord-prelates and lord-princes whom he addressed in the obsequious rhetoric of clerical humility; they make an interesting contrast with the unlordly classicising familiarity of Lupus of Ferrières' letters a century before.[39] A deferential discourse of submissive service, buoyed by an unbroken tradition of precedence in councils, spread through the clergy in the generations before the Investiture Conflict. The bishops and priests who presided over moral deportment amidst multiplying parishes and altars were nurtured in monastic and cathedral liturgies drawn from the psalms, gospels, and epistles in praise of the Lord-God, finding in the parables a conception of official lordship and stewardship.

These ideas, widely and deeply diffused, resonated with characteristic attitudes and procedures of petition and service. One enacted, virtually performed, one's submission in petitioning for a great lord's grace. 'Tearfully prostrate at our feet,' wrote Pope John XIII in 971, Count Borrell of Barcelona 'pleaded with us' to bestow metropolitan status on the bishop of Vic.[40] A generation

---

[37] *Ratherii Veronensis praeloquiorum libri VI*, ed. P. L. D. Reid (Turnhout 1984) iv.15 (119).

[38] *Die Briefe des Bischofs Rather von Verona*, ed. Fritz Weigle (Munich 1949) no. 16 (76–77).

[39] *Praeloquia* i.10.22–29 (22–31); *Briefe*, nos. 2–7, 16, 18, 19. Cf. Loup de Ferrières, *Correspondance*, ed. Léon Levillain, 2 vols. (Paris 1927).

[40] *Diplomatari de la catedral de Vic* . . . , ed. Eduard Junyent i Subirà (Vic 1980–96) no. 405.

later Count Bouchard of Vendôme laboured to persuade Abbot Maieul of Cluny to assume the task of reforming the monastic life at Saint-Maur. 'Again and again he prostrated himself at the feet of the holy man,' we are told, 'asking that the feeling [Latin: *affectus*] of his desire be accepted. Overcome by the many entreaties of the venerable count,' Maieul agreed so to serve. One petitioned for favour, for judgment; the lord-prelate or lord-prince acted or re-acted responsively yet passively. He had the power to act wilfully, but the ritual that renders this mode of official lordship visible gave expression to the rectitude of a quasi-biblical culture.[41]

Not all lordships were up to the dignity of this experience, as we shall see. But that hardly detracts from our estimate of its normative centrality in the ever more populous societies of the eleventh and twelfth centuries. A model of gracious lordship entailing humble or reverential submission probably influenced the construction of vassalic clienteles in the higher aristocracies, as it surely did that of reformed Benedictine congregations. 'The essence of the rite of homage,' wrote F.-L. Ganshof, 'was the self-surrender (*traditio*) of one person to another.'[42] Vassals must often have knelt before lords to do this, as we see in illuminations preserved in the 'Great Book of Fiefs' of Catalonia; but so did peasants in ways of which we know much less before the late twelfth century, when the phenomenon of servile homage, such as in the region of Toulouse, looks like a cultural borrowing from above.[43] Even so, one may suspect that gestural submission was related to the Christian experience of prayer whereby humility in dependence was promoted throughout society. This may have caused difficulty for self-promoting lords. For although the moralist Peter the Chanter (d. 1197) implied that postulants would kneel

[41] Eudes de Saint-Maur, *Vie de Bouchard le Vénérable* . . . , ed. Charles Bourel de la Roncière (Paris 1892) c. 3 (10). See generally Gerd Althoff, *Die Macht der Rituale. Symbolik und Herrschaft im Mittelalter* (Darmstadt 2003) ch. 3.

[42] *Feudalism* 74.

[43] Paul Ourliac, 'L'hommage servile dans la région toulousaine,' *Mélanges* . . . *Louis Halphen* (1951) 551–56.

before tyrants—that is, before anyone at all—, in general his re-flections on prayer are of interest for showing how the virtue of humility, so plausible before God and his official servants, might be diminished before persons of lesser estate as less exalted mo-tives came into play.[44]

This is why new and small lordships matter to the story of power in the (long) twelfth century, in the years from before 1100 to after 1200. They were a facet of demographic expansion and of a vast multiplication of castles, and they were surely more numer-ous than the new centers of command in growing communities. Considered as protectorates, they must have been acceptably functional, although we hear less about good lordships than about troublesome ones. What became of the public obligations of free tenants in new monastic patrimonies, such as at Le Mont-St-Michel or Cluny? We still know too little about the proliferation of be-nign lay lordships. José Angel García de Cortázar likens the ap-pearance of the word *senior* from Catalonia to Galicia to the spread of a blanket across the whole of Christian Spain.[45] The same might be said of Occitania after about 970. The word refers not only to militant or personal dominations but also to elders in familial or ascetic groupings and to delegates of royal power. The monks of Cluny and those in other Benedictine houses were *sen-iores*; in Poland, Duke Boleslaw I was said to have regarded his bishops as 'lords' (*domini*).[46] In Navarre and Aragon the king's retainers were coming to be called *sennores* from the later tenth century, a designation that before much longer became an appel-lative denoting elite status. Towards 1060 the assumption of place-names by knights in the Vendômois points to new claims of local lordship beyond those of landed domain.[47]

[44] *LFM* I, plates iv, ix, xi, xiii, xv–xvii; Peter the Chanter, as cited by Rich-ard C. Trexler, *The Christian at prayer . . .* (Binghamton 1987) 92, 47.

[45] *La sociedad rural en la España medieval* (Madrid 1988) 47.

[46] *Recueil des chartes de l'abbaye de Cluny . . .* , ed. Auguste Bernard, rev. Alex-andre Bruel, 6 vols. (Paris 1876–1903) IV, nos. 2993, 3124; *GpP* i.9 (48).

[47] Dominique Barthélemy, *La société dans le comté de Vendôme de l'an mil au XIVe siècle* (Paris 1993) 773. See also *GpP* i.9 (48); *Documentos reales*

Were people content under their lords; that is, under those of whom we have no record of complaint? Thinking first of the agrarian masses, was not theirs routinely a 'good deal': protection from the noxious forces of a fallen world in exchange for customary services and payments? No doubt many lords did their part; while for those luckier men who were armed or ordained, it seems even likelier that their fidelity secured the rewarding favours of lords with property or endowments to bestow. Such men had plenty of complaints—and plenty of conflicts—, but comparatively few about lordship have come down to us in writing. Bishop Robert Bloet's bitter recollection that King Henry I 'only praises those whom he wishes utterly to destroy' sounds what must have been a familiar theme in the courts of lord-princes.[48] We shall never know whether the vast silences of surviving archives conceal normal experiences of power at variance with those that *can* be documented. This problem will haunt my discussion. But two considerations argue from the outset against any temptation to suppose that what we shall never know about domination was any more benign than what is well recorded. First, there were far more peasants than knights in this turbulent post-Carolingian world: people, that is, capable of being exploited. Second, the prevailing model of lordship through the whole period of this book was what may be called a 'servile' model. Lordship was conceptually likened to the mastership of slaves, a wilful domination to be suffered in patience, not enjoyed. Pope Gregory VII sought to distance himself from a commonplace when in 1075, claiming that submission to papal lordship was that of 'sons,' not of 'slaves' (*servi*), he exhorted Duke Géza of Hungary to faithful obedience.'[49]

Navarro-Aragoneses hasta el año 1004, ed. Antonio Ubieto Arteta (Zaragoza 1986) nos. 54, 64, 65, 75.

[48] Quoted by R. W. Southern, 'King Henry I,' *Medieval humanism and other studies* (Oxford 1970) 225.

[49] *Register* ii.63 (I, 218). Also to the point, *Cartulaire de l'abbaye de Saint Jean de Sorde*, ed. Paul Raymond (Paris 1873) no. 58.

CONSTRAINT, VIOLENCE, AND DISRUPTION

What made this idea commonplace was that the human experience of power in the tenth and eleventh centuries was overwhelmingly that of lordships over growing populations of peasants and townsfolk with no more than their labour to offer. Growing lordships, that is, with little resemblance to the old ones of kings, princes, and bishops. The proliferation of castles, knights, and conditional tenures held by knights was in many parts of France and the Mediterranean an explosive phenomenon. What had begun in the garrisoning of old castles in regions like Provence and Lotharingia vulnerable to external attack was amplified wherever castle-building passed out of control of the old aristocracies. 'The original feature of the tenth century,' writes Robert Fossier, 'was the way in which Europe came to bristle with strengthened buildings . . .'[50]; and while the collaboration of archaeologists and historians in this field is still young, it is already clear that new fortifications multiplied in waves moving from south to north. In Provence more than a hundred new castles went up during the century beginning in 930, over 150 in the Massif Central in the *half*-century after 970.[51] In Anjou and Normandy the starting date for a less frantic proliferation is about 1030, in England and Saxony (in different ways) after 1066, in León after 1109. Every castle, if not quite every fief dependent on it, formed a lordship or (in the castle) a confusion of lordships. In Catalonia the castle's owner and tenant (*castlà*) were normally different persons, each with his rights.[52] Not all castellans were upstarts, yet even those exercising remnants of public jurisdiction were tempted, or constrained, to generalize their powers over dependents of whatever status. So to earlier transformations of rural habitat succeeded a militarizing of

[50] Robert Fossier, 'Rural economy and country life,' *NCMH* III (1999) 47.
[51] J.-P. Poly, *La Provence et la société féodale (879–1166)* . . . (Paris 1976) 126–29; Christian Lauranson-Rosaz, *L'Auvergne et ses marges . . . du VIIIe au XIe siècle* (Le Puy 1987) 371.
[52] Bonnassie, *Catalogne* II, 696–98, 751–52.

powers seized by growing numbers of mounted armed men, their
novel and precarious solidarities requiring them, notably in hilly
zones of incipient fortification but also around old urban castles
adjoining fertile rural patrimonies, to impose intimidating new
dominations on peasants and exchanges.

The impact of this phenomenon, which has been labelled 'feudal revolution,' should not be minimised. However problematic
the concept, it refers unambiguously to a demonstrably massive
multiplication of lay lords *and fiefs* (*feuda, feva*) in the years 950 to
1150. This was sooner or later to transform the map of power almost everywhere. It put thousands of peasants under the lordship
of untitled masters, many of whom tried to impose servile obligations on them; while for further thousands of other people on
older domains belonging to the old aristocracy and the church,
the proximity to penurious knights in threatening castles proved
to be a harsh liability. To be sure, not all was abrasive or violent
in this age of growth when external incursions subsided. A new
world of aristocratic public order was in the making, as we shall
see. But it would be quite as misleading to underestimate as to
exaggerate the problem of disorder, which was clearly perceived
as such by contemporaries. Armed men in or about castles, more
and more of both, and the temptation to constrain by force: these
were elemental realities of power in the age of lordship.

Let us look in on this history. Two problems of interpretation
have arisen: first, whether the violence of ambition and constraint
so often attested in written sources can be accepted as a plausible
representation of 'what happened'; and second, whether evidence
of 'violence' and 'disorder' in the tenth and eleventh centuries
points to disruptive historical change, or even to revolutionary
change.[53] It will be useful to keep both problems in mind, with-

[53] These and related issues were debated under the title 'The "feudal revolution"' in *Past & Present* nos. 142 (T. N. Bisson, 1994), 152 (D. Barthélemy, S. D.
White, 1996), and 155 (T. Reuter, C. Wickham, with Bisson's conclusion,
1997). The debate as such need not be renewed in a book on the twelfth century (however 'long'); what matters here is the evidence (however early) of

out confusing them. What seems beyond dispute is that people living in the heartlands of the old Frankish kingdom in the later tenth century spoke of violence, constraint, and disruption as palpable and deplorable scourges. 'While justice sleeps in the hearts of kings and princes,' wrote the chronicler of Mouzon abbey about conditions in the diocese of Reims in the 970s, 'strong men agitated against [the archbishop . . . and] they began, each as he could, to make himself greater. . . .'[54] In 987 the celebrated teacher and abbot Gerbert of Aurillac put it this way: 'It is rashness itself to be engaged in public affairs these days. For assuredly divine and human laws are there confused because of the enormous greed of excessively wicked men and only what lust and force extort like wild beasts is established as rightful.'[55]

In these testimonies the old order of power was defined by its breach. To be ousted from one's abbey, as Gerbert thought he had been, or from one's land was not simply violence; it was violation. The violators were represented as self-aggrandizing lords with the coercive power to impose their will. They were breaking laws, as was said explicitly of the 'tyrants' in Burgundy after the death of Richard the Justiciar in 921, evoking the absence of a 'king' or 'judge who wished in true justice to resist this wickedness of impious men.'[56] Appalled by the plunderings of Vikings, Saracens, and untitled rebels, chroniclers alleged injuries linked explicitly to order, remedy, or their failure. Their rhetorical excesses hardly

---

exploitative lordship and violence such as long persisted after the year 1000. While the critics have shown that violence in west Frankland was more continuous and more problematic than I first argued, I hold to my contention that the evidence of disruptive change from about 970 to 1030 is irrefutable. Larger issues about the nature, geography, and chronology of power in societal change (Reuter, Wickham) are addressed in chapters below, where the influence of lordship over people is stressed.

[54] *Chronique ou livre de fondation du monastère de Mouzon . . .* , ed., tr. Michel Bur (Paris 1989) i.7 (152).

[55] *Die Briefsammlung Gerberts von Reims*, ed. Fritz Weigle (Weimar 1966) no. 92.

[56] Adso, *Miracula SS. Waldeberti et Eustasii abbatum . . .* , c. 13, PL CXXXVII, 695.

obscure the point that the protections of royal order and justice were seen to be collapsing in Frankland.

What this meant for the human experience of power is less clear in the moralising denunciations. That is because the violent means of the perpetrators were commonplace, habitual: the resort to brute force taking forms already so pervasive in society as to seem of a piece with the old order. Warfare was violent by definition, not only in armed clashes or seizures but especially in requisitioning, maintenance of men and horses, and the wasting of hostile lands. In 945 King Louis IV's Norman allies attacked Duke Hugh in the Vermandois, ravaging crops, seizing or burning villages, violating churches; in 947 a knight pillaged the archiepiscopal vills of Reims from a new-built castle on the Marne.[57] Violence was likewise normal in the feud, a system of customary vengeance rooted in kin right that public authorities could only hope to channel so as to limit the dangers it held for the innocent. 'The mortal hatreds,' wrote Marc Bloch, 'which the ties of kinship engendered ranked undoubtedly among the principal causes of the general disorder.'[58] Customary vengeance had its own dynamic or rationale; unleashed it could only encourage destructive and afflictive impulses such as may often have given rise to disputes in the first place. But violence could take other forms: coercion, fiscal exaction, extortion, for instance. Not all such oppressive behaviour violated societal norms. It looks as if customs and even ransoms connected with Frankish military management were continuous with harsh but lawful practise, even though it was clear that the clergy and unarmed population needed protection against the army's excesses.

In any case, prevalent modes of violence—seizure, intimidation, physical assault, arson, forced exaction—were nurtured in the habits of war as well as of vengeance. People took notice when a band of Muslims captured Abbot Maieul of Cluny in 972 and held him for ransom; it was a dangerous lesson in a society

---

[57] Flodoard, *Annales*, 96, 106.
[58] *Société féodale* I, 199 (*Feudal society* 128).

full of poor knights.[59] And there is timeless poignancy in the depiction stitched into the Bayeux Tapestry of a woman and child escaping a house torched by hefty Norman retainers.[60] But the normal brutalities of war and vengeance could not of themselves have remodeled social order in Frankland or anywhere else. What mattered more was how violent practises came to affect relations of lordship and dependence. For in this respect violence became instrumental as well as customary.

From the tenth century come stories of armed laymen encroaching on peasant holdings so as to enlarge or create lordships. Good lords could surely be found to protect rustics clearing new fields; yet from a biography composed towards 940, in which Count Gerald of Aurillac was represented as saintly for caring for his tenants and not oppressing others, one infers that most lords in the Auvergne behaved otherwise.[61] Such lords had retinues of armed men sometimes, and already since the ninth century, described as 'violence' (*violentia*); men who shared in the lord's take and aspired to fiefs or lordships themselves. 'Violence' in this sense was associated with fortified space. At Conques in Rouergue the monks recalled how Count Raimond III (961–1010) had insisted against their will on fortifying the precipice overhead, declaring that his intention was 'to subjugate by his violence [*violentia sua*] and impose his lordship on those who neglected to render their due submission to him.'[62] It is fair to wonder whether these were *really* Count Raimond's words, for what lord-prince would have cared to admit that a castle had any purpose other than regional defence? Yet what lesser lord would have dared to speak so frankly? Lesser lay lordship without 'violence'—that is, without a castle—became anomalous in many regions of west

---

[59] Lucy M. Smith, *The early history of the monastery of Cluny* (London 1920) 134–36; Bloch, *Société féodale* i, 16 (*Feudal society* 7).

[60] *Bayeux Tapestry*, ed. Musset, scenes 46–47 (216–18). See plate 2.

[61] Odo, *Vita Geraldi*, i.8, *PL* CXXXIII, 647 (tr. Sitwell, 101).

[62] *Liber miraculorum sancte Fidis* ii.5, ed. Luca Robertini (Spoleto 1994) 165. For the concept of *violentia*, see also *La chronique de Nantes . . .* , ed. René Merlet (Paris 1896) c. 10 (29–30).

Frankland by the early eleventh century. Moreover, the old institution of lay advocacy was decisively influenced by the utility of fortified might. Monasteries with extended or isolated domains had little choice but to harness violence at a price. Already in Abbo's day (ca. 995) it could seem that advocates were acting violently like 'lords' (*domini*).[63]

The abrasive self-assertion of castellans and knights became virtually a method of lordship. Violence was nurtured in the economy and sociability of castles. Even when a master's domain sufficed for his upkeep, the support of his knights must have seemed chronically inadequate. The spectacle of prospering peasants was manifestly insufferable; the competition to exploit improving yet ever scarce lands a generator of violence as well as of entrepreneurial collaboration. And for those who would escape their burdens, it could be unsafe to mingle overmuch with peasants. Armed, pretentious, and poor, knights clung to their stoned-off spaces, talking of weapons and deeds, of horses, of strikes and demands; of stratagems and seizures more than of incomes or management. Ransom was a device of the dungeon from the start; notoriously exampled in the coups of Vikings and Saracens, it became a seigneurial as well as a military technique, readily convertible into protection-money.

The lordship of this sort of life was personal and affective: militant, aggressive, but unstable. It aspired to administrative character insofar as it claimed the powers of public command (*bannum*) long associated with Frankish castles. Yet since few of the new castles possessed such a pedigree, banal lordship(s) (*seigneurie banale*) typically fed on the capricious manipulation of powerless people. No evidence whatever survives to show that the castellan elite thought of their lordships in normative terms; they left no surveys of domain, no evidence of accountability. It looks as if their servants shared their predatory outlook, while the cavalcade enforced the abrasive immediacy of personal domination. In social terms this was a quest for status. Only

[63] Abbo of Fleury, *Collectio canonum* c. 2, *PL* cxxxix, 476–77.

lords could be noble, only nobles could govern: could exercise the powers of justice and command that created the presumption of nobility. But two difficulties arose to deflect this aspiration. The swelling masses of armed horsemen had all they could do to avoid being taken for peasants. They needed servants, dependents, suppliants; needed to dominate proprietorially. They needed to replicate the mastership of slaves. Were not unbeaten rustics as free as themselves? It was all the harder because peasants were likely to see through their pretences, an eventuality that may help to explain the beginnings of the Truce of God in Roussillon in the 1020s.[64] Moreover, knights shared with lords possessed of regalian powers a second liability: that judicial powers (other than domestic ones) were losing such sanction in public authority as they had ever had and were becoming occasions for exacting money. Nothing so clearly reveals the novel diffusion of affective lordship as the appearance of the 'customs' (*consuetudines*) in the later tenth century: that is, of demands sanctioned by precedent rather than by regalian concession. In the county of Vendôme around 1005 the customs both domanial and fiscal were pecuniary; there is no sign of courts generating revenues, only of 'vicariate' as a cluster of 'forfeitures' to remedy criminal transgressions. Not even the vestigial survival of public procedures could deflect the landslide towards lordship: towards an unpolitical mode of affective patrimonial power rooted in will instead of consensus. 'You are mine,' Count William V of Poitiers is said to have declared to Hugh lord of Lusignan, 'to do my will.'[65] Would either have said less to his peasants?

---

[64] Bonnassie, *Catalogne* II, 656–60; and for the problematic evidence of peasant unrest in Normandy about 996, Mathieu Arnoux, 'Classe agricole, pouvoir seigneurial et autorité ducale . . . la Normandie féodale d'après le témoignage des chroniqueurs . . . , *Le Moyen Age* XCVIII (1992) 45–55.

[65] The customal of Vendôme may be read in Bourel de la Roncière (Eudes) *Vie de Bouchard* 33–38; also 'Conventum inter Guillelmum Aquitanorum comes et Hugonem Chiliarchum,' ed. Jane Martindale, *EHR* LXXXIV (1969) 543: '. . . quod meus tu es ad facere meam voluntatem.'

In short, it seems beyond reasonable doubt that the multiplication of lay lords, knights, and castles was attended characteristically by coercive violence. Whatever allowance must be made for the self-serving exaggerations and misrepresentations by monks and litigants, an enormous mass of documentary evidence testifies to abrasive lordship during many generations down past 1150. Was this phenomenon, in its beginnings, a disruptive event, a break with the past? Even, as suggested above, a 'feudal revolution'? In light of recent discussion, it now seems possible to suggest better answers to these questions. If the term 'feudal' is employed metaphorically, and if it is defined to refer to fiefs, then the shift from an occasional resort to conditional tenures from public domains to the newly feudalized France of the later eleventh century was phenomenal in quite the same sense as industrialism in the eighteenth and nineteenth centuries. The new societies that resulted, in regions extending far beyond France, as well as a new order of power will be the subject of later chapters. But revolutions are made in their origins; they ought to be incited by subversives if not incendiaries; and the origins of this (quasi) revolution are suspiciously obscure. Perhaps also muddled, for the rise of militant castellan lordships in west Frankland was surely but one manifestation of a massive and ubiquitous implantation of lordships. Whatever its descriptive power (and there remains something to be said about this), the metaphor of revolution lacks explanatory cogency.

To argue against disruption, however, is a different matter. It is true that the experience of power—even that of failing power—was continuous in the tenth and eleventh centuries. But that truth, or truism, won't get us far. All history is continuous. More to the point is that evidence of violence is constant from the ninth century. Yet if we ask of the sources when and where contemporaries were conscious, or became conscious, of violence disruptive of social order, two suggestive responses emerge. First, the eloquent denunciations of disorder from Mouzon and from Gerbert, quoted above, appear to coincide not only with the dynastic crisis of 987, when the Carolingian Charles of Lorraine was thrust aside by the magnates in favour of Prince Hugh Capet,[66] but also—and more tellingly—with a cluster of other events and signs of trouble in late Carolingian Frankland. Second, in the wider historical perspectives available to monks living in the twelfth century, the generations beginning towards 900 in Italy came to be viewed as a disruptive watershed separating an old age of free property and protected patrimony from a new age of lordship and reconstruction.[67] These perspectives can be reconciled: for both, the millennial generation (or about 975–1025) becomes a critical moment when disorder can no longer be contained.

It was just then, in west Frankland, that old authorities and their scribes took new notice of seigneurial violence. The 'customs' make their appearance in records of all kinds after 990, surely because impositions on tenants by lords claiming rights of command were proliferating without sanction other than force or precedent. No doubt, the claims antedated our first records of customs, but the explosion of documentary allusions cannot in the circumstances be explained away. For at just the same time—the first series of programmatic councils dates from 989 to 1014—the peace of unarmed people and the clergy was placed under religious sanctions. First instituted in Poitou and Occitania, the 'Peace of God' was transparently a reaction against violence, perhaps even proof of a collective perception that violence was worsening. And at exactly the same time scribes less professional but more realistic than their elders were beginning to change their vocabulary of power: the word *miles* in an unclassical sense of horseman was introduced, together with a redolent quasi-vernacular equivalent: *caballarius*; while the word *dominus*, hitherto reserved for God, kings, and bishops, and lately applied to counts, was henceforth

---

[66] On which see generally *Le roi de France et son royaume autour de l'an mil*, ed. Michel Parisse, Xavier Barral i Altet (Paris 1992); Dominique Barthélemy, *L'an mil et la paix de Dieu . . .* (Paris 1999).

[67] Pierre Toubert, *Les structures du Latium medieval . . .* , 2 vols. (Rome 1973) I, 330–31; Menant, *Campagnes lombardes*, 409–16, 580–601, places the shift a few years later.

descriptive of masters of castles. Other words for seigneurial power became current: *potestas, dominium, mandamentum* (power, lordship, command). The new vocabulary of lordship was by no means always pejorative, yet at exactly the same time we begin to hear of 'bad customs' (*malae consuetudines*). Denounced in the Council of Le Puy about 994, they figure commonly thereafter in the South, then after 1000 in Champagne, Picardy, and the Mâconnais. All these concurrent events point to the knight as a new subject of anxiety. The earliest extant written oaths to keep the peace, such as were administered in councils, and famously that of Beauvais (ca. 1023), spell out in detail the whole programme of seigneurial violence to be renounced. In graphic language the knight is made to promise not to break into sanctuaries on excuse of protection, not to burn or destroy houses without good reason, and not to destroy mills or seize the grain in them.[68]

Nor is this all. The multiplying signs of newly assertive power and of reaction against it corresponded to apprehensions about the legitimacy of obligations amounting to a crisis of fidelity. Were commended men to be entrusted with conditional tenures no longer sanctioned in public order? Observers of regnal and ecclesiastical affairs in north Frankland became obsessed with faith (*fides*), fidelity, and treachery towards 990. The letters of Gerbert are filled with anguish about his own loyalty and the bad faith of others.[69] His protégé Richer of Reims recounted recent Frankish history as an incessant series of sordid treacheries, some of them his own embellishments on the sober narrations of his predecessor Flodoard.[70] Prelates whose fidelity was crucial to the

[68] Oath printed by Christian Pfister, *Etudes sur le règne de Robert le Pieux* (*996–1031*) (Paris 1885), pp. lx–lxi. See generally Lemarignier, 'Dislocation du "*pagus*"'; Duby, *Trois ordres* 183–205 (*Three orders*, ch. 13); J.-P. Poly, Eric Bournazel, *La mutation féodale* . . . , 3d ed. (Paris 2004; tr. Caroline Higgitt, *The feudal transformation* . . . [NY 1990]) chs. 1–5.

[69] *Briefsammlung Gerberts*, nos. 1, 11, 16, 20, 22, 26, 27, 31, 54, 79, 89, 91, 117, 120, 122, 125, 130, 163, 185, 187; JL 3914.

[70] Cf. Richer, *Histoire* i.64 (I, 122), with Flodoard, *Annales* 53; Richer ii.5 (I, 132–34) with Flodoard 64; but see both narratives passim.

promotion to kingship of Hugh Capet were not deaf to charges of dynastic treachery; they were horrified by the notorious betrayals, both in 991, of Melun castle to Odo of Blois and of the Carolingian Charles of Lorraine by Bishop Adalbero of Laon. According to Richer the recaptured garrison of Melun claimed they were not traitors to the king but 'faithful men' (*fideles*) of their lord-castellan. For his part Count Odo was represented as pleading that he too was no traitor, having quarreled not with the king but with a 'fellow knight' (meaning the king's castellan in Melun).[71] Here the tension between old public order and the new vassalic regime flares into visible conflict: one proof, if needed, that contemporaries experienced the dilemma. Steeped in Carolingian theocratic ideology, Richer may have exaggerated the distinction between fidelities public and personal. What cannot be doubted is that permissible options for solemnly commended men at all levels of society were coming under discussion in north Frankland at the end of the tenth century. The accession of the great duke Hugh, with his own congeries of castles and vassals, could only have encouraged a reshuffling of lesser fidelities and have accentuated the problem of prior or multiple allegiances, a problem worsened by growing temptations to prefer new benefices to old lordships.

That such things were indeed happening is suggested by even more pointed evidence, in the form of three spectacular testimonies: the chapter on 'the king's fidelity' in Abbo of Fleury's *Canons*, the famous letter about fidelity written by Fulbert of Chartres to Duke William V of Aquitaine around 1020, and the *Agreement* (*Conventus*) of about the same time between the same prince William and the castellan of Lusignan. Abbo speaks (in the mid-990s) of the election of kings as a rightful means of securing the 'concord of the whole kingdom,' then urges the right of the 'ordained king' to require 'faith by oath [sworn] to himself, so that discord may not be generated in any parts of his realm,' and goes on to

[71] Richer iv.47,78,80 (II, 216–18, 274–78); Ferdinand Lot, *Etudes sur le règne de Hugues Capet et la fin du Xe siècle* (Paris 1903) 159–63.

warn of the terrors in store for the perfidious ones who fail to keep faith to kings. Even this monk rhetorically evoking the old order seems caught up in current anxieties about fidelity. His chapter helps us to understand Gerbert's testimony that Hugh Capet made some special effort to secure professions of fidelity from prelates and princes.[72] It was a matter of public solidarity.

With Bishop Fulbert we see more concretely how benefices and rewards were muddying the waters of good faith. A 'faithful man,' he wrote (at Duke William's request), must not only 'abstain from wrong [but also] do what is good' if he is to 'deserve his housement [*casamentum*].' This term, while evidently here synonymous with 'benefice,' suggests that Fulbert had knights as well as magnates in mind. It is the word he had applied to the holdings of his subvassal knights at Vendôme and Chartres in 1008, in letters that mark the earliest known attempt by a lord to define the substance of (lesser) knightly fidelity.[73] By 1020 Fulbert was known for his concerned authority in such matters, and we can see from the intriguing details of lordship, vassalage, infidelity, and violence in Aquitaine that fill the *Agreement* what it was that William (here count in Poitou) needed from the bishop. His problem was that Hugh Lord of Lusignan could not be content with a fidelity of submission that left the count free to alter agreements bearing on Hugh's interest without consulting him. When Hugh did the same in reverse, as if his armed and ambitious clientele entitled him to an equal claim to his lord-count's good faith, there was trouble: vengeful seizures and devastations over alleged violations of good faith and sworn commitments relating to the control or inheritance of castles and lordships. All that is left of public order here is the tenacious recognition that complaints should be pleaded openly and procedurally; the *Agreement* has virtually the content of the written charges once required to ini-

---

[72] Abbo, *Canones* iv (PL cxxxix, 478); *Briefsammlung Gerberts*, nos. 107, 112.

[73] *The letters and poems of Fulbert of Chartres*, ed. Frederick Behrends (Oxford 1976) nos. 51, 9, 10.

tiate judicial proceedings in southern lands. The count-duke, for his part, although he retains something of his public prestige, can no longer command officially, can only negotiate with lesser fortified lords on the basis of personal and mutual fidelity of which the rewards, obligations, and rules are still being worked out.[74]

❖

OUR SENSE of a millennial crisis of power in west Frankland—the first of a series of societal crises in the eleventh and twelfth centuries—comes from those who lived through it. Were others elsewhere unaffected? Certainly the Frankish dynastic crisis bore unpleasantly on the Hispanic March, where the failure of their king to defend Barcelona when the Muslims pillaged it in 985 would be remembered as a pivotal event, and where for some years after 987 scribes were unsure who was king. But the violence of multiplying knights and castles was deferred in this region for another generation. The reason for this has important implications for our grasp of the millennial crisis in Frankland, for it has lately been shown that the survival of public justice in the county of Barcelona was far superior to that in northern lands.[75] The disruption, when it came, was of unparalleled violence.

In Italy by that time (ca. 1050), a more protracted crisis of societal change, unaffected by dynastic change, was still in course.

[74] 'Conventum,' *EHR* LXXXIV, 541–48; newly ed. and tr. George Beech, Yves Chauvin, Georges Pon, *Le conventum (vers 1030): un précurseur aquitain des premières épopées* (Geneva 1995). (In BnF MS latin 5927, 265–80 I find no warrant for the reading 'conuentum,' which looks to me like an accusative when it appears. The word is *conventus* in Gerbert's letters, *Briefsammlung*, index, 273.) See also Georges Duby, *Le moyen âge de Hugues Capet à Jeanne d'Arc 987–1460* (Paris 1987) 108–10. Comparable records in procedural form are known from the Midi, *HL* V, 496–502; Bonnassie, *Catalogne* II, 615, 638.

[75] Pierre Bonnassie, 'Sur la genèse de la féodalité catalane: nouvelles approches,' *Il feudalesimo nell'alto medioevo* . . . , 2 vols. (Spoleto 2000) II, 569–606.

What could be seen there with retrospective clarity was that re-settlement around castles (*incastellamento*, in modern usage) begin-ning in the tenth century had put an end to the freedoms of an old regime of protected rural property. A newly militant lordship—was this not what Bishop Raterio had noticed?—was replicated on church lands by the early eleventh century. The militarizing of protection, in lay and clerical patrimonies alike, was, here as in Frankland, at once a 'feudal' and an abrasive pro-cess. Here again it has been called a 'feudal revolution,' and not least because the new regime achieved precocious maturity in much of Italy. Dependency became a privileged status already in 1037, when the knights secured the Emperor Conrad's sanction for the inheritance of benefices conferred from 'public [i.e., im-perial] property' by their lords.[76]

This statute is rightly held to mark the legal recognition of a feudal regime. The first such statute in Europe, it illustrates not simply the progress of elite dependency in quest of status, but also the realization of a fiscal-beneficial feudalism such as had col-lapsed in the demise of Frankish royal power. That it was by no means artificial in Italy is shown by the persistence of pleas (*plac-ita*) of old public order, recorded hearings in which conditional tenures were easily assimilated to property protected by law. Yet by 1100 or soon thereafter the discrepancies of this convergence were creating a new jurisprudence of fiefs.[77]

Even in Italy the regime of fiefs has for us only the importance of proving the diffusion of lordship and dependence. The latter had sprung originally from concessions of fiscal rights by earlier kings, the result of which was to render bishops and abbots vul-nerable competitors for the endowed services of armed men. In

---

[76] *CCr* I, no. 168. See generally Toubert, *Latium* I, 330–38; Aldo A. Settia, *Castelli e villaggi nell'Italia padana: popolamento, potere e sicurezza fra IX e XIII secolo* (Naples 1984) chs. 3–8; Menant, *Campagnes lombardes* 580–671.

[77] *I placiti del 'Regnum Italiae,'* ed. Cesare Manaresi, 5 vols. (Rome 1953–60) IV, V; *UrkMat* nos. 55–56 (1099–1100), with many other citations of 'fiefs' and 'benefices'; Menant 594–601; Philip Jones, *The Italian city-state . . .* (Oxford 1997) 120–30; and compare Reynolds, *Fiefs and vassals* 199–240.

Milan the archbishop and the urban magnates (*capitanei*) came to share patrimonial powers formed from the debris of old comital rights. Spiritual lordship cannot have been foremost for such prelates, as appears from the case of Asti, where in 1041 the episcopal patrimony included thirty-seven castles.[78] That the growth of population and wealth created temptations to impose customs by force is evident from records of all sorts. How this worked in the countrysides can be glimpsed from a remarkable 'inventory of malice' by which the canons of Reggio alleged, about 1040, the defection of their provost

> against Bishop Teuzo's will to the power of Gandulf's sons. And so they might retain him securely against the bishop, he made over to them the castle and domains of Rivalta against the will of the bishop and canons. From that day on their persecutions did not cease,

and the canons found themselves excluded from their own domain. In the messy sequel, various individuals forcibly imposed on tenants, seized houses, and the like. In this case an existing lordship was subverted by the infidelity of a church's servant and worsened by others wanting their pieces of it.[79]

Two other cases bring us closer to the experience of lordship in the making. Around 1090–92 the people of the Valdiserchio near Pisa sought relief from an array of 'bad customs' by enlisting the consuls, bishop, and other notables of Pisa in their defence against some *longubardi*—these were local knights—who were seeking to dominate them. Much the same thing had happened at Casciavola many years before, as people there later (ca. 1100) complained to the church and consuls of Pisa, in a further memorial of altogether singular lucidity and character. What it says is that they had been free men with their own properties, subject to the castellan knights

[78] Giovanni Tabacco, *The struggle for power in medieval Italy. Structures of political rule*, tr. Rosalind Brown Jensen (Cambridge 1989) 161.

[79] Printed in Bruno Andreolli, Massimo Montanari, *L'azienda curtense in Italia . . .* (Bologna 1983) 205–12.

at San Casciano only for their holdings in the castle and for guard-duty. After a lurch for the worse, when these dues were raised, the villagers thought they were off the hook when the castle was destroyed, only to become victims of the knights, now deprived, once again. So they appealed to the Countess Beatrice (that means before 1076), won a favourable settlement, only to have their tormentors lapse into a fully oppressive new domination, assaulting their houses and wives and seizing crops and property. Suspect though it may be for tendentious exaggeration, this memorial preserves an authentic record of contemporary sentiment about a critical contingency of power: the relation between old order and new lordship. 'Afterwards,' it concluded, 'when all power lost effect, and justice died and perished in our land, then they began to do all manner of evils to us, as if [they were] pagans or Saracens.' Here the presumption that pretentious men in quest of lordship were virtually infidels in their midst is explicit. It was an analogy with urgent meaning even in the heartland of Christendom.[80]

The proliferation of coercive (or 'banal') lay lordships was a phenomenon sooner or later attested widely in Europe; an experience of power more or less disruptive depending on local circumstances, pointing to societal transformations, diversely related and phased, by the twelfth century. If this is not quite the whole story of power by then, it is arguably the focal plot that explains what Cardinal Humbert and Pope Paschal were thinking in the epigraphic texts quoted above. This plot, it should be added, is inextricably bound to the craving for nobility that accompanied the rise of lordship. It took lord-princes secure in their allies and castles to preserve some measure of public order, not because of a rebellious disposition resentful of central authority, but because castellans and vicars everywhere were seeking to magnify their lordships at the expense of their offices. Some of the crises that

---

[80] Ruggiero D'Amico, 'Note su alcuni rapporti tra città e campagna nel contado di Pisa . . . ,' *Bollettino storico pisano* XXXIX (1970) 28–29; Wickham, *Community and clientele* 221.

resulted will be examined in other contexts in later chapters. What matters here is to recognize the tendency of events and conjunctures, of which the sketch that follows may be read as a virtual chronology of power.[81]

The most conspicuous, brutally disruptive, and conceptually unproblematic of these transformations took place during the years 1020 to 1060 in the east Pyrenean lands soon thereafter to be known as Catalonia. The failure of the counts of Barcelona to divert the oppressive force of multiplying castellans and knights against the Muslims brought on a terrifying collapse of public justice and the imposition of a new order of coercive lordship over an intimidated peasantry. Literally a 'land of castles'—its very name may be derived from the vernacular *castlà*, meaning master of a castle—Catalonia was fortunate in the survival of enough public strongholds in the count's control to stave off absolute anarchy. The coincidence of events towards 1060, when Count Ramon Berenguer I (1035–76) restored order, is of great comparative interest. This prince's success (in the end) matched that of Duke William (1035–87) in Normandy and probably exceeded that of Duke Kazimierz I (1034–58) in Poland, both of whom overcame dangerous subversions of public order in the same years as the troubles in Barcelona. In Normandy the viscounts came close to imposing a new regime of banal lordships. And in Poland what looks like a lapse of predatory leadership, quite as in the county of Barcelona, led in the 1030s to insurrection in the castles and to a proliferation of new lordships. Known to us only from a chronicle of the early twelfth century, the Polish crisis entailed a reaction against Christianity, then newly imposed, but the violence of men seeking power at the expense of old order is transparent.[82]

---

[81] See the pioneering essay by Pierre Bonnassie, 'From the Rhône to Galicia: origins and modalities of the feudal order' (1980), reprinted in *From slavery to feudalism in south-western Europe*, tr. Jean Birrell (Cambridge 1991) ch. 3.

[82] Bonnassie, *Catalogne* i; D. C. Douglas, *William the Conqueror. The Norman impact upon England* (London 1964) chs. 3, 4; *GpP* i.19 (78–82).

The moment when rulers in the Pyrenees restored princely order—it was around 1060—proved to be the eve of disruptions elsewhere. They were often linked to dynastic crisis, as in Anjou (1060–67) and Flanders (1070–71). These were lands where the spread of violent customs in multiplying castellanies was not new, and where the successions of capable counts put an end to societal disorder. What might be obscured in the unrevealed complexities of such successions may be seen in two further situations of these very years. In England the death of Edward the Confessor (1042–66) brought on a disputed succession and the Norman Conquest; while in Navarre a rarely inept king so totally lost touch with the aristocracy that they murdered him in 1076.[83]

In both these cases new and typically militant lordships multiplied. Old monastic patrimonies in England, notably at Abingdon and Ely, were roughly treated by King William's barons and knights, especially after 1070, when the lord-king himself was often disinclined to restrain their violence. We know this from twelfth-century memorials comparable to those in Italy, likewise making allusion to patrimonies disrupted during the age of Viking invasions but chiefly lamenting the years following the conquest of 1066–67, when Norman lordships sprouted widely.[84] In Navarre the crisis of 1072 masked structural changes already under way and somewhat resembling those in post-Conquest England. Where the elite 'commands' (*tenencias, honores*) had been held by magnates distinctly from the villages (*villae*), the king's control of the latter was now mostly lost, so that peasant communities came under the new lordship of multiplying knights who imposed new customs of command and demand, much as had happened in Italy and Catalonia.

[83] Douglas, *William the Conqueror*, chs. 7, 8; Larrea, *Navarre*, chs. 9, 10; and for Anjou and Flanders, see below, pp. 129–54.

[84] See, e.g., Edward Miller, *The abbey & bishopric of Ely* . . . (Cambridge 1951) 65–74; and Jennifer Ann Paxton, 'Chronicle and community in twelfth-century England,' forthcoming.

In Germany, perhaps the most stable old monarchy down to mid-century, the death of Henry III (1039–56) was a signal for unrest in the aristocracy that ripened into partisan resistance and conflict in the 1070s. Fears for the integral inheritance of great patrimonies were perhaps the major cause of trouble, itself a sign of self-serving insistence on gainful lordship as distinct from service. Neither the king's castellans pressing towards Saxony nor those of the rebels could restrain the knights seeking to maintain themselves or impose on peasants. Castles, castellans, and knights multiplied widely in German lands, obliging subsequent lord-kings to exploit their own patrimonial domains in order to re-build royal power.[85]

An even better example of disrupted dynastic kingship is to be found in Spain. The old monarchy in León held firm past 1100, its cohesion of elite lordships and the church sustained by the dangers and profits of the Moorish frontier. But when Al-fonso VI died in 1109, this balance of forces collapsed, plunging the northwest peninsula into a massive crisis of power. Queen Urraca (1109–26) and her wayward husband Alfonso I of Ara-gon (1104–34), once their incompatibility was recognized, be-came magnets for the disaffected and ambitious, in whose sworn followings sprouted dependencies and commitments of all sorts. Including pretentious ones, for as we shall see the people at Sa-hagún were prepared to submit to anyone who would help them. In so nearly anarchic a predicament there could be little hope that the multiplied professions of vassalage, fidelity, or ser-vice would last; yet of all the disruptive factories of lordship here surveyed, none was so demonstrably productive of feudal lordship and dependence as this one. As conditional tenures proliferated, often from seizures of clerical property, the horri-fied bishops assembled at Burgos in 1117 made explicitly clear

---

[85] Stefan Weinfurter, *Herrschaft und Reich der Salier* . . . (Sigmaringen 1991; tr. Barbara M. Bowlus as *The Salian century* . . . [Philadelphia 1999]) chs. 7, 8. For more on this see below, pp. 213–29.

that they were worried about fiefs: about the '*feodum*, which in Spain they call *prestimonium*.'[86]

What happened in England was quite different. There the Conqueror, having been severely tested in his homeland in the 1040s, had imposed a lord-kingship based not only on baronies held in terms of homage and fidelity but also on the recognition of delegated public powers in local communities. King Henry I (1100–35) presided with consummate skill over a wealthy land dominated by dependents in competition for his patronage. Yet here once again dynastic crisis intervened with disruptive repercussions, casting a bright light on the human liabilities of incipient lesser lordship. Henry's attempt to secure the succession for his daughter Matilda by imposing sworn engagements on his barons ran into deep trouble once the dynastic claim of his nephew Stephen was recognized. The conflict that followed was not unlike that in Spain a generation before. Sworn factions lost control of knights, who could only live off the customary tenants of churches and rival lay lords; new lordships, some of them newly fortified, sprang up like mushrooms.

> When the traitors saw that he [Stephen] was a mild man, and gentle and good, and did no justice, then they perpetrated all manner of horrors. They had done him homage and sworn oaths, but they kept no pledge. . . . For every great man built his castles and held them against him [the king], and filled the land full of castles. They afflicted the wretched people of the country with castle-works [forced labour for building]; and when the castles were built, they filled them with devils and wicked men . . . [they seized, ransomed, imprisoned, tortured] . . . I know not how . . . to tell of all the atrocities nor all the cruelties which they inflicted upon wretched people in this land, and that lasted the nineteen

---

[86] *CAS* c. 19 (22); 'Concilio nacional de Burgos (18 febrero 1117),' ed. Fidel Fita, *BRAH* XLVIII (1906) 394–98; and see generally Bernard F. Reilly, *The kingdom of León-Castilla under King Alfonso VI (1065–1109)* (Princeton 1988). For more on this, see below, pp. 243–59.

winters that Stephen was king, and always it was worse and worse. They levied taxes on the villages every so often, and called it 'tenserie' [protection-money] . . . [seizures, burning, pillage] . . . the land was all ruined by such doings. And they said openly that Christ was asleep with His saints.[87]

So wrote a monk of Peterborough, in a celebrated account that is commonly discounted as self-serving hyperbole. It is, indeed, something like that. But it is, even so, an impressively informative record that has perhaps been less than fully expounded. As a witness to violence it does not stand alone, whether in England at this time, or more generally in twelfth-century Europe. Moreover, what it says about seizures, pillage, intimidation, and protection-money is not only concretely descriptive, categorically if not quantitatively plausible; it is perfectly consistent with other records. For the moment, let one more example serve. We know of a hardworking monastic steward who towards 1105 cleared new land in the Beauce, not far from Paris, for eighty tenants, only to attract 'wicked men,' who

seeing the place prospering, began to impose themselves and make demands. Some of them were menacingly exacting fodder, others a payment in fowl, others protection-money [*tutamentum*], which people call *tensamentum*.[88]

One has only to remember that from 1137 England was swarming with poor knights from across the Channel to recognize that what England then suffered was, among other things, the same phenomenon of incipient coercive lordship as had developed in Frankland. This was clear enough to contemporaries to be summed up in an identical concept of constraint: *tenserie* (in spoken French) and (the clerical) *tensamentum*. In the context of disruptive impulses, the crisis of Stephen's reign was the

[87] *The Peterborough chronicle 1070–1154*, ed. Cecily Clark, 2d ed. (Oxford 1970) 55–57 (*anno* 1137; tr. *EHD* II[2] 210–11, from which I depart slightly); and for more on this, see pp. 269–78, below.

[88] *La chronique de Morigny*, ed. Léon Mirot, 2d ed. (Paris 1912) i.2 (5–6).

last of its kind in a series dating back to the tenth century, though it was by no means the last crisis of power in the twelfth century. Lordships, including feudal-vassalic ones, had multiplied in England since the Conquest, and the permissive disorder under Stephen, when new lordship typically entailed dispossession, was a reaction against the heavy-fisted lordly rectitude of Henry I, a desperate reaction fated soon to be undone.

Nevertheless, the 'feudal revolution,' considered strictly as the multiplication of fiefs, knights, castles, and lordships of constraint, had had a long run. Considered in its meaning for the human experience of power, there is more to be said about it in subsequent chapters. Considered in relation to dynastic crises, it is important to recognize that the disorders were not limited to the imposition of lordship. Much of the violence deplored in Stephen's England was that of ill controlled armies, a phenomenon that would recur in weakly dominated regions of greater France in the later twelfth century. But the craving for lordship by men of new social strata as license to demand lay at the heart of all this. In at least two cases, those of Poland in the 1030s and León-Galicia in the 1110s, we hear of uprisings against constituted lords, perhaps another sign of resentments against allegedly harsh new customs. Violence and constraint had become so normal by the twelfth century as to provoke little repercussion, although they continued to be denounced as wrongful and disruptive where, as in the fiscal domains of Barcelona towards 1150, they could be represented as novel. Abbot Peter of Cluny, writing around 1127, thought it a matter of common knowledge that lay lords dominated their peasant men and women harshly, not content with customary renders but demanding ever more, to the point of pillaging them.[89]

With the growth and furtherance of new patrimonies and with the proliferation of feudal and vassalic dependencies in most of the societies so far mentioned, lordship had achieved a new potential for bypassing official outlets of action. It was—and this

---

[89] *LPV* I, no. 28 (86); and see the records cited and studied in *TV.*

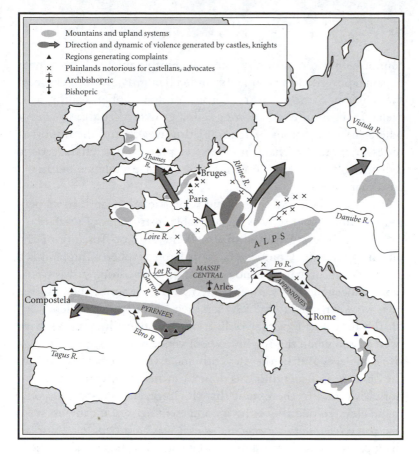

Legend (within map):

- Mountains and upland systems
- Direction and dynamic of violence generated by castles, knights
- ▲ Regions generating complaints
- × Plainlands notorious for castellans, advocates
- ✝ Archbishopric
- ✝ Bishopric

Map labels: Vistula R.; Thames R.; ✝Bruges; Rhine R.; ✝Paris; Danube R.; Loire R.; ALPS; MASSIF CENTRAL; Lot R.; Po R.; Garonne R.; ✝Arles; APPENNINES; Compostela; PYRENEES; Ebro R.; ✝Rome; Tagus R.

1. 'FEUDAL REVOLUTION': HEARTLANDS AND DIFFUSION

This map is as problematic as the concept it illustrates. All that we know, from massive evidence, is that castles beyond princely control sprang up in clusters, especially in hilly regions, associated with multiplied knights and violence during many generations from the ninth century on. While the geography lends itself to a theory of diffusion, perhaps illustrated by the cases of Saxony and England, it also suggests that the phenomenon was as much seismic as revolutionary. It may perhaps be likened to eruptions along fault lines of weakened princely power such as in Burgundy and upland Catalonia. Coincident with the multiplication of fiefs, it nearly corresponds in territorial extent to zones of Carolingian power in the ninth century.

The map attempts, very schematically, to indicate the principal upland and mountainous terrains in relation to river systems, and to suggest that oppressive lordship must often have sprung from relatively new castles in the uplands. Most schematic is the impression that the exploitative lordship associated with advocacies, especially in regions like Flanders and Lotharingia possessed of large ecclesiastical estates, perhaps also in Lombardy and Bavaria, was part of the same phenomenon.

cannot be put too strongly—not inherently vicious. Everywhere personal powers over people expanded benignly, most likely so in the hands of princes, vicars, barons, bishops, abbots, and priors, fueled by economic and demographic growth. Yet almost everywhere the temptations of accumulating wealth and the opportunities afforded by changing habitats promoted a characteristic dynamic of self-promotion in which coercive violence became a customary means.

It is not difficult to understand why. Violence, both in its personnel and its practise, was an adaptable instrument of warfare, so that the pillage we read about in Pomerania or Tuscany or the pilgrims' roads to Compostela or in King Stephen's England is a phenomenon of armed bands as well as of lordship. It was peculiarly associated with status. There had been a time when all free men were expected to fight, when their freedom indeed depended on the fulfillment of that obligation; and there may never have been a time when the imperatives of vengeance became an exclusive privilege. But in the eleventh and twelfth centuries most of the fighting and coercing was done by armed men who arrived on horseback, and to the extent that the freedom to fight and command elevated one above the incompetent masses, it came to seem that force (*violentia* in its special sense) was an attribute of human distinction. Two circumstances contributed to this. The freedom of elite families to fight and to hunt, derived ultimately from their association with or descent from kings, became an enviable emblem of nobility, while a vastly multiplied class of fighting men struggling to achieve the freedom of nobility, seized on its privileged culture of violence as its means. This is why knights, advocates, and bailiffs were disposed to impose afflictively on peasants, to enforce the latters' unfreedom by flaunting their own superiority. The knighthood stigmatized by the early councils of peace looks like a disreputable culture of violence in quest of elusive status, a culture that would in time be co-opted by the church in a refurbished ideology of war in service of Christ. And it was the remodeled knighthood of Christ that induced the higher aristocracy to latch on to the new culture of arms and horsemanship whereby knighthood became ritually central to nobility in the twelfth century.[90]

If lordship was essential to this newly respectable knighthood, it remained problematic for those who, far into the twelfth century, imposed themselves forcibly on peasants, whether their own or others.' Yet the very expressions of disapproval bear witness to the self-justifying persistence of oppressive lordship. To the famous remark by Peter the Venerable, quoted above, may be counterposed the negatively moralised image preserved in the instructions to his son by a repentant Norman knight as he lay dying in 1118:

> Show your men the faith you owe them and dominate them not as a tyrant but as a kind patron. . . . Do not plunder. . . . Care for what is rightfully yours, do not seize the property of others by violence, . . . Honor God's servants . . . Never try to deprive them of their possessions and revenues, nor allow your men to do violence to them.[91]

This looks like good advice, of a sort that must often have been followed. For why, we may ask, should lords of any sort, even the worst, have wished to constrain or abuse peasants who were their productive patrimony? The response must be that penitential counsel should not be confused with economic calculation, of which there is hardly more evidence for the knightly elite in the twelfth century than in the millennial generation. What most lesser men with weapons craved was status, association with the noble free, and this meant putting distance between themselves and peasant tenants. Yet it seems obvious that constraint beyond some tolerable maximum was no way to create lasting lordships, and altogether likely that castellans and advocates learned early to mitigate their demands. Perhaps as a rule they had little to lose in doing so, for in addition to 'bad' or 'new customs,' first mentioned in west Frankland about 990 and attested widely thereafter

---

[90] See Jean Flori, *L'essor de la chevalerie, XIe–XIIe siècles* (Geneva 1986); Crouch, *Birth of nobility*, chs. 2–6.

[91] OV v.19 (III, 194).

past 1150, we begin to hear of new levies, usually called 'tallage' (*tallia, tolta, questa*, etc.), on peasants by the mid-eleventh century. These taxes were understood to be arbitrary by definition; they may often have begun as 'bad customs'; and it must have been in everyone's interest to replace wilfulness with regularity.[92] The commuted tallage will have its place in later chapters; what matters here is that bad customs and tallage are yet another sign of the massive diffusion of lordship everywhere in Europe.

And not only of bad lordship. But in order to understand how power was experienced in the twelfth century, we have to come to terms with the evidence of plunder, consort with pillagers, violent seizures and dispossessions, and depredations of church lands and property, for this is what clerical writers and notaries evoke or echo in many parts of Europe. Historians are, not unreasonably, sceptical of such evidence. It was in the interest of prelates and monks to complain of exactions by lay lords; and since peasants, eager to represent any uncustomary demand as violent, sought to fix obligations in growing economies, a structural tension worked so as to justify seigneurial pressure.[93]

Yet to reject such evidence seems not merely heartless but mistaken. The violence alleged, although sometimes exaggerated, was seldom invented. And what is said about it is reinforced in other ways. People knew of oppressive lords in the twelfth century, knew who they were; they named them—Robert of Bellême

---

[92] Despite Carl Stephenson, 'The origin and nature of the *taille*,' *RBPH* v (1926) 801–70 (reprinted 1954), the early history of this levy remains obscure. Stephenson, perhaps rightly, saw no special significance in the first allusions *ipso nomine* to *tallia*, which he associated with other exactions; but a provisional study of the earliest allusions to *tallia, quista, tolta* (etc.) gives me pause. Cf. *CSPCh* II, 340; and see also Marc Bloch, *Les caractères originaux de l'histoire rurale française*, new ed., 2 vols. (Paris 1955–56) I, 85–86 (tr. Janet Sondheimer, *French rural history* . . . [Berkeley 1966] 82–83); and Georges Duby, *L'économie rurale et la vie des campagnes dans l'Occident médiéval*, 2 vols. (Paris 1962) II, 453–54 (tr. Cynthia Postan, *Rural economy and country life* . . . [London 1968] 225).

[93] Cf., e.g., Barthélemy, *Chevaliers et miracles*; Constance Bouchard, *'Strong of body, brave and noble': chivalry and society in medieval France* (Ithaca, NY, 1998).

and Arnau de Perella, amongst many others—and their deeds in detail. Theirs is a real place in the history of power. The learned John of Salisbury had such men in mind when he wrote of tyranny as wilful not lawful behaviour; moreover, by unhappy coincidence he was himself to witness the spoliation of Archbishop Thomas Becket's property by the knights who murdered him in Canterbury cathedral in 1170.[94] The lord-ruler's claim to confiscate from deceased prelates had become an arbitrary custom of lordship, resented and denounced everywhere in Christian Europe in the twelfth century. Wilfully exploitative lordship, including that addicted to violence, became an institution even as it was discredited. It drew ideological support from the old order it pervaded insofar as it could be likened to slave lordship at a time when agrarian slavery had disappeared from western Europe. Had not the Apostle admonished servants (*servi*) to submit to lords in all fear, 'and not only to the good and gentle but also to the perverse ones'? Where was the line to be drawn between the perversity acceptable to the clergy in the name of order and that they denounced in the name of peace? Beset by tenant unrest at Laon, local lords must have learned with gratitude of the archbishop's sermon on the Petrine text in 1112, dwelling as it did on the sufferance of 'hard and greedy' masters; perhaps not accidentally one of these lords, Thomas de Marle, carried on a singularly ferocious reign of rural terror in the next few years.[95] Such ideas were widely held in these generations when new forms of servility were becoming customary. In bitterly ironic hyperbole King Henry IV denounced Pope Gregory VII for having 'trod under

[94] *Policr.* iv.1 (I, 235); *The letters of John of Salisbury*, ed. and tr. W. J. Millor *et al.*, 2 vols. (Oxford 1979, 1976) II, no. 305; and citations below, p. 281.

[95] Guibert de Nogent, *Autobiographie* [*De vita sua, sive monodiae*], ed. and tr. E.-R. Labande (Paris 1981) iii.10 (358, 360; tr. Paul J. Archambault, *A monk's confession: the memoirs of Guibert of Nogent* [1996] 164–65). On Thomas de Marle, *Monodiae* iii.11,14 (362–72, 396–412; *Memoirs* 166–73, 181–90); Suger, *Vie de Louis VI*, ed. Henri Waquet (Paris 1929) c. 24 (172–78; tr. Richard Cusimano, John Moorhead, *The deeds of Louis the Fat* [Washington 1992] 106–9); there are other sources.

foot' anointed prelates and priests 'like slaves who know not what their lords may do.'[96]

Never had power seemed so personal, so ponderous, so ominous as in the two generations before 1150. It was not just that violence flared about the periphery of instituted lordships, although that was part of it; we shall have to inquire how far princely lordships themselves were immune from violent customs. One at least who was present recalled that at Clermont in 1095 Pope Urban II suggested that violence might better be inflicted on the infidels in the Holy Land than on Christians in France. Lately in Germany, but everywhere else as well, horsed and armed men were all about, men capable of coercing or seizing, and, among them, some exercising or pretending to the power of lordship. Clattering about the towers and moats, like that 'high and terrible' one with which Bishop Gerard II fortified his churches at Cambrai around 1080,[97] such men could no longer be mistaken for poor (or unfree) knights and household retainers; mailed and mounted, they must often have been hard to tell from lords of noble birth. Which was quite as they wished.

Cultures of Lordship

Lordship was nothing new by this time; it was a facet of old order. Yet now it was different. Never had there been so many lords. Never had the bearers of official powers been so tolerant of encroachment on public domination, so ready to share their lordship or commend it to others. Command could be seized or

[96] *Die Briefe Heinrichs IV.*, ed. Carl Erdmann (Stuttgart 1978 [1937]) no. 12 (27 iii 1076): '. . . rectores sancte ecclesie, videlicet archiepiscopos episcopos presbiteros, non modo non tangere, sicut christos domini, timuisti, quin sicut servos nescientes quid faciat domnus eorum, sub pedibus tuis calcasti' (translation in Tierney, *Crisis*, no. 30 [59]).

[97] *Gesta pontificum Cameracensium, continuatio*, ed. L. C. Bethmann, *MGHSS* VII (1846) 499 c. 5.

imposed or, in the perspective of old order, abused, but to many it must have seemed that lordship was a reasonable reward for loyalty and service. Never had there been—in some sense as much qualitative as quantitative—so *much* lordship. It permeated every pore of action in the (relatively) thickly settled zones of European habitation. Without obliterating official conceptions of power, it co-opted or weakened or transformed them. This is why the oaths required of kings at their coronations tended to be fixed in tenth-century forms administered on occasions unrecorded as such.[98] Ecclesiastical offices were notoriously liable to revaluation as mercantile patrimony; and while efforts were duly made to distinguish between the pastoral and temporal facets of episcopal power, it is impossible to believe that prelates like Manasses I of Reims (1070–80) or Ranulf Flambard of Durham (1099–1128), both of whom were accused of exploitative behaviour, paid heed to such niceties.[99] Norman viscounts and Picard *vidâmes* clung to judicial powers as if to a flickering dream of respectability, but one approached them in fear and deference. In Mediterranean lands, where new laws of fidelities and fiefs (that is, of lordship) were arising, the notariate survived in the twelfth century as a customary function: people great and small sought out the priest or monk to write their obligatory memorials of sale or accord or bequest; in some places little more than formulaic literacy remained to activate public lawful authority.[100] It was hardly the Carolingian or Visigothic office that survived, but the claimant—count, vicar, *scabinus*, *judex*, *saio*—to its vestigial prestige; a person, not a function:—a lord. *Miro iudex*: the proud subscription gleams forth from many Catalonian parchments of the

---

[98] Janet L. Nelson, 'The rites of the Conqueror,' *Politics and ritual in early mediaeval Europe* (London 1986) ch. 17. Also Richardson and Sayles, *Governance of mediaeval England* 136–38; Southern, *Making of the Middle Ages* 92–94; cf. P. E. Schramm, *A history of the English coronation*, tr. L. G. W. Legg (Oxford 1937) chs. 2, 3.

[99] See Jaeger, 'Courtliness,' 297–99; Southern, *Medieval humanism*, ch. 10.

[100] *Urban and rural communities in medieval France: Provence and Languedoc, 1000–1500*, ed. Kathryn Reyerson, John Drendel (Leiden 1998); *FAC* I, 156–58.

twelfth century.[101] What did the epithet mean to him, and to those who enlisted him?

The ways in which people experienced power—wielded it, imagined or celebrated it, responded to it—attest to the preponderance of lordship. It became a culture of power, with its characteristic facets of expression, justification, and expectation. Even those without lords knew who had power, for there was nothing private about the claims of many to judge or coerce. Lordship, indeed, created community. Unlike the traditional lay communities of villages, valleys and, in England, hundreds and shires, those who banded together in the eleventh and twelfth centuries were often reacting against the alleged excesses of lordship. Yet even the notables of northern towns who banded in 'communes,' in this respect like the *capitanei* of early Lombard cities, found it impossible to persist in the rejection of the very patrimonial power to which they themselves aspired. What the 'council-men' of the North and the consuls in Mediterranean towns aspired to were exemptions from arbitrary seizures and impositions by external lords, these above all, and seldom much more. They cultivated liberties and (good) customs, not freedom nor (still less) equality. Typically, urban magistrates strove for lordships of their own, so that their chartered solidarities, as at Toulouse in the later twelfth century, somewhat resembled those of vassals.[102]

Lords or would-be lords, those who could command and impose, struggled to secure their dominations as if they were properties. Even the greatest of them. William the Conqueror was quite drastically vigilant in face of Norwegian threats in his late years. They sought to keep order internally, which amounts to the same thing: the justice of Louis VI (1108–37) in the Ile-de-France was an expression of embattled domination. That is, of *noblesse*. The powerful lacking the nobility of worthy domination must strive for it, or become dependent. Let us not yet ask

---

[101] e.g., ACA, Cancelleria, pergamins Alfons I, nos. 249, 278. See plate 7A.
[102] These points are illustrated below, pp. 349–69.

whether lord-princes and lord-castellans had further objectives, let alone common or 'political' ones. Some lords and (or) their servants did try to objectify their purposes rationally, as we shall see. Their eccentricity and ingenuity are of great historical interest. But these people must be approached in their original habitat. What we know of this burgeoning jowly world of elemental constraint—a world of moats, towers, and solemn sworn commitments in candle-lit smoky interiors—suggests that power was habitually wielded, and suffered, as a manifestation, an effluence, of nobility. Something of what this was like can be inferred from works of epic imagination put into writing after 1050. But the elitism of this outlook found justification in an even more capacious culture, that of the Christian faith, bearing on the experience of power.

Secular lordship was sanctioned by God, although perhaps less securely than has been supposed. The strictures of popes and abbots, already noticed, were not limited to categorically bad lordship. Christ's observation that 'the princes of the gentiles lord it over them and they that are greater exercise power over them' was preface to His exhortation to a better way of rule.[103] The Fathers regarded inequality and subjection as a regrettable remedy for sin; and there was talk of humility in ministerial offices amongst eleventh-century reformers. Yet the normal view of power derived from God could only encourage the powerful to think of divine lordship as exemplary, as justification for their imposition of prayerful submission on those rendered safer and freer thereby. 'Liberty' (*libertas*) was an attribute of dependence on God. 'Whether we live or die,' said Saint Paul, 'we are the Lord's.'[104] This was the lesson of Christ in majesty sculpted into monks' portals, as at Conques, Moissac, and Saint-Gilles, in the twelfth century; and the lesson was nowhere so pointed as at

---

[103] Matth. xx.25. See Philippe Buc, '*Principes gentium dominantur eorum*: princely power between legitimacy and illegitimacy in twelfth-century exegesis,' in *Cultures of power*, ch. 13.

[104] Romans xiv.8; Tellenbach, *Church, state, and Christian society* 2–42.

Autun, where in the great art of Gislebert dating from about 1130 a serenely judgmental Christ appears to the agitated damned and saved and the prayerful living.[105]

God the judge, acting by will yet dispensing mercy, was the supreme exemplar of human lordship around 1100. 'Do you not rightly seem to us to act like God / Willingly indulgent even to unasking sinners? . . . / For you alone,' it is predicated of the great king in the German (Latin) epic *Ruodlieb*, 'are our pillar in place of Christ.'[106] The rituals of petition, judgment, and grace not only preserved late Antique conceptions of imperial authority and deference but also replicated liturgical forms of supplication. No wonder that lord-princes laid claim to justice before all else, for in this way they thought to wield God's power; or that vassalage was typically depicted as ritual submission to lords.[107] Such lordship required submission or subjection; rejected dissent. Quoting 1 Peter ii.17, 'Fear God, honor the king,' Orderic Vitalis retold the sad story of Earl Copsi, whose unshakable fidelity to King William provoked his vassals to the rebellion in which he was killed. 'So by his death the famous man affirmed that the majesty of their lord should always be precious to faithful subjects.'[108]

Lordly majesty was attributed as a rule to kings and princes. To defend it required engaging vigilance by a count of Namur towards 1047–64:

[105] Denis Grivot, George Zarnecki, *Gislebertus, sculptor of Autun* (London 1961) ch. 2 and plates; see also Jean-Claude Bonne, 'Depicted gesture, named gesture; postures of the Christ on the Autun tympanum,' *History and Anthropology* 1 (1984) 77–93. See plate 6.

[106] *Ruodlieb. Faksimile-Ausgabe der Codex latinus Monacensis 19486 . . .*, 2 vols. (Wiesbaden 1974–85) I, II, Fragm 4, ll. 146–54.

[107] *Regesto della chiesa di Tivoli*, ed. Luigi Bruzza (Bologna 1983 [Rome 1880]) plate iv; *LFM* I, plates 4, 9, 17; II, plates 5, 10, 14; and Geoffrey Koziol, *Begging pardon and favor: ritual and political order in early medieval France* (Ithaca, NY, 1992) 1–108.

[108] OV iv (II, 206–8); cf. WP ii.48 (184–86).

And so that his justice may be preserved, once a year or when he so orders, he causes one of his servants to ride a high horse bearing a spear from the edge of the town to the summit. If he finds any obstruction in height or breadth, let it be taken down [*deicitur*] by royal authority or remedied by redemption at the count's mercy.[109]

It was from regalian altitude that lord-princes protected churches and monasteries, orphans, widows, and the afflicted, and dispensed alms to the poor; carried on, that is, in the theocratic duties appointed to them since the ninth century. Lesser lords could seldom do more than pretend to such prestigious functions. Majesty was celebrated in great festive occasions such as might be recorded by chroniclers and were lavishly described in *chansons de geste* in the twelfth century. So, for example, the opening scene in the *Coronemenz Looïs*, where the aged Charlemagne arranged for his son's succession in a 'good court . . . such as you will never see,' served fourteen counts on watch in the palace, and was attended by eighteen archbishops and as many bishops, twenty-six abbots, and 'four crowned kings.'

> Poor people went there for justice,
> No one pleaded there without good right,
> One did right there . . . ,

but since then justice has collapsed. 'God is a good man [*prodome*], who governs and supports us,' the wicked will not rise from 'the stinking well.' The pope sang mass, never in France so lovely as in that 'great festival.' The concentration of divinely ordained lordship in the king's justice, inertly attributive, contrasts starkly with the dynamic tension of the action started in their festival court: the infidelity of Arneis of Orléans avenged by William Shortnose, whose promised defence of the child-king is superseded by urgent service to the pope against the Muslims.[110] And this

---

[109] *Actes des comtes de Namur de la première race, 946–1196*, ed. Félix Rousseau (Brussels 1936) 89.

[110] *Couronnement de Louis*, laisses 1–9, ed. Langlois, 1–5 (tr. Joan M. Ferrante, *Guillaume d'Orange: four twelfth-century epics* [NY 1974], 63–67).

action may serve here to evoke a quite different cultural sanction for lordly power.

In the early Middle Ages free men had learned to look upon lords as providers. Fighting lords secured followers by promise and rewards, their lordship amounted to followership. Warlord kings, amassing and distributing wealth, were remembered for the prowess that brought wealth and for generosity. This tradition survived in the homages and oaths that proliferated after the ninth century, in the songs sung about lordly honour and largesse, and vassalic fidelity, as also in the dramas of betrayal, deprivation, and war. For while homage created personal submission, dependence, or even subjection, the oath tended to create reciprocity even as it confirmed submission. Thus Copsi, in the tale related above, could not secure the same measure of fidelity from his followers as he himself reserved to the lord-king. There was discussion, disagreement, and finally rebellion. The dynamic could also work for good. A continuator of the *Miracles of Saint Benedict* wrote of 'a certain noble named Geoffroi, a very powerful man, lord of the castle called Semur,' who suffered the misfortune of losing his memory. 'Whereupon his whole clientele, which did so much in his devoted service,' was in distress, so they decided—these 'illustrious men who by affinity or by friendship or by benefice seemed joined to him'—to recommend that he appeal to the saints at Cluny and other Burgundian shrines. When this remedy failed, they recalled 'great things' Saint Benedict had done at Perrecy, and there Lord Geoffroi was happily restored to health.[111]

Whatever we make of this outcome, two things are striking here: the solidarity of lord and dependents and the diversity of the latter. Geoffroi's lordship was an expression of affective submission and fidelity shared by kinsfolk, friends, servants, and enfeoffed vassals. Among these tenants, and perhaps among the peasants

---

[111] *MSB* viii.42 (346). See also Walter Schlesinger, 'Herrschaft und Gefolgschaft in der germanisch-deutschen Verfassungsgeschichte,' *Historische Zeitschrift* CLXXVI (1953) 225–75 (tr. Fredric Cheyette, *Lordship and community in medieval Europe* [NY 1968] 64–99).

as well, formed the common interest of preserving the stricken lord's power. Status and consensus overtake prerogative; dependents share in the resources of lordship, in its tasks, its habits. Or rather, some of them do, for it is all too evident that the associative interests project a shared lordship of production and constraint. This was a solidarity of 'illustrious men.' Such solidarities in lordship come into better focus in the twelfth century, as the commands of better endowed lords get into writing. Towards 1153–73 Roger de Clare, Earl of Hertford, required 'all his barons and faithful men' to mind the needs and rights of the monks of Stoke in his absence.[112]

Followership, having once determined freedom, had come to define nobility or the aspiration thereto. The lay lord needed companions to realize his power, needed to share his table, needed to be seen with his armed men as well as his servants. One commanded and demanded because of one's freedom from the burdens of command. But the dynamics of elite companionship were changing around 1100 in ways that altered the ethos of lordship. In most regions knighthood was winning enough respectability to influence the ceremonial of noble lordship. If knights wished to celebrate their vocation to the sword, how could their bellicose masters do any less? So to be labelled 'knight' (*miles*) (or 'baron' or 'vassal's vassal') became a sort of entitlement to lordship, carried the presumption of fellowship in that right order in which lordship and servility were not confused.[113] Moreover, it became usual to establish vassals on fiefs or honours that were more than simply shares of lordship, thereby activating the potential of tenure to generate customary rights and creating at a stroke an interest in lordship capable of limiting its power. Here again, shared

---

[112] F. M. Stenton, *The first century of English feudalism, 1066–1166* . . . , 2d ed. (Oxford 1961 [1932]) 76; appendix 19; and ch. 3.

[113] Fears of such confusion were common in the early twelfth century: see, e.g., Hildebert of Lavardin, *Sermones* 23, 35, 37, *PL* CLXXI, 443, 516–17, 533; OV viii.26 (IV, 320). Also Benjamin Arnold, *Princes and territories in medieval Germany* (Cambridge 1991) ch. 1.

elite aspirations shaped what would become a virtual culture of power, placing new stress on familial prestige, patrimony, inheritance, and the knowledge of customary law. Save perhaps in Germany, we hear little of this around 1100, when even in Anglo-Norman domains the inheritance of baronies remained problematic;[114] there was little echo in the early *chansons de geste*. Counsel remained more like a moral obligation than a legal one, an elemental imperative of lordly reputation and submissive solidarity.

Social aspirations and imaginings of divinity, however they may have affected the exercise of power, were not determinants of lordship. No one spoke of 'regalian' or of 'feudal lordship' as such, let alone labelled them godly or otherwise. A lord-bishop or king might judge vassals or peasants or free-holding subjects; what he could not easily do was maintain the quasi-domestic sociability of his festivals and courts for all those he wished to dominate. Trust became critical. In the 1060s a new abbot in the Norman house of Saint-Evroult, knowing too little about his endowment and lacking faith in those on hand to inform him, suffered losses of lands to grasping knights of the environs.[115] How could the cohesion of vassalic lordship be preserved in expanding lordships? The dilemma was felt intensely in agrarian lordships, which, for all their leaning towards benevolent paternalism, were structurally inhumane in reality. Apart from those domestic servile functions, peasants did not frequent the lord's hall, had no claim to familiarity with the one—whether bishop or count or castellan—known as master, not as friend; nor could they share in the knightly and ministerial revels of power. Only monk-lords, said Peter the Venerable, surely with some truth, treated their rustics 'not as serving-men and -women but as

---

[114] J. C. Holt, 'Politics and property in early medieval England,' *Past & Present* no. 57 (1972) 3–52.

[115] OV iii (II, 96–98). Orderic was acutely aware of this problem; see also iv (II, 262) on the 'wise clerks' in Roger of Montgomery's household.

brothers and sisters.'[116] Most peasants could only be subjected, yoked, or exploited by intermediaries. Some of the intimidating presence of lords might thereby be removed, but at high cost for those dependents, surely the vast majority, who could be content to pay for the security of their tenures. Lord's bailiff, monastic steward, king's provost or sheriff: what was his place in the culture of lordship?

This question cannot yet be fully addressed. Service was something less than an articulate pursuit in the early maturity of lordship. What matters here is that domination of the many entailed an objectively defined domain as well as a subjectively experienced command. The lord was to be honoured 'in every place of his domination'; to be petitioned 'in the shadow of [the empress's] lordship'; his (or her) lordship to be realized in his inevitable absence.[117] But the domain, however defined and extended, would have been as various as the elements of lordship themselves: vills, houses, jurisdictions, hunting rights, tolls, and taxes of whatever sort. William Mendel Newman showed how hopeless it is to map the early Capetian royal domain, an incessantly changing crazy quilt of rights, revenues, and tenures. One distinguished between 'power' and 'domain,' a distinction justified by the fact that *dominium* was coming in the eleventh century to refer to lord's land in the lord's hand.[118] Yet as a practical matter, when churches sought confirmation of their material and spiritual wealth or when lord-princes donated to monasteries, they were inclined to articulate their power comprehensively, and in so doing to express their conception of lordship as dominion, as patrimony; to objectify that tangible aspect of lordship most nearly resembling property. When Viscount Aymeri I of Narbonne offered his son

---

[116] *LPV* I, no. 28 (87). See also *GpP* i.12 (58), with reference to Boleslaw I (Chrobry, 992–1025): 'Suos quoque rusticos non ut dominus in angariam coercebat, sed ut pius pater quiete eos vivere permittebat.'

[117] Psalms cii.22; *Die Tegernseer Briefsammlung (Froumund)*, ed. Karl Strecker (Munich 1978) no. 1.

[118] *Le domaine royal sous les premiers capétiens (987–1180)* (Paris 1937) 3–5; John Van Engen, 'Sacred sanctions for lordship,' *Cultures of power* 216.

Berengar to Saint-Pons-de-Thomières in 1103, the pious endowment was summed up as

> all the allod and all power [*potestatem*] and *dominium* of all the aforesaid honor [of Bize, dép. Aude], . . . namely, with villages, with castles, with houses, with courts . . . and with all fief-holders and vicars of both sexes and sergeanties and with the men and women natural to the place, and quests and hospitalities and revenues from pledges and tallages, all actions and justices and all usages and tolls and gate-taxes and hunting rights . . . [119]

Here a distinction between (coercive) power and domain is explicit, yet the items are strung together to describe a lordship that could be more or less enfeoffed or commended in ways of no public concern. As early as 1071 the revenues from pleas, protection, and tenures were compounded in the 'exploit' (*expletum*) that Guillem Falcuç agreed to pay Countess Almodis for the bailiwick (*baiulia*) of Cerver (Old Catalonia); at Osor the countess held pleas in *dominium*, except for one-third of those other than homicide and adultery, which her bailiff was to hold from her.[120] Bailiffs who collected for the lord's protectorate (*baiulia, bailia*) were imposing surrogates by definition, lord-like, projections of the lord's *familia*. 'My servants,' 'my bailiffs,' said Count Fulk Richin of Anjou in records of 1067 and 1090.[121] In 1121 Lord Guilhem V spoke of 'my bailiff Lambert' in providing for his wife and the disposition of revenues at Montpellier, where neither *bailia* nor *dominatio* was to be commended to Jews or Saracens. In 1160 Count Raimond V of Toulouse set limits on collections of

---

[119] *HL* v, no. 417 (785–87). Some of this verbiage figures suspiciously in the endowment charter of Saint-Pons (ibid., no. 67, 175), purporting to date from 936, so it is likely that the beneficiaries produced the description. See also no. 77 (191, April 942).

[120] *FAC* II, no. 139.

[121] 'Le cartulaire de Saint-Maur sur Loire,' ed. Paul Marchegay, *Archives d'Anjou. Recueil de documents et mémoires inédits sur cette province* . . . , 3 vols. (Angers 1843–54) I, nos. 38, 64 (381, 405); see also no. 37 (380).

toll by 'my bailiffs in all my land.'[122] Power was univocal because it was personal, even when it was delegated; it was most commonly lordship sanctioned by God, elite custom, and practical necessity.

THE ATTRIBUTES of seigneurial power were diversely expressive of tradition, situation, and status. Consider what it means to say that the powerful acted (or were expected to act) by will, mercy, and grace. Such behaviour, manifest in rituals of supplication for clemency or the grant of favour, sustained a venerable conception of ministerial kingship: an official theocratic justice resonant with a theology in which humanity was coming to have an enlarged role in the drama of salvation. Representations and rituals of majesty and judgment perpetuated this cultural assimilation, while confirming some in their conviction that they were blessed as well as born to command. But the image of such domination, whatever its relation to 'reality,' was ambivalent. The Lord Who willed human affairs was a merciful lord, doubtless condemning the wicked but surely saving repentant sinners in swelling numbers. Was this just and merciful?—or only merciful? Lord-princes whose mercy was craved were powerful, their will (voluntas) unlimited save by conscience. Could a king who charged for his misericordia, like Henry II of England, be thought either merciful or just? Questions like these surely interested the subjects of this book.[123] But the truth is that written records of petition and clemency seem to project a clerical construct of lofty power. It was prelates or their scribes who thrust on King Philip I of France an iconic language of deference that is seldom found in the charters of his contemporary William the Conqueror. Here we have an at-

---

[122] *HL* v, no. 474 (893); no. 634iii (1234).
[123] e.g., *HC* ii.62.2 (344), quoting St Augustine.

tributive culture of power, variable in incidence and chronology, and not necessarily—or even necessarily not—indicative of common experience.[124]

Lordly will untempered by mercy or grace was thought sinful towards 1100. It was chiefly a moral matter, a wrong in a religious universe of right and wrong. Everywhere people denounced 'tyrants' and bad lords, as we shall see. Peter Abelard wrote of 'bad will' as morally reprehensible, and in one logical context he postulated a genetic disposition to wrongful power, remarking how a father's tyranny recurs in his son.[125] Hugues de Poitiers spoke of 'tyrannical force.'[126] Even the new idea of active resistance to tyrants seems first to have been justified, around 1140, as a remedy for wickedness. That wilful power might also be unlawful was little stressed before the 1150s, when John of Salisbury defined tyranny as 'violent domination' negligent of law.[127] Half a century earlier little was specifically lawful about lordship. Few lawyers could yet be found in princely service, while perhaps only in northern Italy could be discerned the first stirrings of a feudal jurisprudence. Everyday law was a survival of public order, often little distinct from custom. Concepts of law-worthiness and right and the sense of what was penal and not penitential could be found in records of practise and process everywhere. Custom was a novel, sometimes dubious, constraint in societies where the diffusion of banal powers was creating lordship without pretence to majesty. Such dominations moulded custom to their purposes, even to the point of justifying arbitrary practises in the old aristocracies. The best example of this is the widely attested habit of

---

[124] On mercy, justice, and salvation, Hildebert, *Sermo* 11, *PL* CLXXI, 390–91; Koziol, *Begging pardon*, 215–17; Southern, *Making of the Middle Ages*, 95–97, 236–8. See also J. E. A. Jolliffe, *Angevin kingship*, 2d ed. (London 1963) chs. 1–5; *RAPh1* nos. 98, 99, 110, 152; *Regesta regum Anglo-normannorum. The acta of William I*, ed. David Bates (Oxford 1998) nos. 28–31.

[125] *Dialectica* ii.1, ed. L. M. Rijk, 2d ed. (Assen 1970) 168.

[126] Hugues le Poitevin, *Chronique de l'abbaye de Vézelay* ii, in *MV* (419).

[127] *Policraticus* vii.17 (II, 161).

despoiling widowed churches.[128] The *ius spolii* was rooted in traditional resistance to the inclination of (unmarried) prelates to favour kinsfolk in the disposition of clerical property; it had a long history of exploitation by Frankish authorities on pretence of protection. So it was not a new abuse of banal lordship, and since it required and rewarded the collaboration of armed men, it could not be viewed as an exclusively princely scourge. It was amply described in 1050 by Pope Leo IX, who directed the clergy of Auch to excommunicate those who observe that 'perverse and wholly execrable custom of some peoples: namely, that when the bishop dies, they break into the episcopal manse *hostiliter*, pillage his effects, burn his tenants' houses and destroy vineyards with bestial savagery.'[129] This sanction became a staple of conciliar legislation, which prudently held all perpetrators of such violence morally responsible. The custom was nonetheless one of high lordship, confessed to and renounced by Count Raimond IV of Saint-Gilles in 1084, and by Count Guillaume II of Nevers a few years later, in favour of the episcopal churches of Béziers and Auxerre.[130] Yet it was too lucrative a perquisite of comital service to be easily uprooted. The same was true of other coercive practises, such as preemption and distraint.

For the sociability of lay lordship could only encourage collectively rewarding rites and pursuits tending to produce courtly cultures of power. It seems likely that counsel became an attribute of lordship primarily in relation to associative virtue: to consensus about the wisdom of consulting, nourished by biblical precept and clerical experience, rather than to any inherited imperative to limit power. But economic growth and the rooting of patrimonial fortunes worked to deflect collegial talk about shared

---

[128] See generally Fritz Prochnow, *Das Spolienrecht und die Testierfähigkeit der Geistlichen im Abendland bis zum 13. Jahrhundert* (Berlin 1919); 'Spolienrecht,' *Lexikon des Mittelalters* VII (1995) 2131–32.

[129] *BrPD* I, no. 35.

[130] *HL* V, no. 359 (685–87); *Les gestes des évêques d'Auxerre*, ed. Guy Lobrichon et al., 2 vols. (Paris 2002–06) II, 61.

lordship towards the justification of possession or intention, towards definitions of right. Customs of patrimonial inheritance lay at the origins of baronial consultation in England.[131] Counsel was a facet of yet broader values of noble status—honour, fidelity, generosity, prowess—without which majesty was socially useless. The sons of lay lords learned how to manage weapons and horses, and typically, at least in the higher aristocracy, how to enjoy hunting. Before his scandalous election to the bishopric of Laon in 1107, Gaudry had been a court companion of King Henry I. 'He took delight,' wrote Guibert of Nogent, 'in talk about fighting, dogs, and hawks, as he had learned to do among the English.'[132] Such pleasures had their ominous side. To describe the forest as a lordly preserve was to mark off yet another domain of coercive power over people, a domain that came under criticism in the twelfth century. John of Salisbury saw some taint of hunting in tyranny.[133]

Was the culture of clerical lordship so different? Archdeacon Henry of Huntingdon spoke of the misfortunes that overwhelmed Robert Bloet of Lincoln as the normal fate of 'worldly people,' but admitted that he himself had begun by admiring the bishop in his 'glory,' with his 'handsome knights, noble youths, costly horses,' and all the glitter of his clothing and table. 'Everyone deferred to him . . . [who] was regarded as father and god to all . . .'.[134] He was not the only one of this sort. Yet few prelates behaved so, for few had the means of Norman royal favourites. For all we know, the lordship of bishops and abbots did not yet as a rule assume associative or celebratory forms. Prelates managed vassals and peasants much as lay lords did, securing oaths of fidelity from castellans, exploiting jurisdictional powers (or suffering advocates to do so); few can have seen advantage in cultivating the sociability of such lordship. For whatever their tastes, or

---

[131] Stenton, *First century*, ch. 3; John Hudson, *Land, law, and lordship in Anglo-Norman England* (Oxford 1994) ch. 6.

[132] *Monodiae* iii.4 (294; *Memoirs* 135).

[133] *Policr.* viii.20 (II, 373).   [134] HH viii (586–88).

even liabilities when, as often, they had to manage household knights, they could only win respect for a mode of pastoral lordship unsuited to courtly pursuits; an official lordship conceptually akin to that awesome kingship projected by their scribes, and likewise generative of rituals of deference.[135] The interests of those who sought lordly favour—grants of fiefs or benefices or protection—seem to have been increasingly concentrated in courts or lordly receptions of all kinds, so that critics—and the disappointed—came to take a cynical view of 'courtliness' (*curialitas*). John of Salisbury's disdain for flattery and preoccupation with 'trifles' (*nugae*) are sufficient proof that great lords valued affability and caprice, and cultivated them.[136]

Human lordship, like divine, was a house of many mansions. We begin to grasp the limitations of Abbot Peter's categorical denunciation of lay lordship. Those who could be coerced, peasants and the unfree, could be abused. Those who could not—one's vassals and knights—were affectively more like allies than servants; allies, that is, in domination of the many. So were one's ministerial servants—or so they wished to be. Who then, in this culture, was out of order?

---

[135] See *LPV* I, no. 58; cf. II, 339. [136] *Policr.* i–iii and passim.

·III·

Lord-Rulership (1050–1150):
The Experience of Power

OR MOST Europeans living in the century beginning around
1050 the most acute experience of power was that of lordship.
Whatever their other ties and commitments, personal precedence
and deference were insistent realities in their lives, creating or
testing their loyalties, encroaching on official action in restructured societies; dominance and dependence assumed the codified
forms of cultural identity. But did lordship have a history? Can
the phenomenon be deconstructed as sequential experience of the
sort so familiar to us as 'political history'?

Very surely it did have such a history. If one reasons that kingdoms were lordships, the conventional regnal histories of Germany, France, and the rest may seem to be sufficient replies to
these questions. But it should already be clear that a history of
power limited to the doings of lord-kings in France at a time
when several princes were more powerful than the king must be
sadly incomplete. All the more so in view of the countless
micro-histories of petty lay lordship of which such stories should
be compiled, if only we could know them. Few but the greatest
upstart families, such as the Coucy, the Montcada, or the Montmorency, bucking for nobility and bursting with ambition, have
yet found their historians.[1] What is certain is that in the later eleventh and twelfth centuries masses of dependents and subjects

---

[1] Dominique Barthélemy, *Les deux âges de la seigneurie banale. Pouvoir et société
dans la terre des sires de Coucy . . .* (Paris 1984); John C. Shideler, *A medieval Cata-*

looked to princes as well as to kings as their rulers. It was a time when dukes and counts might hope to become kings themselves, either by emulating Duke William's dynastic conquest of England or else by military adventure on the frontiers of Christian Europe. It was also a time when uncrowned princes aspired to the prestige of royalty without fear of subservience to neighbouring kings. If the counts of Aragon and Portugal won titular promotions to kingly status, the duke of Poland towards 1100 and the count of Barcelona half a century later, both well positioned to do the same, made no such claims. This situation began to change in the twelfth century. Symptomatically, while the First Crusade (1096–99) was an enterprise of the princes, the Second (1147–49) was led by lord-kings. What were the circumstances of these rulers? What were their natures, their aims, their means and attainments? In the following pages no attempt can be made to answer these questions systematically, let alone completely, for that would be to depart from the very incomplete records of power; records that are, for this book, the evidence of human designs, impacts, and responses, to be traced selectively through three or four generations.

It is not easy to imagine the aggregate of European lands as their rulers viewed it in the later eleventh century. Counties and castellanies lay thick on the ground; no kingdom, not even England, had very tough or definite boundaries; no lay lord dared overlook his neighbour's power, few could really see beyond it. Perhaps the most illuminating record of ambitious design is the *Register* of Pope Gregory VII (1073–85), with its enticingly attentive addresses to lord-kings, prelates, and lesser powers. No pope had ever claimed so vast a spiritual domain from such exiguous material resources; only he amongst contemporary authorities can have thought seriously about faith, obedience, and security in all these lands. And he lost little time directing such matters. From the earliest hours of his pontificate (April 1073) Gregory

---

lan noble family: the Montcadas, 1000–1230 (Berkeley 1983); Brigitte Bedos, *La châtellenie de Montmorency des origines à 1368 . . .* (Pontoise 1981).

was exhorting French knights to fight the Muslims in Spain on condition that they recognize pontifical suzerainty. Less than a year later he urged the kings of León and Navarre 'to accept the order and ritual of the Roman Church . . . like the other kingdoms of the west and north.'[2] Although such aims must have seemed visionary, they were to be fulfilled in some measure thereafter, and they were sobriety itself compared to epic imaginings of an all-conquering king. The Roland-poet's Charlemagne has his homeland in 'sweet France' while dominating peoples from Scotland, Ireland, and England to Bavaria, Aquitaine, Provence, and Lombardy; he summons to Aix (-la-Chapelle) as to the 'meillor sied de France' to hear the case of Ganilon's treachery. And he campaigns in Spain—'cavalcades' at that perilous distance—for the profit of loyal barons who hold from him that vast patrimony extending from the North Sea to the Pyrenees.[3]

These were visions of authority in a Christian world becoming aware of its frontiers. Very different visions, the administrative and the imaginative. They coincided clumsily for a time when twelfth-century singers depicted the 'lord pope' in embattled alliance with the king to restore the Italian patrimony of Peter.[4] But the courtly culture of the early epics is a fragile guide to the restive elites—the 'Borguignuns / E Peitevins e Normans e Bretuns'[5]—whose aspirations to lordship and expeditions reshaped European frontiers. Their songs celebrated the ideal of faithful vassalage and recorded anxieties about inheritance—matters central to lord-rulership in the twelfth century—while telling us little about their (other) means of power. They rested on traditions of Frankish kingship such as played but feebly about the Norman settlements in Italy or

---

[2] *Register Gregors VII.*, to be cited as continuously paginated in two volumes, (I) i.7,64.

[3] *La Chanson de Roland*, ed. F. Whitehead, 2d ed. (Oxford 1946), ll. 16, 109, 116, 702, 706, 710, 739, 757, 2322–37, 3706.

[4] *Couronnement de Louis*, laisse 18 (13–16).

[5] *Chanson de Roland*, ll. 3701–02 (108).

the ambitions of German-speaking knights in west Slavic lands.
The cultures of these latter societies are even harder to discern
from literary sources, a sign that their transplantations were more
complete. Spain remained a visionary frontier long enough to create a mythology of baronial power in Francophone lands.[6]

The Papacy

The papal outlook of Gregory VII was quite another matter, visionary only in its breathtaking audacity. Spain was but one
point on the full circle of its compass. In his first year Pope
Gregory engaged also with ecclesiastical affairs at Auch, Lyon,
Chartres, Reims, and Lincoln.[7] He wrote a pastoral letter to the
church at Carthage, initiated contact with the Emperor Michael
VII of Constantinople, exhorted Duke Wratislaw II of Bohemia
to support his legates in their case against the simoniac bishop of
Prague, got discreetly into touch with King Henry IV, required
Archbishop Lanfranc to take action against the contumacious
Bishop Arfast, and wrote his first letters to the kings of England,
Aragon, and León.[8] There was nothing slack about these distant
contacts, which opened live negotiations. But there were urgent
concerns in nearer places of Peter's patrimony. From early Sep-
tember 1073, when he moved to Capua for several weeks, Pope
Gregory began to deal with them as well. He sought to promote
an understanding with Abbot Hugh of Cluny, the Countesses
Beatrice and Matilda, the Empress Agnes, and Duke Rudolf of
Swabia against countenancing the simoniac Lombard bishops.[9]
Having notified Prince Gisulf of Salerno (among others) of his

---

[6] See generally Robert Bartlett, *The making of Europe. Conquest, colonization
and cultural change, 950–1350* (Princeton 1993), chs. 1, 2. The crusader lands of
the Levant produced a comparable mythology in historical and literary narratives that must be largely omitted in this book.

[7] *Register* i.13, 32, 34, 36, 52, 55, 76.

[8] ibid., i.17, 18, 22, 29a, 31, 63, 64, 70. [9] ibid., i.11, 14, 19, 20, 25, 40.

election, Gregory demanded sworn and written professions of fidelity to the Roman church from the princes of Benevento and Capua.[10] No less attentive to troubles in Milan, Gregory explained to Erlembald, leader of the *pataria*, that he was tarrying at Capua on account of the Normans who continued to menace the security of the 'public thing and the holy church.'[11]

What was recorded in the *Register* of Pope Gregory VII were the letters and memoranda of official action. No other extant record of this time (in Latin Europe) does it better; or in truth, does this at all.[12] Were it otherwise, the story of power around 1100 would be different. Gregory was unlike most lord-princes in feeling himself elected to office; that is, chosen to exercise the functions his reforming predecessor and he himself in a circle of clerical reformers had laid down. This meant, as his letters show, that he assumed well defined responsibilities—the legatine programmes in France and Bohemia, opposition to simony and clerical marriage, liturgical conformity, among others—and that he was disposed to initiate action in these spheres as well as to respond passively and confirm. It is possible to discern some concentration of despatch in the dating and location of letters, such as those of September 1073 at Capua, and in the Lenten synods of 1075 and after,[13] and this may point to more purposive activity than can be deduced from the lay chanceries to be considered hereafter. A more assured inference is that Gregory was working from the start with sympathetic clerical advisers and scribes whose discussion and consensus based on experience and conviction amounted to a culture of official action.

Whether this was quite a bureaucratic culture is more problematic. It is an irony of this famous moment in history that

---

[10] ibid., i.2, 18a, 21a.

[11] ibid., i.25; also 26, 28. The *pataria* (or *patarini*) were a radicalized sect of reformers.

[12] Surely not even Domesday Book can be counted an exception. The magnitude of Gregory's aims is in stark contrast with the exiguity of a papal patrimony about which next to nothing is said in the *Register*.

[13] ibid., i.19–25; ii.66–68, 69–76.

Archdeacon Hildebrand was irregularly elected pope only a few years after like-minded cardinals had agreed upon a reform of that procedure designed to ensure the 'orderly' promotion of a 'suitable man'—that is, to restore the office of Roman bishop.[14] Few may have doubted Hildebrand's suitability, but in the pressures of the moment influence and enthusiasm overtook deliberation. That Pope Gregory himself understood and regretted this is not the only sign that he thought of his power as rooted in Christian consensus. Nevertheless, there was nothing impersonal about his claims and actions. Gregory VII was deeply self-conscious in his hortatory utterance. He identified viscerally with Saint Peter, whose power he mediated,—and Peter's power was paternal and lordly. In November 1074, Gregory enjoined Archbishop Anno of Cologne to disciplinary action 'on behalf of saint Peter our common father and lord.'[15] In April 1075 he wrote to urge the people of Bohemia to hear the blessed Peter in the pope's exhortation.[16] No doubt, Gregory's vicarial power— for he was often styled 'vicar of Peter'—, like that of terrestrial agents in the eleventh century, was virtually that of his declared lord.[17] And lordship so delegated was assuredly official if not exactly impersonal. Like other Christian prelates, Gregory VII had been promoted to his lordly office. He felt himself a servant invoking, from conviction as well as formula, his unworthiness, protesting his humility in face of charges that he was driven by ambition.[18]

Yet he was addressed as 'lord-pope.'[19] This was an honorific appellation such as Pope Gregory himself applied to his venerated

---

[14] *CAP* I, 539–41.

[15] *Reg.* ii.25, cited by Walter Ullmann, *The growth of papal government . . .* , 3d ed. (London 1970) 277. But Ullmann mistook *pater et dominus*, which refer to Peter, not his vicar. For implied identity between Gregory and Peter, see *Reg.* i.19; ii.40, 72.

[16] *Reg.* ii.72.

[17] ibid., i.68, 72; vii.23; and on the vicariate of Peter, Ullmann, *Papal government* 280.

[18] *Reg.* iii.10a. [19] ibid., i.29; vii.14a.

predecessors in the Petrine office. Likewise, he would have been 'lord' to the clergy and scribes about him; they spoke of him so in their protocols of the Lenten synods.[20] Worded impersonally, these protocols appear to represent official action as arising from the ceremonious expression of Petrine power. The pope is said to have 'celebrated the synod,' somewhat as a lay prince might celebrate his Pentecost court; and in 1078 his order to record the enactments in original forms—depositions of several Italian bishops, renewal of excommunication of Archbishop Guifred of Narbonne, and so on—preserved the first-person (plural) voice of Gregory's decision. In such assemblies, as perhaps also on other exalted occasions, he may have felt himself to be wielding divine power. His impassioned invocation of Saint Peter in the promulgations of excommunication against Henry IV is a case in point.[21] A better example may be found in the *Dictatus papae* (1075), where chapter 23 illustrates the difficulty of understanding papal power in objectively official terms. To claim 'that the Roman pontiff, if canonically ordained, is undoubtedly rendered holy by the merits of saint Peter' was to suggest that popes acted from supernaturally infused power. Can it be said that such power was official in its very nature, analogous to that of a consecrated king? Or should it be regarded an effluence of character, beyond all rules and definitions of office. One scholar has argued for the latter position, seeing in *Dictatus* 23 and the famous justification of the power to depose of March 1081 a claim to act out of subjective sanctity incapable of objective or analytic grasp.[22] This may be so, but it is hard to believe that the Gregorians were always, or even usually, oblivious to regulated behaviour. It was because Gregory was so insistent on the vicarious nature of his power in his extreme mea-

[20] e.g., ibid., iii.10a; v.14a.

[21] ibid., iii.6, and 10a (270): 'Beate Petre apostolorum princeps, inclina, quesumus, pias aures tuas nobis et audi me servum tuum, quem ab infantia nutristi et usque ad hunc diem de manu iniquorum liberasti, qui me pro tua fidelitate oderunt et odiunt . . .' See also vii.14a (*an.* 1080).

[22] ibid., ii.55a; viii.21; Fredric Cheyette 'The invention of the state,' *Essays in medieval civilization*, ed. B. K. Lackner, K. R. Philp (Austin 1978) 162–68.

sures against the king of Germany that he felt compelled to justify them in reasons that do indeed look odd to us but that were nonetheless functional and pertinent. This was official conduct at least to the extent that by conviction and temperament Gregory seems to have been disinclined to interpret the Petrine commission as a spiritual lordship in himself.

Yet circumstances surely forced such an interpretation on him as on others. From his first days in office Gregory tried to secure allies in his campaigns against simony and clerical marriage. These allies were the 'faithful ones,' the *fideles Petri*: to begin with, Abbot Hugh of Cluny, the Countesses Beatrice and Matilda, Count Rudolf of Swabia, and a few others, the people he could count on with or without their sworn adhesions.[23] Theirs was a familiar solidarity, even familial in its affective engagement. Gregory addressed the women as his spiritual daughters. And their collaborative intentions, easily traceable in the registered letters, come near to the sort of principled persuasion that we may wish to regard as political behaviour. Valiantly Gregory tried to extend this quasi-familial cohesion, as can be seen in his letters to Christian princes and his summonses to synods. Abbot Hugh was to exhort those 'who love saint Peter that, if they wish truly to be [Peter's] sons and knights, they should not hold secular princes dearer than he.'[24] In October 1079 Pope Gregory wrote generally to 'saint Peter's faithful' in Germany to urge their fortitude in present adversity.[25] And we should not suppose that the pope was content to think of sympathetic agreement as sufficient to fidelity. Fidelity implied service, and preferably active service.

This is surely one meaning of the pacts and vassalic submissions Gregory VII imposed on Norman princes and such other powers lay and religious as he could persuade. In this respect, at least, he seems to have acted in the fullness of affective personal lordship. The oath imposed on Prince Richard of Capua (dated

---

[23] *Reg.* i.11, 14, 19. [24] ibid., ii.49.
[25] ibid., vii.3; also viii.7, 9; ii.37.

14 September 1073) refers to Gregory in familiar address as 'my lord' while referring to obligations of counsel and aid in the pope's affairs and the reserve of fidelity to the 'Roman church' in respect to imperial fidelity. Robert Guiscard swore in substantially the same terms in June 1080.[26] But these oaths can hardly have created a vassalic solidarity. Patterned on oaths sworn by previous Norman princes to Popes Nicholas II and Alexander II, they amounted to pacts of agreement rather like the one between Gregory VII and Prince Landulf VI of Benevento in August 1073.[27] Moreover, they had the effect of insinuating apostolic power into a perfidious field of territorial lordships where neither the precedents nor the prospects can have seemed encouraging. Pope Leo IX himself had been captured by the Normans in the débâcle of Civitate (June 1053). Gregory VII struggled with Robert Guiscard for years before imposing a lordship that failed catastrophically in 1084, when Robert's army, having driven out the imperial antipope, plundered Rome so badly as to discredit the Gregorian cause. That Pope Gregory had to flee the City with his Norman 'protectors' made a bitter mockery of his claims to terrestrial lordship.[28]

Whether this was an abnormal event in the experience of power we shall see. But Gregory had known better days. His claims were rooted in a functional interpretation of Petrine power whereby all earthly power could be regarded as derivative or subordinate. His proposal to lead an expedition in aid of Christians overseas had drawn on such thinking.[29] So did his claims to suzerainty over Hungary and Aragon, to Peter's 'power' over France, and over England in his (vain) appeal for King William's submissive fidelity.[30] Probably it would be wrong to insist on 'feudal' thinking in the hortatory messages to great princes. What the pope evidently sought was fidelity, sometimes quite explicitly; he understood the nature of beneficial tenure; but it was not

---

[26] ibid., i.21a; viii.1a.   [27] ibid. i.18a.
[28] Morris, *Papal monarchy* 87, 93, 120, 136, 139–40.
[29] *Reg.* ii.31.   [30] ibid.; ii.13, 70; i.63; viii.20; vii.25.

usual for him to liken realms as such to fiefs. Some realms he claimed as Peter's patrimony, so that for a king of Hungary to accept his land as a 'benefice' from Henry IV was to diminish Peter's property, or, as Gregory put it a few months later, effectually to reduce the king himself to 'kinglet.'[31] But the vocabulary of conditional submission sounds diversely through the *Register*, as Pietro Zerbi well showed; it looks as if Gregory VII was disposed to urge it on parties in his presence, as when Prince Jaropolk of Kiev was said to have petitioned to receive his realm 'by Peter's gift . . . through our hands.'[32] The quasi-feudal seigneurial pretensions over princes were by no means categorically distinct from pastoral claims that informed the Gregorian conception of the undivided church. To King Sven II of Denmark the pope appealed for military aid in token of faithful submission to the 'universal government entrusted to us.'[33] Fidelity meant solidarity in pontifical causes as well as subordination.[34]

The habits of pontifical action so clearly delineated in the *Register* of Gregory VII persisted in the practise of his successors. Procedures of synod and consistory continued to project the pope in exalted or sanctified power often, as before, incompletely differentiated from his claims to fidelitarian terrestrial lordships. Whether the quasi-feudal lordship of Gregory VII had any real continuity down to the Besançon incident of 1157, when Pope Hadrian IV represented the imperial crown as a 'benefice,' seems more doubtful; but it is clear that clerks of the curia had little difficulty distinguishing between Peter's spiritual and temporal domains. The essentials of the pope's lordly entitlements were in place long before 1192, when the *Liber censuum* was composed to

---

[31] ibid., ii.13, 70.   [32] ibid., ii.74.

[33] ibid., ii.51; see also i.15, 46.

[34] See generally Karl Jordan, 'Das Eindringen des Lehnswesen in das Rechtsleben der römischen Kurie,' *Archiv für Urkundenforschung* XII (1931) 44–48; Piero Zerbi, 'Il termine "fidelitas" nelle lettere di Gregorio VII,' *Studi Gregoriani* III (1948) 129–48; Ullmann, *Papal government* 299–309; Bartlett, *Making of Europe* 243–50.

register them. What marked the twelfth century was the multi-plication of circles attendant on the popes: of the cardinals as an increasingly privileged element sharing in the pontifical lord-ships, of clerks and scribes concerned with maintenance from seigneurial entitlements, of canon lawyers progressively defining the contingencies of papal prerogative, and of clerks engaged with ceremonial protocol. Walter Ullmann demonstrated the monarchical implications of liturgical practise. Popes were crowned as well as consecrated, occasional symbolic acts that gave point to *Dictatus* 8: 'That he [the pope] alone may use imperial insignia.'[35] By 1179 the canonist bishop Rufinus could liken the pope facing his assembled cardinals, bishops, and abbots to a king before his people.[36]

These circles of interest overlapped in the pope's court, the fo-cus of pleas, petitions, patronage, and flattery in a celebratory culture such as few (lay) kings can have rivaled. Powers earthly as well as divine were visible there, to the extent that many by mid-century believed the favouring means of the 'servant of God's servants' were for sale. The parodist of 'Mark-s of Silver' wrote unflatteringly of doorkeepers and cardinals as well as of the 'lord pope,' while from the sober account by John of Salisbury may be deduced a courtly regime of lordship in which personal stature and influence counted for more than belief in effluent sanctity.[37] Even as impersonal purposes seemed to be served by growing re-spect for competence in management and law the culture of power admitted ever wider scope for patronage and favouritism. Better than any other institution of the twelfth century, the papacy re-veals an abiding confusion between official and affective action.

---

[35] *Register* ii.55a; Ullmann, *Papal government*, ch. 10.

[36] Morris, *Papal monarchy* 205.

[37] *Parodistische Texte. Beispiele zur lateinischen Parodie im Mittelalter*, ed. Paul Lehmann (Munich 1923) no. 1a (tr. Haskins, *Renaissance* 185); John of Salisbury, *Historia pontificalis* cc. 29–45, ed. and tr. Marjorie Chibnall (London 1956) 61–88.

West Mediterranean Realms

For all the efforts of reformer popes, who took great interest in south Frankland and the Hispanic realms, the experience of power was a provincial phenomenon in these lands. People clung to their kings (and queens) in Spain; more so, indeed, than to kingdoms. The latter were too small to matter until two or more of them could be stitched together. In the Pyrenees and in view of them, from the Ebro valley to the Rhône, were the counts and viscounts to whom the vestiges of Frankish royal power had devolved. Theirs was a secondary frontier, oriented to the profitable Moorish frontier, yet ceasing in the twelfth century to be afflicted by Muslim incursions. Some principalities, such as the viscounties of Béarn and Narbonne, achieved some measure of autonomy; others, most remarkably the county of Barcelona, consolidated territorial lordship at the expense of lesser counties; most found it expedient to ally with greater princes in holy wars. Duke William IX of Aquitaine (seventh Count William of Poitiers, 1071–1126) made his only enviable reputation fighting in the campaigns that created a Christian territorial monarchy in Aragon. In right of his wife he tried in vain to secure Toulouse, whose counts for their part were pioneer crusaders to Jerusalem. But in the time of Anfos Jourdain (1112–48) Toulouse fell into dynastic rivalry with Barcelona for hegemony in southern France. Provence was for a time the most centrally strategic and coveted principality in Europe, becoming a dynastic annex of Barcelona in 1112 and barely surviving heavy-handed pretensions to domination by Toulouse and the Hohenstaufen emperors thereafter.

LEÓN AND CASTILE

Spain was the grand European frontier. People north of the Pyrenees—princes, knights, monks, and pilgrims—came to think it the manifest destiny of Christians to secure their co-religionists against the Muslims. The popes, notably Urban II (1088–99) and his successors, in quest of spiritual domain, encouraged military intervention as a pious work meriting the inducements and protections enjoyed by crusaders. This situation, sustained by Muslim pressure—the Almoravid counterattacks after 1080, and raiding thrusts as far as Barcelona—favoured Christian princes in Hispanic lands. The counts of Barcelona and the kings of Aragon, Navarre, and León, to name the most conspicuous ones, could count on alliance with great lords investing profitably in the spoils of conquest. The dominant ruler in the later eleventh century was Alfonso VI of León-Castile (1072–1109), whose capture of Toledo (1085) secured the role of monarchy in Christian Spain even as it provoked the Almoravid assaults. His daughter Urraca married the Burgundian noble Henry who was created Count of Portugal in 1093; their son Alfonso VII (reigned 1126–57) was to be the greatest Hispanic ruler of his day, his claim to hegemony epitomized in an imperial title that lapsed with his death. His mother's stormy marriage to Alfonso I 'the Battler' of Aragon (1104–34) coincided with, if it did not precipitate, the uprisings already mentioned.[38]

The collapse of Toledo in 1085 proved a false hope, for the new incursions by Muslim zealots threatened agrarian settlements in the Duero basin and long postponed the expansionist destiny of the Christian monarchy. People lodged or paid their embattled kings, thereby preserving an order of regalian power that may have impeded seigneurial formation. In a remarkable case of 1050 the villagers of Alvarios resisted the Lord Marina's claim to their services; and she prevailed only by claiming that 'those . . . villagers were of the king's power.'[39] Lordship spread, nonetheless, with the growth of patrimonial wealth and the social escape from

[38] Hilda Grassotti, 'El estado,' in *Los reinos cristianos en los siglos XI y XII . . .* , ed. Reyna Pastor *et al.*, 2 vols. (Madrid 1992) II, 13–186; Reilly, *Kingdom of León-Castilla under King Alfonso VI*; idem *The kingdom of León-Castilla under Queen Urraca, 1109–1126* (Princeton 1982).

[39] *Documentos para la historia de las instituciones de León y Castilla (siglos X–XIII)*, ed. Eduardo de Hinojosa (Madrid 1919) no. 14.

rural subjection. By 1093 knights 'of the better sort who are called *infazones* in common speech' could be described as 'nobles by descent or power.'[40] The aristocracy of 'leaders' (*duces*), 'companions' (*comites*), and prelates wielded powers of regalian concession. But new customs of lordship arose with the quest for status, often coming into conflict with traditions of associative right so conspicuous in peninsular Christian realms. And the kings found it hard to defend peasant autonomy given their need to reward the prelates and magnates who served them.

The king's power remained that of a guarantor of right order. It was 'in the reign of Fernando' (I, 1037–65) or in that of Alfonso VI that disputes were resolved or conveyances approved.[41] Already in 1040 Fernando I could be described as 'our lord the emperor prince Ferdinand reigning in his kingdom.'[42] The imperialist ideology should be neither overlooked nor exaggerated, for while it long persisted, its practical consequences were delayed and ephemeral.[43] Right order was regnal order. Others have power but the king reigns (*regnans*); moreover, he reigns even though he normally acts jointly with the queen.

Royal action was cloaked in traditional forms of reverence and legality. Solemn charters and 'testaments' written by clerical scribes in Visigothic scripts persist far into the twelfth century.[44] Diplomatically enactments in writing by the king and queen, these instruments evoke the atmosphere of their gracious dispensation. Yet they have comparatively little to tell us about deference, petition, and merciful concession. Privileges for

[40] *CDL* IV, no. 1279. On *bene nati*, Hinojosa, *Documentos*, nos. 5, 13; Carlos Estepa Díez, *Estructura social de la ciudad de León* (*siglos XI–XIII*) (León 1977) 256, 258.

[41] *Documentos* no. 14; *CDL* IV, no. 1172.

[42] *CDL* IV, no. 984.

[43] See Claudio Sánchez-Albornoz, *España: un enigma histórico*, 3d ed., 2 vols. (Buenos Aires 1971) II, 373–86; and further below, p. 296.

[44] *Reinos cristianos* II, 46–47; Pilar Blanco Lozano, *CDF1* 10–29; 'Die Urkunden Kaiser Alfons VII. von Spanien,' ed. Peter Rassow, *Archiv für Urkundenforschung* X (1928) 327–414.

churches suggest that the style of Leonese kingship was not so much gesturally as attributively imposing.[45] Charters refer to the king's command in the Visigothic term *iussio*; some of them have the dispositive identity of written commands: *per huius nostre preceptionis serenissimum iussionem* (1049), and the like.[46] The epithet *serenissimus* is frequent and continuous, employed in instruments seeming to stress the king's altitude; yet it also appears in a privilege for the see of León (1043), in which Fernando *princeps* is styled 'exiguus famulus uester' ('your little servant'), a bit of formulaic humility itself recurrent.[47]

Charters were not the only form of recorded decision. In León the survival of law-sanctioned justice is remarkably attested in formulaic notices of disputes and proceedings before appointed judges or notables, sometimes in the *concilium* of neighbours. Many such cases came before the king (or queen); some were heard in enlarged solemn courts.[48] The charters bring us closer to these rulers. Here they speak or act for themselves, even if their voices and assertions are distorted by scribes whose literacy, handwriting, and formulas alike betray a rustic clerical culture unmarked by reform and religion from abroad. Here the rulers begin to sound more like lords than officers. Yet the charters mark no departure from regnal order. On the contrary, the most resoundingly public enactments of the later eleventh century were cast in the form of charters, notably the statutes of Alfonso VI.[49]

Moreover, the charters owed their solemnity to the active engagement of the king's notables in their confection. Typically they bear the names of bishops, abbots, counts, royal kinsmen,

---

[45] Cf. *CDL* iv, no. 1007 (1043).

[46] *CDF1* nos. 39, 51, 53, 71; *CDL* iv, no. 1221. Also no. 1282 (1094): sign of 'Lucius clericus iussionem regis qui notuit.'

[47] *CDF1* no. 20; also nos. 48, 63, 66, 72; *CDL* iv, nos. 1048, 1116.

[48] *CDL* iv, no. 1085 (before king and queen); nos. 1057, 1093; *Documentos*, nos. 14, 26 (before king); *CDL* iv, nos. 1106, 1122 (before queen). See also nos. 1029, 1159, 1202, 1228, 1249, 1272, 1289, 1322.

[49] *CDL* iv, nos. 1256, 1293; *CDF1* nos. 46, 73.

and others untitled, often with the mark *confirmo* following notarial subscriptions disposed in columns. This was no mere formality, for there is plenty to show that it was still normal in the eleventh century to read the completed charter aloud to the assembled *firmatores* and witnesses. The latter were not the *palatium* or *curia* as such, but rather *potestates* or relations or officials in their own right, singly sharers in regnal power, not members or consultants. They confirmed, thus proving their king-supportive fidelity; their presence meant adherence to imposed consensus; their collaboration was procedural, not political. Nor could the scribe be expected to influence a collective ritual of promulgation, for he held no office, and was sometimes himself a beneficiary. The king's command (*iussio*) was ever close to expression, a scribe handy in a local church, and one who knew the rules of royal diplomatic. No doubt, much was concealed by such procedural action, at once ceremonious and passive; a charter was often a settlement bearing on divergent interests. This was surely true of the great charters that purported to regulate weighty matters of societal concern: for example, concessions in November 1072 abolishing violent customs; the confirmation of a judgment guaranteeing the integrity of inheritances in the several categories of lordship (1089); and a regulation of procedures in litigation between Christians and Jews.[50] In all these cases we hear of the attendance, counsel, or consent of notables of the land; in none is the assemblage categorized as such. One may suppose that a 'real' play of power went on behind the ceremonial facade of diplomatic consensus; but this was not the visible king of León.

That is, not to us. The king's subjects—clergy, peasants, townsfolk, and their lords—knew more than we can prove of his devices of influence, coercion, and maintenance. They heard the gossip that trailed the restless retinue eating its ponderous way from León to Sahagún, to Oviedo, to Santiago, even to Toledo,— and always back to León, itself more nearly a capital city since the translation of San Isidoro amidst royalist pomp in 1063. The

---

[50] *CDL* iv, nos. 1182, 1183, 1244, 1256.

king's patronage and influence radiated from his concentration of magnates and servants; this was his 'palace.'[51] But to say how the notables who confirmed with the king were disposed to him, we need to know how they were obligated to him, and this is not easy to find out. For it happens that the rituals of submission in northwestern Spain, lands otherwise well documented, are poorly recorded.

The subject-oath of Visigothic times had disappeared, while the terms of personal submission to the king were not commonly put in writing. Yet the survival of old regnal order surely entailed an obligation of fidelity sanctioned in written law. Allusions to the king as 'natural lord' point to the reservation of an overriding kingship amongst multiplying lordships.[52] Yet no one thought of public order as in conflict with personal tenure. The dynamics of the situation, as can be seen from the deeds of Rodrigo Díaz (El Cid Campeador), favoured the cohesion of an elite group in attendance on the lord-king; and it looks as if by the 1080s a new manner of deference, less official and more invidious, was spreading through the aristocracy. One spoke more of 'holding' one's status or power, more of *tenencias* than of counties. Homage crept into the unwritten rituals of dependence. And the fief, arriving in Spain in the conceptual baggage of Burgundian monks and knights, may well have come to seem something other than a 'loan.'[53] It became easier to wonder why loyalty and its material reward should not be hereditary.

To what extent this tendency affected the lesser ranks of royal and patrimonial servants is unclear. The *maior domus* (also called *seniskalk*, a term surely of French provenance), and the *sayones*) were of Visigothic origin, the latter having become agents of en-

---

[51] Cf. Reilly, *Alfonso VI*, chs. 6, 8, esp. pp. 148–60.

[52] *Leges Visigothorum* ii.1.7, ed. Karl Zeumer (Hanover-Leipzig 1902) 52–54; *Chronica Adefonsi imperatoris* i.8, ed. Antonio Maya Sánchez, *Chronica hispana saeculi XII*, ed. Emma Falque Rey *et al.* (Turnhout 1990) 153.

[53] The equivalence was noted in the decrees of Burgos, 1117: 'feodum, quod in ispania prestimonium vocant . . .' ed. Fita, 'Concilio nacional de Burgos' (*BRAH* xlviii) 395 (facsimile), 397.

forcement, summons, and fiscal collection. Together with the estate-manager (*maiorinus*; Sp. *merino*), such functionaries figured in a written law still in use, their competencies corresponding to real needs in a public regime of justice and protection. Yet questions arise. Little but titles survives to prove an official conception of service; in abundant records we find no allusion to appointments, oaths of faithful service, or tests of competence. The institutes of Coyanza (1055), while recapitulating the *Fuero of León* (1017) for the normative rights of *sayones*, counts, and *merinos*, admonish the latter classes of agent to 'rule the people subject to them justly, [and] not oppress the weak unjustly.'[54] Hardly less telling is a recurrent imprecision of terms. Already the Gothic law supposed that any authority might be called judge, while the *potestates* of the tenth and eleventh centuries were categorically confused. The *merino* could be designated that of the king, of the city, of the region; he was in his way a king's companion, doubtless often face to face, little pressed to distinguish administratively between court and hinterland. In 1093 Alfonso VI favoured his former *maior domus* Pelayo Vellítiz, 'my most faithful and beloved man,' and his wife Mayor with the solemn privilege of holding their whole acquired lordship in Villa Santi in full and immune heredity. With fidelity went omnicompetence, as may be glimpsed in a subscription of the *merino* Pelayo Dominguiz as '*equonomus* of all [the king's] land.'[55] Office was assimilated to lordly patronage. The functions were becoming tenures themselves, symptoms of a regnal order subject to patrimonial pressures to lordship.

The 'perverse men' mentioned early in Fernando I's reign (1037–46)[56] were rebels or violators of churches or murderers, the malefactors normal to regnal order, and their violence was subject

---

[54] *CDL* IV, nos. 1048, 1195, 1213, 1217, 1221, 1316; Estepa Díez, *Estructura social de León* 446–55; and Luis G(arcia) de Valdeavellano, *Curso de historia de las instituciones españolas . . .* , 3d ed. (Madrid 1973) 488–90, 500–5. Also Alfonso Garcia Gallo, 'El concilio de Coyanza . . . ,' *AHDE* XX (1950) 298.

[55] *CDL* IV, no. 1217.

[56] *CDFI* no. 31 (a problematic charter transmitted in late copies).

to legal remedy. Yet customs of violence were becoming known in Spain. When King Fernando visited Sahagún in 1049 and Compostela in 1065, he heard charges against his servants. And when Alfonso VI came to undisputed power in 1072, he learned that *sayones* of the realm were accustomed to engage in retributive violence in cases of stealthy homicide or robbery. They pillaged and devastated neighbouring villages, exacting compensatory payments for homicide, sometimes doubling the fine and imposing it on the innocent with the rest.[57]

The king acted on this complaint, and in so doing defines for us the aims of royal power in León. As had been attested in the Councils of León (1017) and Coyanza (1055), the king functions to promote Christianity and to secure the property of churches and individuals alike. Alfonso's reaction came at a critical early moment, for he was himself a survivor of violence: of the uneasily convenient killing of his elder brother Sancho a few weeks before, and of the insurrection 'of knights and counts and other wicked men' who, according to a later record, 'oppressed churches and God's peoples after King Fernando's death.'[58] Magnates of the several realms, used to bargaining with the king for their loyalty, had exploited the divided succession inflicted on them in 1065. Violence was on his mind when in November 1072 Alfonso convoked prelates and magnates, including those of Galicia–Portugal, to León. The two records by which we know of this grand occasion were statutes in the form of charters directed against customary violence. On 17 November the king acted with his sister Urraca as if in judgment on the *clamor* of pilgrims and travellers to abolish a toll, together with the pillaging for which the toll was an excuse, levied at the castle of Santa María de Autares on the road to Santiago. This was a pious concession, in thanks to God for restoring Alfonso to power 'without bloodshed [and] without

---

[57] Garcia Gallo, 'Concilio de Coyanza,' 298; Antonio López Ferreiro, *Historia de la santa A. M. iglesia de Santiago de Compostela*, 11 vols. (Santiago 1898–1911) II, ap. 233, c. 5; *CDL* IV, no. 1182.

[58] *ES* XL 417–22 (ap. 28).

depredation,' a piety further represented as beneficial not only to Spaniards but even to the people of Italy, France, and Germany. In a second charter (19 November) the king abolished the 'custom' by which *sayones* pillaged villages unable to produce a murderer. Only peasants proven suspect under oath and the ordeal of hot water were henceforth liable to the murder-fine.[59]

These great charter-statutes, records of general address turning on the dispositive word *constituere*, are among the earliest known enactments of royal legislation concerned with the excesses of lordship. For that is what these notorious customs were. There can be no illusion that the easy and lucrative rapacity of mounted armed men was an abuse peculiar to royal servants. It is remarkable that these complaints should have been exploited in a timely celebration of power. It was hardly a moment to press for more, even assuming the vision to do so; the charters were massively confirmed by counts and royal servants as well as by ten bishops of León and Galicia-Portugal and many clerics. The king was struggling to create a new baronial solidarity in three realms. His best device to this end was organized aggression against the Muslim taifas, and Alfonso would exploit it well.

Pressures from within persisted. While disputes over lordship continued to be ventilated in judicial form, one of these, in 1093, referred to local power the bishop of León had lost 'by the violence of knights [*violentia militum*].'[60] *Infanzones* were coming to be termed *milites* by this time,[61] so we cannot be sure when (or even whether) the multiplication of French knights along the roads to León and Santiago affected the rural experience of power in those lands. What seems clear is that the fidelity and methods of castellans were becoming increasingly problematic. Towards 1105

[59] *CDL* IV, nos. 1182, 1183. See also Ramon Menéndez Pidal, *La España del Cid*, 7th ed., 2 vols. (Madrid 1969) I, 190–92, who is overly sceptical about the king's sincerity, although surely right in suspecting that Urraca had some part in the murder of Sancho; and Reilly, *Alfonso VI* 68–72.

[60] *Documentos*, ed. Hinojosa, no. 27.

[61] *ES* XXXVI, ap. 45; also *HC* i.31 (60).

Bishop Diego Gelmírez of Compostela complained to Count Raimond of Galicia that the castellans at San Pelayo de Luto were not only collecting toll but also despoiling travellers—the old custom renewed, in another castle.[62]

IN SIGHT OF THE PYRENEES

'From this hour forward I Gaucelin son of Hermetrude shall not take from Hermengarde daughter of Rangarde the city of Béziers and the towers and the walls and the fortifications there today or to be built henceforth nor take things from it nor violate them nor deceive her about it. And if there is a man or woman, men or women, who take it or take from it, [Gaucelin] will be a helper thereby. . . .' So swore, about 1076, a knight of Béziers to Ermengarde of Carcassonne (viscountess, 1067–1105) in words echoing those of an oath sworn by Count Roger III for Carcassonne city towards 1063.

1122, 13 October: Count Ponç Uc of Empúries, 'son of the late Sancia, woman,' swears to Count Ramon Berenguer III and his son Ramon to be 'faithful . . . from this hour forward . . . for your life and your bodies and for all the honour you now have or henceforth acquire by my counsel, that I shall not take it from you . . . nor anyone [else] for me, but [I shall be your] faithful helper . . . as long as I live. By God and these holy [gospels].' These are virtually the same words in which his grandfather had sworn to Ramon Berenguer I around 1053–71.

1134, vigils of Pentecost: 'I Garin will not take the castle of Randon from you Bishop Guilhem [of Mende] nor undo the fortifications which are there or will be henceforth, nor deceive you . . . And if any man or woman should capture you, I shall have no peace nor association with him or her . . . [on] demand, I shall render [the castle] . . . by these holy gospels.'

---

[62] *HC* i.24 (52); A. G. Biggs, *Diego Gelmirez, first archbishop of Compostela* (Washington 1949) 60–61.

Undated, about 1143: 'Hear ye, Raimond Archbishop of Arles, I Alfonse, Count of Toulouse, Duke of Narbonne and Marquis of Provence, swear to you life, members, and your body and the church and cloister of Arles and the castle of Sello and the castle of Saint-Amantio, which I shall not take from you . . . so help me God and these holy gospels of God. . . .'[63]

Sacramenta, sacramenz, sagrement[al]s: oaths, and ever more oaths, in tumbling, piling, sack-splitting, mouldering profusion; from the Ebro Valley to the Gévaudan a universe of recorded commitments to lords (and others); a written culture of fidelity. Products of the solemnest moment in the recognition of human power, evidently meant to defeat oblivion, the 'writings of fidelity' were nonetheless subject to baffling negligence. Vast numbers of them were undated, a fact that cannot always mean they were drafted for occasions that did not happen. Moreover, their preservation was so inattentive that we must suppose that in Pyrenean lands, *as elsewhere,* written oaths soon perished in large quantities. That so many have survived—over 1100 of them in three great meridional cartularies alone, plus many hundreds of originals—we owe in some part to increasing interest in recording power prescriptively in some princely lordships.[64]

Yet the uncommon survival of oaths in this great Pyrenean world is not entirely illusory. It surely points to the singular importance of specific commitment in the newly sprung feudal societies of this region. Fidelity, as Pierre Bonnassie showed, proved to be a pliantly adaptable instrument for defining security concretely.[65] What must be added is that the articulated oath preserved traces of the public fidelity in which it originated. It is not simply

---

[63] (1) *HL* v, no. 324i; cf. no. 266; (2) *LFM* ii, no. 520; cf. no. 519; (3) *Les plus anciennes chartes en langue provençale . . .* , ed. Clovis Brunel (Paris 1926) no. 26; (4) *HL* v, no. 557.

[64] 'Cartulaire des Trencavel,' Société archéologique de Montpellier, MS 10; *Liber instrumentorum memorialium. Cartulaire des Guillems de Montpellier,* ed. Alexandre Germain (Montpellier, 1884–86); and the 'Liber feudorum maior,' ed. Francisco Miquel Rosell (=*LFM*).

[65] *Catalogne* ii, 742–43.

that formulas such as 'from this hour forward' (*de ista hora in antea*) derived from Frankish oaths of fidelity; more notably, because more revealing of political assumptions, the territorial structures of county and bishopric were reserved in oaths to the counts of Barcelona that guaranteed affectively personal support to public power.[66] It would be mistaken to view the documentary preponderance of Mediterranean oaths as proof that lordship undermined, let alone displaced, an impersonal order of regnal law. What the oaths and conventions suggest is what the *Usatges of Barcelona* say explicitly: that customs of lordship have grown up to supplement the Gothic law where it was silent.[67] There was nothing categorically 'private' about the aims and means of lord-rulership in Pyrenean societies of the eleventh and twelfth centuries.

It is true that there were no kings to cling to—or to fear. One was badly needed in 1108, when Count Ramon Berenguer III called in vain on King Louis VI to help repel an Almoravid invasion that terrorized settlements as far as the hinterlands of Barcelona; his unaided success, replicating an historic ancestral feat, together with impressive counter-thrusts against Valencia and Mallorca confirmed his claim to regalian fidelities.[68] The old upland counties—Urgell, Cerdanya, Besalú, Roussillon—were spared this fright, thanks to Ramon, as were the peoples of Carcassonne, Narbonne, Montpellier, Toulouse, and the Rouergue, whose lord-counts could fairly choose whether to stake their reputations by fighting in Spain or the Holy Land. As for the king of Aragon, few would then have forgotten that he was but a generation removed from ancestral self-promotion. No king of France visited the South before Louis VII's journey to Compostela in 1154.[69] Yet these were thoroughly regalian societies, their

[66] e.g., *LFM* I, no. 150; cf. Santiago Sobrequés i Vidal, *Els grans comtes de Barcelona* (Barcelona 1961) 79.

[67] *Usatges de Barcelona . . .* , ed. Joan Bastardas (Barcelona 1984), US. 1–2 (old 1, 3).

[68] *CPC* I, nos. 45, 46.

[69] A monumental event: "& hoc fuit tempore quo rex Francie venit in partibus istis," *HL* v, no. 629.

lord-princes bearers alike of Visigothic and Frankish traditions. Comital charters of Barcelona and Besalú invoked the *regia potestas* of Gothic law.[70] And scribes everywhere dated records by the Frankish regnal year or else referred to the (Capetian) king in power. This usage marked off the lands of Catalan and Occitan speech as distinct from Hispanic lands, where existent power—the listing of elite tenants—not chronology determined validity. A long frontier of scribal culture was breached in the vicinity of Toulouse, where charters sometimes refer to the count and bishop as empowered together with the reigning principal.[71]

The pretensions and fears of the old elite—counts, viscounts, bishops—are brilliantly illuminated in the famous charges (ca. 1059) by Viscount Berenguer of Narbonne that Archbishop Guifred had wrecked the prelacy his parents had bought for him as a child. The timely appeal to reform-minded clerics hardly obscures an underlying patrimonial dispute between great lineages, the comital house of Cerdanya and the vicecomital house of Narbonne. The complaint refers to the original convention (? ca. 1113) which settled conflicting interests by a payment of 100,000s. for the 'election' of Guifred and to the oath by which the elect (then ten years old!) had engaged not to injure the viscount's family. It also refers to the viscount's father's sharing the payment (*donum*) with the count of Rodez. The viscounty of Narbonne was a public fiscal structure as well as a patrimonial one, an appurtenance of the duchy of Gothia.[72] New families crowded in on this elite: the lords of Montpellier, the counts of Melgueil, the lords of Montcada. But there was no visible resistance to them, for the successes of Barcelona and Toulouse (such as they were) depended on the support of ambitiously loyal families, those with

[70] ACA, Cancelleria, pergamins R.B. III, 20, 104dupl. (=*LFM* II, no. 506).

[71] *HL* v, no. 513; *Cartulaire de l'abbaye de Lézat*, ed. Paul Ourliac, Anne-Marie Magnou, 2 vols. (Paris 1984–87) I, nos. 456, 629, 919 ('dominante Anfusso, comite Tholosa'), 929.

[72] *HL* v, no. 251; Elisabeth Magnou-Nortier, *La société laïque et l'église dans la province ecclésiastique de Narbonne . . .* (Toulouse 1974) 463–68.

but one or a few castles. Nor can we discern much insistence by lord-counts, at least not in Occitania, on their justice of public security or of the peace. No diplomatic of public justice survived, as it did in Spain, although narrations of complaint seem to suggest some procedural formality of *clamor* or *querimonia*. Judges (*judices*) disappeared in Occitania, where scribes variably recorded procedures and judgments, and stressed the presence of notable or noble men; they wrote of awards not of the procedures of official jurisdiction. Regalian initiatives such as those of Alfonso VI as early as 1072 had their parallels in an expanded county of Barcelona, as we shall see, but they were long delayed in Occitania.

There the facade of regnal order and the economic constraints of competitive lordship combined to render violence conspicuous. Victims could try the courts, or rather the magnates (*potentes*) who inspired the occasions sometimes (though seldom) called *curia*, but who could enforce their justice? In 1078 the monks of Conques went to the count of Rodez with a complaint of unjust seizures in a distant domain that had been heard in repeated 'pleas,' and lately in a *judicium* before the bishop of Béziers and 'other nobles,' whose decision the accused had rejected.[73] Normative decisions based on testimony, proof, or law gave way to compromise, of which the unformulaic memorials sometimes bring us close to confrontational power. Guilhem V of Montpellier had to come to terms for his 'invasion of the honour of Saint Peter [of Maguelone]' and 'malefactions,' which had cost him his fief by judgment of bishops, clergy, and lay notables, by swearing a solemn oath of fidelity to Bishop Gotafred of Maguelone and answering his tough question: "'Do you recognize that you hold a better benefice from me and Saint Peter than from [any] other lord and do you recognize that you are my man and Saint Peter's before [any] other lord's?" "I so recognize," replied Guillem.'[74] Recovery of a good fief was on the high side of a variable scale of

[73] *HL* v, no. 333; cf. Jean Dunbabin, *France in the making 843–1180*, 2d ed. (Oxford 2000) 214–15

[74] *Cartulaire des Guillems de Montpellier*, no. 42 (=*HL* v, no. 377 [718]).

rewards for repentance. The tormentors who refused to concede their family's gift of a church to the canons of Béziers had finally, after tortuous efforts to arrive at a 'judgment of truth,' to be bought off in 1053 for 300s. The monks of Lézat did better in 1137, getting Roger de Tersac not only to renounce tithes and first-fruits at Maillan for a mere six sous of Morlaas, but even to recognize that this price was 'unjust.' One might be induced to recognize that lay lordship over churches violated Christ's church, as in a restitution to remedy the 'violence' perpetrated 'by secular knights' in an allod of Le Mas d'Azil (1083), and still exact one's price![75]

Pious restitutions were not uncommon after 1080,[76] yet we sense that God had little better success against seizures and novel exactions than His earthly deputies. There was something more insidious about violence in Occitania, more insistent, than may be deduced from written appeals and settlements. In semi-arid lands and uplands, lordships were more heavily dependent on hospitalities, tools, and justice than elsewhere. The obligatory lodging (*alberga*) of knights and animals must always have been overbearing; it was easily seized by force, commonly suffered in silence, often denounced.[77] To say that only the bishop of Béziers could tax at will (*tolta*, *quista*) at Aspiran was as much as to say that he alone had coercive lordship there.[78] We begin to hear of protectorates (*salvetats*) in lands of Lézat and Comminges; of 'bad customs,' even of 'bad lordship.'[79] 'Bad usages,' opined Count Roger II of Foix in 1111, 'are not to be recited, but rather pondered and abolished.'

---

[75] *HL* v, no. 236; see also no. 371 (1083); *Cart. Lézat* I, no. 253; *HL* v, no. 355.

[76] e.g., *HL* v, nos. 360, 402, 404, 420.

[77] ibid., no. 438; *Cart. Lézat* I, nos. 269, 668; also no. 14; II, no. 1715; see also *HL* v, nos. 333, 387, 503iv. Roger II of Foix gave up his right of *alberga* in Lézat's domains in 1121, *Cart. Lézat* I, no. 919.

[78] *HL* v, no. 531 (*an.* 1135).

[79] *Cart. Lézat* I, nos. 288, 44, 53: 'malum dominium' (1150); Paul Ourliac, 'Les sauvetés du Comminges . . . ,' *Recueil de l'Académie de Législation* XVIII (1947), 23–147; *HL* v, no. 444.

Once in a while? Having renounced 'violence and rapacity' visited on the people and monks of Pamiers by his father and himself, this penitent looter was rewarded with custody of the castle of Pamiers. It was an invitation to more oppression from his son Roger III in the 1120s.[80]

Was there a perceptible tendency, a chronology of violence, in this experience of ponderous power? We have no evidence that contemporaries thought so, which is one reason why historians have debated the nature and extent of feudalizing in southern France.[81] What can be said is that the castral violence attested in the Rouergue in the early eleventh century seems to have spread thereafter, provoking remedial measures in the Gévaudan towards 1050 and 1110, and in the upper Garonne valley in 1139.[82] There was no general crisis, for the brutalities were not linked to disloyalty or the disruption of justice as in the counties dominated by Ramon Berenguer I. The worsening problem in Occitania was that knights, however respectable their allegiance, were multiplying beyond the capacities of orderly maintenance. Hence the visibility of *alberga* and the stress on damage wrought by the force of lords in conflict, even of great lords, as around Narbonne towards 1050 and Montpellier in the 1120s.[83] Violence in the coastal counties may have been chiefly that of warring armies; it was tolerably normal. Something more virulent may have flared along the upland perimeter, from the Massif Central to the Ariège. A curious 'peace,' the *paz de Mende*, apparently reworked around 1100, records the appointment of twelve 'judges' (*iudiciarii*) 'for the stability and observance of peace' by Bishop Raimond (1031–51) and a certain Richard, possibly viscount of Millau.

[80] *HL* v, nos. 438, 503i.

[81] Bonnassie, *From slavery to feudalism* 104–6; and Claudie Duhamel-Amado, *L'aristocratie languedocienne du Xe au XIIe siècle*, 2 vols. (Toulouse 2001–07) I.

[82] Bonnassie, *From slavery to feudalism*, ch. 4; *Les Miracles de Saint-Privat . . .* , ed. Clovis Brunel (Paris 1912) 20–21, 38; 'Vita, Inventio et Miracula Sanctae Enimiae,' ed. Clovis Brunel, *Analecta Bollandiana* LVII (1939) 281–84; the *Breve de paz de Mende*, cited below, note 84; *HL* v, no. 540.

[83] *HL* v, nos. 251, 491.

They were 'to judge quarrels,' probably those such as would arise from the theft of horses, a matter later taken up by a council on the peace at Mende around 1110.[84] It looks as if official authorities had tried in this way to revive public justice while accepting the reality that only magnates of the land(s) in large numbers could be expected to keep the peace. This was the hopeless initiative of a crumbling comital order.

Imperial Lands

Perhaps nowhere in Europe were kings so venerated, or the culture and ceremonial they expressed, as in the lands between the Tuscan Apennines and the Danube river. If traditions of Lombard monarchy were fading in the eleventh century, the Saxon dynastic kings had renewed the Frankish habits of conquest while institutionalizing the German claim to imperial coronation. When the Pavians made King Henry's death (1024) an excuse for tearing down the old palace, they incurred the wrath of Conrad II (1024–39), who declared that the 'king's house' was not theirs to destroy: 'if the king dies, the kingdom remains.'[85] For those on the favoured route from Bamberg or Regensburg across the Brenner Pass through Lombardy, this was dazzling theocracy, the splendours of symbolic display enhanced by the subservience of all who approached a lord-prince suspended between God and man. Easily dominant in Bavaria, where a duke had nominal precedence to go with a vast lordship, the Salian kings (1024–1125) enjoyed authority in Lombardy, which turned into effectual power following their imperial coronations, in 1027 for Conrad II, and 1046 for Henry III (1039–56). They perambulated far beyond this axis—in Franconia, Thuringia, Saxony, Burgundy, and

---

[84] AN, J.304, no. 112, ed. Clovis Brunel, 'Les juges de la paix en Gévaudan . . . ,' *BEC* CIX (1951) 32–41.

[85] Wipo, *Gesta Chuonradi* II, ed. Harry Bresslau, 3d ed. (Hanover-Leipzig 1915) 30.

Lotharingia; and southwards to Tuscany, though seldom beyond. Crowned in Rome, they celebrated feast-days in Utrecht. While it would be a mistake to lose touch with them in their distant pursuits, we may reasonably suppose that people in the cities and churches in sight of the Alps experienced the power of these rulers most intensely.[86]

In 1050 Henry III of Germany was much the strongest king in Europe. That his son Henry IV (1056–1106) surmounted the obstacles of premature succession owed much to his father's prestige. These kings were consecrated to govern. Scribes and monastic annalists spoke easily of the 'kingdom's rule' (*regni gubernacula*) or of the king's direction of 'secular affairs' (*negocia secularia*). They took for granted that kings were attentive to the 'state of the realm' (*status regni*), recording the royal festival courts insistently and sometimes in lavish detail. A Carolingian survival, this scribal perspective was conspicuous in Germany, where it persisted into the twelfth century. The monk-narrators could only think of royal affairs in the liturgical rhythms of the Christian year; could only tell of the king as the talk about him, and around him, the queen and their family, had it; could only, or chiefly, listen in on the public-feastly king. How much scope there was for orderly debate in the princely assemblies is another matter, but the Salians' realm before the Saxon rebellion was, in its way, a solidarity, virtually a 'republic,' of king and princes.[87]

The official solemnity of royal power found expression in a written diplomatic of unparalleled conservatism. Petitioned for his favour or concession, Henry III, like his predecessors, acted without visible constraints. Those who attended him in ceremo-

---

[86] See generally *DDC2*, *DDH3*, and *DDH4*, together with Carlrichard Brühl, *Fodrum, gistum, servitium regis. Studien zu den wirtschaftlichen Grundlagen des Königtums* . . . , 2 vols. (Cologne 1968) 1, 453–577; and Herwig Wolfram, *Conrad II, 990–1039* . . . , tr. Denise A. Kaiser (University Park 2006).

[87] e.g., Thietmar, *Chronik* vii–viii (396–533; *Ottonian Germany*, 306–85); Wipo c. 25 (43–44); *Annales Altahenses maiores*, ed. Edmund von Oefele (Hanover 1891) 48.

nial or ministerial functions are more or less concealed in charters composed according to German formularies, and there was little change in this respect once Henry IV came of age.[88] But the quality of royal prerogative cannot depend on this test. Even in diplomas of grace there may have been affective interventions in the association of the Empress-consort Agnes in acts of her husband or son. Moreover, the ceremonious mercy of lord-kingship is quite as evident in the deferential procedures of the imperial court as in those of León and France. In June 1052, Emperor Henry III acted at Zürich on the petition of Bishop Wido of Volterra and by the 'intervention' of the empress and the chancellor to place clerical tenants of that place under episcopal jurisdiction.[89] Examples of this could be multiplied.[90] Henry IV was more apt than his father to refer to the presence or counsel of bishops, counts, or other notables, but the protocol of sanction remained unchanged. Similar observations apply to the Italian diplomatic of the Salian kings. But one of the inherited forms of royal action in Italy was the *placitum*, whereby the king (or emperor) or his functionaries dispensed justice in accordance with the applicable law. The survival of records of *placita* through the whole period of this book permits us to listen in on people talking about their rights and claims. In May 1055 Emperor Henry III sat with three bishops, twelve 'judges of the sacred palace,' and others at Roncaglia to hear one Gandulf, challenged by Bishop Wido of Luni together with Azo, his church's advocate, renounce his claim to one-third of Castel Aghinolfo. The legal declarations of both parties were quoted verbatim; Gandulf handed over his right by gesture with a stick, which the emperor himself then grasped to place the church and bishop in his ban in case of violation of the judgment.[91] In another case, the very intonation of a bishop's plea—'Oh, Lord my lord Emperor, how often have I

---

[88] *DDH3* nos. 120, 138, 192, 199, 325; *DDH4* I, nos. 25, 94, 97, 100.

[89] *DDH3* no. 291.

[90] e.g., ibid., no. 352; *DDH4* nos. 2, 104, 126.

[91] *DDH3* no. 339.

appealed to you . . .'; and the emperor's questioning of the judges as to the law—preserve the words and atmosphere of such a court.[92] Not all 'pleas' were held in the emperor's presence; indeed, most were not; but their records afford glimpses of the human impact of august power, even as they prove the tenacious survival of public order in this Mediterranean land.

The lord-king acted everywhere in German and Italian lands by virtue of his regnal title. He was styled king (*rex*) in his diplomas from the day of his accession, *imperator* from that of his imperial coronation. By right of inheritance and election, the king behaved officially, dispensing protection and justice according to Carolingian precept. His ministers and servants—chancellor, vice-chancellor, *ministeriales*—were regarded as functionaries responsible to the *res publica* even as they were tempted to prey on 'public property' at the king's disposal.[93] One came to speak of 'ministerials of the realm.'[94] But the laws and offices were not the king's to abrogate, for they had some of the attributes of custom. In support of the Salian regalian itinerary were public obligations to service and maintenance assigned to estates, villages, and palaces, such as at Pavia and Regensburg. Nor was there anything specifically regnal, still less imperial, about the territorial laws the king-emperor was called to uphold. People in Italy lived by laws or customs Roman, Lombard, or Frankish in their transactions and trials. Judgments of right could be presided by counts or bishops as well as by the king or his appointed agents. In German lands the dukes and counts were disinclined to think of themselves as royal agents.[95] It is true that bishops invested by the king or who received comital powers from him were thought of as public functionaries; but their fidelity must have been deter-

---

[92] ibid., no. 188.

[93] Wipo, *Gesta* c. 7 (30); *DDC2* no. 244; *Lamperti annales*, ed. Oswaldus Holder-Egger (Hanover 1894) 88.

[94] *TrSEm* no. 805 (1141).

[95] e.g., Thietmar vii.30 (434; *Ottonian Germany*, 327–28); Lampert, *Annales* 81 (*consuetudo* of precedence, 1062).

mined by alliance and friendship, by personal more than public commitment.[96] The king controlled them by bestowing—or withholding—his *gratia*.[97]

For their ruler was lord-king. His insistence on fidelity and attendance weighed against the princely solidarity implied by the prevailing concept of regnal governance. No wonder he had to press his extra-regnal dominations, so rewarding to his adherents and their retinues; that Henry IV was distracted from his eastern frontiers was not the least of his problems. There was an incessant struggle over access to the king for his favour or patronage. Some of this is perceptible in the diplomas of the emancipated Henry IV, more becomes visible in the hostile accounts from the 1070s. What won favour was service such as the Salians rewarded by grants of lordship in benefice or property. One must guess that such grants, especially those to lay men, were far more numerous than surviving records indicate. The ones we have show the ruler interacting with men of local interests, in far-flung groupings of servants clustered diversely in the regions through which the royal household passed.[98] Moreover, they point to a concept of official lordship in the king's exercise of power that cannot have been peculiar to Germany but that may have been more pronounced in imperial lands than elsewhere. King Henry III's explicit motive in endowing his servile knight Swiggert in 1048 was to encourage faithful service in hopes of such reward.[99] And it was service to the kingdom as well as to the lord-king that made such fidelity an option for knights in Germany. Of the commended men summoned to military service, Henry IV reckoned them bound publicly as well as privately to their lords.[100] Whether he held any such view of the

---

[96] *DDH2* no. 226; *DDH3*, nos. 279–81; Wipo c. 1 (10).

[97] Timothy Reuter, 'The "imperial church system" of the Ottonian and Salian rulers: a reconsideration,' *Journal of Ecclesiastical History* XXXIII (1987) 356 (reprinted *Medieval politics and modern mentalities*, ed. Janet. L. Nelson [Cambridge 2006] 334).

[98] *DDH4* nos. 45, 74, 198, 211. See also *An. Altah.* 35 (1044).

[99] *DDH3* no. 210.   [100] Lampert, *Annales*, 157.

entitlements of royal lordship as his enemies alleged is a matter that will engage us further. Certainly he inherited an austere view of responsible power, as may be inferred from Frutolf's story that when Henry III married Agnes of Poitou and had her anointed in 'kingly' ceremony in 1044, he shooed away a vast crowd of singers and jesters empty-handed.[101]

BAVARIA

They were at their strongest, these kings, in Bavaria, where they enjoyed the steady fidelity of nobles and churches. Yet this was not the crown's land, but a historic duchy with venerable claims to autonomy. Possessed of its customary 'Law of the Bavarians,' it was a prospering society in the eleventh century, habituated to being used as an apanage for the kings' offspring. The dukedom survived as an adjunct office, with its lands and palaces, while the counties seem to have been reduced to vestigial functions of witness to transactions. A quasi-public protectorate remained in effect, if not intact. Towards 1052 Abbot Sifrid of Tegernsee appealed to Henry III's imperial clemency to put an end to the depredations of the counts Henry and Papo, 'who ought to be our defenders [but] are the most rapacious assailants of our grain.'[102]

Here the norm is contrasted with (alleged) reality. No doubt, there had been slippage from official norms. But there is much also to suggest some vitality of jurisdictional order whereby the advocates of clerical lands and the multiplying *ministeriales* carried on in functions of service that can only, however reservedly, be likened to offices. The relation between status and service helps us see how the masses in Bavaria experienced

---

[101] *Frutolfi et Ekkehardi chronica* . . . , ed. Franz-Josef Schmale, Irene Schmale-Ott (Darmstadt 1972) 62–64.

[102] *Tegernseer Briefsammlung* no. 124. Also Wilhelm Störmer, 'Bayern und der bayerische Herzog im 11. Jahrhundert . . . ,' *Die Salier und das Reich*, ed. Stefan Weinfurter, 4 vols. (Sigmaringen 1991) I, 503–29; T. Reuter, *Germany in the early Middle Ages, 800–1056* (London 1991) ch. 7.

power. It was one thing to watch an imperial procession pass by, or to be conscripted in the service of magnate families, quite another to have one's freedom—that is, exemption from servile obligations—questioned. Such a thing happened to descendants of a lady named Guntpirch who had married a serf of Freising around 972; it took considerable litigation for the former to secure recognition of their beneficial status for services clerical, cameral, and courtly around 1050.[103]

The power implied by freedom, however circumscribed, found ritual expression in this society. People who could act were those with the 'power' to act, as the *Traditionsbücher* of Bavarian churches show. Around the middle of the eleventh century the nobleman Minio transacted 'by his empowered hand' the sale of his half-share in the cellar of Bozen castle to the monks of Tegernsee.[104] This gesture, centuries old, and its equally formulaic verbal expression persisted because they focused the solemnity of witnessed action, gave it meaning temporally and lawfully prior to its transcription. Likewise formulaic yet indicative were the expressed fears of 'powerful persons' or, yet more abstractly, of 'wicked power' who or which might infringe stipulated liberties or agreements.[105] Powerfully implicit in this culture was the sense that, while law empowered, lawless power threatened. Yet there was little insistence on law as such; no new edition of the old Bavarian law, the procedural forms of which determined some archaic observances for the interaction of free people. Existing custom sanctioned the ranks in which people partook of the sheltering powers of county and church. And when the property of magnates came to seem vulnerable to the king's will, as in the Saxon risings of the 1070s, the protection of laws assumed new meanings.[106]

How power was routinely experienced in Bavaria is not altogether clear in sources that are incomplete and formulaic. Counts

---

[103] *TrFr* II, no. 1458a.
[104] *TrT* no. 65; see also no. 78 and *TrP* no. 118.
[105] *TrSEm* nos. 651, 753. [106] Lampert, *Annales* 150.

figure in the written peripheries of royal dispensation or clerical regulation; they are seldom visible in enactments, official or patrimonial, of their own.[107] Yet here as elsewhere something like a devolution of official power can be discerned, for the influence of custom on inheritance and the familial interest in consolidating patrimonies or enlarging them by retention of acquisitions tended to redefine power as lordship.

It was a gradual process. There were more and more lords in the eleventh century, but apparently in numbers corresponding to the growth of population, so the habits of lordship and subjection cannot here be seen to weaken those of official action. Counties, advocacies, and ministerial functions persisted even as people recognized proprietary deportment in records of service. Lordship over men holding benefices developed early, as in other west German lands, without losing its expectation of service.[108] No one bothered to distinguish between Count Pilgrim's official status and patrimonial interest when 'his knight Rudolf' took possession of the estate of Mauggen in order to donate it piously to the canons of Freising (1053–78).[109] Knights surely multiplied, yet they figure in our sources more commonly as rewarded dependents than as usurping lords or oppressors.

The persistence of royal and ducal authority prevented any such proliferation of castles and unrewarded knights as in west Frankland. Violence continued to be regarded as the violation of ducal order, constituting a title so designated (*De violentia*) in the written law, as well as distinct titles on theft, arson, and distraint.[110] Prelates expected the lord-king to protect their domains against encroachment, while peasants had chiefly to fear the depredations of

---

[107] *TrP* nos. 117, 181, 285, 435, 445, 483, 546; cf. no. 850; *TrSEm* nos. 195, 952.

[108] *TrP* nos. 13, 31, 89–91, 117, 181, 184; *TrSEm* nos. 191, 196; *TrFr* ii, nos. 1400, 1418, 1536, 1672; cf. no. 1389; *DDH3* nos. 20, 69, 102, 239; *An. Altah.* 40; Lampert, *Annales* 227; Dollinger, *Classes rurales* 45–47; Hans K. Schulze, *Adelsherrschaft und Landesherrschaft* . . . (Graz 1963) 1–22.

[109] *TrFr* ii, no. 1617.

[110] *Lex Baiwariorum* . . . , ed. Ernst von Schwind (Hanover 1926) titles 9–13.

Bohemians or of royal armies themselves.[111] There is nothing in the *Traditionsbücher* to suggest that the violence of lesser lords or of feud was envisaged as normal or novel. It is a point worth pondering, for vigilance against usurpation had been formulaic in the Carolingian diplomatic of land conveyance[112] and was to be revived after 1100. Towards 1126–29 a ministerial named Gottschalk was alleged to have 'oppressed' four peasants 'with the violence of servitude,' an 'unjust subjection' from which they were then dispensed.[113] Reduction to 'servile condition' was a standard sanction for the performance of stipulated obligations in the eleventh century, when, according to Philippe Dollinger, agrarian lordship was customarily benign. The *gistum* continued to be pooled so as to spare individual tenancies; tallage was not yet normal.[114] Oppressive lordship may have been uncommon in Bavaria before the twelfth century, when it becomes visible throughout society. On the eve of the Second Crusade compunction produced at least two illuminating renunciations at Regensburg. A knight named Sighard of Padering restored to the monks of Saint Emmeram a manse he had usurped 'unjustly'; while Bishop Henry dispensed the abbot from the 'bad custom and unjust exaction' of £20 as part of a deal whereby the abbot would compensate episcopal knights on crusade.[115] But it cannot be ruled out that the highly formulaic records of Bavarian churches in the tenth and eleventh centuries conceal much of the sort of incidental and procedural information about lordly practise that is so common in other regions. If there is reason to believe that the survival of the duchy and its law made for better conditions of peasant life in Bavaria than elsewhere, it is equally true that we know next to nothing about lay lordship there in the eleventh century.

[111] *Tegernseer Briefsammlung* no. 68; Wipo, *Gesta* c. 26; Lampert, *Annales* 127 (c. 1071).

[112] *TrSEm* nos. 15, 19; *TrP* no. 73c.

[113] *TrSEm* no. 778; see also nos. 754, 810, 821, 824, 846; and *TrT* no. 171.

[114] *TrT* nos. 75, 151; Dollinger, *Classes rurales* 195–201; and 188–204, 234–63.

[115] *TrSEm* nos. 830, 831. See also nos. 790, 792, 794, 801, 863, 865, 885.

LOMBARDY

In 1043 the king's chancellor-legate Adalger commanded the knights, valvassors, and people in the diocese and county of Cremona to heed the bishop's summons to justice. He prescribed a fine of two pounds, payable half to the king's chamber and half to the bishop, to be levied on those who fail to respond to the summons. He further directed that all must aid the bishop in case he was obliged to coerce a recusant. In closing, Adalger wearily noted that 'in no [other] diocese' had he encountered such complaints that a bishop could not do justice.[116]

Here the scenes have changed. In the Po valley and its Tuscan fringes the king's power mattered because it was distant as well as venerable. The impulse in the matter at Cremona was visibly the bishop's, sprung from the need of external support in a conflictive microcosm of restive interests beyond easy control. It was the situation that, writ large, would favour imperial interests for generations to come. The distinctive element of the legate's mandate was its composite address 'to all knights, valvassors, and all people living in the diocese of Cremona and in the county . . . as well as to all citizens greater and lesser.' To claim jurisdiction over all in the county and town was to reassert the compelling episcopal lordship imposed by Conrad II in 1037 against the interests of knights and merchants who had counted on the kings to favour their autonomy. The command of 1043 was an incident in conflicts that filled Cremona's eleventh century.[117]

The dynamics of local empowerment were of distinctive importance in Lombardy. But there were routines as well as disruptions of power in the turbulent cities and plainland castles and villages, and it is in these that the persistent norms of regalian order and law are best viewed. Here again the usual experience of benign power was associated with the conveyance and securing of possessions, such as

---

[116] *CCr* I, no. 182: 'hanc penam posuimus quia in nullo episcopatu tantas lamentationes invenimus, unde episcopus legem nequaquam facere potuisset.'

[117] See generally Keller, *Adelsherrschaft in Oberitalien*; Menant, *Campagnes lombardes*; and Tabacco, *Power in medieval Italy*, chs. 5, 6, and Appendix.

we read not only in the tenacious Italian practise of *placita* but also in the equally formulaic notices of investiture preserved in Lombard churches. In the weeks of 1043 when he sanctioned the bishop's justice at Cremona the royal *missus* Adalger also held courts at Pavia, Asti, Marengo, and Como. In these he confirmed nuns, bishops, and an abbot in their threatened or contested possessions.[118] The cases show how these prelates put to advantage the royal legate's appearance to secure the protections of law and writing. Such judgments were commonly sanctioned by the king's ban, which could be pronounced even in the king's absence and which imparted an aura of age-old Lombard solemnity to occasions dignified by the presence, carefully recorded, of judges, functionaries, vassals, and others. This was a society of judges (*judices, palatini, causidici*), once the palatine judges of Pavia now progressively dispersed in the localities. Public order was, in the words of a record of 1061, a 'legal order' (*ordo legis*).[119] No doubt the formulaic verbiage of the written notice concealed changes or variations of procedure, but in the century after 1050 it is hard to discern novelty in the options and strategies of those who resorted to this venerable ritual of charter and oath. For it was not so much the king and his surrogates, nor even the prelates and magnates who often held the pleas, and whose lordship made these occasions prestigious, as the conspicuous assemblage of judges, lawyers, and notaries committed to process by law and custom as constraints deemed authoritative in themselves.[120]

---

[118] *CCr* I, no. 182; *Placiti del 'Regnum Italiae,'* III, nos. (356), 357–59. That this was to delimit as well as confirm the bishop's jurisdiction is shown by Rudolf Hübner, 'Gerichtsurkunden . . . Zweite Abtheilung. Die Gerichtsurkunden aus Italien bis zum Jahre 1150,' *ZRG Germ. Abt.* XIV:2 (1893) no. 1339 (c. 1044), a directive freeing the people of Verona from the bishop of Cremona's summons.

[119] *PSVV* no. x. See also Charles M. Radding, *The origins of medieval jurisprudence: Pavia and Bologna, 851–1150* (New Haven 1988) chs. 3–5; and Chris Wickham, 'Justice in the kingdom of Italy in the eleventh century,' *La giustizia nell'alto medioevo (secoli IX–X),* 2 vols. (Spoleto 1997) I, 179–250.

[120] e.g., *Placiti,* V, nos. 467, 469–71, 484; F. M. Fiorentini, *Memorie della gran contessa Matilda,* 2d ed. (Lucca 1756), *Documenti* 172–74, 248–49 (Hübner, nos. 1528, 1555).

This sense of passively empowered legal action is confirmed by the public notices of recognition and conveyance. These could be cast in judicial form. In April 1079 Count Giselbert of Bergamo presided over a 'judgment' whereby three judges, Redulf *legis doctor*, and other magnates attested to the truth of the bishop of Cremona's complaint against the intrusions of one Rusticello di Colognola. They instructed the count to invest the bishop with the rights in question, which he did ritually, stick in hand.[121] More common were investitures of uncontested agrarian rights creating lordships and tenures in carefully attested rituals, such as took place in the castle of Alfiano in April 1103 and in that of Bagnolo in November 1117.[122] In such acts and in countless records of sale, bequest, and settlement in which descriptions of location, verbiage, and attendance tend to be curtailed we can make out the everyday incidents of possession and work in the Lombard countrysides.

Moreover, it is in these records of notarial activity, including the pleas, that lordships below that of the king left traces of their interests and routines. Counts and bishops held great pleas, perhaps increasingly so after 1050. The lay counts (as such) are obscure figures, here too, known to us chiefly in their patrimonial doings. The bishops are visible, though hardly less obscure in their lordly routines. No power in Lombardy, lay or religious, could claim such extended lordship as the marquis Boniface of Tuscany (d. 1052) and his descendants. His wife Countess Beatrice of Lorraine (d. 1076) and their daughter Countess Matilda (1052–1115) achieved autonomy and prestige in their regalian powers and patrimony. Lords of the Apennines and widely endowed with imperial prerogatives, the family had its dynastic seat in Canossa castle and its more concentrated domains and tenures in the counties of Reggio, Modena, and Mantua.

Countess Matilda rose to the role thrust upon her by circumstance as did few other princes of her day. Born to the papal cause of reform, she married first in order to cement the

---

[121] *CCr* II, no. 224.   [122] ibid., no. 249; *CDLaud* I, no. 71.

Tuscan-Lotharingian dynastic inheritance, and a second time to support the anti-Henrician coalition,—and deserted both husbands. She must already have been an imposing lady when her mother and first husband died in the tumultuous months before the king's penitential submission to Gregory VII in her own castle and in her presence. But it was her devotion to the Gregorian programme and her dogged resistance to Henry IV in the terrible years after 1080 that created the lord-princess who would be remembered as the foremost lay ruler of the age in Italy. It was a time of epic struggle. Deprived of her imperial entitlement, Matilda lost the fidelity of vassals everywhere; she was driven out of her Tuscan castles. How she rebuilt her military lordship is hard to discern in the imprecise allusions of chroniclers, but her diplomas of judgment and privilege after about 1085 show a lord-princess attentive to the needs of local order in her inherited counties, especially in those of Reggio and Mantua. Her actions were responsive, arising in the course of peregrinations through her domains from the representations of her patrimonial servants almost entirely hidden from our view or from petitions sometimes ceremonially recorded.[123]

Matilda's career well illustrates the confusion of public and patrimonial attributes characteristic of imperial lands. The princess who presided over pleas or responded to petitions surrounded by judges, counts, and sworn adherents was surely mindful of her quasi-official status. Yet here as elsewhere what the records prove is occasions—spoken words, decisions, festival solemnity—not institutional memory. In September 1104 the countess responded to a personal petition of the abbot of Polirone in the presence of the papal vicar, the judge Adegarius of Nonantola, a lawyer of Panzano, and several of her 'faithful men.'[124] In a diploma of 1114 she spoke of 'treating with our *fideles* about certain matters' when

---

[123] *CDPol* no. 59 (1104); Gina Fasoli, 'Note sulla feudalità canossiana,' *Studi Matildici* (Modena 1964) 75. See generally *I poteri dei Canossa, da Reggio Emilia all'Europa* . . . , ed. Paolo Golinelli (Bologna 1994).

[124] *UrkMat* no. 83.

the bishop of Mantua petitioned her.[125] Matilda was a lord-princess sustained by affective commitments from servants who attended her, who secured her itinerant lodgings, and who maintained her castles and domains; and from vassals (often so-called: *vassi*). She knew how to create faithful service by granting 'benefices' or 'fiefs' to 'vassals' whose tenures were conditioned on services.[126] *Fideles* of her entourage, like the devoted Arduin de Palude, would have kept track of patrimonial possessions and obligations in records none too carefully preserved. A list of castles and parishes held by Matilda's father from the bishop of Reggio may have survived because the bishop felt oppressed by the marquis's expansionist lordship; certainly that precisely was the cause of complaint by Bishop Ubaldo of Mantua around 1090.[127]

Countess Matilda can have had no ambition to enlarge her vast inheritance. Her problem was how to dispose of it. Deeply influenced by Gregorian ideals, she committed her allodial patrimony to the Roman church as early as 1077–78, and confirmed the donation in 1102.[128] But since there was no accommodation with Henry IV in her vulnerable imperial commissions, there must always have been some sentiment in favour of compromise with Matilda's Salian kinsmen. How fully she reversed course in promising her allodial inheritance to Henry V in 1111 is unclear, contributing to the confusions of what became the grand cause of Italy's twelfth century. What is not in doubt is that her life-long commitment to the Gregorian cause had provoked resentments in some towns; she recovered Mantua's fidelity only after the pact with Henry V at the end of her life.[129]

---

[125] ibid., no. 131.   [126] ibid., nos. 113, 138; cf. no. 151.

[127] *Le carte degli archivi reggiani (1051–1060)*, ed. P. Torelli, F. S. Gatta (Reggio-Emilia 1938) no. 9; *UrkMat* no. 42; Vito Fumagalli, 'Mantua al tempo di Matilde di Canossa,' *Sant-Anselmo, Mantova e la lotta per le investiture . . .*, ed. Paolo Golinelli (Bologna 1987) 162.

[128] *UrkMat*, Dep. 37 (415), 73.

[129] Donizo, *Vita Mathildis. . . .*, ii.19; ed. Luigi Simeoni (Bologna 1940) 98–100; Fumagalli, 'Mantua al tempo di Matilde di Canossa,' 164. Her father Boniface had also had trouble at Mantua.

Matilda's lordship, having doubtless grown in stature as she survived the difficult early years, became charismatic at the end. One who knew and mourned her thought posterity would find it 'incredible' how admirable a person she had been. Recalling that princes, counts, magnates, and knights whom she 'ruled' (*gubernabat*) kneeled before her in her counsels, where she was 'highly astute' and 'affable to all,' he also said that 'she greatly honoured the clerks of her castle, had no use for thieves, [and] ruled her peasants.'[130] Without wishing to read too much into these words, I think it likely that Matilda was opposed to the exploitative domination of peasants and townspeople. She had heard plenty about it. Together with Duke Welf, she renounced arbitrary exactions and forced lodging at Mantua in 1090.[131] When the abbot of Polirone complained of violation by her steward in the isle of Zeneure (1101), Matilda acted on the 'reasons and testimony' to confirm her father's donation of exemption.[132] Such concessions multiplied in her later years. Everywhere the countess's agents in the domains were being charged with excesses, with 'bad and unjust usages' such as the men of Monticelli claimed in 1114 had 'never been imposed on their predecessors.' No pushover, Matilda often had such charges investigated before providing remedies limiting the powers of her own agents.[133]

THAT THE German kings retained some powers in Italy through adverse times on either side of 1100 is proof of the historic strength of their claims. Not Gregory VII nor Matilda nor Paschal II could undermine a position that owed so much to civic and regional rivalries, while in Germany circumstances more deeply menacing

---

[130] 'Notae de Mathilda comitissa,' ed. P. E. Schramm, *MGHSS* xxx² (1929) 975.

[131] *UrkMat* no. 43.   [132] *CDPol* no. 55 (*UrkMat* no. 66).

[133] *UrkMat* no. 132; see also *CDPol* nos. 55, 87 (*UrkMat* nos. 66, 137).

forced the later Salian kings to view their Italian interests as something more than entitlement to the imperial crown. Henry IV spent many months in a castle near Verona in the 1090s. Henry V (1106–25) made well-timed journeys to secure the imperial title and succession to Matilda's lands and rights. He demonstrated sagacity in the negotiations that culminated in the Concordat of Worms (September 1122), because the definitive settlement (not to speak of the untenable one of February 1111![134]) secured substantially the king's influence in episcopal elections. But these events must have seemed to many like the expected aftershocks of eruptions long since quieted. Italy was a refuge where the kings and their German retainers had time to think long thoughts about the German realm they had struggled to dominate. Saxony was a troubled cause as well as an historic heartland.[135] Its crisis, anticipating (and resembling) further crises of power elsewhere in the twelfth century, is examined in the next chapter. It arose in distinctly German circumstances.

The routines of royal action persisted unchanged to the end of the Salian epoch (1125) and beyond. All the imposing structures of traditional public kingship may be read in the diplomas, letters, and narratives: the power to command and punish (*bannum*), gracious assent to deferential petitions, the personification of public order in citations of infidelity as treason.[136] One need not suppose that the unsympathetic reportage of Lampert of Hersfeld had official status to see how his annals, among others,' carried on the commemorative tradition of public-festive itinerary.[137] The German church was the king's church, as the reformers saw only too

---

[134] On which, see p. 210 below.

[135] *DDH4* II, nos. 413, 424, 447, 451, 452; Horst Fuhrmann, *Germany in the high Middle Ages, c. 1050–1200*, tr. T. Reuter (Cambridge 1986) 69; *CAP* I, nos. 83–101, 107, 108; Weinfurter, *Herrschaft und Reich der Salier* 147–55 (*Salian century* 170–79).

[136] *DDH4* II, nos. 18, 26, 63, 100, 103, 112, 222, 353; *An. Altah.* 79; *Annales Weissenburgenses*, ed. Oswaldus Holder-Egger, *Lamperti annales* 56; Lampert, *Annales*, 80.

[137] See, e.g., the annals from 1042 to 1073, Lampert, 58–172.

clearly. But the embattled lord-king of the letters and narratives is all but invisible in the charters, which continue to record royal action responsively and so, as in the past, to conceal the patrimonial issues that were effectually resolved in the written dispositives. Perhaps only in charters to secure and reward faithful service can the king's initiative be glimpsed, yet even with these one wonders how far Henry IV himself was engaged in day-to-day negotiation for service and maintenance. The numbers of extant diplomas decline after 1086. Henry V was busier in this sphere, but even for him the average of just over ten surviving diplomas per annum hardly suggests regalian lordship in urgent need or demand.[138]

Justice and the promotion of the church: these were the unswerving professed purposes of Henry IV and his son.[139] But the play of power about the kings, the *familiaritas* of their courtiers, tended to distort, or even to transform, these purposes. The influence of magnates like Archbishop Anno of Cologne was magnified in the minority following the forceful reign of Henry III. It is wholly plausible that Henry IV was reacting against tedious constraints when he recklessly proposed to leave his wife Bertha in 1069.[140] But the real change cannot have lain so much in the king's rejection of counsel as in his understandable resolve to choose the men around him. There is little sign that this Henry was prone to despotic acts as distinct from miscalculations; rather, it looks as if he got used to an associative mode of decision-making that added thump to his more extreme pronouncements. It is hardly likely that he chose alone to carry on his father's aim of extending and fortifying his domain in Saxony. This enterprise became conspicuous in the years after Archbishop Adalbert of Hamburg-Bremen was forced out of the young king's circles

---

[138] *DDH4* I, II; and I, pp. xix–xx; *Die Kaiserurkunden des X., XI. und XII. Jahrhunderts . . .* , ed. Karl Friedrich Stumpf-Brentano (Innsbruck 1865) nos. 3016–3226.

[139] *DDH4* I, nos. 94, 99, 100, 171, 180, 474; *CAP* I, nos. 103–8.

[140] Fuhrmann, *Germany*, 61.

(1066), a spectacular event that shows something of the power of elite consensus; and when the annalist of Niederaltaich grumbled in 1072 about King Henry's new preference for lesser men over the 'powerful' in his management of affairs, it looks as if he had in mind the aggressive programme in Thuringia and Saxony as well as the *ministeriales* who carried it out. He was certainly thinking of the threat to peace posed by the exclusion of *potentes*, referring to the refusal of the dukes of Suabia and Carinthia to come to the king when summoned.[141]

This was a struggle over power for all to see and fear. It would be resolved, transformed into dynastic conflict, only with the accession of Conrad III of Staufer in 1138.

France

Everyone knew who was king in the lands between the Meuse and Loire valleys. But they needed him less than in the South and their scribes easily omitted his regnal year. This was the country of 'Franks'—that is, of (now) those who spoke French; and if these French Franks had a king as always, they looked to lesser lords—to counts, viscounts, castellans, even knights, as well as to bishops, abbots, and priors—for protection and justice. Power was even more diffuse than in Occitania, the solidarities of coercive lordship more diverse and complex. There was more to work with in a warming climate smiling on expanding and prospering peasant societies: more people, more wealth, at rates of growth perhaps by 1050 exceeding those in the South. As fears of devastating incursion receded, the customary spheres of identity forged in provincial action were confirmed: the Franks in their own eyes were Angevins, Burgundians, Normans, Flemings, etc. But these were dynastic peoples, their aspirations bound up with the

---

[141] Lampert, *Annales* 100–102; *An. Weiss.* 53; *An. Altah.* 84; cf. *Brunos Buch vom Sachsenkrieg (Saxonicum bellum)*, ed. Hans-Eberhard Lohmann (Stuttgart 1980 [1937]) c. 10 (19).

visions of princes whose homelands always seemed threatened, who strove for lordships and alliances beyond their borders, who made England part of their French-speaking world with the most ponderous domination of the age; peoples who shared a more nearly uniform culture of lordship, for all its diffusion and dilution, than those of the Mediterranean.

Anjou

Who are they who fight boldly? The Angevins.
Who are they who overcome enemies? The Angevins.
Who are they who spare the vanquished? The Angevins.
Let envy alone deny the illustrious Angevins.
—*Marbod of Rennes*[142]

Highly symptomatic was the experience of Anjou, where ambitious and aggressive counts made a realm for themselves. It is a familiar history, for some of it was told by one of the counts himself, and more was related by admirers of their stunning dynastic successes in the twelfth century. If historians in our day have not always escaped their assumptions of imperial destiny, they have well appreciated the force and fame of Angevin domination. Nowhere save in England was power so reflected upon, so expressly admired, so classically dignified, as in the Loire valley. Few clerks elsewhere were so preoccupied with the procedures of right and remedy; Angevin charters often contain narrations detailing how disputes came to settlement. Nowhere else was expansive domination so precocious as in Anjou.

   That is why our story here begins with the millennium. Who after him could match Fulk Nerra (987–1040) in coercive might? Master of a famously vulnerable Carolingian county, he pressed relentlessly beyond its limits, winning great battles in Brittany and Touraine and building or capturing many castles near or beyond the old borders. These castles were typically centers of

---

[142] *De ornamentis verborum, PL* CLXXI, 1688.

comital lordship, many of them still so in the twelfth century, which is why historians have easily attributed the foundations of Angevin 'government' to the 'military operations of Fulk Nerra.'[143] These were fragile foundations, however, consisting of the vassalic alliances of a singularly aggressive lordship, alliances that weakened after 1050 and had to be reconstructed in the twelfth century. Moreover, a divided succession shook the inherited solidarity of count and castellans; and the inability of Geoffrey Martel's nephew Fulk Richin (1068–1109) to revive his grandfather's military largesse together with the lack of customary safeguards of the lord-count's power to repossess castles encouraged Angevin castellans to claim lordly prerogatives in their own right. We begin to hear of the lordship of Montreuil-Bellay in the years 1068–71 and of that of Malicorne by 1091. And what brought them to notice was transgressions of custom.[144]

People thought counts should deal with such matters in the Anjou of Fulk Richin and his successors. It had been less clear in his grandfather's day. No doubt Fulk Nerra preserved something of Carolingian order. A justiciar-count, he held court in his halls surrounded by servants, vicars, and men on beneficial tenures; loyalty to him retained something functional, or even official; his protectorate of churches, however problematic, was real. Yet by all accounts Fulk Nerra was a brutal lord. Some twenty percent of his extant acts in writing relate to violence and its remedy, mostly his own and that of his servants and vassals: breaches of custom, invasions of churches, novel exactions. His impulsive acts of solemn penitence served to conceal as well as to reveal the count's disposition to exert power wilfully; the monks and clerks of Angers and Saint-Florent who preserved his memory had much to thank him for. Moreover, the 'customs' (*consuetudines*) themselves

---

[143] Southern, *Making of the Middle Ages* 85; see also Kate Norgate, *England under the Angevin kings*, 2 vols. (London 1887) i, chs. 5–11; Louis Halphen, *Le comté d'Anjou au XIe siècle* (Paris 1906) 1–12.

[144] *CSAA* i, nos. 220, 317, 325; Olivier Guillot, *Le comte d'Anjou et son entourage au XIe siècle*, 2 vols. (Paris 1972) i, 460.

were new in Anjou, as elsewhere, in the 990s; not necessarily violent yet presuming a new sanction for obligations no longer justified by law or regalian order. Was not Fulk, having to satisfy grasping knights, as much castellan as count himself? Was not this his example and his legacy? The real lesson of the proliferation of customs is that powers of lordship could no longer be reserved to regalian authorities. The count, as Olivier Guillot well saw, seems not to have noticed what it meant to subject himself—or to permit the scribes of aggrieved churches to do so—to the ominous new norms of customary power. Lordship was virtually equated with custom in the eleventh century.[145]

It was Geoffrey Martel (1040–60) who first anticipated a renewed territorial order in Anjou. He not only completed his father's conquest of Touraine, but was also the first of his line to aim at repressing violent customs as a matter of policy. His 'general court' held at Angers in 1040, although known to us only in a remedial charter for Saint-Florent, surely conveyed a consensus of ecclesiastical lords tired of petitioning singly and repeatedly for relief from 'depredations . . . evil invasions and bad customs in saints' lands.' This was a territorial confirmation of immunities in effect, associating the violence of armed cavalcades such as that reported to have afflicted adjoining Angevin and Poitevin lands in the 1040s with the excesses of lay lords and comital agents.[146] Yet the measure was sadly premature. Succeeding counts had incessantly to redress the grievances of the monastic lordships; worse, at least two of Geoffrey's nephews, Geoffrey and Fulk 'the Goose' of Vendôme, were themselves egregious violators of the peace. The former, labelled a 'new Nero,' diversely antagonized,

---

[145] Halphen, *Comté d'Anjou*, Catalogue des actes, nos. 7–64; Guillot, *Comte d'Anjou* I, 372; idem, 'Administration et gouvernement dans les états du comte d'Anjou au milieu du XIe siècle,' *Histoire comparée de l'administration (IVe–XVIIIe s.)* . . . (Munich 1980) 311–32, p.j. 4 (1051). Bernard S. Bachrach, *Fulk Nerra, the neo-Roman consul, 987–1040* . . . (Berkeley 1993) holds to a different perspective.

[146] AD Maine-et-Loire, H 1840, no. 5; Guillot, *Comte d'Anjou* I, 373; II, no. C80; *Chronica de gestis consulum Andegavorum*, ed. Louis Halphen, René Poupardin (Paris 1913) 59.

then persecuted Berengar of Tours, the monks of Marmoutier, and the archbishop of Tours; while for Fulk's angry rampage in the monastic lands of Vendôme we have a fragmentary letter of grievance from the monks to the dowager countess Agnes that is one of the earliest extant accounts of violence in medieval Europe.[147] Another nephew Fulk, Geoffrey's successor in Anjou, may not have done much better. Orderic Vitalis remembered him as notoriously negligent of the peace in Anjou, alleging that he spared thieves in whose loot he had been content to share. Orderic had hoped for better lordship from this Fulk's lamented son Geoffrey Martel (d. 1106), who initiated the struggle to recover comital lordship over castles.[148] Fulk V (1109–29) persevered in this objective, followed by his son Geoffrey Plantagenet (1129–51).[149]

Incomplete and often ineffectual, the counts' domination remained imposing even so through uneasy times. The consolidation of power in or over Tours, Vendôme, and finally Maine more than made up for the loss of Saintes in 1062. Angevin destinies lay in the north. Loyalty to the kings fostered a tradition of palatine prestige that only underscored the scandal of King Philip's abduction of Fulk Richin's wife in 1092. The family's renown was confirmed when Geoffrey Plantagenet married the Empress Matilda, resulting in events that completed the dynastic victory over Blois at the cost of peace with the Capetians, and when Fulk V was chosen king of Jerusalem.[150]

People deferred to such power. Clerical beneficiaries tactfully represented Geoffrey Martel and his nephew Fulk Richin as august, just, condescending. In 1093 the canons of Saint-Maurice of Angers petitioned Count Fulk's 'serenity' for his concession that the trades in money and spices be confined to the cathedral's pre-

---

[147] Halphen, *Comté d'Anjou* 138–41; *CTV* I, no. 173; cf. Barthélemy, *Société de Vendôme* 396–99.

[148] OV xi.16 (VI, 74–76)

[149] Josèphe Chartrou, *L'Anjou de 1109 à 1151. Foulque de Jérusalem et Geoffroi Plantagenet* (Paris 1928) ch. 2.

[150] Halphen, *Comté d'Anjou*; Guillot, *Comte d'Anjou* I, 39–101; Chartrou, *Anjou*, chs. 1, 2.

cincts. In 1109 the same community blatantly flattered him as a peace-making lord who had promoted the welfare of his people.[151] But the diplomas and notices distort the realities of comital action. As a rule they are at some remove from decisions, the less solemn ones serving to list persons present at (past) events, witnesses or others. Even the privileges alluding to ceremony or assemblage commonly lacked dispositive force, while in lesser conveyances parchments were not usually among the symbolic objects deposited on altars; moreover, the clerks who wished to record which people were present commonly neglected to say when they were present. Of lay action less must have been written, and practically all of it is lost to us. But the charters we have, chiefly recording privileges and the resolution of disputes and written by the scribes of interested clerical parties, are enough to show that the counts were kept busy responding to complaints, proposals, and enticements. About 1118 Fulk V was said to have stopped at Loches castle in order to 'dispose of his affairs.'[152] Many persons would have been there to share in this expression of his lordship.

They formed overlapping circles of family members, baronial companions, managers of estate and domain, and household servants.[153] The count's wife seldom appeared as co-actor before the time of Fulk V, when she was called 'countess,' although her presence was often noticed; the sons were generally on hand. All who attended were bound to the count in fidelity, the barons and greater courtiers, at least, in personal commendation compensated by fiefs. As for the magnates, only their status interested the scribes. Although they attested individually, the collective presence or

---

[151] *CNA* no. 57; also 93: '. . . Fulco piissimus Andecavorum comes . . . sub cujus pacifico dominatu gens in sua terra valde augmentata est. . . .' See also 'Cartulaire de Saint-Maur sur Loire,' no. 23; Koziol, *Begging pardon* 53, 249–50.

[152] Chartrou, *Anjou*, p.j. 16.

[153] See, e.g., *CNA* nos. 22, 27, 57, 91; *CSAA* I, nos. 4, 8; 'Cart. Saint-Maur,' nos. 23, 26, 37, 61; *CMV* no. 65; 'Chartes angevines des onzième et douzième siècles,' ed. Paul Marchegay, *BEC* xxxvi (1875), 421–22, no. 24; Chartrou, *Anjou*, p.j. 33.

consilium of barons was sometimes mentioned, especially under Fulk V.[154] Men called seneschal or constable formed part of this baronial group; together with the chaplains they doubtless kept closer company with the count than other barons. The chaplains wrote charters and one of them may have been the first 'count's chancellor' in the 1080s; but there is nothing to show that the recording of comital acts was thought to be official work as late as 1150.[155] That lesser functionaries attested enactments—chamberlains, cellarers, cooks, huntsmen, foresters—suggests that service to the lord-count promoted some measure of privileged visibility. The emergence of the greater curial functions in the later eleventh century was surely related to the spread of lordship in comital society, to a new insistence on privilege instead of baronial solidarity. No longer able to entrust the castellans with dominical revenues, the counts relied more and more on provosts (*praepositi*) to oversee the old vicars and exploit the comital domain.

This is why the Angevin provosts figure so prominently in comital records. They may have been supervisors in the entourage in Fulk Nerra's time; and their attendance on the counts thereafter suggests that they retained their function even as they became identified with local charges.[156] These were lesser lords on the make seeking to prosper in the lord-count's power and company or even, like knights, in his nobility. They were close to the counts. Fulk Richin rewarded a provost of Angers who had saved his life at the siege of La Flèche (1076) by the gift of a fishery.[157] But they were not much like officials; their accountability, their promises, even their selection seem to have been problematic for the counts. Towards 1050 one Sanctus, the nephew of a provost, asked for the *prepositura* of Loches castle; Count Geoffrey

[154] 'Chartes angevines,' 395–96, no. 7; 405, no. 13; 421–22, no. 24; Chartrou, *Anjou*, *p.j.* 33.

[155] Halphen, *Comté d'Anjou* 193; Chartrou, *Anjou* 108–13.

[156] *CNA* nos. 22, 27; Halphen, *Comté d'Anjou*, *p.j.* 5; *CMV* no. 65; Guillot, 'Administration,' *p.j.* 2; 'Cart. Saint-Maur,' nos. 17, 46; *CTV* 1, no. 245; Chartrou, *Anjou*, *p.j.* 43.

[157] Halphen, *Comté d'Anjou*, Cat. des actes, no. 233.

set a price of 300s., then forgave it when Sanctus promised to stop troubling the monks of Ronceray over a mill![158] *Prepositura* has already here the appearance of an exploitation, of a tenure, like the vicariate in the Midi; once possessed of it a comital servant would not easily give it up. The provostship at Vendôme was hereditary from the start; and the same may have been true at Angers, where the provosts Berno and Geoffroi were father and son in the early eleventh century.[159] If thereafter such charges were cessions for life, as Halphen surmised, it is likely that they tended to be patrimonial. The bishop of Angers resisted this tendency,[160] but there is no sign that the counts did so. The vicariate seems likewise to have become a privileged tenure, this one of relatively declining value in the twelfth century; but the *voyers*, like the *villici* who exploited the count's strictly seigneurial domain, were less visible—and less notorious—than the provosts. In a fable of good lordship composed towards 1170 Jean de Marmoutier aired the allegation that 'provosts, *villici* and other ministers of our lord the count'—but provosts, above all—were guilty of unfaithful violence.[161]

Surely with good reason. On at least three occasions eleventh-century counts of Anjou heard charges against their own provosts encroaching on clerical domains, and judged against them.[162] Around 1074 one Robert the Marshall, provost at Angers, drove a harder bargain with monks of La Trinité, Vendôme: having troubled the priory of Evière, he was well paid to desist. Perhaps this was in character, for he was done to death a year or

[158] Cartulaire de Ronceray, quoted by Louis Halphen, 'Prévôts et voyers du XIe siècle. Région angevine,' in *A travers l'histoire du moyen âge* (Paris 1950 [1902]) 222.
[159] *CSAA* I, no. 5; Halphen, 'Prévôts et voyers,' 221.
[160] *CNA* no. 180. See also AD Indre-et-Loire, H 303, ed. Jacques Boussard, *Le comté d'Anjou sous Henri Plantagenêt et ses fils (1151–1204)* (Paris 1938), p.j. I, 171–72.
[161] *Historia Gaufredi ducis Normannorum et comitis Andegavorum*, ed. Louis Halphen, René Poupardin, *Chroniques des comtes d'Anjou*, 185.
[162] *CSAA* I, no. 5; *CNA* no. 56; Halphen, 'Prévôts et voyers,' 224.

two later in a storm of sticks and stones.[163] Another provost of ill
repute, Aimery who served at Baugé, bore the epithet *Fac malum*
('Do Wrong'); yet another was Gautier *Facit malum*, ex provost of
Loches, who testified around 1115 that the monks of L'Oratoire
paid 100s. each year to the provost of the castle 'not by custom but
by violence.' Nor did such abusive service soon end. Provosts at
Beaufort aroused the protests of four different religious houses in
the years 1120–40.[164]

❖

'NOT BY custom but by violence.' There can be no doubt that
lordship was imposed and exercised coercively in Anjou, perhaps
more so than elsewhere, perhaps not. What is certain is that Angevin records, discursive and garrulous, tell us circumstantially
more about violence than those of any other society north of the
Pyrenees. What is more, they reveal some patches of domination
where wilful force seems to have become an habitual expression
of power, where violence may not so easily have been distinguished from custom. But they also disclose a range of meanings
associated with coercion, enabling us to see how closely violence
was tainted with justice in Anjou.

It was not that people thought laws were being broken. Imperial precepts of redress were long dead in this burgeoning new
society, while regional custom, precocious though it was in Anjou, was slow to develop a jurisprudence of security.[165] Nor was
it that they appealed to courts as such, still less to prelates to impose a territorial pacification. But by resisting the arbitrary imposition of new customs and by holding to comital (and
vicecomital) authority in defence of old immunities, monks and

---

[163] *CTV* I, no. 246; Halphen, 'Prévôts et voyers,' 219–20.

[164] Halphen, 'Prévôts et voyers,' 207n, 213; Chartrou, *Anjou* 118 and *p.j.* 13.
Another perspective in Henk Teunis, . . . *Social justice in Anjou in the eleventh
century* (Hilversum 2006).

[165] See Guillot, *Comte d'Anjou* I, 372–75.

canons (and surely also lay people of whom we have no record) preserved a facade of public order. Fulk Nerra's conspicuous might was recalled in the twelfth century as that of a consummate protector of Saint-Florent's property.[166] But this was personal protection, alliance: one appealed to the lord-count—Geoffrey Martel's testy words about having lost more land to the flooding Loire than to the king of France come through in one case–; and if the 'count's court' (*curia comitis, mea curia*) is often mentioned, it was no more than an ad hoc gathering of notables or the informed, some of whom the count might appoint 'judges' (*judices*). The scribes, quite lacking a diplomatic of justice, faithfully narrated proceedings: *iudicia*, pacifications, before notables, *in curia*; conceptually, all was indistinct.[167] 'I came,' Fulk Richin was made to say some time after 1069, 'to the place of Saint-Maur where I reconciled [*pacificavi*] Eudes de Blaison and his son with Geoffroi son of Fulcher'; this is all we learn of this dispute, its record being incidental to the notice of satisfaction awarded to Saint-Maur in their complaint that comital servants had imposed new customs on their pigs at L'Orme Sainte-Marie.[168]

Almost always, violence was at issue. Much of what these clerical scribes meant by *violentia* hardly mattered, it is true. Petty complaints cannot have moved the count or viscount or bishop, and most may not have reached them; we only hear of them when they were clustered with weightier allegations: dog-keepers showing up too often for meals with the monks of La Trinité, demands and threats by the *voyer* at Montreuil-Bellay.[169] More injurious were abuses of justice—or rather, since the lowliest of servants were prone to exploit it, pretences to lordship. To seize (*distringere*) property for disobedience to commands or summonses arising from banal power was licit violence, normal constraint. Geoffrey the Bearded tried to limit it to vicarial causes in lands of

[166] 'Chartes angevines,' 426–27, no. 28.

[167] *CSAA* i, no. 178; also no. 89; *CMV* i, no. 117; 'Chartes angevines,' 387, no. 3; 396–97, no. 8; *CNA* nos. 53, 94.

[168] 'Cart. Saint-Maur,' no. 38.   [169] *CTV* i, no. 173; *CSAA* i, no. 220.

Saint-Florent; but a mass of unjustified seizures was itemized against the collector Calvin at Montreuil-Bellay towards 1080. When half a century later tenants of Saint-Aubin at Le Chillon refused to serve a local knight in his fighting expeditions, he seized their property, before repenting and settling publicly before the monks.[170] Distraint was rooted in the practise of lordship in Anjou. But seizures (*preda, depredationes*) could also be unexcused, could be undisguised thefts, even of that notoriously destructive sort associated, as in Pyrenean lands, with armed cavalcades.

For there was also a sphere of oppressive violence. About 1080 the lord of Montreuil-Bellay took property from Saint-Aubin's men at Méron 'without any forfeit or cause,' then demanded £60 for its return.[171] In the 1120s the provost of Beaufort and foresters of La Vallée disrupted tenants of the same house seeking to develop cleared land, seized their cattle, and forced them to redeem their animals.[172] Ransoms were frequent, an easy extension of judicial power. Resistance to demands could enrage a tormentor, who might invite his 'men' to help themselves to villagers and their wealth. We hear of lands being ravaged around Saumur and Vendôme in the middle of the eleventh century, even of the desertion of cultivated domains. Violence could even become afflictive, as was alleged at Méron around 1080. The *voyer* threatened to strike the monks who opposed him. One monastic servant was beaten to death, another beaten and robbed.[173]

Violence in Anjou, such as we know it, was perpetrated by lay men, typically the lesser functionaries of lay powers and advocates, in or on the borders of ecclesiastical estates. This suggests that clerical domains were comparatively, perhaps conspicuously,

---

[170] 'Chartes angevines,' 429–30, no. 29. On *distringere* see also Guillot, 'Administration,' *p.j.* 1, 2; *CNA* no. 53; *CSAA* I, nos. 220 (259), 221.

[171] *CSAA* I, no. 220.

[172] 'Chartes angevines,' 429–30, no. 28.

[173] *Chronica de gestis consulum Andegavorum*, 59; 'Chartes angevines,' 429–30, no.29; Guillot, 'Administration,' *p.j.* 2; *CTV* I, no. 173; *CSAA* i, no. 220.

free of the harsh customs that accompanied the spread of lay lordship. It is not hard to imagine that prospering peasants of
Saint-Aubin and Saint-Florent were enticing prey for the count's
provosts and sergeants. But it seems unlikely that tenants of the
count and of castellan lords were more tenderly treated. At most
we may suppose that the greater lords, having long since established heavier obligations, faced the problem of getting the most
from their growing domains without jeopardizing returns
through excessive constraints and taxation. Did the ex-provost
Gautier mean that in his experience custom was normal? —and
that it was (normally) other than violence? Was it only the monks
who called him *Facit malum*? It would later be insinuated that
Count Geoffrey Plantagenet's provosts and stewards were guilty
of self-serving oppression in his own domains.[174] Violence was
normal in the reality of Angevin domination because circumstances long continued to favour the imposition of new customs
by any who could do so. Incipient lordship, far from being peripheral, was central to this experience. This is why the micro-history
of Méron, for all its limitations, is illuminating.

Méron was a domain of Saint-Aubin bordering on that of
Montreuil-Bellay, a castle built by Fulk Nerra, but later in the
lands of an ambitious family creating a new lordship. Its most
aggressive early lord was Renaud, an ally of King Philip I, who
appointed him treasurer of Saint-Martin of Tours and then archbishop of Reims. He was charged around 1080 with numerous
and diverse oppressions against the tenants of Saint-Aubin, and
from the quasi-narrative dossier preserved in that house's cartulary, we can all but relive the terror of Angevin villagers toiling in
the shadow of a new castellan lordship. Renaud's *voyer* had been
distraining tenants at Méron without waiting for the monks' prior
to take cognizance of charges. The castellan had usurped the tenants' rights to usage and firewood from a grove, he had converted
a gracious service in a meadow by the castle into a 'forced custom,'
his collector Calvin had repeatedly extorted money on diverse

---

[174] Jean de Marmoutier, *Historia Gaufredi*, 185.

excuses; and when his *voyer* met resistance to his demand for feed-grain, he dealt brutally (as noted above) with the monastic servants. The *voyer* Baudin and his men broke into monastic buildings, killed the peasants' geese, disrupted their vineyards, imposed uncustomarily on men marrying women from Méron, etc. The list of violations is long, many of them described as amounting to a 'robbery' (*latrocinium*) by the *voyers* of Montreuil against the Saint's people 'with the consent and approval, even by his will and command, of the lord of Montreuil.'[175]

There is no need to defend Renaud on grounds of a biased *clamor*, for he and his nephew Berlai admitted the charges in a great charter of renunciation read out publicly 'in court,' and collected some £135 in coin and value for doing so! Their concessions make clear that vicarial power had been the mainspring of their aggrandisement, for they were permitted to reserve 'by old custom' the six causes of seizure, arson, blood, theft, *lepus* (the hunting of hares), and toll.[176] The castellany flourished under Berlai, who was easily induced—'by counsel of bad men,' according to one record—to violate Méron's new privileges. He extorted 500s. from the free tenants, destroyed the monks' sluices and a mill, and levied an uncustomary tax on wine. The bishop helped undo the first of these encroachments, not without another hefty payoff. We know of no appeal to Fulk Richin during these years (1087–1109), although comital suzerainty over Montreuil seems to have been recognized. But Berlai lapsed into insubordination in the time of Fulk V, who besieged and captured the castle in 1124. At that time he installed his own castellans, leaving only the lordship to Berlai.[177]

This restored suzerainty remained wobbly, and collapsed when Fulk departed for the Holy Land in 1129. At that time Berlai's son Giraud allied with Lisiard de Sablé and other Angevin barons, provoking reprisals by Count Geoffrey, who captured several castles and ravaged domains of Amboise. This violence in service

---

[175] *CSAA* i, no. 220.   [176] ibid., no. 221.
[177] ibid., nos. 222, 223, 233, 235; Chartrou, *Anjou*, 28.

of comital order may help to explain why Giraud Berlai not only relapsed into the oppressive lordship of his father's early days but also became one of the most notorious 'tyrants' of his own time. Once again the people of Méron suffered: Giraud extorted 8s. weekly, demanded redemption-payments for 'false appeals in his court,' and devised nasty ways of charging the monks for permission to bring in their ripe crops. Simpler than in the past, it seems, and more efficiently wicked. This was the sort of violence a determined castellan could hope to render profitably customary; and for all we know Giraud was able to persist in such domination for some years. But his bad lordship went beyond this. 'Together with many strong men infected by the venom of his malice,' Giraud pillaged the surrounding countrysides, ravaging the whole plain from Angers to Saumur to Loudun. 'He was the cruellest of men,' wrote the memorialist of Saint-Aubin, 'serpentine in cunning and guile, canine . . . lupine . . . bovine . . . leonine . . . neronian. . . .'[178]

What may be inferred from the overheated rhetoric is that Giraud Berlai went beyond a tolerable exploitation of his own estates to achieve lucrative violence against outsiders, especially merchants and travellers on the roads. However usual his tolls, he seems to have pushed his castled defiance of princely order to the ultimate in a current norm of domination. Other restive families may have had similar ambitions, there were some alliances, but their cause was not such as to define an estate of baronial interest in Anjou. Giraud made the most of his inherited access to the king's favour, with the bizarre consequence that Louis VII, himself the beneficiary of past royal campaigns against castellans, was his ally during the terrible siege that finally brought him down. Reaction was slow to come. Anjou had no peace movement, its tolerance of violence, even in comital domains, was high. Giraud seems to have ignored an

---

[178] *Chronica vel sermo de rapinis . . . a Giraudo de Mosteriolo exactis*, ed. Emile Mabille, *Chroniques des églises d'Anjou* (Paris 1869) 83–90; *Historia Gaufredi* 215–23.

episcopal excommunication in 1129. Count Geoffrey acted deliberately, building two castles along the vulnerable way from Loudun to Montreuil and two more on that from Saumur to Angers. The final 'campaign of Montreuil' coincided with deteriorating relations with the king, turning into an arduous siege of the castle that Giraud, by this time seneschal of Poitou in the king's pay, had formidably strengthened. The castle fell in May 1151, Giraud and his cronies 'coming out like serpents from a cave' to be led captive to Angers. In a triumphant ceremony held in the chapter-house of Saint-Aubin on 10 June 1151, Count Geoffrey and his sons Geoffroi and Guillaume, at the urging of his barons, declared the bad customs of Méron 'radically quashed.'[179]

FLANDERS

As in Anjou so in Flanders the counts were mighty lord-princes. Their power was conspicuously regalian, coming down to them through Charlemagne's great-granddaughter Judith and first consolidated in programmatically Carolingian terms as early as the reign of Arnulf I (918–65). The later counts who will concern us here retained close ties with the kings of France, including Charles the Good (1119–27), who was the son of King Knut II of Denmark, and who seems to have been the candidate of some to succeed Henry V as emperor in 1125.[180] As in Barcelona and Anjou possession of the county was disrupted in the third quarter of the eleventh century, when the succession of minor sons to Baldwin VI tempted the latter's brother Robert to usurp power in scandalous violence. Robert I ('the Frisian' 1071–93) soon justified himself; 'he held Flanders in great peace and was of great power,' one recalled in the twelfth century, expelling 'all pillagers and thieves from his own land, so that in no region could be found greater

---

[179] *CSAA* II, no. 864. See further about this, below, pp. 310–12.
[180] Galbert of Bruges, *De multro . . .* , c. 4; see also J. B. Ross, *Murder* 90n.

peace and security than in his.'[181] Threatened in the times of
Robert II (1087–1111), an illustrious crusader, and Baldwin VII
(1111–19), and badly shaken by the murder of Charles the Good
on 2 March 1127, the comital peace was restored in an exemplary
princely regime thereafter.

The acts of these counts, bestowing powers, immunities, protection, and justice, were to be commemorated. Their diplomas
and charters, which survive in swelling numbers after about
1050, were remarkably imposing. Diversely written by scribes in
the religious houses that preserved them, they represent the
count's power, 'by God's grace,' as that of a *principatus* or *comita-
tus* or *monarchia* or *regnum*; the count is variously styled *marchio*,
princeps, *consul*, as well as *comes*. 'What the contumacy of the
wicked contrives let the princely power crush' ran the *arenga* to a
diploma of 1090 for the church of Phalempin,[182] and this sentiment was characteristic. One approached these lord-counts in
deference, petitioned them humbly, thereby confirming an image
of condescending grace cultivated by monastic scribes schooled
in the theocratic culture of Saint-Omer, Arras, and Ghent. The
counts doubtless shared the clerical sense that they dominated
officially.

But this written culture is equivocal and incomplete in its revelation of comital power. For all their solemnity, the charters are
voiced subjectively, preserving a semblance of proprietary lordship. Robert II spoke of 'my landed vassal' the noble Enguerrand, lord of Lillers castle, when confirming that lord's foundation
of Ham in 1093; and he and his successors habitually referred to
'my barons' or 'my princes.' According to Hariulf, the Flemish
barons were grateful to Robert I for 'caring for all with paternal affection.'[183] Yet the charters contain little of the colloquial

---

[181] *Herimanni liber de restauratione monasterii sancti Martini Tornacensis*, ed. Georg
Waitz, *MGHSS* XIV (Hanover 1883) cc. 14, 17 (280, 282).

[182] *ACF* no. 10.

[183] ibid., nos. 13, 22, 23, 68, 79, 120; *Vita sancti Arnulfi episcopi Suessionensis . . .*
ii.19, *PL* CLXXIV, 1416.

discourse echoed in Angevin or even in Occitanian diplomatic; convey little sense of comital *voluntas*. They show Robert I and his three successors acting responsively rather than affirmatively; they leave us to imagine how the counts imposed the fidelity on castellans that cemented a territorial domination second only to that of ducal Normandy. Something of this baronial cohesion does filter through the charters, which give expression to festival occasions, courts, and consultations; but the lordly mastery that secured it and the ritual gestures of vassalic submission (such as were exceptionally revealed by Galbert of Bruges) largely escape notice. The baronial peace depended on fear of the count, according to Heriman of Tournai; he thought it a bad omen that in 1111 the young Baldwin VII failed to demand sworn commitments to the peace from his barons, contenting himself with their 'promise.' This must have been a departure from custom, for we can only suppose that the assured lord-counts who so readily associated their baronial allies in recorded recognitions and judgments must have insisted on the attendance of castellans, which *is* attested and is, indeed, one of the striking features of Flemish comital diplomatic. In this curial solidarity intersecting in written and oral cultures the counts could act decisively, while the castellans must as a rule have found it more rewarding to share in the comital domination of productive lands in full *croissance* than to usurp regalian powers. Even the peripheral counts of Saint-Pol, Ponthieu, and Ghisnes, themselves heirs to successful usurpations of advocatorial powers in an earlier day, had fallen into dependence on the counts of Flanders by 1100.

All this said, it must be added that counts and scribes alike were less insistent on lordship than on service and qualifications. This does not mean that lordship was consciously distinguished from office. On the contrary, comital domination in the quasi-scriptural usage of scribes was made up of offices: so Count Robert II, 'among other offices [*officia*] of my dispensation,' as he put it, sought to improve the status of Saint-Donatian in 1101. His father had authorized the monks of Ham in 1093 to collect 100s. annually 'in the office of my *dispensator* Simon' at

Saint-Omer.[184] Office was essential to this realm of power, continuous with traditional public order,[185] and it was rooted in fidelity and consanguinity. Countess Clementia often acted jointly
with her husband after about 1100, normally as his 'wife'; she and
her sons attended, responded, consented, without pretending to
the co-lordship more usual in Mediterranean lands.[186] A specifically ministerial group—the seneschal (often *dapifer*), the butler,
the chamberlains, the constable—becomes visible in the later
eleventh century, when their inherently servile tasks could be
relegated to men dependent on these companions of the count.[187]
As elsewhere, the domestic functionaries had *noblesse* and fidelity
to offer, as did the castellans and advocates who shared in the
proceeds of comital justice and protection. Many would have
been vassals. It was Ingelbert's *feodale ministerium* to collect the
capitation from the serfs of Saint-Vaast together with a monk.[188]
Clerical provosts and canons, often those of Bruges, and notaries
engaged in fiscal collection and accounting were of more distinctly functional value to the count; and if we hear of them more
suggestively—of *Fromoldus inbreviator* in a fiscal donation to Bour-
bourg in 1104, for example—than elsewhere, that is still not very
much. Flemish scribes preferred to identify companions and witnesses functionally, not as sworn dependents; only exceptionally
did they think it necessary to specify that *Onulfus dapifer* was the
'count's seneschal.'[189] Function as well as dependence defined the
quality, the greater or lesser nobility, that justified the association.
Lesser servants understood this—and bore watching. Erembald,

[184] *ACF* nos. 26, 13.

[185] *Diplomata belgica ante annum millesimum centesimum scripta*, ed. M. Gysseling, A. C. F. Koch, 2 parts (Brussels 1950) 1, no. 156.

[186] *ACF* nos. 20, 21, 23, 33–37, 39, 42, 46, 47; see also nos. 54–56, 58, 63.

[187] Charles Verlinden, *Robert Ier le Frison, comte de Flandre. Etude d'histoire politique* (Antwerp-Paris 1935) 138–42; Raymond Monier, *Les institutions centrales
du comté de Flandre de la fin du IXe siècle à 1384* (Paris 1943) 45–47.

[188] *ACF* no. 108 (1122). See also Henri Platelle, *La justice seigneuriale de
l'abbaye de Saint Amand . . .* (Louvain-Paris 1965) p.j. 2 (418–19).

[189] *ACF* nos. 13, 19, 22, 23, 33.

castellan of Bruges, was of servile descent. A society of service took shape, its focus in the count moving with him from one castle or domain to another; and since the work of all the count's men was local—the 'count's seneschal' could be identified as 'seneschal of Aire' (*dapifer Arie*)—the lists of subscribers and witnesses are habitually undifferentiated.[190]

There was no visible routine of domination. If charters were passed or even multiplied on ceremonial occasions, it was for the convenience of publicity or approval, not because the counts reserved access or envisaged problems administratively. Although it appears that the provost of Saint Donatian of Bruges was made count's chancellor in 1089, there is no evidence that he functioned thereafter to systematize decision-making or its commemoration. He or the count continued to rely on local scribes familiar with past privileges. Flemish charters may be said to remember from occasion to occasion, but not to carry on.[191] At most we can make out some tendency to refer to related records, notably fiscal ones, for the inventory of appointed rights.[192] This must have been the chancellor's work, for the *cancellarius* was designated receiver (*exactor*) of comital revenues for the whole 'principality of Flanders' in 1089 (or some time later?), and he was charged also with supervision of the count's notaries and chaplains 'and of all clerks serving in the count's court.'[193]

---

[190] *ACF* no. 13; Ernest Warlop, *The Flemish nobility before 1300*, tr. J. B. Ross, 4 vols. (The Hague 1974) I, 113–17.

[191] See, e.g., *ACF* nos. 47, 52, 69.

[192] ibid., no. 7 (1087): '. . . Hec autem sunt pertinentia ad preposituram: de supradictis Vorslarensis ecclesia cum omnibus nove terre et veteris, cum oblationibus suis et mansum terre et decimatio de Hasleth et advocatio de familia sancte Marie, preter censum, qui est fratrum.' Also nos. 5, 6, 9, 66, 73, 101, 114.

[193] ibid., no. 9; another edition in *Diplomata belgica* I, no. 170; both editions with facsimile. These editors (Vercauteren, Gysseling, and Koch) together with all modern authorities except one have pronounced this celebrated diploma authentic. While not convinced they are wrong, I am doubtful enough to believe it inadvisable to base any argument of institutional chronology on the purported date of the record. As O. Oppermann showed, 'Die unechte

That the count's entourage was conceived as a 'court' (*curia*) already before 1100 is not unlikely. But the usage quoted here is not common in the charters down to 1127. The earliest unequivocal instance dates from 1113, when Lithnot 'minister of our court' rendered his fief so that Count Baldwin VII could pledge it to Saint-Trond; and the 'chaplains of Baldwin's court' subscribed a privilege for Ypres in 1116.[194] The usual meaning of *curia* is that of celebratory assemblage; and in this sense the usage is not only precocious in Flanders but also illustrative of the conceptual ambiguity already seen to attach to comital functions. As early as the 1080s we encounter the count's *curia* either as a possessive manifestation of his lordship or as expressive of Flemish territorial identity. An endowment charter for the canons of Cassel in 1085 refers to the approval of Count Robert's wife and sons 'and the whole court of the Flemings.' On the other hand, 'my court' or 'count's court' figures from 1089, if the diploma for Saint Donatian is genuine, and certainly from 1102.[195] At Epiphany 1093 in Bruges, Robert II provided for the protection of Watten church 'in full court . . . in the presence of great men of the land,' of whom twenty-six are named, including a butler, a constable, a seneschal, a castellan, the provost Bertulf, chaplain, notaries, 'and many others of

---

Urkunde des Grafen Robert II von Flandern fuer S. Donatien zu Bruegge von 1089 . . . ,' *RBPH* xvi (1937) 178–82, the supposed original bears appearances internal and external of twelfth-century redaction. What his critics have shown is only that the paleographical traits in question are attested already in the late eleventh century. Vercauteren's refutation of O's argument that the diploma contradicts Galbert on the chronology of provosts at Saint Donatian is unpersuasive; and I must add for my part that the dispositive clause—'Prepositum sane ejusdem ecclesie, quicumque sit, cancellarium nostrum et omnium successorum nostrorum, susceptorem etiam et exactorem de omnibus reditibus principatus Flandrie, perpetuo constituimus, eique magisterium meorum notariorum et capellanorum et omnium clericorum in curia comitis servientium, potestative concedimus'—looks anachronistic to me.

[194] *ACF* nos. 61, 79. The usage must have been common after 1120; see (Heriman) *Liber de restauratione*, c. 27 (285).

[195] *ACF* no. 6: 'et universa Flandrensium curia'; also nos. 9, 26, 27.

our best men.'[196] What is arresting here is not only the scribal equivocation between objective and possessive reference; this diploma also affords a good example of the conflation of celebratory convocation and routine association. The handy word *curia* lent itself to association with count in different forms. Courts in this county of Flanders were celebrations of the attended count, some fuller and more solemn than others.

The exercise of comital power became self-consciously associative in the early twelfth century. No doubt this owed something to a scribal cult of procedural nicety, but the charters speak in the count's voice. At Saint-Vaast in 1115, when 'my gathered court was seated in the abbot's chamber,' the abbot and monks deposed a 'grave complaint' against the bakers of Arras 'in our hearing.' When the charge had been heard, 'because it was for me to be mindful of the church, I consulted the *échevins* present together with the greater and more trustworthy men of the city about this.' Their testimony, in favour of the monks, was heard 'with the voiced approval of the whole court,' whereupon the count ordered (*precepi*) that the bakers be constrained accordingly.[197] In 1120 Charles the Good assigned a complaint of the abbot of Saint-Pierre of Ghent 'to the judgment of my barons, as the matter required, for discussion.'[198]

What matters here is not that the barons were obligated to counsel and judge by their tenures. That obligation applied everywhere and was seldom mentioned; Flemish scribes took no interest in it. But we can see more clearly in Flanders than elsewhere how the counts, by invoking baronial solidarity on problematic points of tenure, proof, or reproof, in effect permitted customary law to be formulated in their courts. In 1102 Everard de Tournai lost his claim to certain buildings in Saint Donatian's lordship 'not only by ecclesiastical right but even by the law of my [Robert II's] whole court.' The 'law of my court' was cited again in 1111 for Count Robert's regulation of food-render at Saint-Amand. And

---

[196] ibid., no. 12.   [197] ibid., no. 69.
[198] ibid., no. 95; see also no. 120.

in the case of 1120 already mentioned, in which a man of Ghent named Everwacker was charged with seizing land belonging to the monks of Saint-Pierre, the barons 'judged according to general custom anciently constituted in the court of the Frankish kings and of the counts of the Flandrensians.'[199]

Justice, in short, was deliberate in Flanders because it rested on custom—that is, on customary status. Lithnot restored his fief *legaliter* to permit Count Baldwin to dispose of it otherwise. The barons advised the same count to consult the *scabiones* regarding the toll at Saint-Vaast. But one custom could override another, as in the case of 1120 at Ghent, where in the end the persistent anger of the man deprived of his land obliged Count Charles to compromise and amend his judgment so as to permit Everwacker to hold of the abbot on terms of an annual render.[200] The avatars of status, of estate, become visible. But it would be mistaken to conclude that justice had a programmatic place in this lordship. As late as the time of Charles the Good, when records of curial judgments first multiply, there is no diplomatic of justice. Scribes wrote charters recording settlements or judgments, but not *iudicia* per se; nor were their charters the records of courts. Moreover, *iudicia*, however recorded, are very exceptional before about 1111; only two survive from the preceding four decades, nor are they numerous thereafter. Luckily we can see from other records that the charters tell less than the whole story of comital justice.

It was related of Charles the Good that he reproved the abbot of Saint-Bertin for appearing in his Epiphany court at Bergues Saint Winnoc when he ought to have been celebrating the festival mass with his monks. When the abbot explained that he had a grievance to express, Count Charles replied: 'So why didn't you send it to me

---

[199] ibid., nos. 26, 50, 95.   [200] ibid., nos. 61, 52, 95.

through your servant? For it is yours to pray for me, mine indeed to protect and defend churches.'[201]

This invocation of Carolingian political doctrine pointed to a deeper strain of peremptory justice. The count, upon learning that a knight had seized land the monks had held quietly for more than sixty years, condemned him on the spot. Pointing out that the knight's father had kept silence, Charles threatened if he heard further complaint to do what Count Baldwin had done with another delinquent knight: to burn him alive. We learn of this from Heriman of Tournai, who as it happens also wrote of the earlier case and of other comparable incidents. A poor widow had her stolen cow restored when Count Baldwin put aside pressing business with his magnates to hear her case. But the tradition Heriman preserved was that of lord-counts generating salutary fear. His account of how a fully armed knight was thrown into a cauldron of water fired to boiling before an assembled multitude at Bruges is memorably gruesome. 'So great a terror pervaded all present that no one henceforth presumed to seize anything in all Flanders.'[202]

The remedy of violence was summarily just. No one expected the counts to wait on evidence when injustice was manifest. For the barons had sworn to the count's peace, if not in IIII when Baldwin VII was said to have failed to impose oaths at his accession, then in May III4 'in a solemn court at Saint-Omer.'[203] Another anecdote of Heriman evokes an anxious climate of security in these years. When ten knights robbed a merchant going to the market at Thourout, the count was quick to seize and imprison them. Their kinsmen pleaded for mercy: let Baldwin fine the knights in money or horses, but not hang them. His response was to devise a means for the knights to hang themselves, here again prompting Heriman's apostrophe:

---

[201] *Liber de restauratione*, c. 27 (285).   [202] ibid., cc. 22, 23 (283–84).

[203] *ACF* no. 64: 'ea scilicet die qua ab ipso comite cunctisque proceribus Flandrie, pax confirmata est sacramentis.' See also no. 65.

'Flanders might call itself happy if only it had long deserved such a prince!'[204]

The first such prince had been Robert the Frisian. For this we have not only Heriman's assertion that he kept 'peace and security' but also the incidental notice that Count Robert had charged the castellan of Bruges to make a written record of killings at Bruges and its environs in 1084.[205] But it is not clear that Robert I insisted programmatically on the peace. The only statutes imposed in Flanders in his day were the work of a synod at Soissons held by Archbishop Renaud of Reims (1083–93), none other (incidentally) than the former bad lord of Montreuil-Bellay; and these statutes provided that complaints should go to the bishop or archdeacon. Moreover, Robert I was himself a violator of the peace. Charged with seizing the property of deceased clerics, he was reproved by Pope Urban II in 1092; in vain, it seems, for his vassals and servants persisted in violent encroachments. Only when the statutes were reconfirmed ceremonially at Saint-Omer in July 1099 do we find Count Robert II actively engaged, although not even then in such a way as to prove his direction of the peace. The oaths imposed on the 'lords of castles and cities' were to be sworn in the bishop's hand.[206] Perhaps it was only after 1100 that the count assumed the full stature of his protectorate.

The peace was critical to this order because Flanders was a violent land. In a remarkable study based on chiefly hagiographical sources, Henri Platelle concluded that it was conspicuously violent, especially along the coasts, where he discerned a continuity of brutal customs over many generations. He also thought that violence was a consequence of a lately imposed seigneurial regime.[207] Surely he was right. Much of the violence recorded in

---

[204] *Liber de restauratione*, c. 24 (284).

[205] Hariulf, *Vita Arnulfi* ii.19–20 (1416–17).

[206] *Sacrosancta concilia . . .* , ed. Ph. Labbe, Gabriel Cossart, 17 vols. (Paris 1671–72) XII, 961–62, 801–4.

[207] Henri Platelle, 'La violence et ses remèdes en Flandre au XIe siècle,' *Sacris Erudiri* XX (1971) 108–14.

charters as well as narratives took the form of arbitrary seizures, encroachments on clerical lands, oppressive redemption-payments such as were elsewhere symptoms of lordly or proto-lordly ambition or excess.[208] We hear less of baronial insubordination in Flanders than in Catalonia or Anjou; yet when the castellan Everard of Tournai rebelled against Robert I he was said to have seized 'many men rich and poor' and forced them to ransom themselves. Hugues d'Inchy had stormed into the village of Feuchy, burned and looted it, and taken away many wretched men.[209]

These examples suggest that coercive violence in Flanders was often that of armed bands, more like incidents of warfare than of lordship. Thierry, 'a noble and greatly powerful man,' was at war with Count Baldwin of Mons when 'one day, having gathered a considerable militia, he violently entered his land and took from it much plunder'; he even burned two nunneries where the count had installed 'hostile knights.'[210] But the distinction between hostility and domination should not be pressed. Lords in Flanders may well have been tempted to prey on other men's, not their own, peasants or wealth. Frustrated by their failures to win papal support in a dispute over burial rights at Tournai, the canons hired knights to harass the monks of Saint-Martin. Their sergeants (servientes) rode out one evening to the monks' farm at Duissenpierre and pillaged it.[211] Such were the means of men seeking the security of lordly status, of knights as so often in Heriman's stories, but also of the retainers and servants of the counts and prelates. Charges against their own men came to the counts, surely in larger numbers than we know from extant records; the regular clergy attempted to discipline their own provosts and advocates, but had often to appeal to the counts. Expectations

---

[208] ACF nos. 13 (44), 17, 19, 24(?), 50, 68, 81, 82, 85, 92, 100, 106, 107, 119 (274).

[209] Liber de restauratione, c. 66 (305); Le registre de Lambert évêque d'Arras (1093–1115), ed. Claire Giordanengo (Paris 2007) E2 330.

[210] Liber de restauratione, c. 56 (298).   [211] ibid., c. 89 (317).

of violence by lesser agents—*infestatio* is the usual term—pervade the diplomas of protection.[212]

The best evidence of ministerial violence comes from Saint-Amand. Towards 1095–97 one Anselm, who held the *advocatura* of Neuville and other villages in the Saint's domain, imposed forced levies on the peasants, extorted ransom from other tenants, and 'inflicted many other evils.' Abbot Hugh and some monks first pleaded with him to desist and won his penitential renunciation, but Anselm resumed his violent ways. Next the monks appealed to Count Robert II, obtaining a favourable judgment, only to have Anselm relapse yet again in 'increased malice,' building mills in disruption of Saint-Amand's rights. All that was left was for the abbot to excommunicate the tormentor, an ultimate constraint rendered terrible by exposure of the Saint's relics. This was an act of compelling lordship that induced a more solemn amendment: Anselm prostrated himself barefoot before the relics, made his renunciation crucifix in hand, and 'tearfully sought mercy and absolution.' So, 'condescending to his tears and petitions,' the abbot absolved him on condition that in a public gathering of monks and villagers he recognize his unjust exactions and compel his son to relinquish them as well. Not even this was quite the end of it. Anselm having pledged part of the advocacy to one Ramirus, the monks could only avoid that man's devastation of the villages by redeeming the obligation; they hesitated, then decided to pay him off—120 marks of silver, no small sum—in yet another solemn ceremony; and in laboured final clauses, followed by a long list of sworn pledges to the fulfillment of the terms, the monks tried to nail down their shaky success.[213]

What is unsaid here, as always in such ecclesiastical notices, is what the advocate had seriously hoped to salvage of his power. Once it became a test of lordships, the Saint was bound to prevail,

---

[212] *ACF* nos. 50, 55, 81, 85, 89, 99, 107, 119; *Diplomata belgica* I, no. 171.

[213] Platelle, *Justice de Saint-Amand*, p.j. 4 (421–26). See also A. Bocquillet, 'Les prévôts laïques de Saint-Amand du XIᵉ au XIVᵉ siècle,' *Bulletin de la Société des Etudes de la Province de Cambrai* XXVI (1926) 161–87.

even if only in jolting compromise. Fear, threats to the end, compromise: this was the experience of power even in a land where princely authority and the Peace converged. Of office and service there seemed to be no question: what gives this away is the stipulation that Anselm's son swear together with his father to the final agreement. This advocacy was a hereditary lordship.

So was the lay provostship at Saint-Amand—but in this case we can see that it had not always been so. Around 1119–21 Abbot Bovo II noted in a newly undertaken compilation of charters that in the past the people of Saint-Amand were free of the lordship of a lay provost. The abbot and the monk-provost appointed a *ministerialis* to manage the town's affairs; the abbot and his tenants judged him when he was charged; and replaced him when they wished. The situation changed, he went on, when the abbey became subject to the counts of Flanders and Abbot Malbode (1018–62) chose his brother Alain to manage secular affairs. When Alain was assassinated, the abbot appointed his brother Heriman, perhaps already constrained to a choice that in the twelfth century was limited to deciding which son should succeed—or rather, inherit. This function, too, had become virtually a lordship—and a harsh one. Some time before 1076 Abbot Foucart-Lambert brought a plea against his provost Heriman, who was obliged to renounce a cluster of bad practises (*tortitudines*) in the town of Saint-Amand. Chief among these was the 'forced exaction' (*violenta prex*), or what was elsewhere commonly called tallage. But we can see from other settlements that the provost had been exploiting all possible occasions of profit, encroaching on the cellarer's jurisdiction, demanding services and shares in sales, etc. The provost was to keep his promises on pain of losing his benefice together with this function (*ministerium*). But the logic of lordly need could not so easily be overcome. Heriman persisted in his arbitrary ways until a new abbot, Bovo I, recalling the terms of the former settlement, demanded that he make another public renunciation. The struggle long continued.[214]

---

[214] Platelle, *Justice*, p.j. 2, 3 (418–21). See also pp. 71–74.

Northern Kingdoms

Between the venerable principalities just examined lived peoples whose lord-rulers were destined to reduce Anjou and Flanders to provinces of greater kingdoms. That destiny weighs so heavily on our perceptions as to obscure the realities of the later eleventh century, when the ambitions of nobles and knights and the anxieties of peasants and merchants might have seemed little different in Normandy and the Ile-de-France from those in other lands in northern France. Here, too, the norms of castellan lordship and knightly violence are visible, indeed brilliantly illuminated by the monk historians Orderic Vitalis and Suger of Saint-Denis. What did make some difference to the experience of power in these lands, conspicuously so in Normandy (to say nothing of England), was that Duke William conquered England in the years 1066 to 1085, for this event not only created a vastly enhanced principality, it also compelled the lord-kings of France to face up to the liabilities of a territorial lordship virtually confined to the Ile-de-France. The Normans, as mobilised by the Conqueror and his sons, were a formidable power, pressing to extend the Norman Vexin from 1087, and later forcing Louis VI and his allies into a conflict that would become a relentless dynastic rivalry thereafter.[215]

It was not yet that in the eleventh century. The question then facing the northern dynastic rulers was how to dominate, pacify, or exploit their princely neighbours. The surest way was by inter-marriage, always provided that sons were born so as to avoid dynastic disruption or foreign intrusion. The Normans and Ca-petians met this test for two generations, not without some close calls. Flanders figured centrally in their calculations, a trib-ute to the reputations built up by Counts Baldwin IV (988–1037)

---

[215] See OV and Suger, *Vie de Louis VI le Gros*, ed. Henri Waquet (Paris 1929), as cited below, 229–43; and generally Augustin Fliche, *Le règne de Philippe Ier, roi de France (1060–1108)* (Paris 1912); Douglas, *William the Conqueror*; and John Le Patourel, *The Norman empire* (Oxford 1976).

and Baldwin V (1037–67). Duke William married the latter's daughter Matilda at the very time when the courtiers of the child Philip I were choosing her father to assume the tutelage of Philip. Matilda's fertile marriage to a husband of conspicuous fidelity was no small asset in the making of Norman dynastic power. In 1063, Matilda's brother Robert married the widow of the count of Holland, whose daughter Berthe (Robert's stepdaughter) married the young king Philip, probably in 1072. But the Flemish alliance had been disrupted by Robert's violent seizure of Flanders in 1070, when the king had naturally sided with the late Count Baldwin's son and designated successor Arnulf, who died in the battle of Cassel (1071). Philip's marriage to Berthe was part of a settlement with her stepfather, the new count of Flanders. This cannot have been an easy marriage, for while Matilda retired from the ducal-royal scenes of power only for her frequent confinements, Queen Berthe seldom accompanied her husband in his royal enactments, and gave birth to the future Louis VI only after anxious years of waiting and prayer. Having subsequently borne a daughter (and perhaps another son), she was repudiated by Philip in favour of Bertrade de Montfort, the wife of Count Fulk Richin, precipitating a scandal that upset Flemish and Angevin dynastic ties alike. So fragile were such ties; yet the fact remains that Prince Louis survived to validate his quasi-Flemish birth, his very name bearing witness to the Carolingian prestige associated with the Flemish line.[216]

Human power in these northern lands was most visibly experienced in the deeds of lord-kingship, including those of marriage and alliance, in the shifting solidarities of baronial ambition and interest by no means easy to control, and in the personal capacities of lord-kings. Perhaps no comparable stretch of medieval history was so influenced by princely character as the half-century from 1060 to 1110. Historians have not doubted the consequences

---

[216] Dunbabin, *France in the making*, 2d ed. 207–12; Fliche, *Philippe Ier*, 36–46; Andrew W. Lewis, *Royal succession in Capetian France* . . . (Cambridge, M., 1981) 46–52.

of the Conqueror's resolve—and temper—, nor those resulting from the temperamental diversity of his sons. Philip I's weakness lay glaringly in his character. And it took prelates of personal depth and strength—Anselm of Canterbury and Ivo of Chartres—to help their masters ride out the storms called down by reformer popes and their clerical allies.

Yet the lord-kings in France and England, as in other monarchies of the later eleventh century, were far from monopolizing power. When Philip I carried off Bertrade de Montfort he was challenging Anjou for the allegiance of the lesser military aristocracy of the Ile-de-France. The effective solidarity in and about the Capetian court came to be that of the castellans, some of whom, strong and arrogant enough to challenge the most venerable royal protectorates, would require all the prowess of Louis VI to suppress. Likewise, in England and Normandy, where the accumulation of castles by victorious and loyal knights had created fearsome baronies, circumstances favoured the multiplication of lordships of constraint. Only a map of castles and towers, new ones distinguished from old, could represent so much as an impression of the realities of power and lordship in the lands known to Orderic and Suger.

For all their appearances of might, the Norman and Capetian kings suffered from the limitations of circumstance. The euphoria of the Conqueror's success was checked if not reversed in the 1070s. Orderic Vitalis acutely discerned a turning point about 1077, following the execution of Earl Waltheof.[217] It took a modern scholar, J.-Fr. Lemarignier, to show how this same year was critical to the fortunes of Philip I, who had henceforth to do without the support of his prelates.[218] Norman ducal power only became threatening to France when harnessed to English resources, chiefly after the battle of Tinchebrai (1106), but already towards 1097, when William Rufus assaulted Mantes and Chaumont.

---

[217] OV iv (II, 350).

[218] J.-Fr. Lemarignier, *Le gouvernement royal aux premiers temps capétiens (987–1108)* (Paris 1965) ch. 3.

Suger remembered these encounters, perhaps not altogether ten-
dentiously, as a struggle between a rich and ripe spender of England's wealth and a fledgling impecunious Prince Louis who
prevailed by knightly prowess alone.[219] The French under Philip
I could muster no such dynamic solidarity as the Conqueror, having no such epic success to boast, while being vulnerable to the
moral backlash provoked by the king's adulterous union with
Bertrade de Montfort. In both realms new kings brought new
energies to inherited problems in the twelfth century, defining
enlarged conceptions of regal lordship.

CAPETIAN FRANCE

When the child Philip was consecrated king in Reims cathedral
on Pentecost Sunday 1059, a record of the 'order' of ceremony
underscored the archbishop's historic primacy in the ritual. King
Henry I (1031–60), who had assuredly directed the event, was
present; but it was Archbishop Gervais who 'turned towards' the
boy 'before the epistle' and administered the professions of faith,
justice, and defence of the church; and then, 'taking the staff of
Saint-Remi, he explained quietly and peacefully how the election and consecration of the king pertained especially to
him[self]' as successor to the holy Remigius, who had baptized
and consecrated Clovis. 'Then with his father Henry's approval,
he elected him [Philip] king.' Only then were the prelates,
counts, viscounts, knights, and 'people greater and lesser' invited
to ratify the election, 'proclaiming "we approve, we wish, let it
be done"!'[220]

The purpose of this record, it becomes clear at the end, was not
simply to confirm the electoral privilege of Reims, but chiefly to
disclaim any customary obligation to feed and lodge the people
who attended. Officially ecclesiastical in some sense, as the

[219] Suger, *Vie de Louis VI*, c. 1.
[220] *Ordines coronationis Franciae* . . . , ed. Richard A. Jackson, 2 vols. (Philadelphia 1995–2000) I, 217–32.

boy-king's 'profession' suggests, the kingship was conferred ritually, not by record, for the narrative as we have it was manifestly descriptive, not constitutive: an expression of prelatical lordship such as might be expected in a land where a foundation-legend of monarchy so favoured the see of Reims and where patrimonial lordships were in a phase of competitive growth. The old king might have queried the archbishop's tendentious account, which lacked the force of the written 'precept' by which the king-elect confirmed the possessions of Saint-Remi. But the rite of election was evidently a right of power claimed by a bishop, and doubtless recognized as episcopal because it figures so in subsequent French royal coronation *ordines*. What happened at the next coronation, that of Louis VI in 1108, bears out these points. The archbishop of Sens presided, to the dismay of Archbishop Raoul le Vert of Reims, whose own irregular election had failed to gain King Philip's approval; and it required the discreet intervention of Bishop Ivo of Chartres to justify the consecration at Orléans (3 August) while saving the rights of Reims. Here again the office—symbolized by the 'sword . . . to punish malefactors' and the rod and scepter 'for the defence of churches and the poor'—is ecclesiastical, even if the bishops of Sens and Chartres have usurped the right of Reims. Yet here too, once again, the records seem other than concretely official, comprising a circular letter by Bishop Ivo, excusing an irregular coronation at a moment of compelling urgency for the realm, plus the recollections narrated by Hugh of Fleury and Suger. There is no sign that a settled or written order of coronation was yet in use. As Elizabeth Brown has shown, the imprecision of ritual practise persisted down to the 1130s, when in all likelihood the coronation of Louis VII in Bordeaux was the occasion for composing an *ordo* making explicit reference to peoples of west Frankland.[221] Only some reconciliation of dynastic and ecclesiastical interests in king-making could have rendered this early Capetian monarchy an office of record.

---

[221] '*Franks, Burgundians, and Aquitanians*' *and the royal coronation ceremony in France* (Philadelphia 1992) ch. 1.

It was nonetheless an office of transcendent dignity. The 'profession' of 1059 and the *ordines* point insistently to a solemnity of regality such as pervades the diplomas that have come down to us. These are, explicitly in the *arengae* of privileges and implicitly in content and process alike, the memorials of exalted official action. Favouring the church of Laon in 1071, the young King Philip is made to assert that the 'office' of the power (*imperium*) he exercises must not be permitted to lag behind its dignity.[222] A preamble in 1077 alluded to the imperative 'of royal altitude and majesty' to improve the 'state of the realm' with respect to customs and laws while caring for the clergy in return for their prayers.[223] This quasi-Carolingian sentiment figured in one of the last of Philip's diplomas to be subscribed by bishops in any numbers. Yet there was no conceptual diminution of regal office thereafter, the scribes of Louis VI being quite as disposed as their predecessors to invoke the king's 'majesty' as a public 'authority' (*auctoritas*) justifying action, including the punishment of violators branded as traitors.[224] Allusions to 'government of the realm' (*regni gubernacula*) and 'administration' evoke a Ciceronian concept of (republican) public order.[225]

Majesty implied humility in the experience of royal power. People were all about these kings. The diplomas show them responding to petitions as they traversed the castles and palaces of the Ile-de-France. 'Count Gui of Ponthieu came into our presence, pleading that we [King Philip, in 1075 or 1076] should confirm by the authority of our majesty a certain gift he had made . . . to the monks of Cluny' in his county.[226] Around 1120 Abbot Thomas of Morigny 'vehemently urged the serenity of our excellence' that he (Louis VI) confirm donations made by Philip I to the monks.[227] Petitions so described—typically the expression is *adiit presenciam*— were surely formulaic, at least in the sense that the appeal must

---

[222] *RAPh1* no. 61. See plate 1.   [223] ibid., no. 86; cf. no. 87.

[224] *RAL6* I, nos. 135, 170, 173, 177, 186, 189, 191, 231, II, no. 280.

[225] ibid., I, nos. 142, 163, 182, II, no. 342.

[226] *RAPh1* no. 79.   [227] *RAL6* I, no. 173.

commonly have preceded in some other place the royal acquies-
cence recorded by the diploma. The reality was that the king *could*
be approached with due deference doubtless protected by functionaries about him. His informal response is largely concealed from
us, but the charters preserved in churches and often drafted locally
are not so formulaic as to prevent us from glimpsing the usual
events of ceremonial promulgation. In the Ile-de-France as elsewhere the 'corroboration' by persons present of the explicit mention of consultation lent power to the diploma. In 1086 when
Abbot Eustache of Saint-Père of Chartres took advantage of King
Philip's presence to secure his confirmation of a local couple's donation, the petition, judged just by the king 'with our faithful men
who were present,' was approved 'publicly, before Saint Vincent's
gate in the castle of Dreux' and confirmed by the subscriptions of
the king and 'his magnates [*primates nostrí*].'[228] Whether this entailed a ceremonial reading of the diploma, as in León under Alfonso VI, is not clear, and perhaps unlikely, but there was nothing
arbitrary about the written expression of the king's will. Pretentious, ceremonious, the king's action was passive, responsive; it was
expressive of the power of his authority, devoid of active political
or legislative purpose. The 'policies' historians formerly discerned
towards the church or the towns may better be understood as imperatives, even constraints, forced on these kings by the realities of
their lordship.

Philip I and his greater son were, first and last, lord-kings. The
powerfully affective nature of their leadership is hardly concealed
by the official rhetoric of their diplomas. One petitioned the
lord-king in his office, to be sure; but the gestured deference so
characteristic of Capetian diplomatic cannot have been formulaic. 'Begging pardon and favor,' in Geoffrey Koziol's phrase, was
a mechanism of power in a royal entourage which already in the
1030s was creating networks of lordship and dependence that
required the king's personal favour to work. Not that patronage
and favouritism were new, far from it; what was new in France

---

[228] *RAPh1* no. 118.

was the lord-king's engagement, on account of his loss of wider and deeper sanctions, with a petty aristocracy henceforth beyond the royalist discipline of public constraints. This is why the changed form of the royal diploma, elucidated by Lemarignier, was symptomatic, for if the lord-king could no longer sanction his will by the monogram alone, and when he was deserted by the greater magnates who had represented Carolingian order, he was obliged to subject lesser men in personal commendation and to admit them to be guarantors of his power.[229]

Amongst those who prospered in this conjuncture were the functionaries who served the kings: chancellor, seneschal (or dapifer), chamberlain, constable, butler. It was once fashionable to view them as founders of 'public services,' the progressive harbingers of central administration. But there is little to show that they ever functioned much like their namesakes of the Carolingian age, as characterized in Hincmar's *Order of the palace*. What we see in the eleventh century is local families of the Ile-de-France exploiting the lord-kings' favour by securing shares in their lordship; they so prospered in the process that by the end of the reign of Philip I they could claim themselves to constitute the *palatium*, becoming sufficient guarantors of royal enactments even as more illustrious magnates either kept their distance or were excluded. In the time of Louis VI the Garlande family managed so to displace the Rochefort and Senlis as to secure most of the curial functions for themselves. This may have been to aggregate revenues attached to the offices. People learned who counted besides the king, as we see from the diplomas of 1115 granted on the instance of Guillaume de Garlande; from a long string of concessions to Sainte-Croix of Orléans, where the chancellor Etienne de Garlande doubled as dean; and even from Peter Abelard's pursuit of royal favour about 1122.[230]

Likewise close to the kings were the provosts (*praepositi*), who had charge of royal revenues and justice in the localities. It looks

---

[229] *Gouvernement royal*, ch. 2.

[230] e.g., *RAL6* I, nos. 102, 103, 111; and generally Eric Bournazel, *Le gouvernement capétien au XIIe siècle, 1108 1180* . . . (Paris 1975) ch. 2.

as if these agents, virtually courtiers at first, progressively settling in cities, towns, and domains, such as Orléans and Etampes, were recipients of written directives from the king that point to a newly objective concept of administrative service. This appearance bears out an old contention of historians that the provosts were a harbinger of administrative kingship. What has been largely overlooked is that the proliferation of provosts, and doubtless not only of royal ones, coincided with that of castles beyond royal (or princely) control. The vicarial castles of regalian order were slipping from memory; the king's need was for 'supervisors' (*praepositi*) more reliable than castellans. The provosts came, like the household functionaries, from the lesser regional aristocracy, with whom they competed for patrimonial wealth; they may have been disadvantaged by diminished access to the king. They were among the king's sworn men (*fideles*); and it cannot be accidental that we have no evidence of their accountability for service.[231]

Together with his provosts and retainers Louis VI came of age and power in a society of pullulating lordships. Symptomatic of this experience is the multiplication of allusions to tallage (*tallia, tolta*; Fr.: *taille*). That the 'cut' or share, in money or produce, was an arbitrary tax in its origin and essence has long been clear. When first mentioned in or near the Ile-de-France, it is sometimes equated with 'customs' or 'bad customs' or with 'violence.' Towards 1101–06 Philip I forbade his provost of Paris to levy 'tolts or any exactions violently' from the people of Bagneux. In 1114 Louis VI exempted the priory of Saint-Eloi from the imposition of 'tallage or any other bad custom.'[232] But the notion of justified tallage must have been present from the start. The very meanest lords would have found it easier to collect from peasants with an

---

[231] *RAPh1* no. 153; *RAL6* I, nos. 100, 195; II, no. 321. Also Henri Gravier, *Essai sur les prévôts royaux du XIe au XIVe siècle* (Paris 1904) ch. 1; Lemarignier, *Gouvernement royal* 157–63.

[232] *RAPh1* no. 153; *RAL6* I, no. 96; see also II, no. 340 (1133). And in general *RAPh1* no. 114; *CSPCh* II, 483–84; *RAL6* I, nos. 150, 156.

excuse than without. When Raher *de Esarto* renounced his tallage in the monastic patrimony of Saint-Père of Chartres, he promised never to levy it again 'unless for the utility of that land and then only with the consent of our monk there in charge.'[233] On different occasions King Louis VI retained or donated as well as abolished his own rights to tallage; and tallages for cause soon multiplied in this region.[234]

The arbitrariness of tallage points to the exploitative ethos of petty seigneurial life in the Ile-de-France around 1100. But the knightly disposition to coercive action is not to be confused with feudalizing, an equally live facet of this scene. Typically though not always, these were feudal lordships and dependencies; and what matters here is not so much the manipulation of fiefs (*feuda*) in enormous numbers[235] as the affective sociability of enfeoffment and obligation. Around 1110 Abbot Boso of Fleury restored half an allod 'in fief' to the disgruntled son of a late convert-donor, 'wherefore he did homage [to the abbot] and swore fidelity.' That this ritual stands out in its context may be explained by this monastery's recent experience of wasteful enfeoffments, which had been denounced to and undone by the king.[236] The trouble with fiefs was that tenants tended to appropriate them or to ignore reversionary rights. At Châlons-sur-Marne King Louis prohibited efforts to create 'feudal right' (*jus feodale*) in tenures from patrimony conferred on the church by the king.[237] Like lesser lords Louis struggled to retain discretionary power over fiefs. A courtier like Henri le Lorrain could be thankful for the

---

[233] *CSPCh* II, 340.

[234] *RAL6* I, nos. 40, 60, 109, 150, 192; II, nos. 284, 382; *CSPCh* II, 483–84; André Chédeville, *Chartres et ses campagnes (XIe–XIIIe s.)* (Paris 1973) 297.

[235] *Liber testamentorum sancti Martini de Campis . . .* (Paris 1904) nos. 18, 19, 56, 58, 60 (*militis fevum*); *RAPh1* no. 127; *RAL6* I, nos. 27, 32 (*feoda militum*); *CSPCh* II, 312: complex of mills (*molendinaria de Ponte*) 'quam feodaliter suam esse debere' (1119–28). Citations could be multiplied.

[236] *RAL6* I, nos. 44, 27.

[237] ibid., no. 79.

privilege to hold his fiefs in hereditary right from the king.[238] That Louis VI came to entertain a concept of feudal hierarchy culminating in the king[239] is a possibility, as we shall see, but it can have had little if anything to do with his exercise of power down to 1120.

The king and his men were engaged in questions of local order and right of all kinds. When the provosts near Chartres incurred the wrath of Bishop Ivo towards 1112, they informed their lord-king, who ordered the bishop to cease and desist. Ivo had enlisted the pope in what had begun as a complaint about impositions by encroachment on clerical tenants. We happen to possess Provost Foulque's letter to the king, to the effect that by the latter's order to the bishop 'you have made things worse for us than before.' For (he writes) the bishop called off a hearing of us, then got the cardinal-legate Cono to prohibit such a hearing, threatening a summons to Rome. 'And so, having pleaded for your aid and taken refuge in your counsel, now we are injured.' What is striking here is the affective tone of reproach, a point virtually confirmed by Bishop Ivo, who wrote of the provosts 'deceiving the king' in this matter.[240] Here as so often power was deployed strategically in service of conflicting ends—clerical immunity and jurisdiction and royal lordship.

But the proceedings of disputing parties in the Ile-de-France, as elsewhere highly visible in the records,[241] tell us little about the normal experience of power in the early twelfth century. What most people felt as responsive justice and protection can only be imagined for lack of evidence, but may well have fallen short of pleasant routine in the districts of castles or provosts. The prohibition of forced exactions at Bagneux cited above originated in a petition of local people against the provost. What the masses

[238] ibid., nos. 65, 73.
[239] Lemarignier, *Gouvernement royal*, 173–76.
[240] *RAL6* I, no. 100; II, ap. 2, no. 9; *Cartulaire de Notre-Dame de Chartres . . .*, ed. E. de Lépinois, L. Merlet,, 3 vols. (Chartres 1862–65) I, no. 34.
[241] *RAL6* I, nos. 12, 16, 28, 66, 95, etc.

surely experienced were the coercive and abrasive facets of domination and compliance. When Ivo of Chartres insisted that he had no intention of infringing the 'right of provosts' at Chartres, he clearly meant to distinguish their customary impositions from what he called their 'illicit constraints and vexations of the poor.'[242] It is most unlikely that provosts recognized any such distinction.

For the exercise of power by provosts, like that of castellans and newly sprung lay lords, was in ill repute at the turn to the twelfth century. No doubt, this had long been so, but the signs are clear that bad customs in the Ile-de-France were often new customs. Moreover, complaints about the violence of constraint can be associated with the creation or expansion of lordships and settlement. These circumstances of novelty and expansion go together. In 1073 land near Etampes was said to be vacated on account of the 'troubling' (*inquietudo*) by the king's servants. What this 'trouble' was like—and the violence of desertion is often attested in records of the next half century—is revealed in detail in the story of a patrimony, again near Etampes, newly organized for a fledgling house of monks at Morigny. Bad neighbours had muscled in on the peasant tenants with an array of new demands, including protection-money (*tensamentum*). Thanks to the energy of a faithful steward, who fended off these pretenders to new lordship (not quite without paying them off), the monks had reason to remember their deliverance from trouble in their early communal life.[243]

Everywhere in the Ile-de-France castellans and knights, in their quest for lordship, were seeking to impose the customs of servility. One of its venerable customs, an ancient incapacity to testify against free people, seems to have been revived around 1100. Early in his reign Louis VI received appeals from Parisian churches on behalf of their serfs; and in notably solemn diplomas, fortified by

---

[242] ibid. II, ap. 2, no. 9 (460).

[243] *RAPh1* no. 64; *RAL6* I, nos. 15, 54; II, no. 266; *Chronique de Morigny* i.2 (5–6), quoted above, p. 61.

the counsel of imposing magnates, the king decreed that serfs of Notre-Dame and Sainte-Geneviève should have the same procedural rights as free men.[244] These decrees, and more were to follow, cannot have been comforting to lesser lay lords seeking to impose quasi-servile domination on peasants. But what the young king imposed was privileges, not legislation, a form of response that followed naturally from petitions; and much the same kind of response is visible in Louis' attention to a much bigger problem, indeed the defining problem of his reign: the encroachment by castellans (chiefly) on royal and ecclesiastical lordships.

How this problem was resolved in the first quarter of the twelfth century is one of the famous stories of that age. But its celebrity stems from the retrospect of the 1140s, and the dawning of perspectives on power we have not yet reached. What remains to be noticed here is that lord-rulership in the days of Louis VI (1108–37) was continuous with the modes of princely power already sampled in Lombardy, Anjou, and elsewhere. Louis' diplomas exuded the affective solemnity of regalian authority, it is true; yet even in their haughty altitude these documents read much like those of Count Baldwin VII of Flanders. When Orderic Vitalis looked back on this time, he told stories of princely domination in Flanders and Normandy as well as in France. He said little of royal power as categorically superior.[245]

That notion would take years for Louis VI to realize. His judgments—the ones we have typically in favour of churches— afford the illusion of efficacious public protection; his solemn courts and conventions betray his need of alliance.[246] Intermittently at war with the Duke-King Henry I in the Norman borderlands, it looks as if he did neither so well in combat as claimed

---

[244] *RAL6* I, nos. 22, 29; Olivier Guillot, 'La participation au duel judiciaire de témoins de condition serve dans l'Ile-de-France du XIe siècle . . . ,' *Droit privé et institutions régionales. Etudes . . . Jean Yver* (Paris 1976) 347n, 357–60.

[245] OV xi.34–37 (VI, 154–66).

[246] *RAL6* I, nos. 12, 16, 32, 46, 66, 75, 86, 132; Achille Luchaire, *Louis VI le Gros. Annales . . .* (Paris 1890) nos. 28, 73, 78, 87, 92.

by Suger nor so badly as suggested by Anglo-Norman chroni-clers. But he suffered terrible setbacks in his early years, driven out of Paris for a time in 1111, and roundly defeated by King Henry at Brémule in 1119. Moreover, the struggle in the lesser regional aristocracy for royal access rendered the king's entou-rage a focus of contention, a reality of power for people to wit-ness rather than suffer; yet a gripping experience of power not only for those who, like Peter Abelard, needed the king's back-ing, but also for the many who must have been dismayed by the spectacular rise and fall of the Garlande family in the royal ser-vice.[247] What preoccupied this king was not government, but the craving amongst all about him, courtiers and provosts alike, for status and lordship. Louis VI rewarded it, as a lord-prince must. He also subverted it.

NORMAN ENGLAND

The challenges facing William the Conqueror and his sons after him were of a different order. Duke William had already stared down his viscounts in the 1040s, defeating a coalition of rebel magnates at Val-ès-Dunes in 1047 and imposing the Truce of God by way of further limiting their violence. These events went some way to restoring his comital powers in Norman cities and to restraining incipient lineages in the castles. The ducal peace in the 1050s, if little less precarious than the order kept in neigh-bouring principalities, was rooted in revived public powers of command and constraint. Yet one senses from the diplomas and chronicles that its dynamic sprang from affective fidelities in alli-ance with and submission to the lord-count of the Normans that required just such a lordly exploit as the conquest of England to sustain.[248]

---

[247] Robert-Henri Bautier, 'Paris au temps d'Abélard,' *Abélard en son temps* . . . (Paris 1981) 40–71; Bournazel, *Gouvernement capétien au XIIᵉ siècle*, ch. 3.

[248] *Recueil des actes des ducs de Normandie de 911 à 1066*, ed. Marie Fauroux (Caen 1961); David Bates, *Normandy before 1066* (London 1982) ch. 4.

The Norman foundations of Anglo-Norman royal power cannot be fully considered here. What matter for English (even British) history are two points: first, that however much the Normans imposed their lordly order across the Channel, the successes they achieved in conquered lands had only limited resonance in Normandy, where violence was rife in the twelfth century. Second, the problem William faced in England was that of an old kingdom not only much larger than his homeland, but so formed historically as to invite the dissidence that had afflicted the west Frankish and Anglo-Saxon monarchies both, if not quite alike. William had companions-in-arms all too willing to appropriate the ambitions of Godwin of Wessex; but they could not be accommodated without jeopardizing the integrity of Old English local government. In thwarting this tendency William brought together the Frankish-Neustrian institution of the county and the English institutions of shire and hundred; and it proved all but impossible for the magnates of the Conquest to be content with either.[249]

As in León, Germany, and France, the solemn diploma reveals something of the aims and pretensions of Norman kingship. In 1069 William—'victorious *basileus* of the English'—confirmed Bishop Leofric of Exeter in his grant of manses to the canons of St Peter. The original parchment has all the pomposity of an Anglo-Saxon (or an early Norman ducal) diploma, replete with capitals; the personal subscriptions of king, queen (Matilda), and magnates; and a description of bounds in Old English. Yet nothing is said of a petition, unless by implication in reference to the bishop as 'my [William's] *fidelis*.' Nor is this record, such as it is, typical of the Conqueror's diplomatic of concession, which was not only variable and unformulaic but also contaminated with Anglo-Saxon procedure. Wishing from his precarious start to be accepted in the localities, King William permitted his commands and judgments to be conveyed in the tersely fluid form of writs,

---

[249] Douglas, *William the Conqueror*; James Campbell, *The Anglo-Saxon state*, ch. 1.

in Old English as well as Latin (sometimes both); so that among some 160 authentic enactments (*acta*) surviving from the Conqueror, only eighteen are diplomas. Whatever their verbiage may conceal, these point to no particular routine of public petition, hearing, and gracious response. It is rather the old English tradition of written command that flourished under the Norman kings, their writs often attested like charters and typically devoid of formulaic solemnity; the records of decision or judgment variably consented or attested.[250]

William's was a ritually public kingship from the start, based on his claim of dynastic right to succeed Edward the Confessor, loudly declaimed as such, yet insistent on acceptance. The questions put by the presiding prelates to the English and Normans assembled for the crowning at Westminster in 1066 seem to have been new to the rites of English coronation,[251] as was, in a similarly cajoling way, the coronation charter of Henry I (1100), which was virtually renewed at Stephen's accession (1135). The festival crown-wearings of William I and William Rufus were equally characteristic manifestations of public authority, not least in their expression of lordship and royal office combined.[252]

The early Norman kings needed to be visible, and widely obeyed, for a reason without parallel in the other realms here examined. In England the traditional communities of obligation with respect to security and justice remained functional; and since the Conqueror cannot have wished for his knights to impose local lordships heedless of customary proprietors, he lost no time addressing the men of shires. His surviving writs from early in the reign tell not so much of acts in writing as of notifications of (? unwritten) decisions, typically confirmations of ecclesiastical jurisdiction. At first in Old English, then multiplying in Latin verbiage, these writs surely passed for proofs of local right by the

---

[250] *RRAN* I, pp. xi–xii, and calendar; *Acta of William I*, Introduction, no. 138.

[251] WP ii.30 (150); *ASC*, D (1066); Nelson, 'Rites of the Conqueror.'

[252] Green, *Government of England under Henry I*, 20–21.

churches—for example, Saints Peter of Bath and Edmund of Bury around 1067[253]—that preserved them. The hundreds come into our view in the Domesday surveys after 1085 when their witness to tenure and right became needful for social stability; and much evidence thereafter proves that hundreds were liable for the safety of French-speaking men, while being mobilised by sheriffs, even by the king, for varied purposes.[254]

Norman England was a cluster of public institutions and offices lubricated, so to speak, by the king's writ. People were conscious of this customary order, having plausible expectations of justice, exchanging (and amassing) coined money as a guaranteed social utility. They were alive to the spectacle of archbishops in perennial discord over (official) primacy in a Christian church reconceived in Lanfranc's day as including Wales and Scotland.[255] Whatever its incoherence, the anonymous tract known as the 'Laws of Henry I' proves that law and custom were invoked in courts popular, royal, and seigneurial very diversely expressive of Old English practise and Norman innovation.[256]

Yet this public and official order was pervaded by lordship from top to bottom. It is not easy to see how much of this came with the Normans, and impossible to believe that the Conqueror meant to transform the exercise of kingship he claimed to inherit. What is clear is that he acted as lord-king from the start, creating dependents in fidelity, and famously seeking to confirm the vassalage of his magnates and their dependents by imposing homage as well as sworn fidelity in a Lammas-tide assembly at Salisbury in 1086. Although hardly a proof, this event was symptomatic of a massive feudalizing of England by the Normans. Domesday Book, which resulted from surveys ordered in the same year, described England

[253] *Acta of William I*, nos. 11, 34.

[254] *English lawsuits from William I to Richard I*, ed. R. C. Van Caenegem, 2 vols. (London 1990) I, nos. 21–131; *RRAN* II, no. 687; Green, *Government*, 111–12.

[255] Margaret T. Gibson, *Lanfranc of Bec* (Oxford 1978) 121 and ch. 6.

[256] *Leges Henrici primi*, ed. and tr. L. J. Downer (Oxford 1972). On this text see Wormald, *The making of English law* 411–14, 465–76.

as a collection of tenures, including the lord-king's, in boroughs and shires; and while many of these tenures were not strictly fiefs, practically all were holdings in affective dependence on the lord-king and on other great lords.[257]

Lordship, far more than fiefs in this newly feudalized England, was what mattered to the experience of power. And it mattered more than the facades of traditional communal action. Two illustrations may serve. Soon after the Conquest King William conferred the shire of Kent on his half-brother Bishop Odo of Bayeux. This was a prudent concession of (public) defensive authority at a time when the Conqueror had to entrust power in borderlands endangered by his absence to his faithful magnates; arguably wiser than reviving clustered shires such as Earl Godwin and his sons had held in the Confessor's day. That Bishop-Earl Odo exercised official powers is not in doubt: he presided over pleas and mobilised shire courts; he was an admired magnate in the king's circle; and he was later remembered as a prince of overweening power, 'like a second king in England.[258] And what is clear from all sources is that his 'power' (*magna potentia*) was that of a lord grasping for dependents and for the means to reward them. No sooner had Lanfranc arrived in England to assume the see of Canterbury than he discovered how Earl Odo and his men had been encroaching on his church's lands. No doubt, there had been negligence in Archbishop Stigand's uneasy pontificate, but it became clear in the conspicuous trial at Penenden Heath in 1072 that Odo had created tenures for his knights in ecclesiastical lands. No one claimed that Odo had exceeded official powers (as such), only that in his pursuit of lordship he had violated rights and that, as was adjudged against him, he must make restitution.[259]

---

[257] *Peterborough chronicle,* 9; F. M. Stenton, *First century of English feudalism . . . ,* 2d ed. ch. 1; F. W. Maitland, *Domesday Book and beyond. Three essays in the early history of England,* new ed. (Cambridge, 1987 [1897]), Essay I.

[258] OV iv (II, 196, 264).

[259] *English lawsuits* I, no. 5, where the texts are assembled. See also Alan Cooper, 'Extraordinary privilege: the trial of Penenden Heath and the Domesday Inquest,' *EHR* CXVI (2001) 1167–92.

Not all, perhaps not even most, of the Conqueror's companions-in-arms created new lordships by force. It is too bad that the un-disputed baronies left no records, for in their sociability we might come closest to an altered experience of power in Norman England. In this respect Domesday Book is of little help, for in its incomparably lavish description of patrimonies—its allusions to *dominium*, soke, commendation, manors, and tenures—it clings tenaciously to a normative representation of lordship in which slaves, villeins, knights, and greater masters have obligations and rights but little to say to one another. Here the old lordships of personal property (*dominium*) are jumbled inextricably with the newer ones of service; and we can only imagine that the free man of Suffolk commended to Robert Wimarc's son saw more of the latter than of the abbot of Bury, who had him in soke.[260]

A second illustration, or class of examples, will enlarge our sense of how the lordship of personal domination bore on the experience of power in Norman England. On an uncertain date King William Rufus (1087–1100) granted the hundred of Nor-mancros in fee-farm to the abbot and monks of Thorney, payable to the sheriff of Huntingdon.[261] In 1101 Henry I wished 'all my barons and earls to know' that he has confirmed St Martin of Battle in possession of its court.[262] In June 1107 King Henry writes from Cirencester to the bishop and chapter of Bayeux that Godfrey the priest has proven his claim to the church of Saint-Sauveur in the market of Caen 'in my court before my bishops and my clergy.'[263] In 1113 or the next year the king conferred the shrievalty of Worcestershire on Walter de Beauchamp as if it were a fief, enjoining faithful obedience to the bishop and barons of the county.[264] And in 1127 King Henry directed all

---

[260] Maitland, *DBB* 104.

[261] *RRAN* I, Appendix lxxxi (no. 453; =*EHD* II², no. 41).

[262] *RRAN* II, no. 530. [263] ibid., no. 819.

[264] ibid., no. 1034. Cf. William A. Morris, *The medieval English sheriff to 1300* (Manchester 1927) 46: 'The sheriff was appointed for no specified term, and the tendency of the age was to treat offices like fiefs.'

barons holding lands in the hundreds of the bishop of Ely to at-tend pleas of the bishop's hundred-court upon summons of the bishop's sergeant, as in the past.[265] The point of such examples is not to argue that hundreds and shrievalties were other than of-fices. There is evidence to suggest that Henry I managed his sher-iffs and shires so as to preserve royal and communal rights alike.[266] But it looks as if Old English governance, such as it survived, was newly harnessed to lordship after 1066. The confrontation at Penenden Heath was over patrimonial right, not office; the judg-ment in favour of Archbishop Lanfranc limited only by the king's rights of public thoroughfare. And when an anonymous jurist la-boured around 1115 to set down the 'laws' of the realm he saw no need to distinguish the powers of lords and officers (as such), merely listing the venues of their powers: shires, hundreds, *socs*, tithings, and (running out of substantives) the sureties of lords. In another place he implies that men bound to lords need not be in the tithings viewed in hundred courts.[267] The whole discussion of jurisdiction is such as to confirm the normality of lords' courts or boundary settlements of peers alongside the hundreds and shires, to the point of suggesting a historical distinction between hall-moots and lords' courts; cases may be heard, and appropriate cus-toms applied, in any of these courts.

So it would be well not to overrate the tension between official and proprietary power in Norman England. No one thought it anomalous that public order remained the lord-king's to uphold, even as all could see the Conqueror rewarding his warrior-friends with great patrimonial tenures burdened with new customs and services. Nothing like this imposed feudal (public) order had yet happened in continental Europe, although the liabilities of a baronial society for mutual exploitation across the Channel dif-fered only in scale. But the public enterprises of the Conqueror

---

[265] *RRAN* II, no. 1503; see also no. 1865.

[266] See Morris, *Sheriff*, chs. 3, 4; and Judith A. Green, *English sheriffs to 1154* (London 1990).

[267] *Leges Henrici primi*, esp. cc. 6–8, 11, 32, 51–53, 57.

and his sons required a collective understanding that arose from common dangers and temptations of excessive demand and was sustained by alliance with the church.

All this is lighted up by the unprecedented charter of liberties in which, following his hurried coronation on 5 August 1100, Henry I sought to placate a restive people. Addressed in multiple copies to the shires, it is in no other sense popular, although the limits it places on fiscal demands were bound to please the tenants of the lords and king's 'faithful' who paid. It promised (1) a 'free church'; (2) the abolition of 'bad customs by which the kingdom of England was unjustly oppressed'; (3) the institution of 'just and legitimate reliefs' payable for successions to conditional tenures; and it went on to make concessions relating to dowry, coinage, the (king's) forests, justice, and law.[268]

This famous profession of intent is on its face a repudiation of Norman lordship. One may object that its purpose was explicitly to dissociate the new king from the excesses of his rapacious late brother; but that was not its whole purport. The renunciation of *monetagium commune*, which was 'unknown in the time of King Edward,' was meant to undo an imposition of the Conqueror. The 'law of King Edward,' as emended by William I, was to be restored. And when Henry's coronation charter is read together with retrospective narratives, the common experience of power under the early Norman kings comes into clear and unflattering perspective.

Violence was normal in that experience: the violences of conflict, dispossession, and coercive lordship. Orderic Vitalis, writing towards 1115, put it memorably:

> Meanwhile, the English are oppressed under the Norman yoke and were afflicted by the proud lords who were ignoring the king's injunctions. The petty lords who were guarding the castles were troubling native inhabitants of high and lesser status. For Bishop Odo and William fitzOsbern, the king's vicars, were so

---

[268] *Gesetze der Angelsachsen* I, 52 (also in *SC* 117–19; tr. in *EHD* II², no. 19).

swollen with presumption that they would not deign reasonably to hear the pleas of the English and to favour them with impartiality. For they forcibly protected their armed men who indulged in excessive plunder and ugly rape, and inflicted their anger violently on those who complained of the cruel wrongs they suffered. And so the English, having lost their liberty, groaned vehemently and plotted repeatedly how to shake off so intolerable and unaccustomed a yoke.[269]

Every particular of this description can be verified. It is known or recorded of the Conqueror that he imposed a disciplined peace on England, forbidding rapine from the outset, restraining his knights, appointing judges to uphold order even against his knights, and prohibiting theft, violation of property, and other offences.[270] There were, indeed, injunctions to disobey. At his death King William was eulogized for his probity and for 'the good order he kept in his land.[271]

But the character-portrait of the Conqueror is famously mixed.[272] The problem to which this points is not so much that he was prone to violent anger when crossed, as notoriously in his punitive expedition through Yorkshire. The problem is that he was humanly incapable of enforcing his will in a defeated society coming under the domination of several thousand French-speaking knights and barons. As Orderic points out in another place, castles were a novelty in England.[273] The frenetic building of new ones, as at Lincoln and Oxford, and commandeering of the old urban forts, was a prudential measure that subverted the peace of the conquest from the start, because it confirmed the predatory

[269] OV iv (II, 202).
[270] WP ii.2 (102); 34 (158–60); OV iv (II, 192); *Gesetze* I, 486 (*EHD* II², no. 18).
[271] *ASC*, E (1087).
[272] ibid.; see also OV vii.15 (IV, 80–94); *De obitu Willelmi*, ed. and tr. Elisabeth M. C. Van Houts, *The* Gesta Normannorum ducum *of William of Jumièges, Orderic Vitalis, and Robert of Torigni*, 2 vols. (Oxford 1992–95) II, 184–90.
[273] OV iv (II, 218).

instincts of castellans and knights lacking patrimonial resources while antagonizing local peasantries compelled to work on and pay for the fortifying. Orderic's assertion that 'petty lords' in the castles 'were troubling' the natives is borne out in countless records. Penurious armed men in quest of lordships imposed new customs and seized hides and vills where they could. The monks of Ramsey remembered that they had lost donated lands 'by injustice or violence of strong men' after the Conquest.[274] At Abingdon as well as at Ramsey we can see the Conqueror imposing knights on the monastic patrimony with abrasive results.[275] No doubt some effort was made to encourage the peaceable transfer of lands from the defeated or dead to Norman knights; but in the two years following the battle of Hastings unrest brought on insurrection, the lord-king's angry reaction, and a new and stabler phase of sullen acceptance of the Norman regime. It is after 1068 or so that the king's retainers, notably Odo of Bayeux, and the sheriffs become visible. At York a sheriff plundered the archbishop's provisions, only to provoke an indignant and courageous appeal to the king, who put things right.[276] But if, as seems likely, native lords and thegns were depositing valuables in religious houses for safekeeping, it cannot surprise that King William ordered the monasteries to be searched and treasure seized. That this was a violently disruptive enterprise is shown not only by the Old English chronicler's unminced allusion to the king's 'plundering of all the monasteries in England' but also by the account of the impious and violent seizures at Abingdon by the sheriff Froger.[277] The Norman baron Picot, who was sheriff in Cambridgeshire, was notorious for his seizures and oppressions in Ely's lands; and his rapacious underling

---

[274] *Liber benefactorum ecclesiae Rameseiensis*, ed. W. Dunn Macray, *Chronicon abbatiae Rameseiensis* . . . (London 1886) c. 79 (144).

[275] ibid., cc. 80, 89, 90, 105–7 (146, 152–54, 171–76); *Historia ecclesie Abbendonensis* . . . , ed. John Hudson, 2 vols. (Oxford 2002–07) ii.1–8 (II, 2–14).

[276] *English lawsuits* I, no. 1 (1066–69).

[277] *ASC*, DE (1070); JW III, 10 (1070); *Hist. Abbendon.* i.144 (I, 224–28).

Gervase, according to the monks, incurred a just punishment from Saint Aethelthryth herself.[278] Reflecting back on this time, in what seem to be his own words, Henry of Huntingdon put it generally and strongly: 'Sheriffs and reeves, whose office was justice and judgment, were more terrible than thieves and plunderers, and more savage than the most savage.'[279] As for Earl Odo, his encroachments in Kent are more likely to have been characteristic than the competence claimed for him by William of Poitiers; he was later accused by his brother the king himself of oppressing churches and fomenting disloyalty, and was imprisoned.[280]

Orderic was not the only contemporary to opine that the Normans had deprived the English of their liberty, had enslaved them. So it also appeared to Frutolf, writing in a land where the Saxons bemoaned the same fate; and so too to Henry of Huntingdon: 'For God had chosen the Normans to wipe out the English people, because He had seen how they surpassed all other peoples in their exemplary savagery.'[281] It is easy—and, indeed, fashionable—to associate these exaggerations with the allusions to violence that bear out Orderic's commentary quoted above. David Knowles insisted that, for all their lamentation in the twelfth century, the English monasteries suffered few losses that were not compensated in time. His point finds support in Domesday Book, and would be even stronger if we could be sure that the allegations of violation here sampled were untypical.[282] But if we try to imagine the history of vulnerable monks and their tenants in the combustible circumstances recorded in all the chronicles, and set aside anachronistic and inhumane assessments

---

[278] *Liber Eliensis*, ed. E. O. Blake (London 1962) ii.131–32 (210–13).

[279] HH vi.38 (402).

[280] WP ii.37 (166); OV iv (II, 266); vii.8 (IV, 40–44).

[281] *Frutolfi chronica* 78 (x); HH vi.38 (402). See also OV iv (II, 206).

[282] David Knowles, *The monastic order in England* . . . (Cambridge 1950) 116–19.

of long-term corporate health, quite a different scene comes into view. Enslavement was a metaphor for radical dependency in the later eleventh century; that is, for the popular experience of lordship. People were dragooned to build those castles at Huntingdon and Lincoln, their houses destroyed; they were taxed and distrained to heavy labour.[283] What the chronicles attest must surely be read as a sampling of the typical experience of power, not the extent of a newly abrasive lordship introduced by the Normans.

By the time of William Rufus the new customs were in place. The violence of the Domesday Inquest must have seemed a more tolerable imposition than the Conqueror's retaliations and taxes, yet it figures in our sources as an incomparable intrusion on human decency.[284] Forced service, incessant taxation, and the normal violence of castles persisted under Rufus. Orderic remembered how he had failed to protect peasants against knights whose retainers were permitted to ravage working tenures at will.[285] This king's most conspicuously arbitrary practise was to detain the patrimonies of vacant churches. Little of Rufus's wilful domination was new with him, perhaps only his failure to secure the clerical loyalty that rescued his father's reputation.[286] The New Forest, where Rufus was killed while hunting, was yet another imposition of the Conqueror, harshly burdensome on the poor nearby, and a (bad) custom Henry I explicitly reserved.[287]

---

[283] DB fols. 205, 336c.

[284] ASC, E (1085); other sources are cited in conveniently assembled translations in EHD II², nos. 198, 202, 215, 217.

[285] OV viii.8 (IV, 178).

[286] See generally De iniusta vexacione Willelmi episcopi primi per Willelmum regem filium Willelmi magni regis, ed. H. S. Offler et al., Chronology, conquest and conflict in medieval England (Cambridge 1997) 73–100; and Frank Barlow, William Rufus (London 1983) 175–213.

[287] Charter of 1100, c. 10; and Douglas, William the Conqueror 371–73.

IF HENRY had been a governor in his day, we would surely have the evidence of it in ours. What mattered to him, what he perfected once free of the encumbrances of his late father and brother, was an exercise of personal power that must have been the envy of lord-princes everywhere. It depended first on disciplining, or even disinheriting, those who had been unfaithful; second, on cultivating loyalties in those with whom he was content to share the proceeds of his lordship—here, for practical purposes, there was an inner, curial circle of trusted aides, and an outer circle of tenants-in-chief—; and only thirdly on the management of shires and hundreds.[288] This was a formula for early success: the brutal destruction of his elder brother's claim to Normandy, and the jolting arrest of Robert of Bellême; but it tended, and tends to this day, to obscure two liabilities of the situation: (1) mounting tension between the old associative structures of security and justice and the patrimonial interests of the Norman elite; and (2) the unshakable interest of the Anglo-Norman baronage in the dynastic future of the royal lordship on which their status depended.

The first of these problems must have become evident in Henry's early regnal years. The coinage was deteriorating as inexpert Normans succeeded Anglo-Saxon moneyers in the mints. Sheriffs were helping themselves to the proceeds, and no doubt the routines, of the shire courts and hundreds. The royal entourage persisted in virtually plundering the districts through which the lord-king passed, a disgrace that underscored the incompatibility of local order and self-indulgent lordship. King Henry's response to these problems, in remedial measures dating probably to 1108–10,[289] is

---

[288] Some sense of these priorities may be discerned in OV xi (VI, 8–183), and is not contradicted by William of Malmesbury, *Gesta Regum* v.393–449 (I, 715–801). See also C. W. Hollister, *Henry I*, ed. Amanda Clark Frost (New Haven 2001) chs. 3–5.

[289] *Eadmeri historia novorum in Anglia*, ed. Martin Rule (London 1884) 192–93 (iv); SC 122. Also W. L. Warren, *The governance of Norman and Angevin England*

an early landmark in the recognition of a structural failing of lord-rulership becoming visible in many parts of Europe. The baronial interest in dynastic right, given the lord-king's insistence on binding patronage to fidelity, was a problem without remedy. Henry I was at the crest of his power in 1120, when he suffered the cruel loss of his heir in the wreck of the White Ship. His mastery thereafter was matched by his desperation.

1086–1272 (Stanford 1987) 72; and Judith A. Green, *Henry I. King of England and duke of Normandy* (Cambridge 2006) ch. 5 (the reform went further than I have yet indicated).

·IV·

Crises of Power (1060–1150)

THE HISTORY of power in early twelfth-century Europe, read chronologically from the left, has a ragged right margin. It is made up of regional histories whose internal dynamics imply terminal dates scattered from 1105 to 1150. These are dynastic histories, in some cases the new beginnings of national histories, with *raisons d'être* of their own. But the seamless European history violated by such analysis must now be confronted so as to grasp the common pretensions, limitations, and liabilities of lord-rulership on the eve of crises that would transform it.

There was nothing concerted about the crises of the (long) twelfth century. They were the local experience of diverse societies coming into touch in this age of quickening communications, pilgrimage, and crusade, yet whose troubles, when recorded at all, betray the unpoliticised parochialism of futile outrage. Even so, it can hardly be anachronistic to imagine what European travellers surely saw as they left their homelands, such as the author of the *Pilgrims' guide* who contrasted the bellicose vigour of the Poitevins with permissive insecurities in Basque lands;[1] or to suggest that civic violence, as at Milan or Laon, was hardly less notorious for being local than the regional phenomena of bad lordship in the Ile-de-France or the sprouting of illicit castles in Stephen's England. What was familiar to European societies everywhere was a new, and newly intense, experience of lordship and dependence; a transformative expe-

---

[1] *Le Guide du pèlerin de Saint-Jacques de Compostelle*, ed. Jeanne Vielliard, 5th ed. (Paris 1984) c. 7 (16–32).

rience that imposed new obligations on the great families that claimed to rule them.

Uneasy Maturity

So it cannot be surprising to find that commemorations of princely powers composed (mostly) after 1060 sound common themes. Epic successes were their staple, as in the Williams' (of Poitiers and Jumièges) narrations of the Norman Conquest or Fulk Richin's record of his dynastic ancestry. Such texts, with some others to be mentioned, will remind us that troubles in the twelfth century were not so much the failing of princely powers as their affliction. Lord-kings were no luckier than dukes and counts in this respect. Moreover, their liability may help to account for a characteristic unsureness in the normative expression of princely law. On a European view of the incipient twelfth century, it looks as if proud reach was precarious and attended by anxiety.

DYNASTIC ANXIETY

When a self-effacing clerk set about writing the deeds of the princes of the Poles around 1113, he commented on a plurality of rulers whose deeds, although worthy of commemoration, had been 'consigned to silence.' Conscious of 'the spacious universe of the world's lands,' he would try, for Poland at least, to do better.[2] If, to take his word for it, he did not know of commemorative or genealogical texts from his western homelands, he must surely have had some idea of what was being said in princely courts. For on no fewer than three substantial points, his account of the early Polish princes resembles the uniquely personal story of his ancestor-counts composed by Fulk Richin of Anjou in 1096. First, both texts tell of epic heroism a century before, that of

---

[2] *GpP* i (10).

Boleslaw I 'Chrobry' in Poland (992–1025) and that of Fulk Nerra in Anjou (987–1040). Second, in both histories conquests of pagan peoples by Christian princes are represented as foundations of legitimate power, earlier in Anjou than in Poland. Third and most significantly, both writers inform us not only about dynastic succession—they are, in this sense, amplified genealogies—but also about disputed successions, including those attended by violence.[3]

Before returning to this final point, it will be useful to notice related evidence of dynastic commemoration, for it happens that of extant comparable texts relating to dynastic succession composed before 1160, most exhibit the same three characteristics just mentioned. Two further items may be mentioned here: the genealogies of Flanders compiled in religious houses of Saint-Omer in the early twelfth century, and the *Deeds of the counts of Barcelona* (*GcB*), begun about 1152 and (first) completed a decade later.[4] Of these four texts, those from Anjou and Flanders require no further commentary, apart from the point postponed above; for while they are informative about lord-rulership, they add little to what has already been said about their regions. But most of what we know about Poland before 1110 comes from the anonymous *Deeds of the Polish princes* (*GpP*); while in the case of Barcelona the paucity of narrative sources renders the *Deeds of the counts* a precious supplement to archival records that have little to say about dynastic purposes.

These two histories (in both senses) are curiously analogous. During the generations after 1060 the principalities of Poland and Barcelona were both situated in proximity to powerful neighbours with whom they vied for advantage in hostilities against

---

[3] *GpP; Fragmentum historiae Andegavensis*, ed. Louis Halphen, René Poupardin, *Chroniques des comtes d'Anjou et des seigneurs d'Amboise* (Paris 1913) 232–38. See generally T. N. Bisson, 'Princely nobility in an age of ambition (c. 1050–1150),' *Nobles and nobility in medieval Europe . . .*, ed. Anne J. Duggan (Woodbridge 2000) 101–13.

[4] *Genealogiae comitum Flandriae*, ed. L. C. Bethmann, *MGHSS* ix (Hanover 1851) 305–22; *GcB*.

infidel peoples. In both lands the control of knights bent on plunder and patrimonial wealth was critical to the success of lord-princes who were viewed as paragons of nobility. A curious proof of this may be read inversely in the *gesta* of such a knight, the most notoriously successful one, to be sure. In the Muslim hinterlands from Zaragoza to Valencia one Rodrigo Díaz, the Cid (d. 1099), achieved a princely lordship for himself (and married his daughter to Ramon Berenguer III, no less) by selling his services against (normally) the Almoravids to King Alfonso VI and to other princes Christian and Muslim.[5]

In Pyrenean Spain Count Ramon Berenguer III (1096–1131) distinguished himself by renewing anti-Muslim campaigns, notably against Majorca in 1114–15, and reclaiming Tarragona for Christian domination. Moreover, he adroitly secured his own succession to the counties of Besalú and Cerdanya, thereby visibly recreating the principality that had disappeared through fragmentation in the tenth century. These and other such exploits foreshadowed what seemed to an awed monk of Ripoll the yet greater successes of his son, Count Ramon Berenguer IV (1131–62). What is clear, from the *GcB* and many other records, is that princely lordship in the expanded county of Barcelona was an unstable structure of militant alliances with barons and knights who continued to share in the profits of old comital patrimonies and new aggressions.[6]

Much the same may be said of Poland under Boleslaw III ("Wrymouth" 1102–38), of whom we know far less. In the words of his eulogist, he was the miraculously conceived restorer of Poland 'to its pristine state.' A model noble amongst lord-princes, he renewed the aggressive campaigns against Prussians, Pomeranians,

---

[5] *Historia Roderici*, ed. Emma Falque Rey *et al.*, *Chronica hispana saeculi* XII (Turnhout 1990) 47–98. On the problematic dating (before 1125?), see Richard Fletcher, *The world of El Cid. Chronicles of the Spanish reconquest*, ed. Simon Barton, Richard Fletcher (Manchester 2000) 90–98.

[6] *GcB*, first redaction, cc. 4, 5 (6–9). See also charters and conventions of Ramon Berenguer III in *LFM*, as indexed in II, 395–406; and *FAC*, I, ch. 2.

and Bohemians, while defending against Germany. In rivalry for power with his elder brother Zbigniew, Boleslaw resorted to brutality in the end, which may help to explain why the *GpP* breaks off in 1113, when the duke had another twenty-five years to reign.

❈

WHICH BRINGS us back to the darker side of commemorative writing. Virtually all such texts point to the inherent instability of dynastic power. They do so by their very existence. For all their enthusiasm for the epic exploits of princely patrons, they typically gloss over very bad patches without quite concealing them. Every great family, and its provincial tenants no less, dreaded the misfortune of an uncertain or a disputed succession. Who could not envy the good luck of the Capetian kings, who left sons groomed to succeed them in every generation through the thirteenth century?[7] The accident of fortune helps to create an illusion of progressive as well as continuous royal power in France.

For it was otherwise in most principalities. In Anjou Count Fulk Richin recalled how, at his father's death without an heir, he (Fulk) together with his elder brother Geoffrey the Bearded succeeded to the *honor*, and how after years of violence Fulk defeated and imprisoned his brother. And while he failed to make clear that his rival had been designated successor to the comital title, his account accords with other evidence that their late uncle had so favoured his younger nephew as effectually to invite Fulk to seize the inheritance for himself.[8]

The temptation of a covetous brother worked differently in Flanders, where in 1070 Robert I 'the Frisian' usurped comital power from his young nephew Arnulf III, who was then killed in

---

[7] Was Bertrade de Montfort among the envious, towards 1101? See below, p. 190.

[8] *Fragmentum* 237; Guillot, *Comte d'Anjou*, I, 102–11.

the battle of Cassel (1071) in a vain attempt to recover his inheritance. The memory of this event was understandably problematic
in the Flemish genealogies, for Robert proved a forceful count
whose son and grandson succeeded him prior to a second diver-
sion from the main dynastic line in 1119.[9] What rankled in the
1070s, and could be recalled in detail half a century later, was the
treachery by which Robert I had seized power. He had sworn not
to harm his brother Baldwin VI (1067–70), sworn not only to
their father but to that very brother himself.[10]

In Poland the very survival of younger sons in the ducal family
provoked dissident interests in a turbulent aristocracy: first towards 1079, when Boleslaw II was driven out of his land; then
after 1100, when the younger son of Wladyslaw Hermann (d.
1102), thwarted by his elder half-brother Zbigniew, resorted to
the cruel punishment that has been mentioned.[11]

Perhaps the most evocative account of domestic strife over dynastic patrimony is to be found in the *Deeds of the counts of Barcelona*, recalling some sixty years later the succession to Count
Ramon Berenguer I (1035–76):

> Then Ramon Berenguer, the 'Little Old One,' begot Pere Ramon
> and Berenguer Ramon and Ramon Berenguer, count of Barce-
> lona. The two former were like a brood of vipers which, disem-
> bowelled, naturally kill their mothers: for the former, that is Pere
> Ramon, murdered his stepmother Almodis, so that he died a
> penitent in Spain without a son; and the second, that is Berenguer
> Ramon, treacherously killed his brother Ramon Berenguer in the
> place called Perxa. . . .

Here again the fratricide prevailed. Berenguer Ramon II
(1082–96) reigned under a cloud on the understanding that his

[9] *Genealogiae comitum Flandriae* 306, 307, 308, 310, 320–21; Lampert of Hersfeld, *Annales* 120–23.

[10] Galbert of Bruges, *De multro Karoli* c. 69; *Herimanni liber de restauratione
monasterii Sancti Martini Tornacensis* cc. 12, 13 (279–80).

[11] *GpP* i.27, iii.

nephew would succeed him, and he, too, died sonless, as the *GcB* tell us: a penitent pilgrim to Jerusalem.[12]

If practically all extant princely genealogies witness to disputed or violent successions, it is manifestly because dynastic power was, most essentially, patrimonial lordship. The customs of succession to such lordship remained in doubt. And the extent to which this circumstance contributed to prevailing anxiety and to crises can hardly be exaggerated. Taking the period 1060 to 1140 and drawing on sources of all kinds, the European scene may be (incompletely) outlined as follows:

1060–68. Anjou. Succession of two nephews to Count Geoffrey Martel, one of whom prevails by violence (*Fragmentum* 237).[13]

1062–89. Maine. Disputed succession to Count Herbert II, heirless. Norman conquest (1063); Robert entitled count, driven out, restored, and (1089) again expelled (OV, as cited below, note 16).

1067–70. Carcassonne. Disputed succession to Count Roger, deceased without heirs, resulting in a 'sale' of rights to Count Ramon Berenguer I and Countess Almodis of Barcelona, probably to renew its dynastic claim to the county (Cheyette, *Speculum* LXIII [1988], 826–64).

1070. Flanders. Usurpation of comital power by Robert I, whose dispossessed nephew is killed in 1071 (*Genealogiae, MGHSS* IX, 306–21; Heriman, *Liber. SS*, XIV 279–80).

1071. Barcelona. Murder of Countess Almodis by stepson Pere Ramon (*GcB* c. 4 [7]).

1076. Navarre. Treacherous murder of King Sancho IV in a conspiracy of his brothers with others, resulting in seizure of realm by Sancho Ramirez of Aragon (Larrea, *Navarre* 355–60).

1079. Poland. Killing of Bishop Stanislaw and deposition of Boleslaw II (*GpP* ii.27–29)

---

[12] *GcB* c. 4 (7).
[13] Only principal or convenient sources will be cited for this purpose.

1082. Barcelona. Count Ramon Berenguer II is murdered by brother Berenguer Ramon II, to be succeeded by his nephew Ramon Berenguer III (*GcB* c. 4 [7]).

1087. Normandy and England. Uneasy succession to Duke-King William of Robert (eldest) to Normandy, William Rufus to England; Henry otherwise endowed (OV viii [IV, 110–50]).

1090. Maine. Revolt of magnates, who eject castellans and set up a 'new prince' Hugh of Arezzo (OV viii.11 [IV, 192]).

1093–1106. Germany. Revolts of Conrad and Henry against their father Henry IV (Weinfurter, *Salian century* 160).

1097–1112. Poland. Rivalry between Boleslaw III and his elder illegitimate brother Zbigniew, preceding and outlasting their father's (Wladislaw Hermann's) death in 1102, and ending with the capture and blinding of Zbigniew (*GpP* ii.4,7,8,16–24,32,35, 36–41,50; iii).

1100–1106. England and Normandy. Killing of William Rufus, succession of Henry I to exclusion of Robert, followed by conflict and deposition of Robert (OV x.14–16 [v, 282–300]).

1109–20. León-Galicia. Succession of daughter Urraca to Alfonso VI of León, provoking unrest complicated by her problematic remarriage to Alfonso the Battler of Aragon (*HC* i.47–48 [85–87]).

1115. Tuscany. Death of Countess Matilda without heirs, provoking enduring anxiety over succession to patrimonial lands ('Notae,' *MGHSS* xxx² 975).

1120–27. England and Normandy. Death of William in 'Wreck of White Ship' deprives his father Henry I of his only legitimate male heir. Leads to king's decision to prefer daughter (Empress) Matilda to nephew William Clito (1126) and to imposition of oaths of fidelity to Matilda (1127) (OV xii.26 [VI, 294–306]; *Peterborough chronicle* 48 [*an.* 1127]).

1125. Germany. Death of Henry V without heir. Princes 'elect' Lothar of Saxony, provoking resistance of his nephew (grandson of Henry IV) Frederick of Swabia (Otto of Freising, *Gesta Friderici* i.16–18).

1127. Flanders. Murder of Count Charles the Good, followed by crisis and conflict over the succession (Galbert of Bruges, *De multro . . . Karoli*).

1135. England. On death of Henry I his nephew Stephen seizes power in defiance of oaths to Matilda (*GS* cc.1–3; etc.).

1138. Germany. Death of Lothar without male heir. Princes 'elect' Conrad of Swabia, rejecting the plausible claim of Lothar's grandson Henry the Proud of Bavaria (Otto of Freising, *Gesta Friderici* i.23).

Shall we say that this compendium of dynastic anxieties is half full of trouble,—or half empty? Practically every princely house in Europe had its succession crisis in the century after 1060. Practically every region sampled in previous chapters figures in the list. Everywhere power-worthiness flowed in the blood of the legitimate offspring of lord-princes, rendering insufferable the spectacle of designated or arguably unworthy or undivided successions. In view of such continental evidence, it cannot surprise that hereditary right, to say nothing of primogeniture, was slow to develop in the Anglo-Norman elite.[14] The northern princely class was, moreover, a society of cultural familiarity. Was not the mother of the Conqueror's children the sister of the wronged Baldwin VI of Flanders? This was surely the talk in noble courts of the later eleventh century, and spectacles for cowering masses of people everywhere. Prince Louis of France, while in the entourage of King Henry I in 1100–1101, became the endangered object of intrigue by his stepmother Bertrade de Montfort, who had sons of her own to favour.[15] And the Empress Matilda knew of, and escaped, German dynastic problems when she returned to England to face up to her own.

How these dynastic anxieties were implicated in regional troubles will be examined in its turn. What is already clear is that the

---

[14] Holt, 'Politics and property in early medieval England.'

[15] OV xi.9 (VI, 50–52). Like Luchaire and Prou before us, I cannot share Marjorie Chibnall's suspicion that this story 'reads like epic invention.'

security of youthful lord-princes depended on the good will of their baronial allies and on their ability to reward them. Failing these tests, as in Navarre around 1075 and in Poland and Germany at times thereafter, dynastic anxiety might give way to rebellion. Yet for all the attributes of affective domination, the circumstances of dynastic succession had invariably touched a nerve of public or societal interest that was exposed whenever a lord-prince died without issue. In the county of Maine some barons in concert with men of Le Mans claimed to serve this interest on the death of Herbert II; and this initiative had to be renewed in subsequent occasions, notably in 1098 when, in the absence of their imprisoned count, the barons of Maine deliberated on the state of their *res publica*.[16] The most conspicuous occasion of this sort was in Flanders following the murder of Charles the Good in 1127.[17] Doubtless, the claim to be acting in the public interest figured in all baronial deliberations in princely vacancies; talk to this effect was recorded notably of German magnates in the imperial elections of 1125 and 1138. But, just as in papal counsels of these years, it seems likely that familial and patrimonial interests prevailed in post mortem consultations here and everywhere else.[18]

ANXIOUS FULFILLMENTS

The conceptual survival of public interest in the age of lordship has meaning in another perspective of European scope. Not the least of deeds by kings, dukes, and counts to be commemorated were their attempts to define order and security in societies that

---

[16] OV iii (II, 116–18); iv (II, 306–8); vii.10 (IV, 46–48); viii.10–11 (IV, 182–98); x.8,10 (V, 228–32, 252–54).

[17] Galbert, *De multro*.

[18] Otto of Freising, *Gesta Friderici I. imperatoris*, ed. Georg Waitz, Bernhard von Simson, 3d ed. (Hanover 1912) i.17 (31); tr. C.C. Mierow, *Deeds* (NY 1966) 48. In 1125 Archbishop Adalbert prevailed on the princes to choose Lothar of Saxony 'plus familiaris rei, quantum in ipso erat, quam communi commodo consulens.'

had outgrown their inherited norms of rights and obligation. In words attributed to Count Ramon Berenguer I, the *Usatges* of Barcelona put it like this: because 'in . . . cases and business of this land the Gothic laws cannot be observed, and so . . . many complaints and pleas' go unsettled, he and his Countess Almodis had deemed it useful, with due counsel, to impose new usages to cover the new contingencies. That the *Usatges* were the normative expression of a radically transformed feudal society towards 1060 is incontrovertibly clear.[19] Do they stand alone of their kind? Not at all. And the analogues that come to light (without hard digging) not only confirm other evidence for the novelty and growth of other regimes of lordship and dependence but also underscore a characteristic limitation of their princely dominations.

No fewer than five juridical texts of the type here described are known from the years 1060 to 1150: namely, the *Usatges* themselves, of which the first version (ca. 1068) survives only vestigially in a text of ca. 1150; the *Consuetudines et iusticie* of Normandy (ca. 1091, but surely including pre-Conquest matter); the earliest of the so-called *Consuetudines feudorum* by anonymous Lombard jurists (early twelfth century); the *Fors* of Bigorre (ca. 1112); and the 'Laws of Henry I' (*Leges Henrici primi*, ca. 1116).[20] All these texts respond to the problem of new order superimposed on old. Arguably, this is least clear with the Norman *Consuetudines*, which survive as a memorial of ducal rights of justice, command, and security. Even if some of its articles refer to practises antedating 1066, which is likely, the composite impression it affords is that of a society in which baronial fidelities are thoroughly integrated with a public order under ducal control. As for the early Lombard treatises, they represent the com-

---

[19] *Usatges de Barcelona* 2 (Us. 3) 50; Bonnassie, *Catalogne* II, 711–33.

[20] *Usatges*, ed. Bastardas; *Consuetudines et iusticie*, ed. C. H. Haskins, *Norman institutions* (Cambridge, M., 1918) 277–84; *Consuetudines feudorum* I. *Compilatio antiqua*, ed. Karl Lehmann (Göttingen 1892) 8–38 (reprinted by Karl August Eckhardt [Aalen 1971] 32–62); *Fors de Bigorre*, ed. Xavier Ravier, Benoît Cursente, *Le cartulaire de Bigorre* (*XIᵉ–XIIIᵉ siècle*) (Paris 2005) no. 61; *Leges Henrici primi*.

paratively sophisticated expounding of a regime of fiefs already in place by 1100.

Quite a different scene unfolds in the *Fors* of Bigorre, which have the astonishing appearance of a settlement imposed on Count Bernard Centulle by Gregorian prelates steeped in Visigothic ideology. The interest of 'clergy and people' (for 'people' read *nobiles*) in comital successions is of foremost and explicit concern; and the text as a whole, in some forty-three articles, prescribes the count's control of castles and fidelities in such reserved terms as to liken his power to a delegacy of the people. Security is for him to maintain, by the 'law of the land,' who is called 'count,' but not lord-count. Here again public domination is conflated with order, but in terms quite the reverse of those in Normandy.[21] Little more need be said here about the *Leges Henrici*, which, like the other texts mentioned, is an anonymous work aimed at showing (in this case) how Old English and new Norman law worked together in the early twelfth century.

About all these records, two critical points must be understood. First, what they have in common purpose—their witness to the jurisprudence of power in transition—is all that unites them. They represent a common circumstance of change very diversely; so differently, indeed, as to remind us that the juridical cultures of Lombardy, Catalonia, and England, for all their novel obsession with the fief, were driven by the survival of three different laws. Moreover, it is hardly clear what there is to associate these few texts categorically. Why not include the 'Laws of William the Conqueror,' in which precepts of various date are brought together? Or, indeed, the statutes of councils, such as those of Lillebonne (1080) or Burgos (1117) or Cerdanya (1118); to say nothing of charters and statutes like the prohibition of seizures in León (1072) or that of judicial duel in favour of sworn procedure

---

[21] *Cart. de Bigorre*, no. 61. I accept in the main the interpretation of Paul Ourliac, 'Les fors de Bigorre' (1992) in (idem) *Les pays de Garonne vers l'an mil. La société et le droit* (Toulouse 1993) 219–35.

for the burghers of Ypres (1116).[22] All such enactments had normative force, engaged with societal problems in quasi-legislative
form.

Second, what distinguishes these juridical texts is that, in the
forms in which we have them, they purport to address whole
societies without pretending to legislative force. To see this
clearly, we need only consider the constitution of 1037 in which
the Emperor Conrad II regulated the disposition of fiefs in
Lombardy, siding with the lesser knights and vassals in the process.[23] Here is the exception that proves the rule. In Italy before
1050 people could still reasonably expect their emperor to legislate in accordance with social change; and if his regulation dismayed the old establishment, it gave recognition to the
feudalizing that was a reality when, two generations later, lawyers set about writing their commentaries. There was nothing
official about the early *Consuetudines feudorum*; nor were the
Norman *Consuetudines* of 1091 other than an *aide-mémoire* for
courtiers of William Rufus. As for the *Leges Henrici primi*, although it is an extended and learned treatise by no means out of
touch with documented realities, it too lacks the stamp of official status.

In different ways, the same is true of the *Usatges* and the *Fors*.
There is good reason to believe that the former were, indeed, first
promulgated towards 1068 by the counts of Barcelona with legislative force. But that text we do not have. The reason for this can
only be, as Pierre Bonnassie made clear, that the concessions to
feudal-vassalic order that it contained were no longer acceptable
to the courtiers of Ramon Berenguer IV who, about 1150, rewrote the *Usatges* in the spirit of a new ideology of sovereignty.
Even as they destroyed the original version, however, they saw fit
to pretend that the (revised) *Usatges* were the work of the great
count and countess who were remembered for restoring public

---

[22] *SC* 97–99; *LTC* I, no. 22; 'Concilio nacional de Burgos (18 febrero 1117),'
394–98; *LFM* II, no. 691; *CDL* IV, no. 1183; *ACF* no. 79.
[23] *DDC2* no. 244. See generally Tabacco, *Struggle for power* 208–14.

order a century before; and the *Usatges*, as we have them, bear many marks of the new society of lordship and dependence that had arisen in the county of Barcelona in those days. Otherwise, there is nothing in the surviving text to prove public promulgation, while the deceptive attribution to earlier princes, which seems to have taken in the monk of Ripoll who wrote the *Deeds of the Counts of Barcelona*,[24] suggests the contrary.

The case of the *Fors* of Bigorre is like none of the others. Here we have what purports to be a promulgated text in the name of Count Bernard III (d. ca. 1112). But the impulse is said to come from the prelates and 'greater nobles' of the land, 'with the common consent of all the clergy and people'; and there is no sign that either the count or his successors ever imposed the *Fors*, merely that they permitted it to be copied (at some point) together with other comital records.[25]

In short, these compilations of societal customs are unofficial records. They lacked the force of law possessed by the imperial constitution of 1037, although it seems likely that the original *usatges* of ca. 1068 had comparable purpose and impact in their day. But 'office' is surely the wrong test. As late as the times of Henry III and Louis IX there appeared law books without visible courtly sanction, and another century beyond them would pass before rulers publicly ordered the compilation of customs.[26] But lawmaking, if not yet the imposition of customs, revived in the later twelfth century. What mattered in the century before 1150 is that lordship and conditional tenures were being codified in nonlegislative customary forms that had little to do with princely powers, but much to do with wealth, possession, and differentiated status.

This was an impulse of princely power that cannot be made sense of in administrative terms. In each princely entourage, we know—feebly, it is true—of men in the shadows who served in

---

[24] *GcB* c. 4 (7); Bonnassie, *Catalogne* II, 718–28; and see also below, p. 290.

[25] *Cart. de Bigorre*, no. 61; also introduction, pp. xxii–iii.

[26] John Gilissen, *La coutume* (Turnhout 1982) 50–58.

fidelity without guidance from laws or formulas.[27] They were not yet jurists, save possibly in Countess Matilda's court; yet the issue of patronage, inheritance, and privilege surely brought them in touch with those holding pleas, some of whom were tempted or invited to write what they needed recurrently to know. They were grappling with claims to status or exemption arising from the multiplication of knights and vavassors claiming privilege by virtue of homage and vassalage. *Mutatis mutandis*, customary right of status figures in every one of our texts, even if in those of Normandy and England it is firmly subordinated to royal and ducal lordship.[28]

So these customals were the expressions—tentative and problematic—of the *sociétés féodales* in which they were nurtured, and were hardly more uniform than those societies themselves. Nor perhaps more settled. Barcelona in the 1060s was still smoking, so to speak, from the violence of feudal revolution. Around 1100–1120 Lombardy, having weathered the storms of the 1030s, had lately suffered a worse crisis in the civil strife at Milan. And the customs of Normandy and Bigorre together with the *Leges* of England project critical moments of accommodation between regimes of public order and dynastic lordship. It won't do to classify these impulses as immature, or incomplete. On the contrary, they were culminating events of societal change; fulfillments, like the memorials of deeds, and, indeed, anxious fulfillments. They marked in one way or another the resolution of crises of power in their regions: first in Barcelona and Lombardy, then in Normandy in the 1040s, and more obscurely in Bigorre during the years just after 1100. And the dislocations of those crises were far more widely and continuously attested than one would ever guess from a handful of normative compilations.

---

[27] For example, Ranulf Flambard in England under William Rufus; see below, p. 329.

[28] *Consuetudines et iusticie*, ed. Haskins, cc. 8, 10 (283); *Leges Henrici primi* c. 27.

The Church

In 1049 Pope Leo IX began to challenge, and even to depose, bishops and abbots guilty of having purchased their offices. In the 1050s the cardinal-bishops Peter Damiani and Humbert of Silva Candida debated the validity of sacraments performed by simoniac priests. In the Roman synod of April 1059 Nicholas II decreed a new 'order of election,' by which the pope was to be chosen by the cardinal-bishops and clergy; and it was on this occasion that the investiture of churches by lay men was first prohibited. All such measures, notably the first and last, were contrary to the customs and perspective of the king of Germany; so when Pope Gregory VII challenged the episcopal investitures by Henry IV and his predecessors, there ensued a struggle between popes and emperors that assumed epic proportions between 1075 and 1085, and again in the time of Paschal II and Henry V (1111–18). Having become a struggle for temporal supremacy in a nominally Christian realm, it subsided into the dispute over investiture in which it began and was settled by compromise of that issue in the Concordat of Worms in 1122.[29]

No new study of the Investiture Conflict (as such) is required here. It is the best-known crisis of power in the long twelfth century. What is less familiar is the sense in which it is also the first crisis in a period when the reform movement from which it sprang bore profoundly on the secular experience of disruptive and vulnerable powers in what were (as we know them) hardly so much 'lay' societies as superficially sacral ones. Every regional scene to be evoked hereafter was coloured, every local crisis magnified, by clerical interests and liabilities. The *Fors* of Bigorre have the marks

[29] On these famous events, see generally I. S. Robinson, 'Reform and the church, 1073–1122,' *NCMH* iv:1, ch. 9; Friedrich Kempf, *The church in the age of feudalism*, tr. Anselm Biggs (London 1980) chs. 42–54; and Uta-Renata Blumenthal, *The Investiture Conflict. Church and monarchy from the ninth to the twelfth century* (Philadelphia 1988 [1982]).

of a projection of Visigothic clerical ideology promoted by Gascon prelates. Bishops brought complaints of lay violence at their expense to synod after synod; and they themselves were accused of transgressions neither lay nor clerical but just unseemly. In Arezzo the whole order of local power was overturned when, by dint of reformist outrage, the useless 'custodians' in the chapter were ousted from their customary patrimonies in the later eleventh century.[30] That growing numbers of conscientious priests and monks wished to free their doings from worldly attachments was symptomatic.

It is with respect to the church as clergy that the progress from anxiety to crisis is to be traced with whatever precision these concepts admit. Two issues were becoming clear to sensitive clerics towards 1050: that the mysterious efficacy of God's power was threatened by the contamination of spiritual by worldly things; and that (accordingly) patrimonial lordship, even—or especially—when in clerical hands, was problematic or tainted. Contamination was hardly new, to be sure, and was long abetted by reform-minded prelates and popes incapable of distinguishing between the religious and temporal facets of power. But there was a renewed insistence on purity. In the synod of Reims of 1049 we can see how a canny pope who knew about bishops from his own experience put decontamination before all else, requiring personal confessions of innocence in the intimidating glare of the Saint's relics, thereby disqualifying or quarantining the guilty. Having tried to defend the manifestly culpable bishop of Langres, the archbishop of Besançon had to admit that he had been struck speechless by Saint Remigius.[31]

[30] Ourliac, 'Fors de Bigorre'; Charles Joseph Hefele, *Histoire des conciles d'après les documents originaux*, tr. Henri Leclercq, 11 vols. (Paris 1907–52) IV², 995–1204; Jean-Pierre Delumeau, *Arezzo, espace et sociétés . . .* , 2 vols. (Rome 1996) I, ch. 6; William North, '. . . Property, conflict, and public piety in eleventh-century Arezzo,' *Conflict in medieval Europe . . .* , ed. Warren C. Brown, Piotr Górecki (Aldershot 2003) 109–30.

[31] Anselm, *Historia dedicationis ecclesiae S. Remigii apud Remos*, PL CXLII, 1415–40; Southern, *Making of the Middle Ages*, 125–27; JL 4174; Hefele-Leclercq,

All this was a jolting prelude to hearings and decrees moving well beyond simony. Knowing that clerical marriage was pervasive in France, Pope Leo was content to postpone that issue while attending to reports of other failings in discipline and morals. The agenda show clearly—and we have them not only in the report of Deacon Peter's opening sermon but also in that of the synodal decrees—that for these prelates clerical election and deportment, the beliefs and sexual conduct of the laity, and the integrity of clerical patrimony were the elements of a comprehensive programme of Christian direction.[32]

Accordingly, the immorality as well as the injustice of violence remained in the later eleventh century, as in the past, a matter of clerical censure. The Christian reformers witness vividly to the harsh realities of multiplied lordships. In 1049 Bishop Hugues of Langres was charged with unseemly armed action, homicides, extortionate and afflictive collaborations with 'satellites,' and 'tyranny over his clergy.'[33] But the synod inveighed chiefly against the violence of lay lords, not merely by insisting (first of all) on ecclesiastical elections 'by clergy and people,' but notably by a series of eloquent prohibitions: no one but bishops and their servants is to demand payments in churchyards, clergy are not to bear arms and are immune from seizure on the roads, and—not least—'let no one trouble lesser people [*pauperes homines*] by rapine and seizures.'[34]

Violence—for this is not all the evidence—was a central preoccupation in the synod of Reims. It was to remain a leitmotiv in

---

Conciles IV², 1011–26. See also Amy G. Remensnyder, 'Pollution, purity, and peace: an aspect of social reform between the late tenth century and 1076,' *The Peace of God . . .*, ed. Thomas Head, Richard Landes (Ithaca, NY, 1992) 280–307.

[32] Anselm, *Historia*, 1430–40; JL 4176.

[33] *Historia*, 1434. When in the same synod Bishop Ivo of Séez was chastised for burning his own church, his defence was that he was trying thereby to prevent worse crimes by malefactors, *Gesta Normannorum ducum* vii.15 (II, 116–18).

[34] *Historia*, 1437.

all the councils down to 1122 (and beyond), and by no means only those focused on the peace.[35] What is more, the anxiety about arbitrary seizures achieved newly concrete meaning with respect to the spoliation of widowed churches. Already in 1050, writing from the Easter synod in the name of Leo IX, Peter Damiani had protested against the 'perverse' and 'execrable custom of some peoples' of plundering the houses and effects of deceased bishops.[36] A prohibition of such violence upon the deaths of popes or bishops figured in the Lateran Council of April 1059, with a stipulation that throws light on its ancestry. To specify that a prelate's entitlements (*facultates*) were to be 'preserved intact' harkens back to decrees of the early church designed to protect the official or public interest in ecclesiastical property.[37] What had changed by the eleventh century is that opportunity had given way to custom. The reformers stressed custom as well as perversity, and we have seen that in Hispanic and Gallic regions the abuse, as it was branded, was associated with the proliferation of lay lordships and the need to reward knights. So was the encroachment on or seizure of ecclesiastical lands and revenues, which were likewise, if less pointedly, denounced by reformers and stigmatized by councils.[38]

The prevalence of such 'abuses' in reformist discourse points to a symptomatic climate of opinion. In the years after 1050 the church seemed to some a prey to ravenous and depraved appetites. 'All the world just now,' wrote Peter Damiani to Pope Alexander II in 1063, 'is nothing but gluttony, avarice, and lust.'[39]

---

[35] Hefele-Leclercq, *Conciles* iv, 1029–1289; v¹, 13–746; *The councils of Urban II. Volume 1. Decreta Claromontensia*, ed. Robert Somerville (Amsterdam 1972) 73, 78, 81, 82, 106.

[36] *BrPD* I no. 35; cf. no. 20.

[37] *CAP* II, no. 384 (547); and see David Ganz, 'The ideology of sharing: apostolic community and ecclesiastical property in the early middle ages,' *Property and power in the early Middle Ages*, ed. Wendy Davies, Paul Fouracre (Cambridge 1995) 29.

[38] See above, pp. 101–2, 108–10; and Burchard, *Decreta* iii.166–69 (706).

[39] *BrPD* III, no. 96 (57), echoing 1 John ii.16.

Whatever the excess in this steamy rhetoric, two points stand
clear. First, Peter's indignation was current and urgent; here as
often in his writings he seems to refer to *newly* bad or worsened
conditions.[40] Second, in its expressive vehemence this letter
evokes Peter's more specific denunciation of the unspiritual ambitions by which prelates and clerks were lured into the service of
lay princes, in hopes of promotion to religious offices. Not merely
a critique of simony, this was a perceptive probing of prevailing
motives. What ambitious men wanted, in the clergy as in the
world, was the honour of precedence and nobility. 'They desert
churches,' Peter had written about 1060, 'while lusting after
churches; and in order to seize tyranny over citizens, if I may put
it this way, they disdain to be fellow citizens; they flee service
[*militiam*] so as to be set over knights [*militibus*].'[41]

   Here, once again characteristically, Peter Damiani took notice
of the intrusion of lordship upon offices and practise. Others did,
too. Enfeoffments from God's patrimony were questioned, then
prohibited, in councils.[42] But lordship per se was not at issue.
Sprung from the families or circles of Lotharingian and Tuscan
princes, the reformer popes could imagine their powers to be
justly enhanced by the fidelities of lay allies; not even the disastrous defeat of Leo IX at Civitate (1053) diverted Gregory VII
from a course that would render him, too, a victim of the Normans. Pope Nicholas II (1059–61) exploited his lordship over
Richard of Capua so as to secure his temporal power in Rome.
There was no question then of defining temporalities distinctly
from the sacramental facets of ecclesiastical office.

   So a new anxiety about lay investiture arose in the 1050s not
because investiture was a 'feudal' ritual but because some reformers, and chiefly Cardinal Humbert, could not envisage it in other
than religious terms. Once Humbert had decided to question the

[40] ibid. I, nos. 2, 40; II, nos. 65, 87, 88, 96; III, nos. 120, 140.
[41] ibid. II, no. 69.
[42] Anselm, *Historia*, 1431; Hefele-Leclercq, *Conciles* IV², 1111–13 (Narbonne
1054); V¹, 307 and n. 3; *Register Gregors VII.* vi.5b.

sacramental validity of ordinations by simoniac prelates, a perilous
new avenue of doctrinaire reform opened up. His dispute with
Peter Damiani virtually created a party of radicals who triumphed
with the election of Gregory VII in 1073.

Their view was that in a Christian world lay rulers were not
qualified to appoint, let alone invest, to ecclesiastical offices. This
was to press beyond the position of those who boldly confronted
simoniac bishops, but it was the campaign instigated by Leo IX
that imparted logic to Humbert's increasingly intransigent rhetoric. By insisting on intolerable 'disorder' in Christian society, on
the outrageous precedence of lay powers in clerical elections, he
opened the way for the most practical reform of the age. In 1059
a 'new' and 'right order of election' of the popes gave the initiative to the cardinal-bishops, with only a right of consultation reserved to the lesser clergy and laity. This would in time become a
normal principle in canon law. But in 1059 it accompanied a prohibition of lay investiture that must have encouraged some voices
in papal circles to persist in a harsh denunciation of a status quo
wherein Christian souls were at risk in the ministrations of unworthy priests.[43]

The confrontation of Humbert and Peter Damiani in the 1050s
probably looks stormier to us than it did to their contemporaries,
mostly in Italy. This was a regional dispute in which learned
clerks tried to change minds in papal circles. But it laid bare the
conceptual poverty of theocratic thinking, so shockingly tolerant, it seemed, of clerical corruption and incompetence. Moreover, Cardinal Humbert's uncompromising insistence on clerical
sacrality thrust traditional kingship into a defensive posture from
which it never quite recovered. The passionate indignation with
which he and Peter denounced the abuses of religious order and
their familiarity with histories beyond the Alps were harbingers
of polemics in which the discussion of power would be trans-

---

[43] Humbert, *Adversus simoniacos*, *Ldl* I, 95–253; Peter Damiani, *Liber gratissimus*
(1052), *BrPD* I, no. 40; Tellenbach, *Church, state, and Christian society at the time
of the Investiture Contest* 108–12.

formed. And if, as Gerd Tellenbach surmised, something like 'a great revolution' took place in 1058, when the practical consequences of Cardinal Humbert's critique were first contemplated, was it not that he had forced the first crisis of a new world in the making?[44]

'Crisis' was not a common word in the verbiage of the day. But towards 1060 informed Christians could only have viewed events with foreboding. The election of Bishop Anselm of Lucca as Alexander II (1061–73) was followed a month later by that of Bishop Cadalus of Parma, who took the name Honorius II. This schismatic election showed how far religious opinions were tainted by lay alliance, for Roman families threatened by papal alliance with Norman powers were amongst the partisans who joined some royalist bishops to elect the antipope. Cardinal Humbert had died and Pope Alexander, soon confirmed even by the young king Henry, carried on the reform programme without pressing the prohibitions of simony and concubinage to their extreme consequences.

All this changed with the elevation of the radical reformer Hildebrand in April 1073. Himself an architect of electoral reform, he felt obliged repeatedly to deny that the tumultuous popular acclamation by which his candidacy was thrust on the cardinal-bishops invalidated his Petrine power.[45] And it was he who forced the issues of simony and clerical celibacy on reluctant bishops, renewing demands for compliance in councils in France and Germany during 1074–75, and challenging lay rulers in a new way by prohibiting lay investiture. Almost everywhere these demands

---

[44] Tellenbach, *Investiture Contest* 111. Subsequent polemical writings are gathered in *LdL*; and a valuable commentary may be found in I. S. Robinson, *Authority and resistance in the Investiture Contest. The polemical literature of the late eleventh century* (Manchester 1978).

[45] *Reg.* i.3; iii.10a; *Die Briefe Heinrichs IV.*, ed. Carl Erdmann (Stuttgart 1978 [1937]) nos. 10–13; *Briefsammlungen der Zeit Heinrichs IV.*, ed. Carl Erdmann, Norbert Fickermann (Munich 1977 [1950]) no. 20. See generally H. E. J.Cowdrey, *Pope Gregory VII, 1073–1085* (Oxford 1998).

aroused storms of protest. In a synod at Erfurt (October 1074) the clergy rejected outright Archbishop Siegfried's demand to choose between marriage and the altar, threatening violence. At Passau two months later Bishop Altmann faced and capitulated before an equally hostile clergy. Things went no better for the legates in France, where violence erupted in synods at Poitiers (summer 1074), and soon afterwards in Paris and Rouen.[46] The fierce rejection of legatine decrees on marriage must be reckoned amongst the most characteristic experiences of power in later eleventh-century Europe. The lord-pope, if not quite a bad lord,[47] seemed to many a violator of custom, his purveyors ill deserving of protection from assembled angry clerics and their families. And in the year that followed, the crisis flared for all to see.

Henry IV, having first treated Pope Gregory deferentially, assumed an aggressive posture after his victory over the Saxons in June 1075. Consorting with excommunicated courtiers, he simply ignored papal interests by investing a local deacon, Tedald, to the see of Milan. Gregory reproached the king, making reference to his illicit associations, and threatened to excommunicate him. And when Henry assembled with the German bishops at Worms in January 1076, restraint was cast aside. In steamy and intemperate letters the king commanded 'Hildebrand, not now pope but false monk . . . to step down' from the papal throne, being guilty of usurpation of power, tyrannical domination of the church, and outrageous assault on the rights of an anointed king. For all their revelation of the devices of an impetuous ruler, these letters were upstaged in their frenzied genesis by a collective letter from the German bishops present. Claiming to have exercised unrewarded patience with 'Brother Hildebrand,' they denounced him for 'profane innovations,' fomenting disorder, and for arrogant and tyrannical domination. Pope Gregory's public re-

---

[46] Hefele-Leclercq, *Conciles* v¹, 13–114.

[47] Although Wenrich of Trier, for one, would seem to have heard disparagement to that effect, *Epistola, Ldl,* 1, 289, and this was surely the main charge among the bishops gathered at Worms in January 1076.

sponse came a month later in the presence of clergy assembled in the Roman Lenten synod. Invoking his Petrine power to bind and loose in prayer to Saint Peter, he declared Henry's power nullified and his subjects—'all Christians'—absolved from their oaths of fidelity.'[48]

The key factor at this stage, when extravagant claims were diffused in propaganda unexampled in recent history, was that Henry IV had enemies in Germany prepared to exploit the pope's absolution from vows of fidelity. This declaration was, indeed, the most astonishing assertion of arbitrary power of the eleventh century, for besides flying brutally in the face of custom, as royalist critics soon pointed out, it placed masses of people in conscientious anxiety about their souls. Henry, for his part, having overreached himself, was obliged in the course of 1076 to back down. And when it was agreed that Pope Gregory would meet Henry in Germany, the stage was set for the king's second and more temperate coup: his stealthy appearance as a penitent before the Emilian castle of Canossa in January 1077, his wife and child in tow, there at last to secure the absolution Pope Gregory could not withhold.[49]

This was the most conspicuous confrontation of powers—in the medieval sense, *potestates*—of the Middle Ages. It symbolized deeply conflicting conceptions of right order on which neither resolution nor compromise was yet in sight. Or so it came to seem in accelerated discussions that lie mostly beyond the scope of this book. This is not to suggest that ideological claims were somehow above the fray—they were at times the essence of heated debates—but they unfolded as consequences rather than as generators of crisis. It mattered to contemporaries, and not only to

[48] *Briefe Heinrichs IV.*, nos. 10–13; *Briefsammlungen* no. 20; *Reg.* iii.10a; Hefele-Leclercq, *Conciles* v[1], 151–200; Kempf, *Church* 367–74, 380–82; Morris, *Papal monarchy*, 109–18.

[49] *Reg.* iv.12; Lampert, *Annales, an.* 1077 (290–98); Harald Zimmermann, *Der Canossagang von 1077: Wirkungen und Wirklichkeit* (Mainz 1975); Morris, *Papal monarchy*, 114–18.

those wearing crowns, that Gregory VII thought he could depose a king. But the teleological and functionalist implications of Petrine supremacy or the subversive impact of such a programme upon customary theocratic kingship, while not lost on engaged observers, is largely the discovery of modern scholarly exegesis with historical perspectives shared by few of the polemical writers themselves.[50] The confrontation at Canossa projected something of the emotional force of Cardinal Humbert's perception of an outrageous disorder beyond reasonable allowance for custom. The same doctrinaire insistence on righteous order informs Pope Gregory's assertions, not least his claim of the Lord's preference for Truth over Tradition.[51] But the royalist position, however exaggerated in the hyperbolic cant of Worms (January 1076), was hardly less rooted than the Gregorian one, which is why the bishops, pilloried in one synod after another, were deeply provoked. Their anger is a pointer to the immediate impact of the 'worldshaking' struggle[52] between king and pope.

The *ad hominem* fury of this conflict could not last, given the engagement of intelligent souls in need of persuasion about right and precedent. But a deeper anger, perhaps continuous since the challenge to simoniac ordinations, subsisted in the chatter of religious communities, leaving traces in Gregory's own verbiage, but sounding more audibly in polemics of his detractors.[53] In the short term, violence persisted: partisan elections of anti-kings and an antipope, a second deposition of Henry IV in 1080, the latter's bitter success in driving Gregory from Rome in 1084, followed by Gregory's desperate and disastrous appeal to the Normans in

---

[50] See generally Tellenbach, *Investiture Contest*; and Ullmann, *Papal government*.

[51] *The* Epistolae vagantes *of Pope Gregory VII*, ed. and tr. H. E. J. Cowdrey (Oxford 1972) no. 67 (JL 5277).

[52] Frutolf, *Chronica*, an. 1076 (ed. Schmale, Schmale-Ott 84).

[53] e.g., *Reg.* viii.21, to Bishop Hermann of Metz, March 1081; Wenrich of Trier, *Epistola, Ldl* i, 289. A study of anger in the Investiture Conflict would be rewarding; for a normative approach, see Gerd Althoff, 'Ira regis: prolegomena to a history of royal anger,' *Anger's past: The social uses of an emotion in the Middle Ages*, ed. Barbara H. Rosenwein (Ithaca, NY, 1998) 59–74.

1085. In the context of conflict as in that of power, Gregory VII was a lord-prince, so it is hardly accidental that in his letter of 1081 to Bishop Hermann of Metz justifying his depositions of Henry IV, the pope eccentrically deduced the character of secular power in general—a work of the devil, he called it—from that of his adversary. So too, in reverse, Wenrich of Trier likened Gregorian power to that of an arbitrary lordship over peasants.[54]

As the personal crisis eased, the focus of reform was dispersed. Legates carried the Gregorian programme to the provinces, revealing the fervour of those who had been nurtured in circles of righteous indignation, but also the tenacity of regional episcopates in their traditional compromises with lay powers. In the Scandinavian realms, as also in León and Castile, the foremost problem was that of securing reliable metropolitan primacies. Gregory VII found the kings in Denmark and Norway easier to influence than William the Conqueror in England and Normandy, where the best hope of reform of clerical elections and morals lay in the ambitions of the archbishops Lanfranc and Anselm to forge a reformed primacy of Canterbury as free of papal or royal domination as possible. The compromises with Paschal II in France (1106) and England (1107), whereby Philip I and Henry I gave up investiture with ring and staff but not their rites of patrimonial lordship, was the work of prelates, notably Ivo of Chartres, for whom the lord-king's good will was quite as important as moral reform. Yet it may be a sign of conciliar urgings and preaching that restitutions of churches are well attested in northern France.[55]

In Hispanic lands the reformer popes came closer to imposing Roman domination than in the great northern realms. Already

---

[54] Citations in preceding note.

[55] H. E. J. Cowdrey, 'The Gregorian reform in the Anglo-Norman lands and in Scandinavia,' *Studi Gregoriani* XIII (1989) 321–52; Alfons Becker, *Studien zum Investiturproblem in Frankreich* . . . (Saarbrücken 1955); J.-Fr. Lemarignier, *Histoire des institutions françaises au moyen âge*, ed. F. Lot, Robert Fawtier, 3 vols. (Paris 1957–62) III, 78–139.

Alexander II had imagined regions conquered from the Muslims becoming tenures of the pope, and legations under Gregory VII progressively won acceptance of the Roman over the Visigothic liturgy. And there must have been some bite in the conciliar programme of moral reform, for in the council of Besalú (1077) we hear of the count of Besalú collaborating in the deposition of simoniac abbots, and in subsequent councils of the discipline of clerical morals.[56]

But it was in southern France that the reform programme had its most troubling impact, precipitating a crisis of power comparable to that in Germany. It came early and suddenly, for whereas Archbishop Guifred of Narbonne, who had made no appearance at Reims in 1049, had presided over a reaffirmation of the Truce in 1054, the councils of Toulouse in 1056 and 1061 were legatine enterprises that resounded with unprecedented condemnations of simony and clerical marriage. Moreover, the trouble touched a raw nerve. It was clear at once that demands for the divestiture of churches would be taken seriously in a land where the older elite lordships included parishes and tithes in clusters, and at a time when Archbishop Guifred incurred papal censure himself. Soon after these councils, donations to Saint-Victor of Marseille and to other abbeys sound penitential notes. Guifred was vulnerable, for to judge from the complaint against him by Viscount Berenguer (ca. 1059) the *donum* paid at his accession by his noble parents must have looked like blatant simony.[57] But the outcome of the viscount's case eludes us, and in the 1060s the papal campaign doubtless incurred the protests of meridional bishops in favour of their own initiative to reform capitular life and observance.

In the 1070s the Roman, now Gregorian, campaign gained new force, 'by persuasion or menace,' as Paul Ourliac put it, in

---

[56] Odilo Engels, 'Papsttum, Reconquista und spanisches Landeskonzil im Hochmittelalter,' *Annuarium historiae conciliorum* 1 (1969) 37–49, 241–87; Richard Fletcher, *The episcopate in the kingdom of León in the twelfth century* (Oxford 1978) 24–26.

[57] Above, p. 107.

councils presided by the fiercely doctrinaire legates Amat of Ol-
oron and Hugh of Saint-Die; and the new insistence on the evil
of lay investiture shook Occitan society, as in Germany, from the
top. Archbishop Guifred, having reconstructed (so he claimed) a
massive patrimonial lordship in and about Narbonne, died excommunicate in 1079. Gregory VII had been angered by simoniac bishops in Occitania, as elsewhere; his legates on the ground
harangued the 'powers' to free the churches and tithes of their
lordships, and their message got through to the counts of Toulouse, the viscounts of Toulouse and Béziers, and lesser lords.
Their pious restitutions indicate the force of the Gregorian ideology; yet the traffic in churches and tithes by 1100 suggests that,
by then at least, the force of doctrine was giving way to that of
inertia.[58]

In Occitania as elsewhere lordship was revealed not simply as a
subsistent problem in the church but as the best hope for compromise. Reformers might object to prelates trafficking in the Holy
Spirit, but hardly to dominating clerical patrimonies. If ambition
and nepotism, to say nothing of clerical marriage, could not be
abolished, reformers could still hope to limit lay influence in
clerical preferment, and so in time lay investiture came to seem
the most critical issue in religious life. Even so, it took a pope
prepared one last time to insist on the abolition of this ritual to
show how inextricably worldly the church really was. In a furtive
negotiation, characteristically secured by sworn and potentially
armed men, whereby King Henry V agreed with Pope Paschal II
to give up lay investiture in return for the imperial crown, the
bishops were to renounce all revenues except tithes, pastoral dues,
and private gifts; and when the pope had this fantastic scheme

[58] BnF, MS latin 10936, fol. 2r; Magnou-Nortier, *Province de Narbonne*,
447–518; Paul Ourliac, 'La réforme grégorienne à Toulouse: le concile de 1079'
(1979), *Pays de Garonne vers l'an mil* (1993) 51–64, and 52; Jacqueline Caille,
'Origine et développement de la seigneurie temporelle de l'archevêque dans la
ville et le terroir de Narbonne (IXe–XIIe siècles),' *Narbonne. Archéologie et histoire*, 3 vols. (Montpellier 1973) II, 22–30.

read aloud in solemn assemblage in St Peter's, Rome, on 12 February 1111, it was shouted down in a scene of tumultuous violence. When Paschal then refused Henry's demand for the imperial title and the right to invest, Henry seized and imprisoned the pope and the cardinals. The price of their release in April 1111 was a pontifical privilege securing the king's right to invest with ring and staff (following canonical election), exempting Henry from further excommunication, and promising his imperial coronation.[59]

The renewed crisis of power in 1111 was a phenomenon of tactics and compromise, not of visceral fury. It is not unlikely that Henry V saw through the engagements of February 1111, and so negotiated in bad faith. Quite certainly Paschal II, having been defeated in his attempt to impose unconditionally free elections in France and England, miscalculated his chance of success in the even less favourable circumstances in the empire. In the end his successor Calixtus II won back a little of this lost ground in the compromise of 1122 known as the Concordat of Worms. By this time educated opinion had ceased to insist on the (spiritual) unity of altar and patrimony in prelatical power, opening the way to a newly refined recognition of the place of bishops in Christian monarchies.[60]

So to the extent that the crises of the church were impelled by the pressures of lordship, their outcomes fell far short of those envisaged by Leo IX, Cardinal Humbert, and Gregory VII. The phenomenon of clerical lordship—of powers over patrimonies and temporalities—was too deeply rooted in the newly self-searching and aggrieved church of the world. And while this experience points to the failure of radical ideals and to inevitable compromises, it reminds us of what may be called the 'campaign slogan' of restitution. Everywhere in prospering domains from

---

[59] *CAP* I, nos. 83–101; Glauco Maria Cantarella, *Pasquale II e il suo tempo* (Naples 1997); Morris, *Papal monarchy*, ch. 7.

[60] *CAP* nos. 107, 108; S. A. Chodorow, 'Ecclesiastical politics and the ending of the Investiture Conflict,' *Speculum* XLVI (1971) 613–40.

Tuscany to the North Sea there were complaints of seizures from monks, canons, and their patrimonies. The perpetrators came to bad ends in the early *miracula*, although some were said to be rescued by prayers to the Virgin Mary in the twelfth century.[61] Complaints were incessant in councils, where they came, as at Reims in 1049, to be associated with charges of immorality and simony.

What matters here is that such violations were typically recorded when or because they were remedied. 'Considering the evil I was doing and the injustice' to the monks of Psalmody, said Count Raimond IV of Saint-Gilles in 1094, 'I have repented greatly for all such wrongdoing,' and so he renounced much of his jurisdiction in monastic lands.[62] In 1097 one Guillaume d'Assé restored to the monks of Saint-Nicolas of Angers 'the church of Assé which I was holding not without sin.'[63] Bishop Hildebert of Le Mans was extolled for recovering for the capitular domain 'many churches wrested from . . . our church by the violence of lay men.'[64] Examples of expressly penitent renunciations, in north and south alike, appear to respond to the legatine campaign of reform. But in southern domains, at least, guilt is not always easy to distinguish from charity. Many donations to Lézat after 1056 point to familial possessions without reference to usurpation, and to new endowments.[65] J.-Fr. Lemarignier showed how the disposition of lay proprietors to give up churches in their possession was bound up with pious foundations in the eleventh century, when reformers and reformed monks encouraged restitutions of monastic patrimony; and he pointed to a reaction in favour of episcopal lordship beginning in the pontificate of Urban II (1088–99).[66] Suspicion of monastic

[61] *MSB* v.7,13; vi.3,16; viii.6,8,15,35,36,48; ix.1; *Miracula sanctae Virginis Mariae*, ed. Elise F. Dexter (Madison 1927).

[62] *HL* v, no. 387.

[63] Cited by Lemarignier, *Hist. des institutions françaises*, III, 108.

[64] *Actus pontificum Cenomannis in urbe degentium*, ed. G. Busson, A. Ledru. (Le Mans 1901) 420.

[65] Ourliac, 'Réforme grégorienne à Toulouse,' 54–55.

[66] *Hist. des institutions* III, 107–11.

privilege flared in the great council of Reims (October 1119), where Pope Calixtus II heard the bishop of Mâcon denounce encroachments by Cluny, only to provoke a lucid rebuttal by Abbot Pons, and a massive outcry to the contrary.[67]

Restitutions of churches, or at least those motivated by repentance, doubtless helped to mitigate the crises of the church. For the abuse they remedied, although in reality hardly new, had seemed a very symptom of crisis towards 1060. Peter Damiani denounced the seizure of churches 'by violent men' and the 'invasion of sacred property' as one of the 'evils insolently arising in our times.'[68] Yet much as he must have approved of pious restitutions, he would surely have wondered at the muscular ways of prelates building temporal lordships a generation later. Bishop Diego Gelmírez was said to have 'liberated' lands held by knights on his way to augmenting St James's patrimony in Galicia;[69] however typical an exercise of power in his time, as we shall see, it hardly conformed to a spiritual model of prelacy. Theocratic rulership never recovered from the Investiture Conflict. Clerical lordships, one might almost say, had never been healthier,—or ambitions, as Bernard of Clairvaux would soon remark, more deplorable.[70]

Troubled Societies

The reformers' slogan *libertas ecclesiae* was a slur on patrimonial lordships everywhere. But the events of 1111 proved that, unlike simony, it bore little relation to the realities of local power. This was an age of free enterprise in the securing of customs in fields, vineyards, and markets alike; not lordship but lords was the experience, or the problem, of power for most people; and it can hardly be accidental that the evidence of contested or resented powers

[67] OV xii.21 (VI, 268–72).   [68] BrPD II, no. 87 (509); also I, no. 20.
[69] HC i.22 (50–51).
[70] De consideratione . . . iii.5; ed. Jean Leclercq et al., Sancti Bernardi opera, 9 vols. (Rome 1957–77) III, 434.

comes from regions everywhere in Latin Christendom wherein the indicators point to improved human fertility and growing wealth.

THE SAXON REVOLT AND ITS CONSEQUENCES (1073–1125)

The crisis of the church collided with a crisis of power in Germany. When King Henry IV renewed his father's campaign to rebuild royal power in Thuringia and adjoining Saxony, he aroused suspicion that turned, by 1070, into serious resistance. Saxony was virtually an independent society, where a largely free peasantry was only nominally subject to the duke and other nobles, whose protectorates remained largely public in nature. Henry decided to exploit his fiscal domains bordering the Harz mountains, so he built new castles, rather more, it seemed, than were needed for the purpose. Permitting his builders to impose on peasants for these works, he placed loyal knights and *ministeriales* from his secure domains, mostly Swabia, in them. One of these castles, the ominous Harzburg, went up close by the accessible palace of Goslar, and was equipped to accommodate the king himself.[71]

What is remarkable about this situation is that masses of Saxon peasants as well as magnates themselves well fortified were provoked by this royal enterprise. Noble leaders such as the Margrave Dedi and Otto of Northeim easily co-opted lesser free men suffering infringement of their common rights as well as constraints to service and payment, but it was a fragile alliance given the ambitions to lordship of the great men and the unsteady disposition of the masses. Henry IV played skilfully on divergent interests in talks with Saxon leaders, which is why at a point in 1074 when the peasants felt betrayed, a horde of them looted the Harzburg castle, desecrating the king's new dynastic mausoleum. This out-

---

[71] Lampert, *Annales, an.* 1070–75 (111–250); Bruno, *Sachsenkrieg*; and for this section generally Gerold Meyer von Knonau, *Jahrbücher des deutschen Reiches unter Heinrich IV. und Heinrich V.*, 7 vols. (Leipzig 1890–1909); I. S. Robinson, *Henry IV of Germany, 1056–1106* (Cambridge 1999); and Gerd Althoff, *Heinrich IV.*, ed. Peter Herde (Darmstadt 2006) chs. 3–6.

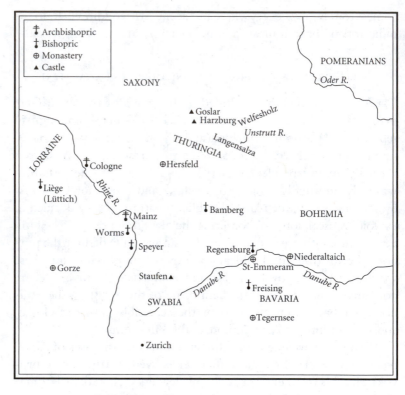

2. THE SAXON REVOLT (ca. 1073–ca. 1230)

rage could only strengthen King Henry's resolve to subjugate the Saxons if not their duchy, and so to reunite his adversaries. On 9 June 1075, at Langensalza on the Unstrutt River, Henry forced the issue in a bloody battle marked by the slaughter of thousands of peasants and the escape of the mounted Saxon elite. In a merciless aftermath the victorious king imprisoned many Saxon leaders and forced a humiliating ritual submission on a mass of his enemies of all ranks (near Speyer, 25 October 1075).[72]

[72]Lampert, *Annales, an.* 1073–75 (140–239); Bruno, cc. 1–56; *Carmen de bello saxonico,* ed. Oswald Holder-Egger (Hanover 1889).

These were the circumstances in which Henry IV incurred the papal censure that goaded him and the bishops to extravagant denunciations of Gregory VII. The king's two conflicts converged in 1077, when embittered Saxon magnates, acting on an impulse that may not have been new, elected Rudolf of Rheinfelden (duke of Swabia) their anti-king. His opposition to Henry weakened with time, though it persisted after his death in battle (1080) in his even feebler successors. By 1085 Henry had regained control of most of the bishoprics while compromising in Saxony, where the magnates had lost the support of the people.[73] No claims to popular liberties had been renounced, and when in 1112 Henry V fell into conflict with Archbishop Adalbert of Mainz over encroachment on royal domains, the smouldering dissent in Saxony flared up anew. But princely powers were by this time too well endowed to be ousted or co-opted, and when Lothar of Supplinburg defeated Henry V in the battle of Welfesholz in 1115, Henry gave up on Saxony,—and indeed, on Germany. Entrusting power to his nephews Conrad and Frederick of Staufen, then struggling, under renewed papal excommunication over investitures, to prevent a new alliance of German rivals and reformers, Henry V was forced into a capitulation to collective princely power such as had seemed unthinkable in 1050. As if in proof of this, strong representations of dynastic propriety in favour of Conrad of Staufen could not prevent the princes from electing the Saxon leader—and victor—Lothar of Supplinburg king of Germany in 1125.[74]

THE ELECTION of a Saxon prince, although not exactly a rebel triumph nor the end of provincial dissidence, marked the defeat of a royal programme of consolidation undertaken by Henry III and

---

[73] Robinson, *Henry IV*, chs. 4–6.
[74] Geoffrey Barraclough, *The origins of modern Germany*, 2d ed. (Oxford 1947) chs. 5, 6; Weinfurter, *Herrschaft (Salian century)* ch. 8.

pressed relentlessly by his son. Generations of historians have seen the setback of strong kingship as an epochal event in German history, by no means (as a rule) for the public good. Given the cries of 'liberty' and 'tyranny' that abound precociously in the sources, the 'crisis of medieval Germany,' as Karl Leyser called it, has been easy to read through republican glasses.[75]

What it meant in its own day is not beyond our means to reconstruct. The nature of the Saxon revolt at its inception was brilliantly expounded by literate clerical observers, including, among others, Lampert of Hersfeld and Bruno the Saxon. Desperately partisan though they mostly are, their narratives preserve something of the gossip of power—its tone and emotion—as do few other witnesses of their age. 'Blessed and greatly blessed it would be,' wrote Bruno in his *Saxon war*, if he [Henry IV] had built those castles against the pagans.'[76] The annalist of Niederaltaich told sparely of King Henry losing faith in magnates who failed to appear on his summons.[77] The chroniclers' anti-Salian bias, often heatedly *ad hominem*, is itself a pointer to the immediacy of the young Henry's temper. People knew what he was like as he came out from under his mother and the archbishop Anno II in the 1060s, and then forced a rigged trial on Otto of Northeim, whose flight and dispossession incited a newly savage phase of the conflict. The anonymous *Life of Henry IV*, which reflects the sobered perspective of a struggling aged king, tends to confirm and correct the adversarial discourse with respect to assemblies, campaigns, and pivotal events.[78]

The Saxons themselves put the matter of castles first among their grievances in 1073. *Montes omnes*, wrote Lampert: Henry 'built up all the mountains and hilltops of Saxony and Thuringia

---

[75] Karl Leyser, 'The crisis of medieval Germany,' *PBA* LXIX (1983), 409–43. Amongst older historians I refer to Wilhelm von Giesebrecht, Karl Hampe, and J. W. Thompson.

[76] *Sachsenkrieg*, c. 16.   [77] *Annales Altahenses*, an. 1072 (84).

[78] ibid., *an.* 1067–73 (72–86); Lampert, *Annales*, an. 1066–73 (100–163); *Vita Heinrici IV. imperatoris*, ed. Wilhelm Eberhard (Hanover 1990 [1899]).

with very well fortified castles, and imposed garrisons in them.'[79] This assertion is borne out by other sources[80] and may be accepted as substantially true; but the larger truth overlooked by most sources is that Saxon magnates had been fortifying their own domains, that the young king had already attacked defiant Saxon lords in their castles, and that for the king to preserve 'peace and justice' in Saxony together with his other duchies he would have to establish a forceful presence there. That larger purpose, beyond the protection of outlier fiscal domains, becomes visible in the later years of Henry IV. Was it really there from the start?[81]

Very likely it was so in concept; but the realities of power after about 1070 surely subverted it. To see this it is necessary to dwell on the forms of action as well as the causes of bitterness in the crisis of 1070–73, and to ask why and to what end the castles were foremost in view. When the texts are reread in this light it becomes clear that violence and lordship—and perhaps in that order—were fundamental to the experience of power in the crisis of the Saxon revolt.

To see this we need only return to the *gravamina* of the Saxon leaders and to the oration of Otto of Northeim (July 1073), as recorded by Bruno. The newly garrisoned castles, whatever their declared purpose, were generators of violence, and *could not* be otherwise. As the texts separately make clear, they were built with the constrained labour of neighbouring rural people.[82] That some of these workers were paid or otherwise remunerated is not unlikely, but there is not the slightest sign that Henry IV tried to mitigate the harsh impact of military building that encroached on the lordships and forest rights of others. On any view, this was non-customary construction for the benefit of armed men from elsewhere bound to the king for safety and profit alike. And the

---

[79] Lampert, *Annales*, an. 1073 (140–41).
[80] *An. Altah.*, an. 1073 (85); Bruno, *Sachsenkrieg* c. 16.
[81] As Weinfurter maintains, *Herrschaft* 118 (*Salian century* 134–35).
[82] Bruno, *Sachsenkrieg* c. 25; Lampert, *Annales*, an. 1073 (146–47).

Saxons made clear that construction was only the beginning of constraint. The very presence of garrison knights and *ministeriales* in the castles was oppressive, for what means of support did they have?[83] New castles on the Saxon borders, as everywhere else, created 'districts': literally, zones of constraint. In Lampert's words:

> Those who were in the aforesaid castles gravely pressed on [*imminebant*] the people of Saxony and Thuringia. In daylight sallies they seized everything to hand in vills and fields, they levied unbearable tributes and taxes on woods and cultivations and often drove off entire flocks on pretext of tithes.[84]

Nor is this all. Lampert goes on to accuse the castellan knights of violating women and the king of rejecting popular appeals on grounds of nonpayment of tithes. Many of these particulars— notably the seizure of property and the abuse of women—figure also in the deposed Duke Otto's war-mongering speech to his Saxon allies.[85]

This indictment as we have it in partisan rhetoric is surely excessive. The new castles were fewer in number than is implied,[86] and nothing is said about the behaviour of castellans in the new-formed districts of the Saxon elite. But the anger that exploded in the peasants' assault on the Harzburg was well founded in a structural reality of fortified coercive power that is massively attested in writing, to say nothing of archaeology.[87] No doubt, the explosion of new castles under Henry IV was epoch-making

---

[83] *An. Altah., an.* 1073 (85): 'Sed quia in vicino ipsarum urbium praedia pauca vel nulla habebat, illi, qui civitates custodiebant, propter inopiam victualium praedas semper faciebant de substanciis provincialium.'

[84] Lampert, *Annales, an.* 1073 (146).

[85] ibid.; cf. *An. Altah.* 85; Bruno c. 25.

[86] Leyser, 'Crisis,' 424 (*Communications . . . Gregorian revolution* 33–34).

[87] In addition to Lampert, Bruno, *Annales Altahenses,* and the *Carmen,* see Frutolf, *Chronica, an.* 1073–75 (82–84); and (with thanks to Joachim Henning) Wolf-Dieter Steinmetz, *Geschichte und Archäologie der Harzburg unter Saliern, Staufern und Welfen 1065–1254* (Bad Harzburg 2001).

in Germany, as historians have long recognized;[88] but if new castles were his means, let us absolve him—and for that matter the Saxon magnates, as well—of blame for the crafty invention of a wicked technology of power. If castles went up on every hill in southeast Saxony, it is surely because by the 1070s they were going up on every unspoilt hillock in western Christendom. That the aggression deplored by the Saxons was in some part a social movement seems possible in light of the circumstances that King Henry's mother Agnes came from Aquitaine, with a French-speaking entourage, to the distaste of the abbot of Gorze; and that the Swabian *ministeriales* on whom Henry relied surely knew of the multiplied castles in Burgundy and Auvergne.[89]

This sort of fortified coercive power was hardly out of keeping with the enforcement of public law. Henry IV would surely have imposed protection and justice on the Saxons had they been willing to accept his vision of restored regnal order. Sources on both sides of a bitter divide resound with the classical rhetoric of republican order. Moreover, the Saxon leaders forged a massive opposition by resort to a tendentious, and probably deceptive, ideology of provincial 'liberty' that may well have owed something to a residual memory of resistance to Frankish subjection three centuries before. Their revolt was argued, it seems, and certainly represented, in a freshly articulate discourse of collective rights in face of tyranny. In the 1070s the Saxons were, according to one authority, 'a political community that had come of age.'[90] This may be so, but only if we allow for a consideration that has been generally overlooked.

In denouncing the king's alleged tyranny, the Saxon nobles were disregarding his lordship—and their own. Or rather, since their chroniclers seldom allude to lordship as such, they were confusing

[88] e.g., Barraclough, *Origins* 135–44.

[89] *Carmen* ii l. 4; iii l. 62; Bruno, *Sachsenkrieg* cc. 36, 37; *An. Altah., an.* 1073 (85). The violence of the king's knights is often noted by Lampert, *Annales, an.* 1070–73 (112, 116, 127, 170–71). Also Southern, *Making of the Middle Ages*, 76.

[90] Leyser, 'Crisis,' 412n, 420–21 (*Gregorian revolution* 24n, 30–31); quotation from 420 (30). See also Lampert, *Annales, an.* 1070 (115); 1073 (152–53, 157, 161–62, 165–66); *Vita Heinrici IV.* cc. 2, 3.

tyranny with lordship. The charge that Henry IV intended to impose a tyrannical domination on the Saxons and Thuringians is overwhelming, even obsessive, in the partisan narrations of revolt. The king, wrote Bruno, organized tributary subjection through castles built by 'free men' compelled to do 'servile labour.'[91] He wished, said Lampert of Hersfeld, to reduce 'all Saxons and Thuringians to servitude.'[92] Taking a longer view, the annalist of St Disibodi said just the same, but added that when the king discovered how hard it would be to achieve this aim, he proposed, advisedly, to begin by despoiling the princes of their honours, and so finally 'to subjugate the other people of the province to his lordship [*dominium*].[93] The fortified heights cast dark shadows.[94] And the contrast between freedom and servility is belaboured so as to underscore the horror of dependence: at Goslar in June 1073 King Henry kept Saxon petitioners waiting in vain, 'like worthless slaves,' whereupon, according to Lampert, the conspirators plotted to throw off the 'yoke of a most wicked domination.'[95] Lordship, so qualified here and elsewhere, seems indistinct from 'tyranny,' a word which itself recurs in these contexts.[96]

What comes through is what people were saying about Henry IV. Behind his back, it seems, for the charge that he meant to impose servility on a free people is veiled in the complaints addressed to the king.[97] Was this charge hypocritical as well as hyperbolic? It is unlikely that royal castellans were the first in Saxony to impose exploitative lordships from the hilltops. The vehemence of the charge—and this is related to the content—is invariable. That the king might have been seeking to impose a harsh lordship short of tyranny, whatever that might be, is an opinion all but invisible in the records. Perhaps it was Bruno who, while clinging to hyper-

[91] *Sachsenkrieg* cc. 16, 24–25, 30, 42.
[92] *Annales, an.* 1073 (147); also *an.* 1075 (236).
[93] *Annales sancti Disibodi*, ed. Georg Waitz (Hanover 1861) 6.
[94] Lampert, *Annales, an.* 1076 (259, 272).
[95] ibid., *an.* 1073 (150).
[96] ibid., *an.* 1073 (141); Bruno, *Sachsenkrieg* c. 56.
[97] Lampert, *Annales, an.* 1073 (152); Bruno cc. 18, 26.

bole, best conveyed realistic fear when he wrote of the renewed pressure on Saxony in 1076 that Henry, 'in order that he be the only lord of all, wished no [other] lord to live in his kingdom.'[98] This was a characteristic overstatement of a well-grounded resentment. Recent research has made clear that dispossessions, of the very sort visited conspicuously on Magnus Billung in 1073, and challenges to proprietary title were the deep cause of the Saxon revolt.[99] Lords, it was held, even the lord-king, may not impugn customary possession, and to the Saxons it looked as if the king was doing so in the same manner as his castellans, who created servitude by uncustomary demands on free men.

Can we be sure they were mistaken about this? No king of the later eleventh century did more than Henry IV, wittingly or otherwise, to promote exploitative coercive lordship over rural people. In most regions the new lordship of castles was self-promoting work of knights in search of patrimony, creating the problem of castellanies that few princes anywhere had yet faced up to. In Germany Henry had to rely on new castles and their garrisons to counter the expanding lordships of Saxon princes; and since any such action was bound to appear oppressive, it is likely that the violence of royal castles and their denizens is exaggerated in the hostile discourse that has come down to us. Few *ministeriales* or 'bad' knights are named in the general lamentations of forced labour and seizures, a circumstance in contrast with those in some other troubled societies. Yet it was the king's purpose of forcing his lordship on a reluctant society that rendered his new castles a bitter contradiction.

❋

SOME PROOF of this may be found in a central purpose of Henry's later years: the enforcement of peace in Germany. It is no accident

---

[98] *Sachsenkrieg* c. 60. On this point see also J. W. Thompson, *Feudal Germany* (Chicago 1928) 194, who wished to distinguish between 'absolute king' and 'tyrant.'

[99] Leyser, 'Crisis,' 423–43 (*Gregorian revolution* 33–49).

that the 'peace movement,' considered as a matter of response rather than of ideology, came to Germany in the last years of the eleventh century. As the crisis of Saxon dissent eased, the problem of castles and the violence of competitive lordships and distraint was left to trouble the everyday reality of power.[100]

Just as in west Frankland two generations before, that reality is visible in the normative evidence of prohibition as well as in discourses of event and complaint. Peace (*pax*) was 'ecclesiastical,' which is why the initiative in Germany came from bishops in 1082–83; the clergy assembled at Cologne in April 1083 alluded to the *novelty* of the church's trouble, thus implicitly associating the crises here distinguished, before proscribing physical violence in detail.[101] Peace was 'public,' at once concept and device, meant to supplement not replace procedures of public justice. King Henry, for whom peace in the 1080s necessarily meant settlement with foes in Saxony and elsewhere, came seriously to grips with disorder in councils at Bamberg (1099) and Mainz (1103).[102] Peace was concrete—'that peace' or 'this peace'—as Archbishop Sigwin of Cologne wrote in 1083, referring thereby to solemn, normally sworn, commitments to observe decrees in detail.[103]

Whether in the forms of peace, or of peace in times of truce, what was prohibited was physical violence: blows to the body with sticks and swords, killings, arson, and assaults.[104] This looks like the normative negation of the violence condemned by Bruno and Lampert; yet while there is little to connect these sanctions with the Saxon revolt, there is no lack of evidence of subverted peace under Henry IV. Some of this relates to the violence of

---

[100] Above, pp. 49, 110; generally Robinson, *Henry IV*, chs. 7–9; and Elmar Wadle, 'Heinrich IV. und die deutsche Friedensbewegung,' *Investitur und Reichsverfassung*, ed. Josef Fleckenstein (Sigmaringen 1973) 141–73.

[101] Lampert, *Annales*, an. 1049 (62); an. 1076 (274).

[102] Bernold of St Blasien, *Chronicon*, ed. G. H. Pertz (Hanover 1844) 457 (Peace of Ulm); Frutolf, *Chronica*, an. 1099 (118); *CAP* I, no. 74.

[103] *CAP* I, no. 424 c. 4; no. 427 c. 1; no. 429 c. 11; Bernold, *Chronicon*, 457.

[104] *CAP* I, no. 424 c. 2 (1083) no. 426 (late s. xi) no. 429 (1094: Wadle, 'Friedensbewegung,' 147–48).

feud, to what seemed disorderly to injured others and to censorious clerks. One may strike one's enemy when meeting face to face, but not pursue him (Mainz 1103), which looks like a weakened version of the sworn undertaking (? Mainz 1085) that during the stipulated time of peace 'no one may harm his enemy.'[105] But there is no reason to suppose that feud was new to the experience of power in German lands, nor that the suffering it caused had worsened.

With lordship it was otherwise. In this respect, all the problems of the Saxon revolt, plus at least one of the Investiture Conflict, were replicated and multiplied, for they were, more or less, the same problems. Henry IV was said to have deplored a new carelessness with fidelity when he commended the duchy of Swabia to Frederick of Staufen in 1079. In a remarkable reminiscence Otto of Freising implied that the trouble was not simply disregard of public oaths but also the betrayal of lords in general.[106] At Liège, where around 1104 an ambitious archdeacon tried to impose new customs on the monks of Saint-Hubert, a canny observer wearily attributed the weakening of judicial institutions to the 'dispute between priesthood and kingdom,' concluding that 'in place of reason, will was lord [dominabatur voluntas].'[107] The arbitrariness of agrarian lordship, however regrettable, was acceptable; like masters with pupils, lords might strike their dependents without violating the peace.[108] But in this connection arose the issue of status. What masters, even newly endowed ones, could do with peasants must have been harder to do in towns, notably those prospering ones in the Rhineland. Troubles at Worms, where the people drove out Bishop Adalbert and his knights and welcomed the king late in 1073, contributed to something worse at Cologne. When Archbishop Anno II, no

---

[105] *CAP* I, nos. 74, 426.

[106] Otto of Freising, *Gesta Friderici I. (Deeds)* i.8.

[107] *La chronique de Saint-Hubert dite Cantatorium*, ed. Karl Hanquet (Brussels 1906) c. 94 (242–44).

[108] *CAP* I, no. 420 c. 2; no. 424 c. 9.

easy lord-prince, tried haughtily to requisition a merchant's ship in Cologne a few months later, the populace rose in fury. The shipowner's son denounced Anno for his 'insolence and severity' in inflammatory speeches, playing on popular emotions, as Lampert put it indignantly, 'like a wind-blown leaf.' Driven out of his city—or was it that the rebels unwarily allowed him to escape?—the archbishop mobilised a 'great force' in the vicinity. The insurgents capitulated at once, offering repentance and even compensation; but when it became clear that Anno would allow his knights to enter the city, many merchants fled to seek the king's protection. In a merciless reprisal against houses and property, some rebels were blinded or killed, leaving this 'head and prince' of cities a desolate 'solitude.' The violence was motivated, Lampert allowed, —but you don't rise up against a great lord.[109]

That troubles in Germany owed something to lordships proliferating beyond their means may be seen in the experience of Lower Lorraine. In 1079 Count Arnulf of Chiny assaulted Bishop Henry of Liège, who was on his way to Rome, brazenly demanding an oath of renunciation of stolen goods from his captive.[110] Towards 1082 'hungry knights' near Liège were said to have become 'public robbers.'[111] A decade later Bishop Otbert of Liège purchased the castle of Couvin 'in the furtherance of peace, because malefactors there were wretchedly disrupting the diocese with seizures, plunder, and other offences.'[112] In 1095 he attacked Clermont castle to put an end to the pillage of boatmen on the Meuse; and the same bishop's purchase of yet a third castle, Bouillon, in 1096 arouses the suspicion that Otbert, by this time called 'pseudo-bishop' by Pope Urban II, was something of a bully himself.[113] He was to the end, however, an adherent to

[109] Lampert, *Annales, an.* 1074 (185–93). Of the harsh penalties, he wrote, 192: 'sed gravior morbus acriori indigebat antidoto.'

[110] *Register Gregors VII.* vii.13.

[111] *Cantatorium* c. 43.

[112] ibid., c. 73; *Cartulaire de la commune de Couvin*, ed. Stanislas Bormans (Namur 1875) no. 1.

[113] *Cantatorium* cc. 82, 91, 96.

Henry IV, in whose last months discontent with the king's rebel son in Cologne and Liège may be viewed as partisan exploits led by burghers in quest of lordship themselves.[114]

Amongst the conspicuous violators of peace were the advocates appointed to secure it. In 1081 the subadvocate Albric of Chauvency 'threatened the ecclesiastical *familia*' of Saint-Hubert by imposing 'uncustomary services' and 'violent exactions.' When his 'inhumanity' came to the ears of the abbot—and this outcome surely points to conflicting cultures of power in this time and space of crisis—a steward who knew the agrarian customs testified against Albric, who lost his claim in a 'public hearing.'[115] Albric must have been small fry in a sizzling pan of would-be lords encroaching on clerical patrimonies. In the end, the Emperor Henry himself took notice, attempting at Bamberg (June 1099) to prevent advocates from appointing surrogates 'to pillage people and churches' and coerce dependents, and subsequently to impress on advocates some sense of office in their work.[116]

Yet here again it is the alleged abuse, not the regulation, that evokes the reality of experienced power. Our informant for the 'peace' of Bamberg adds that the emperor's injunction was ignored from the start 'by princes unwilling to do without their bands of knights,' returning to their old ways. Here the programme of peace converged with smouldering revolt. The betrayal of Henry IV by his (second) crowned son in 1104 moved Germany closer to the princely order first envisaged a generation before, and it built on the widespread acceptance of an order of exploitative and fortified lordship. For the royal biographer, writing soon after the old Henry's death in 1106, this seemed a betrayal of vision as also of person; and the eloquence and withering sarcasm he poured into his account of the Peace of Mainz (1103) and its sequel renders

---

[114] Wolfgang Peters, '*Coniuratio facta est pro libertate*. Zu den *coniurationes* in Mainz, Köln und Lüttich in den Jahren 1105/06,' *Rheinische Vierteljahrsblätter* LI (1987), 303–12.

[115] *Cantatorium* c. 41: 'Huic publice comprobationi interfuerunt . . .'

[116] Frutolf, *Chronica*, 118; diploma cited by Robinson, *Henry IV*, 313–14.

this text our greatest contemporary reflection on the wider crisis of the twelfth century. Through its overblown and tendentious rhetoric may be read just the part of the story Bruno and Lampert had left out: the insistence of the nobles on their retinues and their inability to prevent their own knights, landless and ambitious, from engaging in destructive violence. No wonder they resented the decree of Mainz, which 'profited the miserable and the poor as much as it harmed the perverse and the powerful!' As for those who had squandered their property on knights so as to enlarge their armed retinues, when the 'license to pillage' was snatched from them, 'they toiled in poverty, their storehouses possessed by penury and hunger. He who lately was borne on a frothing steed now had to make do with a rustic draft-horse.' The 'guilt' of the emperor—and the irony here surely evokes the chatter of his partisans' discourse—was to forbid crimes; to restore peace and justice; and to reopen roads, forests, and rivers to safe passage. 'Restore to their fields those you got up in arms, limit the number of dependent knights in conformity with your resources.' Thus exhorting the deprived magnates to a better way for all, the chapter ends with a sigh: 'but it's no use; I invite the donkey to [play] the lyre. A bad custom can seldom or never be removed.'[117]

A safe judgment, those last words? The lordship sprouting everywhere in Germany was a matter of custom: that is, as already in much of west Frankland, of new customs together with the poverty of multiplying knights compelled thereby to seize from stored or peddled wealth as well as to pillage enemy domains. Henry V, given the circumstances of his accession, was in no position to renew his father's pacification. On the contrary, his only course was to permit the princes to fortify their lordships, for he needed their fidelity more than their tenants' welfare. The Staufen brothers Frederick and Conrad, on whom Henry relied after the

---

[117] *Vita Heinrici IV.* c. 8. I have drawn, with a few changes, on the translations by T. E. Mommsen and Karl Morrison, *Imperial lives and letters of the eleventh century* (NY 1962) 120–21.

disaster of Welfesholz, were building quasi-sovereign lordships, as was their adversary Archbishop Adalbert of Mainz; and it was the victory of yet another overmighty prince, Duke Lothar, that put an end to the emperor's renewed attempt to recover crown lands in Saxony. Frederick of Staufen (1105–47) achieved in upper Rhenish lands just what eluded the Salian kings in Saxony: he subjugated settlements (*vicinia*) castle by castle; according to a proverb of the day, 'ever dragging a castle by his horse's tail.'[118]

The ultimate success of the Saxon revolt ratified its astounding consequence: a new regnal order of lord-princes—'heads of the realm,' they called themselves—claiming to act for the kingdom with kingly powers apart from the king.[119] The new regime was more nearly a feudal order than ever before, with the bishops' tenure of *regalia* 'by sceptre' reserved to the lord-king prior to consecration. That this ritual was normally attended by homage and sworn fealty, and the *regalia* treated as a conditional tenure, suggests that in German-speaking peoples 'feudal law' could now be distinguished from 'public law.'[120]

So 'peace' for Henry V came to mean settlement with the powers of church and principality, following a losing struggle to preserve a theocratic monarchy. Less than ever were his efforts to secure regalian rights over clerics and fiscal rights in Saxony matters of moment to the masses of people. All lordships entailed customary services and financial exactions. The most we can say is that the presence of the king-emperor in the years before 1116 imposed some restraint on armed retinues that were foremost in the popular experience of power. What precisely this meant leaps out from Abbot Ekkehard's pages about renewed dissidence and violence in 1123. It was not simply that 'robbers were everywhere, calling themselves knights.' Around Worms battered people imagined armed horsemen 'swarming now here as if to a court,

---

[118] Otto of Freising, *Gesta Friderici* (*Deeds*) i.12.

[119] *Consilium* of Würzburg, *CAP* I, no. 106.

[120] *Cantatorium* c. 5 (17); Concordat of Worms (1122) c. 2, as in *CAP* I, nos. 107–8; also no. 445; and Weinfurter, *Herrschaft* 155 (*Salian century* 179).

now there like a fighting band, to return around the ninth hour
to some hill whence they had seemed to come.' It required an
intrepid witness to the prodigy to learn that these were the 'souls
of knights lately killed. For the arms and attire and horses,' he
was told, 'because they were first our means of sinning, are now
the fuel of our torment, and almost all you see in us is on fire,
although [the flames are] invisible to bodily eyes.'[121]

This is the second of two brilliant passages in which Ekkehard
depicted the horrors visited on German populations after 1116,
when Henry V went to Italy in quest of the Matildine inheritance. There is small danger of misreading these passages. Written with passion and generalizing sweepingly, they stand accused
of exaggeration. But surely not of invention, for apart from the
symbolic truth in the delusion of 1123, the narrations (including
that of the vision) are concretely descriptive, and they refer to
behaviour and circumstances that are explicitly documented
from the earliest days of the Saxon revolt. When the king went
away, we read, the quiet of the preceding decade came to an end.
'Everyone did what he liked, not what was right.' First came the
spoliation of enemy fields and peasants, in the ongoing conflicts
of the Staufen princes against the Saxons and Archbishop Adalbert. Then it was the opportune violence of thieves 'sprouting
up everywhere, careless of times and persons, so to speak, [who]
were kept busy seizing, stealing, assaulting, and killing, doing
nothing useful for their victims.' Mutual slaughters by the
knights of opposed forces, uprisings in several towns, 'castles
built in uncustomary places,' others destroyed, oppression of the
poor and of pilgrims, seizures for ransom: 'it would be tedious,'
pretends Ekkehard, 'to narrate all this.' The 'peace of God' collapsed together with sworn pacts, so that everywhere 'fields were
devastated, villages pillaged, towns and several regions reduced
almost to solitude,' with clergy lacking to perform the religious

---

[121] Ekkehard of Aura, *Chronica*, an. 1123 (362); also Jean-Claude Schmitt, *Les
revenants. Les vivants et les morts dans la société médiévale* (Paris 1992; tr. Teresa
Lavender Fagan, *Ghosts in the Middle Ages* . . . [Chicago 1998]) ch. 5.

offices. The chronicler's shorter account of 1123 is to the same effect.[122]

The crisis of Saxony had ended in a massive failure of public order in Germany. Something of that order—of its judicial procedures, at least—doubtless survived, but new customs and lordships intruded, old titles lost meaning, and multiplied retinues and castles transformed the experience of power. Princes in Lotharingia, once a kingdom, could now be regarded as dukes of Limburg or Louvain.[123] Countless free men subject in fidelity to the early Salian kings were mediatized in new and personal dependencies on lords of all kinds. Did these lordships work? No doubt they were, in some sense, functional. But silence about them is typically the best evidence we have, and for all that is recorded about troubled dependencies in this age, for some of them, too, one must listen hard. In 1112, wrote a local annalist, 'a conjuration for liberty was made at Cologne.'[124] Nothing more. But the sound of this muffled bell is familiar, and bells were ringing elsewhere.

CASTLED FRANCE (CA. 1100–1137)

In one of his early campaigns (1102) Prince Louis of France led an elite army against the lord Ebal of Roucy. According to Abbot Suger, writing a generation later, (1) the 'noble church' of Reims with its dependencies had been assaulted and pillaged by the 'tyranny' of the 'tumultuous baron Ebal' and his son Guiscard; (2) the 'prowess' (*militia*) of Ebal had grown apace with his 'wickedness' (*malitia*), for had he not once led to Spain a 'great army' such as 'befitted only kings'? (3) 'of such a criminous man' a hundred complaints had gone to King Philip, 'and already two or three to his son,' before Prince Louis mobilised his attack. Suger's two

---

[122] Ekkehard, *an.* 1116 (324, 326); followed by *an.* 1123 (362).

[123] Peters, '*Coniuratio*,' 311; Matthias Werner, 'Der Herzog von Lothringen in salischer Zeit,' *Die Salier und das Reich* I, 424–73.

[124] *Chronica regia Coloniensis . . .* , ed. Georg Waitz (Hanover 1880) 52.

further remarks are more complex: (4) in a campaign lasting two months Prince Louis took vengeance for injuries to the churches, devastating the 'tyrant's' lands by fire and rapine. 'What a splendid deed!' commented Suger, 'this plundering of the plunderers, and torturing, equally or even worse, of the torturers.' And yet (5) Louis' campaign, all this notwithstanding, was hardly triumphant. He faced a 'distinguished host,' reinforced by his foe's Lotharingian allies, tried to make peace, was called away to face other 'problems,' and in the end could only secure a sworn promise of 'peace for the churches' from Ebal.[125]

These five points may serve to evoke a troubled scene in the Capetian principality of France. The lamentations of Reims that provoked the young Louis to action were far from exceptional. We know of some twenty-seven places whence allegations of 'bad customs' or violence reached Louis VI before and after his coronation in 1108; and because many other such complaints had come to his father before 1100, Suger's allusion to a 'hundred' from Reims alone, meant to contrast his lethargy with his son's purpose, cannot be altogether hyperbolic.[126] Many of these complaints are known to us from settlements or judgments, but what adds to the impression of trouble they create is the circumstance that the accused often failed to respond to royal summonses, and in some cases disregarded judgments against them.[127] Either way Prince or King Louis was disposed to impose or enforce judgments, which is why we hear of some twenty-five royal campaigns from 1101 to 1132, and of some twenty-three castles captured or besieged during the reign.[128] Complaints, conflicts, and sieges are attested

[125] Suger, *Vie [Vita] de Louis VI le Gros (Deeds)* c. 5.

[126] My figures are compiled from Suger's *Vita* and from *RAL6*. Allegations of bad lordship that may not have reached the lord-kings are known from other sources: e.g., at the castle of Beaugency, Herman of Laon, *De miraculis S. Mariae Laudunensis . . .* i.5, PL CLVI, 968–69.

[127] Suger, *Vita (Deeds)* cc. 2, 3, 5, 18, 19, 25.

[128] ibid., cc. 2–8, 11, 12, 15, 17–19, 21, 22, 24, 25, 29, 31; *Auctarium Laudunense* [continuation of Sigibert of Gembloux], ed. L. C. Bethmann, *MGHSS* VI (1844) 446.

everywhere in the Capetian domains, in some places repeatedly. Most of them fall in the period before 1120, which is surely some indication of the lord-king's success in the remedy of injustice, and, accordingly, of the nature of his society's experience of power.

What Louis VI faced was an incessant clamour of local disturbances over claims to lordship in the vills and towns of growing patrimonies: claims to 'customs' (*consuetudines*) or indeed explicitly 'bad' (*malae, pravae*) customs.[129] The perpetrators were 'tyrants,' such as Ebal of Roucy or Thomas de Marle, in the reproachful vocabulary of our scribes and monastic narrators;[130] but more often lesser men seeking to create or enlarge petty lordships, and notoriously the very provosts and servants of the lord-kings themselves. At Fleury towards 1109 the mayor of the village was accused of imposing 'bad customs' on monastic tenants and 'subjugat[ing] their servants and the mayors of peripheral vills to himself in faith and homage.'[131] What was called an 'infestation of provosts' as early as 1065 was constant in the rhetoric of complaint down to 1119, when it resounds in the Chartrain with the charge, itself recurrent, that people were deserting their holdings by reason of the 'taking of bad customs and the infestation of bad men.'[132] What such malfeasance meant is perfectly conveyed in the charter by which, doubtless about 1110, Louis VI established a 'community' in Mantes. Referring to the 'excessive oppression of the poor,' the lord-king required first of all that 'everyone who shall reside in the community should be lawfully free and immune from all tallage, unjust seizure, [forced] loan, and from every unreasonable exaction, whoever's men they may be.'[133]

[129] Suger, *Vita*, cc. 2, 31; *RAL6* I, nos. 12, 16, 21, 27, 30, 46, 50, 52, 59, 64, 88, 90, 96, 105, 109, 111, 124, 146, 162, 167, 173, 185, 195,197, 239; II, nos. 266, 373, 376, 388, 405, 413.
[130] Suger, cc. 5, 7, 10, 14, 19, 24, 29; OV xi.34 (VI, 156).
[131] *RAL6* I, no. 27.
[132] *RAPh1* no. 20; *RAL6* I, no.146. See also *RAPh1* nos. 52, 61, 64, 77, 114, 145, 153; *RAL6* I, nos. 21, 36, 96, 135, 156.
[133] *RAL6* I no. 47.

This was a list that troublemakers in every weight class could resent. A constant and widespread phenomenon of petty constraint is evoked when the evidence of normative remedy is added to that of complaint. But the problem was worse for King Louis because of the real 'tyrants,' the bad men in possession of castles and banal powers, like Ebal of Roucy, or aspiring to such nobility, like Léon of Meung. When towards 1103 the latter encroached on the bishop of Orléans' share in the castle they jointly held, Prince Louis disposed of him with exemplary violence and despatch.[134] Most of his adversaries were tougher, for the reason adduced by Suger when (point 2) he commented on Ebal's retinue. For Louis VI to mobilise knights, sometimes afforced with baronial allies, was to take sides in local conflicts, to pit his own knights against castellans not so disreputable as to lack allies themselves. The embarrassment of Roucy (point 5) was neither the first nor the last of its kind. A campaign of 1101 against Bouchard de Montmorency, a violator of Saint-Denis' lordship, all but foundered before a coalition of allied castellans, two of whom lost their castles to Prince Louis in further campaigns.[135] The notorious adversaries of King Louis' maturity—his half-brother Philip, Hugues du Puiset, and Thomas de Marle—all relied on retinues of sworn knights in dominations of clustered castles.[136] Moreover, Louis could only respond in kind. His campaigns—and Suger makes no pretence otherwise—were valorous acts of retaliation. His devastation of Montmorency lands in 1101 was explicitly vindictive: fire, hunger, the sword, on the way to 'peace' (*pacavit*).[137] And what is one to make of Suger's enthusiastic irony in recounting the plunder of plunderers in the prince's savage reprisals near Reims a year later? If it reminds us of the Salian biographer reflecting with mock de-

[134] Suger, *Vita* c. 6; cf. c. 5.   [135] ibid., c. 2.
[136] ibid., cc. 18, 19, 24, 31.   [137] ibid., c. 2.

spair on the plight of German knights in the pacification of 1103, Suger's sentiment surely comes off second best.[138]

Louis VI was revealed in his true colours in his exploits of valour and vengeance. That Suger shared this ethos can be seen in his flattering epithets for the prince and his foes alike. He wrote of Louis' 'deeds' (*gesta*) and may have been little less inclined than the Capetian court to see a discrepancy between knightly prowess and the holy protectorate of churches and the weak.[139] But the latter was the explicit purpose of the remedial campaigns in the diplomas and in Suger as well.[140] And it is likely that Louis VI came to share a clerical ideology of peace, for we know that at a critical juncture in his reign—his first capture of Hugues du Puiset and destruction of his castle—he chose not only to mobilise the bishops in support of the campaign but also to mark its triumphant conclusion with a veritable statute of general privilege. The 'possessions of churches and monasteries' were declared to be under 'royal protection' and free 'from oppression and unjust occasions.' And the king added that such a state required the joint action of 'royal right' and 'the sacred authority of bishops.'[141] This privilege coincided not only with a critical event in the history of the Chartrain, but also with news that the people of Laon had formed a sworn commune on their own.

[138] ibid., c. 5; cf. *Vita Heinrici IV.* c. 8.

[139] Suger, *Vita*, prologue, and cc. 1, 2, 5, 19, etc. See also D. Barthélemy, 'Quelques réflexions sur Louis VI, Suger et la chevalerie,' *Liber largitorius: Etudes d'histoire médiévale offertes à Pierre Toubert.* . . . (Geneva 2003) 435–53.

[140] e.g., Suger, *Vita*, c. 2; *RAL6* I, nos. 29, 135.

[141] Suger, c. 19; *RAL6* I, no. 58: 'Non enim res humane aliter tute et incolumes esse possunt, nisi cum in unum conveniunt ad earum defensionem et jus regium et auctoritas sacrata pontificum.' News of the pacts between Paschal II and Henry V must have been fresh in France when these words were written. An anonymous panegyric of about this time (1111) praises Louis VI for rescuing 'sweet France' from the 'wasteland, prey to robbers,' of his father, ed. Jan M. Ziolkowski, Bridget K. Balint *et al.*, *A garland . . . Latin verse from twelfth-century France* . . . (Cambridge, M., 2007) 94–115 (and l. 81).

❖

THAT THIS last was a troubling event we know from an incomparable and nearly contemporary account by the abbot Guibert of
Nogent. In fact, the commune was a comparatively benign incident in a string of catastrophes that Guibert represented as a dra-
matic tragedy. First came the election of one Gaudry (*Galterius,
Waldricus*) as bishop of Laon, probably in 1107. It was a doubly
problematic choice: first, because Gaudry, who was said to be
rich, was a courtier of King Henry I of England without clerical
qualifications; second, because, following two untenable nomi-
nations, Gaudry was publicly opposed by the prestigious Master
Anselm in the cathedral chapter, and privately by several others,
including Guibert. With exemplary candour Guibert told how he
himself attended Gaudry, who paid his expenses, before Pope
Paschal II, who was then at Langres. The pope asked some hard
questions about the election, and received some soft replies, only
to approve it in expectation of pocketing money Gaudry had offered to the papal companions.[142]

In time Bishop Gaudry fell out with a prominent man named
Gérard, who was castellan to the nuns of Saint-Jean. As the dispute worsened, Gaudry plotted with conspirators to kill Gérard
while he himself went to Rome (not to seek the Apostle, as Guibert confided to God). Gérard was at prayer in the cathedral
church of St Mary when he was murdered on 13 January 1111.
Two knights had joined the archdeacons in the crime, which was
instantly notorious. The king's provost incited royal tenants and
those of Saint-Jean to attack the houses of the conspirators, who
were driven from the city.[143]

When word reached him, King Louis suspected Bishop Gaudry's complicity, and ordered that the episcopal palace in Laon be

---

[142] Guibert de Nogent, *Monodiae* (*Memoirs*) iii.1–4. See also Jay Rubenstein,
Guibert of Nogent. Portrait of a medieval mind (NY-London 2002) 101–10.
[143] Guibert iii.5.

sacked. Gaudry returned to the city, not without difficulty, and promptly worsened things by excommunicating those who had attacked the conspirators. While he then absented himself to raise money in England, some notable men in Laon thought of an easier way to do the same by offering to sell their approval to create a sworn commune. 'Now "commune," explained Guibert—'a new and evil name!—works like this: everyone should pay the customary debt of servitude as a head-tax once a year, and if anyone breaks the law, he may pay a lawful fine, while such other renders as are customarily inflicted on serfs are wholly abolished.' So the people, seizing the occasion for gainfully ransoming themselves, paid off the greedy pretenders, who promptly swore their own good faith, and thereby initiated a 'conjuration' of 'clergy, notables, and people.' Returning (rich) from England, Bishop Gaudry professed his indignation with the commune, only to change his mind when compensated. And the king, too, added Guibert, was bribed to approve the commune.[144]

As a result lords, doubtless including the bishop, awoke to find their tenants unwilling to pay or render as accustomed. Gaudry tried to manipulate the coinage for profit, then abused one of his own rural stewards, then brazenly invited the king to Laon in Holy Week 1112 with a view to quashing the commune. This brought a veritable crisis of power to explosive violence. King Louis seems to have succumbed to further bribes—in an astonishing aside, Guibert represented him as a capable king who had suffered a bad lapse of judgment—and, having joined with the bishop to nullify the oaths, left town fast. Social order now collapsed in tumultuous outrage, the powerful having the temerity to demand payments for annulling the conjuration they had sold to begin with; and a new conspiracy was hatched to murder the bishop. Dragged from hiding in his church, Gaudry was seized by a disreputable serving-man known for his brutality as a toll-collector, then savagely murdered by an enraged mob. Other killings ensued, many fled, and we have but a fleeting glimpse of

---

[144] ibid., iii.6–7.

Master Anselm trying to restore sanity by securing decent burial for the dead bishop.[145]

This violence, Guibert makes clear, placed Laon in the king's mercy. In the aftermath, guiltless clergy invited, or permitted, King Louis to impose a new bishop; and when he soon died, one Barthélemy de Jur was chosen in a proper election without simony. But this promising turn of events was subverted by the guilty conspirators who, fearing the royal vengeance, had invited Thomas de Marle, already long notorious in the region, to defend them against the king. So the crisis of Laon became, in the Easter season of 1112, an incident of regional feud, for Thomas found himself in conflict with his own father Enguerrand, who fell on the half-deserted city and plundered it. Nor was this all, 'for besides their murder of priests, a bishop, and an archdeacon [has Guibert forgotten Gaudry's victim, the castellan?], quite recently Raisinde, the abbess of Saint-Jean, a very capable woman from an outstanding family, a benefactor of the church and a native of Laon, was killed by her own serf. . . .' Other killings, and shake-downs followed at Laon. Our informer implies that ransom had become a local institution. But it is time to take leave of Guibert of Nogent, allowing him the last words: 'During that crisis of the city that we have related, the king by whose avarice it had arisen never once came back. Moreover, the royal provost, knowing of the evil to be perpetrated and having sent his concubine and children on ahead, left [Laon] a few hours before the mounting sedition gripped the city. And before he had gone three or four miles, he looked back to see it in flames.'[146]

Was this a fitting farewell? If Guibert's famous narration of the 'trouble' (*malum*) of Laon has a privileged place in this book, it is because it tells us, more directly and fully than any other text, how power was experienced in a historic region of France in the days of Louis VI. It is a powerful corrective to Suger. Govern-

[145] ibid., iii.7–10.   [146] ibid., iii.11–13.

ment in the Laonnais was vestigial, the feeble residue of a royal protectorate nicely evoked in the vignettes of the provost Ivo: at first, helplessly directing the vindictive looting of Gérard's killers; at last, a fugitive from his own city on fire. And every other office of public order was likewise in collapse—the advocacy of Saint-Jean and the bishopric—in a torrent of cascading events that may seem to conceal a 'normal' experience of justice and taxation in Guibert's pages. But surely what Guibert conveys, with stunning clarity, is what life in Laon was like *before* and *between* the murders as well as after them. This was a scene of harshly intrusive banal lordships in competition for shares in mercantile revenues as well as agrarian produce.[147] People seized and ransomed; they allied with others to compel and to profit. Guibert was incensed by the deceitful manipulation of the coinage, a point on which he dwelt at length, concluding: 'No hostility, no plundering, no arson ever damaged this province worse since the Roman walls held the ancient and respected mint of their city.'[148] Following the murder of Gérard, Guibert had preached on God's wrath, 'when with mutual provocations lords moved against burghers and burghers against lords, when with unseemly hostility abbot's men raged against bishop's men,' and the reverse.[149]

Given his contempt for Gaudry and Thomas de Marle, it is remarkable how instinctively Guibert detested the commune. Yet he was of their class, himself a lord of peasants, and could only view the sworn renunciation of servile obligations as subversive of social order. His outlook would long prevail, which is to say that the communes proliferating in his day were in mutation from the outset. It was one thing to abolish 'unreasonable exactions' as the king had done when he chartered a 'community' at Mantes; quite another for local populations to take it on themselves to remodel public life. And according to Guibert, by God's

---

[147] See notably Barthélemy, *Deux âges de la seigneurie banale. Pouvoir et société dans la terre des sires de Coucy*, 76–80.

[148] Guibert, *Monodiae* iii.7 (326; *Memoirs* 149).

[149] ibid., iii.6.

judgment the 'calamity' of Laon, compounded by the squabbling Coucy, soon passed to Amiens. In 1113 the townspeople there plotted with the bishop against Count Enguerrand, whose son Thomas de Marle then joined the conspiracy for a time. Once again, the king is said to have been bribed, and when he did appear (in 1115) in support of the townspeople, he was caught up in a long and perhaps useless siege.[150]

THE LORD-KING'S return to the Laonnais in 1115, following the condemnation of Thomas de Marle by the Council of Beauvais a few weeks before, was in response to multiple complaints of the sort known everywhere in the Ile-de-France. It is time to ask how to interpret these troubles of the early twelfth century. Let us agree that it was hardly a matter of king against knights, let alone against knighthood (*chevalerie*).[151] Louis VI was arguably a castellan himself, albeit a crowned one; and we have seen that his response to violence was tinged, at least, with vengeance. So what truth lies beneath the indignant rhetoric? Was this not a societal crisis of power? Nobody at the time said so, nor even, with due respect to a modern metaphor, anything quite like this. It was well understood that what was lacking around 1100 was the resolution to execute justice against malefactors and 'tyrants,' and that what Philip I could not do his son Louis could and would do.[152] Unlike Germany, which verged on acephalous anarchy at several points in the early twelfth century, France had her kings (although this difference cannot be pressed), so it cannot be mistaken to read her history following Suger as a revival of monarchy.[153]

[150] *RAL6* 1, no. 47; cf. nos. 54 (Compiègne), 61 (Noyon), 62 (Laon) and 85 (Amiens), the two latter known from Guibert. Also Guibert, *Monodiae* iii.13–14; Suger, *Vita*, c. 24.

[151] Barthélemy, 'Quelques réflexions,' 435–37.

[152] OV xi.34–36 (VI, 154–62).

[153] See the essays by Andrew W. Lewis, Eric Bournazel, and Michel Bur in *Abbot Suger and Saint-Denis. A symposium*, ed. Paula Lieber Gerson (NY 1986) 49–75.

But the whole (or better) truth is surely different. Louis VI was in no position to impose justice absolutely, nor did he pretend to do so. All he could do was to combat injustice here, there, and everywhere; that is, to confront what *he* deemed 'unjust' or 'evil,' he together with a newly mobilised clerical interest in patrimonial integrity and in 'peace.' In 1118 King Louis proclaimed it to be the office of 'royal majesty to repress and destroy the oppressive insolence of bad men.'[154] Some of that 'danger' threatened the king of France himself, for the troubles often arose from the self-serving encroachments of provosts and other royal servants. But much of the 'wickedness' the clerical writers deplored was the doing of lesser lords possessed of castles and aspiring to honourable status.

In this connection, two distinct points need to be recognized. First, we should not read Suger to mean that Louis VI put an end to bad customs in the domains of Saint-Denis or other religious houses, or even to the depredations of Hugues du Puiset or Thomas de Marle. What the evidence of remedial action proves is the phenomenon of violence—of new impositions, seizures, ransoms—, its existence, not (necessarily) the end of it. It took repeated forays to rid the Chartrain of Hugues du Puiset, and Thomas de Marle was on the loose till 1132. Moreover, the ineptitude of Louis VI in the crisis of Laon should dispel any temptation to overestimate the lord-king's successes, still less to suppose that the castellanies and lordships Suger fails to mention were havens of peace.[155] King Louis' charters, judgments, and campaigns imposed his order—for how long?—, but they are credible evidence of the experience of suffering in the principality of France.

Second, whatever the limits of his response or of his success in practise, it looks as if Louis VI badly disrupted a new trajectory of power in the fortified banal lordships of the Ile-de-France. Theirs

---

[154] *RAL6* i, no.135.
[155] Such as Beaugency and Tremblay, both troubled places, Herman of Laon, *De miraculis* i.5 (968–69); Suger, *Gesta* [*L'oeuvre administratif*], ed. Francoise Gasparri, *Oeuvres*, 2 vols. (Paris 1996–2001) i, i.2.

was the real crisis of the early twelfth century in this region. For once Philip I and his son had decided to exploit their patrimonial domains, they became formidable competitors of the very knightly families—the Montfort, the Montlhéry, the Garlande, the Senlis, the Coucy, to name no more—with which they allied, into which they married, from which they recruited, against which they struggled.[156] One castle was not enough to secure such families, given growing populations and wealth; two or more were tenable only with the sort of commended servants who were tempted to coerce and encroach, and this was King Louis' dilemma as well as Thomas de Marle's. What the castellans, however devout in their foundations and protections, could not do as well as the lord-king was to collaborate with the bishops in view of peace, and even Louis VI was slow to exploit this resource.

It is tempting simply to dismiss the self-serving testimonies of Guibert, Suger, and the diplomas about the violence of 'wicked men' all about them. This temptation should be firmly resisted. The failing of their evidence is not so much mendacity as tendentious exaggeration; one of its merits, however problematic, is its indignant moralising of motive and event. Evil was a palpable reality in this microcosm of coercive and fortified power, a consciousness the clergy surely shared with the masses of toiling people if they did not derive it from them. Guibert's second thought about the murdered Bishop Gaudry was that 'this evil . . . [was] not in him alone, but arose also from the highest iniquity of others, indeed of the whole populace. For nowhere in all of France occurred such crimes as amongst the people of Laon.'[157] This may look like subjective overstatement, but even when limited to the conspicuous murders it is borne out by our sources, and justified by further examples of violence. Suger blamed the treachery at La Roche Guyon on the castle itself: 'this stronghold detestable to gods and men alike.'[158] Montlhéry was worse yet,

---

[156] See generally Bournazel, *Gouvernement capétien au XIIᵉ siècle*.

[157] Guibert, *Monodiae* iii.11 (372–74; *Memoirs* 171–73).

[158] Suger, *Vita*, c. 17.

the old King Philip telling his son (in Suger's hearing) how 'that tower has all but made an old man of me,' and deploring its 'treachery and wickedness.' Its infidelity was making the faithful unfaithful, and the unfaithful treacherous.[159]

Here again the reified venom may arouse suspicion, but Suger goes on to make a different and wholly plausible point. The reason why the old king rejoiced when Montlhéry came into his hands with the marriage of the heiress to his son Philip was that this castle, in the possession of 'faithless men' preying on the traffic between Paris and Orléans, was critical to the peace of the Ile-de-France, specified within its geographical coordinates. Castles were leverage for the coercive power of the men they sheltered. Montlhéry, added Suger, 'drew together perfidious men from near and far," so that "in the whole kingdom nothing evil was done without their consent or aid.'[160] Once again, manifest exaggeration hardly detracts from the force of a cogent recollection. It is known from other sources that Montlhéry was virtually identified with the knights it housed, whoever their master; and the same was said of Corbeil—Suger called it a 'castle blessed with an old nobility of many knights'—and Sainte-Sévère in Berry.[161] Moreover, just as Montlhéry dominated the Paris-Orléans corridor, so Le Puiset dominated the rich farmlands of the Chartrain, and Montaigu the Laonnais. These were natural habitats of territorial lordship, novel approximations of old *pagi* in which quasi-comital powers seemed within reach of great lords such as Hugues du Puiset and Thomas de Marle, until, in crises of their own making, they were compelled to settle for less.

To our scribes and monastic narrators, they and their kind were 'tyrants' and 'bad men.'[162] Such epithets can only have been popular as well as clerical, even as they served rhetorical and 'strategic'

<hr>

[159] ibid., c. 8. Only such a world of affectively conditional bondedness could have made such a distinction.

[160] ibid.

[161] ibid., cc. 8, 12, 15; and see also *RAPh2* I, no. 29.

[162] Suger, *Vita*, cc. 5, 7, 10, 14, 19, 24, 29; OV xi.34 (VI, 154, 156).

purposes. Peter Abelard spoke of 'tyrants' acting from fallible *voluntas*, not from God's *potestas*; he denounced the habitual tyranny of exactions and seizures by lay princes from their tenants; he even spoke of castles as 'tyrannical fortification.'[163] Much of such talk sounds like rhetorical sparring. There was conceptual space between the notorious murders in Laon and the multiplying 'customs' in demand everywhere by lords of peasants. In his homily following the killing of Castellan Gérard, Guibert opined that 'the place, the crime, and the shame will be talked about everywhere.'[164] Yet our informants saw outrageous violence as symptomatic. A new stridency sounded in their indignation, pointing to a sense of trouble deeper than the ordinary experience of feud, siege, and the devastation of enemy lands. Hugues du Puiset and Thomas de Marle were not merely rivals for public power, like Duke-King Henry I or Count Theobald; they were public trouble-makers. They were described as worse than bad lords, partly in hyperbolic verbiage, but mostly in horrified recitations of violence quite specific enough to enable us to tell them apart. For the moment, it will do to say that Hugues was driven by dynastic ambition, so that 'although few liked [him], many served him'; while Thomas de Marle, likewise striving for territorial lordship, was distinctly prone to impulsive anger, his violence and cruelties quite as excessive as normal.[165] In the perspective of a troubled society of sprouting lordships, these castellan-lords were notorious. They were disruptive enough to provoke a new alliance of king and clergy from 1111 to 1115, a reaction itself pointing to alarm if not crisis. Another test of 'tyranny' was the seizure of church lands, no new problem, and one with which councils in (greater) France were preoccupied from 1095 to 1119; but the most urgent decrees and sanctions

---

[163] Citations in T. N. Bisson, 'L'expérience du pouvoir chez Pierre Abélard . . . ,' *Pierre Abélard. Colloque international de Nantes*, ed. Jean Jolivet, Henri Habrias (Rennes 2003) 93, 103–5 (and generally 91–108).

[164] *Monodiae* iii.6 (308; *Memoirs* 141).

[165] Suger, *Vita*, cc. 19–22 (Hugues); 7, 24, 31 (Thomas).

on the matter were formulated at Beauvais (1114) and Reims (1119).[166]

It follows that the crisis of the castellans in France persisted beyond the setbacks of some of them. Neither Hugues du Puiset nor Thomas de Marle were crushed; indeed, their lordships survived Louis VI, by no means fully compliant. Theirs is a microhistory of power all but concealed in the records of their conquerors. By continuing to act as protector-justiciar and by not seeming over-eager to seize castles, King Louis had undercut the defiance if not the oppressive habits of the castellans. We know of no royal effort to subjugate them in vassalic dependence, nor may the famous journeys to the Auvergne in 1122 and 1126 be construed as much more than an extension of his campaign of remedial justice.[167] What troubled France in the days of Louis VI were the growing pains of a contagious exploitative lordship. Men nurtured in arms and the hunt, like Bishop Gaudry, were questing for local power and status while arrogating or pretending to banal powers, an anxious and risky quest—treachery was its symptom—sometimes bursting into wilfully coercive violence. Tyranny was a reality in this society. It was not rebellion.[168]

TROUBLES ON THE PILGRIMS' ROAD (1109–36)

> They wish to reign, but by treachery; they wish to
> command, but by violence.
> —*Historia Compostellana* i.114.15

It would be mistaken to suppose that the troubles in Spain replicated those in France. As we shall see, they more nearly resembled

---

[166] ibid., cc. 19, 24; Hefele-Leclercq, *Conciles* v¹, 388–592; and for the texts of 1114 Robert Somerville, 'The council of Beauvais, 1114,' *Traditio* XXIV (1968) 493–503.

[167] See Suger, *Vita*, cc. 29, 31; and cf. Lemarignier, *Gouvernement royal* 165–76.

[168] OV to the contrary, xi.34 (VI, 154). Orderic's own commentary (VI, 156) suggests that *rebellare* was the wrong word.

those in contemporary Germany. But the pilgrim towns on the way to Compostela were full of Frenchmen in the early twelfth century, many of them must have been sorely tempted to compare the scenes,—and at least one of them virtually did so. The canon Girard, writing of one of the most desperate moments in a communal uprising at Compostela in 1116, admitted that 'I was afraid, and wished I were back in Beauvais.'[169] Girard had come from France to serve Bishop Diego Gelmírez (1100–1140); he had lived in the cathedral community of Saint James for at least a decade before he became the newly promoted archbishop's chronicler (ca. 1120); his account of those years is in every way comparable to Suger's, and in some respects superior; and his words referring to the Galicians, quoted above, imply some comparison, and perhaps some contrast, with France. That the story of power was different in Spain we know not only from Girard's chapters in the *Historia Compostellana*, but also from the *Crónicas anónimas* of Sahagún (whatever the latter's limitations). From these texts[170]—and they are not the only sources—can be reconstructed a critical *tournant* in the histories of lordship and kingship in Galicia and León.

Modern historians have not hesitated to speak of a time of 'crisis' in these societies, and they are surely right to do so.[171] Here

---

[169] *HC* i.109.4.

[170] On which see Bernard F. Reilly, 'The *Historia Compostelana*: the genesis and composition of a twelfth-century Spanish *Gesta*,' *Speculum* XLIX (1969) 78–85; Fernando López Alsina, *La ciudad de Santiago de Compostela en la alta Edad Media* (Santiago 1988) 46–93; Ana Maria Barrero, 'Los fueros de Sahagún,' *AHDE* XLII (1972) 407–13; and critical work (in progress) by Charles Garcia. See below, p. 251.

[171] Reyna Pastor de Togneri, *Conflictos sociales y estancamiento económico en la España medieval* (Barcelona 1973) 22–23; Bonnassie, *Slavery to feudalism* 123–24; Reilly, *Kingdom of León-Castilla under Queen Urraca*, ch. 2. See also Carlos Estepa Díez, 'Sobre las revueltas burguesas en el siglo XII en el reino de León,' *Archivos Leoneses* XXVIII (1974) 295; Reyna Pastor, *Resistencias y luchas campesinas en la época del crecimiento y consolidación de la formación feudal. Castilla y León, siglos X–XIII*, 3d ed. (Madrid 1993) 13–16 and ch. 4; Ermelindo Portela, Ma. Carmen Pallares, 'Revueltas feudales en el camino de Santiago. Compostela y

the disruption is quite as palpable as in Salian Germany, the chroniclers even more relentlessly horrified by it than elsewhere. Indeed, it will be useful to begin with their descriptions, not simply so as to judge their conformity with detailed evidence, but also because it is from them that the weightiest point of this story becomes clear. The conspicuous uprisings in Sahagún and Compostela were, as contemporaries themselves could see, incidents of widely experienced and tenacious disorder.

IN A sermon preached at Burgos in June 1113 Bishop Diego Gelmírez recalled the glories of Spain under the late King Alfonso VI, when the church 'flourished,' when the Moors were subjugated, and when 'laws, rights, peace, [and] notably justice prospered.' Since his death, under Queen Urraca and her son, 'discord sprang up at once. Ecclesiastical rights were blatantly violated, the dukes, princes, and all the magnates of Spain reduced to impotence [i.e., as protectors]. Their former virtue is wholly hidden.' And while the queen and her son have an inalienable right to their kingdom, the rest of us, 'once triumphant, . . . now find ourselves dominated by a few.'[172] The Anonymous of Sahagún put it more strongly still, viewing the 'accursed union' (*maldita cópula*) of Urraca and Alfonso of Aragon the 'occasion for all the evils that were born in Spain,' the massive killings followed by 'robberies, adulteries'; and 'almost all the laws and ecclesiastical virtues were diminished and humiliated.'[173] In another place the same writer extolled the 'peace and security' under 'the king don Alfonso, may whose soul enjoy the wealth of Paradise,'

Sahagún,' *Las peregrinaciones a Santiago de Compostela* . . . (Oviedo 1993) 313–33; H. Salvador Martínez, *La rebelión de los burgos. Crisis de estado y coyuntura social* (Madrid 1992).

[172] *HC* i.86.2.

[173] *CAS* c. 19 (22). In this case by exception, parenthetical citations refer to chapters in the edition by Ubieto Arteta (Textos Medievales 75 [1987]).

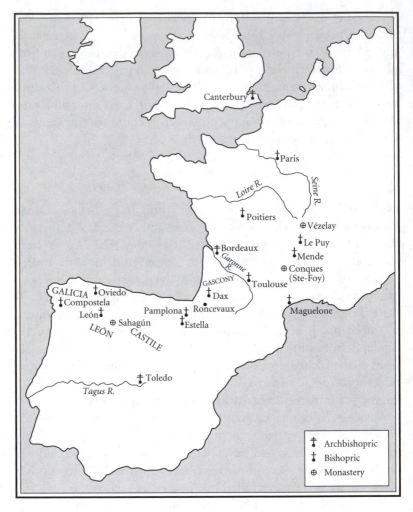

3. The Pilgrims' Road (ca. 1050–1150)

when 'no village or place needed walls,' when the old and young alike could relax and dance in peace.[174] And in yet another chapter the vexations of local burghers are said to afflict 'not only the

---

[174] *CAS* c. 40 (43).

church of Sahagún, but even, as we have said, all of Spain we live in.'[175]

This was the disorder of dynastic failure. One needed a male heir in this abrasive world of aspiring noble lordship, or, failing that, a well secured male consort for one's daughter. With two years to live (summer 1107) the ageing King Alfonso VI might have expected the succession to be safe either way; yet in the very moment when Louis VI took his father's place in France, Alfonso's hopes were dashed: his son-in-law Raimund of Burgundy died, followed by his son own Sancho in battle against the Almoravids. Alfonso lived his last days knowing that his daughter Urraca would succeed as the mother and (remarried) wife of formidable male rivals. In the event her new husband Alfonso of Aragon and her son Alfonso Raimundez became magnets for all the disaffected and ambitious elements of Christian Spain. The newlyweds, second cousins and married in face of clerical dissent, got on badly, perhaps in some part owing to Alfonso's ambitions. By 1110 he was enticing allies from Castile to Galicia, and his repeated thrusts, at first together with his wife and later with support of the townspeople of Sahagún, accounted for much of the violence deplored by the chroniclers. Urraca's problem was that by remarrying she had lost her original claim to the succession in Galicia, which could only encourage those barons who favoured her son Alfonso as their defender against a foreign invader. The boy's guardian was Pedro Froiláz de Traba, no friend to the bishops of Compostela, on whose domains the Traba had long encroached; and it points to the disorder of elite consensus that, while the 'Battler' king of Aragon antagonized his wife by gratuitous brutality in their joint campaign, by 1111 Bishop Diego was moving warily and perilously towards the recognition of the younger Alfonso as king in Galicia.[176]

---

[175] ibid., c. 53 (56).

[176] ibid., c. 18 (20); and in general Biggs, *Diego Gelmirez, first archbishop of Compostela*, ch. 3; Reilly, *Queen Urraca*, ch. 2; R. A. Fletcher, *Saint James's catapult. The life and times of Diego Gelmírez of Santiago de Compostela* (Oxford 1984) ch. 6.

Crowned at Compostela in September 1111, Alfonso Raimundez came of age in the dynastic contest that followed, gaining his mother's recognition, and finally the support of magnates outside Galicia to deflect the larger ambitions of Alfonso of Aragon. As for Urraca, her marriage challenged by the church, her husband cranky, inhumane, and perhaps from the start unstable, herself by no means guileless and assuredly resourceful, she struggled through a tumultuous reign to secure for her son (Alfonso VII, king 1126–57) the power so few of her subjects believed a woman could exercise. 'She reigned tyrannically and womanishly [*muliebriter*],' opined one chronicler, who added that she 'ended her unhappy life' in adulterous childbirth.[177]

This touch of slander doubtless evokes a prevalent attitude in her day. Otherwise worthless, it contrasts starkly with massive evidence of the afflictions suffered by her people, for those who told of them cannot have viewed them as 'womanish' but only as an appalling consequence of her father's death. She was no more—or less—responsible for them than those with whom she struggled for power: her son, her Aragonese husband, even at times Bishop Diego Gelmírez. All were 'tyrants,' not quite in the same sense as applied to defiant barons in France, but in that of mobilising armies they found it hard to control.[178]

The violence was not only that of unrestrained fighting men in alien prospering lands. But it was just their habitual mode of disdainful savagery that, in Galicia as elsewhere in Europe, proved contagious amongst knights seeking to dominate people. Bishop Diego, for example, charged Pedro Froiláz with pillaging episcopal tenants 'according to military custom,' and there is other evidence to support Canon Girard's weary comment that 'command' entailed 'violence.'[179] Alfonso of Aragon, when he heard that 'some Moors and infidels' in his pillaging army had broken into a religious house and violated nuns before the altar, is said to have replied, 'I

---

[177] *Chronicon Compostellanum*, ed. Henrique Flórez, *ES* xx (1765) 611.
[178] *HC* i.64.3; *CAS* c. 20 (23).
[179] *HC* i.31.8; 114.8; also i.95; *ES* xxxvi, ap. 45; xxxiv, ap. 46.

don't care what my army and my warriors do.'[180] Yet with respect to the general disorder what shocked Girard quite as much as the suffering of peasants, merchants, and pilgrims, and others perhaps even more, was the inconstancy of the princes and lords set over them. Treachery was in plentiful supply. On a notorious occasion in IIII, when Pedro Froiláz, whose wife and ward were besieged in the remote Castrelo do Miño, was trying to secure a Galician consensus to crown Alfonso Raimundez, the barons in opposition persuaded Bishop Diego to help secure a compromise. Following deeply perfidious negotiations, in which rumours of betrayal were constant, the bishop, Mayor de Froiláz, and the child-prince were indeed seized at the moment of settlement by men sworn to the bishop, yet desperately opposed to Pedro Froiláz. It was a grim morality tale for Canon Girard, prolonged by the pillage of the bishop's religious effects—no wonder Girard came to associate betrayal with violence—and remedied by Diego's compact with Pedro to crown Alfonso Raimundez, which was a stinging rebuke to the traitors.[181] The leader of this conspiracy, Pedro Arias, having long since violated his oath of 1107 to Urraca and her son, was by no means done with betraying Bishop Diego. Likewise, with respect to unrest at Sahagún, the Anonymous wrote of the deliverance of the town to Alfonso of Aragon as a betrayal of the lord-abbot.[182] Everywhere, the stress of reward and defeat subverted the sanctity of oaths. Girard came finally to vilify the treachery he knew as an ethnic failing. 'What can I make of the habits of all these Galicians? They are companions to fortune, aroused by success, crushed by adversity. A mere breath of air blows them anywhere; they hold it their highest liberty to change lords and to be rebellious to their lords. They pursue wealth not justice.' They say what the powerful like to hear while putting down their lords. Notable for the 'art of flattering,' they cultivate 'perjury and treachery.'[183]

[180] CAS c. 18 (20).   [181] HC i.48–61.
[182] CAS c. 28 (31).   [183] HC i.108.3.

Once again truth filters through the exaggerated rhetoric. Girard admits as much: 'But these things I have wished to say *pace* the good people of Galicia.'[184] The equally impassioned narrative of Sahagún has a comparable (far from identical) story to tell; and to the extent that oaths of burghers and peasants could be violated like those of knights, it follows that the leitmotiv of treachery in our sources points to a massive crisis of lordship in Queen Urraca's lands. Traitors and 'manifest perjurers' were condemned in a synod at León in October 1114 in chapters adopted by Diego Gelmírez in his own synod a few weeks later.[185]

Here, as in earlier times in France and the eastern Pyrenees, we glimpse the novelty of banal lordship. Knights multiplied in the followings of the dynastic protagonists, and were tempted to exploit the distraints and profits of public power. One revealing sign of this may be read in accounts of the pretensions of rebels. It is true that we know of these assertions only as transmitted by unsympathetic chroniclers. But when both major sources record repeatedly that conspirators wish to rule 'like kings,' it looks as if snatches of plausible gossip are getting through. It was said of the peasants around Sahagún that if some noble happened to favour them, 'they wanted him for their king and lord.'[186] Kingship remained normative in this rustic discourse of power. While lately lordship had *been* kingship, or some form of dominance in agrarian order, the tumultuous circumstances of competing princely armies enabled lords and knights to bargain for their service, settling for no less than the rewards only public 'powers' could offer.

Impulses of defiance, conspiracy, infidelity, and pretentious ambition were widespread along the pilgrims' road in the early twelfth century: in Lugo, Carrión, Burgos, and Palencia between 1110

---

[184]ibid.   [185]Mansi XXI, 113; *HC* i.101.

[186] *CAS* c. 19 (22): 'a tal como aqueste deseauan que fuesse su rrei e señor'; also *HC* i.113.2, 114.3. See also i.114.15, quoted above, p. 243.

and 1117, as well as in Sahagún and Compostela.[187] That they bear witness to broadly societal dislocation continuing thereafter follows from the accounts of dynastic disorder sampled above and has been well shown by modern historians. In the best recorded of these uprisings, those at Sahagún and Compostela, it is possible to discern some distinctive traits of this culture of power.

Sahagún. The troubles that erupted around Sahagún in 1111 lasted until 1117, when Queen Urraca finally won a bitter struggle for the allegiance of the townspeople. They were obliged to renounce their expedient alliance with King Alfonso of Aragon, who had attempted to secure Sahagún with his Aragonese knights and vicars, as a strategic position in León. The failure of his design owed something to Urraca's resourceful resistance, the growing strength of her position once she allied with her young son; but it owed quite as much or more to the nature of the domination the 'Battler' king tried to impose. These events together with much else about the experience of power were narrated by a monk of Sahagún close to the beleaguered abbots in a text that survives today only in a Castilian version made centuries later. Problematic not only in its transmission but also in its silence about the chronology of uprisings, negotiations, and settlements, this first of the 'Anonymous Chronicles of Sahagún' nonetheless informs us about a rebellious society in incomparable detail.[188]

Sahagún was a conspicuous prize for its lord-abbot as well as for the *reyes.* A prestigious Benedictine affiliate of Cluny teeming with merchants and pilgrims, it was the lately consecrated mausoleum of its benefactors, Urraca's parents Alfonso VI and Constança. Their charter of 1085 virtually created the abbatial lordship of Sahagún that was repudiated a few years later. This privilege had done for the abbot what lay castellans had to do for themselves, hence normally by violence: it conveyed regalian powers,

---

[187] *CAS* c. 28 (31); Pastor, *Conflictos sociales* 29–32; Estepa, 'Revueltas burguesas,' 291–95.

[188] *CAS* cc. 18–75 (20–78); Barrero, 'Fueros de Sahagún,' 407–13.

a modest annual levy on householders, and the profits of justice. Disguised as a concession of customs (*foros*) to the people, its clause 'you shall have no lord except the abbot and monks' invites a second reading.[189] Urban interests grew apace with the lordship down to 1109, not without friction, adjustment, and signs of Abbot Diego's enterprise in rural and urban spaces alike.[190]

With the passing of the old king, the blighted marriage of his daughter, and the first signs of her husband's brutality, all this changed. It was surely around Sahagún in 1110 that a violent rebellion broke out. The Anonymous wrote of 'peasants,' workers, and little people' conspiring in a 'brotherhood' (*hermandad*) against their lords, withholding payments and services, compelling adhesion to their union, attacking 'vicars' and other agents, breaking into royal 'palaces' and noble 'houses,' even killing Jews. This rebellion, while it seems to have fizzled for want of allies, revealed the weakness of the abbot's lordship. Confronted by the conspirators when he visited a rural domain, he found the city gates shut against him when he came back, and had to flee to León.[191] A faction of burghers now allied with Alfonso of Aragon, whose knights and camp-followers became notorious pillagers in hostile lands. A capable monk Domingo succeeded Abbot Diego in the convent's poorly defended lordship, a situation worsened when Alfonso of Aragon sent two knights to Sahagún, said now to be well fortified, nominally to defend his allies, in reality to seize patrimonial villages with all necessary force. By 1112 the burghers were emboldened to stir new enmities by demanding conformity to their collective, violating all who resisted, including the monks, and proposing that their princely lords be obliged to swear upon first appearance to uphold new customs of the town's devising.[192]

---

[189] *CDS* III, no. 823.

[190] ibid., nos. 830, 911, 914, 915, 974, 977, 1015, 1064, 1065, etc. See also Romualdo Escalona, *Historia del Real Monasterio de Sahagun* (Madrid 1782 [facsimile reprint 1982]) 80–103.

[191] *CAS* c. 19 (22).   [192] ibid., cc. 23, 24 (26, 27).

After Easter 1112—it was the very Easter when Bishop Gaudry was killed—King Alfonso drove Abbot Domingo out of Sahagún, placed yet another crony knight, Sanchianes, over the monastic lordship, and saw to the distribution of patrimonial units to Aragonese knights. Moreover, the king invited his brother Ramiro—our chronicler calls him a 'false and bad monk'—to come to Sahagún and 'lord it over [se enseñorease] the monks.'[193] Worse, the urban conspiracy now extended to Burgos and Carrión, the townsmen themselves devastating what had been a 'delightful garden-land,' while the dispossessed abbot sought out the queen in distant Aragon.[194] So by 1113 the people of Sahagún, located in a coveted zone of Aragonese ambitions, became the prey of armies in conflict.

From then until 1117 it is even harder to discern a course of local events than before. Possibly the writer himself lost heart or direction, for he seems thereafter to elaborate on the urban conspirators' violence of 1112–13, adding details from later times, but unsure just when Abbot Domingo returned and was again expelled from Sahagún. During his absence in 1114 'all the burghers' trooped into the chapter house and tried in vain to secure the monks' adhesion to their 'charter' of new customs. As late as 1115 King Alfonso came and imposed yet another notable ally to enforce his domination on the town; but reaction then set in, and the burghers lost the support of people they had abused. Many now viewed the abbot and the queen as their protectors; and when Abbot Domingo returned from Rome with papal privileges condemning the uprising, the restoration of old order was in sight.

One point stands clear from this story of local conflict. Plenty of people in Sahagún were eager to undo the abbot's lordship. It is less easy to see why, for the Anonymous understandably says nothing about excesses in the exercise of this power. It is likely that the enhanced monastic domination after 1085 contrasted

[193] ibid., c. 27 (30).
[194] ibid., c. 28 (31). Sanchianes has been identified with the Aragonese baron Sancho Juanes by Ubieto Arteta, c. 31 (54n).

with the relaxed royal oversight it replaced, and all but certain that the abbot moved beyond his chartered rights in imposing on markets, merchants, and pilgrims. His was, in any case, a new lordship in a society swarming with men in need of dependents and shares in their produce.

A brilliant glimpse of this scene figures in chapter 19 of the Anonymous. The ephemeral rural conjuration was aimed at 'lords' and their enabling personnel: *señores* and mayors, vicars, *mayordomos* and *façedores*. Everything that is said of their doings— about services, payments, markets, granges, bread and wine— points to new and more exacting lordships, including the abbot's, as well as the productivity to sustain them. No wonder the Aragonese leaders thought of billeting their knights on these farmlands. Repeatedly, their former fertility and prosperity are mentioned with regret.[195]

All this notwithstanding, it seems to have been lords rather than lordship that stirred unrest. When the burghers of Sahagún, spurning the queen's lordship, called in the Aragonese knights to secure the town, they are said to have exclaimed: 'Who says that the abbot and monks should lord it over such noble barons and such great *burgeses*? Who says they ought to possess such and so big lands, fields, vineyards, and orchards'?[196] To possess lands and vineyards was to possess people, and there is reason to believe that the flattering words just quoted echoed the rebels' attitude. This would explain why we hear nothing of a commune as such, despite some manifest consensus over replacing the abbot's charter with their own 'laws and customs'—perhaps also why many of their urban allies deserted them in the end. Some of the latter must have been the 'very lowly persons,' like smiths and shoemakers, said to have joined the 'rich and, if you like, noble burghers' in one of the insurrections against the abbot and monks. Disparagement of monastic lordship was partisan talk by aspirants to lordship, designed to exploit the most nearly common interest

---

[195] ibid., c. 19 (22); also cc. 28, 33 (31, 36).
[196] ibid., c. 33 (36).

available: reduction of the monastic share in rents, tolls, and the market.[197]

Less salient but equally important matters follow from this preoccupation with lordship. The Anonymous was keenly alert to the problem of ministerial fidelity. He has much to say about vicars, those of the abbot and the queen as well as of Alfonso of Aragon. They together with *caualleros* untitled exemplified coercive force, a mounted police privileged to exploit and distrain; a fearsome, feebly accountable, abrasive intermediary in elite lordships. Only the abbot's vicars were (once) represented as victims; and it is all but certain that the named deputies of Alfonso of Aragon held vicarial (or banal) powers.[198] These men notoriously, but also the rebels, were said to have indulged in violence described in grisly detail in pages that not only form the most astonishing facet of the anonymous monk's record but also pose a considerable problem of interpretation.

What may be called the 'normal violence' of revolt is constantly in evidence: the pillaging of farmlands, sacking of houses, etc. This is what armies did and, if the Anonymous can be trusted, insurgents great and small found the means and allies to do the same.[199] But after 1112—or from chapter 40 in the narrative—his allusions to habitual bellicosity are overtaken by those to angry or vindictive violence, which may be why he wrote, for once reminded of the face of violence the monk of Sahagún recounted brutalities in digressive and obsessive detail.[200] Much of this attached to the hated knights the 'Battler' king sent to dominate the abbey-town. Pelayo Garcia was a 'noble knight but very cruel and without piety or mercy.' Giraldo, who came in 1114, was worse: 'notorious [*torpe*] in all he did, brutal in the will . . . Hideous' to look at, worse yet 'in heart and will . . . Giraldo the Devil he was

---

[197] ibid., cc. 35 (38), 51 (54), 34 (37). A tradition of associative privilege (*fuero*) in León may likewise have mattered.

[198] ibid., cc. 19 (22), 24 (27), 27 (30), 28 (31), 30 (33), 33 (36), 39 (42).

[199] ibid., cc. 19 (22), 24 (27).   [200] ibid., cc. 40–49 (43–52), 66 (69).

called.' He was said to be merciless with indigent captives, who could not pay to avoid afflictive punishments and torture.[201]

But many burghers were complicit in the brutalities associated with this precarious social control. While the Anonymous recalled much about Giraldo's reign of terror, his account of worsening atrocities from 1112–13 is plural and impersonal. Captives were (said to be) physically abused and tortured to the extent of grotesque indecency, and starved. Some they ransomed, for 'in truth many whom they persecuted in these ways were nobles and knights,' but one could not even buy release with assurance. 'Others were middling folk and rich ones and many of those they tortured died.'[202]

It is hard fully to trust an account of such extreme and sustained violence, impossible to reject it. The same note of outrage over much the same behaviour sounds in the records from contemporary Germany and France already sampled, nor is this the last we shall hear of it. Around Sahagún as elsewhere force and pretence converged as mounted armed men multiplied beyond the limits of old public order in a vulnerable prosperity both agrarian and commercial. The swift and seemingly bloodless suppression of dissidence under the monastic lordship is proof in its way that the disposition to abuse *mezquinos*,[203] however inhumane, was not altogether wrong in this seething pool of power.

Compostela. The rising at Compostela was rooted in a natural tension between Queen Urraca and Bishop Diego Gelmírez. Both were claimants to the territorial lordship of Galicia, and there had been signs before 1116 that the bishop's efforts to dominate and pacify were resented by the barons. Even so, some felt safer with his lordship and control of the young Alfonso Raimundez than with the queen's determination to mobilise her realm against the Arago-

[201] ibid., cc. 23 (26), 56 (59). Yet another Giraldo, Viscount Guerau I of Ager (ca. 1068–1131), served Alfonso at Sahagún, c. 23 (26, p. 47n).
[202] ibid., c. 45 (48), and other citations in note 199.
[203] ibid., c. 48 (51).

nese. During a perfidious negotiation with Diego, Urraca lost his trust so as to face a formidable alliance of her son, crowned by the bishop, and Diego himself. At this point the spiraling inconstancy of all parties wrecked a fragile peace. The queen incited a faction of townspeople, including dissident canons and priests, to resist the bishop, whose lordship was badly disrupted in 1116.[204] When Diego attempted to exploit his acquisition of the head of Saint James, a radicalized element of the opposition refused to confuse religious and temporal powers. Along with other provocations this turned the rebels against the queen and bishop together. In the spring of 1117 they were virtually besieged in a bell-tower of the cathedral. Urraca, betrayed by the people and her fellow captive alike, was physically abused in retreat from the tower; while Diego, in a tale echoing that of Bishop Gaudry's ill-fated flight in the cathedral of Laon, barely eluded his captors.[205]

In the following hours the rebels lost control of the mob they had incited, yet still tried to secure the queen's approval for a settlement at the bishop's expense. Canon Girard was well informed about deliberations within a *hermandad* to which some of Diego's unfaithful men adhered. Their failure to capture the bishop was critical, for once he and Urraca were safely outside the city, the rebels faced newly antagonized armies that encouraged reaction and imposed submission. The queen urged vengeance in view of the violence—some notables had been killed, including Diego's brother and several officials, and she herself abused—but Diego had his way with a deliberate settlement: abolition of the brotherhood, a biggish indemnity of 1100 silver marks, and the restitution of property. Rebel leaders were expelled, their property confiscated—a consequence not without bearing on the future, and one resembling the near simultaneous outcome at Sahagún.[206]

This revolt was more like the communal risings in France than that of Sahagún. The oath was central, and associative purpose is

---

[204] *HC* i.111.1,2. [205] ibid. i.112–14.
[206] ibid. i.114.8,13; 115, 116; ii.53.6; Fletcher, *Saint James's catapult* 185–89.

visible in the efforts to secure episcopal revenues, to fortify, to enforce collective loyalty. But Girard's account, for all its partisan excess, very plausibly—indeed, all but helplessly—represents the rebels as wishing to take over the bishop's lordship. Perfidious men do not destroy lordship, they—like the Galicians—change lords. That the contradiction in such behaviour occurred to some in the heady moments of associative resolve is altogether likely; but nothing of that slipped through our partisan source.

While it had its perilous moments, this was not a desperate rebellion. It lacked the savagery of Sahagún, perhaps because its leaders were less tempted to exploit peasants. The exiles lived to cause the bishop further headaches; and what may be more instructive, Diego, who achieved metropolitan status in 1120, became the subject of further discontent in 1127 and more seriously in 1136. Twice again urban notables and clergy in Compostela challenged the ageing prelate, going so far in 1136 as to deprive him of his lordship and drive him nastily out of his city. The later events confirm our sense of 1116–17, that what motivated rebels in this pilgrim city was the reality of a lord-bishop imposing heavily on urban trades and revenues, the spectacle of an enormously ambitious, vain, and clever climber exploiting religious power in service of a thoroughly worldly lordship.[207]

THESE STRUGGLES on the pilgrims' road have defied efforts to categorize them. Formerly viewed as 'communal' or 'anti-feudal' revolts, they can now be grasped as consequences rather than creative enterprises.[208] They were the growing pains of societies wherein lordship, dependence, and the fragility of fidelity were even more novel and threatening than in France after 1100. In

[207] HC iii.46–47; Fletcher 189–91.

[208] Luis Vázquez de Parga, 'La revolución comunal de Compostela en los años 1116 y 1117,' AHDE xvi (1945), 685–703; Estepa, 'Revueltas burguesas'; and Portella and Pallares, 'Revueltas feudales.'

Spain the old public order lay in a more recent past. It was symptomatic that when in 1110, according to the monk of Sahagún, Alfonso of Aragon came to Astorga on his way out of Galicia the 'counts and nobles' met him in arms 'and warned that, as he valued his life, he should stick to the public road and not enter any castle or stronghold' of theirs.[209] What happened at Sahagún was not class warfare, nor were the solidarities in Compostela, not even the 'brotherhood' (*germanitas*), more than flickering alliances. Kingship persisted even as it lapsed: were not the conspirators in the chapter-house exerting power over all 'as if they were kings'? Perhaps not accidentally the identities of ringleaders and purposes, in both Compostela and Sahagún, are obscure. What is recorded were structural 'crises' of power in which temptations and dangers abounded. If these were 'feudal societies,' then the uprisings, so far from being 'anti-feudal,' were precisely '(pro-)feudal' revolts.[210] Oppression and suppression, as well as the fief,[211] were in the air. Here as elsewhere there was something abrasive about the experience of lordship. On her way to Compostela in 1116, Queen Urraca took time out 'to crack down on the arrogance' of the castellan Menendo Núñez, who was pillaging the district.[212]

FLANDERS: THE MURDER OF CHARLES THE GOOD (1127–28)

> What madness, Oh serfs, drove you to this?
> Like Judas you have betrayed your lord.
> —*A monk's 'sad song'*[213]

On 2 March 1127, while alone in prayer in his castle-chapel of Saint Donatian in Bruges, Count Charles of Flanders was brutally

---

[209] *CAS* c. 21 (24). Intimidated, the king chose two of them to get him out.
[210] As Portella and Pallares well saw, 333.
[211] Above, p. 100.   [212] *HC* i.107.1.
[213] ed. Henri Pirenne, *Histoire du meurtre de Charles le Bon, comte de Flandre (1127–1128), par Galbert de Bruges suivie de poésies latines contemporaines* (Paris 1891) 188.

murdered. The killer was one Borsiard, who, however, was far from acting alone; he was the nephew of the count's provost Bertulf and one of a flock of 'nephews' descended from Erembald, formerly castellan of Bruges (ca. 1067–ca. 1089). From the beginning few doubted the complicity of the Erembald clan. Their crime, matched in notoriety only by—perhaps not even by—the murder of Thomas Becket in 1170 precipitated the most tumultuous crisis of power in the twelfth century. It plunged Flemish society into terrifying disorder marked by reprisals and the struggle of rival claimants to secure the succession to Count Charles.[214]

Yet it should now be evident that, however disruptive its consequences, this was a 'normal' crisis in its day. As in Maine (1062), Carcassonne (1067), León (1109), and Tuscany (1115), the death of a lord-prince without heir was enough to incite a foreigner to help himself to power. As late as 1125, the Flemings could share such anxiety with the English and the Germans; and the English crisis was hardly so much resolved as renewed when, only a few weeks before the murder of Count Charles, King Henry I compelled his barons to swear recognition of his daughter Matilda. Yet it is only in the perspective of history that the dynastic crisis in Flanders can be seen to have preceded the death of the Lord-Count Charles.

For contemporaries, to take them at their word, lived through it diversely; and their despair sounds for once in so many written accounts as to bring us close, indeed, to *their* experience of power. What rings through their lamentations is the sheer horror of a crime that can only put older readers of this page in mind of 22 November 1963. This was the Kennedy assassination of the twelfth century: a young, proven, and popular ruler perfidiously cut down in his prime. But no modern parallel can quite measure

---

[214] Walter of Thérouanne, *Vita Karoli comitis . . .* , ed. R. Köpke (Hanover 1856), cc. 1, 25; Galbert of Bruges (to be cited by chapter from editions by Pirenne and Jeff Rider, and the translation-edition by J. B. Ross, q.v. in bibliography) cc. 15, 12; Heriman of Tournai, *Liber de restauratione* cc. 28–30; and generally Warlop, *Flemish nobility* 1, ch. 4.

the dimensions of the Flemings' revulsion in March 1127. 'In the second week of Lent,' wrote a monk in Ghent, 'when Count Charles was kneeling before his altar, his servants killed him. He was succeeded by William, son of Count Robert of Normandy.' The annalist was less verbose about 1128: 'Count William died. Thierry succeeded.'[215]

In these few words the monk summed up the crisis as well as the crime that precipitated it; summed up, that is, a story that took one Galbert, a notary of Bruges who lived through the turmoil, some 175 vibrant pages to tell. Yet Galbert's account of the crime is not only substantially the same as that of the monk-annalist; with respect to its emotional force it is identical. And that is what must be underscored, for only so can we recover the truth of this past so profoundly unlike our own. The horror of March 1127 was not simply that the lamented lord-count was a good prince, was not simply that his murder was an outrageous violation of sanctuary. Beyond these lay something else that even the reticent notice of Ghent made clear: Count Charles of Flanders was murdered *by his 'servants'* (*servi*)! No mere breach of law and public order, this was to shatter a social order, to strike at the God-ordained hierarchy of power and status.[216]

So it is permissible to distinguish, with the afflicted Flemings, between the misfortune of dynastic crisis and the outrage of murderous infidelity. These were systemic dislocations situated on either side of nobility, suffered by some, craved by others. The first task of those who were outraged was to identify, corner, capture, and punish the 'traitors' (as they called them, *traditores*). And because their need of executive force coincided with the desire to restore public order, the story of retribution merged with that of

---

[215] *Annales Blandinienses*, ed. Philip Grierson, *Les annales de Saint-Pierre de Gand et de Saint-Amand* (Brussels 1937) 39. See also Galbert, cc. 1–16; Walter of Thérouanne, cc. 26–27; *Liber de restauratione* cc. 28–29.

[216] Galbert; Walter of Thérouanne, *Vita Karoli*; *An. Bland.* 39; *Liber de restauratione* c. 30, who stress the violence; plus poems and epitaphs, ed. Pirenne 177–91.

succession. By the time this happened—Galbert was far along in his journal of events before he began to think historically—both stories were in process of eclipsing that of the genesis of the crisis arising from a murder.[217]

The events of this crisis, rendered famous to modern readers by Galbert's incomparable journal, need detain us hardly longer than they did the monk of Ghent. Once the custody of the count's venerated body was assured and the aggrieved people of Bruges had secured allies for tracking down the murderers, interest shifted to the succession (May–June 1127). King Louis VI moved circumspectly—might he have remembered his own futility in the crisis of Laon?—and won recognition of William Clito, the grandson of Matilda of Flanders and William the Conqueror, as count.[218] This was to thwart the ambitions of William of Ypres and Thierry of Alsace, both of whom claimed descent in the co-mital family, and was undone when William Clito, insensitive to the pleas of his townspeople, forfeited his advantage. Lapsing into conflict with Thierry, Count William was mortally wounded in a skirmish at Aalst in July 1128, opening the way to Thierry's succession.[219]

Considered as a crisis of power, the murder of Charles the Good and its aftermath exhibited two profoundly novel features. Neither was born of the moment but only revealed; this for once was true revelation. First, the guilty Erembalds were exposed by the excess of their ambitions as an extended family of immense patrimonial wealth. They had prospered in service to the counts of Flanders since the 1070s, when the castellan Erembald was said to have been engaged on fiscal work in the palace of Bruges.[220] The generation of his sons, foremost among them Bertulf the provost, had been so enriched by patrimonial favour as to enable

---

[217] Galbert cc. 15–67, 72–85; Pirenne, *Histoire du meurtre*, p. x. See also Ross, *Galbert of Bruges . . .* 63–75.

[218] Galbert cc. 47–53; Walter cc. 44–48.

[219] Galbert cc. 88–122; Walter cc. 48–49.

[220] Hariulf, *Vita Arnulfi* ii.19 (1416–17).

them to form followings of their own. In a brilliant brush-stroke, as if from life, Galbert described Bertulf's haughty manner with newcomers to his presence; and while the notary's animus against the clan distorts his characterization, his account of their methods and cohesion conforms with much other evidence.[221] By Bertulf's day they were an affective force, at once a lordship and a *familia*, the nephews and brothers (Borsiard, Isaac, Didier Hackett) nurtured in knighthood, but comprising also friends and servants; and if it cannot be shown that a conspiracy was sworn as such, the dependencies grounded in patrimonial favour were surely sworn and in some cases even vassalic.[222] The Erembalds, counting allies not of their blood, were a lordship wholly characteristic of the age. What we know of Bertulf's simony is of a piece with the ambitions deplored by the reformers a generation before. These people were tolerable if not quite respectable, their names peeking forth from records that let us glimpse their service in an upwardly mobile society.[223]

What goaded them into defiant cohesion was the charge that they were of unfree status. This cannot have been new in 1127, but it took on ominous meaning when a free knight declined a challenge to single combat against a knight named Robert of Creques who was married to a niece of Bertulf the provost. The count may have worsened matters by subjecting the Erembalds to a judicial inquiry resulting in a finding of their servitude. A hint of what was at stake may be glimpsed in Galbert's commentary. First, he told how the disparaged knight (Robert) was grieved to learn that a marriage he had supposed would make him 'freer' (*liberior*) was turning out to do the reverse. Was this not—whether on the knight's part or on Galbert's—virtually to equate freedom with power and wealth? Galbert goes on to describe Bertulf's 'arrogant'

---

[221] Galbert cc. 13 and (on Erembald's sinful ways) 71; Warlop, *Flemish nobility*, I, ch. 4.

[222] Galbert c. 13; Walter c. 14.

[223] Galbert cc. 7–13, 15–21, 25, 30, 36–39, 46, 48, 57, 71, 73, 80, 84, 92; Walter cc. 11, 14–19; *ACF* pp. lii, liv, lxxxii; nos. 25, 33, 76, etc.

and blustering insistence on his family's freedom. And once the count, perhaps characteristically open in his rectitude, had revealed his intention to impose new discipline on his overmighty servants, a murderous conspiracy ripened.[224]

The Erembalds were by no means the only lineage bucking for power in their way and their day. In France knights of the Garlande family had come so to dominate the royal household functions as to precipitate a crisis in the same year as the Flemish plot. When Etienne de Garlande attempted to endow a niece when she married Amaury IV of Montfort with his proprietary claim to the seneschalsy, King Louis VI reacted swiftly by dismissing him, confiscating his tenures, and capturing his stronghold of Livry. Unheard of amongst this king's favourites, this was treatment hitherto reserved for bad castellans; and from the little we know of this emergency, Louis would seem to have been acting on the lesson he had lately learned about the disastrous ambitions of Bertulf in Flanders. The disgrace of Seneschal Etienne can be dated to the later months of 1127. The analogy runs deep, for the Garlandes like the Erembalds had trafficked in clerical patrimonies, touching off murderous feuds in France; it extends even to the violent proscription of the Garlandes. Yet there, too, the analogy ends. Louis VI remembered the service and fidelity of ambitious knights who were neither murderous nor serfs. Etienne de Garlande recovered the chancery in 1132, but that was all.[225] In England the rise—and fall—of an episcopal 'dynasty' under Roger of Salisbury (1102–39) was altogether comparable, as will soon appear.[226]

A second novelty of the Flemish crisis relates to its settlement. The glory of Galbert's record is its sustained witness to the play of

---

[224] Galbert cc. 7, 8, 25; Walter cc. 14–15.

[225] Suger, *Vita* c. 31; Chronique de Morigny ii.12 (43–47); Luchaire, *Louis VI*, nos. 399, 426, 505, 519 (and index for Etienne de G.); Bournazel, *Gouvernement capétien* 35–40, 112, and ch. 3.

[226] Edward J. Kealey, *Roger of Salisbury viceroy of England* (Berkeley 1972), esp. 272–76; and below, pp. 284–85.

human forces in the absence of 'natural lordship.'[227] Here for once the interests of the afflicted and the fugitives alike were laid bare as they scrambled for allies and as their expedient aims changed. Not that the vacuum of power was new as such; it could be glimpsed in Maine before 1100, more than once, and was indeed an occupational hazard of dynastic failure everywhere. Yet only Flanders had its Galbert, and by the 1120s this scene of manifest urban prosperity may have lent itself to the strategies of collaborative action that look so new in Galbert's pages.

That we should avoid the temptation of locating the origins of political behaviour in the Flemish crisis was made clear by Jan Dhondt half a century ago in articles that retain all their value.[228] The 'powers' (*puissances*) he discerned were quite diversely 'solid,' and perhaps most typically fragile. Foremost was the *potentia* of the prince with his dependent barons, knights, merchants, and towns. This was a lordship, its vitality inherent in binding fidelities, and its newly associative dynamic unleashed upon the lord-count's death. Seemingly more coherent was an urban solidarity manifest notably in the preferences of individual towns for this or that claimant to the principality: the Brugeois for Thierry (son of the countess of Holland), the people of Oudenaarde for Baldwin IV of Hainaut, those of Ghent for Thierry of Alsace, and so on. Yet theirs was a cohesion rooted in local communities—some of them communes of associatively sworn members—none too durable in the first place and prone to factional division. Only once or twice do we read of allied towns, never of all the towns, as a representation of Flanders. Still less were the Flemish clergy a 'power' as such, although Galbert is explicit about the fiercely protective interest of the community of Saint Donatian in their possession of the count's body.[229]

---

[227] Such as Count Charles had exercised, Galbert, prologue: 'naturalis noster dominus et princeps.'

[228] Jan Dhondt, 'Les "solidarités" médiévales. Une société en transition: la Flandre en 1127–1128,' *Annales: E.S.C.* XII (1957), 529–60; idem, ' "Ordres" ou "puissances," L'exemple des états de Flandre,' *Annales* . . . V (1950) 289–305.

[229] Galbert cc. 22–25; Dhondt, ' "Solidarités" ' 537–45.

It follows that the most cohesive and energized solidarity of all was that of the lineage and, concretely, that of the Erembalds. Their enemies the Straten were forced into their own desperate cohesion, their alliance with the castellan of Dixmude, the lord of Woumen, pointing to a confrontation of forces under the lordship yet beyond the control of Count Charles. The disintegration of these solidarities following the murder is one of Galbert's themes.[230]

These solidarities of interest only work (for us) conceptually as they once worked in practise: as bondings nurtured in lordship. It is in this sense that the murder of Charles the Good precipitated (or worsened) a crisis of lordship, not a political experiment. One chronicler noted that Count William succeeded 'by the election of the princes and the connivance of King Louis.'[231] As the German election of 1125 had shown, with Count Charles himself in the wings, princely 'solidarity' was a house of cards in a draughty waiting-room; it masked dissensions themselves forming new and equally vulnerable compacts of fidelity. The count's lordship of vassals, an element of what Dhondt called the 'princely solidarity,' was more secure, its ritual significance stunningly lighted up by Galbert's record of the homages-with-fealty tendered to William Clito on 6–8 April 1127.[232] Yet the successive counts' castellans and tenants in homage and fidelity seem to have been a flimsy solidarity at best, and no community at all. It was expedient for these lords on the take to serve the count, hardly a collective interest, still less a quasi-public obligation. Barons came to the siege of Bruges with their own followings.[233]

By contrast, lordship over the conspirators and sworn dependence on them were in conformity with their interest. It was the

---

[230] Galbert cc. 7–11, 16–92; Walter cc. 14–26, 40–42.

[231] [Sigiberti Gemblacensis] Continuatio Praemonstratensis, ed. L. C. Bethmann, MGHSS VI (1844) 450. On the king as lord of the Flemish barons, see also Galbert cc. 47, 59, 60.

[232] Galbert cc. 55, 56; see also c. 104.

[233] ibid., c. 31; Walter cc. 33, 36.

Erembalds' fidelity that enriched them, its breach that aroused unsettling horror.[234] On 17 March 1127 the castellan Hackett, pleading for mercy before men of the siege, admitted that his sympathy of 'blood-kinship' was in conflict with his recognition of the killers' guilt; he was promptly rebutted by his knight Walter, who defied him and them as men 'without faith [or] law,' whereupon many others of the siege ritually cast off their homage and loyalty to the besieged.[235] Galbert reflectively dilated on the irony of the situation when, having violated the sanctuary of Saint Donatian, 'those serfs who had impudently and fraudulently betrayed the most worthy consul of the land, were shut in with their lord [that is, besieged with his corpse], although against their will to be confined with their lord consul.'[236] Terror and danger worked to reinforce familial bonds that had first prospered in faithful dependence; they had nothing to offer a crumbling following.

WHAT HAD begun as a crisis of disrupted lordship ended in 1128 with a crisis of renewed lordship. Were the townsfolk right to see, or at least suspect, that William Clito was no Charles the Good? They alleged that Count William or his castellans had imposed new exactions or otherwise mistreated them. It is striking that, whereas Charles in his known enactments had been settling disputes and confirming rights, Count William was pressed from the start to confirm or grant urban customs. His charters to Aardenburg and Saint-Omer (April 1127) responded foremost to fears of arbitrary demands;[237] and when the burghers of Saint-Omer and Ghent rebelled by turns in February 1128, the grievance in both cases was of allegedly brutal castellans imposed

---

[234] The breach occurred long before March 1127, according to Heriman of Tournai, *Liber* c. 29.

[235] Galbert c. 38.   [236] ibid., c. 43.

[237] ibid., cc. 55, 66; that of Bruges almost certainly likewise, c. 55.

or to be imposed by the count.[238] If this is all that Galbert says about arbitrary lordship, it is enough to remind us of the violence so close to the surfaces of power even in this firmly dominated land.[239]

Of lord-princes who evoked associative responses in Flanders, King Louis VI was the most conspicuous. He twice convoked the magnates, first in March 1127 to urge the election of William Clito, then again a year later in a futile effort to rescue his foundering ally.[240] But these interventions did little to foster territorial cohesion; the effectual groupings arose from shoulder-to-shoulder deeds in the siege and prosecution of the traitors and from dissatisfactions with Count William. The latter had been a strategic choice for the king in his larger conflict with Henry I, yet one could hardly have asked for more than Louis offered: to help the Flemish elite to elect a suitable count so as to remedy the real and worsening dangers in the land. Whatever the subsequent suspicions of his Flemish intervention,[241] in March 1127 he had acted to secure the succession, not to claim it.

The Flemish crisis of 1127–28 was one of lordship, not of polity. Associative commitments lacked the solemnity of personal ones; infidelity was treachery, the murderers insistently 'traitors.' The ease with which lesser men had renounced their lords during the siege of Bruges must have been contagious. When disputes arose over the jurisdiction of delicts, the men of Bruges were quick to claim their right; even in one heated moment, says Galbert, to disclaim the lordship of anyone at all.[242] Very likely the concessions of urban tribunals to Bruges and Saint-Omer in April 1127 were prompted by seizures in the name of the count or king at this moment when urgency induced self-reliance.[243] Charters

[238] ibid., cc. 94, 95. Lille had rebelled in August 1127, c. 93; and the Brugeois were soon thereafter in conflict with Count William, c. 88.

[239] See above, pp. 151–52.

[240] Galbert cc. 47, 106; Walter c. 44; *Liber de restauratione* c. 32.

[241] See below, p. 301.   [242] Galbert c. 59.

[243] ibid., cc. 59, 66; *ACF* no. 127.

remained concessions, nonetheless. Once William's lordship was contested and the mythic aura of Caroline domination faded, pretenders easily found supporters. 'It was wonderful,' observed Galbert of Bruges in March 1128, 'that Flanders could take on so many lords at once, the boy from Mons [Baldwin of Hainaut] and Arnold [nephew of Count Charles], the one now waiting at Ghent [Thierry], and that oppressive count of ours [William].'[244] Wonderful, indeed!

ENGLAND (1135–54): 'WHEN CHRIST AND HIS SAINTS SLEPT'

Was it so different in England? Only a few years later Abbot Gilbert of Gloucester would exclaim: 'we suffer from as many kings as strongholds to oppress us'; and William of Newburgh was to echo the idea: 'There were as many kings, or rather tyrants, as there were lords of castles.'[245] Was it so different, after all, *anywhere* else? In Burgundy Peter the Venerable lamented the state of a land 'without king or prince' in 1138; while the Normandy of Robert seemed to Orderic Vitalis, writing in 1133–35, to have been an 'Israel without king or duke.'[246] The proliferation of fortified dominations was a generic phenomenon by the third decade of the twelfth century. A consequence of crises, as we have seen, yet not only that. No contested succession was required for the castellans in Capetian France to assert themselves.

Nor, it may be argued here, was it necessary in England. It is true that the reign of Stephen resulted from a dynastic crisis—yet another, and not least, in our series—and to the extent that conflicting claims on fickle loyalties brought on the violence of warfare, we may attribute a troubled experience of power after

---

[244] Galbert c. 96; the same point in cc. 99, 121.

[245] *The letters and charters of Gilbert Foliot . . .* , ed. Z. N. Brooke, Adrian Morey, C. N. L. Brooke (Cambridge 1967) no. 26; William of Newburgh, *Historia rerum Anglicarum* i.22; ed. Richard Howlett, *Chronicles of the reigns of Stephen, Henry II, and Richard I*, 4 vols. (London 1884–89) I, 69.

[246] *LPV* I, no. 21; OV viii.15 (IV, 228).

1135 to the death of King Henry's legitimate male heir and to a failure of baronial consensus in recognition of Matilda. When Stephen of Blois invaded England in December 1135, he instantly challenged the barons and prelates who had sworn recognition of Matilda. Plausibly justifying his seizure of the crown and treasure, the pretender promised good lord-kingship; he pressed dissident barons; undercut the positions of bishop-barons, notably Roger of Salisbury, and others who owed much to the late king; resisted Matilda's legitimist Angevin invasion; gradually prevailed in a 'dynastic' conflict, thanks in part to Matilda's insufferable affectations of domination; then settled in the end for recognition of Matilda's son Henry as the rightful successor to Anglo-Norman power.[247]

This history of events is well known. Stephen's reign is a favourite subject of historians. Some have argued that, in spite of evidence to the contrary, Stephen ruled, indeed governed, throughout his reign, and that the routines of exchequer and shires persisted, however disrupted. Few have doubted, however, and one or two have lately urged, that the celebrated lamentations of disorder in contemporary records have some basis in historical experience.[248] And once this subject is approached by way of continental European history, it can be seen that the 'anarchy' under Stephen— and this venerable concept dates *from* the reign, we now know— differs from 'disorders' elsewhere chiefly in the abundance of its contemporary testimonies.

The most celebrated of these, a post-regnal lamentation by the Old English annalist of Peterborough, has been quoted above (p. 60). It is arguably the consummate medieval expression of 'feudal revolution.' What matters here is that its indignant allegations of forsworn violence, unlicensed fortification, constraints of service

[247] On the reign of Stephen see David Crouch, *The reign of King Stephen, 1135–1154* (Harlow 2000); and *The anarchy of King Stephen's reign*, ed. Edmund King (Oxford 1994).

[248] Besides Crouch, see Donald Matthew, *King Stephen* (London 2002), and chiefly *Anarchy*, ed. King, 1–6 (King), and ch. 1 (C. W. Hollister).

(including castle-building) and payment, extortions, and cruelties are replicated in many other English records. The Peterborough monk drew on one or more of these, notably that of William of Malmesbury writing in 1142; and the latter's sense of the 'asperity of war' in 1140—multiplying castles, seizures for ransom, pillage—figures in other early accounts by John of Worcester, the anonymous author of the *Gesta Stephani*, and Orderic Vitalis.[249]

These accounts take on added meaning in comparative perspectives. They resonate with continental expressions of dismay in face of crises of power and violence in Saxony, León, and Normandy during the years just past. English writers could generalize (and exaggerate) with the best of their counterparts, such as Ekkehard of Aura, and say much the same things, because they were living through the same wider crisis of multiplied knights and castles. The worst of it in England, indeed, was imported. William of Malmesbury deplored the influx of 'knights of every description, and lightly armed men, especially from Flanders and Brittany . . . men of the most rapacious and violent sort. . . .' It is no accident that protection-money, a scourge of the time almost everywhere in Latin Europe, came to England in its French dress: *tenserie* (=*tensamentum*).[250]

In England as elsewhere castle-building, seizures and imprisonments for ransom, and protection-money became normal after 1137. Widely experienced and deplored at the time, they were not

[249] For good samplings of the evidence see Edmund King, 'The anarchy of King Stephen's reign,' *TRHS* 5th ser. XXXIV (1984), 133–53; and Robert Bartlett, *England under the Norman and Angevin kings, 1075–1225* (Oxford 2000) 283–86. Also *HN* c. 483; JW III, 216–18; *GS* c. 78 (et passim); OV xiii.19 (VI, 450, 452).

[250] See above, pp. 60–61; *HN* c. 463; and on *tensamentum*, *Chronique de Morigny* i.2 (6); *RAL6* I, no. 124; II, no. 409; *PUE* II, no. 36; *RRAN* III, no. 233; *C&S* i:2, 823. See also J. H. Round, *Geoffrey de Mondeville. A study of the anarchy* (London 1892) 414–16; and Flach, *Origines de l'ancienne France* I, 402–5. Fuller discussion in T. N. Bisson, 'The lure of Stephen's England: *tenserie*, Flemings, and a crisis of circumstance,' *King Stephen's reign*, ed. Dalton, White (2008) 171–81.

soon forgotten. What is distinctive about the generalized indignation in England is that it long reverberated as the recollection of a crisis that had passed. No doubt this owed something to the determination of Henry II (1154–89) to promote his restorationist image, but the recurrent tales of violence in dreadful days past have the looks of authentic local traditions. In the 1170s a clerk of Beverley wrote of the magnate Robert de Stuteville imprisoning the son of a Lincoln man for ransom, while the monk Reginald of Durham recalled how knights in Nottingham had been incited by their lord to pillage and steal cattle in Saint Cuthbert's patrimony; and both writers went out of their ways to explain, at some length, that it was *like* this during the reign of Stephen.[251]

The English laments bear a peculiar relation to traditions of disorder in Normandy. Although Orderic Vitalis wrote incessantly about the troubles of 'unhappy Normandy,'[252] he clung stubbornly to his belief that the violence generated by Norman barons and castellans was disorderly and rebellious. Repeatedly, Henry I is said to restore the 'peace' in Normandy—in 1107, 1119, 1124, 1128—and so to lose it when he died in 1135.[253] This belief, while it cannot have been wholly mistaken, is surely misleading. For Orderic also insisted that in the duke-king's absence the Normans lapsed repeatedly into self-destructive violence. At Easter 1105 Henry arrived in Carentan to find a besieged church full of peasant belongings. In 1119 Hugh of Gournay, while undoubtedly betraying the lord-duke who had knighted him, found the support of no fewer than eighteen castellans in a resistance that looks more like truculent seigneurial aggrandisement than rebel-

---

[251] [William Ketell], *Alia miracula* [*S. Johannis episcopi*] . . . , ed. James Raine, *The historians of the church of York and its archbishops*, 3 vols. (London 1879–94) I, 302–3; Reginald of Durham, . . . *Libellus de admirandis beati Cuthberti virtutibus*, ed. James Raine (London 1835) c. 67, and see also cc. 49, 50 (my thanks to R. Bartlett for these references); and for Selby's experience of a bad castle, Bartlett, *England* 284–85.

[252] OV xi.11, xiii.32 (VI, 60, 492).

[253] ibid. xi.11, 21–23; xii.39, 45–46; xiii.19 (VI, 60, 92–98, 346–56, 368–80, 448–52).

lion. The lapse of Waleran of Beaumont in 1124, replete with gratuitous brutality towards peasants, has the same appearance.[254] Accordingly, Orderic's flights of lamentation referred mostly to the regimes of Robert (1087–97, 1101–06) and of Stephen after 1135. This is what misleads, for the constant subtext of this great chronicle is that not even Henry I succeeded in mastering the Normans after the Conqueror's death.[255] Seldom was he without rivals to local power in the viscounties and castellanies, nor were the churches fully secure; for what Orderic virtually proves is that, in Normandy as in France and every other northern province except Flanders, many barons and castellans, struggling to secure and consolidate patrimonies and lordships, were prepared to defy lord-princes to that end. It is the duke-king who *returns* to rescue and pacify, not the absent one, whom Orderic commends; and while Hollister was surely right to identify a solidarity of great baronial support in Normandy, rendering the overthrow of Robert of Bellême in 1112 a critical event of the reign, this was, nonetheless, as Stenton well saw, an 'enforced obedience.'[256]

※

IN THE end Orderic's voice sounded his weariness of war. His regret for the collapse of peace under Stephen is full of military noise, full of the abrasive to-and-fro of hungry, brutal retinues and armies, of the cruel tactic of pillaging an adversary's tenants. That was how he remembered his Norman past, making no explicit

---

[254] ibid. xi.11, xii.3, 39 (VI, 60–62, 190–92, 346–48); David Crouch, *The Beaumont twins . . .* (Cambridge 1986) 17–18.

[255] Nor does Orderic really claim so in his hexameter eulogy of Henry, xiii.19 (VI, 450–52). See the earlier lamentations in (OV) viii.1, 4, 9, 12 (IV, 112–14, 146–48, 178, 198); x.17 (V, 300); xi.23 (VI, 98).

[256] On lawless violence in a ruler's absence see OV xi.11, 16, 22 (VI, 60, 74, 96), etc. Also viii.2 (IV, 132); C. W. Hollister, 'Henry I and the Anglo-Norman magnates,' in *Monarchy, magnates, and institutions in the Anglo-Norman world* (London 1986) ch. 10; and Stenton, *First century* 257.

distinction between the violences of lordship and war. Exaggerating the merits of King Henry's protectorate, he overlooked the persistence of magnate ambitions.[257] Plenty of men were ready to try their luck where Robert of Bellême and Waleran of Meulan had (finally) failed (and the former's years of success may have been as exemplary as his downfall), although of this perspective little has filtered through to us.[258] One of the chroniclers, however, saw more clearly than the others what the succession crisis meant for the exercise and experience of power in England.

This chronicler was the author of the *Gesta Stephani*, most likely Bishop Robert of Bath, and what he saw was that the conflict of fidelities was an invitation to the ambitious to enlarge and consolidate their lordships. Their resistance to Stephen, in whom they could see something of themselves, was not simply depraved insurgency, for it was touched as well with plausible if luckless initiatives. There is grudging admiration in the *Gesta*'s depiction of Richard fitz Gilbert's massive lordship in Wales, replete with vassals and castles; and regret for Miles de Beauchamp, castellan of Bedford, who was goaded by the king's demands—the author implies that they were less than tactful—into 'shamelessly robbing the townsmen and their neighbours, whom formerly he had spared as his own dependants.'[259]

What impresses most is the severely realistic treatment of Stephen's baronial adversaries, whose styles and methods of domination are described in nuanced detail. Payn fitz John and Miles of Gloucester, having risen thanks to Henry I, had created border lordships along the Severn exploiting judicial means and forced services. The self-indulgent knight Robert of Bampton (North Devon) tried to dominate by violent constraints from his castle;

---

[257] OV viii.8 (IV, 178), xii.39 (VI, 346, 348), xiii.19 (VI, 452): 'Tollere quisque cupit iam passim res alienas, / Rebus in iniustis en quisque relaxat habenas'; xiii.32 (VI, 492, 494).

[258] See generally Le Patourel, *Norman empire* 77, 84–85, 293; and Crouch, *Beaumont twins*, ch. 1.

[259] *GS* cc. 9, 23. JW recorded Stephen's assaults on Exeter and Bedford with no mention of the rebel lordships there established, III, 218, 234–36.

in this case, for once, we learn that he was convicted at law and lost his castle. King Stephen had been obliged to suppress William fitz Odo, 'a man richly endowed . . . who lived very frugally in peacetime, never taking provisions from neighbours in the customary way,' but who when strife arose in the realm, joined others in revolt.[260] A model of soldiers of fortune deploying violence in service of new lordship is found in the story of the Flemings Henry de Caldret and his brother Ralph, who raged oppressively in Gloucestershire. Securing castles, they 'imposed a yoke of the most dreadful servitude on all by imposing forced labour of diverse kinds and by many other sorts of exaction,' and perpetrating thefts, pillage, and killings.[261]

This mode of 'bad lordship' cannot have been universal in Stephen's England, nor does the *Gesta Stephani* imply that it was. But the latter is one of the testimonies that bears out the Peterborough lamentation with respect to forced levies and protection-money, which are indeed widely attested and may well have been associated with foreign knights. The association is likewise explicit in the *Gesta*'s own chapter of general lament, which has the further interest of defining a veritable typology of militant dominations. Foremost was that of opposed and passing armies, inevitably destructive of the economic adjustment of existing lordships. Geoffrey de Mandeville, once stripped of the Tower of London and other castles, was no less conspicuous than Robert of Gloucester or Matilda; gathering up knights 'in faith and homage' as well as 'thieves' from all over, he exercised a moveable destructive domination in the Fenlands, pillaging Cambridge, desecrating churches, and turning Ramsey abbey into 'a castle for himself.' There was the zealous expansionist lordship of rebel barons who, like William de Mohun in 1139, made insurgency the excuse to raid inland from his coastal castle, compelling submission by cruel force. The most intractable of such magnates was Baldwin de Redvers at

---

[260] *GS* c. 12; see also cc. 42, 44, and cc. 14 and 38.
[261] ibid., c. 96; *Letters of Gilbert Foliot*, no. 27. See generally Crouch, *Reign of King Stephen* 112, 150, 152–54 on baronial purposes.

Exeter (1136), for whom the moment of truth in staring down King Stephen seems to have turned his head. In a few crisply engaging words the *Gesta* tells how Baldwin affected a new arrogance, as peacemaker surrounded by knights, demanding submissions to his 'lordship' (*dominium*) from townsfolk and villagers alike; provisioning the royal castle as if it were his own; and threatening all who failed to yield to his 'presumption.'[262] The worst of the scourges was that of 'a savage crowd of barbarians,' by which the author meant the 'pitiless mercenaries' who had 'swarmed to England' as (no fewer than) a 'herd' (*grex*), and made for the 'castles everywhere.'[263]

'Castles everywhere.' They were critical to the experience of power 'when Christ and His saints slept.' 'Castles multiplied throughout England,' wrote William of Malmesbury, looking back on the year 1140 when the alarm was fresh, 'each defending its own space, or indeed, to say it more truthfully, plundering it.'[264] It would be hard to say more succinctly what is recorded concretely in all the sources. The subsequent Peterborough annal exonerates the *castles*, it is true, attributing the violence of forced labour to 'devils and wicked men' placed *in* them by rebellious magnates.[265] While the narratives refer to upwards of seventy castles by name,[266] it is their allusions to literally countless ones *not* named that matter most to the crisis. Whatever their failings, the monk-writers were not so heartless as to suppose that it was enough to mention the old public forts, such as in Exeter or Winchester. No wonder they could not name the rest: the 'devils,' weak in social graces, had failed to invite the monks; and if the new castles remain countless to us—were they somewhere between twenty-seven and forty?—it is because they were hasty,

---

[262] *GS*, c. 78; also cc. 37, 38, 82, 83, 15–19; and on Matilda, cc. 58-[59]; and Robert of Gloucester, c. 75.

[263] ibid., c. 78.

[264] *HN* c. 483; Stenton, *First century* 203–4.

[265] *Peterborough chronicle, an.* 1137 (55–57).

[266] For this purpose, JW, *HN*, *GS*, HH, and *ASC*.

ephemeral, and vulnerable to the destructive justice of Henry II.[267] 'Everywhere in England'? This is the sort of exaggeration that rings truly. No single chronicler can have known the extent of abrasive castle-building; but to judge from the *Gesta Stephani*, whose author knew southern and southwestern England well, the violence was notorious in Gloucestershire (notably along the Severn); in Devon, Cornwall, and parts of the south coastal hinterlands; and only slightly less so in the zone marked off by Hereford, Oxford, Winchester, and Exeter, where the problem was chiefly that of fidelity in existing castles. The arrest of the bishops in 1139 was driven by resentment of episcopal castles sited ominously over much of central England. Evidence from Durham and York points to veritable routines of castle-generated coercive violence in those regions, where such trouble was represented as characteristic of Stephen's reign.[268]

The war together with the loss of control over castellans and knightly retinues amounted to a national crisis of power, which was a mark in its way of Old English durability under Norman dominations. That is why the castles were so widely experienced and feared, why they should be as focal to our historical sense of the crisis as they were to the immediate suffering of the working people within sight of castles—that is, of most people. This was not, of course, the whole story of power in Stephen's England. Institutional life surely carried on, however disrupted. We happen to know that the abbots of Battle and Peterborough struggled to preserve and secure their communities.[269] Princely charters and notices tell of the play of royal and elite patronage for which

---

[267] See Charles Coulson, 'The castles of the anarchy,' in *Anarchy*, ch. 2, and at p. 70.

[268] *GS*, virtually the whole text. On the bishops, cc. 34–36, 46, 47. Also 'The miracles of St Bega,' *The register of the priory of St Bees*, ed. James Wilson (London 1915) 512–15; *Historia monasterii Selebiensis*, in *The Coucher Book of Selby*, ed. J. T. Fowler, 2 vols. (York 1891–93), i.4, 5, 13; and citations in note 251 above.

[269] *The chronicle of Battle Abbey*, ed. and tr. Eleanor Searle (Oxford 1980) 140–52; *Peterborough chronicle*, an. 1137.

privileged bodies competed as ever.[270] Access to the lord-king
and the privilege of his favour in offices had its price, as the bishops, including Henry of Winchester, found out; and it surely bore
on the abrasive tenor of local life that Stephen's concessions could
not always satisfy former servants, such as Miles de Beauchamp at
Bedford and Geoffrey Talbot at Hereford. The routine works of
shires and hundreds, perhaps more portentously than in the past,
are known to us chiefly from the cessions and exemptions that
bespeak lordship and favour.[271] And the silence of the written
exchequer, whatever it means, is deafening.[272]

There is one thing more. Recurrent allusions to the requisitioning and fortifying of English churches should not be ignored. They
are a precious pointer to an uneasy reality we can only imagine:
the dynamic of power set off when armed strangers and their horses
swarmed uncastled into resentful settlements, in need of public shelter, and of stone.[273] Again in this bad dream England experienced
what Europeans had suffered elsewhere. And there is symptomatic
irony in the spectacle of men armed to coerce seeking asylum.

An Age of Tyranny?

For the Devil by the defect of his perversity is a lover of
power, and a desertor and assailant of justice, in respect to
which great men imitate him.
—*Hildebert of Lavardin, Sermo 32*[274]

---

[270] *RRAN* III, nos. 543, 672, 675, 870, et passim; *Historia ecclesie Abbendonensis*
II, no. 264C.

[271] See the items indexed for hundred and shire in *RRAN* III, 420, 421.

[272] H. A. Cronne, *The reign of Stephen 1135–54. Anarchy in England* (London
1970) ch. 8; R. H. C Davis, *King Stephen*, 3d ed. (London 1990) 82–88; Crouch,
Reign of King Stephen 327–29; Matthew, *King Stephen*, 133–37, 216–19.

[273] *Letters of Gilbert Foliot*, nos. 1, 2, 5; JW III, 272; *HN* c. 468; HH x.22 (744);
GS cc. 43, 53, 65, 74, 83. Cf. Pierre Bonnassie, 'Les *sagreres* catalanes . . . ,'
L'environnement des églises . . . , ed. M. Fixot, E. Zadora-Rio (Paris 1994) 68–94.

[274] *Sermones de tempore, PL* CLXXI, 501–2.

And so the crises played out. Not all of them have been addressed, nor were they at an end towards 1150. In Italy the ambitions of great families of Milan contributed to a violent conflict
ending in the destruction of Como and Lodi (1118–27). In southern France an uprising of knights shook the incipient Trencavel
domination of Carcassonne in 1125. In Germany the uneasy
elections of 1125 and 1138 pointed to the untypical success of
magnate clienteles in preventing purely dynastic successions at
their expense. And when the Norman dynasty in Sicily achieved
papal recognition in the coronation of Roger II (1130), the ideal
of princely ambition was realized once again.[275] In Mediterranean lands, at least, the multiplication of local lordships figured
in tensions less bound to dynastic claims than in the north; yet it
looks as if the pressures of expansionist lordship together with
the relative poverty of recruited knights worked everywhere to
refashion urban and rural communities quite as abrasively as in
France, Lorraine, or Saxony.[276]

The 'crises' of 'troubled societies' were, indeed, hardly less normal in the early twelfth century than the routines of transaction
and justice they disrupted. The violence of magnates and knights
in Germany after 1103 could be spoken of as a 'bad custom.'[277]
That benign routines mattered to the common experience of
power cannot be doubted. Jurisdictional claims everywhere gave
expression to a vestigial sense of procedural and remedial order, of
which the satisfactory practise largely eludes us. It has become
clear that courts and judgments were subverted (and averted) by
customary constraints, including patronage; we can only guess
how well or widely jurisdictions public or popular, which kept no

[275] Tabacco, *Struggle for power* 192–93, 237; G. A. Loud, *Church and society in
the Norman principality of Capua, 1058–1197* (Oxford 1985) chs. 3, 4; *HL* v, no.
489i; Hélène Débax, *La féodalité languedocienne XIᵉ–XIIᵉ siècles. Serments, hommages et fiefs dans le Languedoc des Trencavel* (Toulouse 2003) 72–85; Otto of Freising, *Gesta Friderici (Deeds)* i.15–23.
[276] Wickham, *Community and clientele in Tuscany* chs. 4, 5; Larrea, *Navarre* chs.
8–11; Martínez Sopena, *Tierra de Campos occidental* 181–566.
[277] Above, pp. 225–26.

records as such, responded to people's needs.[278] But about one testimony produced by the troubled societies of this age no guesswork is required. Everywhere people noticed and spoke up about 'bad lords,' 'bad lordship,' and 'tyranny.'

This evidence, like that of violence, of which it may be said to form a part, has been strenuously denounced by recent historians.[279] Yet it is innocent, on the whole, of all but one minor charge: exaggeration. Are we really to believe, on one hand, that 'many thousands [of people] starved to death' in the dungeons of 'wicked men' in the new castles of Stephen's England?—or that the 'devils' in those castles were other than castellans and knights?[280] On the other hand, much of the brutality ascribed to individuals unnamed by the Peterborough chronicler is imputed to well identified men in the *Gesta Stephani* and in other narratives of the English crisis; and what lends credence to this evidence is its conformity with records from continental lands far beyond the Anglo-Norman world. What is more, it looks as if towards mid-century the violence of some magnates was becoming widely notorious. When Henry of Huntingdon thought back over the fortunes and fates of powerful lay men, his first example was the French baron Thomas de Marle, who so far as we know never set foot in England. What the chronicler had heard of Thomas, doubtless from clerical gossip in councils going back to that of Beauvais (1114) in which Thomas had been condemned, had to do with his excessive cruelties to captives and his seizure of church lands. In a similar perspective of moral censure, John of Salisbury listed some of the magnates who had terrorized the English in Stephen's time: the king's own son Eustace, who had

---

[278] The *Leges Henrici primi* are almost alone as a guide to norms of local procedure in this period. See also Chris Wickham, *Courts and conflict in twelfth-century Tuscany* (Oxford 2003).

[279] Dominique Barthélemy, 'La mutation féodale a-t-elle eu lieu? Note critique,' *Annales: E.S.C.* (1992) 767–77; 'Debate: the "feudal revolution,"' comments by Barthélemy and Stephen White, *Past & Present* no. 152 (1997) 196–223; *Conflict in medieval Europe*, ed. Brown, Górecki; Matthew, *King Stephen*, ch. 6.

[280] *Peterborough chronicle, an.* 1137 (55–56).

allegedly seized clerical lands to pay his knights; and the earls Geoffrey de Mandeville, Milo of Hereford, Ranulf of Chester, Alan of Brittany, Simon of Senlis, and Gilbert de Clare. 'Where are they now,' John queried, 'not so much earls of the realm as public enemies'?[281]

Such men, said John, were 'tyrants' (*tiranni*). The epithet was hardly new, having been used by Peter Abelard with some precision, and sometimes before him with polemical force. Pope Gregory VII had referred to Kings Philip I and Henry IV as 'tyrant(s),' which helps to explain why John of Salisbury has been supposed to have had evil kings in mind.[282] But there was nothing technical in the use of this emotive term, which often corresponded to circumlocutions for violent or coercive power of equal rhetorical force. Orderic wrote of Hugh of Avranches (d. 1101) and Robert of Bellême (d. ca. 1132) as monsters of violence quite in a class with Thomas de Marle, yet with only a single passing allusion to the 'tyranny' of Robert.[283] Nevertheless, it would hardly be mistaken to refer to the lifetimes of Orderic and Abelard, which nearly coincided, as an age of tyranny, for no other *contemporary* concept in such general use so well summed up the prevailing experience of power that resounds in complaints, petitions, and the renunciations in normative texts.

In this respect Henry of Huntingdon and John of Salisbury summed up a passing epoch better than they can have known. What Henry said of Thomas de Marle was that he belonged to the category of those who attain the 'felicity of a great name.' 'Yet in our times,' he added sourly, 'no one arrives at a great name save by the highest crimes.'[284] John's comment in the same context was more searching: he wondered why anyone would wish to oppress

---

[281] John of Salisbury, *Policraticus* viii.21 (II, 394–96).

[282] *Register Gregors VII.* ii.5 (I, 33), iv.12 (313); see also Richard and Mary Rouse, 'John of Salisbury and the doctrine of tyrannicide,' *Speculum* XLII (1967) 693–709.

[283] OV iv (II, 260–62); viii.2,24 (IV,132, 296–300).

[284] HH viii.10 (600–602).

God's people by the yoke of servitude, unless perhaps 'they seek power [*potentiam appetunt*] so as powerfully to produce the torments of misery.' The 'will of a tyrant' is 'to dominate' (*dominari*), not to rule (*regere*), for to rule is to assume a 'burden of office' uncongenial to the tyrant.[285] Not all, nor even most, of the new dominations of the early twelfth century conform to these definitions. For all we know, the pushy entrepreneur selling his protection to tenants of Morigny around 1100 would have settled for some modest enlargement of his little lordship.[286] But by naming names of the predatory barons of the late wars in England, John of Salisbury evoked a whole class of great lords in quest of 'great names.'

They must, indeed, have been widely notorious. They included Hugues du Puiset as well as the arch-tyrant Thomas de Marle in France; Sanchianes, a climber on the organized violence of Alfonso of Aragon in Urraca's León, soon to be outdone by Giraldo 'the Devil' in the patrimonies of Sahagún; Emicho, a Rhineland count who sought to extend his dominations by terror and violence in 1099–1100; Robert the simoniac abbot of Saint-Pierre-sur-Dive, who in 1106 'built a castle in the monastery and assembled a family of knights, and so turned God's temple into a robbers' cave'; and Bertulf the Fleming, whose familial dynasty came crashing down in 1127.[287] Another Fleming, Robert fitz Hubert, outdid most others for cruelty and blasphemy in Stephen's time. Having captured Devizes and bragged that he would soon dominate the region from Winchester to London, he was said to ransom captives or to expose them inhumanely, to have approved the burning of eighty monks in his homeland, and to have well earned his own capture and spectacular execution by hanging before his castle's walls.[288] But the list of men who built and collected castles while resorting to terror and intimidation in

---

[285] *Policraticus* vii.22 (II, 396–97).   [286] See above, pp. 61, 166.

[287] Above, pp. 67, 234–43; on Emicho, Ekkehard, *Chronica* (I) 146; and on Abbot Robert, OV xi.14 (VI, 72, 74).

[288] *HN* cc. 479, 485; *GS* i.43, 50, 52 (92, 104–8).

quest of great lordship is far longer than this, notably in England, where the *Gesta Stephani* mentions no fewer than twenty magnates (not counting Matilda and her half-brother Robert) who meet the test of tyranny laid down by the moralists. Suger, more interested in fidelity than power, has a different perspective on the bad castellanies, and it seems likely that the more constricted fortified spaces in the Ile-de-France placed natural limits on the ambitions of the Montmorency and the Rochefort, if not also those of the lords of Coucy and Le Puiset.

The alleged iniquities of great men matter to the experience of power because they coincided with those, far less conspicuous, of lesser 'bad lords,' of those everywhere who *would* be lords. Like the 'perverse men' of Compiègne who, towards 1060, built a tower in Saint-Corneille's immunity; or the 'invaders' in the diocese of Freising who tried to reduce the priest Ernost and his brother to servitude 'by tyrannical domination.'[289] In the old fiscal domains of Catalonia a veritable portrait gallery of heartless pretenders to lordship can be assembled from written memorials of complaint submitted to the count (and successive count-kings) of Barcelona from about 1150. To mention but two of their tormentors, indignant peasants singled out Raimund de Ribes as a specialist in greedy intimidation and Berenguer de Bleda for his oppressive swagger amongst villagers at Font-rubí; and one anonymous scribe outdid the rest in his rendition of Arnau de Perella, a 'little tyrant of his fields' at Caldes de Malavella and Llagostera. Seeking to put distance between himself and his (fellow!) peasants, Arnau was a cruel manipulator of justice and credit, a conspicuous profiteer living it up in a make-believe lordship shared by cronies in fidelity. For an incipient sociability of self-promoting domination, this representation is unmatched in twelfth-century Europe. That such evidence survives at all points to a change in mid-century, as will appear; to a change in evidence, that is, not of behaviour.[290]

---

[289] *RAPh1* no. 125; *TrFr* II, no. 1535.
[290] ACA, Cancelleria, pergamins extrainventaris 3433, 3217, 3409, 3141, 3288; (T. N. Bisson) *TV* 80–94, 166–69.

A spectre of enslavement haunts this world of burgeoning lordships, in rhetorical usage at least, a matter not so much of custom
(still less of law) as of moral and social presumption on the part of
those in need of being served. And for the rest, the experience of
power relates to 'badness'—like 'tyranny' a soft and elusive term
in the sources (but nonetheless, be it understood, a twelfth-century
concept, not ours)—in at least one further problematic way. For
the 'bad' (*perversi, pravi*) might be, or come to be, admired. People were fascinated by power-building men. Some seemed to be
bad to the end, like Thomas de Marle; others to be reprehensible,
or violent, only so long as they had to be. Ranulf Flambard may
have been too canny to violate people afflictively, yet for his work
enabling King William II to profit from episcopal vacancies he
was charged with 'cruelty,' 'rapacity,' and 'oppressive' taxation.
What counted in this case was ambition, for as William of Malmesbury was to put it, memorably, who but Flambard could so
'incur the hatred of others while pleasing his lord[-king]'?[291]
Who was the 'bad lord' here? Rewarded with the see of Durham,
Ranulf Flambard did more to serve his church than to prove any
innate wickedness. He had 'made it' in the kings' favour. Yet this
was not quite all. After his death the prior of Saint Cuthbert's of
Durham secured the king's remedy of the 'wrongs and acts of
violence that Bishop Ranulf committed against them in his
lifetime.'[292]

Another Anglo-Norman clerk of humble origins in search of a
'great name' was Roger, who rose to be 'justiciar' under Henry I,
yet to the puzzlement of historians was less touted by contemporaries for his fiscal wizardry than for his ambition to great lordship. Yet it could be that those who knew him had things the

---

[291] *Willelmi Malmesbiriensis monachi de gestis pontificum Anglorum libri quinque*,
ed. N. E. S. A. Hamilton (London 1870) iii.134 (274); OV viii.8 (IV, 170–78);
Peterborough chronicle, an. 1100 (27–29); HH viii.15 (612).

[292] *RRAN* II, no. 1574. See also J. O. Prestwich, 'The career of Ranulf
Flambard,' *Anglo-Norman Durham, 1093–1193*, ed. David Rollason *et al.* (Woodbridge 1994) 299–310.

right way around, with his technical expertise merely the unwritten means to the satisfactions of affective and conspicuous
power. What we know best about Roger is the massive lordship
he came to enjoy as bishop of Salisbury, about his quasi-dynastic
outlook in securing bishoprics for his nephews Alexander and
Nigel, and about his vulnerable passion for building castles. Like
Flambard, Roger was accused of violent encroachments, but the
charge that brought him down in 1139, in partisan counsels of
King Stephen, was surely his domineering ways: the retinue of
armed men as well as his stones of security.[293]

Karl Leyser rightly likened the nepotism of Bishop Roger to
that of the provost Bertulf in Flanders; yet if account be taken of
the militant elements of such clerical lordship, an even more
compelling analogy lies with episcopal lordships on the continent. In Galicia Diego Gelmírez (ca. 1068–1140), Roger's exact
contemporary, became a princely lord of sworn knights and
castles on his way to securing metropolitan status for the see
of Compostela. His may well have been the greatest success of
any of these lord-prelates. In Germany the two Archbishops
Adalbert—of Bremen (1043–72) and of Mainz (1109–37)—likewise parlayed royal favour into territorial power. The failings alleged of these prelates were not those of devilish iniquity, yet all
were practised in violence and constraint, and resented for warped
ambitions. Heedless of canonical reform, they exemplified the
habitus of militant princely lordship at its height.[294]

That the predatory lord-prelates just mentioned lived *through*
the crises of power cannot be accidental. Allegedly 'bad lordship'
was not so much cause as symptom in the early twelfth century,

[293] *HN* cc. 469–75; *OV* xiii.40 (VI, 530, 532); *GS* i.35–36,46; *HH* viii.15 (610):
'Rogerus, uir magnus in secularibus'; and see generally Kealey, *Roger of Salisbury* chs. 2, 5–7.
[294] *HC* i.15,20,33,117; ii.23,25; iii.119; and generally Fletcher, *Saint James's
catapult*, chs. 5, 9. Also Adam of Bremen, . . . *Gesta Hammaburgensis ecclesiae
pontificum*, ed. Bernhard Schmeidler, 3d ed. (Hanover 1917) iii (142–226); and
Mainzer Urkundenbuch (Darmstadt 1932) no. 451 (358–59); Ekkehard, *Chronica*
(iv), 348.

cresting and (doubtless) subsiding like the breakers of a windy sea.
Few stopped the action of such experience, or savoured its dis-
agreeable images, so well as two monks who, although living in
times, places, and ascetic cultures remote from each other, wrote
of bad lordship in the same years 1123 to 1133. The 'first continuator' of Peterborough lost no time denouncing one Henry of
Poitou, whom King Henry had imposed as their abbot, and found
nothing at all to write once he was removed in 1133. And just at
that moment a bad castellan in the deep south of France named
Pons of Léras had repented of his late wicked ways, leading to a
fully ascetic conversion and to the writing, around 1160, of a Cistercian foundation-story from which we learn of the wild oats he
had sown.

Amongst people striving for power in his day few can have
matched Henry of Poitou. He was said to be related to both King
Henry I and Duke William IX, and was assuredly well connected. Bishop of Soissons in the 1080s, then monk and prior of
Cluny and prior of Souvigny, he became abbot of Saint-Jean-
d'Angély about 1103. He spent the rest of his life trying to improve on this, without giving up the abbey. There was a bold stab
at the archbishopric of Besançon around 1109, a bid for the see of
Saintes (1111–13?), before England came into his sights. There he
presented himself as a pushy legate before securing the king's designation (1127) as abbot of Peterborough, where, according to the
outraged annalist, 'he stayed exactly as do drones in a hive.' Looting the movables, he 'did nothing good there and left nothing
good there.' Henry clung to Peterborough, promising vainly to
give up Saint-Jean, until in 1132 King Henry had heard enough
of him and forced him out. So the monks spoke of him in a historically informed lamentation—on *this* huckster's background
they had done some research!—that is arguably the most acutely
passionate response to power-seeking tyranny that we have from
Norman England. Quite arresting in this text is the representation of Abbot Henry's excuses and pretences, together with the
withering disparagement they provoked. Moreover, one may peer
through this text to see why Abbot Henry's English reputation

was so confined to the notice of one afflicted house, which is that
he was canny and experienced enough by the time of his last ca-
per to limit his prey to the patrimony of Peterborough.[295]
    The experience of Pons of Léras, of himself and his victims as
well, was different. Only the depth and permanence of his religious conversion, rendering him the pious founder of a new con-
gregation such as would have lacked even the slightest appeal to
an entrepreneur like Henry of Poitou, here permits us to glimpse
the anxious life of peasants who looked apprehensively up the
hills. Pons grew to adulthood around 1120, and although he was
the master of an 'impregnable' castle, he was enticed by 'worldly
desires' and began to threaten, encroach upon, and oppress his
neighbours. Some he deceived, 'others he disrupted by the violence of armed men, while seizing the property of everyone he
could,' incessantly pressing his greed. If this seems a stereotyped
account, which by no means detracts from its plausibility, the
story of the castellan's penitential renunciations that follows holds
even greater interest. Pons is said to have convoked people of all
sorts with a view not only to selling his possessions pursuant to
Matthew xix.21 and giving to the poor, churches, pilgrims, widows, etc.; not only to restoring to all whatever 'he had seized by
force'; but also to organizing a judicial session, in the second
week of Easter, where all those he had injured might appeal to
him *as judge* against *himself* as defendant(!). When an astonished
shepherd standing by seemed reluctant to press charges, willing
even to thank his 'lord' for small favours, Pons had to insist that
he himself was, indeed, the culprit, the perpetrator of theft. 'I did
this, said Pons, I did it all with my vassals and pals. So I beg you
to forgive me, so that I may then restore to you what I stole.'[296]

---

[295] *Peterborough chronicle, an.* 1123–32 (43, 48–50, 52–54). See also Cecily
Clark, ' "This ecclesiastical adventurer": Henry of Saint-Jean d'Angély,' *EHR*
LXXXIV (1969), 548–60. Henry was not the only monk of Cluny promoted to
power in England in the 1120s, nor even the only Henry; and the relation of
Henry of Blois to his namesake raises questions.
[296] *Chronique de Silvanès*, ed. P.-A. Verlaguet, *Cartulaire de l'abbaye de Silvanès*
(Rodez 1910) no. 470: '. . . Ego, inquit Pontius, illud feci, per satellites et

❖

'WITH MY vassals and pals!' Something in those words rings free of the clerical template that distorts them in a parable of repentance. Petty lordships of constraint were the prevailing reality of power even in the regional societies that escaped the troubles of dynastic crisis. If Abbot Henry's tyranny at Peterborough was short-lived, it was because he lacked the solidarity of commended men. His way to power, long since stigmatized by the reformers, was only as secure as a lord-prince's favour, as Etienne de Garlande and Ranulf Flambard well knew; but the prosperity of new power in this age fed on followership and fidelity as well as new wealth. The phenomenon remained disruptive while ceasing to be revolutionary: everywhere old units of public power survived even as they too—for example, the viscounties of Lombardy and Normandy, advocacies in German-speaking lands, and vicariates in Poitou—assumed new sanctions in custom; moreover, the patrimonial value of old offices made it tempting to encroach on their resources or attack. If the fear of bellicose depredations is counted among popular anxieties, as of course it should be, the experience of power in local conflicts was even more troubled than we yet know. Was not this, too, a consequence of multiplied lordships? Crises of power arose from compounded constraints of custom, status, and wealth. While few lord-princes could long master these constraints, knights trading in prowess and fidelity could only aspire to—and seldom attain—a nobility that required social superiority and the service of people beneath. It was a cold and draughty vestibule, this aspiration; indeed, a lordship dynamic and unstable to which tradespeople of other sorts were to be drawn in growing numbers.

---

complices meos totum egi . . .' See also Constable, *Reformation of the twelfth century* 81, 237, and ch. 3.

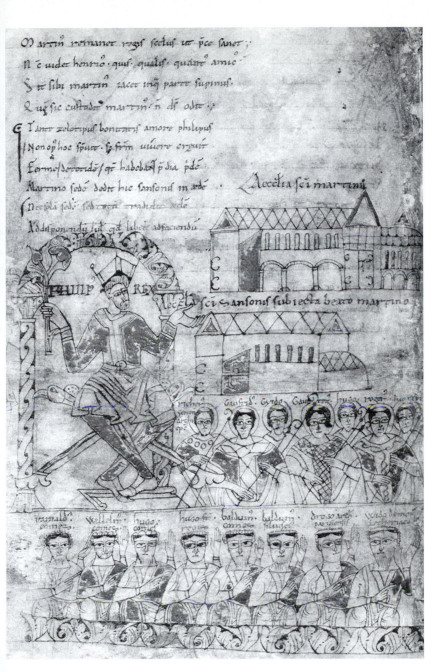

PLATE 1. King Philip I of France with retainers: bishops, counts, and the lord-castellan of Montlhéry (extreme lower right). Illumination of late eleventh century, depicting the king's donation to the canons of Saint-Martin-des-Champs in an early copy of their chronicle. (© British Library Board. All rights reserved, Additional MSS 11662, fol. 5v.)

PLATE 2. Bayeux Tapestry, ca. 1080. Woman and child escaping house torched by Norman knights, fall 1066. Embroidery of ca. 1080 (Photo by Eric Lessing/Art Resource, New York.)

Opposite: PLATE 3.

Top: Oxford Castle, viewed from the west. Built 1171 by the Norman baron Robert d'Oyly, the motte (structural mound) is visible much as it first appeared. Many castles of this age were built on natural elevations, often called *puig* or *puy* in southern lands. (Photograph by author.)

Bottom: This view, from the south, shows not the original tower or keep, but simply what such a structure on the motte might first have looked like. Until recently Oxford Castle served as a public prison; it is now renovated as a museum and hotel. (Photograph by author.)

PLATE 4. Henry IV of Germany flanked by his sons Henry (V) and Conrad, with three abbo of Saint Emmeram shown below. (St Emmeram Gospels, Kraków Cathedral MS 208, fol. 2v By Permission.)

M. ATHILDIS LUCENS. PRECOR HOC CAPE CARA VOLUMEN

PLATE 5. Countess Matilda of Tuscany. Illumination of ca. 1115 in an early manuscript of Donizo's *Life of Matilda*. (Vatican MS latinus 4922, fol. 7v. Reproduced by permission of the Biblioteca Apostolica Vaticana.)

PLATE 6. Tympanum of the west portal of Ste-Foy of Conques, Rouergue (c. 1130-35). Above, on Christ's right hand figures the blessed order of Paradise, contrasted with demonic disorder on his left (the viewer's right). Below, Christ welcomes the rising dead to beatitude while to his left the beastly jaws of Hell swallow the damned. (Vanni/Art Resource, New York.)

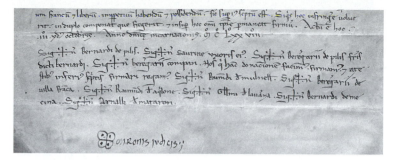

PLATE 8A. The Count-King Alfons I addresses the prelates, magnates, knights, and townspeople of Catalonia in a great charter of imposed peace passed at Barbastro (in Aragon!) in November 1192. Of the many charters of peace and truce issued in Catalonia from 1172 to 1214, this is the only surviving original. (Ministerio de Cultura, Archivo de Corona de Aragón, Canc. pergamins Alfons I 639. Reproduced by permission.)

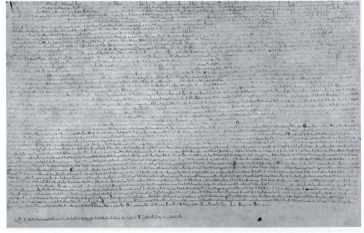

PLATE 8B. Magna Carta, June 1215. This is one of four extant originals, the others being a badly damaged copy also in the British Library, and ones at Lincoln and Salisbury. (© British Library Board. All rights reserved, MS Cott. Aug.II.33.)

· V ·

Resolution: Intrusions of Government

(1150–1215)

IN 1152 the 'common council of the town and suburb of Toulouse' imposed an ordinance (*stabilimentum*) intended to clarify
the relations between the townspeople and their extramural
neighbours. Concretely, the purpose was to secure people from
arbitrary seizures and 'harm' (*malum*). So described, this regulation can be seen to remedy an old complaint in a new way. Half a
century later, when the *capitouls* of Toulouse collected the muni-
ments of their rise to civic power, they found no earlier prescript
than this one. Yet what it describes is an existing order of local
powers whereby seizures for debt are reserved to creditors, injuries to Toulousans inflicted by people outside the walls are to be
settled by the lords of suspect castles or villages, so that the seizure of chattels is warranted only in default of such process (*rec-
tum*), and so on. And what resonates here is that the petty violence
envisaged in the first articles of the earliest communal regulation
at Toulouse was not only normal, but a threat (equally normal) to
local peace.[1]

Such regimes must have seemed tolerable almost everywhere
in Latin Europe in the later twelfth century. Yet it was just such a
regime that King Henry II was to challenge in England a few
years later; and it was arguably the routine violence of distraint
and dispossession that prompted a revival of the peace movement
in southern France, its early transmission to León, and its renewal

---

[1] *HL* v, no. 595; Roger Limouzin-Lamothe, *La commune de Toulouse . . .*
(Toulouse 1932) 7–14, 261–71.

in new forms in all the Iberian realms in the 1180s. Toulouse was not in crisis in 1152, nor England in the 1160s, yet in those places, as almost everywhere else, possession remained precarious and peaceful prosperity an elusive dream. And there are signs that some people, quietly, obscurely, and out of phase with 'critical events' or visible touch with one another were beginning to react against the easy violence, no longer to think of it as simply disorderly or regrettable, and some few of them at least to do things differently.

Yet the violent tenor of life, for all its oppressive familiarity, was no match for the illusions that nurtured the masses. Power was greatness in the ripening twelfth century, the conspicuous greatness of exploit and spectacle. The deeds of Frederick Barbarossa, already in his earliest years as king and would-be emperor, and those of Count-Prince Ramon Berenguer IV, commemorated in narratives of triumphalist rhetoric, resounded in the aftermath of the failed Second Crusade. 'I offer my history to your nobility,' wrote Bishop Otto to Barbarossa, his nephew, in 1157, although in fact the latter had put him up to it, listing his own feats of power and lordship.[2] Even as the routines of lavish patronage played out in the yearly rounds of festival observance, where singers of deeds and romancers alike found reward and inspiration, some such events seemed memorable: the great court of Würzburg in which Barbarossa married Beatrice of Burgundy (1156); that of Huesca (1162) in which the dynastic union of Catalonia and Aragon was confirmed; the prodigious diet of Mainz (1184) in which, following the downfall of Duke Henry the Lion, was celebrated what seemed like the grandest royal success in German lands since the time of Charlemagne.[3] Swelling numbers of people looked on in wonder—peasants, merchants, pilgrims, the working poor clinging to courtly largesse and clerical alms—;

---

[2] Otto of Freising, *Gesta Friderici* 1–5 (*Deeds* 17–20); *GcB*.

[3] Otto, *Gesta* (*Deeds*) ii.48; *LFM* I, no. 494; *Die Chronik* [*Chronica*] *Ottos von St. Blasien*, ed. Franz-Josef Schmale (Darmstadt 1998) c. 26.

felt their low-born smallness in the glitter of noble pageantry; experienced through the senses the power of superiority.

As time passed, such events were offset by dynastic misfortunes, equally visible. The fruitful marriage of Henry of Anjou to Eleanor of Aquitaine (1152), having at first encouraged lavish schemes of marital alliance, turned sour with the revolt of their sons in the 1170s, followed by continued domestic dissent. In the Anglo-Norman realms as in Poland a century before, the principle of familial condominium proved difficult to realize in practise. A worse accident befell the empire in 1197, when the premature death of Henry VI (1190–97) left power to his three-year-old son, ushering in a long period of conflict. The Hispanic realms, France, and England were spared such mischances, or mostly so, down to 1250; while in Italy the diminished imperial presence after the Peace of Constance (1183) encouraged urban lordships in an equally precarious competition.[4] It was a commonplace reflection, and perhaps for many a consoling one, that the powers of this world rode an ever-turning wheel of fortune.[5]

In the later twelfth century dynastic constraints were overtaken by changed circumstances of population, wealth, and religious change, creating new perspectives of interest and action, and new challenges. Every original impulse of the century bore on the popular experience of power. A vastly strengthened papal lordship reached into distant localities through judges-delegate imposing and enforcing rules of Christian conduct of unprecedented scope. The power of the keys began to lose something of its lordly absolutism in towns, like Lyon or Bologna, where lay persons troubled by clerical vice seemed to encourage unorthodox commitments in faith and morals. When a gifted demagogue

---

[4] *CAP* I, nos. 293–95.

[5] Walter Map, *De nugis curialium*, ed. and tr. M. R. James, rev. C. N. L. Brooke, R. A. B. Mynors (Oxford 1983) i.1–5; Petrus de Ebulo, *Liber ad honorem Augusti sive de rebus Siculis . . .* , ed. Theo Kölzer, Marlis Stähli, tr. (German) Gereon Becht-Jördens (Sigmaringen 1994) fols. 146–47.

like Arnold of Brescia tapped into this strain of dissent, in Rome, the world's greatest rulers had no trouble agreeing to squash him.[6] Heresy seemed doubly threatening to those cajoled to fear and others to assault the infidel. No fewer than four major crusades from 1146 to 1209 taxed the ingenuity of their organizers and the means of their subject peoples.[7]

Less visible than such manifestations yet hardly less consequential were new currents in lordly purposes, resources, law, learning, patrimonial exploitation, and associative experience. If these currents flowed through enterprises at all levels, though less evident, as ever, in lesser lordships, the novelties they brought mattered most in princely and royal dominations. People who had learned how to think about concepts and numbers turn up in entourages of power coming to be called 'court' (curia). Everywhere the inherited liabilities of lordship—the insubordination and violence of castellans and advocates, knightly desperation or greed, and a poorly functional prescriptive accountability grounded in face-to-face trust—were recognized and countered. It became harder to defend profits of exploitation in tenures of service, easier to distinguish between affective entitlement and functional service. Moreover, interests defined deferentially as rights and obligations to payments and services were at once so pressed and so multiplied in growing societies as to invite associative redefinitions of interest. The talk of men convoked to great courts began to sound and mean differently.

How or when such changes happened is not easy to say. Much of the history of power in the later twelfth century is bound up with dynastic and customary lordship. Yet the instabilities of

---

[6] G. W. Greenaway, Arnold of Brescia (Cambridge 1931) chs. 6–9; Robert L. Benson, 'Political renovatio: two models from Roman antiquity,' Renaissance and renewal in the twelfth century, ed. R. L. Benson, Giles Constable (Cambridge, M., 1982) 341–50.

[7] Jonathan Riley-Smith, 'The crusades, 1095–1198,' NCMH iv¹, 534–63; Norman Housley and Bernard Hamilton in ibid., v, 569–72, 164–68; or Christopher Tyerman, God's war: A new history of the crusades (Cambridge, M., 2006) chs. 9–18.

unaccountable dominations and services in the hands of multiplied aspirants to power surely exerted pressures in need of release. In this perspective three shifts or adjustments look not
merely responsive but auspicious: justice and accountability, in
this context virtually a single topic; new stirrings of official conduct; and the recognition of social purpose amongst those serving
lord-princes and urban communities.

Great Lordship in Prosperity and Crisis

None of these changes detracted from the normative excellence
of lordship. It became clearer than ever that men and women
were born to the great lordships that went with nobility, making
it harder than ever for upstarts to forge new powers over people
in respectable ways. Roger II of Sicily (1102–54), himself descended from the most successful lordly plantation of its age,
struggled to limit the pretensions of his princely peers. Lesser
lords with instituted powers, such as advocates, ministeriales, and
judges, prospered in the later twelfth century. Appointed imperial *podestà* of Milan in 1164, Markward of Grumbach got rich
from the new taxes he imposed. In Flanders the advocate Walter
of Tournai, who had married the castellan's daughter, 'amplified
the goods of his land, and having founded many new villages,
settled and endowed it.'[8] But such nobility of action became increasingly problematic for castellans and younger sons of limited
inheritance.

The consummate bearers of noble lordship continued to be the
kings (and queens). They ruled some fifteen realms of Latin Europe, a number lately augmented by two—Sicily since 1130 and
Portugal since 1140—and lessened by the lapse of the royal title in
Poland. The vital events in royal families were the real news of

---

[8] Hubert Houben, *Roger II of Sicily . . .* , tr. G. A. Loud (Cambridge 2002)
chs. 2, 3; Peter Munz, *Frederick Barbarossa . . .* (London 1969) 274–75; Gislebert
of Mons, *Chronicon Hanoniense* c. 43.

the day, as already noted, because they projected the ambitions of an expansionist nobility as well as the ideals of the masses; and because they intermarried. The first kings of Sicily and Portugal were the descendants of (respectively) Norman knights and Burgundian dukes; Louis VII of France (1137–80) married Constance of Castile; his daughter Margaret married King Bela of Hungary following the death of her first husband Prince Henry Plantagenet. That the latter's parents Henry and Eleanor could have imagined their children binding much of Europe in a dynastic empire of marriage was famously evident by the 1170s. Such ties meant more than superficial glitter, for they brought practised retainers in different lands into contact.

Yet apart from the celebrated Thomas Brown of England and Sicily, of whom more will be said, it is hard to see that royal lordships of the later twelfth century had people or purposes they could usefully share. All were bound by patrimonial customs difficult to adjust, let alone change. None save Sicily and (from 1155?) England had record-making offices during the years 1152–62, when new kings came to power in Germany, England, Sicily, León, Castile, and Catalonia-Aragon. Moreover, all lord-kings, without exception, persisted in rounds of ceremonial audience, concession, and settlement, the records of which, typically preserved by beneficiaries, were routinely dispensed. The diplomas and charters tell us about the ruler's lordship of favour and command, about those in attendance upon him; often little more. Many of Henry II's instruments are undated. The power of such lordship could still be exerted by word of mouth or concession. On the other hand, King Henry's charters are far more numerous (as we have them) than those of Frederick Barbarossa, which *are* dated and which are models of ideologically charged imperious expression.[9] This comparison has unexpected significance, as we

---

[9] Compare *DDFr1* with *Acta of Henry II and Richard I*, ed. J. C. Holt, Richard Martino (1986–96); and see Karl Leyser, 'Frederick Barbarossa and the Hohenstaufen polity' (1988) in idem, *The Gregorian revolution and beyond*, ed. Timothy Reuter (London 1994) 118–22.

shall see. It is less easy at present to extend the comparison to include the extant records of Louis VII of France, Fernando II of León (1157–88), Alfonso VIII of Castile (1158–1214), Alfons I of Catalonia-Aragon (1162–96), and Williams I (1154–66) and II (1166–89) of Sicily. What can safely be said from the editions available is that these lord-kings exercised their chancellors and scribes much as Anglo-Norman and German rulers did; that they, too, were called upon to endow, confirm, and regulate.[10] The lord-kings profited from two cultural facets of power reserved to them. First, their ritual consecrations virtually enacted for witnessing masses—as in the coronations of Frederick I and Alfons(o) I(I) in 1152 and 1162—the regal mediation of God's power. This was, as the *ordines* of the empire, France, England, and Sicily continue to say, official power; not so much a tenancy of God's lordship as an execution of it.[11] It follows, secondly, that royal lordship reached out for its own customary sanction in affective expression and pretence. In greater or lesser measure the lord-kings of León, Catalonia, Aragon, France, England, Germany, and Sicily claimed to dominate tenants in homage and fidelity, typically those holding fiefs. In his first Diet of Roncaglia (1154) Frederick Barbarossa confirmed the Italian custom of fiefs, by which lords were assured of feudal services.[12] Less concretely

[10] In default of new or better editions see respectively: Achille Luchaire, *Etudes sur les actes de Louis VII* (Paris 1885), Catalogue analytique (798 pieces); *Regesta de Fernando II*, ed. Julio González (Madrid 1943), 623 pieces (unnumbered!); Julio González, *El reino de Castilla en la época de Alfonso VIII*, 3 vols. (Madrid 1960) ii. Documentos 1145–1190 (563 pieces); *Alfonso II rey de Aragón, conde de Barcelona y marqués de Provenza. Documentos (1162–1196)*, ed. Ana Isabel Sánchez Casabón (Zaragoza 1995), 726 pieces (but this edition omits most of the 100-odd fiscal accounts of this reign, printed in FAC). For Sicily see *Guillelmi I. regis diplomata*, ed Horst Enzensberger (Cologne 1996), 94 pieces. I have not attempted to count William II's extant records.

[11] Schramm, *English coronation* chs. 2, 3; Reinhard Elze, 'The ordo for the coronation of King Roger II of Sicily: an example of dating from internal evidence,' in *Coronations: medieval and early modern monarchic ritual*, ed. János M. Bak (Berkeley 1990) 170–78.

[12] *DDFrI* I, no. 91.

yet more tellingly feudal-vassalic lordship lent itself to claims of precedence and hierarchy. The Abbot Suger is known to have encouraged a concept that could only flatter the lord-king; and the wispy reality that attached to this idea is visible everywhere in Latin Europe. In Spain Alfonso VII of León-Castile (1126–57) had based his claim to *imperium* (no less) on a notion of overlordship of other peninsular kings and princes. The fragility of this claim was evident at once upon his death, at a moment when Barbarossa's revived imperialism was to generate a more plausible version of feudal hierarchy that became current with Henry VI (1190–97).[13]

A more nearly realistic expression of feudal lordship may be discerned in the experience of the lesser noble elites. Theirs is an unwritten history, a comparative history of regions such as Castile, Occitania, Saxony, and England that may one day improve our grasp of what is conventionally represented as 'political' history. It was in the high aristocracy that the experience of power changed most critically after 1150. But this was not at once obvious in the routines of prosperity. It was said of Gautier of Tournai that 'he never presumed to oppose himself to his lord' (the Count of Hainaut).[14] One waited on counts and dukes as well as kings, as also on bishops and popes, for favour or remedy; it helped to have intercessors, whose numbers in the greater entourages seemed incessantly to grow. The uncrowned powers in society were like kings, some of whom had themselves been titled princes before their coronations. If the duke of Burgundy or the earl of Chester was less favoured in royal courts than the lords of Lara or the counts of Champagne and Flanders, they were nonetheless prestigious guarantors of public order in their lands. Never had the Flemish countlets and castellans been so ambitious, their powers

---

[13] Lemarignier, *Gouvernement royal* 175–76; *Chronique de Robert de Torigni . . .*, ed. Léopold Delisle, 2 vols. (Rouen 1872) I, 282; Bernard F. Reilly, *The kingdom of León-Castilla under King Alfonso VII, 1126–1157* (Philadelphia 1998) 234–38.

[14] Gislebert, *Chronicon Hanoniense* c. 43.

so feudal.[15] No prince came closer to forging a kingdom within a kingdom than Henry the Lion in Saxony; none had so far to fall when he was condemned as a contumacious vassal and stripped of his titles in 1180.[16]

Yet their kingly potential and resemblance to kings looks to have been a liability for lord-princes. They never cultivated a self-sufficient ideology of power, their apologists of deeds content to echo biblical precepts of royalist obligation found in liturgies of consecration and to claim descent from kings. To this day some Catalans grieve that Ramon Berenguer IV failed to style himself king when he married the heiress to the kingdom of Aragon; the truth is that his Catalan servants *did* speak of him as king in the county of Barcelona as well as in Aragon, and it was only the pride of later generations in the comital title as it figured in the venerable customs of Catalonia that stood in the way of such a promotion. Likewise in Normandy the ducal title survived in customary law, which the Capetian kings were too canny to abrogate after conquering the duchy in 1204. In Sicily, where the ruler was precociously said to dominate lands rather than peoples, the *ducatus* of Apulia and the *principatus* of Capua survived in the royal intitulature after 1135.[17]

Custom worked in another way to depress the ambitions of lord-princes. The convenience of ceding patrimonial wealth in return for the fidelity and service of noble knights and their followers was found almost everywhere by 1150. In some regions

[15] To judge from *Lamberti Ardensis historia comitum Ghisnensium*, ed. Johann Heller, *MGHSS* xxiv (1879) 550–642.

[16] *Historia Welforum*, ed. and tr. Erich König, 2d ed. (Sigmaringen 1978); Simon Doubleday, *The Lara family: crown and nobility in medieval Spain* (Cambridge, M., 2001) ch. 1; Shideler, *The Montcadas*; Theodore Evergates, *Feudal society in the bailliage of Troyes under the counts of Campagne, 1152–1284* (Baltimore 1975); Karl Jordan, *Henry the Lion: a biography*, tr. P. S. Falla (Oxford 1986).

[17] *FAC* ii, no. 156; Joseph R. Strayer, *The administration of Normandy under Saint Louis* (Cambridge, M., 1932) ch. 2; Houben, *Roger II of Sicily* 132. My term 'prince' (or 'lord-prince'), as in contemporary usage, refers (in context) to kings as well as to dukes, counts, and viscounts.

such relationships doubled as virtual alliances, in which the dependence implied by fidelity was resisted.[18] But everywhere mounting sensitivity to personal status together with the ceremonial attributes of the oath of fidelity encouraged lords to insist on their superiority. Much depended on the play of mutual respect, and since this is hard to read between written lines, it was (and is) well to be careful with the word 'vassal.' It denoted a status diversely understood and often unstipulated. Count Ramon Berenguer IV subscribed charters of King Alfonso VII as 'emperor's vassal' towards 1151, and a few years later Count Ermengol VII of Urgell was openly addressed as 'vassal' by King Fernando II; in both cases vassalic status was equated with princely rulership.[19] In a treaty of 1162 wherein Ramon Berenguer IV accepted Provence as a fief (*feodum*) and promised to do homage and swear fidelity to Frederick Barbarossa, the nature of his dependency was nowhere defined.[20] It is safe to say that lord-princes were eager to define alliance as dependency in respect to lesser men and women while reserving their own nobility in respect to lord-kings. The craving for nobility was overtaken by impulses to classify people, to differentiate the privileges of status.[21] But the dynamic of tenurial custom was working everywhere to underscore the nobility of fidelity, making it easier for princes to accept honorific dependency (and the gifts that came with it). Count Baldwin V of Hainaut, responding 'on account of his inheritance' to Barbaros-

---

[18] J.-Fr. Lemarignier, *Recherches sur l'hommage en marche et les frontières féodales* (Lille 1945); *LFM* I, nos. 14, 27–45 (variably pertinent); and generally Adam Kosto, *Making agreements in medieval Catalonia. Power, order, and the written word, 1000–1200* (Cambridge 2002) ch. 5.

[19] *LFM* I, no. 31; González, *Alfonso VIII* II, nos. 6, 8, 10, 11, 13; José-Luis Martín Rodríguez, 'Un vasallo de Alfonso el Casto en el reino de León: Armengol VII, conde de Urgel,' *VII Congreso de História de la Corona de Aragón* (1962), 3 vols. (Barcelona 1964) II, 223–33.

[20] *DDFr1* II, no. 378.

[21] See generally *Libellus de diversis ordinibus* . . . , ed. Giles Constable, Bernard Smith (Oxford 1972); *Usatges de Barcelona*; and *Le Très ancien Coutumier de Normandie*, ed. Ernest-Joseph Tardif (Rouen 1881).

sa's summons to the court of Mainz (Pentecost 1184), was proud to be recognized there as one of the richest of the imperial princes.[22]

So it would be mistaken to suppose that vassalage to lord-kings was feared. It was an honourable status for all who could achieve it. In the little realm of Aragon every free man was expected to do homage and fealty to the king, a hand-to-hand experience of affective power perhaps the more notable for the disinclination of Pyrenean rulers to flaunt their regality.[23] What did arouse concern in princely courts was the spectacle of kings redefining tenures and fidelities schematically so as to turn precedence into command. This was not a wholly new concern. Indeed, it was a lost cause in England, where the Norman kings had attempted to reserve the fidelities of important subtenants and to prohibit, as they had done in Normandy, the building of new castles. But even in England this vassalic-feudal structure, so premature in the all-European perspective, was shaken during the troubles of Stephen's reign, thereby postponing as elsewhere a definitive baronial subordination to the lord-king. Mediterranean lord-princes had long since stipulated the 'power' of castles in the hands of 'faithful men' and subtenants, that is, the right to repossess them, however briefly, on demand; and the principle of preferred, or 'liege,' lordship spread widely after 1100. Perhaps the most coherently realized feudal polity of castles was that of Trencavel Occitania, where it was characteristic of a culture of fidelity that pervaded a whole society in the generations before the Albigensian crusades.[24]

In these circumstances it is hardly surprising to find lord-princes prescribing their claims to provincial domination. The records we possess, by no means surely the first of their kind, had known precedents in lists of knights and fiefs held of lesser lords and

---

[22] Gislebert, *Chronicon Hanoniense* c. 109 (154–63).

[23] *DI* iv, nos. 24, 25, 159.

[24] *Consuetudines et iusticie*; Stenton, *English feudalism*; Charles Coulson, *Castles in medieval society . . .* (Oxford 2003); Débax, *Féodalité languedocienne*.

churches. Bigger than these in every way were the inquiries imposed by King Roger II of Sicily in 1150 and by Count Henry of Troyes in 1172. The latter's clerks recorded the obligations of some 1900 lords and knights in Champagne, thereby confirming the count's lordship and overlordship of fiefs and castles. What looks like a similar record of comital power 'in the fidelities and securities of all castles and fortifications in the whole county and lordship of Hainaut' underlies an entry in the chronicle of Gislebert of Mons about 1196.[25]

Rather different in nature if similar in effect were the enterprises of Kings Roger II (1150 and after) and Henry II (1166). While the first of these was little more than a survey of military obligations in Apulia and Capua, it gave concrete expression to the feudal basis of coercive power that was more fully probed a few years later in England. What King Henry required was that his tenants-in-chief inform him what and how many knights they had enfeoffed on their estates before and after the death of his grandfather (1135). Nothing could show better how emphatically public was this Anglo-Norman feudalism based explicitly on 'enfeoffments' (*feffamenta*) old and new: the command of realm-wide scope was administered through the sheriffs. Yet the affective dependence persists. The written returns (known as 'Charters of the barons,' *cartae baronum*) reveal something of the deferential fear in which even the greatest of tenants complied, many of them addressing Henry as 'dearest lord' or confirming tenure by the king's grace.[26]

Sicily apart, no such declarations were yet forthcoming in the continental realms. The princes of Champagne or Bavaria or Urgell could still claim some measure of independence beyond

---

[25] *Catalogus baronum*, ed. Evelyn Jamison (Rome 1972); *Documents relatifs au comté de Champagne et de Brie, 1172–1361*, ed. A. Longnon, 3 vols. (Paris 1901–14) I; Gislebert, *Chronicon Hanoniense* c. 43.

[26] *Cat. baronum*, whose editor (Jamison) rightly draws attention to the *public*-feudal obligation there in question; '*Cartae baronum*,' *The Red Book of the Exchequer*, ed. Hubert Hall, 3 vols. (London 1896) I, 186–445.

the hopes of most English barons, no matter how princely their internal designs. Not impossibly, Count Henry the Liberal knew of the *Cartae baronum* when ordering his own survey six years later. But the magnates of every land were experiencing pressures from lord-kings as never before. King Louis VI had claimed lordship over Aquitaine as early as 1124, and his heavy-handed intervention in the Flemish succession-crisis three years later almost certainly provoked the ideological cause of independence already noticed. In the next few years Roger II decisively annexed Apulia and Capua, provoking not so much their long suppressed Lombard peoples as the popes and emperors. The most spectacular reaction of all followed from the marriage of Eleanor of Aquitaine to Henry of Anjou in 1152, resulting in the potential consolidation of her vast inheritance, plus Anjou, Maine, and Normandy. Shaken by this coup, Capetian claims to overlordship in greater France were set back for another generation. The Peace of Soissons, sworn by the greater magnates of the realm upon King Louis VII's summons in 1155, looks like a reactive measure in this perspective. Meanwhile, the scene of pressing elite confrontation shifted to Germany, where the Emperor Frederick, having parried the pope's pretence to feudal lordship in a celebrated incident at Besançon in 1157, made a conspicuous bid to impose his own on the German princes.[27]

In these years the notional potential of feudal custom for the empowerment of lord-kings came to stunning fulfillment. From the start of his reign Frederick Barbarossa (1152–90) had been compelled to rely on the fidelities of stem princes to compensate for a much reduced fiscal domain. But it was not fully clear in what manner of obligation those fidelities were sanctioned, and for those princes who profited from Frederick's successes and good will, there can have been little reason to resist the implications of a feudal view of their entitlements. Yet when Henry the Lion was charged with dereliction of service in the Italian campaign of 1174,

---

[27] Suger, *Vita* (*Deeds*) cc. 29, 30; Houben, *Roger II*, ch. 2; W. L. Warren, *Henry II* (Berkeley 1973) part I; Fuhrmann, *Germany in the high middle ages*, ch. 5.

the emperor acted according to the procedural requirement of *Landrecht*, entailing a judgment by Henry's Swabian peers. Twice Frederick tried and failed to secure Henry's adhesion to this procedure; then, turning the tables on his formidable adversary, he convoked a court of German princes bound in homage and fealty at Würzburg in January 1180. Even there the charges, alleged by the emperor in person, were by no means all 'feudal,' for it was far from clear that the obligations of homage, fidelity, and dependent tenure constituted a valid alternative to the old public law. Nevertheless, what the court judged was that Henry the Lion had not only violated the rights of magnates and churches as charged, but had also exhibited treasonous contempt of the emperor, as shown notably (but not only) by his failure to respond to three summonses 'under feudal law [*sub iure feodali*]'; wherefore Henry was deprived of his imperial 'benefices,' including the duchies of Bavaria, Westphalia, and Angaria (or Saxony).[28]

What gave force to this decision, and consummated the fall of Henry the Lion, was the understanding between the emperor and a number of princes threatened more by Henry than by Frederick. There could be no defence of princely order personified by an over-powerful dynast who, moreover, had aspired to kingly status in North Germany. The judgment had to be enforced by an invasion of Henry's Saxon lands, a campaign that not only confirmed the judgment but secured the tenurial fidelity of a new group of magnates who were invested with the Lion's fiefs. Little was left of the ancient principalities in a new Germany. Her leaders found cohesion in an incipient custom that seemed protective of tenure and inheritance at small cost, for the aids and incidents of western lands were unknown there; while Barbarossa for his part had only to justify to them the causes and expeditions that required their collaboration.[29]

Now fully king in Germany as well as in Burgundy and (with setbacks) Italy, Barbarossa had achieved a pinnacle of imperial

---

[28] *DDFri* III, nos. 795–97; *CAP* I, no. 279; Otto of St Blasien, *Chronica* c. 24.
[29] Fuhrmann, *Germany* 167–71; Leyser, 'Frederick Barbarossa' 135–40.

power. This power found consummate expression as lordship in a spectacular court held to celebrate the knighting of the emperor's sons Henry and Frederick near Mainz at Pentecost 1184. Literally a world's fair—many thousands of men in the retinues of princes and magnates 'from the whole Roman world' assembled in the temporary buildings—this was also a make-believe household of honorary submission in which kings and dukes served as dapifer, cupbearer, chamberlain, and marshall. Nor was this cultural manifestation at variance with royal purpose. So far from insisting on official power and imperial welfare, as was formerly thought, Barbarossa was by this time deeply engaged in a dynastic policy devised to secure Hohenstaufen patrimonial supremacy over the Welfs and all other competitors. Not least of these schemes, though untypical, was the betrothal of Prince Henry to Constance of Sicily in 1184, for she became unexpectedly the heiress to Sicily (1189) and the mother (1193) of Barbarossa's real successor. Henry VI (1190–97) died young, followed by his wife a year later, leaving all their realms to their child Frederick, whose tumultuous reign (1212–50) was preceded by a civil strife. The newly partisan solidarity of Staufer feudal monarchy was challenged by a partisan reaction in favour of the Welfs. The liability of Barbarossa's attempt to restore dynastic succession was the accident of premature succession; so when in 1201 Pope Innocent III threw his support to Otto of Brunswick, the son of Henry the Lion, a renewed inducement to electoral monarchy was floated that exposed the fragility of German princely submission. Frederick II pursued a Salian–Italian–Sicilian programme at the price of concessions that confirmed an estate of princes in later medieval Germany virtually created by his grandfather.[30]

In France King Philip Augustus (1180–1223) set out to do what Barbarossa had attempted, with more nearly permanent results. This was not easy, for his princely rival wore a crown while holding

---

[30] Otto of St Blasien, *Chronica* c. 26; *Die Cronik des propstes Burchard von Ursberg*, ed. Oswald Holder-Egger, Bernhard von Simson, 2d ed. (Hanover-Leipzig 1916) 56–57.

vast contiguous domains from the Channel to the Pyrenees. Under Louis VII the homages of dukes and counts, often in borderlands, had tended to define alliance rather than submission. What led to a newly insistent exercise of royal lordship was a series of problematic successions to counties followed by King John's neglect of a summons to King Philip's court. Beginning with Flanders in 1192, heirs or claimants were required to pay vast reliefs, as if for fiefs, to secure the royal permission to inherit. This is surely why Philip had already worked to redefine counties and duchies as fiefs, while urging his 'faithful men,' such as bishops, to perform homage as well as swear fidelity. But only practise and precedent could turn such events into princely custom; the lord-king had to negotiate, and sometimes to compromise. The counts of Toulouse and Burgundy seem to have resisted efforts to impose on their holdings as fiefs, while the county of Barcelona, where scribes had been instructed in 1180 to discontinue dating charters by the regnal year of France, was distant and prestigious enough to secure full independence in the later twelfth century.

Accordingly, the disinheritment of King-Duke John (1199–1216), following judgment in 1202 by a court of peers, was fully comparable to that of Henry the Lion two decades before. But the grounds in 1202 were strictly feudal, for John had already recognized Philip's lordship and jurisdiction for various fiefs inherited in his French domains when a plea from John's tenant Hugh of La Marche went to John's lord King Philip. John had wronged Hugh by seizing his betrothed Isabelle of Angoulême for himself. John's blunder in ignoring Philip's summons became the excuse for a conquest of principalities that might otherwise have long survived. Nevertheless, the feudal monarchy Philip Augustus virtually created, even if it was little more than suzerainty in some regions of a vast territory, put an end to princely independence such as had been formerly cultivated in Flanders and Anjou.[31]

---

[31] T. N. Bisson, 'The problem of feudal monarchy: Aragon, Catalonia and France,' *Speculum* LIII (1978) 460–78 (*MFrPN* ch. 12); John W. Baldwin, *The government of Philip Augustus* . . . (Berkeley 1986; tr. Béatrice Bonne, *Philippe-Auguste* . . . [Paris 1991]) chs. 1, 5, 9; Jacques Boussard, *Le gouvernement d'Henri*

❖

'FEUDAL MONARCHY': is this the right concept? Few scholars, if any, have ever denied it, for it seems so perfectly expressive of appearances around 1200. If Frederick Barbarossa rejected tenurial dependence on the pope in 1157, King John was willing to accept it in 1213, to the point of performing homage and fealty for his 'kingdoms' as the condition of peace with Pope Innocent III. After 1150 European kings and princes everywhere sought to maximize their lordships by claiming to influence or profit from successions to great patrimonies, by pretending that professions of fidelity implied the homage of vassals, and above all by urging that dependent tenures created customary obligations on which lords were entitled to insist. So Philip Augustus justified his invasion of Normandy as the execution of a judgment according to feudal custom. In other ways Alfonso VII (d. 1157) in León and Castile, Alfons I in Catalonia and Aragon, as well as Henry II, Frederick Barbarossa, and Philip Augustus himself, worked deliberately to put feudal custom to their own uses, and in so doing effectually to establish tenurial service and fidelity as the realm-wide norm it had long been in England.[32]

Yet it cannot be said that feudal *monarchy*, as distinct from lordship, was ever a juridical norm, let alone a logical one. There was something doctrinaire about it, as in the spreading notion that lord-kings should not hold of lesser men.[33] It remained a style of action, if not quite an ideal, rooted in the sentimental and traditional morality of fidelity. None of the enlarged thirteenth-century customals, apart from the peculiar one in Magna Carta, sanctioned kingly domination of fiefs as a normative end in itself. On the other hand, the management of vassals, fiefs, and tenurial

---

II Plantagenêt (Paris 1956) 280–82; J. C. Holt, *Magna Carta*, 2d ed. (Cambridge 1992 [1965]) chs. 2–6 (1st, chs. 2–5).

[32] Bisson, 'Problem of feudal monarchy'; Reilly, *Alfonso VII* 234–38.

[33] Louis Halphen, 'La place de la royauté dans le système féodal,' *A travers l'histoire du moyen âge . . .* (Paris 1950) 266–74.

obligations could easily be integrated with new techniques of power. 'Feudal monarchy' remained an implement of power, surviving only insofar as it served the reviving purposes of public defence, taxation, and crusade.

'SHADOWS OF PEACE'

Clearly it would be wrong to imagine that the great people of the later twelfth century knew only success and happiness. Amongst monarchs alone the crises of power were spectacular and by no means altogether ephemeral. Yet it may be said that, with few exceptions—the crisis of Magna Carta (still to be examined) and the judgments against Henry the Lion and John Lackland (mentioned above)—, their historical import is out of proportion to the attention scholars have lavished on them. The confrontation of pope and emperor at Besançon (1157), for all its ideological (and juristic) interest, was an inconsequential echo of dated and futile pretences. The uprising of Plantagenet sons in the 1170s was a noisy replay of earlier dynastic conflicts without so much disruption in society. The snarling violence amongst Sicilian courtiers after about 1160 had small repercussion among working people. And while modern historians of the empire rightly viewed the minority of Frederick II as a critical time for Germany, theirs was in some measure an elitist-'political' view distorted by royalist anachronism.[34]

The (better) truth would seem to be that, whereas crises of power affecting whole societies were fewer after 1150 than before, they were accompanied in many lands by the same pressures of exploitative lordship and militant ambition that had boiled over in Saxony, León, England, and elsewhere. This point may not

[34] Fuhrmann, *Germany* 145–47; Bartlett, *England* 54–57; *La historia o Liber de regno di Ugo Falcando . . .* , ed. Giovanni Battista Siragusa (Rome 1897), together with the fine commentary and translation in *The history of the tyrants of Sicily by 'Hugo Falcandus,' 1154–69*, tr. Graham A. Loud, Thomas Wiedemann (Manchester 1998).

seem obvious to readers nurtured on the demolition of 'feudalism,' and in fairness to their authorities it has nothing to do with feudalism. It has to do with the experience of power. As Abbot Stephen of Cluny remarked towards 1165, 'castellans and knights of the land batter one another; but only the churches suffer their evils and madness, only the poor experience [them, *soli pauperes sentiunt*].'[35] Abbot Stephen had Burgundy in view, yet it can hardly be doubted that the abrasive style of everyday persuasion persisted widely in his day. This persistence was out of phase with new impulses and devices of power, which themselves coincided with changing expressions of self-promoting domination. But it was more than simply coincidence. While few yet addressed the reality of violence and constraint, some now held lord-kings responsible.[36]

The phenomenon is best recorded in France, Catalonia, and Lorraine, which may not be accidental. These were zones of 'feudal revolution' in its more salient manifestations; it was here if anywhere that a knightly ethos of self-serving violence subsisted. The canons of Toul seem to have grasped this historically when, about 1151 in an astounding memorandum of appeal to the archbishop of Trier, they explained that Count Renaud II of Bar (1150–70) was guilty of violent lordship and encroachments in their lands in a pattern of hereditary 'tyranny' that had originated in the tenth century! The record is explicit about the 'usurpation' by which the church's lordship had been violated, new exactions subsequently imposed together with forced service in the count's castles. It looks like a reliable, if tendentious, account of the aggressive expansion of a one-time public lordship.[37]

---

[35] *HF* XVI, 130 (no. 398).

[36] ibid., 87 (no. 266), 130 (no. 399).

[37] *Chronique et chartes de l'abbaye de Saint-Mihiel*, ed. André Lesort (Paris 1909–12) no. 99. See also Marcel Grosdidier de Matons, *Le comté de Bar des origines . . .* (Paris 1922) 159–78; and on hereditary tyranny in Peter Abelard, citations in Bisson, 'L'expérience du pouvoir chez Pierre Abélard,' 104–5.

It is, to be sure, only one part of a local story, the only part we have. One may reasonably imagine that in an earlier generation the tenants of Saint-Mihiel had been more accepting of what had become an exploitative customary lordship. But the record of Toul could be rejected as fictional and still serve to illustrate two essential points: (1) a harshly exploitative lordship troubled large numbers of people even when it was customary; and (2) as late as 1150 people of the old social elite could be infected with the aggressive habits or ambitions of landless knights.

These were realities, indeed, in much of (greater) France; as notorious in their day as they are obscure in ours. Let us look in on several scenes, of which the representations tend not merely to confirm that of Saint-Mihiel but also to underscore the durability of an old order of power.

Aquitaine: Princes of Ill Repute. In 1137 the newly crowned Louis VII, fresh from his wedding trip to Bordeaux, received 'tearful complaints' from the monks of La Réole. They alleged that since Louis' departure their 'neighbour' lords, in violation of their oaths to the prince, had perpetrated ever worsening violence against them. The viscount of Bezeaumes had seized monks for ransom, then 'worse than ever' had extorted money from a prosperous monastic servant, and had seized two churches and a village. One Ramon Wilelm had helped himself to two estates the monks held of the king. Others of 'our neighbours . . . have imposed uncustomary tolls' in the abbey town 'contrary to your prohibition.' The complaint as we have it breaks off incomplete, but not before the monks allege that the viscount and his brother had seized the monastic lordship of Saint-Eyrard, forcing the people to resettle in a new castle nearby, imposing tolls in the marketplace of the 'desolate town,' and 'violently' forcing two of 'our townsmen' to pay ransom.[38]

[38] 'Cartulaire du prieuré de Saint-Pierre de la Réole,' ed. Ch. Grellet-Balguerie, *Archives historiques de la Gironde* v (1864) 173–74 (no. 137).

Here on display are all the elements of a petty regional tyranny: local lords, one of princely rank with his castle; seizing, imposing, and encroaching so as to create or enlarge their lordships; and it is explicitly violence in the protector-lord-king's absence that is deplored. The outcome of this plea is not known. Louis VII was soon caught up in the intrigues of his own court, favouring Raoul of Vermandois over Suger for a time, promoting his crony Cadurc to the point of antagonizing Pope Innocent II, and the like. Marcel Pacaut wrote of Louis' *politique de grandeur et d'illusion*,[39] yet if the buffetings of great-courtly lordship seemed absorbing to King Louis, some hundreds of people in the Bordelais surely had other cares. They were not alone.

Much the same profile of harshly exploitative lordship may be read in other complaints to Louis VII. They filled his reign. Princes were stigmatized: the counts of Auvergne and the viscounts of Polignac during many years; successive counts of Nevers; and the counts of Rodez, Montferrand, Mâcon, and Troyes, among others. Perhaps most notoriously violent were the viscounts of Polignac, who for decades, with brief pauses to swear amendment, plundered tenants and travellers and resorted to arbitrary demands and seizures; that is, engaged in the violence of lordship as well as the dynamic of feud.[40] The complaints point also, and perhaps progressively, to the brutalities of warfare. Depredations as recorded—denounced, renounced, not necessarily disrupted—tend to sound like the violence of armies. We begin

[39] *Louis VII et son royaume* (Paris 1964) ch. 2.

[40] Auvergne, counts and viscounts: Etienne Baluze, *Histoire généalogique de la maison d'Auvergne . . .* , 2 vols. (Paris 1708) I, 59–67; II, 57–69; *HF* XV, 707 (no. II); XVI, 43–48, 110 (339), 111 (340–42), 146 (442), 161 (476); *De glorioso rege Ludovico, Ludovici filio*, ed. Auguste Molinier, *Vie de Louis le Gros par Suger suivie de l'histoire de Louis VII* (Paris 1887) c. 22; *HL* III, 824–26; VI, 8–9 (c. 6). Also: Troyes: *HF* XVI, 119 (no. 366); Nevers: *HF* XVI, 182–83 (81); Hugues le Poitevin, *Chronique de Vézelay* ii, *MV* 419, 427, 431, 433–34, 440; *Brève histoire des premiers comtes de Nevers*, *MV* 239; Burgundy: *HF* XVI, 131 (nos. 399, 401); Georges Duby, *La société aux XIe et XIIe siècles dans la région mâconnaise* (Paris 1953), 3e partie, ch. 2. Also *HF* XVI, 57 (188), 92 (283).

to hear of *routiers*, of the ravages of 'Germans, whom they call Brabançons,' and to suspect that the bonding of unendowed knights was becoming a problem quite generally for lesser princes.[41] Yet it was for lords to protect their tenants. So it is startling to find that as late as 1170 the lord-king's biographer thought it axiomatic that without royal protection 'the stronger [men] would overly oppress the powerless.'[42] Seizures from pilgrims and merchants in the roads to Le Puy had been repeatedly condemned and renounced, and King Louis had twice made punitive expeditions to Auvergne, when in 1173 Bishop Aldebert III of Mende wearily tried again to secure the abolition of 'toll and rapine . . . unjustly' exacted in those roads. Admitting failure, he wrote bitterly to the king that the bishop (Peire) of Le Puy and the viscount (Pons) of Polignac had agreed cynically to share in the plunder for which the former had once excommunicated the latter; 'and so a shadow of peace [*umbra pacis*] was made between them.'[43]

Anjou: The Tyranny of Giraud Berlai. It was harder to exercise oppressive lordship in Anjou, but not impossible. When Giraud Berlai conspired against Count Geoffrey IV (1126–51) towards 1150, the latter put down the revolt, imprisoned the rebel, and seized his castle of Montreuil. This tyrant we have met.[44] It remains to see how his bad end marked a beginning, for what had looked like rebellion was revealed as iniquity liable to arouse princely indignation in a new way. It is engaging to speculate that Giraud's ally Louis VII may have missed the point. Surely he knew less about Giraud's lordship than the monks and tenants of Saint-Aubin. And it came out—this was represented as a miraculous revelation of their patron-saint himself to Count Geoffrey—that the prisoner had done worse

[41] HF xvi, 130 (398); *Chronicon breve de gestis Aldeberti*, ed. Clovis Brunel, *Les Miracles de Saint-Privat . . .* (Paris 1912) c. 2 (126).

[42] *De glorioso rege Ludovico* c. 22.   [43] HF xvi, 161 (no. 476).

[44] Above, pp. 140–42.

than conspire. 'Good to no one,' fearing 'neither God nor man,' he had afflicted the monks 'among others' with injuries, seized property, pillaged, and imprisoned people for ransom. The monks had appealed to the bishop of Le Mans in vain, then to the count, only to see the 'tyrant' besiege him in his castle. So with 'nowhere' (they said) to turn for 'protection,' the monks had wearily decided 'to give up part so as not to lose all.' They agreed to pay tribute to Giraud and, what is more, to do so on terms recorded in *his* charter, bearing the seals of the abbot, the count and the oppressor himself! When Giraud then attacked the count, the events already related took place. Plus one more. Once persuaded that infidelity was hardly his prisoner's only offence, Geoffrey was enraged, demanded to see Giraud's chirograph, and heard the prior of Saint-Aubin plead to recover for the church this record by which their tormentor had tried 'to turn' the deprivation of their 'liberty by tyrannical violence into a right.' So it was that in the end, Count Geoffrey staged a veritable 'triumph' of victory: by way of returning the offending document to the monks, he led his captive in chains into the cheering city of Le Mans, then came into the chapter, told the monks of his visions, and in the sight of all, solemnly tore the parchment to shreds, and tossed them into the fire.[45]

So much we learn from a thoroughly partisan account, which proves at least how deeply this ritual savaging of bad lordship struck the contemporary imagination. But this story is substantially confirmed by other texts, including the solemn diploma (dated Angers 11 June 1151) by which Count Geoffrey referred to the 'intolerable savagery' of Giraud Berlai, quashed the 'customs and exactions' he had imposed in the patrimony of Méron, and confirmed the ancient privileges of Saint-Aubin. Apart from the irony of a chartered bad lordship, there remains one further

---

[45] Jean de Marmoutier, *Historia Gaufredi* 215–23; also *Chronica vel sermo de rapinis* 83–90. All the regional annalists noticed the fall of Montreuil; see generally Chartrou, *L'Anjou de 1109 à 1151*, ch. 4.

arresting detail. The young Duke Henry attested the charter of June 1151.[46] Less than a year later he was married to Eleanor; less than four years later he was king of England. His new realm was full of baronial strongholds, and still, so it was said, of foreign knights. Henry's first public proclamation, in the Christmas court at Bermondsey 1154, was to banish the Flemings and to destroy the castles 'built to plunder the poor.' And the barons who submitted in 1155, even those formerly known to Henry, bore some resemblance to Giraud Berlai.[47]

A Tyrannical Bishop(?): Aldebert III of Mende (1151–87). Around 1170 an anonymous clerk of Mende wrote a laudatory précis of the deeds of his bishop, none other than the very prelate who was serving as the lord-king's intermediary in Auvergne. It is an astonishing text, for in and between its lines may be read not only the ecclesiastical norms of peace for which the author believed Bishop Aldebert was striving in his diocese, substantially the Gévaudan, but also something of the indignation he had aroused in those who held out for a wholly different order of power. Nor is this all, for the Anonymous cannot quite conceal that since Aldelbert was himself of the lesser castled elite—and was, indeed, as activist bishop, in conflict with his own brother, the lord-castellan of Tournel—there was something equivocal, if not quite unfaithful, about his behaviour.[48]

The story is that of a lord-bishop constructing his church's patrimony. Aldebert built a wall around the 'city of Mende, which [had been] a rustic village.' He set about ridding his cathedral of the fortified lordships of four magnates, including the count of Barcelona, that encroached physically on the church from all sides. Although the count's power was of fully public character, the bishop is said to have bought out his rights 'just and unjust.'

---

[46] *RAH2* I, no. 18* (*RRAN* III, no. 19). See also *CSAA* II, 339 (no. 865).

[47] Gervase of Canterbury, *The chronicle of the reigns of Stephen, Henry II, and Richard I . . .* , ed. William Stubbs, 2 vols. (London 1879) I, 154–61.

[48] *Chronicon breve de gestis Aldeberti* 126–34.

He got rid of the 'bad custom' by which knights of the city had their own 'prince of the kitchen' in the bishop's house. He recovered a village appropriated by the castellans of Planiol, regained a lordship seized by vicars of the lord of Doulan, acquired three castles and built another, and reclaimed revenues siphoned off by a citizen and a castellan. Having vainly censured Ricard de Peire, who was unjustly taxing tenants of Saint-Privat, and the bad castellans of La Garde-Guérin, who pillaged and beat travellers below their lair—for it was *non castrum sed spelunca*[49]—, he forced compliance on both by armed force.

In all this Bishop Aldebert surely had the masses of people with him. The 'day of reckoning' for the defeated castellans of La Garde was a public celebration in which the malefactors 're-linquished their bad customs' with solemn oaths in the presence of knights and their children, dependents [*servi*], young people and old, 'in full view of the whole people.'[50] Some other deeds were (differently) problematic. When the bishop claimed a tithe on revenues from the regional silver mines, and was canny enough to bring this matter (too) before an assembly, the people—'not very happy about his profits'—rejected the claim, evidently on grounds of its regalian nature, and consulted the count of Barcelona, who agreed with them and prohibited the imposition. Even so, Bishop Aldebert decided to levy the tax, the proceeds of which amounted to 400 marks of silver (a huge sum) per year.[51]

He did this in the belief that he himself now held regalian power from the king of France. And indeed the people of Gévaudan surely knew that in 1161 Aldebert had gone to Paris, explained to Louis VII all he was doing in his diocese to prove his fidelity to the lord-king, and had returned bearing his reward: the so-called 'golden bull' by which King Louis VII, in the presence of his 'whole baronage,' had granted to Aldebert and his successors

---

[49] 'Not a castle but a cave,' echoing the synoptic gospels on the 'cave of robbers.'

[50] *Chron. breve* c. 15.   [51] ibid., c. 8.

tenure of the bishopric of Mende together with the 'justice of the material sword.'[52]

Coming as it did in the midst of Aldebert's quest for peace—or was it, perhaps, for power?—this coup must have caused consternation in the castles of Gévaudan. Although the Anonymous could only view opposition to the bishop in moral terms, as a malicious rejection of the bishop's pastoral care, his conclusion was realistic and clear: 'for from that day when his subjects learned that the bishop had received royal power, they turned their heart to hate him and to trouble the Lord's bishop.'[53] What was left inexplicit was the cleavage between peasant tenants and masters, for it cannot have been the former who opposed Aldebert on the matter of jurisdiction. In Gévaudan as elsewhere the massive experience of exploitative lordship can only be glimpsed beyond recorded moments of renunciation. But the bishop's bid for refashioned public lordship doubled as a campaign, much resented, to impose peace on the castles. A work of the 1150s, it was amongst the earliest such enterprises in Europe. No wonder Louis VII called upon Bishop Aldebert for help in Auvergne.[54] Yet their way was premature, their efforts largely futile, for the prevailing power in all these lands was of another order.

THAT SUCH power prevailed in other European lands down to 1180 or later is as hard to deny as it is to prove. No such epistolary archive of complaint as for Louis VII survives in León-Castile or in Sicily. Whether this points to more benign regimes of rural lordship is impossible to say; everywhere fortified lordships were suffered in silence as well as complained of, yet it may be that newly exploitative dominations were ill suited to the open lands

---

[52] ibid., c. 16; and for the text, *LTC* I, no. 168 (*HL* v, no. 642).

[53] *Chron. breve* c. 17; and for the bishop's words, *HF* XVI, 160–61 (nos. 474–76).

[54] *HF* XVI, 43–44 (nos. 140, 141); 160–61 (474–76).

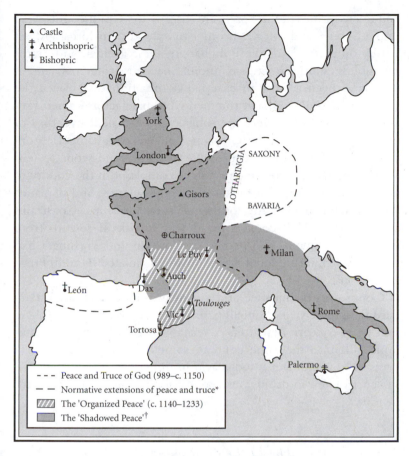

Legend:
- ▲ Castle
- ☨ Archbishopric
- ✝ Bishopric

- – – – Peace and Truce of God (989–c. 1150)
- – – Normative extensions of peace and truce*
- ▨ The 'Organized Peace' (c. 1140–1233)
- ▓ The 'Shadowed Peace'†

4. ZONES OF CONCEPTUALLY DIFFERENTIATED PEACE

*Normative extensions of peace and truce to Rhineland Germany (1090s to 1106) and to Christian Spain (1120s).

†Purely conceptual, this notion applied to all Christian Europe. The writers who echoed it had in mind French-, English-, and Italian-speaking zones, perhaps especially those associated with the Capetian-Plantagenet wars after 1150. The shading conveys no more than the implications of their moralising.

and micro-properties in Spain. In Tuscany the Guidi counts were prone to seize and violate in order to extend their lordships, yet hardly on the scale of the Polignac. In these accidented terrains resembling southern France, monks needed protectors, and it may have been a lapse in external domination that placed the community of Prataglia at the mercy of 'malefactors.' Their ravages of around 1160 were the subject of a detailed inventory of complaints to the bishop (Girolamo) of Arezzo (as imperial surrogate) that is not only comparable in nature and scope to (exactly) contemporaneous memorials of complaint in the county of Barcelona, but that also makes clear how seizures and demands were instrumental to the forging of rural lordships. Constraint was foremost. Half-cooked bread was at risk of seizure from frightened women. The people of Corezzo and Frassineta had been invaded, intimidated. Orlandino had violated Piero di Freggina's house.[55]

Complaints of injustice and violence came to Frederick Barbarossa in these years from all parts of his empire.[56] Some of these will be of concern hereafter. A veritable crisis of power in Catalonia falls into the same context, something rather less than a crisis in England. But it looks as if in imperial lands, at least, the violence of new lordships was in remission during the later twelfth century.

The Justice of Accountability

Yet the shadowed peace, to borrow Bishop Aldebert's expression, remained normal in Europe. Whatever the iniquities or failings of princely lords or the occasional violence that stalked

---

[55] *Regesto di Camaldoli*, ed. Luigi Schiaparelli *et al.*, 4 vols. (Rome 1907–22) II, no. 1193; Wickham, *Courts and conflict in Tuscany*, ch. 5; and for the setting, idem, 'La signoria rurale in Toscana,' *Strutture e trasformazioni della signoria rurale . . .* , ed. Gerhard Dilcher, Cinzio Violante (Bologna 1996) 343–409.

[56] *DDFr1* I, nos. 60, 160, 166–68, 178; cf. II, no. 222.

the customs of vengeance in walled-off streets as in countrysides, the cause of most sustained and widespread distress was the deportment of agents or commended persons in service to greater lords of all stations. In England Thomas of Monmouth thought of the sheriff as a terrifying lord with a castle.[57] At about the same time the Emperor Frederick reacted against the violence of advocates at Augsburg and Tegernsee.[58] In Champagne itemized complaints went from one R. to the abbot of Saint-Denis against the malefactions of Thibaut, 'our advocate, nay our oppressor.'[59] Everywhere allegations about harsh or extortionate surrogates were so constant and continuous that in 1159 John of Salisbury could only denounce the ones he spoke of as 'tax collectors [*publicani*]' in classically generic terms. They were worse than thieves, he said, for the thief at least felt some guilt in his transgression.[60] Yet given as he was to reflections on types, in this matter John overlooked not only current events in support of his denunciation but also some early signs of remedy. That it was a matter bearing on the experience of power in his day may be illustrated from two considerable scenes.

First, in Italy where, following the siege and destruction of Milan in 1162, Frederick Barbarossa had several towns formerly allied with her at his mercy. This was an abnormal situation, for it was in the emperor's interest to reward his retainers with the *regalia* of conquered towns without subverting the fidelity of their people. But here for a time he resorted to an exploitative domination, and for one town, Piacenza, we are informed exactly what this meant. Besides submitting to stringent terms of submission, including an indemnity of 6000 marks of silver, the citizens came under the command of a series of German magnates, of whom the most notorious was one Arnold of Dorstadt. Known colloquially as *Barbavaria*, Arnold was *podestà* from 1162 to 1164, and

---

[57] *The life and miracles of St William of Norwich* . . . , ed. Augustus Jessopp, M. R. James (Cambridge 1896) i.8,16.

[58] *DDFri* I, nos. 147, 160.

[59] *HF* XVI, 170 (no. 500).   [60] *Policraticus* vi.1 (II, 3–4).

then became the subject of a sworn inquiry relating to his regime. Some sixty-seven men and women deposed that while some of the payments they had made to Arnold's collectors (*missi*) were shares in the communal mulct (*estimum*), many others had been exacted unwillingly. What results is the resentful collective image of a (regalian) lordship in action. Here we see the 'lord Arnold,' for so he is called, and his agents exploiting justice for profit, selling 'offices' (*offitia*) as if the functions of retailing wine or making pots were theirs to license, imposing tolls in markets and gates, as well as seizing and demanding for no stated purpose. Tetavillana Scorpianus, having suffered her land to be requisitioned in her(?) absence at Pavia, had redeemed it for the substantial payment of 35*s*. 'Item, for fear of him [lord Arnold], so that he not do me harm, I sent him three pounds. And for the same fear, that he help me, I sent money totaling 45*s*. to five men by 'my messenger.'[61]

This was an authorized civic tyranny. Arnold had his own men handy to press the people; they pressed hard, expanding into the *contado* with their claims; and there is no sign of reprimand from above. Arnold remained in the emperor's favour. But if this was an altered policy of imperial domination, aimed at exploiting the rebelliousness of prospering towns, the impress it left in this sworn inquest, conceivably initiated in clerical circles, is a valid representation of exactly that mode of oppressive lordship so commonly attested elsewhere. That it could be imposed as 'public policy,' not unlike the recent attempt of an Angevin baron to have his bad lordship certified by charter, can only strengthen the appearance of normality of what might in the Italian case be termed 'fearsome lordship.' The lordly facet must be underscored, for the *podestà* came draped in the legality of an imperial official. One related to Arnold and his cronies affectively, as Tetavillana learned to her sorrow. Their lordship muscled out beyond the

---

[61] Archivio di S. Antonino di Piacenza, original (s. xii), ed. Ferdinando Güterbock, 'Alla vigilia della Lega Lombarda. Il dispotismo dei vicari imperiali a Piacenza,' *Archivio storico italiano* XCV:1 (1937) 188–217; XCV:2 (1937), 64–77.

walls, where one Gerardo Enurardo and his nephew had to give up a third of their rights over peasants and swear fidelity to Arnold in order to secure *any* of their customary renders; and because Alberto Paucaterra and his 'people [*socii*] had the domination over villagers and distrained them for crops, we [they said] gave them five sous.' And in hopes of securing Arnold's support in a judicial plea, Lanfranc Prelopanis gave up his alod and received it back in fief, 'wherefore he swore fidelity to him.'[62]

A second scene of discontent with princely servants comes into view in the county of Barcelona. There during a period extending from about 1150 to 1190 peasants subject to the lord-count Ramon Berenguer IV and his son Count-King Alfons I (1162–96) were invited to testify about the deportment of the vicars and bailiffs set over them. The resulting memorials of complaint, of which some one hundred survive for the twelfth century (extending a little beyond 1200), most still unprinted, contain evidence for the experience of power unmatched in Latin Europe before about 1250.[63]

What is revealed here looks on first sight like the reverse of the Lombard situation: an *un*-authorized rural tyranny. On closer reading the contrast weakens, without vanishing. Like Barbarossa in the 1150s Ramon Berenguer IV was trying to nail down conquests; he was, indeed, the more successful conqueror, for the captures of Lleida and Tortosa (1148–49), however uneasy, proved definitive. His problem lay in the rural domains left behind the new frontier: how to secure the bailiwicks entrusted to companions-in-arms and creditors at once aware of the rewarding frontier and less easily managed by a lord-count with widened horizons. As early as 1151 the latter had ordered a survey of old Catalonian domains, which may point to his knowledge of rural discontent, for the earliest extant memorials of complaint

---

[62] ibid., xcv:2 ('Documenti'), 69, 71; and for the contexts, Piero Castignoli, *Storia di Piacenza*, 6 vols. (Piacenza 1984–2003) II, 146–51.

[63] Introduced in my book *TV*, ch. 1; and registered from unprinted originals, 165–71.

appear to antedate, while some others are demonstrably related to, the survey-charters of 1151.[64] Both the charters of description and the memorials relate to rural patrimony, notably to domains near Girona, Barcelona, and Vic, together with others in the Ribes valley, the Penedès, and lands stretching into the new western frontier.

The memorials of complaint bring us close, indeed, to the feelings of working people subject to castellans, vicars, and bailiffs entrusted to exercise the lord-count's jurisdiction, to collect his renders, —or just to keep clear. Guillem of Sant Martí was an ambitious rising castellan when he was charged in about 1150 with 'breaking into' the count's villages of Gavà, Sant Climent, and Viladecans ('Dogtown'). He and his squires allegedly seized donkeys and grain and imposed labour services on the peasants. Deusde ('God-given'!) was a castellan at Terrassa who seized from his people, they said, and beat them. In what may be the most extraordinary of the surviving memorials, this one likewise dating from near the time of the survey of bailiwicks (1151), one Arnau de Perella was represented as a pretentious village tyrant at Caldes de Malavella and Llagostera. Making uncustomary demands on peasants and neglecting his own service to the count, he lived a lordly life of conspicuous consumption, usurping judicial payments, driving out (the count's) bailiffs, and creating his own clientele of favoured men to the 'great injury' of the count and his people. Together with much else of unflattering interest there follows a long list of itemized seizures and forced payments from men, women, and clerics. At Font-rubí to the west of Barcelona, in multiple records of complaint extending to the years 1162–65, we hear of a vicar named Berenguer de Bleda and his castellans who not only seized and taxed in uncustomary ways, but pulled beards, and outrageously ousted a prosperous villager from his house. In the Ribes valley towards 1162–70 a heartless vicar named Ramon preyed on villagers from his castle by demanding

[64] FAC II, no. 1.

money or animals on all conceivable pretexts.[65] People at Caldes and later at Argençola were said to have fled from their homes. Impassioned collective outcries against injustice were voiced at Font-rubí, bringing us as close to the popular experience of power in the twelfth century as the evidence anywhere permits. And as the peasants themselves sometimes claimed, the violence they specified was far from being the whole story of oppression they had to tell.[66] They were pointing to regimes as well as to violators.

Why and by whom were the peasants invited to make such charges? The initiative can only have come from the lord–count, whose scribes wrote the parchment originals that we possess. Quite possibly they sought oral testimony in local sessions like those in which the survey charters of 1151 were drawn up. Traces of a questionnaire, or order of questions, can be discerned, as in Piacenza. Unlike the inquest of Piacenza, however, it is categorically clear that the purpose of the Catalan scribes and their witnesses alike was justice. 'May the lord–king know,' exclaimed the people of Ribes, 'that the things we have reported are true . and we shall bring [them] to truth in his court by judgment or oath . . .'![67]

Was justice forthcoming? It is (for Catalonia) a critical question, to which there is no clear answer. All we know for sure is that the memorials of complaint were retained amongst the count-king's records when they were first classified around 1190, possibly because they corresponded to none of the judgments (iu-dicia) then on hand. And it is hard indeed to see how the complaints as such could have been judged other than by compromise or charter. For the unvoiced ones in counties and lay castellanies beyond royal control must have be been equally numerous and abiding, as we shall see.

[65] ACA, Cancelleria, pergamins extrainventaris 3451, 3275, 3409, 3141, 3288, 3433, 3217; Ramon Berenguer IV extrainv. 2501.
[66] ACA, perg. R.B IV extrainv. 2501, extrainv. 3145, 3409.
[67] ACA, perg. extrainv. 3433.

THE ACCOUNTABILITY OF FIDELITY (1075–1150)

What must be underscored about these Catalan and Lombard scenes is that the mode of power there described (and alleged) was insistently that of lordship. The 'Lord Arnold' forced people in and near Piacenza into submission, imposing oaths of fealty, creating feudal dependencies at the expense of proprietary right. Most of the accused in the domains of Barcelona—Arnau de Perella, Berenguer de Bleda, Ramon de Ribes, and others—were doing the same. Whatever the resentments they aroused, these were fresh and vital lordships sustained, like less coercive ones, by the ambitions of lesser men and knights. Lordship as a viable way of power distinct from kingship reached its apex in much of Europe in the third quarter of the twelfth century. But the truth in this assertion needs to be pried loose from the problematic irony that surrounds it.

Consider once again these people denounced by exploited populations: were they not officials bearing the public powers of the exalted rulers who appointed them? Officials, not lords? Was not the remedy for their transgressions an improved accountability? Traitors one brought to justice, but these vicars hardly look like traitors. At worst, they were violators of fidelity. What remedy could their victims have hoped for in this world of affective dependencies?

The pertinence of these questions may be illustrated by two texts from northern Europe. The first, dating from around 1180 but recalling the exploits of Count Geoffrey le Bel of Anjou (d. 1151), is a fable of good lordship narrated by the monk Jean de Marmoutier. The count, having lost his way in the forest, falls in with a peasant who, not recognizing him, is induced to comment on Geoffrey's reputation. In this telling the count comes off far better than his agents, who are described, indeed, as enemies of the people. They are said to requisition, preempt, seize and demand from, and ransom the peasants. At harvest-time the provosts 'go out to the villages where, forcing the peasants to assemble, by a new law—or rather, violence—they impose a grain-tax on them.' Also in their bag of tricks were false charges and false summonses, to be redeemed at a price. In the end, the count's identity is revealed, the peasant-informer is rewarded, and in a final lively scene the count's provosts are convoked together with his creditors. It is virtually a trial, in which the count, 'diligently hearing the cases of each, learned from them what was owed to each.' The drama mounts as the count exclaims: 'I thought I was keeping peace—and behold, such disturbance [*turbatio*]!' The provosts confess, they are ordered to make restitution, and the good count directs his agents to swear to restore illicit collections before giving up their posts.[68]

For all its literary veneer, this story cannot be dismissed as a caricature. Not only does it lend plausible support to a mass of like testimonies, including ones relating to a prevailing ethos of power in Anjou;[69] it is explicitly informative about ministerial accountability. Indeed, it may be said to respond to the question what might have become of the Catalonian memorials of complaint, for it suggests (1) that detailed charges might, indeed, be heard and settled by a lord-prince; and (2) that such a hearing might be the very trial in court that the peasants of Ribes had sought. Jean de Marmoutier, he too well read in the classics, provides what is missing in John of Salisbury: a perceptive view, one of the first we have, of the functional relation between a territorial lord and his agents.

Less perceptive but more symptomatic were the reflections of another monk. Guimann of Saint-Vaast was directed in 1170 to put new order into the accumulated fiscal records of his monastery. Drawing on a Carolingian survey dated 866(!), he had found, or decided, that Saint-Vaast had lost patrimony owing to the 'neglect of the mayors' and the 'perfidy of the stewards and lay men' to whom the custody of domains had been committed. He assured the abbot that he had done his best to collect the old titles and bring fiscal control up to date, while preserving the old survey

---

[68] Jean de Marmoutier, *Historia Gaufredi* 183–91.
[69] See above, pp. 136–42.

intact; and he urged that, while current records of patrimony be adjusted as needed, his new compilation of charters should have the venerable immutability attaching to lists of God's elect.[70]

Guimann is understandably preoccupied with the records before him. He has a strong suspicion of what they imply about past service to the abbey. But he is hardly more interested than the monk of Marmoutier in the procedural accountability of agents. For both writers it is fidelity that counts, not competence; a fidelity that is, indeed (like treachery), subject to judicial review. There is no trace of written verification here, none of periodic audits. When the count asks his provosts how much money he has, they can reply (orally); when the count hears a bad report of his provosts he summons them and demands an (oral) accounting. Some elemental notion of administrative service may be lurking here, but it is bound up with fidelity, not with office. And the real test of a servant's fidelity is reputation, hearsay. Accountability is not administrative; it is moral, remedial, judicial, —and it is occasional.

It was deeply rooted in biblical culture. This is not to claim that the influence of Scripture was decisive, for we may be sure that the New Testament parables of stewardship were as widely ignored as they were reiterated. Yet it is no accident that the act of account, of whatever sort, is represented habitually in the Vulgate Latin: *reddere rationem* (to render account).[71] These words evoke judgment, judgments, of every sort, including the Last one. By the third quarter of the twelfth century the Last Judgment, while hardly original in iconography, seemed freshly threatening, not least in the lands of pilgrimage and crusade. Great sculptors in the Massif and Burgundy had rendered it overhead in tympana of fearful power: at Conques (Rouergue) the damned and elect re-

---

[70] *Cartulaire de l'abbaye de Saint-Vaast d'Arras* . . . , ed. Eugène van Drival (Arras 1875) 3–8.

[71] Sigibert of Gembloux, *Chronica, an.* 1062, ed. L. C. Bethmann (Hanover 1844) 360; OV v.3 (III, 14); Landulph Senior, *Historia* iii.5 (88); John of Salisbury, *Policraticus* vii.21 (II, 197).

spectively writhe and rejoice following the verdicts of Christ Judge.[72] Like some scary film, opening (so to speak) all over southern France, this novelty coincided with new stress on compunction. Hildebert of Le Mans had preached of God's Second Coming as a judgment of diversely accountable people; while Peter Abelard found wisdom in the unfaithful steward (Luke xvi) by likening the unrighteous mammon to alms incumbent on Christians as God's stewards.[73] This resonance in religious culture matters chronologically as well as conceptually, for accountability is a topic—the first of three major topics in this book—that takes us back some two generations in order to grasp the conjunctures of the later twelfth century.

The concept of audit was indistinct from that of judgment. It is true that towards 1178 Richard fitz Nigel had no difficulty with the distinction, yet even he spoke of sheriffs being judged (iudicantur) in the exchequer.[74] Closer to popular belief was the contemporary Catalan homilist of Organyà, when he wrote that for our sinful words 'we shall have to render account [redre radó] on Judgment Day.'[75] And it was this way of thinking that helped to define the accountability of office, such as derived from the Rule of Saint Benedict and the Pastoral Care of Saint Gregory. Abbot Martin surely had the former (at least) in mind when he commissioned the monk Guimann to reform the patrimonial records of Saint-Vaast.

Prescriptive Accountancy. The practise of accounting for fiscal domains was, as for several centuries past, more or less in conformity with these biblical, patristic, and monastic (and baronial) ideas. The fable from Anjou shows how it worked; the story may

---

[72] Plate 6; *Rouergue roman*, ed. Jean-Claude Fau, 3d ed. (Zodiaque 1990) planches 12–13; Grivot and Zarnecki, *Gislebertus*, plate B. Last Judgments figure on tympana at Beaulieu and Saint-Martin (Saint-Gilles).

[73] PL CLXXI, 350; Abelard, *Sermo 30*, PL CLXXVIII, 564–66.

[74] *Dialogus de scaccario* . . . , ed. and tr. Charles Johnson, corrected ed. (Oxford 1983) i.4 (15); ii.1,4,7 (69, 84–85, 87).

[75] *Homilies d'Organyà*, ed. d'Amadeu-J. Soberanas *et al.* (Barcelona 2001) 99–100.

be apocryphal or embellished, but it is not a parody. Occasional or informal audits of stewards or bailiffs must have been the rule on monastic and episcopal lands as well as princely ones in the eleventh and twelfth centuries. For these audits, as also in their absence, the only written instrument of account would have been the survey of domains; that is, a static description of the lord's tenants, their wealth, and their obligations. For example, here is the beginning of one of the survey-charters for the comital domains in Catalonia (2 April 1151):

> This is a commemoration of all this *honor* and usages which the count of Barcelona has in Caldes de Malavella and in its limits. The count has indeed 115 manses in this *honor*. And there go out in rents from this *honor* 169 and a half pigs and 88 pairs of chickens and 61 quarters of feedgrain as provision, and this is the vicar's fief . . . and the count receives in all this *honor* taschs and a quarter of the tithe . . . [etc.].[76]

This was a prescriptive accountancy in its essence: it responds to the question: what do I have. (or should I have)? 'How much money do I have?' asks the Count of Anjou. 'Lord,' says the provost, '1000 sous of your revenues are on hand.'[77] It is an inventory, not the active reckoning of a balance or profit. And when the monk Guimann discovered a Carolingian survey for Saint-Vaast, he was eager to preserve it—intact.

Does it seem odd to speak of such activity as accountancy? Are not the polyptychs and surveys of medieval Europe the very sources of social and economic history? Surely they are so, yet here for once we may have mistaken the trees for the forest. For the astonishing truth seems to be that historians of institutions have never considered the possibility that accounting might once have taken this form; that it might therefore have changed in purpose in the Middle Ages. To put it another way: that when Charlemagne ordered his servants to inventory his estates in about 800 he was quite as much engaged in accounting as when

---

[76] *FAC* II, no. 1G. [77] *Historia Gaufredi* 188.

barons of the English exchequer ordered records of income and expense to be written annually on rolls of parchment four centuries later. In fact, there are strong reasons for believing that the surveys of fiscal domains that survive abundantly for every medieval century after the eighth were thought of *as accounts* by contemporaries, who spoke of them as *brevia, descriptiones, rationes,* polyptychs, and the like, including Domesday Book.

One of these reasons is that surveys of monastic lands in Flanders in the tenth century were called *ratio(nes)*; and this is the very Latin word Saint Jerome had used to translate the Greek word for account (*logos*) in the New Testament parables. *Ratio* continued to be used in twelfth-century Flanders to refer to those periodic records of income and expense that every historian regards as accounts. A second reason is of a different order: if we understand that lords were chiefly interested in testing fidelity, and less concerned about precise balances of credit/debit, then it is hard to see what more they needed in writing. Plenty of mercenaries must have been paid without record. For the masses of people the survey showed what was out there; the steward served up what was due, or did not. What more was needed?

Only the merest wave at mountainous survivals need be made here to prove the normal persistence of prescriptive accountability in the period of this book. 'This is a breviary [*breviarium*] of Saint Columban's [of Bobbio] lands. In the court of Saint Martin . . . [tenth or eleventh century].' The 'benefices' are specified.[78] 'Here is a description of the lands of Peterborough Abbey in Lincolnshire. 1. Walcot by Threekingham 2 1/2 carucates is demesne and 2 1/2 carucates in socage . . . [ca. 1083–87].'[79] 'If anyone wants to know how many peasants Saint-Jean [de Sorde] should have in Sen-Cric and what each one ought to give, he will find a full notice here. The house [*Lo casau*] of Doat de La Barrere ought to

---

[78] *Inventari altomedievali di terre, coloni e redditi,* ed. Andrea Castagnetti *et al.* (Rome 1979) no. 8:4 (176–92).

[79] David Roffe, 'The *descriptio terrarum* of Peterborough abbey,' *Bulletin of the Institute of Historical Research* LXV (1992) 15–16.

give 10 loaves, 2 *concae* of grain, a hen . . . [1150–67].'[80] Audits
sometimes occurred, like that of a Gascon steward (late eleventh
century) summoned 'to render account for certain matters un-
faithfully [*infideliter*] managed by him.'[81] A century later Caesar of
Heisterbach told of some jealous servants of Utrecht who tattled to
the bishop about a steward managing the patrimony *non fideliter*:
'we advise you,' they say, 'to account with him.'[82] It rather looks as
if—and the fable of Anjou points the same way—lords who trusted
their servants were unlikely to insist on auditing them with regularity. Accounting was the remedy for malfeasance. It becomes
easier to understand why hardly so much as a scrap of written evidence of balances of account survives from before 1100.

Most lords in early medieval Europe thought of their patrimonies as fixed assets. They accounted for them accordingly. The
written survey resembled some ornate reliquary or gospel book.
It contained the estate exactly, took account of it in that represen-
tational sense. It was a prescriptive account against which the fidelity of servants (stewards, bailiffs) could be tested. And it was
easy for the servants of distant masters to imagine themselves in a
state of lordship rather than of managerial fidelity. We have met
some of them.

Towards an Accountability of Office (1085–1200)

One of the problems faced by Ramon Berenguer IV around 1150
and Frederick Barbarossa a decade later is that neither had devices
of account adequate to his needs. The *regalia* were prescribed in
charters or treaties, but not so as to guide or limit collectors in the
streets or households of Lombard towns; nor had the lord-emperor
any useful, let alone official, survey of German domains he was

---

[80] *Cartulaire de Saint Jean de Sorde*, no. 143.

[81] *MSB* viii.22 (310–12).

[82] *Dialogus miraculorum* xii.23, ed. Josephus Strange, *Caesarii Heisterbacensis* . . . ,
2 vols. (Cologne 1851) II, 332–35. See also *Chronicle of Battle* 108.

having himself to reorganize.[83] The only fiscal account to survive from this time in German royal archives is an undated memorandum detailing the obligations of towns to service in imperial campaigns; its latest editors place it in the first months of Frederick Barbarossa (1152–53).[84] For the count-prince of Barcelona the solution was to revive an inherited prescriptive regime, which becomes visible in a well-preserved roll of parchment that contains the survey-charters for bailiwicks of 1151. Both rulers were behind the times. While both were faced with the constraints induced by unfaithful service, neither had yet been obliged to reckon with economic pressures as such.

A Dynamic of Fiscal Growth (ca. 1090–1160). It was otherwise in the lands bordering the English Channel and the North Sea. There the limitations of prescriptive accountability had long since become apparent, even if obscured by the celebrity and originality of personages, events, and ideas. This was a cluster of growing societies around 1100: of expanding and multiplying villages and churches; of prospering towns, such as Rouen, Bruges, and Winchester; of church building; everywhere more people, more horses. Yet it was an old world in its sensibilities, imperatives, and techniques, which is why Eadmer of Canterbury exclaimed about the 'strange new changes we have seen.'[85] Lords expected fidelity of servants, some of whom were good, some bad; but competence still counted for less than fidelity in the management of affairs. And it was just in the most prosperous, buoyant, and turbulent places that we begin to hear of new men handling domains and revenues—of new men doing things differently. The problem is to figure out what exactly they *were* doing.

Take Ranulf Flambard, for example. Ambitious, unprincipled, perhaps the most hugely successful of social climbers in Norman

---

[83] *DDFr1* I, nos. 88, 94 119; II, nos. 224, 229–43.

[84] *Das Tafelgüterverzeichnis des römischen Königs* (MS. *Bonn S.1559*), ed. Carlrichard Brühl, Theo Kölzer (Cologne-Vienna 1979).

[85] *The life of St Anselm . . .* , ed. R. W. Southern (London 1962) 1.

England, he began in the 1080s and 1090s tending the lord-king's revenues. As far as we know he did nothing to alter ways in which sheriffs accounted; he invented no new techniques, had no worries about balancing books. What he certainly did was to manage ecclesiastical vacancies so as to enable William Rufus to profit lavishly from them; and he probably did something even more interesting than that. Apparently Flambard copied out of Domesday Book some assessments for the midlands, then made experimental measurements with a view to multiplying fiscal and taxable tenures. The evidence is problematic, but it supports the conjecture that Flambard, who could see that the values of those lands were increasing, imposed new assessments on them. Orderic speaks also of 'new taxation' and adds that by all such measures Flambard 'brutally oppressed the king's people.' One is reminded of the *Peterborough chronicle* which, in its entries for 1094–1105, has a relentless indictment of fiscal rapacity by kings' men.[86]

It is not hard to imagine how well it worked for the lord-king: this affective-fidelitarian mode of management. His new men produce more and more revenue; who is he to worry overmuch how it is produced?—to worry about accountability in this heady time of overflow? But there must have been uneasiness amongst those serving William Rufus, to say nothing of bitterness in the localities, such as Keyston (Hunts.), where the sheriff Eustace had been accused of seizures.[87] The inquiries of 1085 had produced a flood of complaints about evictions and encroachments, and many people would have known about the discrepancy between the swelling incomes of sheriffs and the fixed totals of obligations and entitlements, as defined in Domesday Book and other surveys.[88]

---

[86] OV viii.8 (IV, 170–74); *Peterborough chronicle, an.* 1094–1105; R. W. Southern, 'Ranulf Flambard,' *Medieval humanism and other studies* (Oxford 1970) ch. 10.

[87] DB fol. 208 (Hunts.).

[88] DB for Hunts., Lincs, Yorks.; *Historia ecclesie Abbendonensis* ii.4 (II, 4); BL, MS Cotton Tib. A xiii, fol. 39 (ed. Thomas Hearne, *Hemingi chartularium ecclesie Wigorniensis*, 2 vols. [Oxford 1723] I, 83–84); BL MS Cotton. Vesp. B xxiv, fols.

That this problem was noticed in England in the 1080s—earlier there than anywhere else in Europe—is all but proven by the structure of the Domesday inquiries. Domesday Book itself is not simply the greatest of all medieval surveys, it is also untypical of its genre in one crucial respect. It aimed to take account of change, by prescribing a chronology of valuations in its questionnaire: 'in the time of King Edward [TRE],' when King William gave the [land], and the present.[89] This was arguably a promotional device in the circumstances of the Conqueror's last years, but the economic implications cannot have been lost on men like Ranulf Flambard. Domesday Book was a fiscal account for a conquered public order reorganized in lordships and dependencies. Its inadequacy as an account, and its incongruity with Old English devices of public reckoning, were almost at once apparent.[90]

Turning next to France, two situations may be distinguished. At Cluny in the 1120s Abbot Peter the Venerable was trying to pick up the pieces of a patrimonial lordship badly neglected in prosperous times of dependency on Spanish gold. Having consulted 'informed brothers' about the economic crisis, he reorganized the patrimony in deaneries of monthly responsibility (mesatica). In time this system required adjustments. We hear of second and third ordinances in which functional responsibilities were shifted and resources redeployed. It was prudent economy, for example, to reassign the deanery of Mazille, which was productive of oats, to the maintenance of horsely retinues. Whatever the improvements, among which nothing is said about audits, they could not prevent the abbey from falling badly into debt in the 1140s. Whereupon Abbot Peter and the monks, taking advantage of Henry of Winchester's willingness to bestow

---

57v–62 (ed. H. B. Clarke, 'The early surveys of Evesham abbey . . . ,' PhD thesis, Birmingham, 246–70, which I have not seen); etc.

[89] SC 101.

[90] Dialogus i.4 (14); ii.14–16 (61–64); Reginald L. Poole, The exchequer in the twelfth century . . . (Oxford 1912) 27–31, 36. For other views, Domesday studies . . . , ed. J. C. Holt (Woodbridge 1987); David Roffe, Domesday. The inquest and the book (Oxford 2000); and works cited below.

his own money and valuables on the house in which he had been
nurtured, entrusted to Bishop Henry a further task of fiscal
reform.[91]

Henry proceeded to survey the monastic patrimony of Cluny,
much as, we may suppose, he had done at Glastonbury some
thirty years before.[92] His results at Cluny, probably in 1155, may
be read in a remarkable record that he himself (it seems) spoke of
as a *constitucio expense* for Cluny. As this term implies and the contents show, this was a prescriptive fiscal account. It responds to
the questions what do the monks possess and where? Four points
about it stand out. (1) The account has an old-fashioned appearance, to the extent of resembling a Carolingian polyptych, for it
is neatly organized by deaneries and bears summations for the
customary renders of each. (2) Yet it has also the marks of adap-
tive flexibility. It takes notice of change over time, like Domesday Book; it refers to variable returns owing to seasonal change;
and it mentions incremental change without seeming to notice
the difficulties this poses for prescriptive evaluation. Most remarkably, as Georges Duby stressed half a century ago, it appears
to invite a more intense exploitation of the direct domain, because the summations are repeatedly said to be exclusive of returns (*lucracio*) from the domain. (3) Accordingly, the purpose of
the 'constitution' is not so much to evaluate Cluny's lordship in
total as to establish the minimum yield of customary assets while
setting no limit on collections from the direct domain. How the
latter were to be realized is quite as inexplicit as it is crucial.
Was this perhaps Bishop Henry's challenge to the monks? At
any rate (4) in the absence of written audits, Henry's survey
could only have been used to verify collections from customary
tenancies, mills, fisheries, and the like. That such an operation

---

[91] *Chartes de Cluny* v, no. 4132; Georges Duby, 'Le budget de l'abbaye de
Cluny entre 1080 et 1155. Economie domaniale et économie monétaire,' *Annales: E.S.C.* VII (1952) 155–71.

[92] N. E. Stacy, 'Henry of Blois and the lordship of Glastonbury,' *EHR* CXIV
(1999) 1–33.

might be confused conveniently with current audits is suggested by an entry for the deanery of Malay that 'in this year were collected there 200 *panals* of wheat, 200 of barley, and two *carrats* of wine.'[93]

The story of the Abbot Suger at Saint-Denis shows even more explicitly what was happening in fiscal domains. It relates to a period beginning around 1110 or even before. About 1145 Suger wrote an account (the word is apt) of his own service to the monks, first as provost in local domains, then (from 1122) as abbot. This text has the appearance of something genuinely new in the history of accounting. At the request of his assembled monks Suger reviewed the condition of the Saint's domains in a kind of narrative survey that not only tells us what the villages are worth, but also what they *were* worth before he set to work. Suger is not modest. What he wrote is an account of entrepreneurial energy, a veritable litany on the Latin words *augmentare* and *incrementum*. At Saint-Denis itself Suger has increased the render from £12 to £20, 'wherefore,' as he says, '£8 of increase' (or as we might say, 67 percent). At Tremblay, where the count of Dammartin had imposed an arbitrary tallage, Suger bought him off with a money-fief of £10 in return for his homage, and achieved for the abbey an increment in revenues from grain of 90 modes. At Argenteuil he claims to have doubled the old rents to £40, while 'from the render in grain, which used to be 6 modes, we now receive 15.' For some domains Suger has much else to say about his achievement; for all of them he stresses growth, and for several the *incrementum* is the sole element of account. So, 'at Sannois £4 increment of the new rent, and of the old 100s.' Likewise for Montigny, where the numbers are respectively 50s. and 10(s.), and where the word *incrementum* is omitted as superfluous.[94]

---

[93] *Chartes de Cluny* v, no. 4143.

[94] *Gesta Suggerii abbatis*, ed. and tr. Françoise Gasparri, *Suger, oeuvres* i.1–30 (i, 54–110). In his edition-translation titled *Abbot Suger on the abbey church of Saint-Denis*, 2d ed. (Princeton 1979), Erwin Panofsky omitted most of this material.

What is happening here is of great interest. The procedural novelty is not merely formal; it affects the whole conception of fiscal control. Suger has restored the abbey's lordship by the expedient of taking it into his own hands. This is an arbitrary act that has the effect of shifting fiscal defendancy from himself to the castellans, advocates, and provosts whom the abbot has called to local account or with whom he has negotiated. Suger tells us how this worked. At Le Tremblay he converted an arbitrary castellany into a feudal dependency, thereby securing incremental revenues for Saint-Denis. At Toury Suger *himself* took on the provostship, struggled to free the domain from demands by castellans of Le Puiset, and had a new survey put into writing.[95]

Everywhere in the twelfth century there are signs of this abrasive, quasi-judicial accountability of growth. Suger's is the rare voice of a medieval provost who became a great man and a prestigious writer. Yet he was not alone in his purpose. Listen to Bernat Bou, a one-time bailiff for Count Ramon Berenguer IV of Barcelona, addressing the court of Ramon's child-successor about 1165:

> I Bernat Bou of Girona for the love and profit of my late lord-count . . . have sought all his well-being and profit and increase for Girona and Palafrugell [and other places], as is written here below, without imposing any new usage in those places by the grace of God. First, on the day when I bought the bailiwick of Girona the bailiff . . . gave the lord-count only 800s. from tolls and customs and I give my lord from those tolls and customs 1500s. each year. Formerly, the lord-count received only 5 1/2 modes of wheat from the measuring tax and I give him 7. . . . [etc.]

Everywhere Bernat has increased the old renders. He insists on his achievement with pride and pain, feeling obliged in the end to accuse a rival bailiff of trying to conceal his (Bernat's) success.[96]

[95] *Gesta Suggerii* c. 2 (60, 62), c. 18 (82–88).
[96] *FAC* II, no. 18.

Rulers and their courtiers begin to face up to their agents, summoning them as defendants, like the count of Anjou in his biographer's tale. Just here two narratives may be said to converge, for Bernat Bou's account can, indeed, be associated with the memorial of complaint for Caldes and Llagostera already mentioned. When we first catch sight of sheriffs accounting in England, or provosts in France, or notaries in Flanders, or bailiffs in Catalonia: wherever we look, as the mist of our ignorance clears, the accountants for fiscal domains are defendants in justice. The accountability of growth remains remedial, like that of salvation; and as will soon appear, these two cultural spheres are bound up by a curious coincidence in the early twelfth century.

But the lord-rulers of that time were labouring under a severe handicap, for they and their servants continued to rely on surveys or inventories that went out of date almost as fast as they were written. That Sicily was in advance of other lands in respect to accountancy, as has sometimes been thought, now seems most unlikely; for to judge from the surviving fiscal archives, the registers of the *dīwān* were not conceptually different from the surveys and fiscal lists known everywhere else in Latin Europe.[97] And if there was one thing that prescriptive accounting could *not* do well, it was to keep pace with fiscal growth: if every new tenant, every new manse, every new toll required a revision in the survey (or worse, a rewriting) then the whole idea of fidelity to a fixed domain was shaken. One lesson of Domesday Book must have been learned bitterly soon after it was made: that one could neither use it for accounting with sheriffs nor rewrite it.[98] This, too, was a crisis in the twelfth century, a sustained crisis of outlook and technique that forced new contrivances on men

---

[97] Cf. C. H. Haskins, *The Normans in European history* (Boston 1915) 22, 226, 228–29; Doris May Stenton, 'England: Henry II,' *Cambridge medieval history* v (1926), 574. See below, p. 343.

[98] The known attempts to rewrite it hardly prove the contrary. See, e.g., *The Lincolnshire Domesday and Lindsey survey*, ed. C. W. Foster, T. Longley (Lincoln 1921); and *Hereford Domesday, circa 1160–1170 . . .*, ed. V. H. Galbraith, James Tait (London 1950).

behind courtly facades, and that was hardly better recognized by Richard fitz Nigel than by the monk Guimann in the 1170s. Economic growth could no longer be ignored. There was a spreading realization that to maintain great estate one must exploit domains profitably; *manage* them, not simply live off them; and that to profit from lordships one must achieve the capability of calculating profit by means of periodic audits.

Towards a New Technique (ca. 1110–75). This capability required nothing other than a new attitude towards patrimonial domains together with a correspondingly new technique in accounting. What linked attitude and technique was the realization that fidelity might not always entail competence. So in the course of the twelfth century a new sort of written account comes into view: a record devised to prove rather than prescribe, one that literally takes account of current balances of revenue and expenditure.

ENGLAND: PIPE ROLLS AND EXCHEQUER. Possibly the earliest and certainly the most famous of these new records were the pipe rolls of England, in which accounts of shire-revenues were written down annually after the sheriffs were audited at Michaelmas (29 September) by the lord-king's courtiers. Strips of parchment bound at their heads and rolled into pipes, these records survive in a continuous series from 1155 to the nineteenth century, the greatest deposit of fiscal records in the world. But they originated in the reign of Henry I, and it is clear from the lone extant pipe roll from that time—for the year 1129–30—that it was already the product of collaborative expertise in the royal court. By 1127 the king himself could refer to 'my barons of the exchequer' as the locus of that expertise, and there are good reasons for dating the exchequer as a recognized body of audit to about 1110.[99]

As everywhere else the audit in this body was judicial. This means not only that the sheriff sought quittance for his year's ac-

---

[99] *RRAN* II, no. 1538. See generally Poole, *Exchequer*; and Mark Hagger, 'A pipe roll for 25 Henry I,' *EHR* CXXII (2007) 133–40, regarding a new-found fragment from 1126.

count, but also that unprescribed obligations, disputes, and violence might exercise the men hearing the sheriff, as they did the sheriff himself. It is likely that the violence of purveyors for the lord-king had provoked some regulation of the royal household already towards 1108–10; the decision, quite plausibly by Bishop Roger of Salisbury, to regularize audits on the model of a chessboard may be connected with this reform. The son of Bishop Roger's protégé, fitz Nigel, had heard it said that the English exchequer was copied from a Norman one, which is not inconceivable given the diffusion of chess in continental elites in the eleventh century. But the Norman exchequer is not otherwise recorded so early, so that the more interesting analogy relates to the abacus. It is very suggestive that the monk Turchil, who wrote about this device for counting, probably before 1117, was acquainted with the sheriff Hugh of Buckland.[100]

The pipe rolls were, so far as we are informed, a novelty in the early twelfth century. Already in 1129, and so thereafter, the sheriff accounts for the farm of his revenues and other receipts in relation to his expenses, resulting in a balance that doubtless varies from year to year. It is true that fixed revenues are entered on the roll, which remains thereby a prescriptive account. But the essence of the audit lies in the state of mutable account, receipts, and obligations.[101] How had this come about?

Almost a century ago R. L. Poole argued that the appearance of the exchequer, both word and thing, marked 'a revolution in the method of auditing the accounts.' He stressed the capability of the abacus for easing the arithmetic difficulties in accounting,

---

[100] *Dialogus* i.4 (14); Poole, *Exchequer*, ch. 7; C. H. Haskins, 'The abacus and the exchequer,' *Studies in the history of mediaeval science* (Cambridge, M., 1924) 327–35; Green, *Government under Henry I* chs. 3–5. For the troubles of 1108, Eadmer, *Historia novorum in Anglia* iv (192–93); William of Malmesbury, *Gesta regum Anglorum* v.411, ed. R. A. B. Mynors *et al.*, 2 vols. (Oxford 1998–99) i, 742. On influences and derivation, *Dialogus* i.4 (14); Pierre Bonnassie, 'Descriptions of fortresses in the Book of Miracles of Sainte-Foy of Conques,' *From slavery to feudalism* 142–43; and for Hugh of Buckland, Poole, *Exchequer* 46–50.

[101] *Magnus rotulus scaccarii, 31 Henry I*, ed. Joseph Hunter (London 1833).

which was as much as to suggest that numeracy and literacy were becoming new prerequisites for fiscal service. Later scholars have questioned this interpretation, while stressing the self-evident aim of improving accountability. 'The whole point of the court,' writes Judith Green, 'was to make sure financial officials discharged their obligations in full, and to impose penalties on those who failed to do so.'[102] All these views, including Poole's, may now be regarded as acceptable within unacceptable limits. Fully to verify fiscal service would indeed have signaled a revolution in accountancy, but surely not because the chess-board enabled a better arithmetic. What must be recognized is that the abacus was a device for counting, not for accounting. One cannot explain the pipe roll simply by explaining the exchequer. It is good to ask why people wished to count better, and the answer is hardly beyond comprehension for any who have tried to add or multiply Roman numerals. But let us also ask why royal clerks began to record the king's revenue in relation to expenditure in such a way as to produce summations or balances of receipts, payments, and debts.

For England these questions remain unanswered, perhaps even, to some extent, unasked. The troubles with sheriffs under Rufus, the facts that Domesday Book was organized by lordships (and compiled by hundreds) and was first preserved and consulted in the treasury at Winchester, the profusion of (prescriptive) inventories and lists for taxation and lordships alike, and the absolute lack of records of audit: all these matters (and the last of them only with the others) taken together point to a subversion of Old English written accountancy after the Conquest. Not all was lost, to be sure. Anglo-Saxon lists of possessions or books sometimes include summations or declarations of value, always a pointer to the sufficiency of prescriptive accounts. The Northamptonshire Geld Roll refers to payments as well as possession; the flyleaf to a post-Conquest gospels preserves a list of payments by Worcester

---

[102] Poole, *Exchequer* 40; Richardson and Sayles, *Governance* 279–82; Green, *Government* 40.

church to King William I; and the (Latin) geld rolls that figure in the Exon Domesday were clearly designed to further the work of collection.[103] Nor is this all that we have. For the later twelfth century it has been surmised that writs, lists, and memoranda of every sort were being routinely destroyed in vast amounts,[104] but by that time we may be sure of what is lost, for not all was destroyed. It is otherwise with the post–Conquest generations, when amongst diverse fiscal survivals there is not the slightest trace of written audits. Fidelity was on trial in early Norman England, where sheriffs, reeves, and moneyers must often have been reproached with the fading ideal of bureaucratic purpose. In this respect Domesday Book was more the problem than the solution.[105] When fiscal accountancy is viewed in European perspective, it looks as if the revolution that produced the exchequer was not so much technological as conceptual.

FLANDERS: THE *GROTE BRIEF* AND ITS ORIGINS. For that is, indeed, what we find on the continent. If, as historians now reasonably suppose, the new accountancy of the exchequer dates from about 1108–10, then we cannot be sure that the English invention was the first of its kind. For one thing it is altogether likely that an exchequer audit was instituted at the same time in Normandy, where it was cited as a functional operation in 1130.[106]

---

[103] *Anglo-Saxon charters*, ed. and tr. A. J. Robertson, 2d ed. (Cambridge 1956) 230–36, 242 and 493; Exeter, Library of the Dean and Chapter, MS 3500, fols. 1–12; and for a fine conspectus of records, H. B. Clarke, 'The Domesday satellites,' in *Domesday Book. A reassessment*, ed. Peter Sawyer (London 1985) ch. 4. See also James Campbell, 'The significance of the Anglo-Norman state in the administrative history of western Europe,' reprinted in (idem) *Essays in Anglo-Saxon history* (London 1986) 174. For a good example of an unitemized survey and its difficulties, see BL, MS Cotton. Vesp. B xxiv, fols. 57v–62 ('Evesham K.' Clarke's edition is cited in his 'Satellites,' 62–63.).

[104] Nicholas Vincent, 'Why 1199? Bureaucracy and enrolment under John and his contemporaries,' *English government in the thirteenth century*, ed. Adrian Jobson (Woodbridge 2004) 29, 33, 44–48.

[105] See also M. T. Clanchy, *From memory to written record. England 1066–1307*, 2d ed. (Oxford 1993) 32–35.

[106] *RRAN* II, no. 1584; Richardson and Sayles, *Governance* 165–66.

None of its early records survive. Secondly, there is notable if problematic evidence of a public fiscal accountancy in Flanders, likewise in the early twelfth century, and conceivably antedating 1100. Yet the earliest known example of a Flemish fiscal account comparable to the pipe roll of 31 Henry I—that is, a probatory record of audit—dates from 1187. This is the so-called *Grote Brief*, literally 'great account,' which is a record of payments and charges in the comital domains of Flanders. Reconstructed from dispersed parchments once stitched end to end, the *Grote Brief* sought, like the pipe roll, to represent income and expenses in relation to fixed obligations. It organizes balances of debt by locality, making no attempt to totalize for all domains. As with the pipe roll of 1130, the *Grote Brief* of 1187 has already a regularity of form that points to practised routine. And there is a further point of likeness, for in Flanders, too, the earliest extant composite account of audit stands alone, no doubt (in this case) by accident; no further rolls survive until 1255.[107]

When and how did this Flemish accountancy begin? Once again we are in the dark, surely because, here again, creative people were departing from tradition and written forms. But the traces in Flanders are engaging and curious. By a famous charter dated 31 October 1089, Count Robert I granted major fiscal privileges to the canons of Saint Donatian of Bruges. Their provost, he went on to declare, was henceforth to have charge 'of all the revenues of the principality of Flanders'; he was to be 'our chancellor' as well as 'receiver and collector,' and was to have the 'supervision of all my notaries and chaplains of all clergy serving in the count's court.'[108]

These words appear to mark the foundation of a probatory accountancy of audit. Indeed, it is tempting to suppose that the *Grote Brief* of 1187, wherein the notaries of Flanders are accountants

---

[107] *Le compte général de 1187, connu sous le nom de 'Gros Brief'* . . . , ed. Adriaan Verhulst, Maurits Gysseling (Brussels 1962).

[108] *ACF*, no. 9; and for the problematic nature of this charter, above, p. 146n.

for local revenues, was produced from a *Redeninge* with the provost-chancellor in the manner here projected.[109] This appearance cannot, in the present state of knowledge, simply be rejected. It is just possible that Flanders was the first European principality to adopt a new accountancy of periodic review. But any such conclusion faces two objections. First, the authenticity of the Robertian charter has been seriously disputed. One of the suspicious elements is precisely the clause relating to the provost's charge, which is arguably anachronistic. Second, even if the eminent defenders of its integrity are correct, the charter as we have it is inexplicit as to the fiscal work of the *magisterium* of provost and notaries. What were they doing in the 1090s? All that can safely be said, taking account of these difficulties, is that a probatory review of Flemish comital revenues is first attested by Galbert of Bruges in his record of the crisis of 1127–28. Having first mentioned *brevia et notationes* 'of the count's revenues,' he says that in May 1128 Count William Clito had to summon an informed notary before whom the 'keepers of estates and revenues would appear to render account [*rationem . . . reddituri*] of their obligations.'[110] This can only refer to a procedure of audit. It is the earliest such evidence anywhere in the twelfth century. In Flanders this novel practise would seem to have originated in or before the time of Charles the Good (1119–27), and so perhaps at the same time as the incipient exchequer(s).

And there is one further gleam in the pre-Caroline obscurity, a tantalizing gleam. Towards 1117 the monk Lambert of Saint-Omer was at work on his encyclopaedic *Liber floridus* when he ran out of parchment. So he made do with a discarded fiscal record of revenues on comital estates, stitched it together with other blank membranes, and did his best to erase the unwanted

---

[109] The editors of the *Grote Brief* (cited in note 107) assume so.

[110] *De multro* cc. 35, 112. The latter chapter reads in part: '. . . comes Willelmus precipiens notario suo Basilio ut ad se festinaret, eo quod in presentiam suam berquarii et custodes curtium et reddituum suorum rationem debitorum suorum reddituri venissent.'

writing. His best, luckily for us, was not quite perfect. Just in the middle, where the folio folds, some of the old lettering escaped his pumice, where it can be read today in Lambert's original.[111]

Now, since it is known that Lambert wrote these folios about 1118, the fiscal account he requisitioned was older than that; and if we imagine that the piece had been thrown out or superseded, it could have been written as early as 1100 or so. That it was indeed a fiscal account there can be no doubt whatsoever. Here it is, all that we have of it:

RATIO DE CVRTIBUS COMITIS; GALLINE ET OV . . .

d   cap cccc

Ratio: literally, 'account.' But of what kind? In Flanders *ratio* was the traditional word for survey, having been so from Carolingian times onwards, and the very same word was applied to the transformed records of audit in the twelfth century. Each one of the forty-odd accounts that make up the *Grote Brief* in 1187 was termed *ratio*. There could be no clearer proof of functional continuity in accounting even as accounting was conceptually reoriented to economic growth in the twelfth century. The account that survived for a monk-scribe to cannibalize, although no probatory element is visible in what little is left of it, *could* nonetheless have been a record of momentary balance; that is, of a sort of account more eligible for destruction than a survey. Only one (other) such account has survived in Flanders from before 1187: a local collector's record of *fodermolt* (a maintenance-tax) at Saint-Winoksbergen in 1140.[112] As for Lambert of Saint-Omer, it only remains to add that he was, unwittingly, a cultural intermediary. What he was writing, over a wasted and

---

[111] *Lamberti S. Audomari canonici Liber floridus*, ed. Albert Derolez (Ghent 1968) fol. 147v (298).

[112] 'Het Fragment van een grafelijke Rekening van Vlaanderen uit 1140,' ed. Egied I. Strubbe, *Mededelingen van de koninklijke Vlaamse Academie voor Wetenshappen, Klasse der Letteren . . .* XII:9 (Brussels 1950) 25–26.

scraped fiscal account, was the first known copy of a famous treatise on the accountability of redemption: none other than Saint Anselm's *Cur Deus homo.*

SICILY: PLURI-CULTURAL CONSERVATORY? Of cultural bearings on accountability a salient example is to be found in Norman Sicily. Here if anywhere we should expect to find evidence of fiscal ingenuity. Master Thomas Brown was a renowned political refugee when sometime around 1160 he was assigned a prestigious place in the English exchequer; renowned, that is, for his expertise in Sicilian royal service. So it was said in the *Dialogue of the Exchequer,* and since this testimony implies familiarity with written records, modern scholars have exclaimed over the wealth of Sicilian fiscal records and the supposed refinement of the 'administration' to which it testifies.[113] Yet to an astonishing extent the evidence of this treasure consists of allusions to lost records. What is known for sure and by inference is that prescriptive accounts of fiscal and patrimonial domains were made by masters Greek and Muslim prior to the Norman conquests of the eleventh century. What is now even clearer, thanks to the work of Jeremy Johns, is that fiscal management by local knowledge and recording of properties and tenancies persisted strongly under Duke and King Roger II (1102–54) and his successors. This was marked by successive revivals of Greek and Arabic record-making, which is why by the end of the century people thought routinely of notaries Greek, 'Saracen,' and Latin in the royal *dīwān*. But since the ascendancy of George of Antioch in the 1130s, the royal dominations had come under the influence of Fatimid practise, which is why surviving records of royal accountability are thenceforth mainly in Arabic.[114]

[113] Haskins, *Normans* 226–29; David Abulafia, 'The crown and the economy under Roger II and his successors,' *Dumbarton Oaks Papers* XXXVII (1983) 2; Houben, *Roger II* 147–59.

[114] Petrus de Ebulo, *Liber ad honorem Augusti*, fol. 101r; Jeremy Johns, *Arabic administration in Norman Sicily. The royal dīwān* (Cambridge 2002) chs. 4–10.

Amongst distinctive features of this Mediterranean scene, two points of comparative interest stand out. First, the exclusive survival of prescriptive records of account, and the allusions to lost fiscal documents of no other sort, create the impression of an exceedingly conservative, not to say archaic, fiscal regime in Sicily. Is this an illusion? According to Johns, 'accounts of income and expenditure' figure together with other records that 'have disappeared practically without trace.'[115] Nevertheless, what is known today about records of the *dīwān* suggests no transformation of conceptual focus in the twelfth century such as is attested in England and Flanders. A detectable shift in practise from about 1145 relates not so much to the fidelity or failings of local managers as to the reformed registration of properties and tenants. To judge from the impressive *jarāʾid* it produced, the reorganized *dīwān* under Williams I (1154–66) and II (1166–89) thought of 'control' rather more in legal than in financial terms.

Second, if this is so it can only be related to a quite distinctive structure of power in Sicily. The records of people and boundaries that are central to twelfth-century accountability were venerable (indeed) because they were elements of a neoclassical fiscal and patrimonial order. That they could be reorganized under Roger II points to the pervasive vitality—and venality?—of this order, in which the quest for status among managers was not as a rule at the expense of peasants. In this quasi-classical regime agents must surely have been required to account, even perhaps in writing. In his glowing history of Roger II, Abbot Alexander of Telese not only extolled his subject's devotion to public affairs and justice but also laid stress on his engagement with accounting. Roger wanted to know what was *paid* as well as owed 'in public taxation,' the quoted words probably referring to renders as well as taxes; and when this assertion is taken with the biblical phrase *sub cirographorum ratiociniis*, it seems hard to doubt that the experienced prince who became king in 1130 took interest in

---

[115] *Arabic administration* 144.

receipts and expenses as well as in possession. He was insistent, wrote Alexander, on written precision in all fiscal affairs.[116]

If it follows that official expertise in patrimonial management was more deeply rooted in greater Sicily than in lands to the north and west, then the remedy of violence must have figured less in Sicilian accounting than elsewhere. The *dīwāni* records relate sometimes to boundary disputes and local violence, but hardly so as to bear decisively on accountability. In Capua complaints against bailiffs and judges comparable to those in Lombardy and Catalonia multiply only after 1150.[117] In one respect comparable to the English exchequer from the 1160s, the Sicilian accountability projected by Roger II took on a bureaucratic life of its own. Yet less, it seems, for reasons of efficiency or economic constraint than to project an image of august kingship.[118]

CATALONIA: FROM EXPLOITATION TO AGENCY. What is distinctive about the Sicilian experience cannot be explained simply by its Mediterranean location. For Catalonia had a history equally its own, unlike Sicily's; one unique, indeed, in Latin Europe. There and there alone we can trace an evolution from prescriptive to probatory accounting such as can only be inferred elsewhere. We can see it happening under our noses, happening with breathtaking speed; and we can date the change quite exactly to the years 1155–60.

Things begin here with the prescriptive accountancy of 1151, for the survey (already noticed) by the knight Bertran de Castellet on behalf of the lord-count of Barcelona marked an attempt to bring new order to the control of his old patrimony. Some sixteen bailiwicks or clusters of domain in every part of what was later called Old Catalonia were recorded, one charter (*carta*) for each, the information on obligations and renders having been

---

[116] *Alexandri Telesini abbatis ystoria Rogerii regis Sicilie . . .* , ed. Ludovica De Nava (Rome 1991) iv.3 (82).

[117] Johns, *Arabic administration* 103, 108, 132, 150, 170–71, 190, 250; Loud, *Church and society in Capua* 21, 189.

[118] Johns, *Arabic administration*, makes a good case to this effect.

collected by Bertran and his scribes in assemblies of bailiffs and local notables. Ultimately, one scribe copied the charters so produced, all but one now lost as originals, on a roll of parchment that somewhat resembles the assemblage of *rationes* in the *Grote Brief* of 1187.

These survey-charters must soon have been found wanting. As we have them, they contain little or no annotation, which doubtless means they were superseded by further surveys; and these, it is safe to conjecture, were copied in registers—the earliest known registers of the Crown of Aragon—that are mentioned in the 1180s, but are lost today. From the mid-1150s come lists of revenues and disbursements followed in 1157–58 by three anomalous accounts for bailiwicks. The first of these, for the new frontier domain of Estopanyà, begins thus: 'This is a memorial [*Hec est memoria*] of the tithe of millet. . . .' It goes on prescriptively for five lines: 'from Miravet 3 *fa*[*neques*] . . . from Estopanyà 6 *fa* . . . from first-fruits 12 *almuds* . . .'; then, following a space, the record turns into a list of receipts from the mill and of expenditures. In a space following the prescriptive entries a second scribe has entered totals for these; and in the same hand farther below figure totals for the receipts and first set of expenditures. A second account for Estopanyà of the same time lists receipts from tenants in grain, expenditures for maintenance and seed, and concludes with a statement of what (the bailiff) G. Agela has received and what he 'ought to render' in millet, tithes, and proceeds of the mill.[119]

These records may be said to confuse prescriptive and probatory thinking. One need not speak of a contamination of forms, for it is clear that scribes found it easy to combine surveys with audits. What forms for the latter they possessed by 1157 we cannot know; what is striking is that already by 1158 we find written notice of an audit for the bailiwicks of Molló, Prats de Molló, and Ribes in the very form of account (*computavit*) that was to be formulaic by the 1170s. Yet the work of the 1150s was demonstrably tentative, and

[119] *FAC* II, nos. 5, 6.

the experimentation was not yet over. The writer of the account of 1158 was the very man who had annotated the hybrid memorials of Estopanyà, the count's scribe Ponç; and it was he again who, ten months later in the heart of Old Catalonian domains, having first written the *computavit*, subsequently added prescriptive notations about values, possessions, and unpaid obligations in Mollò and Ribes. 'There are 22 mills in Prats, whence are paid 3s. from each.' And so on. There follows, again (very probably) in the hand of Ponç, a third account for Estopanyà, this one evidently for 1158–59 on a yearly cycle: 'We had this year in Estopanyà 5 *cafisses* of barley and 6 *cafisses* of wheat . . . ,' this entry followed by items of receipt only in a newly orderly pattern. This looks like the earliest extant account of fully probatory nature for Catalonian domains, yet even here the attitude of the accountant-scribe seems to be that of one reviewing the value of a domain. But the day of the audit had come. From the autumn of 1160 the archives preserve a single parchment bearing no fewer than four records of audit passed successively in Tuïr, Vilafranca de Conflent (two audits), and Llagostera a week later; all this followed by yet another record telling of the sale of a bailiwick (probably that of Llagostera) to two local men for 26 modes of grain.[120]

This is an illuminating parchment, for the accountant summoning to audit and to sell bailiwicks was none other than Bertran de Castellet, the very retainer-knight who had carried out the survey of comital domains a decade before. He for one had seen what was needed. Experimentation doubtless continued into the reign of Alfons I. The concern of his regent-courtiers towards 1165 is visible in the account of his service given by the bailiff Bernat Bou of Girona. His testimony has the importance of revealing the economic interest in improved accountability that surely underlay the whole fiscal enterprise of the 1150s. Yet it is unclear how the new accountancy of Bertran and Ponç was carried on thereafter. Certainly the retainers of Alfons were borrowing money on the security of fiscal revenues, and it is likely that

[120] ibid., nos. 7, 9, 10.

the bailiffs we hear of after 1178 had begun as creditors of the count-king. From 1179 to 1213 the probatory audit of bailiffs in the comital domains of Barcelona was regular, next to the English the best—indeed, the only other— documented routine of regalian accountancy then known in Latin Europe.[121]

Quite as with the sheriffs in England, the defendancy (so to call it) of bailiffs persists. The new accountancy is judicial in the twelfth century, probably everywhere; yet in one respect, very specially so in Catalonia. For it is only in this region that the historian can read in the records how the alleged delinquency of local agents came to be judged in a new way. Not accidentally the early *computa* resemble the memorials of complaint, having (so to speak) barely outgrown them. It was a question of distinguishing between charges against and charges delegated, and then of a convergence of interests popular and regalian. Ponç the Scribe was in the thick of it, for it was he who wrote up the violence alleged against Guillem de Sant Martí as well as those accounts for Estopanyà and Molló-Ribes. Moreover, in at least two cases the bailiffs mentioned in the early accounts can be identified with the rogues charged by the peasants.

SIGNS OF a newly searching and flexible accountability were widespread in the third quarter of the twelfth century. Something resembling audits of public revenue may have survived in Tuscan and Lombard cities; yet when the practise comes into view, as at Pisa only in the 1160s, it looks as new as the consular programme in which it figures.[122] In most places and most lordships it cannot yet have been clear that one must audit local officials to secure power in growing economies. The Catalonian system lapsed after

[121] ibid., nos. 8, 11–18, and (for 1179–1213, nos. 34–138).

[122] *I brevi dei consoli del comune di Pisa degli anni 1162 e 1164 . . .* , ed. Ottavio Banti (Rome 1997) 51, c. 7 (1162); 82–83, c. 17 (1164). See also below, p. 369.

1213, as we shall see; and in France, where the monks of Saint-Denis and Cluny were assuredly alert to the implications of *croissance*, there is no evidence of change until after 1200. They saw no need to revise their prescriptive method. In Germany the curial personnel under the Hohenstaufen are highly visible, yet the only written survival of their work in the twelfth century is a prescriptive list of public obligations that cannot be securely dated. So too in Spain, where, as in France and Germany, one finds nothing in the plentiful archives of responsive lord-kingship to prove an altered engagement with patrimonial service.

Almost everywhere fidelity and tenurial obligations still counted, and perhaps were accounted, more than money. This is why taxation in support of crusades was momentous and resented; not by chance the financing of the Third Crusade coincided with further initiatives in accountancy. Nor is this all. Mathematically speaking, accountability remained prescriptive; that is, a matter of realizing values more than profit. Lords continued to survey their lands and list their rights, even if the substance of those lists changed with the status of those in dependence.[123] And what did not change, in fiscal accounts of all sorts, was the reliance on Roman numerals. Although Arabic ciphers are widely attested by 1200, they make no appearance in the Catalonian and English records that are by far the fullest evidence of accountancy in the period of this book, nor for long afterwards.[124]

Constraint, Compromise, and Office

The prevalence of exploitative lordship posed a further problem for accountants, and not only for them. How was a provost or

---

[123] Robert Fossier, *Polyptyques et censiers* (Turnhout 1978); P. D. A. Harvey, *Manorial records*, rev. ed. (London 1999).

[124] Murray, *Reason and society* 166–74; and for examples: *Surveys of the estates of Glastonbury abbey c. 1135–1201*, ed. N. E. Stacy (Oxford-NY 2001); and *FAC* I, 152; II, passim.

bailiff to acknowledge, let alone represent, the proceeds of un-consented taxes? Whose were those proceeds, if not simply the lord's way of remunerating his servants? Were they legitimate? What is certain is that they could not easily be thought official. And if a provost, bailiff, or ministerial were accountable only for fidelity, was this the extent of his office? Was it 'official' service in any sense?

In these questions two issues may be said to meet, their conver-gence marking a characteristic phase in the history of power in the twelfth century. The first is that of the nature and extent of arbitrary lordship. That the latter was a more widespread phe-nomenon than 'bad lordship' should already be clear. 'Bad lords' were conspicuous in this permissive age not only because they were notably worse behaved than most lords, which they were, but also because they exemplified to excess a habitual mode of domination. The second issue is whether this habitus of lordship, with its egoistic penchant for affective superiority, was compatible with what Pierre Bourdieu has termed 'officializing strategies.'[125] Was an accountability of fidelity ultimately self-contradictory?

CHARTERS OF FRANCHISE: SOME LESSONS

Another class of documentary evidence has now to be introduced. 'Charters of liberties,' as they are often called, became famous in the hands of Henri Pirenne, who viewed them as a gateway to a transformed world of urbanized prosperity. A century on this in-terpretation, although much qualified, seems beyond challenge. Sir James Holt showed how one class of these charters gave nor-mative expression to new structures of associative power.[126] An-other class created or recognized sworn communes in France and Italy; yet another served to encourage or attract settlers, the Iberian

---

[125] Pierre Bourdieu, *Outline of a theory of practice*, tr. Richard Nice (Cam-bridge 1977) 40.

[126] Henri Pirenne, *Medieval cities. Their origins and the revival of trade*, tr. Frank D. Halsey (Princeton 1925); Holt, *Magna Carta* (2d ed.) chs. 1–3.

charters of *población(n)* and of *fueros* being notable subsets of these. Charters of all sorts were, more or less, instruments of lordship. Whether they resulted from petitions, impulse, or—perhaps most often—preliminary discussion, they projected normatively the outcomes of local confrontation. They multiplied massively after 1050; and what matters here is that of the many hundreds of privileging charters issued down to about 1225, a substantial proportion date from the first three quarters of the twelfth century, and that, taken as a whole, these represent the earliest perceptible impulse of cultural reaction against the institution of exploitative lordship. By defining privilege collectively and by limiting the more wilful or arbitrary prerogatives, the charters promoted such communal interests—security, justice, freedom—as demanded competence in the agents deputed to uphold them. They created officials.

To say it so is, of course, to exaggerate in the interest of clarity. (This is the place to observe that a strictly Weberian analysis of incipient bureaucratic power misses the historical reality, for there is no sign that European people in the twelfth century thought of lordship and office as contrasting categories, only that, so to speak, while these categories got on together, they were bad for each other. A concept of corruptible office was held by Gregorian reformers, as we have seen;[127] and in the twelfth century no one can have doubted that lords of whatever status held 'offices' (*officia*) of power.[128] Yet towards 1125–38 the provost of Sammarçolles could be questioned by his Lord-Bishop Ulger

---

[127] Above, pp. 197–203. On Gregorian ideas, see, e.g., *De ordinando pontifice auctor Gallicus*, ed. Ernestus Dümmler, *Ldl* I, 14; Peter Damiani, *Liber gratissimus* c. 4, *BrPD* I, no. 40 (396); Humbert, *Adversus simoniacos* iii.9, *Ldl* I, 208; Lampert of Hersfeld, *Annales, an.* 1071 (126–28).

[128] Hildebert, *Moralis philosophia*, Questio I, c. 42, *PL* CLXXI, 1038; *CCr* II, no. 282; *HC* iii.33.2; Heriman of Tournai, *Liber de restauratione* c. 38 (290); *PUE* II, no. 19; Assizes of Roger II i.25–26, ed. G. M. Monti, 'Il testo e la storia esterna delle assise normanne,' *Studi di storia e di diretto in onore di Carlo Calisse*, 3 vols. (Milan 1940) I, 326–27 (i.8); *DDFr1* II (see index, 715); John of Salisbury, *Policraticus* v.4 (I, 290), and he described *tirannia* as virtually official, viii.17 (II,

of Angers whether his *praepositura* was a hereditary tenure or was held at the bishop's pleasure.[129] Countless examples to the same effect could be cited.)

The charters helped to create officials by limiting the lordship—or more exactly, the normal arbitrariness thereof—in their deportment. This was true even of the most famous, although least typical specimens of the genre: for example, the 'coronation charter' granted by Henry I to the English in August 1100. In this text the 'oppression' of 'unjust exactions' figures at the head of the first article, coming even before the stirring promise of a 'free church,' and the same article returns twice more to the words 'bad customs,' which are 'therewith abolished.' Arbitrary demands for money are not the only 'bad customs' renounced, but they come first and they pose for us the question: who lost most by this concession: the lord-king or his officials?[130]

Both the fact and the question prove deeply pertinent. Countless charters have the renunciation of arbitrary taxes foremost among their concessions, many more include this concession, while few indeed fail to raise the question of impact on prerogatives. When King Pedro I of Aragon sought to entice settlers to his frontier castle of Barbastro in 1099, he promised them freedom from all exactions other than a tenth and first-fruits 'to God' and one ninth to himself.[131] When King Louis VI of France authorized a commune at Mantes in 1110, he declared that his purpose was to remedy 'the excessive oppression of the poor,' and specified first of all that residents of the community be 'free and exempt from all tallage, unjust seizure, *creditio*, and from every unreasonable exaction.'[132] It is safe to suppose that neither king had much to lose by giving up arbitrary taxation. Not they but their local agents, the *merinos* in Aragon and the

345–58); Adam de Perseigne, *Lettres* I, ed. Jean Bouvet (Paris 1960) no. 14 (cc. 148, 153); *TrFr* II, no. 1569 (1196–99).

[129] *CNA*, no. 180.   [130] *SC* 117–19.
[131] *CPA*, no. 15.   [132] *RAL6* I, no. 47.

provosts in France, were the men constrained by the charters. And not only they, to be sure, for local communities of interest were freed from the exactions of other lords as well as those of the lord-kings.[133] Something of their resentment may be heard in the loathing for communes voiced by Guibert of Nogent around 1115. In 1140 Louis VII reminded the mayor and people of Reims that if he had granted them a commune (modeled on that of Laon), it was not to invite them to infringe on the customary rights of local churches. As late as the early thirteenth century Jacques de Vitry was fulminating against the 'confusion' of 'violent and pestilent communities' bent on 'oppressing knights' and seizing their jurisdictions. Through this weary hyperbole resounds the abiding resentment of lesser lords in bitter defeat.[134]

The charters of franchise tell—incidentally—of *their* crisis in the twelfth century. But also, let us not forget, of their means to and exercise of power. The renunciations or deprivation of arbitrary taxation and seizures marked (at best) the *end* of unwritten local histories of coercive lordships. Moreover, when taken together with petitions, complaints, and penitential renunciations of tallage and other 'bad customs,' the incidence of charters in space and time tends to confirm that banal or arbitrary lordships flourished best in the old west Frankish lands between the Ebro and Rhine valleys. Over five hundred charters of associative privilege dating from the long twelfth century, mostly for towns, are readily accessible in collections of printed records for these regions. Here too the notion of spreading privilege 'took off' in the countrysides in the later twelfth century. The royal charter of Lorris (as reissued in 1155) became the model for some eighty-five other villages in the Ile-de-France; the charter of Prisches (1158) was borrowed for some forty places in Hainaut, Champagne, and the Vermandois; while that of Beaumont-en-Argonne (1182), promulgated by Archbishop

---

[133] ibid., II, no. 380: 'gravamina . . . quae a dominis suis patiebantur.'

[134] Guibert, *Monodiae* iii.7 (320; *Memoirs* 167); *Recueil de textes d'histoire urbaine française des origines . . .* , ed. A.-M. Lemasson *et al.* (Arras 1996) nos. 33, 90.

Guillaume of Reims, gave rise to no fewer than five hundred other charters for places in Champagne, Burgundy, Lorraine, and elsewhere.[135] And while this matter resists a categorical precision that was alien to contemporaries, it can be said that (1) enfranchisements were fewer and later in Germany, England, and Atlantic France; (2) they were perhaps equally numerous in León and Castile, yet significantly divergent in nature; and that (3) rural charters, often indistinct from 'urban' ones with respect to the character of the community envisaged, multiplied enormously in the thirteenth century, notably in Occitania and Savoy, as well as in Lorraine and Picardy. In Italy the 'rural commune' can be discerned after about 1100, as in Tuscany and the Padovano, in records less generically characteristic than charters of franchise.[136]

Everywhere the charters point to compromises with lords over powers to protect, seize (or distrain), and tax. This huge subject, still far from mastered, can only be touched on here.[137] It has two lessons for us: the remedy of arbitrary impositions, and the reaffirmation of official action in localities. In both respects the charters of franchise, which are by no means the only evidence, help to mark off zones of variable sociability in which the pressures of lordship cannot have been the same. West of the Ebro valley, where the protective role of monarchy was hardly in question, the persistence of customary communities not only invited definitions of collective rights in the early *fueros* but also shows the coherence of *concejos* in practise. Yet even here, in charters as early

---

[135] [Lorris] Maurice Prou, 'Les coutumes de Lorris et leur propagation aux XIIᵉ et XIIIᵉ siècles,' *NRHDFE* VIII (1884); [Prisches] Léo Verriest, 'La fameuse charte-loi de Prisches,' *RBPH* II (1923) 327–49; [Beaumont] *LTC* I, no. 314. See also *La charte de Beaumont et les franchises municipales entre Loire et Rhin . . .* (Nancy 1988).

[136] This rough estimate (see next note) is based on documentary collections cited in notes following. See also Robert Fossier, *Enfance de l'Europe Xᵉ–XIIᵉ siècles. Aspects économiques et sociaux*, 2 vols. (Paris 1982) I, part 2, ch. 2; and Wickham, *Community and clientele in twelfth-century Tuscany* chs. 7, 8.

[137] No one has yet counted the charters, by whatever definition. Cf. Georges Duby, *L'économie rurale* II, 477–91 (*Rural economy* 242–52).

as elsewhere, security of life and possessions generally comes first, as appears in Queen Urraca's concessions of 1109.[138] New pressures of lordship, visible in troubles in Galicia and around Sahagún, are reflected in subsequent charters of *población*.[139] In Tuscany, where agrarian interests were denatured by looming towns, an oppressive lord might simply disappear in face of complaints from villagers whose successors were consuls (that is, officials). Yet here, too, as in much of Italy, the remodeling of traditional rural communities coincided with mounting seigneurial pressures, a general phenomenon even where not the only impetus to associative organizing.[140] Even in Germany, where mercantile needs moulded charters of liberties, the stress on peace and safety points constantly to the permissive violence of lordship, or indeed, of protection. Duke Conrad of Zähringen, whose powers in the Breisgau arose from compounded rights of advocacy, promised 'peace and security of the road to all persons seeking my market' at Freiburg in 1120.[141] And when a lordship was imposed with the customs, as happened in 1159 when Archbishop Wichmann gave the law of Magdeburg to the colonists at Grosswusterwitz, the exemption from forced labour on castles (*burgwere*) evokes an abiding climate of constraint in Germany.[142] In England, by contrast, the burgesses of Beverley received quittance (*liberi et quieti*) from toll as well as a *hans-hus* but little more in

---

[138] *Diplomatario de la reina Urraca de Castilla y León, 1109–1126*, ed. Cristina Monterde Albiac (Zaragoza 1996) nos. 1–3; *Coleccion de fueros municipales y cartas pueblas . . .* , ed. Tomás Muñoz y Romero (Madrid 1847) 96–98. The Muñoz collection remains fundamental.

[139] e.g., *Documentos*, ed. Hinojosa, no. 40.

[140] Wickham, *Community* 221; and generally 209–31. See also Jean-Marie Martin, *La Pouille du VIe au XIIe siècle* (Rome 1993) 301–28, 748–68, who writes (768) of the 'brutalité des transformations,' but says nothing about the prevailing experience of power.

[141] *Quellensammlung zur Frühgeschichte der deutschen Stadt (bis 1250)*, ed. Bernhard Diestelkamp (Leiden 1967) no. 55; Theodor Mayer, 'The state of the dukes of Zähringen,' tr. Geoffrey Barraclough, *Mediaeval Germany, 911–1250 . . .* , 2 vols. (Oxford 1938) II, 189–91.

[142] *Quellensammlung* no. 72 art. 4.

their charter of about 1130; while in the customs of Newcastle ascribed to the same period the only allusion to violence is the license freely to distrain people not of the town, and one another, only with leave of the reeve.[143]

France was the place—that older, larger Frankland extending to the Muslim borders—where the violence of knights, castellans, advocates, and the makers of banal lordships became the cause and content of charters of franchise. The charters of Barbastro and Mantes already mentioned were but two amongst a profusion of comparable enactments from about 1075 to 1140 that prove in *their* way a new and insufferable experience of power. This is a history one can read charter by charter, taking care not to miss the sense of the concessions as well as their verbiage. In 1077, founding a 'city in my village called Jaca,' King Sancho Ramirez renounced 'all bad *fueros* which you had until now.'[144] Towards 1089–90 Count Guillem Ramon of Cerdanya (1068–95) chartered a 'free town' (*villa libera*; the modern Villefranche de Conflent) as a place of 'freedom from servitude'; that is, from the arbitrary exactions thereof.[145] Not accidentally, the word 'tallage' (*tallia, tallagium*) creeps into these concessions; this is a new word associated from the outset with uncustomary exactions, compulsion, and violence.[146] Sometimes equated with 'bad customs,'[147] *tallia* was more or less synonymous with *tolta, forcia,* and *quest(i)a,* terms more common in Mediterranean lands.[148]

---

[143] *SC* 130–34.

[144] *CPA*, no. 2.

[145] *CPC* I¹, no. 41.

[146] '. . . quod vulgo dicitur tallia,' Cartulaire de Quimperlé, fol. 34v, quoted by Flach, *Ancienne France* I, 392; 'exactio . . . que vulgo tallia vocatur,' *CSPCh* II, 433–34 (before 1111); and for *tallea* 'extorted by royal officials,' *RAL6* II, no. 340 (1133).

[147] *RAL6* I, no. 96; *Cartulaire de Sauxillanges*, ed. Henry Doniol (Clermont 1864) no. 949; *De oorkonden der graven van Vlaanderen (juli 1128–september 1191)*, ed. Thérèse de Hemptinne *et al.* (Brussels 1988) II.1, no. 96.

[148] *RAPh1*, nos. 114, 133; *Recueil des chartes de l'abbaye de La Grasse*, ed. Elisabeth Magnou-Nortier *et al.*, 2 vols. (Paris 1996) I, no. 138; ACA, Cancelleria, perg. R.B. III, 39; *CPA*, no. 117; *CPC* I¹, nos. 42, 65, 76; *HL* v, nos. 515i, 531;

Tallage as a device of lordship has a facet yet to be addressed. What is clear from charters and complaints alike is that tallage as a resented abuse—for that is how it is first known to us—was tenacious and long-lived. It was still widespread, if somewhat mitigated, in the thirteenth century, when masses of new charters were granted.[149] It looks as if Louis VI had thought of it as an abuse to be remedied. He addressed it explicitly in his charter for Mantes; he frequently exempted peasants on clerical lands (evidently from his own men's seizures); and it was he who first promulgated the charter of franchise for Lorris, in which immunity from tallage is explicit.[150] The region in which this village lay was notorious for oppressive lordship. Yet the real significance of these famous 'liberties' is that most of their influence in the spread of privilege came after 1155, when Louis VII reissued them; and that, indeed, his decision to renew the charter resulted from appeals from people, even lords, in the domains.[151] As late as 1186 the people of Saint-Denis (no less) had to plead with their Lord-Abbot Hugh for liberation from the 'customs of tallage and tolt, and indeed of all rapine.' In so doing they generated a rare glimpse into the collective psychology of fear brought on by an 'odious custom' that deterred outsiders from coming to trade while driving natives away from their homes. Whereupon the abbot abolished all tallages and forced exactions, on condition that the townspeople pay an annual tax of 123 pounds of Paris. To assess this levy the abbot and townspeople were to choose ten men of good reputation. And these

---

Cartulaires des Templiers de Douzens, ed. Pierre Gérard, Elisabeth Magnou (Paris 1965), A, nos. 116, 203. See generally Duby, *L'économie rurale* (*Rural economy*) iii.2.2.

[149] Ch.-E. Perrin, 'Chartes de franchise et rapports de droits en Lorraine,' *Le Moyen Age* XL (1946) 11–42; *Chartes de coutume en Picardie: XIIe–XIIIe siècle*, ed. Robert Fossier (Paris 1974); Ruth Mariotte-Löber, *Ville et seigneurie. Les chartes de franchises des comtes de Savoie, fin XIIe siècle–1343* (Annecy 1973) 53–56.

[150] *RAL6* I, nos. 96, 104, 109, 150, 156, 195; Prou, 'Coutumes de Lorris,' art. 9 (448).

[151] Prou, 'Coutumes de Lorris,' 148–55, 267–70, 303–18.

deputies were to promise under oath to conduct the assessment 'faithfully.'[152]

THRESHOLDS OF OFFICE

Here we are in on the makings of official conduct aimed at social purpose. It is true that the abbot's motive is not stated, so the only certain inference can be that he was a lord in need of money. But the new deal was so manifestly a compromise in the interest of both parties that it must have been the outcome of negotiation about needs 'useful to us and them' both (as the abbot himself put it); that is, about things beyond his lordship.

This event, though it may look timely for its date, was long overdue in northern France. For if tallage originated as an arbitrary levy, perhaps routinely the seizure of crops by armed retinues, it had been contested from the start. This appears not only from pejorative allusions in the records but also from hints of local resistance or questioning of purpose or justification. To return to an event we have met, when Raher *de Esarto* renounced the tallage he shared with the canons of Chartres, around 1100, he reserved the contingency of a levy for the 'utility of that land,' which would require the consent of the monk in charge, who would be entitled further to share in the proceeds.[153] Around the same time and locale we hear of a knight's tallage permissible in case his wife's daughter marries or he wishes to buy a castle or needs to raise a ransom for release from captivity, etc.[154] And when King Philip I forbade his provost of Bagneux to demand 'tolts or exactions . . . violently,' was this not to allow for acceptable impositions?[155] Even the worst of tallages, it is safe to imag-

---

[152] *GXa* VII, *inst.*, 75, cited perceptively by Carl Stephenson, 'The origin and nature of the *taille*' (1926), reprinted in idem, *Mediaeval institutions . . .* , ed. Bryce Lyon (Ithaca, NY, 1954) 41–42.

[153] *CSPCh* II, 340 (no. 110). See also *RAPh1*, no. 114; *RAL6* I, nos. 96, 109.

[154] *CSPCh* II, 484.   [155] *RAPh1*, no.153.

ine, were attended by words of justification; moreover, many lords succeeded in rendering their tallage customary.[156]

What eludes us in all this is the talk about tallage. To collect arbitrarily from peasants was easier than from townsfolk, but was unaccountable either way. The way of superiority was non-negotiable and it was of necessity unofficial. Yet the returns from armed constraint must have been problematic enough to induce the sorts of compromise that would salvage tallage for lords willing to commute pretence and violence into customary fixed revenue. Tallage as well as violence was up front in the communal charter of Mantes towards 1110. At Laon debate over tallage must have begun around 1112, when the people secured their first communal charter, but the troubles of that turbulent juncture evidently led to a more radical initiative in the years ahead. In 1128, the provision that every man owing tallage should henceforth pay 4*d.* at prescribed intervals, for all its originality, is overshadowed by the recognition that a mayor and sworn men (*jurati*) now have the power to keep order in Laon. No fewer than seventeen of the thirty-three articles of this 'institution of peace' suggest that seizures and unavenged injuries had been the prevailing reality.[157] Justice in all matters not naturally in the jurisdiction of other lords, including the king and bishop, now fell to the mayor and jurates. Although it seemed unnecessary to specify, they or *their* assessors would surely have had a hand in the newly commuted tallage.[158]

To regulate taxation and justice in these ways: was this as much as to open new offices of power? People can hardly have thought so. Mayors must have seemed like village foremen (*villici*) writ large, their very designation (*major*) evoking precedence. In all these charters the lord-king confirms more than he institutes. Mayors and sworn men arose in communities of circumstance where vengeance and lordship were losing relevance. They

---

[156] e.g., *CSAA* I, no. 120; *RAL6* II, no. 382; *HL* v, no. 531.
[157] *RAL6* II, no. 277. [158] ibid., I, no. 47; ii, no. 277.

entered into settlements in which nothing was yet specified about election, qualifications, or commitments. And if now we turn back to the pact of Saint-Denis in 1186 and compare it with earlier charters, an impression of conceptual inertia is confirmed. In this respect, as for the whole problem of office, the evidence of sworn commitments is critical.

To begin with, the oath of 1186 is an oath of fidelity. It is the abbot, not the sworn men of Saint-Denis, whom he merely consults, who appoints assessors; their oath is to collect 'faithfully' (*fideliter*). While they might have been chosen by reason of experience or expertise, nothing is said of that, which suggests that the oath was submissively oriented to the lord-abbot.[159] Quite as usual, it can be said. In 1089 the mayor of a village given to Saint-Martin-des-Champs (Paris) was to swear fidelity to the prior and monks to render the divided revenues to each. Early in the twelfth century some villagers of Saint-Père, Chartres, had an oven keeper who was to swear fidelity for the revenues to the church and the parishioners.[160] The social meaning of such rites could be made explicit. In 1118 the seven men representing Cremona for its share in the castle of Soncino were to be faithful to the 'community' of constituent people 'as a vassal to a lord.'[161] When Count Thierry of Flanders granted a vill to the monks of Saint-Trond in 1146, he prescribed the obligation of the *villicus* to do homage and swear fealty to the abbot.[162] In all such cases, the commitment is for services, more or less analogous to those of knights on military tenure, conceived more in terms of loyalty than of functional competence. 'Our provost,' declares Louis VI in his *paréage* with the bishop of Paris (1136) shall do 'fidelity' to the bishop; and his provost reciprocally to the king.[163] It is a deal about trust, not accountability.

[159] *GXa* VII, *inst.*, 75.
[160] *Liber testamentorum*, no. 72; *CSPCh* II, 307–8.
[161] *CCr* II, no. 273; cf. no. 296.   [162] *Oorkonden der graven* II.1, no. 95.
[163] *RAL6* II, no. 381.

So it should come as no surprise that the first known communal engagements look like oaths of fidelity. To judge from their *établissements* (first granted before 1180), the people of Saint-Quentin lived by a tissue of oaths, 'saving *feuté* to God, the Saint, and the count and countess,' that are not so much mutual as multiple. 'Common' (*quemune*) oaths of security, ad hoc, they resemble the sworn engagements over castles in Mediterranean lands.[164] It must have been because the communal oath commonly lacked such specificity that it was often omitted, or left inexplicit, as in the charter for Noyon (1108–12). In that for Soissons a few years later the oath to the commune (*communiam jurent*) is a proof of fidelity that places non-jurors in jeopardy.[165] It is true, however, that oaths 'to the community' or, as at Valenciennes and Laon, to the peace, soon seemed suspect to the lord-bishops (typically) who began to equate fidelity to utilitarian purposes as infidelity to themselves.[166] So in Italy we begin to hear of oaths 'which have been made *against* bishops.'[167] Sworn communes in Compostela (1116) and Bruges (1127) as well as in Italy and France were so easily likened to conspiracies as to help explain why objectively defined social purposes were slow to catch on as the defensible content of oaths. Nor was it always clear where the general interest lay, as in 1159 when the *ministeriales* of Utrecht opposed the bishop 'in defence of their right' in a 'very strong conjuration.'[168] The fidelitarian model of engagement remained more respectable, if increasingly strained by reality. It was arguably a 'faithful' discharge of duties for mayors, consuls, and *scabini* to work for utilitarian projects that served lords and communities alike. But there was no such theory of official service at hand.

---

[164] ed. Arthur Giry, *Etude sur les origines de la commune de Saint-Quentin* (Saint-Quentin 1887) 68–78.

[165] *RAL6* II, no. 244, art. 16.

[166] *Recueil de textes d'histoire urbaine française,* nos. 26, 28.

[167] *Chronica monasterii Casinensis*, ed. Hartmut Hoffmann (Hanover 1980) iv.35 (500, *an.* 1111).

[168] *Recueil de textes d'histoire urbaine néerlandaise des origines au milieu du XIIIᵉ siècle*, ed. C. Van de Kieft (Leiden 1967) no. 25.

The closest we get to the recognition of conceptual maladjust-
ment is the recurrent concern in some places to redefine functions as non-feudal or non-hereditary. And this look like a
pragmatic *pis aller*, not so much like a claim that functions should
be appointive or accountable.

In Sight of Our Lady's Towers. Given the argument set out above
that patrimonial agents were unaccountable seekers of personal
power, it will be useful here to notice one further instance, this
one with a differently pertinent outcome. Around 1150 Bishop
Goslin of Chartres received complaints from his canons about the
misconduct of their provosts, of the sergeants (*servientes*) under
them, and of the mayors of their villages. These are recorded in
two undated charters, of which the earlier (in all likelihood) tells
of 'many and grievous abuses which the mayors of their villages
and the provosts' sergeants have inflicted on the peasants.' The
bishop accepted this complaint, noting that it had already reached
his predecessor, and required that the oaths sworn by the mayors
and peasants were to be renewed every two years. Here there is
no pointed reference to the capitular provosts, who can have been
far from blameless themselves.[169] This must be why a further petition from the canons induced Bishop Goslin to engage with patrimonial management in a second charter recording what appears
to be a different solution. Here the allegations, all too familiar,
are set out as the justification for a statutory remedy. The provosts' sergeants, sometimes mounted, traverse the districts, imposing themselves for food and shelter on the peasants, and
making demands long since prohibited (it is now clarified) by
Bishops Ivo and Geoffrey, and by Pope Paschal II. The provosts
trouble the tenants with summonses and other requisitions, until
they are paid off. They pervert the good old custom of the church
by demanding reliefs from the successors to deceased mayors.
And the provosts wrongly insist on having their own houses in
the provostships.

---

[169] *Cart. Notre-Dame de Chartres* i, no. 58.

This time the bishop's response was to turn the hearing into a settlement acceptable to the provosts, and then, with their assent and the counsel of his retinue, to decree (*statuimus*) the abolition of each and every transgression charged. Not merely reiterating the allegations, the prohibitions amplify them with a view to showing that the bishop meant to do away with the lordship claimed by his provosts.[170]

Was this tantamount to rendering them officials? This may be going too fast. Nothing whatever is said about their accountability. What is more puzzling, there is no mention of a provost's oath in the bishop's statute, although it had good precedent.[171] Had it been resisted, or, perhaps more likely, been lost or left unwritten? Either way the oaths written into the first charter hold special interest. The 'oath of the mayors' renounces in detail seizures and exactions of all sorts, including reliefs and the sufferance of provosts' sergeants in *their* impositions. What is more, it explicitly defines the responsibility 'of collecting and paying your revenues,' of renders due at term and payable a fortnight thereafter in the treasury of Notre Dame.[172]

This orientation to service in detail, notably the prescriptive definition of accountancy, is something new in France. Yet it hardly affirms the autonomy of official service, because its express purpose is to certify fidelity to the mayor's 'lords' (*domini*), the canons; because it has the traditional form of the oath of fealty;[173] and because personal fidelity—'I shall henceforth be faithful to you'—is all that is promised with respect to the management of revenues. And the lordly cast of it all is confirmed by the otherwise inexplicable 'oath of the peasants,' likewise to be tendered in

---

[170] ibid., no. 57. The interventions of Ivo and Pascal II (1114) figure in nos. 33, 34 (JL 4741; 2d ed. 6403).

[171] A provost's sworn renunciation of 'bad customs' (ca.1070) figures in *Un manuscrit chartrain du XIᵉ siècle . . .*, ed. René Merlet, Alexandre Clerval (Chartres 1893) 188–89. See also 191, another such oath of ca. 1100.

[172] *Cart. Notre-Dame de Chartres* I, no. 58.

[173] ibid.: 'Hoc audiatis, domini, quod ab hac hora in antea a rusticis mee majorie non exigam . . . [etc.].'

the chapter. This is substantially a commitment, with God's help 'and these holy [gospels],' to the canons not to connive in the malfeasance of mayors and sergeants.[174] In its way it is yet another oath of fidelity.

❖

SIMILAR STORIES could doubtless be culled from the archives of old churches elsewhere, particularly in Mediterranean lands.[175] What they suggest is that the normal temptations in patrimonial habitats seldom broke into writing. It points as much to the past as to the future that the mayorship (*majoria*) was represented as a function. But it was in towns more than countrysides that associative experience was redirected, to judge from such written oaths as have survived. What these suggest is that the template of personal fidelity, while constant, is progressively denatured by enlarged attention to the specifics of public interest. The *Historia Compostellana* preserves an illuminating cluster of early oaths. In 1102, the canons' oath to Bishop Diego Gelmírez conforms to the original (Frankish) model of fidelity.[176] But two decades later this embattled prelate, now archbishop and legate, was himself 'promising' in assembly at Compostela that the steward of the city shall swear to keep justice, not deviating from it for love, hate, nor money . . .'; and the same oath, including also the preservation of 'good customs of the city,' was to be imposed on the judges.[177] A more singular focus of public interest figures in the oath of judges at Bruges (27 March 1127) to elect as count of Flanders one who will defend the land, help the poor, and 'work for the common utility of the land.'[178] Here the king's office is transmuted to a quasi-civic imperative.

---

[174] ibid.

[175] Further evidence from northern regions may be found in Robert F. Berkhofer III, *Day of reckoning. Power and accountability in medieval France* (Philadelphia 2004).

[176] *HC* i.20.4 (47–48). See also ii.39 (283); 59.2 (337–38).

[177] ibid., ii.68.2 (365–66).   [178] Galbert, *De multro* c. 51.

The oaths in Italy can only be explained in their settings. By this time the notables of Italian towns were acting associatively with or without elected consuls. The very concept of *consul(es)*, it is clear, points to public and official authority, as in Roman law. Yet it would be wide of the mark to assume that early Italian consular bodies, as in Milan or Genoa before 1100 and then Pisa and Mantua, were more nearly official bodies than the jurates of northern communes. The oath of fidelity being ubiquitous, we can be no surer of the content of lost inaugural oaths in Italy and southern France than of those of Noyon or Laon. Oaths of consuls as we first see them show these persons at work, such as at Genoa in 1143 and Pisa a year later. What looks like the form of an inceptive oath figures as a simple promise by the individual consul to uphold the statutes preceding.[179] At Pisa the *consulatus* is mentioned as a non-proprietary function even before the earliest known oaths to serve it; and the 'office of the consulate' figures explicitly there in the 1160s. By 1162 the whole complex of civic responsibilities has become the sworn commitment of each consul upon taking office; an annual programme in the written form of an oath.[180]

Amongst other records coming to resemble oaths of office, one of the earliest comes from Provence. Probably it was Archbishop Raimond I of Arles (1142–60) who, late in his pontificate, reformed what he spoke of as a 'good, legal, and communal consulate' in his city. Figuring in an (undated) charter of customs, his enactment reads like a foundation, and it was, indeed, copied early and often. As here prescribed, the *consulatus* of Arles corresponded to the whole sworn populace as well as to the consuls, who were to be a body of twelve made up of four knights, four burghers, and two men each from the market and the new

---

[179] *Statuta consulatus Ianuensis*, ed. G. B. F. Raggio, *Monumenta historiae patriae . . .* ii:1 (Turin 1838) cols. 241–52, and c. 73. Ottavio Banti takes a different view, *Brevi di Pisa* 9n.

[180] *Brevi di Pisa*, appendix 7, 116–17; also 91, and the whole texts of the *brevi* 43–101.

bourg. Here characteristically the remedy of violence was of foremost concern; and the charter seeks to redefine jurisdictions so as not to disrupt the lordships of others. The lord-archbishop was at pains, however, to reserve his cognizance of egregious malfeasance. The elected consuls were to have power to judge and to execute judgments. They were to be chosen by electors sworn to choose the most 'suitable [men] . . . for governing the city,' in consultation with the archbishop; and the new consuls were to swear, according to a formula set down verbatim, to 'rule and govern' according to the best available counsel, not quitting their posts until replaced. They were to settle internal disputes with the advice of the (larger) consulate and the archbishop.[181]

The charter and the oath of Arles mark a new stage in the history of power. Fidelity to public lords is either assumed or overlooked, or both. 'Governing' (so worded) is articulated in clauses that appear central. It is true that the talons of local lords with honorial claims hover ominously; yet in this place for once the public order is foregrounded. Could this point to the input of Romanist lawyers at Arles? It is also true that Arles preserved no written evidence of the routines of governance instituted probably in the 1150s, of what were spoken of as *publica consilia* and *negocia* in its charter. Few other consulates or communes achieved any such recognition of autonomy in the later twelfth century. One place that came to regret this was Saint-Antonin in Rouergue, which in about 1143 had received a stirring charter, in the vernacular, of exemption from 'that bad custom which is called *questa*' together with much else from its Viscount-Lord Isarn and his brothers. What it omitted was precisely what the charter of Arles contained about the election and offices of twelve consuls;

[181] *Cartulaire de Trinquetaille*, ed. P.-A. Amargier (Aix-en-Provence 1972) no. 308, not the best of extant texts. A similar programme was soon instituted at Avignon. See André Gouron, 'Sur les plus anciennes rédactions coutumières du Midi: les "chartes" consulaires d'Arles et d'Avignon,' *Annales du Midi* CIX (1997) 189–200.

and when, two or three generations later someone rewrote this charter in Latin, apparently pretending that it was the original, new articles of exactly this content were added.[182] In the meantime the inadequacies and excesses of lordly power became visible in other circles. The oaths of royal provosts turn up in Capetian records.[183] In England the justiciars and sergeants appointed to manage the Assize of the Forest (1184) were to swear to uphold it.[184] Services in European monarchies, long sanctioned in personal fidelities, inched their ways towards an official status of accountability.

WHAT THE charters achieved was the rejection, the widespread rejection, of arbitrary lordship. They became in consequence a window, however clouded, into unrecorded debates over the just disposition of enlarged material resources. And while those debates promoted new alignments of interests, the avatars of local governments, they did not in principle reject, let alone oust, the old official dominations by which lords-king, count, bishop (etc.) became their partners in the renovation of public powers subverted by lordship. Charters not only veiled, they doubtless suppressed, the struggles in which they originated. But it can no longer be maintained that the proto-governments of the twelfth century were the work of a revolutionary *bourgeoisie*. If the famous uprisings of Laon, Compostela, and (after all) Bruges have been placed in their settings, others equally startling—notably Le Mans, Milan, Vézelay—have hardly been mentioned. Their histories were not so different. In a vast majority of places such disruptions were avoided when bishops and counts saw the point of

---

[182] 'La coutume originale de Saint-Antonin [Tarn-et-Garonne] (1140–1144),' ed. Robert Latouche, *Bulletin philologique et historique (jusqu'à 1715) du Comité des Travaux historiques et scientifiques* (1920) 257–62; *LTC* I, no. 86. On jurists at Arles, see below p. 469.

[183] e.g., *HF* XVI, 155, no. 464.   [184] *GrH* I, 323–24.

renouncing the chronically arbitrary elements of their lordship while clinging to the profits of jurisdiction and markets.

This is why, at Toulouse, where very exceptionally for its time the 'common council' of notables is legislating already in 1152, it (or they) do(es) so with Count Raimund's counsel.[185] A generation later, it is true, the consuls tried to shake free of the same ageing count's lordship, yet even at the height of their autonomous power they stood in the relation of mutual fidelity with the count. In January 1189 a settlement took place in the church of Saint-Pierre-des-Cuisines whereby the count and the consuls—he claiming to be their 'good lord'—swore reciprocal oaths of fidelity in concrete terms of governance such as were elsewhere ascribed to consulates.[186] What is more, the Toulousan consuls of these years, more insistent on their individual, named identities than on their official solidarity, were altogether cosy with the lordly status they themselves so manifestly craved.[187] Count Raimund VI (1194–1222) did even better at Nîmes, where his regulation of the urban consulate in 1198 is a glittering showcase of the precocity of civic initiative together with the tenacity of old public lordship.[188] By this time Italian towns were turning to external lords, the *podestà*, to keep order. One can sense from the oath of the *podestà* Gerardo Cortevecchia at Pisa in 1206–07 how the pressure to pacify factions and feuds was subverting the revived interests of civic order.[189] Much the same urgencies help to explain the restoration of comital domination over Toulouse during and after the Albigensian crusades.[190]

---

[185] Cartulaire du Bourg, no. 4, ed. Limouzin-Lamothe, *Commune de Toulouse* 266–69.

[186] ibid., no. 8, *Commune* 275–76. See also John Hine Mundy, *Liberty and political power in Toulouse, 1050–1230* (NY 1954) chs. 4–6.

[187] T. N. Bisson, 'Pouvoir et consuls à Toulouse (1150–1205),' *Les sociétés méridionales à l'âge féodal . . . Hommage à Pierre Bonnassie*, ed. Hélène Débax (Toulouse 1999) 197–202.

[188] *LTC* I, no. 483.   [189] *Brevi di Pisa*, ap. 10 (122).

[190] Laurent Macé, *Les comtes de Toulouse et leur entourage, XIIe–XIIIe siècles . . .* (Toulouse 2000) part 3.

What is arresting about this tendency is that in and after the 1140s Genoa and Pisa had already known communal governments: that is, record-making agencies of collective purpose, more or less autonomous. Their consuls were then officials in the usual sense of public service; their work was recorded in their own statements of commitment (*brevi*), to the city not lords, such as are found practically nowhere else.[191] After about 1150 there were hundreds of places, north and south in Europe, possessed of jurates, *scabini* (those transformed functionaries of Carolingian origin), judges, alcaldes, and the like. For extremely few of these places have we the slightest evidence of their routines of work. Rural mayorships continued to be claimed as hereditary property.[192]

So the trajectory towards office is only visible within an ampler narrative of lordship, an institution with its own credentials of social purpose. The chronologies and dynamics of power seem more accidental than purposive, more out of phase than progressive. Contemporaries surely had some sense of them. Yet what they talked about, one imagines, was violence and its remedy, and the shifting, problematic uses of sworn fidelity.

Working with Power

Such preoccupations were slow to disappear. The greater lord-kings feasted on the violence their peoples suffered, for having now the means to suppress it they first won applause for doing so. Just as Henry II began by assaulting defiant castellans in Anjou and England, so did Philip Augustus with decisive campaigns against barons of Berry and Burgundy.[193] These campaigns, like

---

[191] *Statuta consulatus Ianuensis*, cols. 241–52; *Brevi di Pisa* 43–101; and see further, below, pp. 494–97.

[192] e.g., *CSPCh* II, 718 (*an.* 1281).

[193] Rigord, *Gesta Philippi Augusti*, ed. H. François Delaborde, *Oeuvres de Rigord et de Guillaume le Breton, historiens de Philippe-Auguste*, 2 vols. (Paris 1882–85) I, cc. 7, 8, 34–35.

the less successful ones of Alfons I in upper Catalonia a few years later, were not simply expansionist enterprises. They were quite in the nature of deeds to be celebrated, which is why the Occitanian monk Rigord, writing of King Philip after 1196, often reads like Suger half a century before. Yet the tradition of heroic commemoration was itself in confusion in the later twelfth century. While narratives of dynastic and militant success could easily accommodate the dynastic and crusading exploits that so starkly recoloured the map of power from about 1170 to the Battle of Bouvines (1214), their authors were perplexed by what look to us like equally momentous changes behind the scenes of conflict, submission, and treaty.[194]

The story of these changes is that of lord-princes beginning to work with the power they had. This is not to say that their prior lives of conspicuous nobility were devoid of social purpose. Of course not. Their oaths of office imposed duties of protection and justice that they carried out with the variable success flowing from their natures and circumstances. Yet their normally passive response to petitioners for grace and favour required no visible adherence to routine, while the new impulses of accountancy arose silently in the ill documented experiments of patrimonial servants. The delegated management of the king's justice that Roger of Salisbury had held under Henry I was not an 'office' so designated, nor did it keep records as such.

This was to change under Henry II. But it is unlikely that the spread of official conceptions of public service, first manifest in charters of franchise and in Mediterranean towns, had much influence in the monarchies anywhere. What mattered to them was the experience of notables and clerks serving—and promoted by—the lord-kings whose exploits they recorded. And

---

[194] In addition to Rigord and Guillaume le Breton, see *GcB*, first redaction, cc. 1–11; *Chronica latina regum Castellae*, ed. L. Charlo Brea, *Chronica hispana saeculi XIII* (Turnhout 1997) cc. 6–50; *Roderici Ximenii de Rada historia de rebus Hispanie*, ed. Juan Fernández Valverde (Turnhout 1987) vi.3, 4; vii.1–36; viii.1–12.

their records, taken as a whole, came to be tainted with a new conception of power still lacking official status or documentation of its own. To see this, however dimly, requires attention to a disparate array of evidence arising from diverse conjunctures in the several kingdoms of Europe. In three instances, to be examined below, the evidence points to significant if not quite irreversible change. A fourth conjuncture, that of the Roman church, displays a lordship, wholly untypical because elective, that is coming to recover its natural status as a religious administration.

CATALONIA

In Mediterranean realms the normative declarations of assizes and *Usatges* around 1140–50 redefined public regimes of prescriptive order. Yet there is little in their diplomas and charters to show that lord-kings in Sicily and the county of Barcelona were moving from passively responsive action towards engaged domination. Nor was it otherwise in the (other) Hispanic kingdoms or the counties of Toulouse and Provence. Yet the suggestive evidence of other sorts from Catalonia not only bears up in comparison with that of new impulses in northern realms; it can also be associated in some respects with similarly creative enterprise in Spain and southern France.

According to the continuator of the *Deeds of the counts of Barcelona*, Alfons I 'powerfully ruled his kingdom while he lived.' But this was a detached monastic account of a great lordship; and when in 1194 the same lord-king convoked other Hispanic monarchs to join in an anti-Muslim campaign, little came of it but a pilgrimage to Compostela. Yet by 1212, when his son Pere I took a valiant part in the Christian triumph of Las Navas de Tolosa, his realm from the Ebro to the Rhône seemed hardly inferior to England or France in size and potential.[195] The 'deeds' that made for this were all but unknown to the chroniclers.

[195] *GcB* (first version) cc. 9, 10.

They can be reconstructed from the problematic survival of records of justice and fiscal management dating back to the 1150s. What these show is that by 1175–80, soon after King Alfons came of age, the multiplication and accumulation of titles to castles, conventions, and oaths had reached a point of self-defeating confusion. A big bundle of such parchments had been pawned to a Jewish moneylender, their value as collateral evidently exceeding that of legal utility. The redemption of these records in 1178 by the notary Guillem de Bassa, followed two years later by the lord-king's successful prosecution of the castellan Pere de Lluçà for the right to repossess two castles, marked not simply the foundation of a major European public archive but even a new departure in written lordship. The earliest dorsal marks of classification on surviving originals date from these years. Moreover, from the later 1170s to at least 1194 Guillem de Bassa worked with another notary, Ramon de Caldes, in the newly routine work of auditing the bailiffs in the count's fiscal domains; and this activity coincided with the notary Ramon's engagement with the records of castles, the task of classifying and transcribing them in 'two volumes' called (at first) 'Book of the Lord-King' (*Liber domini regis*).[196]

The pride with which Ramon de Caldes dedicated this work to 'his' lord-king Alfons conveys not only awareness of his own role in conceptually augmented notarial service, but also the fitting magnitude of the regal achievement in consolidating power over massive and dispersed lands, counties, fiefs, and castles. Now the 'Lord-King's Book' represented that achievement with singular precision. Evoking sacks and stacks of useless mouldering

---

[196] For all these points, *FAC* i; and see also Anscari M. Mundó, 'El pacte de Cazola del 1179 i el "Liber feudorum maior." Notes paleogràfiques i diplomatiques,' *Jaime I y su época*, 3 vols. (Zaragoza 1979–82) ii Comunicaciones i, 119–29; and Adam Kosto, 'The *Liber feudorum maior* of the counts of Barcelona: the cartulary as an expression of power,' *Journal of Medieval History* xxvii (2001) 1–22. The records of 1178 and 1180 are: ACA, Cancelleria, perg. R.B. IV 258; and *LFM* i, no. 225. The *liber domini regis* came long afterwards to be called *liber feudorum maior*, and was printed as such; hence my citations of *LFM*.

parchments lately classified by region and recopied for easy consultation, the prologue is perfectly illustrated by an initial illumination that must have been conceived by Ramon de Caldes
himself when he finished the work towards 1192, even if its execution was delayed for some time. What it shows, in stunningly
original iconography, is the compiler Ramon in his decanal habit
holding a parchment for the seated king to inspect, with a copyist
at work to Ramon's side. 'Shall we include this one?' the dean
seems to ask; yet as Adam Kosto has acutely noticed, this may not
be just right. Neither the dean nor the king is quite centered in
the canon-tabular frame; indeed, the king looks nearly as mar-
ginal as the scribe. What *is* exactly centered is a single legible (!)
parchment in Ramon's hands, with some ten other parchments
jumbled below, evidently suggestive of the useless bundles now
freshly mobilised. One parchment over many, the control of possessions and their records: that is what this illumination says. It
conveys not so much spoken words as an eloquent gesture: 'Here,
lord-king, is your power.'[197]

Do the words and images of Ramon de Caldes point further to
a literacy of government? There are two reasons for thinking so.
First, Ramon says explicitly that his compilation was intended to
serve (that is, to help the king serve) the 'utility of subjects,' to
establish the rights of 'your men' as well as your own; and a study
of the contents and rubrics of the *Liber feudorum maior* shows that
the reconstructed dossiers of records it contains are by no means
only briefs for contested royal rights. The iconography of parchment, dean, and (unexalted) king supports this point. Second, the
frontispiece miniature in Ramon's register provides a more important clue that justice was at the heart of the king's and the
dean's conception of power.

These reasons open an ampler historical perspective. The parchment in Ramon's hand happens to be a 'judgment' (*iudicium*) that

---

[197] ACA, Cancelleria, Registre 1, fol. 1, reproduced in plate 7, and in *FAC* I,
frontispiece. Also Kosto, '*Liber feudorum maior*,' 20. Mundó identified the chief
copyist from lettering as Ramon de Sitges, "Pacte de Cazola,' 122–28.

is easily identified from its legible wording. An undated compendium of decisions from about 1157 relating to alleged malfeasance by the Catalan baron Galceran de Sales, it was, indeed, copied in the register. It is the only judgment depicted, the other visible parchments being oaths, conventions, and charters, such as in fact make up the bulk of the *LFM*.[198] Moreover, this was the only written judgment (in the form *iudicium*) from a court of Ramon Berenguer IV to be included in the register, although the compilers knew of at least eight others. Could they have noticed, what has not escaped the attention of modern scholars, that amongst all these records, only the judgment depicted in the center of their frontispiece makes explicit reference to the *Usatges of Barcelona*?[199]

What this connection means is that a new campaign of comital justice in the post-conquest 1150s was associated with a code of manifestly regalian character. At just the same time, let us recall, Count Ramon Berenguer IV had launched an inquiry into complaints against his own patrimonial servants, charges apparently meant to be heard in his 'court' (*curia*). And the extant judgments of these years, settlements between great churches and nobles and the count or with each other, are remarkable in two respects. They are decisions by the lord-count's court or its 'judges,' not by the count himself; and they exhibit the count as defendant as well as accuser. Where written law could not be invoked, oral testimony or charters were required.[200]

In this engaging situation even the peasants were appealing to public order. Legislation, judges, accountability: these amounted to renewal in Catalan-speaking lands, not invention. Yet quite certainly some of the lord-count's retainers and notaries were bringing a new spirit to his service; and it looks as if

[198] 'liber secundus,' fol. 10 (=*LFM* II, no. 511). The original survives, ACA, perg. R.B. IV s.d. 12 (printed [also] in *DI* IV, no. 146). Again, plate 7.

[199] Adam J. Kosto, 'The limited impact of the *Usatges de Barcelona* in twelfth-centruy Catalonia,' *Traditio* LVI (2001) 64–65.

[200] ACA, Canc., perg extrainventaris 3433, 3217; cf. 3409; and generally *TV* chs. 1, 3.

the unexpected death of Ramon Berenguer IV in August 1162 disrupted a promising new adjustment between castellan families and the count. What survived of necessity, under the five-year-old Alfons who succeeded his father, was an entourage of notables, also called *curia*, that virtually ruled the child's bi-regnal inheritance for the next decade. Their ill-advised seizure of Provence in 1166 brought on conflict with Toulouse, manageable in time only because of the young king's sensible accommodation with Castile.[201]

Comparatively well known, this dynastic history seems almost beside the point. What happened down to 1175 to sustain the new impulses of territorial justice? The answer must be conjectural in part, for want of evidence of activity lacking its scribal forms. Judgments persist, although taking variable written forms no longer stressing the court's autonomy. The *Usatges* drop out of sight, as if the expertise required to hold castellans to observance of the lawful requirements of 'power' of castles and service were in short supply. And it looks as if the claims of great lordships were having to be resisted in the royal entourage during these years, as if some of the novel impetus of the 1150s was lost.[202]

The work of power devolved upon literate courtiers, among whom Ponç the Scribe (d. 1168), Ramon de Caldes (d. 1199), and his brother Bernat were foremost. These were clerics earning promotion through competence as well as fidelity, notably the Caldes brothers in the cathedral chapter of Barcelona. As so often in the twelfth century, fidelity may have come first, for Ramon and Bernat were sons of Porcell, the comital bailiff of Caldes, as was another Porcell who may have taken over his father's bailiwick. These men were nurtured in the very circles of which peasants were complaining since the 1140s. Ponç, at least, had written experimental accounts in the 1150s; the brothers Caldes

[201] *GcB* (first) c. 9; Ferran Soldevila, *Història de Catalunya*, 2d ed. (Barcelona 1963) ch. 9.

[202] *Alfonso II . . . documentos*, nos. 10, 18, 23, 27, 33, 36, 40, 45, 52, 53, 59, 60, 63, 65, 74.

were amongst those engaged with a new system of fiscal audits of bailiffs by 1173; and from 1178 to 1194, Ramon de Caldes and Guillem de Bassa virtually directed, while auditing and writing themselves, a new fiscal accountancy. Their operation became as routine as the exchequer's. The lord-king's accountants met with the bailiffs to arrive at current balances of debit and receipt, their settlement being recorded in original parchment chirographs, one for each party. Their routine entailed a further innovation surely meant to remedy the chief failing of the old prescriptive methods. The scribes created registers of fiscal information against which the audits could be tested. It is no accident that their operation began in the very year when the defiance of powerful castellans incited a new departure in record-keeping. The accountants retained the king's copies (and doubtless the registers) as well as the charters and conventions for the lord-king. Ramon de Caldes was the key figure in both enterprises.[203]

There is no sign that contemporaries noticed the reformed accountancy, still less that they applauded (or resented) the new custom imposed on them. The service of Ramon and his associates was manifestly in the public interest because it effectually defanged the bailiffs and vicars, yet no such opinion survived in the written evidence, including their own words. Their work conformed to a Mediterranean tradition of patrimonial enhancement through improved record-keeping proclaimed as such. The pride of Ramon de Caldes in 1192 had been anticipated some thirty years before in one Canon Bernardo's preface to a vast compilation—this one also, though more traditionally, illuminated—of the privileges of Santiago of Compostela. The great cartularies for the viscounty of Béziers (1186–88) and for the Lords Guillem of Montpellier (ca. 1202, with preface) were very

---

[203] *FAC* I and II. The scribes and accountants are identified in I, 234–50. A fuller study of Ramon de Caldes is T. N. Bisson, 'Ramon de Caldes (c. 1135–1199): dean of Barcelona and king's minister,' *Law, church and society: essays in honor of Stephan Kuttner*, ed. Kenneth Pennington, Robert Somerville (Philadelphia 1977) 281–92.

comparable in impetus and purpose to the *LFM*, the preparatory work for which may well have been known in Occitania.[204]

What the courtier-scribes contributed to their lord-king's power was a viable solution to challenges of the 1160s: how to mobilise patrimonial resources and secure titles to castles and the fidelity of castellans. Ramon de Caldes and Guillem de Bassa look for all the world like administrators, like functionaries in an incipient territorial government. Yet their functions seem to have been hardly more 'official' than a cook's. They held or earned no titled offices, were rewarded with no bishoprics. Moreover, it is likely that their works provoked dissent in the lord-king's retinue. It had been usual for creditors to repay themselves from the baili-wicks they purchased, and while most bailiffs held their functions as conditional tenures, some of those who figure in the early au-dits were surely creditors.[205] It is a murky question how the ex-pert scribes viewed the persistent allegations against vicars and bailiffs, none of which, to our knowledge, came to trial.[206] To-gether with some others in Barcelona, Ramon de Caldes must be credited with preserving the memorials of complaint as well as the judgments, silently passionate witnesses in their discrepancy to functional incoherence in the exercise of power. Moreover, clinging as they did to the conventions, oaths, and charters, these men would have viewed with dismay the mounting opposition of castellans and barons to the lord-king's peace. It was the pro-grammatic peace, as we shall see, that pushed aside any serious insistence on the *Usatges* as the basis of public order.

---

[204] *Tumbo A de la catedral de Santiago. Estudio y edición*, ed. Manuel Lucas Alva-rez (Santiago 1998) 47–48; together with notice of the important critical work by José María Fernández Catón, 30–39. See also Hélène Débax, 'Le cartulaire des Trencavel (*Liber instrumentorum vicecomitalium*),' *Les cartulaires*, ed. Olivier Guyotjeannin *et al.* (Paris 1993) 291–99; and *Liber instrumentorum memorialium. Cartulaire des Guillems de Montpellier*, ed. Alexandre Germain (Montpellier 1884–86).

[205] *FAC* II, nos. 1, 31, 33, 35, 45, 49.

[206] Sixteen of the memorials of complaint are registered in *TV* 165–71; others are cited in that book, but I know of no full list of them.

So the curial works of the scribes were and remained bound up with princely patrimonial lordship. With the passing of Ramon de Caldes and Guillem de Bassa, both by 1200, the fiscal audits sputtered intermittently under Pere I. By 1204 the Templars of Palau-solità were in charge of the accounts, which soon degenerated into reckonings of the new king's increasingly imprudent credit. No more is heard of the fiscal registers, which for their prescriptive content may already have been out of date by 1200. Regularity of account was entirely lost under Jaume I (1213–76), to be restored only after the conquest of Valencia in the 1240s.[207]

THESE INNER workings were not the whole story of power in the counties becoming known as *Catalonia* in the later twelfth century. But they will serve in this chapter to caution against any presumption of progressive change. In their obsessive fidelities the king's scribes may not have foreseen the potential of the new implements of power they had created. Those judgments from the 1150s—finely detailed about procedures of allegation, rebuttal, and informed decision—marked a high point of quasi-legislative order that came to be fiercely resisted in the baronies, castellanies, and upland viscounties. Territorial justice, for all the initiatives to recreate accountable delegations of power, remained elusive for another century.

ENGLAND

Was it so different in England? This question is not posed lightly, nor is the answer so easy as might first appear. In some famous ways King Henry II and his sons (and grandson) presided over a uniquely experimental and articulated regime of justice. Much of

---

[207] *FAC* II, nos. 102–38; T. N. Bisson, 'The finances of the young James I (1213–1228)' in (idem) *MFrPN* ch. 19.

this regime survived the troubles of King John (1199–1216) to become the foundation of royal government in the thirteenth century. By then some hundreds of English families and thousands of people had tested their claims and rights in procedural instead of coercive ways. Nor was this the extent of insular singularity, for the earlier survival of Old English local institutions made for generalized expectations of public order that were never silenced. Yet for all this the English society to which Henry Plantagenet laid claim at the end of 1154 was hardly more 'governed,' hardly less dominated, than the turbulent Anjou whence he sprang.

Henry had done much to change this by 1178, when a cleric close to the royal court named Roger of Howden summed up his latest exercise of power as follows: 'Staying in England, the lord-king questioned the justices he had appointed in England whether they had treated the people of the realm with decent restraint.' And when he learned that the people were 'overly oppressed' by an 'excessive multitude' of justices, the king took 'counsel with competent men' and decided to reduce the number of justices from eighteen to five,

> namely, two clerics and three laymen, all chosen from his private entourage [*familia*]. And he decreed that these five should hear all pleas [*clamores*] of the realm and do right; and that they should not leave the court, but stay there to hear pleas of the people, so that if any question arises to prevent a settlement, it may be presented to the royal hearing, and so be decided as he and the wiser men of the realm see fit.[208]

This celebrated evidence, like some lighthouse on the rocky coastline of Angevin experience, illuminates past and future alike. For the lord-king to 'stay' in England was premonitory, seeing that the previous visits of this French-speaking prince (1154–55, 1157, 1163–66, 1170–71, 1174, 1175–76) had witnessed to his attentive engagement with power. In 1178 he meets and

---

[208] *GrH* i, 207–8.

challenges the appointed justices, tests their success by resort to a notion of public interest—the people's satisfaction—, finds it wanting, takes counsel, and imposes a reduced team of justices henceforth to work in the king's court. Here, as F. W. Maitland well surmised, we have the beginnings of a *curia regis* that governs.[209] Quite as in Catalonia justice is central in a redefinition of responsive lordship. Here as there, complaints (*clamores*) of the people—and in the very same years—compel the prince's ingenuity. Yet the situations are merely schematically alike, for it is only in England that we are privileged to glimpse a process of experimentation with justice that is comparable to that of the Catalan notaries with patrimonial management in the 1150s and 1160s.

The *clamores* of 1178 are not much like those of the Catalan peasants. The English already have justices at work whose summonses are proving inconvenient or disruptive; the complaints are lodged against utilitarian works of power threatening to become arbitrary in new ways. Yet those justices were themselves part of the lord-king's response to allegations of injustice that went back to the beginnings of his reign. The same may be said of the chronicler's words, which conceivably reproduce the king's question verbatim: 'whether they have treated the people of the realm with decent restraint [*si bene et modeste tractaverunt homines regni*].'

How early or eagerly Henry Plantagenet embraced the concept of public utility is hard to say. Neither he nor his chroniclers insist on the point, although he was surrounded by literate courtiers familiar with it.[210] From the start his restorative intention was that of the good lord-prince confirming good old laws (and renouncing bad ones), confirming patrimonial titles, and 'renewing the peace.' Yet his most urgent early deed was the securing of castles, which makes it likely that this intention, known to have been voiced in the inaugural assemblies of December 1154, was

[209] P&M I, 153–54.
[210] e.g., *Letters and charters of Gilbert Foliot*, no. 125.

already responsive to petitions and *clamores*. If so, King Henry may have been nudged by practical experience into an exercise of administrative lordship. Yet even if we suppose that he was more angered by infidelity than by violence, he had long since pressed Stephen to destroy the new castles put to bad uses; and he pursued a campaign against fortified lordships deep into his reign, unwilling to put up for long with baronial intransigence or self-serving castellans. The surrenders of Hugh Bigod and William of Blois in 1157 were not the last of their kind.[211]

Less threatening (to the king) but more deeply and pervasively troubling was the petty violence in the English countrysides: usurpations, seizures, dispossessions. That Henry understood this to be an inherited disorder is proven by his early directive to rid England of Flemish knights.[212] Complaints against petty violence must have been quite as numerous in England at this time as in France and Catalonia, though recorded differently; they normally survive only in the lord-king's writs of response. In (probably) spring 1155 he directed the sheriff of Lincoln to restore the land of Threckingham to the abbot of Ramsey; land 'of which he has been disseised unjustly and without judgment, and if you do not, my justice should do this so that I hear no further complaint about it for lack of right or justice.'[213] In cases of 1155–57 relating to the monks of Abingdon and Athelney, Henry and his courtiers ordered the sheriffs of Oxford and Berkshire to determine whether they had been unjustly disseised.[214] Functionaries and procedures were in place, requiring only to be activated, but the young monarch can hardly have been content with the order in England he left his retainers to manage. In 1159 bandits were said to fall in with travellers in the disguise of monks who enticed their

---

[211] HH x.38 (772); *SC* 151–52, 158; Graeme J. White, *Restoration and reform, 1153–1165* . . . (Cambridge 2000) 4–8; Warren, *Henry II* 66–68.

[212] Warren 59.

[213] R. C. Van Caenegem, *Royal writs in England from the Conquest to Glanvill* . . . (London 1959) no. 90.

[214] *The acta of King Henry II, 1154–1189*, ed. Nicholas Vincent *et al.* (forthcoming) nos. 5, 6.

victims into ambushes.[215] By this time Henry was hearing about clerics claiming judicial immunity for acts of violence. Things were no better in Anjou and Aquitaine, where little pretence of public justice survived; and the more the duke-king attended to his continental castles, the more he had to rely on surrogates in England.[216] So once again, as a half-century before, men behind the scenes were tempted—and doubtless encouraged—to experiment with their devices of power.

Their work was, by the 1160s if not before then, an expression of King Henry's response to complaints that he and his justiciars can only have viewed as signs of insufferable disorder. From the writs that survived mostly in ecclesiastical collections, it is clear that appeals for justice were falling into the classes of right, status, possession (etc.) that were soon to be codified; so it looks as if procedural convenience in the face of multiplying instances in the king's absences prompted the novel remedies wherewith to expedite justice. These remedies seem not to have figured in legislative proclamations; it was enough for the justices to agree on the reformed verbiage instituting the processes of *utrum* ('whether' lay fee or alms), first mentioned in the *Constitutions of Clarendon* in 1164, and novel disseisin, which though not cited in the *Assize of Clarendon* (1166) is evidently associated with it. The written monuments just mentioned, while different in genesis and nature, have to do with jurisdiction—they are proof of better rooted courts of justice than in other lands—and the remedy of crime and violence.[217] And while the *Constitutions* may seem on first sight unrelated to public order, in fact the dispute over the liability of 'criminous clerks' was far from abstract. It had arisen soon after the promotion of Thomas Becket (1162) as the lord-king was led to suppose that if his once-favoured chancellor could be unfaithful as well as ungrateful, so might clerics of his

[215] *Chronique de Robert de Torigni* II. *Continuatio Beccensis*, 173.

[216] Boussard, *Gouvernement d'Henri II* 285–338, 427–35, who surely overestimates Henry's success in France.

[217] Van Caenegem, *Royal writs* 195–346, 405–515; SC 163–67, 170–73.

new order be guilty of the violence of violation in the same ways as lay men. It had been alleged in the Council of Westminster (October 1163) that archdeacons were exerting power 'not with prelatical modesty but with tyranny, troubling lay people with calumnies and clerics with undue exactions.'[218] A forceful presence to secure these efforts at administrative justice was required; yet while in England King Henry's response to easy and habitual violence had reached this new stage, it was otherwise in his homelands and Aquitaine. Henry spent the next four years there in a more elementary exercise of power, managing Normandy himself, facing up to a king of France emboldened by the birth of a son and heir in 1165, but chiefly engaged in subjugating the castles and baronies that stood in the way of his territorial domination.[219]

Those four years became the test of a more searching and stringent initiative in the use of royal power. When Henry returned to England in the spring of 1170, surviving a bad storm in the Channel crossing, he demanded an accounting from and about the sheriffs as well as from all others possessed of power. He wanted to know what—exactly what and how much—lords of every kind had collected from their tenants since his last crossing to Normandy. Imposed in a council at London convoked 'concerning conditions of the realm' and to plan the crowning of the young Henry, this command must have struck with terrifying force. Gervase of Canterbury called it 'astounding,' while Roger of Howden claims that the lord-king 'deposed almost all the sheriffs.' Setting a short term of nine weeks for the return of written response, it surely stirred the English masses while jolting their masters as never before.[220]

The *Inquest of Sheriffs*, although sometimes underestimated amongst Henry II's measures, was arguably the most symptomatic of them all. Here is the lord-king acting in something like vindictive rage (one is reminded of Henry I with the moneyers),

---

[218] *C&S* I², 851. [219] Warren, *Henry II* 100–110.
[220] *GrH* I, 3–5; Gervase, *Chronicle* I, 216–19.

but the vehemence here is of a new order. Obscure experimentation with summary procedures of right gives way to openly engaged interaction with courtiers to enlarge the existing structure
of accountability. Whatever happened—and although Howden
surely exaggerated, no fewer than seventeen or more sheriffs
were, indeed, displaced in 1170—Henry II served notice that
quittance for county farms was no longer sufficient proof of fidelity in face of a constant volume of complaints. Foremost in
the articles of inquiry, as undoubtedly in the grievances they
echoed, were seizures, exactions, and (unwarranted) distraints.
Robert of Torigni summed things up as the king's 'rebuke' to
'the sheriffs of England who had afflicted [people] by exactions
and plunder.' Yet it looks as if sheriffs were but a conspicuous category of great lords with the power to oppress. Not only were
prelates, barons, and knights subject to the same inquiry; from
the scraps of written returns that survive it also appears that the
lord-king's men had in view the 'financial exploitation of the
country and the manner of it, in whosoever's interest, whether
just or unjust.'[221]

The justice and violence thereby exposed needs to be read in
its wide perspectives of space and time. Better than any other text
from Latin Europe, the *Inquest of Sheriffs* witnesses to a problematic experience of power in the 1170s, to the fragile balance between habitual impulses of domination and the renewed discipline
of official and accountable service. Provoked to wilful response,
the lord-Henry does what Count Ramon Berenguer IV has done
two decades before in the old Pyrenean realm. In both lands, and
in Catalonia still in the 1170s, princely initiatives in face of insur-
gent claims to public powers have an aspect of institutional nov-

---

[221] Quotation from Warren, *Henry II* 289. See also Julia Boorman, 'The sheriffs of Henry II and the significance of 1170,' *Law and government in medieval
England and Normandy . . .* , ed. George Garnett, John Hudson (Cambridge
1994) 255–75; *SC* 176; Robert of Torigni, *Chronique* II, 17; *Red Book of the Exchequer* II, pp. cclxii–cclxxxiv.

elty; the suppression of violence, even as it ceases to be the only impulse of collective interest, remains elemental.

Yet the inquest of 1170 was considerably more than a reaction against perceived disorder. It emphatically reiterated previous initiatives on two points that had been responsive to complaint: dissatisfaction with the deportment of sheriffs, and reliance on barons-errant to bear the king's justice to localities. Already in the years 1159–64 sheriffs had been dismissed in large numbers; at a time, that is, when unlawful violence was said to have peaked. In 1166 the *Assize of Clarendon* defined a new procedure of public accusation against violators of social order to be carried out by itinerant judges; and on one matter, the disposition of fugitives' property, the Inquest referred explicitly to the *assisa de Clarendune*. In other ways, too, the *Inquest of Sheriffs* refers to mechanisms and emoluments of justice and service as to ongoing functions of royal power. That those functions were coming to be thought of as 'official,' in our words if not theirs, is suggested by a marked antipathy to perversions of right and to bribes in ministerial conduct. Assemblies in the hundreds and shires are mobilised at the king's beckoning. What the people possess or pay interests Henry II, doubtless because he has had, and will have, projects for which he wishes to tax their wealth himself.[222]

So in England the passivity of lord-kingship is subverted by the 1170s. The new engagement is not quite legislative, although it remains judicial quite as in contemporary Barcelona. What is distinctive in England is the experience of procedural expertise proliferating obscurely, beyond the exchequer, with only the imperative of utility. Having now to respond as of custom, no longer simply as of grace, Henry, or more usually his justiciar or his justices, seeks to manage complaints and petitions, to channel them; and so pressed to respond, they innovate. Declarations or commands are—or, more exactly, may be—put into writing; the new writs become customary before they become formulaic: unwritten writing, one might almost say. By 1176 the *Assize of*

---

[222] Boorman, 'Sheriffs,' 258–59; *SC* 170–73, 175–78; and 177 c. 8.

Northampton could refer to novel disseisin as a previously sanctioned remedy newly pertinent by reason of the late rebellion of
the king's sons. Violence yet again! And it was this measure that
so multiplied the justices as to require the reform of 1178 that set
a term to a remarkable stage of procedural invention.[223]

The innovations of this stage go beyond anything of the sort
known to have happened in the monarchies of continental Europe. That this was not accidental is proven by another circumstance peculiar to England, perhaps the most remarkable one of
all. The royal outreach for responsible territorial mastery was a
working *with* power by men about the lord-king who *came*, on
the job, *to recognize what was happening.* One can virtually date this
recognition to the early 1170s, when a chronicler began to write
about Henry II's affairs, and dated his subject not from the Creation, Christ, or the Conquest; not even from 1154, but from
Christmas 1170 (or 1169, as we count). This was the start of a tumultuous year, that of the great Inquest preceded by a terrifying
storm and followed by the murder of Thomas Becket. From these
events the writer, who was almost certainly the secular clerk
Roger of Howden, carried forward a near-current narrative focused closely on royal power. He may even then have been working for the king, as he surely was in 1174–75, for in the conventional
chronicle he surely wrote later he included letters and records
from the 1160s.[224]

Howden reoriented a traditional discourse of dynastic power
by focusing in a new way on the lord-king's purposes and commands. It is from his copies that we possess the *Assizes* of Clarendon (1166), Northampton (1176), Arms (1181), and the Forest
(1184), as well as the *Inquest of Sheriffs* (1170). The text of an important assize on coinage passed in January 1180 at Oxford not

---

[223] *GrH* I, 108–11.

[224] ibid., with the introduction by Stubbs; see also J. C. Holt, 'The assizes of
Henry II: the texts,' *The study of medieval records. Essays in honour of Kathleen
Major*, ed. D. A. Bullough, R. L. Storey (Oxford 1971) 85–92; *Chronica magistri
Rogeri de Houedene*, ed. William Stubbs, 4 vols. (London 1868–71) I, 215–82.

only eluded Howden but apparently all other collectors; from fiscal allusions and numismatic evidence we know that it imposed a new currency while separating the operations of striking and exchanging money.[225] The texts of 1166 and 1170 must have been in Howden's possession, or accessible, when he began to write his history, which began with an extended account of the *Inquest of Sheriffs*; and he habitually incorporated such normative records as if they were the very events—indeed, the 'deeds' (*gesta*) to which an early copyist referred—in need of his attention.[226] No other scheme to collect such records of command is yet perceptible, although utilitarian copies may well date from Howden's time and circle. No 'archive' as such is mentioned. Howden is not a directed archivist, like Ramon de Caldes, but more like a facilitator engaged with written directives being replicated for local purposes. As with others incorporating injunctive material in their narratives—for example, the monk Gervase and the chronicler(s) of Battle Abbey[227]—the impulse was public yet not quite official. Some of the assizes were preserved by no other hand than that of a clerk whose very identity remains problematic.

Nor is this all. It happens that Howden was far from alone amongst (to us) obscure clerks about the lord-king, and the human interest in their competencies could not easily be concealed, even in these pre-bureaucratic circumstances. In the very years (1177–89) when Howden represents Henry II energetically directing teams of justices coping with amplified demands for royal justice, men familiar with the workings of this power wrote two books of stunning originality: the *Dialogue of the exchequer* (1177–79), and the *Treatise on the laws and customs of the kingdom of*

---

[225] D. F. Allen, *A catalogue of English coins in the British Museum: the cross and crosslet type of Henry II* (London 1951) pp. lxxxviii–xcv; Gilbert Stack, 'A lost law of Henry II: the Assize of Oxford and monetary reform,' *Haskins Society Journal* XVI (2005) 95–103.

[226] *GrH* I, 4–5, 108, 278; Roger of Howden, *Chronica* II, 245; also 248–52 for Roger's text of the *Assize of Clarendon*.

[227] Antonia Gransden, *Historical writing in England c. 55–c. 1307* (London 1996) 253–59, 277–78.

England (1187–89). These were the works of experts, and it is fair to say that the subject they have in common is expertise with power. The *Dialogue* was the work of Richard fitz Nigel, treasurer in the exchequer (ca. 1160–98) and finally bishop of London. The *Treatise on the laws* goes by the name Glanvill, although no one believes today that Ranulf de Glanvill (justiciar 1180–89) was its author; the identity of the justice who doubtless wrote it remains in question. Moreover, the skills of these writers on accountability and justice were mediated in a curial culture of which yet a third book, Walter Map's *On courtiers' trifles*, affords a less technical but more humane—and far less sanguine—commentary. A secular clerk in the king's service from about 1173, when he was himself a royal justice, Walter knew at first hand how the life of royal lordship was changing. The anecdotes he began to compile in 1181–82 evoke the personnel of justice and the exchequer as an inscrutable 'court' given as much to sordid ambition as to useful competence.[228]

The cluster of normative records copied mostly (as we have them) by Roger of Howden come from the years 1166 to 1181, when Henry II was most engaged with internal order in his kingdom. They committed the king's clerks, justices, and sheriffs, even as they confirmed the barons of the exchequer, to the execution of prescriptive direction extending over much of English life: local peace and order, new remedies for common complaints, coinage, military obligation, and the forests. What provision was made for record-keeping in this ferment is hard to discern, but should not be minimised. Clerks began again to collect assizes and lists, not quite all of which were lost as they were superseded in the thirteenth century. Moreover, the clerical perception of newly coordinated powers in the 1170s is borne out by the likelihood that from just then on the exchequer was receiving rolls of fines and copies of writs (*contrabrevia*). Not literacy but record-keeping for

---

[228] Walter Map, *De nugis curialium* i.1, v.7. Also Richard fitz Nigel, *Dialogus de scaccario*; *Tractatus de legibus* . . . , ed. G. D. G. Hall, revised (Oxford 1993 [1965]).

newly routine work is at issue here. As Nicholas Vincent has stressed, countless multiples related to extant records were written, deployed, and destroyed by petitioners, litigants, sellers, etc., in the twelfth century.[229] And one novelty of the years when Roger of Howden, Richard fitz Nigel, and the author of *Glanvill* were chiefly at work was the mounting pressure to coordinate runaway specialties in expert service. It may be well to avoid assumptions about the nature of works under the chancellor. The exchequer was, indeed, something like an office. Its routines of enrolment and the protocols attested by the *Dialogue* are sufficient proof of that. Successive justiciars, Richard de Lucy (1154–79) and Ranulf de Glanvill (1180–89), were noted for competence as well as fidelity. But Thomas Becket (1154–62) had been, or became, a lord-chancellor in every sense, and there is little sign that his inconspicuous successors were expected, or permitted, to innovate. No chancellor was appointed for a decade after Becket. It was enough for Geoffrey Ridel, untitled, to carry on with other expert scribes in a function at the service of justice and accountancy; the chancellors Ralph (1173–82) and Geoffrey (the king's bastard son, 1182–89) had their sights on ecclesiastical promotion. There was no 'Dialogue of the Chancery.'[230]

Yet the more significant changes had occurred in works outside the exchequer. Henry II had presided over a remodeling of the judicial prerogatives of his lordly power. What we may speak of as 'government,' something culturally distinct from lordship, has intruded, pervasively so, even brutally. The prevailing outlook from Walter Map's *curia* is territorial-regnal in a sense more nearly objective than is possible in Henry's ancestral and acquired domains.[231] The peace of possession begins to work against the

---

[229] Vincent, 'Why 1199? Bureaucracy and enrolment under John' 29; see also 25, and Holt, 'Assizes of Henry II' 86.

[230] As Vincent has pointed out, 'Why 1199?' 17. See also T. F. Tout, *Chapters in the administrative history of mediaeval England . . .* , 6 vols. (Manchester 1920–33) I, 132–34; and Clanchy, *Memory*, ch. 2.

[231] Walter Map, *De nugis* i.1, v.6.

self-serving powers of lesser lords.[232] The lord-king's justice assumes new reality even as more and more commands in the king's name are spoken or written and executed out of his sight. Local men sworn to declare or determine in accordance with the *Assizes* of Clarendon and Northampton were working for a social purpose.[233] Yet the power of affective presence persists, not always for the good. King Henry did little to inhibit such behaviour, least of all his own; his son Richard famously exploited it for profit.[234] Nor can we suppose that these lord-kings saw the slightest discrepancy between lordship and government. Still less their servants, for whom the nature of royal power held little meaning apart from contexts of legality and customary procedure. And the 'reasons' of the new law were far from transparent. Local juries sent suspects to ordeals by battle.[235] Richard fitz Nigel wrote (bravely) that with respect to the forests the lord-king reserved arbitrary powers at variance with the 'common law.'[236] This conceptual wobble may help to explain why the assizes of Henry II as we have them do little to help the barons and clerks think of their prescribed works in official ways or to anticipate the managerial problems they entail. Even less is said of public function in Plantagenet England than in contemporary Italy. As in Toulouse, it took a generation for authorities to face up to the confusions created by lost charters, misplaced writs, and useless sacks of parchments. The English solution of enrolling records of right, procedure, and decision was one of the ways in which ad hoc functions—for instance, the supervision of accords in the king's court—became offices

---

[232] S. F. C. Milsom, *The legal framework of English feudalism* . . . (Cambridge 1976) chs. 1–3.

[233] *SC* 170, 179, 180 c. 5.

[234] *The chronicle of Richard of Devizes* . . . , ed. John T. Appleby (London 1963) 4–5; John Gillingham, *Richard I* (New Haven 1999) 114–16.

[235] Paul R. Hyams, 'Trial by ordeal: the key to proof in the early common law,' *On the laws and customs of England. Essays in honor of Samuel E. Thorne* (Chapel Hill 1981) 90–126.

[236] *Dialogus* i.11 (59–60).

under Henry II and his sons.[237] It was unfinished business when Richard succeeded his father in July 1189.

What chiefly impeded the 'reason' of efficiency during the reign of Richard I ('Lionheart' 1189–99) was a resurgence of lordship in office. According to the monk Richard, 'William Longchamp, who had been chancellor to the count of the Poitevins . . . , once the count had been crowned king, felt that his function had been augmented by as much as a kingdom is greater than a county.' More remarkably, Archbishop Hubert Walter, who succeeded Longchamp as justiciar (1194–98) and became chancellor under John (1199–1205) was himself a worldly profiteer in his multiple functions. A trusted and competent surrogate for a lord-king seldom in England, he was largely responsible for the changes required to secure the procedural innovations under Henry II. Yet he was not above—or should we not say that it came naturally to him?—enriching himself from justice, then from the seals he controlled, and by patrimonial encroachments as archbishop.[238]

Such temptations were the rule under Richard and John. The story of self-promotion barges in on us here because its human subjects, whatever their altitude, were engaged with the less conspicuous courtiers whose devices in justice and finance were to be decisive in the bureaucratic monarchy to come. King Richard began as a needy crusader selling power and status to would-be sheriffs and towns as well as to the courtly elite. Roger of Howden, ever the close observer, put it strongly: 'To him [Richard] all things were for sale, namely powers, lordships, earldoms, castles, vills, lands, and the like.' Once again the story of government is drowned out by that of lordship and dependence. Howden refers

---

[237] See generally Clanchy, *Memory to written record* 57–68; Vincent, 'Why 1199?' 20–34.

[238] *Chronicle of Richard of Devizes* 4; Roger of Howden, *Chronica* III, 240: 'Eboracensis archiepiscopus [Geoffrey] obtinuit vicecomitatum Eboracensem et ita factus est regis serviens et praecipitavit se in potentias regias'; IV, 35; C. R. Cheney, *Hubert Walter* (London 1967) 49–50, 92–114, 178–79.

to the delegations from which the justiciar and 'almost all the sheriffs' were dismissed in 1189 as *bailliae*, an equivocal word evoking exploitative power as readily as office. Richard thought it more important to placate his brother John with immensely augmented lordships in England than to maximize his own patrimonial domains. That this was mistaken, as many people thought, was proven when rebellion broke out during Richard's first long absence from England as crusader and captive.[239]

Yet Richard meant to dominate with social purpose. The lord-king who virtually legislated a new structure of command, obligation, and remedy for his crusading fleet in 1190 proved equally fit to deal firmly with anti-Jewish rioters in London soon after his accession, and attend thereafter to appointments of sheriffs and bishops with foresight and care.[240] With his release from captivity by Emperor Henry VI and the capture of John's castles, Richard could come to England briefly in 1194 and entrust the realm to his new justiciar Hubert Walter. But it was Richard himself who presided over a council at Nottingham that has all the looks of an executive session setting policies: a new round of shrieval appointments, judicial process against John, the finance of a campaign in Normandy, and the advisability—for the king had to be persuaded—of a new coronation at Winchester.[241] Two further measures left to others to implement were surely Richard's: the imposition of a customs-tax in the port towns, and a shrewd decree of August 1194 instituting licensed tournaments in five midland towns as a device for improving English horsemanship in conflict with French knights and for raising money.[242] By that

---

[239] SC 260–62; GrH II, 90; Gillingham, *Richard I* 113–22, 239–44, 269–70.

[240] GrH II, 110–11; Roger of Howden, *Chronica* IV, 5–6; William Alfred Morris, *The medieval English sheriff to 1300* (Manchester 1927) 138; Gillingham, *Richard I* 270.

[241] Roger of Howden, *Chronica* III, 240–42.

[242] Gillingham, *Richard I*, 277–79; William Stubbs, introduction to *The historical works of Master Ralph de Diceto . . .* , 2 vols. (London 1876) II, pp. lxxx–lxxxi; William of Newburgh, *Historia rerum Anglicarum*, ed. Richard Howlett, *Chronicles . . .* II (London 1884) v.4.

time Hubert Walter was wholly in charge. It was he who issued a 'form' for the judicial eyre (summer 1194) of the highest interest for what it says of the lord-king's purpose, and a 'royal edict' for the peace in 1195. The *forma* of 1194 sets up a grand jury of representative knights to hear 'pleas of the king's crown,' including recognitions and pleas brought by the king's writ relating to wards, escheats and other royal rights, counterfeiters, and violence against Jews; much of the process of securing information on these matters and about values is to be written down. A revised assize on forests and another on weights and measures date from 1197.[243]

These are the externals of a history of purposive routine that can by this time be probed more deeply. The problem for us is how to make sense of fragmentary survivals, to know when they cease to be accidental. So with respect to the king's justice, a roll listing persons who placed themselves on the 'grand assize' to determine proprietary right belongs to 1190 'following Richard's coronation,' according to its rubric, and it is not obvious how it was to be used.[244] Another roll, abbreviated in ways that point to recurrent practise, bears summations of pleas from Wiltshire in autumn 1194, quite in accordance with the *forma* of judicial eyre of several months before.[245] Records of the eyre, at least, may, by Richard's later years, have achieved a regularity beyond adequate means of retention and consultation.

But the problem for the king's clerks was that of fiscal utility. How were those in the exchequer to know what payments or promises of value to the lord-king had been made apart from those on the sheriffs' accounts? This very question implies a measure of institutional complexity of routine beyond the capability of Catalan auditors in the 1180s and 1190s; or for that matter, of

---

[243] Roger of Howden, *Chronica* III, 262–67, 299–300 (=SC 252–58); IV, 63–66.

[244] *Curia regis rolls . . . of Richard I and John*, ed. C. T. Flower, 7 vols. (London 1922–35) I, 1–14 (Roll 12).

[245] ed. F. W. Maitland, *Three rolls of the king's court . . .* (London 1891) 65–118.

English ones in the 1150s. As early as 1166–67, and plainly associated with the *Assize of Clarendon*, the pipe rolls bear notations of
'pleas' (*placita*) that imply the transference of information about
judgments to the exchequer.[246] Copied seriatim on strips of parchment (for this was a different operation from the analytic-formulaic
record of the sheriff's liability), such records might be devoted to
debts owing to the lord-king or to charges or concessions payable
by him. From the former class evolved the fine rolls, of which the
earliest traces date from 1175; the latter became the 'close rolls,' so
called already in 1203. Related conveniences of access explain the
rolls of 'ancient charters,' forming a series under Richard; and of
memoranda, of which the earliest extant example (Michaelmas
1199) alludes to *memoranda* of earlier dates.[247]

The subject of this proliferation of records was justice, because
the king's scribes had even less occupational identity than those of
the court then taking root at Westminster. Almost all that the
scribes wrote had its place in the larger accountability then in full
gestation; this was an ampler, more resonant justice than had prevailed under Henry I. The establishment of seisin or title (*jus*),
settlements of disputes and reconciliations of animosities, the review of fallible memory: all these might now be documented as
well as enacted; and while the peacemaking of settlement need
not necessarily exercise the justices, it was the exchequer court
that gave focus to the recording of intention. But those early rolls
so destined are mostly lost, which suggests that the retention and
classification of parchments was hardly more expert at Westminster in the 1180s than it was in Barcelona.

In the final decade of the twelfth century three events evoke
the dilemmas of this *innerkurialische* experience. Around 1190

---

[246] *The great roll of the pipe for the twelfth year of the reign of King Henry the Second* . . . (London 1884) 7–10, 14–15, 46–49, 57–58, etc.

[247] See generally H. G. Richardson, introduction to *The memoranda roll for the
Michaelmas term of the first year of the reign of King John (1199–1200)* . . . (London
1943), pp. xiii–xcviij; and (making important revisions) Vincent, 'Why
1199?' 17–48.

scribes serving King Richard began to date his letters and charters with new precision. H. G. Richardson was surely right to attribute this change to the influence of papal diplomatic as well as to the legal learning of William Longchamp;[248] yet beyond this one must suspect that the piling up of undated parchments was producing helpless and irritating confusion. Then on 15 July 1195 there turns up that rarest of welcome sports, a self-consciously innovative record. In labelling a concord in the 'lord-king's court at Westminster' securing the feudal tenancy of one William *Heruci* to Theobald Walter (who happened to be the archbishop's brother), a clerk noted that 'this is the first chirograph that was made in the lord-king's court in the form of three chirographs' as directed (he went on) by Archbishop Hubert Walter and the barons present 'so that by this form a record can be made . . . to be placed in the treasury. . . .' And so henceforth the 'foot' (*pes*) of the written fine, the lowest of three copies (the upper two for the interested parties), was preserved by the king's men, who might refer to it, as *Glanvill* explains, in case of further litigation on the matter.[249]

Although convenience has no name here, it looks as if this event marked the recognition of an archive of judicial accords. That some copies before this one were on hand (because they survive) permits the inference that third copies *not* enrolled now seemed advisable at whatever cost. And this inference (if justified) would seem further to imply that the lord-king might now think it useful to help his litigious people keep track of their own commitments; that, indeed, this might be some part of the public service purchased by the principals.

Yet a third symptomatic event happened shortly after King John's accession in spring 1199 and may likely be credited to his newly appointed chancellor Hubert Walter: the decision henceforth to

[248] *Memoranda roll . . .* (*1199–1200*) pp. lx–lxii.
[249] *Feet of fines . . . A.D. 1182 to A.D. 1196* (London 1894) 21; *Glanvill* viii (94–103); P&M I, 169; II , 97; Clanchy, *Memory* 68–73; Vincent, 'Why 1199?' 30–43.

enrol (and retain) copies of charters, letters of certain kinds, writs ordering payment (*liberate*), and notices of fines and offerings. That such records might prove helpful in justice and finance is hardly in doubt; but the novelty here was for the scribes writing the king's concessions and directives to retain his records for themselves. It is possible to exaggerate the self-assertion of the chancery (as such) in all this, yet it is only from 1199 that whatever it was that historians understand by that term meets one test of official status: it keeps records. And what we know of King John, who as lord-prince had worked with his own chancellor and justices, suggests that enhanced control of records written in his name made for hard bargaining for his favour.[250]

Bear each other's burdens and you will thereby
fulfill the law of the exchequer.
—*Memoranda roll* 1 John[251]

Was this an ironic comment by a tired clerk writing above his own list of items left unsettled in the Michaelmas Exchequer of 1199? In England there was no backsliding at this time. King John, whatever his failings with power, never lost interest in the works of his clerks, never undercut the delegacies of his command. His evident contentment in the push and pull of cases, claims, means, and promises helped to secure the new remedies of a common law and the reformed accountability of sheriffs. Old and new, the rolls under John leave us in no doubt that while the lord-king profits from these mechanics, they are self-propelled because the obligations to be enforced are balanced by the private interests they serve. Under the rubric quoted above sheriffs are disclaiming liability for the unpaid charges of men—like the Glastonbury knight Robert Malerbe,

---

[250] Holt, *Magna Carta* 180; Vincent, 'Why 1199?' 30–43.
[251] ed. Richardson 32.

who owes 20s. for a false claim—of other counties; in this case, says the sheriff of Wiltshire, the bill should go to Somerset. The list of *communia memoranda* in which this item appears not only bears out the rubric but shows how the justice of lordship is becoming publicly territorial.[252]

Contemporaries seem to have been less astonished by the new remedies, procedures, and records than modern historians have been. This should come as no surprise, for whatever these events portend for English government, they were essentially the transformation of lord-kingship. Two great books have blazed trails into this historical old growth—those by J. E. A. Jolliffe (1955) and S. F. C. Milsom (1976)[253]—yet the forest they prospected, vastly documented, has more to reveal. What already seems clear is that the Angevin kings did not think they were promoting a new mode of power. They wished for servants high and low who would be competently as well as loyally responsive. They came to grasp the inadequacy of shrieval farms in a growing society, even of old patrimonies in general, resorting to new fiscal devices and taxation, of which the relation to tenurial obligation and to public service was problematic from the start. And in their well advised acts they promoted an accountability that burst the fetters of venerable exchequer justice. Yet while they evidently resisted claims to seisin in delegated functions, they made no effort to impose oaths such as might have defined conceptions of office. No new ideology of power overtook that of traditional kingship, visible in the oaths sworn by Richard I at his accession.[254] And while the incipient common law offered concrete benefits, it remained a live issue whether the sheriffs, like the justices, were expected to do more than 'treat the people with decent restraint.'

---

[252] ibid., 33; *The great roll of the pipe for the first year of the reign of King John* . . . , ed. Doris M. Stenton (London 1933) 176, 235, 241.

[253] Respectively, *Angevin kingship*, 2d ed. (London 1963); and *The legal framework of English feudalism*.

[254] *GrH* II, 81–82.

FRANCE

In the spring of 1184 King Philip II ('Augustus' 1179–1223) wrote to Pope Lucius III that 'powerful men assail our [my] youth and trouble themselves to disrupt the start of our reign.' There was a clerical tinge to these words, which were in fact composed for the young king by the canonist-abbot Etienne de Tournai by way of countering a papal request for the services of Archbishop Guillaume ('White Hands') of Reims. The latter was close to King Philip's exercise of power. Maternal uncle to Philip, he was implicated in the Champagnard-Flemish conflict that resulted from the king's inscrutable threat to divorce Isabelle of Hainaut. It is likely that Philip had this 'crisis' (*discrimen*) in mind when he wrote to the pope.[255]

As with England and Catalonia the story of Capetian power is easily traced on the elite level of courtly-dynastic experience. Archbishop Guillaume, whatever his role in furthering causes by which Philip II secured new domains at the expense of Flanders, was to remain the mentor of choice; he and his sister the Queen Mother Adèle were entrusted with the lordship of France when Philip went off on crusade in 1190. Yet Philip, having already tasted success in dynastic enterprise, soon returned to France, never to leave it again. His way of putting feudal custom to work against Richard and John was no small part of his deployment of power.[256] He was to dominate his courtiers as well as his subject peoples for the rest of his long reign. He appointed no successor to his titled chancellor in 1185 and allowed the seneschalsy to lapse at the death of Thibaut V of Blois in 1191.[257]

This means that in France as elsewhere, untitled servants and clerks worked with royal power. No more than in England or Germany did chroniclers take interest in their devices. Nor for

---

[255] *RAPh2* I, no. 109.   [256] Above, pp. 303–4.
[257] Baldwin, *Government of Philip Augustus* 31–35 (*Philippe-Auguste* 56–61).

some time did Philip himself, for in carrying on his father's kingship he was caught up in the unfinished business of protective justice. The 'deeds' that first aroused the monk Rigord to write of him were punitive expeditions against the perpetrators of violence in clerical lands. Those 'powerful men' who 'disrupt . . . our reign' surely included the castellan-lords of Charenton and Beaujeu, both stigmatized with 'tyrannical' offences, and both losers in decisive campaigns ending in settlements on the king's terms. Nor was this merely an adolescent interest. Royal intervention in Burgundy had begun under Louis VII, and when King Philip was invited to intercede in the war of Vergy (1185–86) the violence of predatory armies was added to that of 'tyrannical' castellans as a grievance subject to the lord-king's remedial power.[258] Philip already knew how to seize castles when he began to do so for strategic reasons.[259] His tireless receptiveness to complaints defined an ever widening zone of royal protection extending far beyond the Ile-de-France; and he continued to assail allegedly 'tyrannical' castles throughout his reign.[260] As in every other European land where the process is visible, this royal (or public) suppression of fortified lordships was a precondition for the delordified exercise of royal power.

The latter was retarded in France, not because the king was weak, but because Philip's ambition was to extend the enterprise of his grandfather to the vastly larger realm inherited from the Carolingians, an option only Barbarossa could share in the later twelfth century. The young Philip II was rich enough in patrimonial resources that he could judge, campaign, and decree without regard to means; and it was only when that situation changed in the 1190s that the inadequacy of the old prescriptive accountability—an inheritance from Suger—prompted changes of technique long since familiar in several other lands.

---

[258] Rigord cc. 7, 8; Duby, *Société mâconnaise* (1953) 535–51.

[259] As in Berry, Rigord c. 51.

[260] *RAPh2* 1, nos. 235, 253, 337, 425; Rigord c. 137; Guillaume le Breton, *Gesta Philippi Augusti*, ed. H.-Fr. Delaborde, *Oeuvres . . .* 1, cc. 150, 156.

Yet there is reason to think that the young Philip thought in officially entrepreneurial terms from the start. Almost certainly the defence of clergy and churches figured in his coronation oath; the urgent accountability for him was that of justice. Even if his early measures in an itinerant entourage were prompted by petition and complaint—for example, the edict of 1182 expelling the Jews from the realm—, they have also, without exception, the appearance of resolute decisions from personal conviction. Indeed, they look like declarations of policy, for in the case of the decree just mentioned there is no sign that it lacked support from prelates and barons who knew that indebtedness to Jews had mounted so as to invite the intervention of an impressionable Christian lord-king.[261] Philip's even earlier edict against blasphemy and gaming in the royal court reflects an immature piety nurtured in his father's household.[262] A gathering sense of social utility may be discerned not only in the anti-Jewish decree, however bizarre this act looks to us, for it had perceptible fall-out in the real-estate market; it appears undiluted in King Philip's decision to pave the muddy streets of Paris. As Rigord told the story, in 1185 Philip was busy in the 'royal hall' with 'affairs of the realm' brought by others—this must have been the habitual posture of royal power—when his own offended nose rendered the king himself at once plaintiff and judge. His directive was made (even so) in consultation with the townspeople and the provost of the city.[263]

What may be called local utilities were not confined to Paris. As early as 1181 the young King Philip had responded to a petition from the people of Montlhéry by abolishing as 'contrary to reason' the abusive custom by which knights of the castellany confiscated the springtime crop of hay in certain fields. Although

---

[261] Rigord cc. 15, 19; *RAPh2* i, nos. 12–16 (see also nos. 62, 90, 94, 95, 99, 133, 134, etc.); Gavin I. Langmuir, ' "Judei nostri" and the beginning of Capetian legislation,' *Traditio* xvi (1960) 209–10.

[262] Rigord c. 5.

[263] ibid., c. 37; and citations in note 260.

he came to favour urban communes, Philip refused to permit the burghers of Soissons to enclose the (king's) tower in their own defences; and in 1199 he quashed the commune of Etampes on grounds that the clergy and knights had suffered encroachments on their rights from the sworn men.[264]

How Philip II and his servants groped towards—or with—an objective concept of public purpose cannot be explored here. The distinction between domination and government, well recognized by contemporaries, has been easy to obscure in this reign whose very actors ignored it.[265] Courtiers and scribes working typically out of the king's sight would have experienced a sense of depersonalized service, as at Westminster, that was harder to inculcate amongst the provosts charged with patrimonial management and local justice. No one in Capetian circles is known to have trumpeted such ideas, although on at least one public occasion—the assembly in Paris (spring 1190) in which Philip ordained for the custody of France during his absence on crusade—a Romanist ideology of official service rings out in the preamble: 'It is the royal office to provide for the needs of subjects in every way and to prefer the public to its private utility.' Yet even this text, the most spectacular normative record of its kind to survive from any land of Europe in its day, is tainted with conceptual ambiguity. It is a 'testament' as well as an 'ordinance,' according to Rigord, whose transcription is the only copy of it to survive; moreover, the realm is the king's (*regnum noster*), the 'officials' are *his* men (*baillivi nostri*), and Philip's personal vow of 'pilgrimage' is the justification for visiting the inconvenience of

---

[264] *RAPh2* I, nos. 29 (Montlhéry), 44; II, no. 616. On Etampes see also Ch. Petit Dutaillis, *Les communes françaises . . .* (Paris 1947) 143–44 (tr. Joan Vickers, *The French communes in the Middle Ages* [Amsterdam 1978] 87–88).

[265] See the verbal play on *prodesse* and *preesse* in the *Dialogue* of Philip Augustus and Peter the Chanter, ed. Léopold Delisle, 'Etienne de Gallardon, clerc de la chancellerie de Philippe-Auguste, chanoine de Bourges,' *BEC* LX (1899) 24. This was a commonplace in clerical cultures: *Chartes de Cluny* IV, nos. 3030, 3111; *Actus pontif. Cenomannis* 456; John Baldwin, 'Philippe Auguste, Pierre le Chantre et Etienne de Gallardon . . . ,' *CRAIBL* (2000) 450n.

his absence on his people. This is the place to stress, moreover, that the ideology of public and official kingship seems to have had limited currency in Philip's France. The testament of 1190 was, like all previous edicts of this king, preserved only in a chronicle; so that, as also in England, one cannot yet argue for official, or legislative, record-keeping.[266]

Yet the impression of novelty in the exercise of royal power in France cannot be false. To make this clear it will be useful to examine three questions: (1) How did Philip's courtiers keep track of his possessions and concessions? (2) What did this lord-king ask or expect of his appointed servants? (3) How do these questions explain the new fiscal accountancy first visible to us in 1202?

(1) The chancery inherited by Philip II was little more than a titled function (*cancellaria*). Beneficiaries could still virtually write their own privileges, a practise in decline, to be sure; but even as the king's scribes imposed a virtual template of royal power on written concessions and commands, the most characteristic mark of authenticity was the listing of titled courtiers *other* than the chancellor. The 'chancery' was never so conspicuous as during the many years of its nullity, when charters were given *cancellaria vacante*. Yet no curial function can have interested Philip more, for the unnamed scribes (seventeen distinct hands have been discerned) who wrote his judgments, concessions, and commands were the guarantors of his inimitable will in protocols tending to become fixed even in different hands. 'Petits fonctionnaires,' Françoise Gasparri calls them; men following orders—but whose orders?[267]

The last visibly engaged chancellor before 1185 had been Hugues de Champfleuri, bishop of Soissons (1159–75), who had retired

---

[266] *RAPh2* I, no. 345. If Rigord drew on the court's copy, he must still have possessed it after the loss of records at Fréteval in 1194. No other copy appears in the reconstituted archive in Register A. For earlier ordinances, Rigord cc. 5, 15, 37, 47, 58.

[267] See generally *RAPh2* I and II; Françoise Gasparri, *L'écriture des actes de Louis VI, Louis VII et Philippe Auguste* (Geneva-Paris 1973) ch. 4; quotation from p. 78.

to the abbey of Saint-Victor. There, it seems, he caused to be copied a mass of letters to and from Louis VII; and because these were classified by recipients and writers, the manuscript bears some resemblance to registers undertaken by Philip's clerks beginning in 1212.[268] But there must have been perplexity over the use of such copies in the 1180s when drafts, duplicate originals, and fiscal records were multiplying; when the 'chancery' fell vacant; and when the documents to be lugged by the itinerant king must have spilled out of their sacks. Until 5 July 1194, that is, when King Richard's mobile force caught up with Philip's vulnerable rear-guard at Fréteval and plundered the baggage-carts, causing major damage to the royal household treasure, and seized or destroyed written records. In time this would prove something worse than a setback in a summer campaign of variable success; what must at first have aroused consternation was the loss of compromising documentary evidence of support for Philip and John against Richard.[269] And if there were any who had warned of the risk in a portable collection containing unduplicated parchments, their day had come. A handful of potentially embarrassing pieces survived the débâcle, whether because they were in Philip's personal possession or because a repository had already been organized, is not known. What is certain is that the royal archives later called the *trésor des chartes* originated in consequence of Fréteval in 1194 and were located in the king's palace in Paris. The household chamberlain Gautier (the younger) was entrusted with the task of reconstituting the lost records.[270]

---

[268] Bibliotheca Vaticana, MS Reg. lat. 179, substantially printed by André Duchesne, *Historiae Francorum scriptores* . . . , 5 vols. (Paris 1636–49) IV, 557–762. See also Françoise Gasparri, 'Manuscrit monastique ou registre de chancellerie? A propos d'un recueil épistolaire de l'abbaye de Saint-Victor,' *Journal des Savants* (1976) 131–40.

[269] Roger of Howden, *Chronica* III, 255–56.

[270] Besides Howden, Guillaume le Breton, *Philippide* iv ll. 530–82 (ed. Delaborde II, 118–21); Teulet, *LTC* I, pp. v–xxiv; and Baldwin, *Government* 405–12 (*Ph-Aug.* 510–18).

This cannot have been easy, nor was it completed (whatever the nature of the lost portable collection). Two points about this work seem clear. First, it must have been next to impossible to replicate the fiscal records. No accounts of any sort antedating 1200 figure in the registers produced in and after 1204. Gautier's only apparent success lay in the recovery of charters prior to 1194, some thirty-one of which found their way into the new registers while (by one estimate) another twenty-eight originals from Philip's France survived in the Trésor des Chartes.[271] Second, one may not exaggerate the official nature of this work. What was lost at Fréteval was the glitter, furnishing, and proofs of Philip's lordships feudal and patrimonial. The chamberlain Gautier was the son of a favoured servant close to the lord-king, one whose fidelity probably exceeded his competence. New mechanisms of control at Paris may already have resulted from the public accountability stipulated in 1190. At some point after 1194 the incessant routines of scribes must have eclipsed the work of restoration; and by the spring of 1204 the initiation of a (new) register of copies with several scribes at work points to a quasi-bureaucratic operation. Moreover, from 1201 the appearance of the Hospitaller Guérin 'giving' charters in the still vacant chancery heralded the rise of a conspicuously competent, though still unspecialised, servant who was to be second only to the king.[272]

(2) As to what the lord-king expected of his servants, the first thing to understand is that the ordinance of 1190 is quite strictly limited to the accountability of personnel whose relation to the king is *not*—and in this respect, at variance with Philip's own prefatory declaration—explicitly official. Nothing is specified about the appointments of the dowager queen and the archbishop;

---

[271] *Les registres de Philippe Auguste*, ed. John W. Baldwin (Paris 1992) 21–24; Baldwin, *Government* 410 (516).

[272] Baldwin, *Government* 412–18 (518–25); and see also Léopold Delisle, introduction to *Catalogue des actes de Philippe-Auguste . . .* (Paris 1856) pp. vi–xxx; Françoise Gasparri, 'Note sur le *Registrum veterius*: le plus ancien registre de la chancellerie de Philippe-Auguste,' *Mélanges de l'Ecole française de Rome* LXXXIII (1971) 363–88.

neither for them nor for the provosts and bailiffs do we hear of oaths, let alone of the virtual auctions in which some at least of the provostships (*prévôtés*) were sold at farm. What is known from other sources is that the management of rights in royal patrimonies, such as Lorris or Montargis, as well as in towns by this time from Bourges to Laon, was entrusted to some sixty-two provosts, which points to a considerable expansion of the domain in late years; also that the bailiffs, more substantial men drawn from the lord-king's entourage, were of quite recent institution. The ordinance represents bailiffs as virtual supervisors of the provosts, whether for the first time is unclear.[273]

The ordinance of 1190 surely innovated on several substantial matters, in the following order. It provided for four local men (six in Paris) to counsel the provosts in 'affairs of the town.' It required the bailiffs to hold monthly sessions, called *assisia*, for the settlement of cases in the king's justice (*nostra justitia*). It turned the royal prerogative of justice into a thrice-yearly 'day at Paris' when and where the regents were to 'hear the grievances [*clamores*] of the kingdom's people.' On that day the bailiffs were also to appear to give their account of the 'business of our land.' Finally, the king directed that all royal revenues were to be brought to Paris at three terms now fixed as Saint-Remi (1 October), the Purification, and Pentecost, and paid to specified receivers; and they were to be recorded by Adam the clerk.[274]

For all we know (including the loss of records in 1194), one or more of these directives may have been tried out before they were imposed in June 1190. Philip II would surely have heard of Angevin initiatives in curial and itinerant justice, for he was personally acquainted with Henry II and his sons. He and his courtiers

---

[273] *RAPh2* I, no. 345 (from Rigord c. 70); Baldwin, *Government* 44–45, 125–8, 155–58 (71–72, 172–76, 210–12). Although it is customary for scholars writing in English to refer to provost and bailiff as *prévôt* and *bailli*, presumably so as to distinguish them from lesser patrimonial officials called *prepositus* and *ba(i)llivus* in the records, in the context of this book it seems advisable to avoid a distinction all but unnoticed in the twelfth century.

[274] *RAPh2* I, no. 345.

would have known something about consultation with local men on public affairs, about the Norman *assises*. Philip was seeking to renovate his control of patrimony, to bridge the gulf between exploitative provosts and his men of court by appointing the latter as bailiffs to mediate and supervise, but also to bring the king's justice to localities. The injunction to that effect was implemented and persisted, as appears in cases at Etampes (1192) and Orléans (1203); and the hitherto unexampled resort to sworn inquiries to establish right would seem to spring from the same institute.[275] In every way the ordinance-testament defines a royal lordship more objective in its purposes than in the past, more attentive to associative interests, less self-interestedly subjective.

Yet it looks as if these tendencies were the outcome of a more resolute insistence on remedial justice. The ordinance of 1190 should be read in the abiding perspective of 'complaints' (*clamores*) such as figure in the most salient chapters of the text, for this was objectively the prevailing experience of power. In France as in other lands the subjects of complaint continued to be the very functionaries entrusted with powers to resist the encroachments of fortified lords as well as to tax and defend. By the 1150s, to judge from some letters collected by Hugues de Champfleuri, the provosts were as likely to be protested as vicars in the South or sheriffs in England. Abbot Roger of Saint-Euverte (Orléans) pleaded with Louis VII for relief from an 'infestation' of 'your provosts' towards 1165–66.[276] Their powers of distraint were all but indistinct from unjustified self-serving violence. So in 1190, as in England two decades before, the king of France wanted to be informed *even in his absence* of charges against provosts, and against bailiffs as well. The latter were to be denounced to the queen and archbishop in the appointed seasonal sessions for violence, venality, or incompetence; and their reports, and those of the bailiffs on provosts, were to be sent to Philip. Whatever the efficacy of this measure, it was hardly a device for improving the

---

[275] Baldwin, *Government* 137 (Ph.-Aug. 185); *Registres* 37–180.

[276] *Historiae Francorum scriptores*, ed. Duchesne, IV, 669; see also 666, 679.

king's touch with patrimonial management. As a rule Philip II addressed 'his' provosts, and even his bailiffs, impersonally, yet as late as 1200 his charters of protection, often sent to provosts to enforce, could presume their penchant to unlicensed violence or constraint.[277]

(3) Yet it was precisely during the critical decade when Philip II left France, then returned to mobilise costly wars with Duke-Kings Richard and John, that the king undertook to improve the fiscal accountability for his expanding realm. Quite surely this arose in some part from suspicion of the provosts, for when we first encounter a written fiscal audit in 1202–3 the provosts figure as accountant-defendants seeking quittance for their farms, receipts, payments, and expenses. Moreover, one sees in this record that bailiffs are accountable for a range of functions expanding on that of the old (and inflexible) *prévôtés*.[278] The bailiffs, to repeat, doubtless antedate the ordinance of 1190; and it would seem plausible, even if proof is lacking, to associate a new stress on these curial functionaries, perhaps towards 1185, with a reform of fiscal accountancy.

Something like a reform there must have been, because the famous first-known *exercice* for three terms of 1202–03 is like no fiscal record of France known or extant before then. It has long been assumed that previous accounts (of this sort) are simply lost; and since we learn from a near contemporary chronicler that 'accounts' (more exactly, books thereof: *libelli computorum*) were confiscated or destroyed in the assault at Fréteval,[279] the prevailing assumption has been bolstered as well as nurtured by negative evidence. This assumption is untenable. Capetian records prior to the 1190s afford no evidence of fiscal audits of the sort progressively attested in England, Normandy, Flanders, and Catalonia. In those lands, and perhaps also in Sicily and the empire, an old

---

[277] *RAPh2* II, no. 615; see also nos. 518, 533, 541, 567, 727, 833.

[278] *Le premier budget de la monarchie française. Le compte général de 1202–1203*, ed. Ferdinand Lot, Robert Fawtier (Paris 1932).

[279] Guillaume le Breton, *Gesta* c. 74 (197).

prescriptive accountability of patrimonial assets was overtaken by the novel practise of challenging accountants for their receipts, expenses, and balances; and this experience had eluded France as late as the early years of Philip Augustus. The most likely explanation for this procedural lag must be economic. When in 1190 Philip prescribed for an accountancy of provosts and bailiffs during his absence on crusade, his expectation was that they would pay in revenues at Paris, of which some portion would be available to the lord-king as he needed and requested.[280] If this expectation was then normal, the French royal domain would have been prosperous before the Angevin wars and crusade became a serious drain on resources. Already by the mid-1180s Philip was renegotiating farms by making communes responsible for their own *prévôtés*; and other signs, too, point to his vastly larger lordship taking the same interest in *incrementum* as Suger and Bernat Bou had done.[281]

So it would not be far-fetched to suppose that the young Philip, well schooled in the ill repute of provosts and fast learning about supply, may have encouraged some experimentation by his and his seneschal's clerks. The men of Compiègne had evidently been summoned elsewhere 'to account' for royal revenues, an uncustomary practise the king was willing to renounce in his charter of 1186. And in the ordinance of 1190 it is the convocation to account, once again, that catches our eye, for this is the real novelty in question.[282]

Does not this ordinance itself mark the origin of a new accountancy? The command that provosts and bailiffs are to bring their revenues to Paris at appointed terms and that these payments are to be recorded by a king's clerk looks enticingly like the recorded accounts of 1202–03. On closer reading, however, doubts arise, for all that is certainly shown is that the concept of such an accountancy dates from 1190 (or before). The bald prescription of 1190 differs in

---

[280] *RAPh2* I, no. 345 (419 ll. 15–23).
[281] ibid., no. 116; II, nos. 642, 706; above, pp. 333–34.
[282] ibid., I, nos. 168, 345.

Cartoon dated 16 November 1980, at the time of an international conference commemorating the accession of King Philip Augustus eight centuries before. (Morgan, Le Monde, 16 November 1980, by permission).

some ways from the accounts recorded in 1202. The former points not to farms, receipts, and expenses, but rather to a collector's list of taxation-payments at a place of dispensation. Was the king or his clerk merely generalizing in 1190, heedless of the real experience of accounting for *prévôtés*? And there is a further difficulty, for no trace survives of any accounting corresponding to the template of 1190 prior to 1202. One could imagine a roll or two being lost at Fréteval, to be sure; it is harder to see why nothing is known of rolls after 1194, just when the *trésor des chartes* was taking form.

The key to explaining the new accountancy first manifest in 1202 lies in the evidence that documents were lost at Fréteval. Of the several narrative sources, none contradicts another. Guillaume le Breton in different works refers to 'books of accounts of the fisc' and to 'records of renders' (*scripta tributorum*) and fiscal obligations. No one mentions rolls or any other sort of probatory account. These allusions, *and others*, in the remarkably concrete passages of the *Philippide*, witness surely to the well-nigh catastrophic loss of the prescriptive accounts of the lord-king's domains.[283] Preserved typically in registers (*libelli*), like those created for the comital domains of Barcelona, these listed tenants and fiscal obligations primarily in the old Capetian patrimonies. The challenge to Gautier the younger and his colleagues was that of restoring such information for the use of accountant-clerks, whether itinerant or in Paris. If the central accountancy known from a few years later was already in effect, the disruption would have been minimal, because the placement of farms and fixed assets and expenses at the heads of rolls (whenever it happened) effectually transferred the prescriptive values of account into the newly flexible form of the written audit.

Whether this transference took place before July 1194 or—as seems more likely—as a consequence of the losses, it cannot have been easy to do. It would have required some manner of coordination of *prévôtés* in different hands and different stages of account.[284] But once done, it would have obviated the need to replace the lost registers as such. This is surely why, with few exceptions, the only surveys incorporated in Register A were those for newly acquired domains on the periphery of the old *prévôtés*.[285] The conclusion to

---

[283] Howden, *Chronica* III, 255–56; Guillaume le Breton, *Gesta* c. 74 (197); *Philippide* iv ll. 530–82 (Delaborde II, 118–21).

[284] That this indeed happened is suggested by *RAPh2* III, no. 1030 (1208).

[285] *Registres*, chiefly 183–264.

be drawn is not *post hoc ergo propter hoc.* It is rather that a process of change owing to economic growth and accompanied by some disposition to redefine service in official terms, finally produced in the lord-kingship of France the new accountancy of periodic audit that had been pioneered in other lands.[286]

The accounts of 1202–03 survived in the Chambre des Comptes, escaping the fire that destroyed *those* archives in 1737 only thanks to the fine copy made by the king's auditor Nicholas Brussel a decade before. What place this record may have had amongst other fiscal matter in the restitution undertaken by the younger Gautier can only be guessed. But this work went on in or near the chancery, for around 1207 surveys of no fewer than thirty-three domains—some lately secured in Normandy, others in (peripheral) northern lands, yet others restored from the late Queen Adèle's dowry—were copied into Register A. These accounts— for such indeed they are, in the old prescriptive form—would seem to have been solicited in the *prévôtés,* first written in analogous summary forms, and then collected in Paris. Some or most of them may already have been obsolete when, perhaps simply to dispose of clustered parchments no longer current, they were transcribed by a single expert scribe on consecutive folios. The information they contained had already been recomputed as farms such as figure in the roll of 1202 for places of the Norman Vexin that had fallen to Philip II in 1195 and after, as well as for Amiens, Compiègne, and Montdidier.[287]

The probatory form of account was becoming current, as may be seen from Brother Guérin's audits of the chamberlain Eudes for household valuables and receipts in jewels in February 1206. Records of these audits were transcribed in what became the first *cahier* of Register A; they are the more interesting for being preceded by

---

[286] For the procedural comparison of the new Capetian accountancy with Flanders, Normandy, and England, see Baldwin, *Government* 144–52 (*Ph.-Aug.* 195–204).

[287] Registre A, fols. 86r–89r (facsimile ed. Léopold Delisle, *Le premier registre de Philippe-Auguste* . . . [Paris 1883]; re-edited by Baldwin, *Registres* 207–28).

a normative declaration of the jewels held by the butlers and cooks, which is followed by an attestation, cancelled, of the chamberlain's receipt of gems from the lord-king.[288] Yet the solemnity of these audits underscores not so much the king's concern for accountable offices as his interest, here well seconded by Brother Guérin, in realizing and securing his wealth. For the two decades from Fréteval to Bouvines (1214) money and military obligations had precedence in accounts of whatever sort. Summations of value become common; moreover, just as in Catalonia, and at the *very* same moment, the audits of 1202 were put in the custody of Templars who received and dispensed money. Accountancy was part of a war effort, fragile. The *Prisia servientum*, a record first got up in 1194 as a normative list of quotas of footmen imposed on communities, was reworked a decade later as a probatory account transcribed in Register A.[289] No accounts of coinage have survived, which is one reason why modern efforts to estimate King Philip's wealth, however well intentioned, are problematic. Philip wanted to know, too. It wasn't easy, for his services were dispersed. From fragmentary survivals (Candlemas 1213, All Saints 1221) it looks as if his clerks were trying to represent receipts and balances in ways more readily visible, perhaps even comparable from year to year, than in the accounts of domain rendered in Paris.[290]

EARLY IN 1206 someone close to the king drafted a memorandum in the very words a messenger was to put to Count Raoul of Eu in order to persuade him to accept appointment as royal deputy

[288] Registre A, fols. 5vr, 4v, 12rv (*Registres* 229–37).

[289] Printed by Edouard Audouin, *Essai sur l'armée royale au temps de Philippe Auguste* (Paris 1913) 123–29; Registre A, fol. 91v (*Registres* 259–62); with the commentary of T. N. Bisson, 'Les comptes des domaines au temps de Philippe-Auguste: essai comparatif,' *La France de Philippe Auguste* . . . (Paris 1982) 526.

[290] See generally Lot, *Compte général* 15–27, 53, 104–10, 113–39; Baldwin, *Government* 163–75 (219–33); Bisson, 'Comptes des domaines,' 521–38.

in Poitou. 'The king sends me to you,' this spiel begins, 'because he knows that you are one of the most powerful barons of Poitou and [one] who would know how and be able to manage his affairs in the land of Poitou.' Gentle flattery gives way to terms: the king would like to give you his Poitevin domain for five years, plus money, knights, and sergeants 'to carry on the war' (against John), but he requires that you give him your lands and castles in Normandy 'to secure' your own service, and that you order your own men 'to do fidelity to him.' The king would engage to restore your land to your wife and children, according to Norman custom, in case of your death. He would like to talk with you about all this, but will look for someone else if he must. 'For the land of Poitou is so remote and distant from him that he cannot go to or provide for it as the land requires.'[291]

These words bring us close to Philip Augustus, ring with the very sound of his politic talk. And they illustrate three aspects of the deployment of power in his reign. First, he had arrived at a mode of domination that was habitually managerial, not exploitative. 'His affairs [*negocia sua*]' in Poitou refer to order, justice, and the acceptance of royal power; they imply a territorial interest that required the acceptability of a native baron (for Raoul was a Lusignan) as well as familiarity to achieve. The same sense of 'affairs' informed Philip's dealing with towns. He needed to know what had been granted or confirmed at Laon and Soissons before reviewing or imposing customs at Amiens and Arras; not accidentally the assemblage of communal charters was the first preoccupation of those compiling Register A.[292] As for Raoul in Poitou, he seems not to have responded, nor does it appear that the king found anyone else to serve as his seneschal in a land still far from reconciled to Capetian rule.[293]

Second, Philip's setback in this matter illustrates the dilemma created by his major conquests and wider ambitions. Where he

---

[291] Registre A, fol. 96r (*RAPh2* II, no. 926).

[292] Registre A, fols. 11r–26v.   [293] Baldwin, *Government* 239 (308).

could not govern, he could fall back on feudal custom, yet only when he could credibly offer protection. And while he was in no position to require Raoul's vassalage, Philip did seek to bind that baron's men in a fidelity of security that was soon to become a favoured device. From about 1200, and especially after 1209, clerks produced and preserved mountains of parchments bearing the personal engagements or oaths of countless persons committed to the lord-king's conventions and judgments.[294] It was a device for promoting the solidarities of affective power such as might inform utilitarian purposes, as in communes, but that were chiefly bound up with elite customs of lordship and dependence. So the binding of men was a constant preoccupation of Philip's, one his clerks understood as they listed 'his' men and fiefs and castles. They must have been content to transcribe the written homages of distant magnates: the count of Périgord for his county, no less; the bishops of Limoges and Cahors.[295] Such parties could be the lord-king's friendly allies, though hardly the administrators Philip meant for his territorial seneschals to be. For the many as well as the few, vassalic dependency made sense, especially following the conquest of Normandy; their charters of commendation, recording incessant rituals of recognition, flooded the newly formed archives.[296] The negotiation over Poitou not only projected the utilitarian solicitude Philip had shown towards the Parisians; it betrayed the shackles of the lord-kingship thrust upon him.

Finally, it should not be overlooked that Philip's appeal for help in Poitou was borne by a nameless intermediary, and rescued (in Register A) from an odd (indeed!) parchment that might have been disposed of as obsolete. In his later years the 'august Philip,' as he was already known to many, dominated his vastly augmented realm as no Capetian king before him. Yet it would be mistaken to identify

[294] See *LTC* I, nos. 562–71, 581–87, 666–73; and comprehensively nos. 879–1590. Also *Registres* 385–437.

[295] *RAPh2* II, nos. 799, 856; III, no. 1206.

[296] *LTC* I, nos. 448–50, 473–74, 504; *RAPh2* III, nos. 959, 960, 971, 975, 989, 995, 996, 1001.

his power with his plumage. He himself worked at victory and success more than at government, while favouring those who made them possible. Nurturing expectation and rewarding competence, he secured long and faithful service. Almost without trying, one is tempted to think; and that is the point. Philip thought that someone else would take on a demanding task if Raoul refused, and said so. It looks as if there were enough men about the king engaged with his commitments—to the peace of churches, to the crusade, to the mobilising of armed force on hostile frontiers, to the campaign of Bouvines—to enable Philip to carry on a domination little changed conceptually from the past. It was tendencies imposed *on* him as much as the reverse that modified this conception in ways that few of Philip's dependents of any rank would have thought inevitable. There was new talk about order in churches and lay communities, about qualifications, elections, and the absurdity of despoiling deceased bishops in regalian churches; also about the generalizing of immunity from arbitrary tallage, the utility of reserving criminal offences for a royal justice ever more widely dispensed, and the promotion of quasi-official accountability.[297] A provision for auditing the accounts of outgoing magistrates in the charter for Péronne (1207), for all its resemblance to Italian civic practise a half century before, may owe something to thinking in King Philip's circles.[298] Public order had been more deeply subverted in France than in England. Yet in France, as well, we begin to read of a 'common law.'[299]

THE ROMAN CHURCH

The notion that power might be actively deployed in objectively defined or even official purposes was widespread by 1200.

[297] *RAPh2* I, nos. 40, 59, 73; II, nos. 637, 727; III, nos. 977 (and 1067, c. 23), 1000, 1052, 1060.

[298] ibid., III no. 977.

[299] ibid., II, no. 727, and this in the deeply pertinent context of the lord-king's claim to regalian right in churches everywhere. As a rule Philip responded to churches one by one, each with it own right.

Commonplace in urban records, it is perceptible in the royal diplomas of every realm of Christendom.[300] What is less easy to trace is evidence of altered methods or techniques amongst the personnel serving lord-kings west of the Ebro valley or east of the Rhône. One need only place Roger of Howden and Rigord alongside the chroniclers of Castile or the empire to see how distinctive were the former in attending to novelties in justice and normative matter.[301] Sparing as well as distinctive, however, so that the managers of royal lordships in England and France were hardly less reluctant than those elsewhere to prescribe in statutory form or to preserve their institutes when they did so.

To these observations the Roman church may look like an exception. Popes and cardinals had worked like a government since the 1130s, if not before, carrying forward purposes of reform while claiming the spiritual powers of Universal Ordinary. There was collegial insistence on the programmatic peace such as would become a seminal influence on the making of secular states. Yet as Colin Morris has remarked, 'the agenda for papal business was written by interested parties in Christendom as a whole.'[302] The popes were like lord-kings and -princes, in this sense, responsive to petitions, yet quite without the financial resources to ensure an independent, let alone impartial, outlook on the people for whose souls they claimed to care. By the 1120s access to the curia was, if not quite openly venal, subject to just such partiality of interest to be expected in the elite circles of privilege and lordship whence the popes themselves had sprung. It would be mistaken, to be sure, to equate the corrupt exercise of official power with lordship, for in this context 'corruption' itself may be the conceptual anachronism; yet perhaps equally mistaken to overlook what is

---

[300] e.g., from among countless examples, *LTC* I, no. 935; *Documentos 1191–1217*, ed. Julio Gonzalez, *Castilla en la época de Alfonso VIII* III, nos. 732, 809; *DDFr2* I, nos. 41, 43, 52.

[301] Besides Howden and Rigord, as cited above, see *Chronica latina regum Castellae*; Rodericus Ximenius de Rada, *De rebus Hispanie* vii–ix.

[302] *Papal monarchy* 217; and for the papal peace, below, ch. 6.

essential to the expression of affective power by consecrated persons in societies where power over people counted most.[303] Like the kingdoms, the papacy remained a lordship as it modernized in a chronology distinctly its own.

What have been described above as intrusions of government elsewhere look like precocious infusions of the same in the Roman See, manifestations of interest in the resources and mechanisms of power that span the twelfth century. As early as 1087 Cardinal Deusdedit had assembled texts in proof of the possessions of the Roman church, both spiritual and patrimonial, as well as of its lordships over lay men, prelates, and churches, and of its claims against the empire. Much of this content remained serviceable. Charters, privileges, and an array of oaths were taken from the *Collection of canons* without substantial change for use in new compilations by Cardinal Albinus in 1187 and by Cencius the chamberlain in 1192. Their works also drew upon a survey of rights (*liber politicus*) produced by one canon Benedict around 1140–43; and upon new biographies of Popes Hadrian IV (1154–59) and Alexander III (1159–81). By about 1190, the papal curia or chamber was in possession not only of the registers (now lost) of recent popes, but also of utilitarian compilations of miscellaneous texts and proofs relating to the works and purposes of the popes.[304]

Yet this array was not up to the needs of papal clerks. In 1192 the *Book of Renders* (*Liber censuum*) was undertaken, according to its compiler Cencius, so as to remedy the incompleteness and the inconvenience of existing 'memorials.' He claimed that, despite the efforts begun under Pope Eugenius III (1145–53), the 'Roman church has suffered no slight injury and loss' with respect to

---

[303] e.g., *Peterborough chronicle, an.* 1123 (42–45); Hugh the Chanter, *History of the church of York* 90–222; John of Salisbury, *Historia pontificalis* cc. 21, 40, 42.

[304] Paul Fabre, *Etude sur le Liber censuum de l'église romaine* (Paris 1892); Thérèse Montecchi Palazzi, 'Censius camerarius et la formation du "Liber censuum" de 1192,' *Mélanges de l'Ecole française de Rome: Moyen Age, Temps modernes* XCVI (1984) 49–93.

'Saint Peter's right and propriety' over churches, cities, castles, villages, even over kings and princes, which (or who) 'ought to be dues payers [censuales] and pay what they owe.'[305] Even if these words fully describe its purpose, the *Liber censuum* was a new departure. Cencius had done the research required to expand the scope of prescriptive entitlement beyond the suburbicarian and Italian churches. Also included in Saint Peter's domain were now, in this order, Hungary, Poland, Germany, Burgundy, France, Gascony, Spain (beginning with the province of Tarragona), England, Wales, Dacia, Norway, Sweden, Scotland, Ireland, Sardinia, and *Outremer*. No conceptual differentiation appears between the Italian, let alone concretely patrimonial, entries and the rest. The pope is a lord-protector of all Europe entitled to recognitive payments for his 'right and property' in a domain no longer cognizant of the original juridical status of churches. However presumptuous the appearance, the dynamic vision of Cencius was borne out, for the register he created became, indeed, a work in progress, with new entries added down to and long past his own pontificate as Honorius III (1216–27).[306]

In its original design as a list of contributory churches and persons, the *Liber censuum* resembles the great lay cartularies of the Pyrenees composed at the same time. Their prologues sound the same imperative to reorganize archives; Ramon de Caldes may have written his in the same year (1192) as Cencius.[307] But the contents of the *Liber censuum* soon outgrew the stated fiscal purpose. Cencius himself as well as his successors in the chamber added other elements to the fiscal provincial (so to call it), some drawn from prior collections, notably the *Marvels of the city of Rome* (*Mirabilia urbis Romae*) and Deusdedit's charters, others original with Cencius. So the register became more nearly like the princely cartularies and indeed, in its dynamic receptivity, more

---

[305] *LC* I, 1–5; conveniently reprinted by Montecchi Palazzi, 'Cencius camerarius' 83–84.

[306] *LC* I, 5–240.

[307] *LFM* I, 1–2; *Cart. des Guillems* (*Liber instrumentorum*) 1–4.

like the Parisian Register A of a decade later. Whatever Cencius thought of this, the *Liber censuum*, as deconstructed by modern scholars, bears witness to an adjusted but hardly novel conception of papal power.[308]

Least original, it turns out, was the fiscal design. So far from renovating papal finance, as was once argued, what Cencius produced was an updated (albeit incomplete) prescriptive account of pontifical sources of revenue. No doubt the revised and amplified list facilitated the recovery of delinquent payments, as Cencius claimed; but the result was no more like a current account than the new Catalan registers of the 1180s, assuredly used for the same purpose as the Roman one, or the Capetian surveys lost in 1194. Still less was the *Liber censuum* a budget, for the effort to bring the record of obligations up to date remained incomplete, nor were the different currencies of different epochs reconciled.[309]

For the rest the *Liber* describes papal works without defining them. Ceremonial had become more important since the return of popes from exile, and it was articulated in an amplified 'order' of liturgical observance with respect to obligations and payments in the chamber. The *Mirabilia* points to practical public experience with petitioners and pilgrims, as does the recycled evidence of papal claims to allegiance and payments.[310] These were tools of reference for papal servants in charge of ceremony, provisioning, and travel. And their mediation was specialized to the extent of excluding the sort of legal works that had sprung up outside the curia in the 1120s, had found spectacular fulfillment in Gratian's *Concordance of discordant canons* (ca. 1140 or before), and was becoming a new learned industry by the 1170s.[311]

---

[308] *LC* I, with the analytic abstract by Montecchi Palazzi, 84–88.

[309] See above, pp. 376, 404; *FAC* I, 100–101; and Toubert, *Structures du Latium médiéval* II, 1064–68.

[310] *LC* I, nos. 31–164.

[311] Morris, *Papal monarchy* 182–88, 400–403; André Gouron, 'Une école ou des écoles? Sur les canonistes français (vers 1150–vers 1210),' *Proceedings of the*

It was in these para-pontifical tasks of organizing its norms and laws and settling disputes rather more than in its updated accountancy that the Roman church recovered something of its official purposes after mid-century. The popes were mostly lawyers by this time, aware of the elemental qualifications required of men serving in the offices prescribed by the newly assembled canons; they were also aware of the need for updating Gratian's summation of old law in changing societies. Their decretals—that is, written responses to litigants and judges on problematic points of law or custom—multiplied, especially those of Alexander III, to the point of requiring themselves to be codified. Already in 1190 Bernard of Pavia's 'First Compilation'—intended to expedite justice 'for the honour of God and the holy Roman church and the utility of students'—nearly coincided with Cencius's enterprise in the chamber.[312] The popes were doing bishops' work by encouraging appeals that were typically heard and settled by judges-delegate chosen from local prelates. Bishop Roger of Worcester (1164–79) was repeatedly engaged as judge-delegate. The common resort to investigative questioning coincided easily with the casework of itinerant justices in England and Normandy.[313]

A resourceful deployment of its means, the new pontifical justice was hardly an administrative system, still less a centralized one. Accountability, here too, was the focal issue. 'Judge justly,' exhorted Bernard of Pavia, '. . . having Him before the heart's eyes Who renders to each according to his works.'[314] New law sprouted from cases that were as far-flung in space as the fiscal provincial of 1192. Moreover, the popes and cardinal-priests drew on the experience of judges and litigants as well as prelates,

---

sixth international conference of medieval canon law . . . , ed. Stephan Kuttner, Kenneth Pennington (Vatican City 1985) 223–40.

[312] Quinque compilationes antiquae . . . , ed. Aemilius Friedberg (Leipzig 1882) 1.

[313] See Compilatio I. 23, Compilationes antiquae 9; and generally Jane E. Sayers, Papal judges delegate in the province of Canterbury 1198–1254 (Oxford 1971) ch. 1 (and p. 10).

[314] Comp. I, Compilationes antiquae 1.

curates, monks, and the faithful in their great Lateran councils of 1179 and 1215. Here the Petrine authority was exalted in ways open to no other lord-princes in their assemblies; and it was on these occasions that the contradictions of office and lordship were fully exposed. The scandalous play of affective influence in the promotion of Innocent II had not been forgotten when it was laid down in 1179 that a two-thirds majority of cardinals would henceforth suffice to elect to the 'apostolic office.' By canon 4 the horsed retinues of prelates on visitation in the provinces were to be reduced in numbers—archbishops, for instance, to be attended by no more than forty to fifty horse!—'nor shall they travel with hunting dogs and hawks,' nor demand sumptuous meals. Whatever the sense of this age-old injunction in the past, its meaning in the Alexandrine papacy is clear: prelates are officers, not lords, and should behave accordingly. Nor may 'bishops presume to afflict their tenants with tallages or exactions,' nor archdeacons their clergy; and the text pointedly contrasts exploitative with pastoral prelacy.[315] Countless decretals rest on the presumption that service is official.[316] That writing went with official conduct, being its test and its record, may have been progressive in the work of judges-delegate. Only under Innocent III was it required that attendant clerks write all phases of delegated justice.[317]

❖

It is not likely that Pope Innocent III (1198–1216) thought of governance as an end in itself, but he surely wished to promote

---

[315] *COD* 211–14 (1179, canons 1, 4); cf. *Papal decretals relating to the diocese of Lincoln in the twelfth century*, ed. Walther Holtzmann, Eric W. Kemp (Hereford 1954) nos. 13, 15.

[316] *Decretals of Lincoln* nos. 1, 3, 4, 13, 16, 20, 21; and *Compilationes antiquae*, passim.

[317] Kemp, *Decretals of Lincoln*, p. xxx.

official services. As in France and every other realm we know about, increasingly expert clerks were doing the work that produced the first extant papal registers. The letters of Pope Innocent that fill these registers give insistent expression—for instance, against Philip Augustus on a marriage that could only be viewed as binding in a Christian world—to a rhetoric of papal supremacy that informs his decretals.[318] Ideology, for once, outstripped the real power that is the subject of this book.

But on one point the popes were better placed than the lord-kings of this epoch to press the exercise of material power beyond the conceptual limits of lordship. The Third and Fourth Lateran Councils not only regulated procedures and deportment; they promoted something resembling (in our terms) policies. Just as lords and towns acted on collective purposes—witness the scene at Toulouse in 1202, when just as the consuls saw fit to create an archive of their power they also set out to conquer their countrysides—so the popes and cardinals came to consensus on yet larger issues of collective challenge. And causes like heresy could not arise from partisan agreements, could not be invented; they could only be captured as their social logic took hold in provincial consensus and social change. Heresy was already a challenge in the Lateran Council of 1179, where it was addressed in the final canon; in 1215 it was *the* challenge above all others, the subject of canons 1–3, where it evokes the trinitarian theology of orthodoxy that pervades the whole. Likewise, one may suppose that recognition of the mendicant enterprises of Francis of Assisi and Dominic of Caleruega was thrust upon Innocent III by irresistible circumstances, a virtual cause he could only lead or lose.[319]

---

[318] *Die Register Innocenz' III.*, ed. Othmar Hageneder, Anton Haidacher, 10(?) vols. to date (Graz-Cologne 1964–) I, nos. 4, 171; Morris, *Papal monarchy* 426–33.

[319] Mundy, *Toulouse*, chs. 6, 10; above, p. 289; and *COD* 224–25 (1179, c. 27), 230–35 (1215, cc. 1–4); Morris, *Papal monarchy* 444–45.

This enlargement of societal imperatives was a general phe-nomenon in Europe. Its symptoms, impossible to date precisely, were everywhere in evidence after 1150. We can begin to guess why. The inadequacy of prescriptive accountability in growing domains and a contagious resentment of arbitrary taxation were newly urgent circumstances. But there is more to the story than this, for it remains to see how whole peoples became engaged with power. Was kingly dynastic right comparable to pontifical visions of Christian orthodoxy? Even more visible in the big and well recorded schemes of Innocent III than in secular realms, principalities, and towns, interests that begin to look like causes had one feature in common: they were costly far beyond the ac-ceptable bounds of customary aids, payments, and renders. Noth-ing so jolted lordships of all sorts as the rise of public taxation in the later twelfth century. Was not any new imposition a bad cus-tom? This event, too, was bound up with the prevalence of arbi-trary lordships, which proved incapable of withstanding the 'reason' of social purpose in their insistence on imposing and co-ercing as of customary right. It is in towns everywhere that this confrontation comes into clearest view, their statutes empower-ing collective purpose whatever the concessions to lords. 'Fishing is public,' we read in the customs of Montpellier of 1204, and wonder whether the embattled pope could have said the same about heresy or crusades. In fact, the charter of Montpellier goes further than most enactments of its day to define a veritable con-dominium of administrative power. The lord-king's (Pere's) bai-liff is explicitly accountable 'to him whom the lord shall appoint'; other local bailiffs are answerable to him; appointive 'good men and wise' of the town are to serve in the lord's court upon oath not to accept bribes; and amongst much else the bailiff and court-men alike are qualified by a sworn promise to the lord of Montpellier that is no longer an oath of fidelity, but a concretely detailed oath of office. And yet, so thoroughly Romanist in its legal provisions as it is, enacted before 'nearly the whole people of Montpellier' assembled 'in common colloquium,' this charter of public government is filled with traces of suspicion. And not only traces: in chapter 60 the lord of Montpellier explicitly and absolutely renounces 'tolt or quist or forced gift or any forced exaction.'[320]

Were not the greater powers exempt from this dynamic, given their residually public and official faces? It was not so. Yet it was in the crises at the end of the twelfth century that the avatars of government became tenacious heralds of the state.

[320] *LTC* I, no, 721, and c. 51: 'Piscatio est publica.'

·VI·

Celebration and Persuasion (1160–1225)

JACQUES DE VITRY was on his way to the Holy Land, having been elected bishop of Acre. Boarding ship in Genoa in October 1216 he wrote vividly of his experiences in quest of allies in Italy. His adversary was the Devil; his 'weapons, namely my books,' and other possessions had been all but lost while crossing a flooding river. He had preached against heretics in Milan, where the *Humiliati* had impressed him. In Perugia, where Innocent III had just died, he viewed the pope's body despoiled of its vestments by thieves. There, Jacques attended the new pope's consecration and secured recognition of himself as bishop from Honorius III. And he says that Honorius treated him 'kindly and *familiariter*,' offering him easy access while responsive to the bishop's requests. One of the latter, however, the pope refused: he would not cede 'special power' to the preacher-bishop to defend French crusaders against 'oppressive' taxation as he had promised them. There were others about the pope, Jacques had heard, who aspired themselves to the 'legation' of France. Lingering in the *curia*, Jacques de Vitry found it preoccupied with secular affairs—with 'kings and kingdoms, with litigation and disputes—so that hardly anything could be said about spiritual matters.' He took comfort from what he saw and heard about the 'Lesser Friars,' and provided one of our best early accounts of the Franciscans as they began to disperse beyond Tuscany and Lombardy. By late September Jacques had arrived in Genoa, where he arranged for passage to Acre. And while his horses were seized by Genoese men for their military assault on a neighbouring castle—a local custom, they had told him—in their absence

Bishop Jacques induced their wives and sons to take the cross, a vow in which (he claims) they were joined by the fighting citizens on their return.[1]

Readable, circumstantial, and chatty, this letter conveys the scents and sounds of its day. It makes no mention of Frederick II, then in the first flush of threatening manhood; nor of Philip Augustus, for whom heresy was now the only challenge; nor of the Templar-papal regency for the child Jaume I; nor still less of King John, who died in the very days when the bishop boarded ship; yet these were the lord-kings, theirs the 'realms' (*regna*), of which Jacques found the papal court preoccupied.[2] Never had defence of the faith seemed so urgent to Christians; and if the Fourth Lateran Council likewise passed unmentioned by Bishop Jacques, it was because everything that mattered to him resonated in the charged atmosphere of religious enterprise created by the great pope whose forsaken corpse becomes the most shocking image of the letter. People were muttering that while most prelates were like 'mute and unbarking dogs' (Isaiah lvi.10), the Lord[-God] wished to save souls 'before the world's end' by resort to 'simple and poor men' like the friars.[3] For all its biblical texture this letter has a colloquial directness and narrative force that seem new. It shows a solicitude for women characteristic of Jacques de Vitry, as well as his shrewd engagement with the details of travel.

His outlook being that of a Christian warrior locked in combat with the Devil, his travelogue has the further interest of evoking the experience of power in newly symptomatic ways. Jacques speaks of the papal court as worldly but not patrimonial. It is a place of debate on public affairs, on something like policies (as lately codified in the Lateran Council). And while this served the ambitions of adviser-prelates, what the bishop of Acre attests is some willingness in papal circles to hear him out, to be persuaded; and even on Jacques' self-favouring account it looks as if

[1] *Lettres de Jacques de Vitry (1160/1170–1240) évêque de Saint-Jean-d'Acre*, ed. R. B. C. Huygens (Leiden 1960) no. 1 (71–78).
[2] ibid., 75 ll. 103–7.   [3] ibid., 76 ll. 132–35; 73 ll. 61–65.

CELEBRATION AND PERSUASION 427

resistance to his enthusiastic offer to take sole charge of recruitment for crusade in France was a reasonable response by Honorius III. Moreover, Jacques wrote of the incipient Franciscan custom of periodic assemblage explicitly in terms of celebratory as well as constitutive consensus. 'For the men of that religion [the Friars Minor] convene once yearly with great profit in a designated place, so that united in the Lord they might rejoice and feast, and by the counsel of good men devise and promulgate their holy institutes' to be confirmed by the pope. Only on one point relating to habitual power did Jacques de Vitry sound an old and discordant note. What did he mean by writing of his fear for the French crusaders he wished to defend 'that almost everywhere they are oppressed [*opprimuntur*] by tallages and other exactions, their very bodies in many places imprisoned'?[4] This is the rhetoric of bad lordship, by no means outdated in the early thirteenth century, yet here surely pointing to a canny strategy of this dedicated preacher of crusade. At a time when new demands on patrimonies were multiplying, when even taxes *for crusade* could be viewed as arbitrary, the assurance of ecclesiastical protection for the domains of absent crusaders was as timely as ever.[5]

It would be wrong to represent Jacques de Vitry as a sufficient witness to the works of power in his day. He is merely a good one, all the better when judged by his histories and sermons as well as his first letter,[6] yet quite as oblivious to all that lay beyond the cares of literate Christians as most of the others whose writings we have. Robert Moore has well shown how pressures for Christian conformities were building in the decades around 1200.[7] Amongst

---

[4] ibid., 74–75, 76 ll. 124–28; 74 ll. 83–90.

[5] And perhaps rather new in practise: see James A. Brundage, *Medieval canon law and the crusader* (Madison 1969) 12–14, and ch. 6.

[6] *The Historia occidentalis of Jacques de Vitry* . . . , ed. John Frederick Hinnebusch (Fribourg 1972); and *Die Exempla aus den* Sermones feriales et communes *des Jakob von Vitry*, ed. Joseph Greven (Heidelberg 1914).

[7] R. I. Moore, *The formation of a persecuting society* . . . , 2d ed. (Malden 2007).

heretics, agnostics, and Jews the words of priests and preachers must often have fallen like the blows or threats of knights, a mode of moral intimidation mediated by fear. The requirements of 1215 that Jews wear distinctive dress and be prohibited from holding 'public offices' can only have encouraged many to think of triumphant Christianity as rightful order.[8] Justly coercive order, as Jacques de Vitry insisted, and as successive droves of knights felt assured. Lost to view is the experience of power beyond their perimeter of certitude, in the murky pasts of heretics, unbelievers, and nominally Christian peasants and shepherds; people in typically undocumented bondings (before about 1225) of family and friendship coming under new constraints of a Christian parochial regime fostered by canonist teaching and papalist conciliar decrees.

However incomplete or tendentious one may judge the Latin Christian sources, they surely reveal what may be called a normal sense of prevailing public order continuous with the past. All contemporaries—not least, the Jews of those buffeted communities in Capetian France and England—knew about those lord-kings who so engaged Popes Innocent III, Honorius III, and Gregory IX (1227–41). Three decisive battles had effectually rearranged their relations: Las Navas de Tolosa (1212), which not only secured Castilian-Leonese claims to mastery of a Christian Spain but fairly invited the papal leadership of extra-European crusades to come; Muret (1213), in which the prospects for a Catalan dynastic power straddling the Pyrenees were definitively checked; and Bouvines (1214), which opened the ways towards the Capetian domination of French-speaking societies. In these perspectives it can readily be seen that Frederick II was bucking an adverse trend in seeking to dominate Sicily and Germany both. The cost of the Sicilian crown was not simply the implacable hostility of successive popes but also the virtual abandonment of Germany to the princes. For the latter this would have seemed as natural as it was welcome, the recovery of their pre-Staufer ascendancy.

[8] *COD* 266–67, cc. 68–69.

In every land at every level patrimonial lordship remained critical to the disposition and experience of power in the early thirteenth century. Yet few lords, least of all the princely ones, could now prosper without subjecting or allying with communities. This was to be a major cause of major transformation. In Italy, where communes had prospered while wresting liberties from bishops and emperors, this was when the *podestà* first flourished: lords called in to mediate, defend, and exploit what some communities helplessly possessed. In the closing years of this book the Lombard League revived against an emperor whose marshalled forces not even Milan could withstand; yet it was precarious power founded on alliances with such as the tyrant Ezzelino da Romano with ever more ephemeral interests exploited or betrayed.[9] Elsewhere, alliance shaded into fidelity, simply more focused forms of commitment, in a crazy quilt of diversely constituted dependencies—those of villagers in Aragon or of knights and burgesses in England—with purposes wavering between the defence of custom and the discovery of common interests. The summons of village consuls in the lower Garonne valley to the princely court of the Agenais some time before 1221 seemed so easily untried as to leave no trace in the records.[10] But it was an uneasy time for lords with single castles lacking dynastic or customary status. Rising costs of fighting afflicted them, too. Everywhere campaigns like those of Philip Augustus in the 1180s—or of Genoa in late summer 1216—reduced the numbers of castellan lordships still free to aggrandize or encroach. This phenomenon, associated with the successes of princely and royal dominations, was general towards 1175–1225.

This chapter carries forward a story of power in which the works of lord-kings are foremost because the claims and pretences of castellans remain insistent, the accountability of agents and servants problematic. How people variously thought about power comes next, followed by evidence of intensified violence,

---

[9] Ph. Jones, *Italian city-state* 408–19, 628–31.
[10] See below, pp. 563–65.

renewed efforts to pacify, and the incipient politicising of peace and other 'causes.' Kings, princes, even urban potentates found it needful to engage with their peoples, harder to persist in the wilful lordship that was their own inheritance from the castles; and these new circumstances help to explain crises of power in Catalonia and England that were at once characteristic and auspicious. All but insensibly the engagement with people is found associated, then identified, with assemblies, which become the expression of interests no longer their lord-prince's alone to argue. Status and persuasion begin to compete with celebratory lordship, alongside accountability, office, and the recognition of social purpose.

Cultures of Power

Lay lords possessed of patrimonies and ambitions tended to become cogs in the exercise of public powers. Their cultures were increasingly those of functional dependence, service, and fidelity. While the castellans around 1100 could reasonably aspire to the values of noble lordship, their successors a century later were more likely to feel like retainers. Even more insistently than Philip Augustus the young Frederick II imposed his own faithful castellans in the Regno; and in the statutes of Capua (1220) they are subjected to something like official accountability.[11] Reflections on power shift from concern with ideals of valour, prowess, and largesse to the modalities of command, management, and competence; to the changing realities by which justice and protection were coming to be secured and theorised. People in service to those with means and public purposes multiplied from about 1140; and what bore critically on the shift here in view was that their patrons—notables like Archbishop Theobald and King Henry II—were close to the new devices of justice and finance

[11] *Ryccardi de Sancto Germano notarii chronica*, ed. C. A. Garufi (Bologna 1938) 89, 92 (cc. 7, 19), 109.

examined in the preceding chapter, and were disposed to favour educated men, even as they saw no reason to propagate the talents and expertise they nurtured. The patrons were, indeed, 'used' by secular clerks in quest of ecclesiastical preferments: John of Salisbury, Walter Map, and Gerald of Wales, to name but three. These are famous names to modern historians, and with reason, for their competencies were symptomatic of new and distinct impulses in the exercise of power.[12] Yet they were the contemporaries of people surely better known, more widely known, who thought very diversely about power. A sampling of their experience will help us to get the conceptual novelties of the later twelfth century into better perspective.

SUNG FIDELITY

Guilhem de Cabestanh was a Catalan lord-castellan who wrote and most likely sang songs about love and longing in the early thirteenth century. He may well have fought the Almohads under his Lord-King Pere I in 1212. Seven or eight of his songs were soon famous enough to be copied in anthologies of such inventions, together with a capsule biography of the knight-poet composed before all memory of his life had faded and itself soon embellished and enlarged in further copies.[13]

The fame of this 'inventor' (*trobador*) need not be exaggerated. He was one of some 460 troubadours whose songs have come down to us in song-books copied in the thirteenth and fourteenth centuries. But if Guilhem de Cabestanh fell below the line marking off the most celebrated poet-singers of his day, he made the 'second cut' of those from his region to be recopied, perhaps as early as the 1220s, and he must already have been recognized in his lifetime. As we can tell from his own songs as well as from the

---

[12] Much discussed: Egbert Türk, Nugae curialium. *Le règne d'Henri II Plantagenêt (1145–1189) et l'éthique politique* (Geneva 1977); Turner, *Men raised from the dust*; Martin Aurell, *L'empire des Plantagenêt, 1154–1224* (Perrin 2003).

[13] *Les chansons de Guilhem de Cabestanh*, ed. Arthur Långfors (Paris 1924).

explicit assertion of his biographer, he was a man of castles. His love (he said) was the best 'there is from Le Puy to Lerida,' the merits of 'my lady' like a 'high dungeon' such as rose on every *puig* from *the* Puy (en-Velay) southwest to the Ebro River. And when his baronial neighbour Raimon of Castellrosselló learned that his own wife Seremonda was the object of Guilhem's devotion, he murdered his rival, and then—if the sequel is not wholly imagined—served his victim's heart to his wife, who, upon learning what she had eaten, refused ever to eat again.[14]

The 'legend of the eaten heart' belongs to the same stratum of mythologising memory as the story that Peire Vidal, a more celebrated troubadour, had his tongue cut out by the cuckolded husband—he too of noble status—of a lady of Saint-Gilles.[15] Such men and women were famous among the castles. Theirs was a culture of unsevered tongues wagging about people and their failings, yet mostly about power in the metaphor of love, or of love as power; and of love *and* power within a tenacious paradigm of dependence, fidelity, and the largesse of lordship. 'E car vos am, dompna,' wrote Guilhem de Cabestanh, 'tan finamen / Que d'autr'amar no·m don' Amors poder.'[16] Such sentiments would have been understood widely in later twelfth-century Europe; perhaps, indeed, wherever lordly courts enticed—or did not banish—poet-musicians and *joglars*. Arnaut Daniel (fl. 1180–1210), who came from a little castle in Périgord, was said to have been well known in Prince Richard's courts, and to have attended the coronation of Philip Augustus (1180).[17] A remarkable further indicator of the breadth and diffusion of this imaginative culture may be found in the versified 'Instruction' (*ensenhamen*) by which

---

[14] ibid., 1.4–5, ll. 29–34; and pp. 31–33; also chapters by Miriam Cabré and Sylvia Huot in *The troubadours: an introduction*, ed. Simon Gaunt, Sarah Kay (Cambridge 1999) 134, 274.

[15] Peire Vidal, *Poesie*, ed. D'Arco Silvio Avalle, 2 vols. (Milan 1960) I, 9–11.

[16] *Chansons* VI.3, ll. 15–16: 'And because I love you, Lady, so faithfully / that Love denies me the power to love another. . . .'

[17] *Biographies des troubadours* . . . , ed. Jean Boutière *et al.* (Paris 1964) no. 9 (A, B).

around 1150–55 the Catalan troubadour-baron Guiraut de Cabreira affected to chastise his *juglar* Cabra for his ignorance of a mass of literary texts, including no fewer than fifteen *chansons de geste*. It is a veritable catalogue of songs, heroes, and singers, including Raoul de Cambrai, Girart de Rossilho, and the troubadours Jaufré Rudel and Marcabru, from *north* of the Pyrenees.[18]

What such courtly entertainments meant to the experience of power is more problematic than first appears. With few exceptions the troubadours are mere names to us, their works transmitted by copies made from variably performative versions long after they were composed. Yet the recognition that this transmission was a cultural survival dates from the period of this chapter, when troubadours like Peire Vidal proclaimed their fidelity to *chant e solatz*.[19] As early as ca.1200–1210 Raimon Vidal of Besalú wrote a grammar of *provençal*, the *Razos de trobar*, with a view to securing good practise and teaching beginners in an artificial language distinct from everyday speech (*parladura*). That this writer was himself a Catalan may not be accidental. The singers had first multiplied in Aquitaine, which is why their contrived language was first identified with Limoges (*limousin*). But Catalans had to learn this language, needed to seek out teachers, in ways that must have drawn these would-be singers into touch with themselves as well as with the admired singers.[20]

So their culture of castles was by no means confined to Catalonia. The count-king Alfons I of Barcelona-Aragon, himself an initiate, welcomed troubadours from near and far. Whether he used this creative clientele to further his aims in southern France, as Martí de Riquer argued, is problematic, for apart from winning the approval of many troubadours there is nothing to suggest that

---

[18] '"L'Ensenhamen" de Guiraut de Cabrera,' ed. Martin de Riquer, *Les chansons de geste françaises*, tr. Irénée Cluzel, 2d ed. (Paris n.d. [1957]) 342–51.

[19] *Poesie* XXIV.3, l. 19 (II,192).

[20] *The Razos de trobar of Raimon Vidal and associated texts*, ed. J. H. Marshall (London 1972) 1–25. See also *Les poesies del trobador Guillem de Berguedà . . .*, ed. Martí de Riquer (Barcelona 1996) 9, 63.

Alfons courted popularity or acted politically. He mediated a courtly discourse of love, service, and benevolence that came and went with its transpyrenean language of lordship and fidelity.[21] This was the default mode, so to speak, even for truculent spirits like Guillem de Berguedà and Bertran de Born, both of whom composed in this way.[22] The tension between fidelity and wilful power cannot have been lost on them. Yet it is these two untypical troubadours who bring us closest to the life of power in the castles.

Both of them were castellans actively engaged with the lordships of their castles. Less deferential than the singer-sons of furriers and merchants, caught up in ugly realities of accusation and dispossession, unreluctant to put their worst suspicions into words, their *sirventes* convey emotions—anger, exultation, contempt—colloquially. In the early 1170s Guillem de Berguedà bragged of cuckolding all his neighbouring castellans.[23] In 1183 Bertran de Born gloated when Henry II restored his natal castle of Hautefort, although this was merely to ratify Bertran's eviction of his brother. In capturing this castle, an incident of the baronial revolt in which Bertran was implicated, Prince Richard had help from King Alfons, who thereby earned the troubadour's biting contempt.[24] Extolling violence, Bertran de Born was outdone by Guillem de Berguedà, who practised it. Having murdered his enemy Viscount Ramon Folc of Cardona in 1176, he was forced into a long exile during which he seems to have met and exchanged songs with Bertran de Born. And while the latter subsided into the religion of crusades and convent, Guillem never gave up his venomous singing upon return to his castles, dying—by the hand of a nobody, it would be remembered—a

---

[21] Martin de Riquer, 'La littérature provençale à la cour d'Alphonse II d'Aragon,' *Cahiers de Civilisation médiévale* II (1959) 177–201; *Poesies de Guillem de Berguedà*; and *The poems of the troubadour Bertran de Born*, ed. William D. Paden *et al.* (Berkeley 1986).

[22] Guillem's most copied song went on abstractly about his beloved Senyora, *Poesies* XXVI; *Poems of Bertran de Born*, nos. 4, 5.

[23] *Poesies* IV. [24] *Poems*, nos. 17, 19, 21, 22.

rebel against the lord-king who had been slandered by them both.[25]

What can be overheard in these troubadours, however distorted, is the coarse chatter of their castles. Power is moral, not political; people are judged for what they are, not what they think. The invective goes beyond this, to be sure; but Guillem's ironic pretence that he means not to injure Ponç de Mataplana by vilifying him, only to vent his own 'natural desire,' serves as rhetorical cover for the *vilania* of his victim's words in contrast to the 'artfully invented *cortesia*' of his own.[26] Words sting in this culture. Arguably, the verbal virtuosos were often giving expression to commonplaces of contempt or envy; that whatever the slant, this is how people around them talked. Despising peasants, Bertran de Born warns against misguided efforts to coddle them.[27]

If it is hard to read such prejudices in other troubadours, so it is harder to hear real voices. But the pervasive stress on love and fidelity, shared by their vindictive fellows, likewise sprang from the castles; from the tradition still nourished, in its third generation, by the genius of William IX of Aquitaine (1071–1126).[28] That this soon spread to the Pyrenees is clear from the *Ensenhamen* of Guiraut de Cabreira, he too a master of castles. As were, in the following generation, Guillem de Berguedà, Ponç de la Guàrdia, Uc de Mataplana, and Guillem de Cabestanh. Of the earliest known Catalan troubadours all but one or two were castellans and indeed, so far as we know, actively engaged with the lordships of their strongholds. Of the far more numerous troubadours from Provence, Occitania, and Aquitaine, while many

---

[25] Riquer, introduction to *Poesies*; also 78 (*Vida*), and I–XXXI; and *Poems of Bertran de Born*, nos. 36–47.

[26] *Poesies* XI.I (182).

[27] *Poems*, no. 28.2,3 (321).

[28] See generally *Les chansons de Guillaume IX* . . . , ed. Alfred Jeanroy, 2d ed. (Paris 1927); *The songs of Jaufré Rudel*, ed. Rupert T. Pickens (Toronto 1978); Peire Vidal, *Poesie*; and *Le troubadour Folquet de Marseille* . . . , ed. Stanisław Stroński (Cracow 1910).

seem to have been nurtured in castles, few of them are known to have lived the militant life, like Bertran de Born, in search of coercive power. Ademar lo Negre was disinherited by Count Raimond VI of Toulouse (1194–1222). Raimon de Miraval, 'a poor knight from the *Carcasses*, had only a quarter-part in the castle of Miraval [which had] fewer than forty people in it!' Not a few troubadours from these lands were escaping or rejecting the knightly dominations in which they had been nurtured, including those fathered by merchants (Peire Vidal, Folquet de Marseille) or working people (Bernart de Ventadorn, Guillem Figueira).[29]

So the cultural perspective brings full circle the problem of castles. One reason for leaving castles—or for contenting oneself with one's lone 'high fort'—was that the cost of securing multi-castle dominations became prohibitive after 1160. To dismiss Bertran de Born as a pretentious blowhard is therefore to miss the point.[30] That he lacked the resources to cut a figure in Plantagenet courts may seem little more than his personal crisis of ambition; but other Aquitanian lords less witty would have understood. That is why the arrogance, the hyperbolic vulgarities, matter, for however absurd or distorted, they seem to betray a strain of desperation in this culture of power. Must one now be someone *else's* castellan?

Not yet, it appears, in upland Catalonia. This was a land of troubadour castles, where to sing cleverly was to proclaim one's power. Here if anywhere the inherent ambiguity of sung fidelity figured in the honouring of Marquesa, granddaughter of the count of Urgell allied with the count-king in the interest of peace, and wife of Ponç of Cabrera, the rebel son of a troubadour favoured by Guillem de Berguedà. In her the interest of lineage

[29] *Biographies*, nos. 1, 87, plus the whole collection; and (Gaunt and Kay) *Troubadours*, ch. 5. For the Catalan troubadours, István Frank, 'Pons de la Guardia, troubadour catalan du XIIᵉ siècle,' *BRABLB* XXII (1949) 229–327.

[30] Warren, *Henry II* 577–79, who then sees the point himself; cf. Gillingham, *Richard I* 74–77.

ran up against an inchoate ideology without the slightest cultural expression of it own. The later songs of Guillem de Berguedà, caustic as ever and with a subtext yet to be examined, play on his obsessive sense of honour and his resentments. Guillem cultivated other singers, more devoted to his art, it seems, than anxious about current challenges to his lordship.[31]

IT WOULD not have occurred to the troubadours that they were a southern culture. Arnaut Daniel was hardly the only one to visit northern courts, nor were the themes and tales of epic and romance unknown to them. Modern research has sensibly eschewed a categorical geography, while justly discerning some formal and thematic preferences among *trouvères*, even those who, like the Châtelain de Coucy or Gace Brulé, seem influenced by the troubadours. Here we find a more articulate sensibility in composers distinguishing better between stories and opinions; a more nuanced subjectivity even when the resonance is occitanian, as in Conon de Béthune's opener: 'Chançon legiere a entendre / Ferai, que bien m'est mestiers / Ke chascuns le puist aprendre. . . .'[32]

Fidelity and the castle?—yes, there they are, there to be sure, yet somehow receding in a distance. Not even the paradigmatic metaphor of vassalage, constant though it is in these lands of customary and conditioned tenures, quite fully survives, tending to slip into the semantic field of civility.[33] In France, Champagne, and Picardy sociability was gaining on sensibility. If Jean Bodel

[31] *Poesies de Guillem de Berguedà* XXIII; also pp. 59, 63, and (nos.) XI–XXXI. See more fully, below, pp. 499–514.

[32] *Les chansons de Conon de Béthune*, ed. Axel Wallensköld (Paris 1968) I.I: 'I'll make a song easy to understand / for I want everyone to know it'; and for generic comparison *Songs of the troubadours and trouvères. An anthology of poems and melodies*, ed. Samuel N. Rosenberg *et al.* (NY 1998).

[33] As in *Chansons de Conon* VI.4 line 25; Jean Bodel, *Le jeu de Saint Nicolas*, ed. Alfred Jeanroy (Paris 1925), ll. 190, 312, 1294; and Jean Renart, *Le Roman de la Rose ou de Guillaume de Dole*, ed. Félix Lecoy (Paris 1979), ll. 78, 2976.

(ca. 1165–1210) can be called a 'professional writer of Arras,'[34] he cannot have been much like his contemporary troubadours. Indeed, as courtly performance and lyric esprit gave way to advocacy in the greater northern courts, the 'cultures' here in view came into rivalry with 'discourses' of tendentious ideas. Contributing to this, more visibly in the North than the South, was some growing suspicion of verse as a medium for (truthful) persuasion. The anxiety of dynastic elites up against an expanding Capetian domination, though hardly new in Philip II's day and with some analogy to the failing struggles of castellans in their times of sung fidelity, assumed a new discursive form in vernacular prose histories, as Gabrielle Spiegel has shown. For all its lay patronage and presumable stimulus to lay literacy, this was virtually a clerical culture to be distinguished from that of the poet-composers.[35]

COURTLY TALK

These ways of thought and expression verged on educated or trained cultures of power that were generically distinct. When Walter Map affected to be lost in the very 'court' of his own experience, he gave utterance to a sentiment often felt by courtiers whose frustrations, not altogether unlike those of the troubadours, were grounded in other commitments and realized in new expectations. Their ideas, argumentative rather than performative, came from the schools, which is not to deny the recreative purposes served by the memorials of Walter Map and Gervase of Tilbury and the letters of Peter of Blois. Like the troubadours, these writers cultivated power with envy and disdain, not so much their subject per se as their passion.[36]

---

[34] Songs 265.

[35] See generally Gabrielle M. Spiegel, Romancing the past. The rise of vernacular prose historiography in thirteenth-century France (Berkeley 1993); John W. Baldwin, The language of sex. Five voices from northern France around 1200 (Chicago 1994).

[36] Walter Map, De nugis curialium i.1 (2), v.7 (498, 500). See generally Türk, Nugae curialium; and Aurell, L'Empire des Plantagenêt.

While the values and discourses of courts were hardly novel in the later twelfth century,[37] it was only from the 1150s that they found a voice of their own. That was when the tone, topics, and accents—the commonplaces—of a newly organized sociability of power began to matter, reshaping the competitive outlook of those seeking clerical lordships. The chronology of power essayed in this book supports the familiar view that princely courts proved alluring to ambitious literate clerics. John of Salisbury, having experienced the papal court of Eugenius III (1145–53) and the needs of royal service under Thomas Becket, was moved to think about power philosophically in the *Policraticus* (1159), and was promoted bishop of Chartres in 1176. Yet he had been passed over when English sees fell vacant, doubtless by reason of his devotion to Becket; and his younger contemporaries Peter of Blois and Gerald of Wales wrote their letters and books in near total frustration of their ambitions.[38] That such witnesses to courtly service were critical of those they knew or envied has been well shown; but what preconceptions or originality did they bring to their critique? Was the court a new experience of power? Or was it an alternative experience of lordship?

It was more like the first of these things. The 'court' (*curia*) was Walter Map's springbow for flights of allegorical fancy and opinionated history that fill his pages without quite escaping the conceptual gravity of an obsessive reality: the common experience of 'courtiers' (*curiales*).[39] Whatever this was, it looks new. Peter of Blois told of courtiers serving 'now' or 'today' as if their vanities were a deplorable innovation: 'it is beyond me,' he wrote, 'how

---

[37] See C. S. Jaeger, *The origins of courtliness: civilizing trends and the formation of courtly ideals, 939–1210* (Philadelphia 1985).

[38] For background, Christopher Brooke, 'John of Salisbury and his world,' *The world of John of Salisbury*, ed. Michael Wilks (Oxford 1984) 1–20; R. W. Southern, 'Peter of Blois: a twelfth-century humanist?' in his *Medieval humanism . . .* , ch. 7 (Southern's severe judgment of Peter's character has small bearing on my view of his reminiscences); and F. M. Powicke, 'Gerald of Wales,' *The Christian life in the Middle Ages . . .* (Oxford 1935) 107–29.

[39] *De nugis* i–iii (2–278).

the courtier can put up with vexations which for so long afflicted the services of schools and castles.'[40] To Walter Map the court seemed to be a manifestation of degenerate 'modernity,' and he implied that what courtiers talked about were ominous novelties, such as the appearance of heretics.[41] Novelties were the 'news' of the day, to be sure. It was hardly a failing of courts to voice prevailing moral concerns. But courts as such were powerless to direct such concerns, nor did the courtiers engage in political behaviour, whether to further causes or deplore them. Their causes were themselves. 'Led by ambition, I immersed myself wholly in worldly waves,' recalled Peter of Blois. 'And I knew that courtly life is death to the soul.'[42] Later Peter felt compelled to admit that his critique of courtly life had gone too far. 'Indeed, I confess that it is holy to attend the lord king. . . . Nor do I condemn the life of courtiers, who, while not giving up prayer and contemplation, are engaged even so with public utilities and often do good works of salvation.'[43]

This was grudging (and passing) praise from a frustrated courtier, virtually the only sort of informer we have. Power was not the court's to impart, save as an implement of access for those who had or wanted it: for ambitious and qualified men seeking favour from the lord-prince and preferment in his patrimonial lordship. The court, as evoked, was not a delegacy. Perpetuating a competition for patronage, it fostered a play of interests that was hardly new. Was the court (after all) much more than the talk it cultivated, the gossip that, once leaked, named the court as its source? It generated its own decorum, its own *curialitas*, according to Gerald of Wales, who recalled speaking '*satis curialiter and elegantly*' to Prince Rhys in a session at Hereford in 1184.[44]

---

[40] *Petri Blesensis epistolae*, PL CCVII, *epp.* 14, 25.

[41] *De nugis* i.30 (120, 122).

[42] Peter of Blois, *ep.* 14.   [43] *Ep.* 150.

[44] Gerald of Wales, *De rebus a se gestis* i.6,9 ed. J. S. Brewer, *Giraldi Cambrensis opera*, 8 vols. (London, 1861–91) I, 38, 58. Same chapters in *The autobiography of Gerald of Wales*, tr. H. E. Butler, new ed. (2005).

Yet there was something different about this experience of power. For the first time we can overhear from its verbiage, as it filters through the imaginative and epistolary discourse of disillusioned retainers, some commonplace tenets of order and lordship. That Walter Map was baffled by the 'court' suggests that for him lord-kingship, ordained of God, remained the normative institution of human power. Doubtless, all courtiers shared this view, which as it figures in the letters of Peter of Blois comes as close to ideology as the courtly talk admits. But in this culture lordship was a problematic institution, not simply because it was conceptually indistinct from office, but chiefly because, in its lesser, tainted manifestations, it was characteristically oppressive. Fulminating against a bishop's *officialis* at Chartres, Peter feared that he would succumb to the 'lust for dominating [*dominandi libido*]' and to the temptations to violence and seizure that attached to such posts. In another letter Peter justified his desertion of law for theology by denouncing advocacy as an oppressive practise at variance with the Roman legal requirement that the advocate gratuitously serve the minor or widow 'for the utility of the republic.'[45]

Much of the talk about unworthy officials relates to the church, where the courtiers typically looked for advancement. Yet they thought of lordship quite as much as service, to the extent of seeming to ignore a distinction between office and affective power. They could refer easily to their own dominations of 'clients' or to clerical dependencies in sworn fidelity.[46] Although they felt uneasy in the clumsy exploitative entourages of lord-princes—this, indeed, was a foremost guise of the inscrutable *curia*—, they had little to say about lesser lay lordships, save to denounce their violence in sweeping terms.[47] It would be quite as mistaken to ignore this passing interest of theirs in arbitrary

---

[45] *Epp.* 25, 26.

[46] John of Salisbury, *Policraticus* i prologue (1,16); Gerald of Wales, *De rebus a se gestis* i.6 (37).

[47] Peter of Blois, *epp.* 16, 147.

lordship—they got it from the schools, as we shall see—as to overrate it. It echoes in every courtier whose writings we have.

Perhaps closer to current events was the courtly interest in patrimonial service to lords. This was the context for indignant censures of harsh or afflictive conduct and 'tyrannical exactions.' Having portrayed Henry II as an admirable lord-king, Peter of Blois could tell him on another occasion about the very outrages of sheriffs and foresters that led to the statutes of 1166–76. This is an illuminating letter, for in appealing to a ruler who could not be expected to know the failings of his servants everywhere in his 'spacious regions,' Peter exhibited an innocence of the new accountability that is characteristic of the courtiers.[48] As for the monk Nigel, even when he displays some grasp of local valuations and *incrementum*, berating clerics who seek out churches for wealth instead of spiritual need, his context is religious fidelity. He could not think it acceptable for English bishops to serve in the king's court and exchequer, as if they 'were ordained to the service of the fisc rather than to mysteries of God's church.'[49] Readier to deplore injustice than incompetence, the sometime courtiers were more like preachers than whistle-blowers. Power lay in great lordship and faithful service thereto as (they supposed) in ancient Hebraic kingship, requiring vigilance and exhortation. Such power was official insofar as it was public, which is why, after all, the courtiers were familiar with a concept of service at least rhetorically distinct from the self-inflating power so commonly attached to lordship. They often punned with the words *praeesse* and *prodesse*, meaning respectively 'to dominate' and 'to serve usefully,' a pairing once again known from the schools.[50]

---

[48] *Epp.* 66, 95.

[49] Nigellus de Longchamp, *Tractatus contra curiales et officiales clericos*, ed. A. Boutemy (Paris 1959) 168–69, 190.

[50] See citations above, p. 401 note 265; also Peter of Blois, *epp.* 120, 134, 233; *The later letters of Peter of Blois*, ed. Elizabeth Revell (Oxford 1993) no. 43 l. 9; Gerald of Wales, *De rebus a se gestis* ii.14 (69); idem, *Gemma ecclesiastica* ii.34, ed. Brewer, *Giraldi Cambrensis opera* II, 33.

The dichotomy between exploitative power and official service was constant in this discourse. This was 'familiar' talk, to repeat, meant at best as useful counsel, seldom authoritative, typically self-serving, lurching at times into slander. Peter of Blois thought it 'a common vice of courtiers' that they spoke or advised intemperately or unwisely.[51] But as it is known to us, theirs was a para-curial culture of servants and seekers in which the princely queries of the past have been displaced by more or less formulaic echoes. This was hardly an experience of lordship, let alone a viable one, for the coherence of collective fidelity and dependency has vanished. What was left was a culture of fragile association, at least in Plantagenet France and England. Was it confined to those lands?

It would be misplaced concreteness to claim so. Books bearing on behaviour in courts have survived from the realms of Sicily, the empire, and Castile. But none of these works much resembles those mentioned above. The pseudonymous *History of the tyrants of Sicily* (before 1189) is a venomous exposé of a royal court allegedly rent by conspiracies.[52] Gervase of Tilbury's *Otia imperialia* (1211–15) consists of stories and marvels compiled to entertain the emperor Otto IV;[53] and in 1218 the Castilian chancellor Diego Garcia produced his *Planeta*, which is a prolix and abstractly analytic theological meditation on *Christus vincit . . . regnat . . . imperat*. Its long epistolary prologue, a dedication to Archbishop Rodrigo Ximénez de Rada of Toledo, is full of opprobrious talk, castigating prelates for worldly ambitions, caricaturing all the peoples of Europe, and affording ample hints that courtly talk (*curialitas*), 'free of rusticity,' was the spring whence flowed this torrent.[54]

[51] *Ep.* 150.

[52] [Hugo Falcandus] *Historia o Liber de regno Sicilie*, to be consulted with the commentary by Graham A. Loud in his translation (with Thomas Wiedemann, Manchester 1998).

[53] ed. S. F. Banks and J. W. Binns (Oxford 2002).

[54] Diego Garcia, *Planeta*, ed. Manuel Alonso (Madrid 1943) 164, 185–203. My thanks to Janna Wasilewski for suggesting this text.

These books are further proof that power, its means and de-
ceits, deeply informed the gossip of princely courts everywhere.
But it hardly follows that such a 'culture' was the same as that of
Plantagenet courts, still less that the new exigencies of courtly
service were uniform in Europe. On the contrary, what is striking is how diversely writers with experience of princely powers
gave expression to their perceptions. This is so even when Pietro
of Eboli is excluded: his *Liber ad honorem Augusti* (1195–97), dedicated to the emperor Henry VI, contains fine depictions of courtiers while reeking of an obsequious ideology.[55] Amongst the
writers here sampled only Walter Map was self-consciously engaged with the 'court,' although John of Salisbury, Peter of Blois,
and Gerald of Wales so far share in his ironic critique as to form a
Plantagenet circle.[56] Their sort of originality may have been contagious, for Gervase of Tilbury had written a book (it is lost) to
amuse the young King Henry before 1183, while Diego Garcia
had studied theology at Paris before writing *Planeta*.[57] But there
was nothing generic about this culture. No two of the works
mentioned (save possibly those by Gervase) have the same form or
intention; what they have in common is familiarity with conver-
sational topics—ambition, injustice, violence—sounded on the
peripheries of courtly service. Words may have been recalled as
smarter or less wounded than in situ. Still, the whole experience
surely made for better calibrated speech. Peter of Blois thought it
well for men in power to know the difference between flattery
and praise.[58]

The courtiers were unsuitably placed to see themselves whole.
Cultivating possibility (and disappointment), they wrote for others more than for themselves about power. And since most others

---

[55] ed. Kölzer, Stähli (1994).

[56] In addition to citations above, see John of Salisbury, *Policraticus* vii.16,24 (II,
157–59, 216–17); Walter Map, *De nugis* i.10 (12), iii.1 (210), iv.2 (284); Nigellus,
Tractatus 173–76, 192, 198–200; Gerald of Wales, *De rebus a se gestis* ii.8 (*Opera* I,
57), iii.5 (99), 7 (104).

[57] *Otia imperialia*, p. xxvii; *Planeta* 80–83.

[58] *Ep.* 77. As did surely, yet distinctly, the singers.

could see more clearly what these men were not, it happens that the best definitions of the courtiers' dilemma came from lawyers and theologians. Already before 1160 Rufinus (and Gratian) had examined the concept of *curialis* analytically, distinguishing types of service more or less problematic for ordained men.[59] A generation later Huguccio refined this taxonomy, naming knights (*milites*) together with 'officers' of court (*officiales*) and entertainers (*ystriones*), while reserving a stricter differentiation between 'respectable' offices in the court and those tainted by blood.[60] And towards 1210 Robert of Courson drew on this juristic analysis even as he assembled his own proofs for and—more persuasively—against the promotion of *curiales* to prelacies.[61] All these writers worried about the practical consequences of restricting clerical services on moral grounds, a sign perhaps that they saw useful purposes as well as dangers in commended powers. Yet it was not for them to expound the relative merits of fiscal, judicial, and domestic needs.

Learned Moralising

For they were doing something else. It was these writers with some others—readers, teachers, students—who arrived at a new model of consensus grounded in the authority to discipline Christians. Once it was discovered, in the wreckage of Abelard's career, how to question without subverting doctrines from scripture and canon law, literate novice clerics were enticed to bond with like-thinking masters. This pedagogy was not so much about controverted beliefs, as in Saint Anselm's day, as about newly accumulated questions in theology and law on which sourcebooks

---

[59] *Die Summa decretorum des Magister Rufinus*, ed. Heinrich Singer (Paderborn 1902), to D. 51, 133–35.

[60] Quoted by John W. Baldwin, *Masters, princes and merchants. The social views of Peter the Chanter & his circle*, 2 vols. (Princeton 1970) II, 118 n. 25; see also I, 178–79.

[61] BnF, MS latin 14524, fols. 179ra–180ra, partly quoted by Baldwin II, 119 n. 28.

and textbooks alike were becoming accessible, if hardly afford-able. Typically useful for priests and confessors, these questions often extended to issues arising from the everyday experiences of justice and princely power. One may read them analytically, as they must have been heard in disputations; but they were not so much 'disputed questions' as academic formulations progressively adjusted and improved. Repeatedly, Robert of Courson refines or enlarges upon pronouncements of Peter the Chanter, as for instance in the matter of pious alms from usurious or ill-gotten profits. This issue was a crux of moralising theology, for by un-packing good intentions it complicated penitential practise and theory alike.[62]

What can it mean to speak of such activity as a culture? The courtiers, closer to the exercise of power, had common ground in a spectacle bound up with their hopes and resentments. The mor-alists were only contingently engaged with power, yet they were habituated to reflecting on its place in a religious universe. In do-ing so they promoted academic talk, and debate, such as the courtiers had known in the schools; but the academic culture of power is best expressed in writings more systematic than the playthings and reminiscences of princely courts. Their authors, readers, and auditors were surely more numerous than the 'circle' of clerics John Baldwin discerned in Peter the Chanter's orbit, yet this was virtually a Parisian learned culture, however far its con-centric waves may have spread with prelates who had attended the Third Lateran Council (1179) or knew of its statutes.[63] It was, moreover, a culture of the converted, whose numbers and com-mitment in the later twelfth century should not be exaggerated. Heresy and unbelief went with the new penitential theology,

[62] BnF, MS latin 14524 (Robert's 'Summa') xi.14 (fol. 54vb); Peter the Chanter, *Verbum adbreviatum*, ed. Monique Boutry (Turnhout 2004) i.44 (295–99), ii.16 (661–63); Baldwin, *Masters* I, 279, 303, 307–11; and the whole book for the subject of this section.

[63] See generally I. S. Robinson, 'The papacy, 1122–1198,' in *NCMH* IV:2, 329–43.

enough so as to account for a persistent stress on sin, salvation, and sacramental truth in the texts and sermons.[64] So the masters treated power typically in its shortcomings, abuses, and failings. God's to institute, power was man's to exploit in all the snares and delusions of original sin. Alan of Lille, Simon of Tournai, Peter the Chanter, and the latter's disciples, like their less learned contemporaries, thought not so much of government as of power. No civic or curial revolution was at hand to remedy the failings of rapacious agents or greedy prelates. God's power was good, to be sure, in its circles of ordered hierarchy. Following John Scotus Eriugena, Alan of Lille defined hierarchy as the 'lordship of deiform nature legitimated by order, knowledge, and action.' Without 'order,' he added, lordship is 'foolhardy' (or 'accidental,' *temerarium*), but it fails in the absence of any of these attributes.[65] Whether it was God's to institute or to suffer was highly problematic.

What Alan stresses is not so much God's triumph as the ferocity of prolonged conflict. That was the theological story of past and present. Preaching on the gospel for Palm Sunday *Ite in castello quod contra vos est*, he imagined the Incarnation as the building of a castle over against the bad one planted in Eve by the Devil following the betrayal of God's own castle by fallen angels. This

---

[64] The account that follows draws chiefly on Alanus de Insulis, *Liber poenitentialis*, ed. Jean Longère, 2 vols. (Louvain 1965); *Summa de arte praedicatoria, PL* CCX, 109–98; . . . *Textes inédits*, ed. M.-Th. d'Alverny (Paris 1965); *Les disputationes de Simon de Tournai . . .* , ed. Joseph Warichez (Louvain 1932); Petrus Cantor, *Summa de sacramentis et animae consiliis*, ed. Jean-Albert Dugauquier, 5 vols. (Louvain 1954–67); *Verbum adbreviatum*, cited note 62; the same work in its 'short version,' *PL* CCV, 21–370; Robert of Courson, 'Summa de sacramentis,' BnF MS latin 14524, partly ed. Georges Lefèvre as *Le traité 'de usura' de Robert de Courçon* (Lille 1902); and Vincent L. Kennedy, 'Robert Courson on penance,' *Mediaeval Studies* VII (1945) 291–336; Robert of Flamborough, *Liber poenitentialis*, ed. J. J. Francis Firth (Toronto 1971); Stephen Langton, *Commentary on the Book of Chronicles*, ed. Avrom Saltman (Ramat-Gan 1978); *Selected sermons of Stephen Langton*, ed. Phyllis B. Roberts (Toronto 1980); and Thomas de Chobham, *Summa confessorum*, ed. F. Broomfield (Louvain 1968).

[65] *Hierarchia Alani*, in *(Alain de Lille) textes inédits* 223.

scenario had disrupted a quasi-civic order in which knights protected people in useful pursuits, but for Alan's hearers the message
evoked infidelity and violence.[66] The Englishman Ralph Niger,
who may have heard Alan in the schools, made the same point
more subtly towards 1187. Writing of the perils of crusade, he
described the 'vices of military status': how 'by violence and coercive power' instead of by agreement the armed man injures
his better self as much as his foes. Well armed and attired, he
was no model of deportment for the clergy and people; all decency
failed in tournaments, where cupidity and jousting produce 'much
badness.'[67]

All the masters spoke or thought like this. Not all the time,
to be sure, but their sense of evil—and of arbitrariness and
violence—was, in our terms, a default mode of cognition. Their
injunctions, amounting to a theology of rescue from the predica-
ments of fallen people, followed easily from prevailing realities. It
was remembered how Alan of Lille, when his classroom at Montpellier was disrupted by knights eager to know what he thought
about nobility, cannily undid them in debate. Granted that
knights habitually seize from peasants, he got them to see that
what marked the 'greatest courtliness' was generosity, and he required them in turn to define for him the 'highest rusticity.'
When the knights failed to agree about this, Master Alan pointed
out that since they were necessarily looking for the contrary of
liberality, it followed that the 'most rustic' (translate: boorish?)
behaviour possible could only be the seizure from and abuse of
peasants.[68]

This was a received view, as we know. Yet Peter the Chanter
could write as if the lapse of knights from protectors to 'thieves

---

[66] *Textes inédits* 246–49: 'Go to the castle that is over there [against you].' Alan
surely enlarged on Jerome's rendering of Matth. xxi.2

[67] Radulfus Niger, *De re militari et triplici via peregrinationis Ierosolimitane*
(*1187/88*), ed. Ludwig Schmugge (Berlin 1977) iv.49–50 (222).

[68] A tradition twice recorded by Etienne de Bourbon, *Anecdotes historiques* . . . ,
ed. Albert Lecoy de la Marche (Paris 1877) iv.293 (246), 426 (370–71).

and violators' was a phenomenon of his time.[69] Could that be why rapine, itself no new scourge, assumes enlarged importance for the masters?[70] What they well saw was that the giving of alms by lords and knights was likely to be tainted by wrongful possession, and so to be subject to penitential remedy. This was to expose the strictures of Hildebert and Stephen of Grandmont,[71] to mention no others, to a more searching exploration of fraud and intention. For example, Peter the Chanter discerned rapine wherever temptation or covert pressures threatened to subvert justice. Like the chronicler of Anjou he got up a scenario, in this case that of a prelate *in extremis* convoking his agents and requiring them to confess under oath to the 'excesses, injuries, and enormities' they had inflicted on their charges.[72] But the Master's original point was that because the perpetrators shared the guilt thus brought into public exposure, the dying prelate could not fully confess *unless* he brought his servants to account. Their sin was also his. And where the Chanter explored rapine in relation to giving, bribery, and delegated powers, Robert of Courson in the years 1210–13 devoted a whole book of his summa on penitence to rapine.[73]

Enlarging on discussions of the past quarter-century, Master Robert defined rapine as 'the violent usurpation or taking away of someone else's belonging or of an honour or dignity possessed or expected. There are many sorts of plundering,' he wrote: those 'of movables on real property, present and future'—one feels again the sensitivity to the plight of minors in a rapacious world; 'some by violence, others by bad custom, others by fraud, others by slander.' Claiming that he had already addressed the sort of

---

[69] *De oratione et speciebus illius*, ed. Trexler, *The Christian at prayer. An illustrated prayer manual attributed to Peter the Chanter . . .* (1987) 226.

[70] e.g., *Sermons of Stephen Langton* ii.19 (48); Thomas de Chobham, *Summa* Q.11, 306. It figures in virtually all the texts cited in note 64.

[71] Hildebert, *Sermo 25*, PL CLXXI, 461–62; *Liber de doctrina*, ed. Jean Becquet, *Scriptores ordinis Grandimontensis* (Turnhout 1968), ci (48–49).

[72] *Verbum abbreviatum* (ed. Boutry) i.18 (171).

[73] BnF, MS latin 14524 (to be cited as 'Summa'), fols. 63vb–69ra.

rapine that 'may not seem violent'—usury, simony, fraudulent dealing—Robert proposes to consider the coercive rapine by princes and prelates, notably the 'unjust customs of kingdoms,' such as tolls and seizures of flotsam. Even this class of rapine is deconstructed so as to expose, distinctly, the guilt of courtiers who 'suggest to princes and prelates that they impose tallages and exactions,' and that of flatterers and detractors. All such people, to achieve a 'worthy' repentance, must restore all they have seized, even to the utmost clod.[74]

These opinions may be seen to frame two concerns characteristic of the masters. One is that moral responsibility for the exercise of coercive power was so contagious in their society that the age-old habit of blaming servants for malfeasance became problematic. The spectre of lesser 'bad' lords is overtaken in (northern) France and England by that of lord-kings imposing with arbitrary force, thereby putting at risk not only their own souls but also those of men in their service. How could knights accept wages manifestly paid from usury or rapine? An impulse to fix responsibility for armed violence exposed the greater powers in society, inviting comparison with Hebrew leadership; and so arose, although not only for this reason, an academic cult of biblical kingship.[75] But the casuistry was timely. Courson says that contemporary kings and princes could behave like castellans, imposing bad customs on the people they dominated.[76] A second concern arose from the growth of wealth, for in order to make sense of bad customs the masters undertook a newly searching examination of taxation, the most pervasive form of rapine of all.[77]

If rapine was a 'vice of the military condition,' could there be any hope of remedy? If so, in whose interest: that of suffering

---

[74] 'Summa' xv.1, fols. 63vb–64ra (partly quoted by Baldwin, *Masters* II, 171).

[75] Citation in note 73; and in general Philippe Buc, *L'ambiguïté du livre: prince, pouvoir, et peuple dans les commentaires de la Bible au moyen âge* (Paris 1994), parts 2, 3.

[76] 'Summa' xv.1–3, fols. 63vb–65ra.

[77] Peter the Chanter, *Verbum adbreviatum* i.17 (139); *Summa* ii.75 (II, 14), 129 (272); Baldwin, *Masters* I, 215–20.

peasants, or that of the knights' salvation? This would have seemed a false dilemma to the masters, for whom restitution seemed the only option for knights and princes whatever its value to peasants. Was Alan of Lille's lesson to the knights anything other than a studied insult? Yet one senses that the masters were taking new interest in welfare as well as damnation. Take the matter of tallage. They used the words *tallia* and *exactio* loosely, although they knew that the former, at least, referred to unconsented impositions. Anticipating Robert of Courson, Peter the Chanter viewed tallage as rapine, associating it with theft, 'exactions,' and 'extortions' of money.[78] But the resonance of these terms worried the masters. Alan of Lille once felt obliged to qualify an 'exaction' as 'violent,' as if the word *exactio* remained benign or equivocal in ordinary usage.[79] The Chanter went out of his way to define 'exaction' as 'violent and importune extortion,'[80] which is what it seemed widely to mean in the practise of his day.

Tallage was more problematic. Everywhere in northern Europe, perhaps especially in ecclesiastical domains and towns, efforts were being made to justify tallage. Either that, or to impose new taxes *not* tainted with the equation: uncustomary equals bad. But since any *new* exaction could be deemed wrongful, prevailing values created a practical as well as conceptual dilemma. While Master Robert denounced tallage as unjust, it was he who reflected on the excuses of those who resisted the penitential sanctions. For one thing, there were serfs, as (he thought) in Sicily, who were so fully their masters' property that to tallage them was no abuse. Then there were lords and prelates whose uncustomary impositions could be excused, if not justified, by reason of famine or need, or by demands placed on prelates and other lords by princes alleging the necessities of war. Moreover, there were knights (and 'ladies') who claimed that, having no renders

---

[78] *Verbum adbreviatum* i.17 (139); *Summa* ii.75 (II, 14); also *De oratione* (ed. Trexler) 226.

[79] *Liber poen.* ii.11 (II, 53).   [80] *Verbum adbreviatum* i.45 (309).

(*census*) in their villages, they could only live by tallage. Much it seems depended on context, as if some of the excuses were getting through. Excuses, to be sure, of the powerful. Robert could be acerbic about tallage. When it meant the seizure from the peasant tenants (*pauperes*) of churches whom prelates were bound to protect, he scolded prelates who failed to resist the 'tyrannies of princes' trying to tax clerical domains, for whatever purpose. Pressed by demands for war subsidy, abbots and bishops could be forced to 'violate' their people 'in order to pay the exactor.' If nothing good can come from doing wrong, then rapine is no way to restore the church's peace.[81] Yet when the question was whether tallages are ever justified, Robert noted that in his statute *Cum apostolus* of 1179 Pope Alexander III had made allowance for 'necessities' and 'reasonable cause' to justify a 'moderate aid with charity.' This position had led to a distinction between 'tallages of violence . . . [which] are never warranted]' and 'tallages of pretended benignity, which some claim to be licit.' Impatient with this distinction, Robert would merely allow that gratuitous aids were not tallage, and reiterate that 'all tallage is a species of rapine.'[82]

This was a curious instance of exaggerated nominalism. Robert of Courson and his fellow masters of penitence surely understood that tallage could be confused with taxation. But having no vocabulary of public service, they could only speak of taxation in the untechnical verbiage of common usage—aids, customs, subventions—that had at least the merit of corresponding to the indefinite conceptual categories of everyday life. The distinction between public and private spheres of power was no less clear to these men than to their predecessors; but since the lordships they knew of straddled both spheres, they had no more to say about public order than about lordship. They knew about feudal lordship as a contemporary, sometimes deplorable, reality. One of Courson's most striking examples of rapine is that of a conquering lord-king who seizes a realm for the benefit of his

---

[81] 'Summa' xv.13 (fol. 66va).   [82] 'Summa' xv.14 (fol. 66va).

fief-holding knights; and the old issue of sworn fidelity to a prince under religious censure likewise had some urgency for him.[83] Not accidentally, these illustrations of great lordship also point up commonplaces about public order: necessity or defence of the realm, protection of the church. In other contexts we read about the king's sworn engagement to avenge wrongdoing, and about just wars, subjects' fidelity (as distinct from vassalic), just price, and the defence of merchants on dangerous roads.[84] A quite special place in debate was reserved for the public need of stable coinages together with practical solutions for the monetary problems arising from customary renders and credit.[85]

What is hard to find in this academic culture, doubtless because it posed no moral issue, and perhaps also for another reason, is any normal conception of aggregative social utilities, any disposition to define theoretically the incipient purposes of public and civic powers. Were they not aspiring lords themselves, these masters, creating affective followings of intellectual fidelity?[86] Could they think of power impersonally? Alan of Lille defined the power of those 'who justly rule subjects' as a 'regime' (*regimen*), to be contrasted with 'tyranny,' associating them with lordships of, respectively, utility or domination.[87] Yet even if neither he nor his colleagues spell out the requisites of a utilitarian lordship, let alone define government explicitly, their passing reflections on power and justice have new resonance. To the problem posed by knights inflicting bad customs to the distress of their

[83] 'Summa' xv.2–3 (fols. 63vb–64ra); iv (fol. 29rv).

[84] 'Summa' xv.18 (fol. 67rb), iv.12 (fol. 29rv), x.11 (fol. 49ra), i.30 (fol. 11ra), iv.4 (27rab), x.15 (50ra), xv.4 (64rb–65ra).

[85] Baldwin, *Masters* 1, 241–44; T. N. Bisson, *Conservation of coinage* . . . (Oxford 1979; abbrev: *CC*) 172–83.

[86] Duby put this strongly, *Trois ordres* 372 (*Three orders* 309): 'Une nouvelle forme de domination s'instaura, celle des docteurs, sachant, parlant, subjuguant des auditeurs.'

[87] *Hierarchia Alani* 233. With the 'demons' of tyranny will be those 'qui suis subditis potius preesse quam prodesse volunt.'

people, Robert of Courson proposed that these might be redeemed by the institution of 'some public conveniences in common, such as a house where the citizens' poor [sic] are received, or
a public pasture, or aqueduct, or something like that.' Those last
words—*aut aliquid consimile*—have emotional as well as conceptual sweep. The subject masses (*subditi*), according to Robert,
were a *status*, a condition vulnerable to the bad customs; and this
status—it is the 'state' peeking through, as we shall see—, although it hardly arouses compassion from the masters, affords a
rare glimpse of a social dynamic otherwise obscured by the analytic serenity pervading their works.[88]

To oppose arbitrary (lordly) powers in the interest of princely
salvation was bound to look like connivance with peasants and la-
bourers, especially those with the visibly improving means to respond to tax collectors. Yet the masters, who could not doubt that
some people were their lords' property, were no more democratic
than the knights they chastised. Within the same cocoon of lordship they simply thought differently about the cultures of arms and
money. And it was hard to stigmatize rapine and tallage without
labelling such violence as oppressive, quite as injurious to the 'poor'
as to the otherworldly hopes of their knightly tormentors.[89]

In short, the moralising postures of the masters thrust them
into a problematic defence of the peace and security of the labouring masses. It could hardly be otherwise, given prevailing
levels of coercive and recreational violence and the abrasive tenor
of life. Whether the Parisian masters were drawn into renewed
ideological debate, as Georges Duby suggested, is hard to discern
in their writings; but it does appear that Peter the Chanter and
Stephen Langton were inclined to widen and deepen the human
circles of consultation and collective action.[90] It also looks as if

[88] 'Summa' xv.6 (fol. 65vb).

[89] Alan of Lille, *Liber poen.* i.28 (II, 34); Peter the Chanter, *Summa* ii.129 (II,
272); Robert of Courson, 'Summa' xv.6 (fol. 65rb–va), 13 (66va).

[90] Duby, *Trois ordres* 384–86 (*Three orders* 320–21); and see also Buc, *L'ambiguïté
du livre* 312–408.

this was extra-curricular activity, nonetheless important historically for escaping the eyesight of modern readers of penitential
theology.

REFLECTIVE NEIGHBOURS of the powers of their day, the masters
of the later twelfth century brought an academic mode of persuasion to the needs of the Roman church. They would put reason
into the lordships whose tenants were no less subjects than sworn
men. For Alan of Lille those earthly ones 'who rule their subjects
reasonably' were of an angelic princely order.[91] The moralists emphatically denounced spoliation, the most starkly outrageous
proof of lordship's arbitrary *praeesse*.[92] Concepts of office, administration, sworn commitments, and accountability likewise fell
into problematic zones of moral volition noticed by the masters.[93]
What have been called their 'social teachings' brought the maps
of those zones up to date without supplanting them. This was an
academic culture skilled at unmasking the moral failings of lordship, perceptive of motive, ambition, and the moral impact of
trade, money, and credit, yet without the vision to spell out what

[91] *Sermo in die sancti Michaelis, Textes inédits* 251: 'De hoc ordine erunt qui
subditos rationabiliter regunt.'

[92] Peter the Chanter, *Summa* ii.124 (II, 253); *Verbum adbreviatum* i.54 (361–72);
ii.36 (739–43); Robert of Courson, 'Summa' i.30 (fol. 11ra), 33 (fol. 12rb); x.11
(fol. 49ra).

[93] Office: Alan of Lille, *Sermo in die sancti Michaelis*, in *Textes inédits* 251; Peter
the Chanter, *Verbum adbreviatum* i.17 (149–50), 18 (161), 49 (329–30), 50 (335);
short version, *PL* CCV, c. 54 (165–68); *Summa* ii.81 (52). Administration: *Disputationes de Simon de Tournai* iv.2 (28); Peter the Chanter, *Verbum adbreviatum* i.21
(184); short version, *PL* CCV, c. 22 (81–82), c. 25 (95–96); Robert of Courson,
'Summa' xv.9 (fols. 65vb–66ra), 18 (fols. 67rb–va). Oaths: Alan of Lille, *De
poen.* i.82–5 (II, 90–91); Peter the Chanter, *Summa* ii.76 (II, 20–22), 122 (246–47);
Verbum adbreviatum (short), *PL* CCV, c. 127 (322–23); Robert of Courson,
'Summa' iv.4 (fol. 27rab), 12 (fols. 29rab–va); Stephen Langton, 'Questiones,'
St John's College (Cambridge), MS 57, fols. 235v–36v, no. 91. Accounts: Peter
the Chanter, *Verbum adbreviatum* ii.36 (741).

the rejection of rapine and tallage would require of its society. They were (of course) men of their age, healers not builders, better grounded in the Bible and the fathers than in the laws, and non-politically suspicious of causes. It was remembered in the king's court that Peter the Chanter, in an exchange with Philip Augustus himself, had opined that if prelates of his day were less likely than those of old to serve their people, it was because an uninvited counsellor—the Devil—had intruded to impose his values, including the 'lust to dominate,' in elections.[94] To 'rule their subjects reasonably': Alan's assertion lingers as a question. Could human beings learn to do the work of angels?

EXPERTISE: TWO FACETS

It is hard to see that anyone thought so, let alone meant to try. Whatever their differences the singers, courtiers, and moralists had much in common. They shared assumptions about the origins and nature of power; they understood that fallible men were prone to sordid and brutal behaviour that was the Devil's own work; and they fully accepted that lordships good and bad were the way of this world. Even after 1200 it remained a world of abrasive force and constraint, morally as well as physically. Stephen Langton preached that gluttony and abstinence were castles, the latter under siege.[95]

If few amongst those who entertained, served, or professed thought of power per se as problematic, some others, differently oriented, found themselves in demand for reasons beyond all control of their masters. Caught up in the pressures of convergent forces, they too could see, like the masters and courtiers with whom they had studied, how the moral strictures against arbitrary taxation coincided with enlarged princely ambitions from about 1185. It cannot have been lost on them how custom, so to speak, sided with those strictures; and because custom made no

---

[94] Citations above, p. 401 n. 265.
[95] *Sermons* ii.16 (45).

allowance for increasing wealth, yet another coincident pressure, the conflict between custom and need, produced a tension in courtly and scholastic debates that invited the attention of resourceful men. For there were some who could take satisfaction from the challenge of technicalities, men in whom competence came to rival fidelity as a qualification for service. They were *periti* in new ways, 'experts.' Stephen Langton exemplifies a coupling of theological and courtly expertise, for as he mediated between King John and English barons and clerks pressing for concessions, he knew of the latters' efforts to found their cause on records and precedent.[96] But this was neither the first nor the best instance of a cultural phenomenon that becomes perceptible in the 1160s, and of which two facets may be discerned.

Knowing. First, and most prolonged, was the multiplication of lawyers. Men trained in the laws were not a new breed, to be sure. In southern France, Romanist teachings derived from Bologna flourished for a generation after 1120 without securing much influence in practical applications. When the prospering knight Berenguer de Puisserguier defied his lord Viscountess Ermengarde with the input of a lawyer citing the *Code* on the incapacity of slaves and women, his cause failed because King Louis VII could cite customary law to the contrary.[97] Precocious though they were, the southern jurists were slow to buy into a new canonist jurisprudence,[98] so that as experience with customary jurisprudence gave way to familiarity with the two learned laws, the meaning of expertise changed. One either knew Gratian, whose 'Concordance of discordant canons' became available in the 1140s, or did not; and only those familiar with the canons and

[96] F. M. Powicke, *Stephen Langton* . . . (Oxford 1928) 113–16; Holt, *Magna Carta*, 222–26, 280–82.

[97] *HF* xvi, 88–92, nos. 271–81 (notably 280); and for contexts, André Gouron, 'L'entourage de Louis VII face aux droits savants: Giraud de Bourges et son *ordo*,' *BEC* cxlvi (1988) 25–28; and Cheyette, *Ermengard* 213–16.

[98] Gouron, 'Canonistes français (vers 1150–vers 1210),' 230–34.

decretals assembled in the massive *distinctiones* and *causae* of Parts One and Two could hope to interpret and apply the new conciliar statutes in lately mobilised episcopal courts. The situation was complicated by the accelerated multiplication of decretals, especially under Pope Alexander III, together with a snowballing increase of commissions to papal judges-delegate. All this entailed learned expertise—erudition in normative writings, a grasp of technicalities—such as was inevitable with the proliferation of suits at law.[99]

It would be mistaken to suppose that this numerical growth was driven by the recognition of expertise in or about church courts. The jurists versed in decretist and decretalist learning were, like the courtiers, a self-serving lot. Their ambitions had little to do with visionary ideals. Yet it was surely understood that their reading stood opposed to the violence of marital repudiation and the arbitrariness of dispossession and disinheritance. So their outlook served the procedural safeguards of justice; indeed, of a papal justice that could only enlist the envy of greater lay lords and princes. But juridical expertise arose from experience as well as learning. Bishop Bartholomew of Exeter (1161–84) was appointed and reappointed judge-delegate some seventy times, most often in his later years; and it was during his working lifetime that the papal court came to stress local experience and expertise in the assignment of cases everywhere. Why English cases of delegated jurisdiction outnumber those from other regions is a debated problem not to be examined here; yet it follows from our visits to other cultures that, since the training of lawyers in Bologna, Montpellier, and Paris brought them together with men in

---

[99] See in general Stephan Kuttner, 'The revival of jurisprudence,' *Renaissance and renewal in the twelfth century*, ed. Robert L. Benson, Giles Constable (Cambridge, M., 1982) 299–323; Walther Holtzmann, *Studies in the collections of twelfth-century decretals* . . . , ed. C. R. Cheney, Mary G. Cheney (Vatican City 1979); Peter Landau, 'Die Entstehung der systematischen Dekretalsammlungen und die europäische Kanonistik des 12. Jahrhunderts,' *ZRG Kan. Abt.* xcvi (1979), 120–48; and on Gratian Anders Winroth, *The making of Gratian's Decretum* (Cambridge 2000).

theology who were often trained or employed in northwestern Europe, the naming of those educated in the laws is understandably concentrated there. Peter of Blois epitomizes the convergence of theological and legal cultures, and for all we know it was the anti-stylistic technicality of the law that aroused less challenging courtly ambitions in him.[100]

All this said, the reader may still wonder whether 'expertise' is quite the right concept for grasping the place of law and lawyers in the remodeling of power after 1160. Assuredly they were influential, these literate men whose book learning proved welcome in princely entourages, chanceries, and courts of judicial action. Customary procedures devoid of intellectual justification yielded to the reasoning that informed the Roman law of sale or the new canon law of marriage. Something similar happened with the incipient jurisprudence of fiefs in Italy, where by the 1150s Romanist lawyers were making a place for it in their teaching and settlements.[101] Their work coincided with a deepened engagement with Roman law such as was, around 1200, only possible in Italy and which tended for a time to marginalize French practitioners in the two laws. What mattered more to princely power, and still more to the remodeling of associative life in regions like Lombardy, Aragon, Flanders, and England, was how the new legal learnings bore on the exercise of command, coercive force, and justice. Pitting law against law, as in the issue of the Viscountess Ermengarde's capacity, was not unheard of in later times, but it ceased to matter once the possibilities for adjusting customary rules and procedures by reference to equity and (Roman) reason were tried. Jurists steeped in the two laws sharpened

[100] Adrian Morey, *Bartholomew of Exeter, bishop and canonist* . . . (Cambridge 1937) ch. 4; Sayers, *Papal judges delegate,* ch. 1; Southern, 'Peter of Blois,' 107–9.

[101] *Compilatio antiqua,* ed. Lehmann, *Consuetudines feudorum* 1–38; and see generally Johannes Fried, *Die Entstehung des Juristenstandes im 12. Jahrhundert* (Cologne 1974); Peter Classen, 'Richterstand und Rechtswissenschaft in italienischen Kommunen des 12. Jahrhunderts,' *Studium und Gesellschaft im Mittelalter* (Stuttgart 1983) 27–126; Reynolds, *Fiefs and vassals* 215–40.

prevailing understandings of community, rights sole and collective, interests, and decision-making with reference to counsel and consent. This was not so much expertise as ideology, for what it fostered was an intellectual approach to power, even potentially an educated critique of lordship. Here again the jurists were compatible with the moralists, some of whose tenets, like that of Robert of Courson on the admissibility of tallage, drew on the new canon law. Most of the ideas mentioned above arose together with newly self-conscious communities towards the end of the twelfth century, yet their full impact in Europe was delayed for several generations thereafter.[102]

Even so, most people must have regarded educated lawyers as experts. Were they not in a 'lucrative science,' to use the dismissive words of theologians, including Gerald of Wales, who once taught canon law at Paris? What worried some masters was that law became preferable to letters and theology as qualification for courtly service.[103] But it was popes, whether directly or indirectly, quite as much as princes who employed lawyers. This fact is fundamental to grasping the place of legal culture in the experience of power from about 1160. What is remarkable about Pope Alexander III and his successors is that they were jurists themselves. Unlike other lord-princes of the twelfth century they could bring their own knowledge of case-law to bear on specific problems—such as Alexander III on hereditary successions to benefices or Innocent III on elections[104]—and so to create the precedents or even frame policies that could be expected to bind their successors or determine judgments. Whether from the pope

[102] Robert of Courson, 'Summa,' xv.14 (66va). Also André Gouron, 'L'inaliénabilité du domaine public: à l'origine du principe,' *CRAIBL* (2001) 818; and in general Brian Tierney, *Foundations of the conciliar theory. The contribution of the medieval canonists from Gratian to the Great Schism*, new ed. (Leiden-NY 1998), part 2.

[103] Baldwin, *Masters* I, 84–86.

[104] JL 12254 (Mary G. Cheney, *Roger bishop of Worcester, 1164–1179* [Oxford 1980], appendix ii, no. 61); Comp 3 (i.6), ed. Friedberg, *Quinque compilationes antiquae* 106–7.

himself or from his advisers, decretals of appointment of judges-delegate commonly stated the church's law applicable to the case.[105] What is more, since Pope Alexander made no effort to codify, or legislate, his pronouncements, he was often, it seems, virtually serving as a consultant to bishops, like Roger of Worcester, who addressed him. And since it was pointless to appeal for his judgment while doubting his competence (in either sense), least of all at a time when proprietary complexities were outstripping applicable norms, a distinctive dynamic of lawmaking under Alexander III created yet another cultural novelty: the proliferation of anonymous collections of papal decretals.

It might seem digressive to pause over this highly problematic by-way in the history of canon law were it not for one salient truth. Here for once in this book the evidence permits us to glimpse the reality of an ungoverned society appealing prematurely for the sort of justice no lordship in Christian Europe was yet equipped to provide. The demand for workable principles and precedents in populations bursting with tenures, claims, and moral liabilities ill comprehended by a jurisprudence itself in transformation, far exceeded supply. As the trickle of appeals to Rome swelled to a flood under Alexander III, the proliferation of decretals on like topics created local needs to know how the multiplying cases and judgments implied new norms; to know whether new cases required new appeals or further consultation. The need was met by collecting decretals and written decisions, the work of expert jurists close to judges-delegate and with access to their fragile files. In some such way a compiler, possibly Master David of London, copied papal letters addressed to Bishop Roger of Worcester, for his transcript found its way into a compilation of such copies now preserved in Portugal. These uncommissioned compilations multiplied from the 1160s, for the judges ad hoc kept no archives in these very years when expert papal declarations were creating new law in fields and topics beyond Gratian's scope. The compilers of Pope Alexander's time—mostly anonymous, as

---

[105] Morey, *Bartholomew* 51.

was characteristic of twelfth-century innovators—brought literate and technical expertise to the hopeless labour of keeping up with an activist lord-pope. Their work laid the foundation for a better classified series of officially sanctioned compilations after 1190, culminating in the *Liber extra* of 1234. Otherwise known as the *Decretals of Gregory IX*, this work directed by the Catalan jurist Ramon de Penyafort brought to mature fruition a convergence of provincial ingenuity with curial direction that was the achievement of Pope Innocent III.[106]

Knowing How. The recognition of expertise arose silently in a widening culture of knowledge. By no means confined to opaque scenes of delegated papal justice, it can be traced in the 'tracts of judicial order' (*ordines iudiciarii*), which began to appear in the later twelfth century as helps to procedure in courts.[107] It also figures in some contemporary treatises on law, of which *Glanvill* (1188–89) is the most notable. Here a justiciar's expert knowledge of the English common law is on admirable display. To do the law of right writ by writ, so to speak, is to flaunt the certainties of precedent and written form the papal judges-delegate had lately lacked. But what is of interest here is how visibly the expert who knows, has achieved an expertise of knowing how. Complaints to the lord-king concerning fiefs or free holdings, if eligible for royal jurisdiction, begin with a writ of summons, continue when the person summoned comes or fails to come, and if he fails to come . . . (etc.). This is how you do the king's justice: it is complicated, technical, here are the steps to take, the forms you need.[108]

---

[106] Charles Duggan, *Twelfth-century decretal collections and their importance in English history* (London 1963), chs. 3–5; Sayers, *Papal judges delegate* 25–54; Cheney, *Roger*, ch. 4, and 206–8; G. Le Bras *et al.*, *L'âge classique 1140–1378. Sources et théories du droit* [of the church] (Paris 1965) 222–43.

[107] e.g., *Pilii, Tancredi, Gratiae libri de iudiciorum ordine*, ed. Fridericus Bergmann (Göttingen 1842); and in general Linda Fowler-Magerl, Ordines iudiciarii *and* Libelli de ordine iudiciorum (*from the middle of the twelfth to the end of the fifteenth century*) (Turnhout 1994).

[108] *Glanvill* i.5–12 (5–8).

Now much of this how-to-do-it was an updating of older, equally technical procedures such as few would presently need or remember. *Glanvill's* expertise was assuredly shared, or diffused; one needed to know how the writs worked in English courts by 1190, and the treatise was copied early and often, even revised. Yet the text, which is insistently normative and didactic, contains little to suggest a shared culture of legal know-how. Only in its eloquent prologue on royal power, which bears some resemblance to that in the *Dialogue of the Exchequer,* can we overhear notes of that royalist ideology that was pervasive amongst royal servants everywhere in these years.[109] What better reveals the cultural impact of new techniques is the evidence of fiscal management. For this it will be useful to return once more to Barcelona (with the reminder that we have nowhere else to turn for parallel evidence), before taking up the incomparable testimony of the *Dialogue.*

In Catalonia the critical phase of fiscal invention fell in the 1150s. It looks as if Bertran de Castellet, Ponç the Scribe, and one or two others collaborated like a team engaged in improving the lord-count's patrimonial value in the wake of military expenditures and conquests. But it was only towards 1175–78 that the auditing of bailiffs' accounts took on a semblance of regularity. For the next thirty years a group of royal courtiers apparently organized by the scribes Ramon de Caldes and Guillem de Bassa, who were succeeded under King Pere I (1196–1213) by the Templars of Palau-solità, accounted routinely with vicars and bailiffs for the fiscal domains of Catalonia.[110]

Theirs was assuredly an expertise of practise. This is clear from the records these men produced; and because some of the latter were trained scribes, we can discern in their work a characteristically notarial culture. Their fiscal work was hardly exclusive. They were quite as conversant with the forms for sales, conventions, and pledges as with that for accounts (*computum, computavit*), which one of them would employ so as to write up the balance of

---

[109] ibid., 1–2; cf. *Dialogus* 1–3; and citations above, pp. 387–88.
[110] Above, pp. 345–48.

revenues and expenses declared in the audit. Bailiffs themselves, including Jewish ones in Girona, Barcelona, and Lleida, might act as assessors when not defending their own accounts. Responsive to memoranda and charters, this work was fully literate (and numerate), which is not to claim that scribes and bailiffs were well educated. None of them appears to have attended the schools of noted masters, not even the dean of Barcelona cathedral (Ramon de Caldes).[111]

So it would seem reasonable to question whether these Catalan functionaries achieved self-conscious fiscal expertise. As we saw in the preceding chapter, their fiscal work was part of a thoroughgoing reform of their masters' patrimonial domination. Yet even in their fiscal supervision, the known accountants and auditors were a cohesive group; they were known to one another and were to some extent interchangeable in their roles of account and audition. By selling bailiwicks on terms of periodic account, they manifestly preferred administration to credit, a preference that may have amounted to a problematic reversal of prevailing practise. Moreover, they devised a new means of testing current accounts against (prescriptive) records of the count-king's domains. It is unlikely that these registers, which did not long survive, and may have been lost during the Valencian war of Jaume the Conqueror, were meant to include the ephemeral sums of current account, many of which survive as originals. For in yet another initiative of the courtier-scribes, some one hundred or more of these parchments were bound, or sacked, together, and labelled in dorsal scripts easily legible today.[112]

In short, the evidence points to an organizing of accountability with a minimum of committed specialisation. Selling and accounting periodically for local exploitations, a subset of courtier-scribes and entrepreneurs functioned so as to perpetuate if not also to ameliorate a mode of patrimonial service that, but for its writtenness—and it is a huge exception—, may have been widely

---

[111] *FAC* I 156–57; II passim.   [112] ibid., I, ch. 3; II, 424, word *liber.*

prevalent in Europe towards 1200.[113] If in 1203–04 Bishop Wolfger of Passau could have his travel expenses precisely recorded, in
accounts of exactly the sort attested for the count of Barcelona
half a century before, who can doubt that his men also accounted
for his domains?[114] What Ramon de Caldes and his associates got
up was an inchoate culture of expertise that persisted under King
Pere, only to be disrupted by novel fiscal demands that resulted in
enormous borrowing and new taxation. The day of fundraisers
had arrived; and in circumstances yet to be examined, one Guillem Durfort took the place of Ramon de Caldes.[115]

Lest it seem that practical expertise amongst those engaged
with power in the twelfth century was in short supply, the case
of England beckons once again. The *Dialogue of the Exchequer*,
composed by Richard fitz Nigel in the years 1177–79, is of such
blinding interest in this context as to threaten some misrepre-
sentation of the contrast between his circle and continental
ones. The Catalan scene was simpler and Ramon de Caldes
wrote no such manual; but he was even busier in his way than
Richard the Treasurer (and, as it happens, in the very years
when the *Dialogue* was written). He wrote clearly of his project
to reorganize the comital archives, and he understood the
mechanisms of an administrative accountability.[116] The real
question is why nothing of *this* description survives for most
other continental lands. And the answer must surely be that, as
in Capetian France, a traditional *gestion patrimoniale* persisted
almost everywhere as late as the 1190s. In these prescriptive regimes only the fiscal surveys were in writing, in rolls and registers constantly going out of date, vulnerable to loss by fire,
neglect, or violence. Current estates of account, if in writing at

---

[113] For speculation on its origin in England, *Dialogus* i.7 (40).

[114] ed. Hedwig Heger, *Das Lebenszeugnis Walthers von der Vogelweide. Die
Reiserechnungen des Passauer Bischofs Wolfger von Erla* (Vienna 1970) 77–146; cf.
FAC II, no. 4.

[115] *FAC* I, ch. 4, and see below, pp. 511–13.

[116] *LFM* I, 1–2; Bisson, 'Ramon de Caldes,' 283–88 (*MFrPN* 190–98).

all, were absolutely ephemeral. 'Cultures' there must have been, as in Normandy and Flanders, the exceptional regions in which we know for sure that records of account were lost.[117] In *this* context the Catalan experiment is startling: symptomatic of new princely needs, yet deeply vulnerable to tenacious habits of hand-to-mouth exploitation.

In England fitz Nigel had heard it said that accountability—he means, an accountancy of tallies—antedated the Norman Conquest.[118] The practise he describes, largely worked out under the Norman kings and disrupted after 1139, was revived after 1154. The *Dialogue* is a record of this revival, recast so as to make the accountability of sheriffs seem self-justifiably timeless, written by the experienced and well-read son of Bishop Nigel, to whom Henry II had commended the rescue of royal and patrimonial revenue towards 1155. Humanely literate, powerfully descriptive and analytic, it is not only a masterpiece of the 'renaissance' of its age; it is the consummate manual of expertise of the twelfth century.

In the voiced conceit of a Master teaching his Pupil, the *Dialogue of the Exchequer* disassembles an institution the way a master mechanic might pull apart an automotive engine to show how it works. And the point of this analogy is that pride in a complicated human device is there from the start. Designed (or built?) to secure the rights of individuals and the revenues justly accruing to the king's fisc, 'the exchequer has its own rules not by chance but by the deliberate wish of great men.'[119] There is a 'knowledge of the exchequer' that one must grasp to make it work. The Master is made to promise that he will explain 'not subtleties but useful things' (no need of a professor in this machine shop). Yet the

---

[117] *Pipe rolls of the exchequer of Normandy for the reign of Henry II, 1180 and 1184*, ed. Vincent Moss (London 2004), and further volumes in progress; *Gros brief* 77–138.

[118] *Dialogus* i.1–4 (7–14). A quite differently original manual of courtly expertise may be found in Andreas Capellanus, *De amore*, ed. Graziano Ruffini (Milan 1980).

[119] *Dialogus* pp. 3, 5.

Dialogue is full of recondite detail, much of it highly technical, like the discussions of tale and scale, assay, assart, and *foresta*.[120] Nor does lowly lore preclude conceptual sophistication: the very word 'exchequer' (*scaccarium*) refers to an occasion as well as a chessboard.[121]

The exchequer as court epitomises the functional utility some contemporaries found wanting in princely services. Here is a place where clerics need have no fear for their vocation. The summons brings together officers who preside, judge, and review; they associate with men of greater or (mostly) lesser status who are nonetheless equally requisite, like meters and bolts in a machine. The Master implies that all business would be held up if the chancellor's clerk were not present from 'the beginning of the accounts to the end.'[122] Yet if *ratio* is the moving principle of this assemblage,[123] it is compromised in some ways. It is not withheld from the Pupil that official order is contaminated by privilege. The Master conveys his creator's embarassment in having to justify the exemption from dues on their lands enjoyed by barons of the exchequer; and the spectacular anomaly of the forest law, administered not with absolute justice but in accordance with the king's will, is represented with clear-headed patience.[124]

Yet the prevailing dynamic of procedure in the exchequer lies in the functional coordination of competencies. What defines these 'competencies,' it becomes clear (even if the Pupil fails to ask), is experience as much as skill. Indeed, it would appear that the more menial the task—like those of cutting the tallies or preparing the parchments—the more expertise was required. But the great men of the exchequer enjoyed something like tenure—or rather, tenures?—in their posts. They held offices, to be sure, in

---

[120] ibid., i.5 (25, 30), 6 (36–38), 7 (41–43), 11–13 (56–61); ii.11 (104).

[121] ibid., i.1 (6–7). [122] ibid., i.6 (33–34).

[123] ibid., preface, 3: 'scarrarium suis legibus . . . cuius ratio si seruetur . . .'; cf. i.11 (59): 'forestarum ratio.'

[124] ibid., i.8 (45–47), 11–13 (59–61).

the usual sense of endowed or privileged functions: the treasurer (Richard himself), the chancellor. But the functions of the bishop of Winchester and Thomas Brown could only be described with reference to themselves. Brown was said to have 'faith and discretion,' which are about what a lord-prince might look for in a commended baron. When pressed to explain why King Henry II had intruded on settled procedure to make a place at the board for such a man, the Master could only add that Brown was reputed to have occupied a place of great prominence in the royal court of Sicily.[125] In short, the imposing 'dignity and knowledge'[126] of the exchequer owed much to the lord-king's interest and favour, not much to his personal engagement with fiscal technology. They derived from traditions passing from member to member, also from its quasi-genealogical interest in its own antiquities.

So that even in England expertise remains incompletely free of fidelity. Lacking fiefs of its own, the exchequer cannot be called a lordship, yet its sociability remains that of magnates obliged and privileged to serve the lord-king in a restructured accountability of justice and service. Probably fitz Nigel exaggerated its cohesion. What would we not give for a 'secret history' of the exchequer in these years? But the achievement claimed by the *Dialogue* may not be minimised. Persons of competence, including expert technicians in written accountancy, worked proudly for a social interest manifestly wider than the royal lordship in which it was disguised. The privileges mentioned were seen to be embarassing as well as anomalous. Over time pride and proprietary precision would become rigidity, inviting (though hardly causing) disruption and reform during the early years of Henry III.[127] But something resembling professionalism had been achieved when the restoration of the

---

[125] ibid., i.5 (26–27), 6 (35–36).   [126] ibid., prologue (5); ii.4 (84), 28 (127).
[127] Robert C. Stacey, *Politics, policy, and finance under Henry III 1216–1245* (Oxford 1987) 8–9; and D. A. Carpenter, *The minority of Henry III* (London 1990) 109–12.

exchequer (ca. 1158–80) created the first associative institution of territorial government in Europe.

❈

THE PEOPLE of these cultures served themselves as well as the princely courts, churches, and towns to which they were drawn. Purveyors of old values, they made no claims to originality, not even the fiscal and judicial technicians. Yet perhaps this assertion is too sweeping. If our task is to imagine what these gifted or skilled men *thought* as they worked, a few more words about one of these cultures might help.

The Romanist lawyers were not merely learned and expert; by virtue of their uniquely challenging resource they stood in a special relation to circles of power of whatever sort. Their commentaries on Justinian's *Code, Digest,* and *Institutes* contain much the sort of guidance to procedure as *Glanvill,* even if they are unspecific about the jurisdictions to which the Roman rules apply.[128] The Bolognese masters' engagement with the Roman law was competitively academic, to the extent of defining philosophical approaches that appealed to students who carried forward the divergent teachings of Bulgarus (d. ca. 1165) and Martinus (d. ?1166). Together with their followers in southern France—notably the authors of the *Summa Trecensis* and the *Exceptiones Petri*—these were men who knew and knew how. The 'Peter' of the *Exceptiones,* lately identified convincingly with one Pierre de Cabannes, was a learned practitioner amongst amateurs, visible in records in and about Arles in the years 1150–58, servant of the archbishop and then of the count of Provence. But it cannot be said that men who knew Roman law flooded the courts of those who found their learning useful.[129]

---

[128] e.g., *Summa Trecensis* iii.1–6, ed. Hermann Fitting, *Summa Codicis des Irnerius* (Berlin 1894) 46–52; *Placentini summa 'Cum essem Mantue' siue de accionum uarietatibus,* ed. Gustav Pescatore (Greifswald 1897).

[129] See Fried, *Entstehung des Juristenstandes,* ch. 2; André Gouron, *La science du droit dans le Midi de la France au Moyen Age* (London 1984), esp. chs. 1, 3, 7–9, 14;

For they had, so to speak, no courts of their own. They were in no position to impose themselves on the managers of customary or ecclesiastical jurisdictions. Yet they were closer to the realities of everyday life than anyone else, habituated to reading about commonplace experience—marriage, inheritance, property and theft, privilege and disability—in the terms, often in the very words, of habitual speech or notarial representation. It seemed obvious to them, if technically complicated, that lordship was (in some sense) proprietary right or that freedoms were as problematic as they were desirable. 'Whatever the slave [servus] acquires is his lord's,' wrote Pierre de Cabannes, 'and so cannot pass to his successor.'[130] Master Roger pointed to the difficulty, surely contemporary in its reverberation, posed by men attached to the glebe (Roman terms): were they free, or merely free of the lord?[131] In a breviary of the Roman law, another commentator wrote that 'of humanly lawful things some are public,' such as rivers and seashores; 'some are communal, like the marketplace . . .'; some are personal, and others impersonally proprietary, 'like wild beasts and fish.'[132] By defining obligations objectively, and justice as public, the glossators gave voice to the deeply subverted presumption that public order was right order. Moreover, this outlook was precisely that of the notaries who brought newly formulaic regularity to the recording of all that was most ordinary in the settled life of southern France and Italy.[133]

---

and for Gouron's identification of author Pierre, 'Petrus "démasqué",' Revue d'Histoire de Droit LXXXII (2004) 577–88.

[130] Exceptiones Petri i.21, ed. C. G. Mor, 2 vols. Scritti giuridici preirneriani 3,10 (Milan 1935–80) II, 68; cf. Brachylogus i.3.5, 8.3, ed. Eduardus Böcking (Berlin 1829) 7, 11.

[131] Rogerii quaestiones super Institutis iii, ed. Hermann Kantorowicz, Studies in the glossators of the Roman law . . . (Cambridge 1938) 279.

[132] Brachylogus ii.1.10–13 (31–32).

[133] See, e.g., Formularium tabellionum di Irnerio . . . , ed. G. B. Palmieri, Appunti e documenti per la storia dei glossatori I (Bologna 1892); and on the notariate, André Gouron, 'Diffusion des consulats méridionaux et expansion du droit romain . . . ,' BEC CXXI (1963) 54–67.

There was no need to reimpose Roman imperial order, even if Barbarossa set out to do so with expert help; nor even for the professors to insist on Roman over against customary law.[134] What Justinian had codified was a massive consensus about right and reason that was destined to prevail in Latin Europe once revived and, towards 1140–75, diffused. This was one meaning of *aequitas*, as insisted upon by Martinus and his followers and by the early French commentators.[135] 'Equity is a coming together of things in which all is equivalent in like causes requiring like rules.'[136] Law, they taught, is something bigger than right.

Pacification

Alan of Lille distinguished three species of peace: the peace of the times, that of human intention, and that of eternity. For him as for others the first of these was a 'shadow of peace,' illusory, 'slippery'; an 'exterior peace' in contrast with the 'interior peace' of moral exertion, and with God's peace. One must strive for the latter while trampling the former; so that, if the shadowed peace was a deplorable norm even of princely power, the 'peace of conscience' was a laudable battleground of virtues and vices, the scene of a dynamic quest for untroubled goodness.[137]

The dynamic of this homiletic theology resonated in Alan's society. Peace was breaking out all over after 1150, which is to say, in Alan's terms, the rejection of shadowed reality. In June 1155 Louis VII got the 'baronage' of France to confirm under oath a

[134] Hermann Lange, *Römisches Recht im Mittelalter* I (Munich 1997) 77–79.

[135] *Vetus collectio*, ed. Gustav Haenel, *Dissensiones dominorum* . . . (Leipzig 1834) 1–70; Kantorowicz, *Studies*, 86–88; *Exceptiones Petri*, prologue, ed. Mor, *Scritti giuridici* II, 47–48; *Brachylogus* i.i.3, 3 (1, 6–7).

[136] *La Summa Institutionum 'Justiniani est in hoc opere,'* ed. Pierre Legendre (Frankfurt 1973) i.1, 23.

[137] *Summa de arte praedicatoria* i.22, PL CCX, 155–57.

'peace of the whole realm.'[138] The idea for this probably came from southern France, where the king had lately travelled and where shortly before that the metropolitans of Narbonne and Bordeaux had joined with their bishops and magnates to impose new statutes of peace. An assembly celebrated at Mimizan (Bordelais) on Assumption Day 1148 (or 1149) may have been the occasion of a peace for Gascony of which the statutes have only recently come to light. In both provinces the Templars were to receive a tax on oxen in support of peace; and in the form imposed by Archbishop Arnaud I of Narbonne, this was to become a privilege confirmed by Pope Hadrian IV, then repeatedly by Alexander III and again as late as 1190. But the statute as well as the privilege caught on, so that from about 1148 to 1195 normative institutes of peace were promulgated in almost every county and diocese between the Pyrenees and the Alps. In 1173 the count-king Alfons I revived the peace of Roussillon in a newly injunctive form that was promptly extended to the whole range of his Catalan-speaking counties.[139] And in 1179 the Third Lateran Council, while reiterating old rules about the truce, added the explicitly 'innovative' injunction that clergy, merchants, and peasants be secure from new exactions.[140]

These statutes mark a new stage in the history of the medieval peace. But this point is far from self-evident. Normative and prescriptive, the texts cannot, with one exception, be linked to known specific causes or outrages. Verbally, even conceptually, they stand in a tradition dating from the tenth century. Moreover, because they are proof of the violence they aim to remedy, they point to an incessant failure of territorial justice in the regions where the Peace of God had originated: the hilly lands

[138] Records printed by André Duchesne, *Historiae Francorum scriptores* IV, 583–84.

[139] In addition to T. N. Bisson, 'The organized peace in southern France and Catalonia (c. 1140–1223),' *AHR* LXXXII (1977) 296–97 (*MFrPN* 221–22), see *Cartulaire de la cathédrale de Dax . . .* , ed. and tr. (French) Georges Pon, Jean Cabanot (Dax 2004) no. 142, referring to work by Frédéric Boutoulle.

[140] *COD* 222, cc. 21–22.

extending from the upper Loire valley to the Ebro. The violence of roads and fields was hardly confined to this space, as the exceptional sworn peace of Soissons (1155) reminds us; some consequence of that event may be read in appeals to King Louis VII, to his successor, and to other northern princes, that multiplied from the 1160s.[141] Indeed, the novelty of the Mediterranean statutes can only be grasped in wider perspectives of peace after mid-century. In England a wholly distinct though equally venerable tradition of the king's peace was revived in the Assize of Clarendon (1166) and reaffirmed in Hubert Walter's 'royal edict' of 1195.[142] In the empire Frederick Barbarossa renewed the *Landfrieden*, which dated from the troubles of the later eleventh century, in the edict of Roncaglia (1158).[143] In both instances peace had become a facet of royal justice, in need of local enforcement in England, and a mandatory alternative to violence in Germany. By comparison, the papal initiatives look retrograde. Like the Lateran councils of 1123 and 1139, that of 1179 dealt with the Truce, reiterating old rules of enforcement, and it seems likely that Alexander III had heard some complaint from prelates bent on more forceful measures when a chapter correctly claiming novelty was added to that relating to *treugae*. 'We innovate,' the text reads, in requiring that priests, monks, pilgrims, merchants, and peasants on the roads and in their fields, even their animals bearing seed, be secure, and suffer no 'new exaction of tolls without the authority of kings and the consent of princes.'[144] Here was a decree in support of public powers, reserving for the clergy only the sanction of excommunication.

Those powers had been there first. Already in the eleventh century the popes were confirming local initiatives without

---

[141] *HF* XVI, 130–31 (nos. 399, 401); Rigord cc. 23, 34–35 (I, 36, 51–52); *Gestes des évêques d'Auxerre* II, 115–21; Platelle, *Justice seigneuriale de Saint-Amand* 431–33.

[142] *SC* 170–73, 257–58.   [143] *DDFrI* II, no. 241.

[144] *COD* 193 c. 15; 199 c. 12; 222 cc. 21–22; and for canonist commentary Hoffmann, *Gottesfriede* 231–40.

proclaiming them; and it was from the proclamation of 1095 that the twelfth-century Lateran decrees descend. So the novelty in 1179 lay not so much in a redefined programmatic peace as in an endorsement of regional measures. In the very next year Pope Alexander was content to commend Duke Kazimierz II of Poland for renouncing the custom of despoiling deceased prelates and their churches.[145] So it happened that, whatever his intention—and he had but a few more months to live—, Alexander III presided over the convergence and diffusion of two traditions of violence long known yet normatively distinct in west European lands: the brutalities suffered from their lords by peasants and those suffered by clerical communities.

By a sort of conceptual inertia, spoliation had not figured in the Peace of God. It remained under attack in the later twelfth century and may fairly be regarded an element of the general disorder the popes sought to remedy in prospect of a new crusade.[146] But the papal strategists were slow to recognize that to pacify dynastic combatants might be to release multiplied knights and mercenaries from the discipline of elite command. Their violence was like an eruption bursting through the crust of customary castellan brutality around 1150–60. Achille Luchaire was (doubly) mistaken to write of the 'habitual brigandage of the feudal class [*féodalité*],'[147] for there is nothing in earlier records to match the indignant denunciations of armed bands living by plunder that fill the local narratives of the later twelfth century. The violence in the Gévaudan stared down by the eccentric Bishop Aldebert in the 1160s was not simply that of arbitrary demands on peasants and seizures from travellers passing below a bandit-castle; he had fortified his 'rural village' of Mende so as to resist the attacks of

---

[145] Vincent Kadłubek, *Chronica Polonorum* iv.8–9, ed. Marian Plezia (Kraków 1994) 147–50; *Alexandri III . . . epistolae et privilegia*, PL CC, no. 1512 (1304–05). See further, about this, p. 575, below

[146] I. S. Robinson in *NCMH* iv:1, 419.

[147] *La société française au temps de Philippe-Auguste* (Paris 1909) 17, quoted in my translation.

'faithless' Gascons, Aragonese, and 'Germans.'[148] Allusions to 'Brabançons' and *coterelli* multiply thereafter. Already in 1171 Frederick I and Louis VII had agreed not to retain 'such wicked men,' which can hardly have eased the scourge; and about 1180 Walter Map wrote that the 'Brabançons,' having begun as 'robbers,' had become so numerous 'that they settle in safety or wander through provinces and kingdoms, hated by God and the people.'[149]

Such men, said to be violators of the peace, became the targets of some of the local initiatives. By Rigord's account the coterels in Berry were guilty of the same offences as bad lords and castellans: seizing people for ransom, beating men and violating wives, despoiling churches.[150] And it was in this context that this southern-born chronicler of Philip Augustus introduced the story of a poor carpenter at Le Puy-en-Velay.[151] This man's response to local violence in the Massif Central became famous overnight. It is the only incident that we can associate with the proliferating institutes of peace that have been mentioned, and it is deeply illuminating for the study of power.

THE CAPUCHINS OF VELAY

No fewer than seven or eight near contemporary accounts have survived, incontestable proof of the story's impact.[152] What is more, these records are sufficiently independent that one need only hold to what they have in common, or to what they disagree about least, to reconstruct the likely course of events. On about Saint Andrew's day (30 November) 1182 a humble carpenter

---

[148] *Chronicon breve de gestis Aldeberti* c. 2 (126).

[149] Robert of Torigni, *Chronique* II, 42–43, 50–51, 81–82; *CAP* I, no. 237; Walter Map, *De nugis* i.29.

[150] *Gesta* cc. 23–24. See also *GrH* II, 120.

[151] Rigord cc. 23–25.

[152] The texts to be used here are Geoffroi de Vigeois, Robert of Torigni, Rigord, Gervase of Canterbury, Robert of Auxerre, the *Gesta pontificum Autissiodorensium*, the 'Anonymous of Laon,' and Guiot de Provins. Acute modern commentary in Duby, *Trois ordres* 393–402 (*Three orders* 327–36).

named Durand went before Bishop Peire of Le Puy and urged that he do something 'to reform the peace.' Rebuffed by the bishop, Durand found many supporters, of whom more than four hundred swore to a first pact of peace soon after Christmas. By Easter their swelling numbers, having surpassed five thousand, could no longer be counted. All this according to the Limousin prior Geoffroi de Vigeois, who wrote within a year of these events. He goes on to say that Durand 'instituted institutes [*instituit instituta*] of peace.' These consisted of a uniform code of dress, a solemn oath preceded by confession of sins, an annual payment of six pennies at Pentecost 'in' [or 'to?'] the brotherhood,' a once-for-life payment of one *poyes* in a leaden receptacle, and the commitment of the sworn men to fight when summoned. Canons and monks who swore were dispensed from fighting on condition of praying. Conspicuous in white capes, with cloth pendants front and back resembling the woolen pallium worn by archbishops, the sworn brothers were a visible moral force if not quite a rival clergy. Over their breasts hung an image of the Virgin and Son bearing the circular inscription *Agnus Dei, qui tollis peccata mundi, dona nobis pacem*. Durand's institutes were confirmed by his bishop in a festival assembly on Assumption Day (15 August) 1183. At that time knights were joined in the cause by 'princes, bishops, abbots, monks, clerics, and women without husbands'; and the assault on Castle-*dun* a few days later resulted in the killing of a 'prince of robbers' together with many hundreds of coterels.[153]

What happened next is harder to reconstruct, for none of the other sources were so close (in time or space) to the experience as Geoffroi, who wrote no more. But Robert of Torigni and Rigord, writing in the 1180s, largely confirm his account of the first year, while setting the Capuchins in a wider context of explanation. Both represented Durand as motivated by the miraculous

---

[153] Geoffroi de Vigeois, *Chronica*, ed. Philippe Labbe, *Nova bibliotheca manuscriptorum . . .* , 2 vols. (Paris 1657) II, 339, c. 22 (to be read together with the corrected text in *HF* XVIII, 219).

apparition of the Virgin Mary, while Rigord, having noted the atrocities that had provoked the poor carpenter, saw him and his movement as God's choice to relieve the suffering caused by the war between the king of Aragon and the count of Toulouse.[154] Robert of Auxerre, whose annals for 1183 and 1184 may have been first written in those years, is the first to describe the Capuchin campaigns; he was also the first to record a massive reaction against this motley force of (mostly) lesser men pretending to do without lords. Their arrival in 'France' (regions north of Velay) and their 'insolent' refusal to submit to their betters ended in their 'destruction' by the French princes. Conceding that they had begun well, Robert thought that the Capuchins had been overtaken by the 'angel of Satan.'[155]

Other texts carry this disapproval much further. Their authors knew that the Capuchins had a cause, knew that many regions of (greater) France had been infested by desperate and violent men—*rouergats*, Aragonese, Gascons, Brabançons–; men who looked and spoke differently (from us); mercenaries all.[156] But these writers could no longer say anything to justify an association of men so manifestly subversive of lordship. For Guiot de Provins Durand was a venal impostor; for the 'Anonymous of Laon' a simple man deceived by a malicious canon disguised as the Virgin. Brilliantly opinionated, the 'Anonymous' touches on all the points known from other texts and distorts them mercilessly, save for one alone that takes us to the very heart of the matter. The Capuchins, he wrote, were madmen from the start. For him the enabling assembly of the Assumption (August 1183), so far from being the ratification of a grand impulse, was a self-indulgent orgy of worldly and (worse) mercantile opulence, its corruptly overheated materialism nurturing the foul trick

---

[154] Robert of Torigni, *Chronique* II, 126; Rigord cc. 23–24 (36–37).

[155] Robert of Auxerre, *Chronicon*, ed. O. Holder-Egger, *MGHSS* XXVI, 247–48.

[156] Gervase of Canterbury, *Chronicle* I, 300–302; *Gestes des évêques d'Auxerre* II, 179–83; and citations in next note.

played on Durand. Next comes an account of the conjuration, of which the commitments and pieties are made to look suspiciously unorthodox. The oath of the brethren fares no better: it was said to associate the 'princes' with brigand-knights as enemies of the peace. And the peace-tax, plausibly amounting to 6*d.* in Geoffroi's account, is doubled to 12*d.* in this version, resulting (it was claimed) in an ugly swollen treasury of abuse soon amounting to £400,000![157]

Overblown rhetoric? At its close this narrative sounds a different note, in two sentences, separated by a muddled account of Capuchin military successes. Here they are: 'Everywhere the princes trembled, not daring to impose anything unjust on their people, nor presuming to require any exactions or impositions from them except their customary renders . . . [with these successes to boast of] their insane folly drove these foolish and undisciplined people to command counts and viscounts, and other princes as well, to treat their subjects more gently than was customary if they wished not to incur their indignation.'[158]

HERE WAS exposed the raw nerve of a clumsy aggregate of fortified societies that was hardly yet France. Nothing less than lordship itself seemed threatened by the hooded men of 'peace.' Outrageous that princes should be limited to just or customary impositions! In their pernicious solidarity, wrote the chronicler of the bishops of Auxerre, the hoods 'had no fear, no reverence for higher powers,' forgetting that servitude had been the just consequence of the sin by which people had lost their primal liberty. When Bishop Hugues and his knights captured some Capuchins

---

[157] Guiot de Provins, *La Bible*, in *Les oeuvres de Guiot de Provins* . . . , ed. John Orr (Manchester 1915) ll. 1927–88 (70–71); Anonymous of Laon, ed. Alexander Cartellieri, Wolf Stechele, *Chronicon universale Anonymi Laudunensis* . . . (Leipzig 1909) 37–40.

[158] *Chronicon*, 39.

in his patrimonial village of Gy, he deliberately reduced them to elemental poverty, so 'that they learn that serfs may not rise against their lords.'[159] The norm of power, even in kingless lands of castles and princes, was lordship: a precedence of affective superiority—indeed, of nobility—as well as of armed might. And by this plausible account, when the Capuchins saw, with the pity of an archbishop of Sens, that they could not prevail against instituted lordships, however violent, their movement collapsed.

Were the frightened magnates right about the hoods? Had these people lost faith in local lords? No more fundamental question can be raised in this book. And because we may be sure of the fright, it is possible to answer that some Capuchins, at least, must have relished the idea of 'getting even.' For it is all but certain that from the moment when Durand's institutes were agreed upon, some distinction must have been made between the violence of coterels and Brabançons and that of lords. The early enlistment of magnates could only have rested on that consideration. Once that distinction was lost, the cause was lost.

Whatever their fears, the critics of the Capuchins were surely mistaken about one thing: the initial purpose. Geoffroi de Vigeois got it right when, with honest plausibility, he described an original pact of associative action. Such events are not unheard of in previous generations, but they typically proved ephemeral or else, as in the organizing of urban utilities, went unrecorded. Durand's 'institutes of peace' do not survive in writing, and may never have been written, but they are, as we know them, rational and socially purposive: the solemn oath, surely bound to the commitment to fight when summoned, the pecuniary assessment, and the uniform.

The Capuchins of Velay illustrate a wider phenomenon that may be spoken of as the organized peace.[160] The early Peace of

---

[159] *Gestes* II, 181, 183.

[160] If I am not mistaken, this concept originated with my article of 1977 ('The organized peace . . .' *AHR* LXXXII); it is borrowed by Alan Harding, *Medieval law and the foundations of the state* (2002) ch. 4, where it is used to similar

God had deployed relics so as to evoke repentance in the violent, and this mode of affective pacification persisted in the Gévaudan in the twelfth century.[161] But this was not Bishop Aldebert's way at first, nor was it Durand's a few years later; it was symptomatic that a pseudo-apparition of the Virgin was concocted to discredit the Capuchins at Le Puy. What matters about the social planning described above is that it corresponds to other institutes of peace in Durand's time. Prior Geoffroi's very word *institutum* rings bells, for the peace of Narbonne (1155) had been termed *institutio*, and many other statutes from 1148 to 1226 in regions extending from the Ebro valley to the Provençal Alps show that peace as a matter of enforcement had become a mode of power competitive with princely and castellan lordships. Mechanisms specific to the peace were routinely provided for: oaths to secure the peace, armies of enforcement, taxation to support such armies or to compensate the victims of violence, even (after 1200) officers to police the peace.[162]

All this was new in Durand's day. There had been written institutes to accompany the sanctified peace, to be sure, even precedents for oaths and armies; but no such obligations had been secured in the early instituted peace. It was only when the new scourge of rootless knights arose around 1140–60 that the peace was reorganized in concretely functional ways; so it comes as no surprise that the newly printed Gascon peace of ca. 1148 is the first to specify a remedial army of enforcement together with a financial subsidy. Whereas the old oaths had been passively negative, like oaths of fidelity, the new ones such as appear

---

effect yet without notice of the chronological divide around 1140–60 that it implies.

[161] *Les Miracles de Saint-Privat . . .* 8, 38, 54, 105.

[162] *Papsturkunden für Templer und Johanniter . . .* , ed. Rudolf Hiestand (Göttingen 1972) no. 27; BnF, Collection Moreau 68, fols. 1–2, 4–5v; *HL* VIII, *preuves* no. 6 (275–76); *CPT* no. 14; *Cartulaire de l'église collégiale Saint-Seurin de Bordeaux*, ed. J.-A. Brutails (Bordeaux 1897) no. 24; *ACP* no. 102 art. 28. Fuller discussion in Bisson, 'Organized peace.'

in the statutes of Elne (1156) and Tarascon (1226) included positive commitments to serve in the peace-force and to pay the peace-tax.[163]

Moreover, circumstances worked to widen the scope of the peace. The security of rural property had been identified as a focal category of concern in Pyrenean counties, where it was known as the 'peace of beasts' (*pax bestiarum*; *bovaticum*), and in the province of Narbonne; and an old disposition to shelter the stability of coinage under the peace was confirmed.[164] But the most pregnant change in peace-making after 1150 was of another and more problematic sort.

It was a liability of the Capuchins that their impulse was grounded in penitential devotion. Guiot de Provins viewed them as yet another troublesome religious order; but much worse, and very early, the hoods were likened to heretics. An oath to Bishop Gaucelm of Lodève from the 1160s not only renounces dicing, as did the sectarians of Velay, but lumps malefactors with heretics.[165] In the *Deeds of the bishops of Auxerre* the peace-men were seen as endangering the unity of the faith.[166] And what was getting back to the Holy See about suspicious deviants from Catholic practise, especially after scares in the 1160s when Pope Alexander was in France, carried more weight in the church than anxiety about human suffering. What came to be known as the 'business of the peace and faith' (*negotium pacis et fidei*) not only exacerbated local religious tensions; it weakened efforts to suppress the ravages of unpaid knights, let alone to mitigate the prevailing arbitrariness of lordships. None of these problems had been resolved when Pope Innocent III threw his energies into promoting the crusade and combating heretics. Perhaps not everyone in southern France welcomed the *negotium pacis et fidei* when hundreds of people were

---

[163] *Cart. Dax*, no. 142; BnF, Moreau 68, fols. 1–2; *ACP* no. 102.

[164] *LFM* II, no. 691; *CC* 50–64.

[165] *Cartulaire de Béziers* (*Livre noir*), ed. J. Rouquette (Paris 1918) no. 223.

[166] *Gestes* II, 179, 181.

massacred at Béziers in October 1209, followed by uncompre-
hending, oppressive violence in years to come.[167]

To suggest that an effort is futile is not, of course, to deny the
effort, nor even to doubt its impact. It bears repeating that the Lateran decrees of 1179 went everywhere in Latin Europe; that the
spoliation of widowed churches in Poland was prohibited by a great
territorial prince in 1180, a measure unique of its kind that was
promptly confirmed by Alexander III; and that a cardinal-legate
with long experience in the Hispanic realms served as Pope Celes-
tine III in the 1190s.[168] Yet it would be mistaken to conclude that
the lawyer-popes were bent on pacifying a troubled Europe. For
all their familiarity with turbulent homelands (Tuscany, the Lazio),
they did little to prove the slightest awareness of the 'shadowed
peace' and its torments. Responsive to the noisy yelps of those
thought worthy of God's help, anxious to subvert distractions from
crusading, they tried fitfully to mediate the Capetian-Plantagenet
conflicts. To suppress bands of violent knights was equally useful
(and futile). What they could not do, and never tried, was to side
with the suffering masses against their masters. It can hardly be
doubted that the elite reaction against the Capuchins of Velay was
congenial to the successors of Alexander III.

It follows that pacification was a local or regional phenomenon.
About the geography there need be no cavil. The institutes and
statutes of peace, those here overlooked as well as those cited,
relate to vast stretches of Europe where it was found useful to
prescribe solemn constraints on violence and even coercive remedial action. How such norms were realized in practise largely es-
capes our view, because peace-making was not bureaucratic; it
was contrivances ad hoc, not government. Even so, it seems safe
to conclude that the organized peace was something more than
peace-making, more than the justice of rights or the stifling of

---

[167] M.-H. Vicaire, '"L'affaire de paix et de foi" du Midi de la France,' *Paix de
Dieu et guerre sainte en Languedoc au XIII* siècle* (Toulouse 1969) 102–27; Bernard
Hamilton in *NCMH* v (1999) ch. 6.

[168] V. Pfaff, 'Papst Coelestin III.,' *ZRG Kan. Abt.* XLVII (1961) 109–28.

feuds or wars. Dissuasion from violence or the changing of hearts:
were not these within its limits? This is another critical question.
And the evidence about this, if problematic, is hardly equivocal.
The Capuchins, by several accounts, devised a penitential culture
of peace. In the turbulent mountains of Old Catalonia the
preacher of Organyà (ca. 1180–1200) taught love as well as resig-
nation; and for him charity (*caritad*) was *abstinència de mal*.[169] That
malefactors could be softened in the awful presence of holy relics
cannot have been forgotten in the twelfth century. If few founded
monasteries, like Pons of Léras,[170] others too must have given up
the bad life in unrecorded repentance. Was not shame, too, a
mode of pacification? Our best proofs may be yet to come, but
this scene is already familiar. Could the bad castellan of La Garde
Guérin (ca. 1166–68) have suffered any worse fate than to be
hauled before 'the whole populace' of Mende to relinquish his
bad customs?[171]

But the sacramental phenomenon of peace was overtaken by
princely justice after about 1160. The institutes of southern France
coincided with the Assize of Clarendon and the Inquest of Sheriffs
in England (1166, 1170), with the imposition of a royal territorial
peace in Catalonia (for the first time defined geographically as
such, 1173–1214), and with the promulgation of fully secular statutes of the lord-kings' justice over violence at once in Aragon and
León in 1188. Yet even in these manifestations, compassion—the
affective comprehension of human suffering—played some part. In
Catalonia the priority of memorials of rural complaint suggest that
the new statutory peace was responsive to the experience of power.
Moreover, the sworn adhesion of barons and knights brought a
conspicuous element of religious compunction to the recognition
of this peace; and the statutes of León were likewise sworn.[172]

[169] *Homilies d'Organyà* 42. [170] Above, p. 287.
[171] *Chronicon breve* c. 15 (133).
[172] *TV* 104–11; *CPT*, nos. 14–21; Julio González, *Alfonso IX*, 2 vols. (Madrid
1944) II, nos. 11, 12.

However local, however disjointed the consensus, the repression of violence in later twelfth-century Europe was, indeed, something like pacification. Religious motives remained in play, not only because the compunction of violent men was involved, or because the suffering of afflicted people could be heard here or there, but also because the mature statutes of peace were invested with the biblical ideology of kingship. In the peace of Urgell (May 1187) the same invocations of peace known to preachers instructed by Alan of Lille echo Proverbs on the 'divine majesty by which kings reign . . .'[173] But it cannot be claimed that the church, as such, had a policy of peace. Policies of any sort were still in short supply in Latin Europe towards 1200.

Politicised Power

On 29 December 1170 four knights violated the sanctuary of Canterbury cathedral, seized the archbishop, and hacked him to death with their swords. Leaving the body alone for a time, they returned to plunder the dead prelate's rooms, carrying off money, precious objects, liturgical vestments, and movables of all sorts. Local mourners, shocked and cowed, held back in horror.[174]

The murder of Thomas Becket was instantly notorious. Miracles about his tomb led to his canonization as early as 1173; dedications and graphic representations of his martyrdom spread about Europe; and in all ages from then to now this act of violence is remembered as the most heinous crime of the European twelfth century.[175] The murder, that is, for the plunder, being a recognized custom of the age, was a less memorable event. Although it

---

[173] *CPT*, no. 16; Prov. viii.15.

[174] Willliam Fitzstephen, *Vita sancti Thomae* . . . cc. 136–45, *Materials* III, 135–46; Herbert of Bosham, *Vita sancti Thomae* . . . vi.1–16, *Materials* III, 491–514; John of Salisbury, *Letters* . . . , ed. W. J. Millor *et al.*, 2 vols. (Oxford 1979, 1986) II, no. 305.

[175] Frontispiece. See generally Warren, *Henry II* 509–19; Frank Barlow, *Thomas Becket* (Berkeley 1986) ch. 12.

figured in detail in the memoirs of outraged contemporaries, it is nowhere to be found in Eliot's *Murder in the cathedral*. Yet in the human experience of its moment—and there were witnesses both famous and obscure, to say nothing of people far, wide, and lowly who, having heard of Thomas Becket, could reasonably hope to invoke his saintly power—the plunder went with the murder. For the murder was deeply symptomatic of a mode of power in which plunder was of the essence. Had not the brutal knights foregathered at Saltwood castle, where in view of Canterbury Ranulf de Broc acted the very part of a predatory castellan? Moreover, Henry II had lately been reminded that the spoliation of deceased prelates was a 'bad custom' of whole kingdoms, including England. The king, as we have seen, was not himself the bad castellan he had often assaulted—far from it. But neither was he an ideologue, and this was so to the extent of refusing to engage with Becket's insistence on high principle. For his part, Becket fell short of persuading his bishops that the 'freedom of the church' was a defensible position. So for both there lurked an insistence on obedience together with the possibility that its failure might mean infidelity—the violation of a solemn oath—or, worse, betrayal. This murder in the cathedral was yet another breach of peace, this one his lord-king's peace twice sought by Becket in preceding months, yet to the end ominously lacking the king's kiss.[176]

The conflict that resulted in the murder was a crisis of lordship. It was above all else a matter of customs, rights, (personal) fidelity (and suspicion and distrust); and it originated in a wilful act of the lord-king. That King Henry acted out his lordship can have surprised no one in the 1160s; what is critical to understand is that Thomas Becket did the same. Both men were officers in an ideological order: that was not in question. Neither saw the slightest discrepancy between their public commitments and their personal dominations. Becket's penchant for hunting and pompous

---

[176] Fitzstephen, *Vita* cc. 97, 107, 125, 128, 132 (100, 108–11, 126, 129–32); Herbert of Bosham, *Vita* iv.26 (418–22).

adulation had marked him out as a would-be noble lord from his time in service to Archbishop Theobald; and his biographers leave us in no doubt that Archbishop Thomas never gave up his quasi-noble deportment. Like the lord-king, he had his own dependents in homage and fealty, not only as chancellor but still as archbishop, and it was critical to his status in the conflict that he considered the suffragan bishops his 'men' in their sworn fidelity to him.[177]

If ever a medieval conflict cried out for a 'political solution' it was this one. Given the visibly increasing activity of lay courts, few can have misunderstood when Henry II sought an agreement with the English bishops about the customary limits of secular and clerical jurisdictions. But he had been incautious—impolitic, shall we say; un-political?—in springing something on the prelates and barons assembled with him at Clarendon in January 1164: his wish to have the customs of jurisdiction put in writing and approved under oath by the magnates. Becket had sided with the bishops in opposing this approval, which posed serious issues of commitment, custom, and canon law; then under fierce pressure from the king, he had given in. Moreover, just as King Henry had seemingly made no effort to explain to the bishops why he thought it needful to ratchet up his proposal about the customs, so Becket was said to have neglected in the assembly or behind closed doors to explain his own change of mind or heart to the bishops. 'He neither took their counsel nor advised them,' wrote W. L. Warren; 'his capitulation was as impetuous and wilful as his resistance.' Worse yet, it left Archbishop Thomas vulnerable to the king's festering suspicions about his fidelity. Knowing that the prelate had repented of his oath to uphold the Constitutions, Henry moved adroitly to impose his royal lordship harshly. An appeal to the king against the archbishop became the occasion for summoning Becket to justify his judgment against a

---

[177] Fitzstephen cc. 10–12 (20–22), 18 (29), 53 (63), 63 (72), 66 (74), 122 (124), 125 (126–27); Herbert of Bosham iii.15 (227–28), 19 (251), 20 (254), 25 (275); v.7 (478–79).

tenant and then (November 1164) to a condemnation of Becket for his unwary response to the summons. Underscoring the solemn affectivity of the bond Becket had allegedly betrayed, the bishops and barons referred not merely to his oath of fidelity but also to the 'tie of liege homage.' Becket was judged contumacious, and he stood to lose his lands and lordships.[178]

It was a hollow success for the king. Not only were the bishops and barons unsure of their own judgment, but Becket's predictable appeal to the pope was bound to delay any execution of the sentence. The occasion for the judgment was a council at Northampton marked less by leadership than by posturing. Having found little to say about the council at Clarendon, Becket's biographers kept veritable journals of this one. In fairness to Becket, he could only have rallied the bishops to his cause by foreseeing how arbitrary would be the condemnation imposed by the lord-king. Yet his reasonable protest thereafter, that his alleged infraction was minor, was made to rest on a recitation of Canterbury's privileges unlikely to win over the bishops. The king did no better with them. Rather than comforting the men who had given him the judgment he demanded, he brought further charges against Becket, yet another sign of the lordly posture he was taking. As was customary, Henry had cultivated allies in the episcopate without having created a following, let alone settled on a policy that more than two or three of them could accept.[179]

King Henry had assembled his bishops and barons not to persuade but to applaud while, day after day, he brought new charges. The inert perplexity of these men had been fully exposed when, on the first day, before the king's demand that they pronounce the sentence, they had associated long enough to disclaim the obligation. The barons would have gladly left it to the bishops to

---

[178] Warren, *Henry II* 473–88; quotation from 474. The Constitutions of Clarendon are in *SC* 163–67. On fidelity and homage, clearly distinguished, Fitzstephen c. 40 (52).

[179] Fitzstephen cc. 38–61 (49–70); Herbert of Bosham iii.32–38 (296–312).

attaint one of their own, while the bishops retorted that they sat in this 'secular judgment' not as bishops but as barons. In the end, the king prevailed on the aged Bishop Henry of Winchester to say what everyone knew the other bishops had agreed to. And when on the final day King Henry learned from them that Archbishop Thomas had chastised them for daring to judge him in a secular proceeding, and had appealed to the pope against them, Henry understandably demanded that they join the barons in a further condemnation. The bishops this time put it to Becket that he had placed them in the impossible situation of having to disobey either him or the lord-king. Striking a deal with the king, they were prepared to appeal to Rome against their archbishop, who when the climactic moment arrived, refused even to hear the verdict; who asked that night for the king's safe-conduct; and who then slipped away before daybreak.[180] So the crisis went on—and on—marked by patience on both sides as well as intransigeance, a 'shadowed peace,' this one, that would end in violence.

What William Fitzstephen and Herbert of Bosham reveal in narratives well nigh unique of their kind in the twelfth century is not so much the failure of 'political action' as its continued irrelevance. Already at Northampton and increasingly during his exile in France, Thomas Becket was disposed to argue for the 'liberty of the church.' At the end he famously contended that this could not be compromised. It was a matter of right, not policy. Moreover, he cast about for allies quite as all lord-princes were used to doing. At some points his 'case' might thus have become a 'cause,' yet there is no sign that he thought it negotiable. As for King Henry, his anger as ever was overtaken by reconsiderations; yet with him the violated vow of obedience became an absolute. At once naturally and ironically, this was an absolute the doomed archbishop could understand.[181]

---

[180] Fitzstephen cc. 40–54 (52–64).

[181] ibid., c. 107 (108–11); David Knowles, 'Archbishop Thomas Becket: a character study,' *PBA* xxxv (1949) 198–205.

※

IF THE principals in this epic dispute could not recognize their causes as negotiable, it was because they were born and bred in cultures of lordship and nobility that prevailed widely and deeply in the twelfth century. It is not because it was unthinkable in the 1160s to hold 'political views' such as would become common-place in later centuries. Unlike the moralists of a few years later Thomas Becket saw no conflict between *praeese* and *prodesse*;[182] neither he nor his great adversary could have doubted that power is rightly oriented towards the social needs of people. Like other princely lords they surely supposed that they were 'governing' as well as dominating their peoples. They clung to the presumption of a public order challenged or violated by others. Writing after 1165 in support of Archbishop Thomas, John of Salisbury often referred to King Henry's regime as a 'public power.'[183]

Whatever this implied for John's feelings about his lord-king, it betrayed conceptual poverty: John had no word for 'government,' indeed scarcely even euphemisms. What he wrote about was power, its modalities, excesses, and limitations. He wrote in near constant disillusionment, holding up the 'political constitution of the ancients' for commendation in contrast with the immoderate self-indulgence of modern hunter-lords.[184] He once wrote of the *res publica* as a 'mundane polity [*polisi*],' one of his few allusions to the 'political' in any form of the word.[185] Nor were those ideologists of public order, the lawyers, much more inventive. At least one of them, however, by virtue of familiarity with Ciceronian ethics, may be cited to confirm that a classical notion of polity was indeed in the air. Writing about 1130 in southern France, an

---

[182] Fitzstephen c. 53 (64).

[183] *The correspondence of Thomas Becket archbishop of Canterbury (1162–1170)*, ed. Anne J. Duggan, 2 vols. (Oxford 2000) I, no. 7; *Letters of John of Salisbury* II, nos. 246, 262, 300.

[184] *Policraticus* v.1 (I, 281), 5 (298); and passim.

[185] *Letters* II, no. 288; see also *Policraticus* i.3 (I, 20); vii.23 (II, 209).

anonymous jurist defined 'political [things, *politice*]' with reference to prudence before virtually concluding that all four cardinal virtues inform social order, or the 'public thing' (*res publica*). 'Political virtues,' he wrote, 'pertain to those charged with governing the public thing. . . . Political [ones] are of man because he is a social animal.' And 'just as peace is acquired by arms so it can only be preserved by laws.'[186] John of Salisbury shared this view. His organic conception of society implies as much. Yet that very metaphor, together with John's fixation on power, blinded him to the convenience of categorizing power for the public good as government, let alone to recognize 'political government' as something other than a tautology. The changes of interest to this book did not wholly escape him. He knew about offices, and—characteristically—how they were abused; yet could not see how the forms of their abuse were of a piece with his society.[187] What lay beyond him was the 'politicising' of cause and interest. And for this point to become clear a longer perspective is required.

That power in medieval Europe could have been anything other than 'political' has seldom been questioned. All societies, it is said, have governments, however rudimentary, and governments are political by nature. Joseph R. Strayer wrote of feudalism as 'government reduced to lowest terms,' as 'a way of accomplishing certain essential political acts.'[188] He had justice in mind, and there is, to be sure, a sense in which any power that seeks to legitimate itself and therefore to judge those whom it subjects may be regarded as political. Susan Reynolds refers to 'political collectivity' and to 'political units' within which medieval peoples assumed objective identities.[189] In such capacious senses as these it would be pointless to deny that medieval societ-

---

[186] *Summa 'Justiniani est in hoc opere'* i.1 (23); also (p.) 21.

[187] *Policraticus* v.4, 11, 12, 16 (1, 290, 330, 334, 354).

[188] J. R. Strayer, *Medieval statecraft and the perspectives of history* (Princeton 1971) 63, 65, 77.

[189] 'Government and community,' *NCMH* IV:1, 86–87.

ies have a continuous political history. Moreover, it is in this perspective that government may be viewed as conceptually continuous. When dealing with dynastic disruption, as in Maine (1098), Germany (1125), and Flanders (1127), the chroniclers were wont to refer to public affairs (or the like) falling into the hands of magnates, as if these 'natural representatives' of territorial polities had *agenda* other than their late prince's lordship. Towards 1131 Bishop Hildebert spoke of Count Geoffrey's *administratio* in exhorting him to be steadfast in service to his people.[190]

But these understandings of 'political' action and 'government' are less innocent than they appear. They not only tend to confuse government with public order—a mistake no intelligent peasant in the twelfth century could have made—; they also tend to identify political behaviour with dynastic events, judgments, wars, and taxation. They obscure the problem of historical change while perpetuating conceptual anachronism. The very possibility that judgments or impositions might be better understood as familial or friendly or proprietary is excluded. Think of the 'political histories' of France and other European lands in which events of the 'political' are set forth, but not the modalities![191] Ways of doing things, of talking, evolve. If we choose to regard any exercise of power as political, we are in danger—as was John of Salisbury, who had a better excuse—of overlooking some all but imperceptible changes in the associative life of the twelfth century that appear in retrospect to have been fundamental to European state-building. For two reasons. First, because the very idea of political behaviour seems to have been new in the thirteenth century, being a revival of Aristotelian social theory together with the utilitarian precepts from Roman law and letters. The doctrine

---

[190] OV x.18 (V, 304–6); Otto of Freising, *Gesta* i.17; Galbert of Bruges, *De multro*; *PL* CLXXI, 282.

[191] The point holds notably with respect to older national and collaborative histories, such as those by Georg Waitz, Gustave Glotz, the old *Cambridge medieval history*, ed. J. B. Bury (1912–36; chapters by Corbett, Halphen, Powicke, and Petit-Dutaillis); but also to the *NCMH* IV:2.

that people interact socially for legitimate this-worldly ends evidently corresponded to realities in contemporary secular life; and if we speak of those realities as 'political' then that word would seem to denote something new in the history of power. This is not to argue that associative action was unprecedented, but rather that the burgeoning of collective enterprise in towns and estates was (even so) a salient novelty in the twelfth century.

Second, it is not enough for historians to record the foundations of urban communities, administrative institutions, and estates if they do not also inquire how people interacted in these new agencies and settings. If in all ages officials resist accountability, the devices for exploiting delegated powers seem almost everywhere, well into the thirteenth century, to betray ambitions to noble lordship.[192] Do we yet have the least idea how, and how well, the early oaths of office, such as those introduced in chapter V, were observed?—and violated? What is yet securely known about the attitudes of incipient European bureaucracies?

These reasons and questions need not preclude a 'political' approach to the twelfth century. They merely suggest that research into 'societal' circumstances will teach us more about authority and constraint amongst peoples different from ourselves. What resonates in their records is (coercive) power. Those who possess it may be labelled 'power(s),' which is how John of Salisbury referred to Henry II.[193] Writing about *pouvoirs*, French scholars of the past generation were close to the sources; and their conceptual distinction between *pouvoirs* and *puissances* helpfully evokes a problematic reality of the twelfth century. The 'forces' (*puissances*) that Jan Dhondt discerned in the Flemish crisis of 1127–28 were heralds of those collective powers that would later inform the politicised societies of estates.[194] What would it take for a

---

[192] For one instance, see below, p. 581. Arguably, some exceptions may be found in Italian cities before 1200.

[193] *Letters* II, no. 246; cf. nos. 262, 300, 304.

[194] Duby, *Société mâconnaise; De Toulouse à Tripoli. La puissance toulousaine au XIIᵉ siècle* (Toulouse 1989) 15, 70; Dhondt, ' "Ordres" ou "puissances." '

cause like theirs to outlive their acceptance of a new count? Already there were more durable causes, even if half a century later Thomas Becket still could not impose his own. The stability of coinage was a matter of regional consensus as early as 1118 in Cerdanya, while the exemption from uncustomary exactions was a Europe-wide movement if not yet a cause throughout the twelfth century.[195]

All such issues were envisaged as matters of right. Rights or claims might be bargained for, to be sure, but the negotiations leading to settlements between townspeople and their lord-princes, as at Laon in 1128 or at Augsburg in 1152, are seldom visible in the resultant charters.[196] This means that the most fervent solidarities largely escape us in a diplomatic meant to conceal them. And it is in this perspective that a stark contrast comes into view: the rarity with which the word or concept of 'political' is found before 1200 together with a choking profusion of allusions to conjurations and conspiracies in records of every sort.[197] That these words (*coniuratio, conspirare*) often misrepresent peaceable initiatives cannot be doubted; the very term *pax* surely took on new meaning from conceptual compromise. But it is the pejorative sense of 'conspiracy' that prevailed in the twelfth century, the normative reaction of lord-princes who felt themselves to be wrongfully challenged.

What had been lacking before the thirteenth century was a *normal* conception of associative (that is, in Aristotelian terms, political) power, rooted in practise, and distinct from lordship. The natural communities of valley and vill, where they survived at all,

---

[195] *LFM* II, no. 691; and generally *CC*, chs. 4, 5. On the renunciation of exactions, above, pp. 350–58.

[196] e.g., *RAL6* II, no. 277; *Quellensammlung der deutschen Stadt*, no. 65. For the remarkable turbulence at Reims in 1167, John of Salisbury, *Letters* II, no. 223.

[197] Only the tiniest of samples is possible: *HC* i.72 (111–12), ii.53 (321–22); Guibert de Nogent, *Monodiae* iii.5 (302; *Memoirs* 138), 7 (320; *Mem.* 146); John of Salisbury, *Policraticus* vi.25 (II, 75–77); *Oberti cancellarii annales . . .* , ed. L. T. Belgrano, *Annali genovesi di Caffaro e de' suoi continuatori . . .* , 5 vols. (Rome 1890–1901) I, 219–20; JL 4978; Mansi XXII, 949–50.

were too distant or too weak (and many of them too elevated) to impose their sociabilities as such. What Max Weber theorised as patrimonial domination was the prevalent mode of power in post-Carolingian societies; and lordship, sanctioned by fidelity and legitimated by protection, was a social-relational rather than a behavioural structure. It was sociologically personal, affective, and unpolitical in nature.[198] Counsel and (especially) consent were not political functions but devices for ensuring and imposing the lord's will; for creating affective solidarities, typically in ritually ceremonious ways, in lord-kingships, principalities, even in ecclesiastical lordships. Accordingly, the historical problem is how this prevalent mode of lordly power begins to lose its passively affective character: not only how it becomes progressively institutionalized, as seems to have happened with accountability and office, but also how, in courts, causes, consultations, and parleys, a new kind of discourse emerged; a talking less ceremonious and deferential than engaged with issues, in which interests as distinct from rights came to be articulated. Taken together these changes may be spoken of as 'politicising.'

There is reason to believe that this phenomenon became general in the years around 1200. If historians have seldom noticed this, it is because the evidence is unsatisfactory. 'Politicising' should not be confused with what has been called the 'invention of the state.'[199] The resort to 'verbalized rules' instead of custom, the recognition that power resides in law(s) rather than in an 'effluence of character,' may have been stimulated by the Investiture Conflict, and was widely diffused by the clergy in the twelfth century. The *Historia pontificalis* is the work of a courtier-cleric 'listening in' on a newly intense institutional life rooted in argument about rights, offices, and claims. To secure such things the clergy knew how to make friends, how to exert influence.[200] That ecclesiastical jurisdictions promoted rational, rule-bound

---

[198] See Weber, *Economy and society* I part I, ch. 3; II, chs. 9, 10.
[199] Cheyette, 'Invention of the state.'
[200] Colin Morris, *The discovery of the individual 1050–1200* (London 1972) 104.

spheres of discourse is evident from the records of papal judges–delegate.[201] But there is nothing in all this to show that political talk was yet common.

For in reality the Christian clergy and lawyers lived in a chiefly seigneurial world. They were the sons and brothers of barons and knights; they were all too familiar with the imperatives of lordship. They did not easily give up lordly habits of approbatory consultation. Synods were held by bishops and legates who were respected and addressed as lords. Preoccupied by rights and wrongs the prelates in such assemblies were in no hurry, nor did they feel pressed, to reformulate their concerns as social causes worthy of autonomous debate and regulation. So that even in the church neither the formal adherence to written rules nor the presumably sharpened precision of curial discourse seem to have hastened the politicising of power. In 1215 the constitutions of the Fourth Lateran Council were promulgated as the lord-pope's programme, contrived to conceal objections that may have arisen in its formulation; only for the dogmatic decrees on the Trinity and against heretical teachings did Innocent III so much as request the assembly's approval.[202]

Still less do the records of lay power suggest that the interaction in conventions, courts, and assemblies was other than deferential, ceremonial, or juridically procedural towards 1200. As a rule the charters and diplomas of lord-kings in Castile, León, Sicily, and the empire mention the court (*curia*) only as the locus of power or justice, leaving it to the chroniclers to refer to, and sometimes dilate upon, great courts noted for the numbers and

[201] *Decretales ineditae saeculi* XII, ed. Walther Holtzmann *et al.* (Vatican City 1982), nos. 7, 12, 28, 43a, 46, 53, 82; *Letters of John of Salisbury* I, nos. 4, 53, 70, 71, 83; *The letters of Arnulf of Lisieux*, ed. Frank Barlow (London 1939), nos. 65, 77, 78, 91. See also Mary G. Cheney, *Roger, bishop of Worcester*, ch. 2. This is problematic evidence on a point still little investigated. Were proceedings in lay courts so different?

[202] *COD* 230–71; 'A new eyewitness account of the Fourth Lateran Council,' ed. Stephan Kuttner, Antonio García y García, *Traditio* XX (1964) 127–28. See also below, pp. 541–48.

altitudes of those in attendance.[203] It is true that in England the chroniclers become more expansive on elections and treaties, suggesting some recognition of associative interests bearing on the lord-king's decisions. The abbatial elections to Bury-St-Edmunds in 1182 and 1211 are famous cases in point, and the local issues in dispute are visible in successions in many other churches. Yet typically, as in the conciliar discussion (August 1184) of an election at Canterbury, rights not policy are at issue.[204] Indeed, what has been observed about Lateran conciliar statutes is even more characteristic of secular records. Produced by or for lord-princes or descriptive of their activity, they normally conceal whatever happened contrary to deferential approval of the lordly agenda. Where this proves impossible, adversarial conduct and speech are easily condemned as conspiratorial.[205]

The more one reads such records the more suspicious one becomes. How much is surely left out! What are we to make of the commitments of Italian communes to the Guelf cause, like that of Brescia, or to the Ghibellines, like Pisa's? Yet the interested powers—let not *us* call them 'parties,' for they themselves did not—cultivated alliances with communes, not causes (as such).[206] The civic chroniclers of Genoa and Pisa were as reluctant as princes to identify the hawks and doves in the councils and 'parliaments' in which decisions to commit collective manpower and

---

[203] Among countless examples, *Regesta de Fernando II, Selección diplomática* nos. 54, 57; González, *Reino de Alfonso VIII*, III, nos. 573, 574; *Chronica latina regum Castellae* c. 11 (44); *Chronica regia Coloniensis* 130, 133, 147, 154; *DDFr2* I, nos. 11, 21, 26; *CAP* II, no. 52.

[204] Ralph of Diceto, *Ymagines historiarum*, ed. Stubbs, *Historical works* II, 23; see also 12–13, 14. On the Canterbury election see also *GrH* I, 319–21. And for Bury *The chronicle of Jocelin of Brakelond . . .* , ed. and tr. H. E. Butler (London 1949); and *The chronicle of the election of Hugh abbot of Bury St. Edmunds . . .* , ed. and tr. R. M. Thomson (Oxford 1974).

[205] OV viii.23 (IV, 284); *Chronicle of Richard of Devizes* 20–21, 33–34, 45, 48–49; *CPT*, nos. 14–17 (see below, pp. 499–514).

[206] See generally Jones, *Italian city-state*, 288–423.

wealth were routinely made. What look to us like the real issues in Genoa from about 1165—the defiant self-promotion of local oligarchs and the destructive violence of their feuds—must have been suppressed in consular debates. The lord-consuls themselves were implicated. When their suspect efforts to impose themselves as pacifiers in the 1180s collapsed in lethal conflict, they agreed to try something new. Their first *podestà*, 'lord Mane-gold of Brescia,' was literally a 'power' (*potestas*) from outside. And while he and his successors faced no lack of civic problems—defence and aggression, coinage, building—there is little in the great consular reports carried on by Caffaro's continuators to reveal how the Genoese came to consensus. As also in Toulouse around 1200, government was more programmatic than politicised.[207]

Or so the records suggest. Nothing is written about alternative positions or votes, which could simply mean that there was no diplomatic form by which to convey them. Talk about rights and interests surely happened in Italian consular towns in the twelfth century. But the palpable changes of regime in Genoa after 1190 and in Toulouse a decade later have the looks of factional action sprung from affective alliance rather than from principled commitment. In other circumstances records could be more informative. If it had long been necessary for crusading leaders to seek consensus on ways, means, and tactics through debate, the enlarged problems of mobilisation and costs imparted new urgency to decision-making at the end of the twelfth century. The promotion of the Fourth Crusade was attended by a rarely explicit interaction amongst lord-barons and knights incapable of succeeding on their own. Geoffroi de Villehard-ouin wrote of the assembly at Soissons in 1200 to decide when and where the expedition should go; then of the assembly at Compiègne where 'all the counts and barons who had taken the Cross were present [and] many counsels were there taken and

[207] *Otoboni scribae annales . . .* , in *Annali genovesi di Caffaro* II, 3–66; *Ogerii panis annales*, in ibid., II, 67–117; Mundy, *Toulouse*, chs. 5, 6.

given' and agreement was reached to send envoys to negotiate the logistics.[208] Villehardouin then records how the doge of Venice resorted to intelligent persuasion to win the consent of his *grant conseil* to the covenant proposed by the French barons: 'So he cajoled them, then a hundred, then two hundred, then a thousand, so that everyone trusted him and approved.'[209] Villehardouin himself served as envoy and returned to present the Venetian offer to the barons reassembled at Soissons. Urging them to accept Boniface of Montferrat in place of the deceased Count Thibaut, he records that 'many words were said in one sense or another, but as the discussion turned out, all came to agreement, the great and the lesser men.'[210]

It becomes clear that the originality of these narrations of engaged debate and decision-making is due to the singularly detached view of Villehardouin. His accounts of further assemblies—of the dissensions following the siege of Zara (November 1202), of the army's assent to baronial agreements with the (Greek) emperor (January 1203), and of the election of Baldwin IX as (Latin) emperor (spring 1204)—are so vividly circumstantial as to suggest that Villehardouin was routinely noticing a sort of social conduct most scribes and narrators habitually overlooked.[211] Yet consultation on matters touching the variable interests of greater and lesser men cannot yet have been so frequent. The predicament of financially pressed crusading barons was no everyday situation. For all his testimony to engaged debate about decisions and policy, Villehardouin is far

---

[208] Villehardouin, *La conquête de Constantinople*, ed. Edmond Faral, 2 vols. (Paris 1961) c. 11 (I, 14).

[209] ibid., cc. 15–25 (I, 18–26); c. 25 (26): 'Ensi les mist, puis .c., puis .cc., puis .m., tant que tuit le creanterent et loerent.'

[210] ibid., c. 42 (I, 42). See also Robert de Clari, *La conquête de Constantinople*, ed. Philippe Lauer (Paris 1927) cc. 3–5 (4–6).

[211] Villehardouin, cc. 80–87 (I, 81–85, 87–89), 91–99 (I, 91–100), 256–61 (II, 60–68).

from doubting the preponderance of lordship and nobility in his experience.[212]

This remained the norm towards 1200. In the parliament of Pamiers (1212), wherein Simon de Montfort consulted prelates and barons before ordaining on the legal settlement of lower Languedoc, a commission consisting of clergy, northern and southern knights, and burghers was appointed to discuss and to draft. How precociously modern it looks! Yet such matters of policy as arose are concealed in the lordly diplomatic of Montfort's imperious statute. The commissioners functioned as assessors on issues of right and custom.[213]

THE CRISIS OF CATALONIA (1173–1205)

All these tendencies, including that of a sluggish diplomatic, come out in an episode rooted in the whole history addressed by this book. Nowhere in Europe can we see so clearly as in Catalonia the procedural contradiction between ceremonial decision-making and spontaneous or engaged opposition. In 1173 the count-king Alfons I, acting in concert with the archbishop of Tarragona, revived the old programme of the Peace and Truce of God. Barons and castellans were now required to observe comprehensive prohibitions of violence. These statutes, lacking explicit devices of enforcement, betrayed the weakness of the old religious sanctions; so in the later 1170s the count-king instituted a vicarial, that is, royal, jurisdiction of remedy; and in August 1188 he tried to promulgate an altogether tougher version of the peace-and-truce of 1173.[214] What happened in 1188 brought on a stormy crisis of power.

---

[212] Boniface de Montferrat was elected to 'la seingneurie de l'ost,' c. 41 (I, 42); also c. 44 (I, 44). The army's leaders are spoken of and to as lords, cc. 16, 20, 41, 59, etc. (I, 18, 22, 42, 61, etc.).

[213] *HL* VIII, no. 165.   [214] *CPT* nos. 14–18, examined below.

To make sense of this requires another visit to the circumstances. Peasants in the fiscal domains of Barcelona had made serious complaints against the harsh deportment of vicars and bailiffs, alleging an exploitative, even afflictive, manipulation of justice and credit that was likewise becoming customary in baronial domains from which no written memorials survive. Hardly less pressing was the princely control of castles, which was challenged in the courts of Urgell and Barcelona in the 1170s: the rendering of 'power' in castles on demand, in accordance with the *Usatges* of Barcelona.[215] And these issues could only fester behind a spectacular outbreak of defiant crime in the aristocracy. Archbishops were no safer in Catalonia! It was eerily symptomatic that Alfons I came of age just after his own metropolitan and mentor Hug de Cervelló (1163–71) was assassinated. All Christian Europe was then in shock following the murder of Thomas Becket, whose cult found its way to Catalonia at once.[216] Yet it was different here. No cult arose for Hug, nor two decades later would the killing of Archbishop Berenguer de Vilademuls (1174–94) make a martyr of him. These two murders were acts of vengeance, the first of them at least resulting from thwarted ambitions to great lordship, the second having possibly another explanation.[217] Nor was the renovated peace much of a deterrent to this brutality of the castles, to judge from the murder of Viscount Ramon Folc in 1176. His killer, the castellan-singer Guillem de Berguedà, wanted no part of the king's peace, and he had plenty of company in the upland counties and viscounties.[218]

[215] ACA, Cancelleria, pergamins Alfons I, 144; *LFM* I, no. 225.

[216] Frontispiece. One of the earliest and most graphic depictions of the martyrdom of Saint Thomas of Canterbury, this fresco (late s. xii) survives in Santa Maria of Terrassa. See also *Catalogne romane*, ed. Eduard Junyent, 2 vols. (Zodiaque 1960–61) II, 194–95.

[217] Related to the baronial war of 1190–94, below, p. 505.

[218] Emilio Morera y Llauradó, *Tarragona christiana . . .*, 2 vols. (Tarragona 1897–1901) I, chs. 16, 17; Miquel Coll i Alentorn, *La llegenda de Guillem Ramon de Montcada* (Barcelona 1958); Riquer, *Poesies [de] Guillem de Berguedà* 19; and *Vida*, 78.

To such as these the peace now seemed deeply threatening. Two decades had passed since their lord-prince had led the barons in lucrative campaigns against the Muslims. Few can have supposed that the seizure of Provence following the death of Count Ramon Berenguer III in 1166 could offer a compensating frontier; nor did the dynastic settlement effected by the count-king's marriage to Sancha of Castile in 1174 bear visibly on what may now be called the deeper history of power in Catalonia.[219] And if the boy-king's regents could no longer enforce the social discipline of the *Usatges* in face of persistent complaints from peasants and of baronial reluctance to submit to solemn judgments, it hardly mattered that the right of magnates to kill one another was intact.[220] Word of a worse regime must have leaked from the court, for it can hardly be doubted that the doomed Archbishop Hug first floated the idea of renewing the old peace and truce by rewriting the *Usatges* in a statutory form. If this was known in Catalonia it would help to explain why the count-king and his courtiers, including Bishop Guillem de Torroja of Barcelona (1146–71) and a few other Catalan followers, spent more than two years continuously in Aragon before moving back to Girona in April 1171.[221] Was this when the crisis began? If so, the murder of Hug de Cervelló only weeks before the king's return was its first casualty. Producing a backlash of public revulsion, almost simultaneously with King Henry's penitent concession to the church in England,[222] this outrage enabled a new archbishop (and papal legate), none other than Guillem de Torroja (1171–74), to urge with new resolve.

---

[219] *FAC* I, 79–86; ACA perg. Alfons I, 146 (ed. Sánchez Casabon, *Alfonso II . . . documentos,* no. 161).

[220] *CPT* nos. 14–18; ACA, perg. Alfons I, 86; *Alfonso II . . . documentos,* no. 59.

[221] Jaime Caruana, 'Itinerario de Alfonso II de Aragón,' *Estudios de Edad media de la Corona de Aragón* VII (1962) 104–26.

[222] Morera, *Tarragona christiana,* I, 474–76; and for papal indignation JL 11895, 12133–36.

What happened next may have been determined by the (natural) death of Count Guinard II of Roussillon in July 1172. In a will dating from his mortal illness this childless prince not only bequeathed his county to the lord-king but also revealed himself to be an exploitative lord with much on his conscience. Within days of his death King Alfons came to Perpignan to secure the homage and fidelity of the free men of the town and of the barons (*militares*) of Roussillon. A few months later he returned to impose a new charter of the peace and truce. In its solemn arenga, adorned with all his titles (now including 'count of Roussillon'), Alfons referred to the 'public utility of all our land' and to 'debate [*tractatus*] and deliberation' with archbishop-legate Guillem, the bishops of Barcelona and Elne, and 'all the barons of Roussillon county as well as with many magnates and barons of my court.' And he claimed that by the 'consent and intention of all the aforesaid,' he meant by these provisions to 'institute' a peace and truce and to 'exterminate the wicked audacity of violent men and thieves.' At the end Alfons recorded his own oath to uphold the 'aforesaid truce and peace,' and the text (as we have it) closes with a list of thirteen barons of Roussillon.[223]

Whatever its local impact, this event rumbled across the mountains. Only a few weeks later Alfons I imposed substantially the same charter on *all* his Catalan-speaking lands, including Roussillon, employing the same arenga *mutatis mutandis*, but containing two or three suspicious anomalies. It bears only a year date, as if the month and day had been left vacant in a prepared parchment; and its location is not a city but (in all probability) the tiny village of Fondarella in the arid plain east of Lleida. Only eleven barons are listed at the end, although in this case it is explicit that they have sworn with the king.[224]

The trouble with these great charters, whatever *we* make of them, is that they were emphatically enactments of government. They were designed to pry into every lordship of the land(s) to

---

[223] *LFM* II, nos. 792, 793; *CPT*, no. 14.
[224] *CPT*, no. 15.

protect and to judge. They are not to be confused with prior versions of the peace, even if no fewer than ten of the fifteen provisions of Perpignan derive from the *tregua et pax* of Toulouges (1062–66),[225] of which the count-king's men had a copy. Virtually all the provisions of Perpignan had precedents in texts of public princely lordship reserving episcopal collaboration; none of these had the kingly *arengae* of 1173, for which the regalian *Usatges* of about 1150 afforded the nearest analogue. In the new statutes, moreover, associative purpose was linked to territorial scope without the slightest allowance for baronial immunities.[226]

Taking the new statutes together, two further points stand out. First, almost every provision common to both would have antagonized the needy castellans and petty princes of upland Catalonia. Whether it was the intimidating abuse of clergy, nuns, and peasants (cc. 2, 4, 6), petty seizures, pillage, and invasion of clerical domains (1, 3, 5, 7, 9–13), or the safety of plunder in fortified churches (2!), virtually their whole practise of lordship and warfare is assailed in statutes that purport to have been promulgated with their consent.[227] Second, there are signs that the barons' dissent had been grasped as well as ignored. A prohibition against the destruction or firing of peasant dwellings was omitted in the charter of Fondarella.[228] On the other hand, the latter contains, among three new articles, an exclusion from 'this peace' of 'betrayers of their lords.'[229]

What can their authors have expected of these programmatic charters of statute? There is one further indication: the lists of names appended to the copies of each text. Here we encounter the obstacle of having only copies to work with. In the charter of Perpignan the appended names appear as an unadorned list; in that of Fondarella it is explicit that each listed baron has

---

[225] Cf. *LFM* II, no. 708.
[226] *CPT*, nos. 3–15; *Usatges de Barcelona*, 9–13.
[227] *CPT*, no. 15; cf. no. 14.   [228] ibid., no. 14 c. 8.
[229] ibid., no. 15 cc. 13–15.

joined the lord-king in *his* oath, which is recorded explicitly in both texts.[230] There can be no doubt that oaths to uphold the peace were sworn in both assemblies; that a copyist simply omitted the words '[we] who swear this' in the charter of Perpignan. Indeed, it is all but certain that the original intention was to carry copies of the charters throughout Catalonia in order to seek the written sworn adhesions of barons and knights everywhere.

This aim was surely frustrated. An ominous silence surrounds the instituted peace of 1173, punctuated by outbreaks of violence and dissent. In 1176 the murder of Ramon Folc III of Cardona, who had sworn with the lord-king at Fondarella, deprived Alfons of one of his few upland allies. The murderer Guillem de Berguedà, once returned from exile in the 1180s, fell out with his neighbours as well as the king; yet his snarling invective animated a progressively regional dissent. Had not Pere de Lluçà set a bad example for the viscounts and castellans by submitting to the lord-king when challenged in 1180 for the power of his castles?[231] From 1173 to 1186, when Alfons was busy securing castles and allies in his coastal domains, he lost touch with the viscounts of Cabrera-Ager and Castellbò and their dependents.[232] There is good reason to doubt that these men were in conformity with the instituted peace. For the period 1178–88 at least three explicitly alleged violators in Urgell and Cerdanya are known by name, including Arnau de Castellbò.[233] Alfons did not force the issue, but by entering into their own game sought to pry apart his big-

---

[230] ibid., nos. 14, 15. An early copyist of no. 15 wrote 'qui hec iuramus' with every subscription.

[231] *LFM* I, no. 225.

[232] Caruana, 'Itinerario,' 138–232; Armand de Fluvià, *Els primitius comtats i vescomtats de Catalunya* . . . (Barcelona 1989) 122, 128, 147, 158–59, 169; Viader, *L'Andorre* 117–24; and Th. N. Bisson, 'The war of the two Arnaus: a memorial of the broken peace in Cerdanya (1188),' *Miscel.lània en homenatge al P. Agustí Altisent* (Tarragona 1991) 95–107.

[233] ACA, perg. Alfons I, 303, ed. *FAC* II, no. 38; perg. extrainv. 3465, ed. Bisson, 'War of the two Arnaus,' 103–4.

gest adversaries and their allies. By securing the release of Ponç III of Cabrera from prison in Castile, he imposed a settlement by which the viscount conceded the power of several castles (1186).[234] In 1190 Alfons allied with the count and bishop of Urgell against Arnau Viscount of Castellbò and a powerful retainer.[235] Not until 1194, however, was the lord-king able to concert with his most powerful princely ally, Count Ermengol VIII of Urgell (1184–?1209) fully to suppress this resistance, imposing settlements in a 'full court' at Poblet in August 1194.[236]

By that time the struggle for peace, although far from over, had been politicised. The problem lay not so much in the new royalist ideology—not yet—as in the practical consequences of the statutes of 1173. Their authors had made no realistic provision for their enforcement. Allegations of violation were to be in the bishop's jurisdiction (Fondarella, cc. 1, 4, and implicitly others), or else to be judged by the bishop together with the king or his bailiff (cc. 2, 9, 10, 14, 16).[237] Such measures cannot seriously have deterred oppressive baronial lords. So it was decided—perhaps quietly in the king's entourage, for no record of it survived—to reform the old lay vicariate and to entrust the management of the peace to vicars accountable to the king. As it appears in revised statutes of 1188 this reform empowered vicars and bishops to convoke householders in the dioceses to combat recalcitrant malefactors.[238] That this measure antedated 1188 (in Catalonia as well as in the Gévaudan) is all but proven by another new measure. The revised statutes also contained the lord-king's promise henceforth to appoint only Catalans as vicars.[239] This provision betrays one baronial complaint explicitly, while throwing welcome

[234] ACA, perg. Alfons I, 412, transcribed in *Alfonso II . . . documentos*, no. 423.

[235] ACA, perg. Alfons I, 547, ed. Charles Baudon de Mony, *Relations politiques des comtes de Foix avec la Catalogne jusqu'au commencement du XIVᵉ siècle*, 2 vols. (Paris 1896) II, no. 23.

[236] Baudon de Mony, *Relations politiques* II, nos. 24, 25; *LFM* I, nos. 412–14.

[237] *CPT* no. 15. [238] ibid., no. 17, c. 16.

[239] c. 23. For the bishop's army in Gévaudan, above, p. 313.

light on King Alfons's efforts to tame his insubordinate magnates in the Pyrenees. For in 1183 Alfons had appointed an Aragonese knight named Pedro Jimenez vicar in charge of royal patrimony in Cerdanya; and when two years later he became the king's feudatory for the lordship of the Querol valley, Pedro must have seemed an intimidating ally. In August 1188 this vicar-magnate subscribed a royal license to Guillem de So to build a castle in the Capcir.[240]

This last was part of a design by the lord-king to encircle his adversaries by strengthening his hold on the valleys Tet and Segre. The trouble with this scheme was that Count Ermengol VIII, who was father-in-law to the obstreperous Ponç, had neither consented nor sworn to the statutes of Fondarella (a place on the border of Urgell). Seemingly, this was not because he resented their tenor, but because he claimed the same regalian status as Alfons. And in May 1187 he acted on that claim in a singularly appropriate way by promulgating his own charter of 'truce and peace' in a form contrived to reassert his lordship over Viscount Ponç III. This great charter invites comparison with the royal statutes in every way. It was patterned on that of Fondarella, while being in no sense a copy of it. Invoking the theology of peace more fully than its model, it refers to consultation with 'my magnates' together with Archbishop Berenguer and Bishop Arnau of Urgell. It is the first of these great charters to provide for a remedial army against 'him who breaks the peace and refuses to make amend.' And it purports to have been passed with the oaths of those present, first in Agramunt, the southern capital of Urgell, and then at Castelló de Farfanya, in the vicecomital domains of Ager, where Ponç swore 'to you, my lord E,' to uphold the peace. Both principals are said to have required their followers to confirm by oath; and there follows the longest list of names by far to be found in any of these records of the peace. They are

---

[240] *FAC* II, nos. 45, 47, 60; *Los documentos del Pilar, siglo XII,* ed. Luis Rubio (Zaragoza 1971) no. 199; ACA, Monacals, Sant Llorenç de Munt 353; Archivo historico provincial, Zaragoza, Hijar II.52.1 (August 1188).

the names, mostly, of baronial followers of Ager and Urgell who must have subscribed the statutes on an original parchment that survived when, towards 1190–1200, our oldest extant copy was made.[241]

The huge pertinence of this last detail will now appear. In August 1188 King Alfons summoned *his* magnates to Girona in order to renew the peace. Of the text that resulted the only medieval version we possess begins like a copy of Fondarella, but then diverges. No fewer than eleven of its twenty-three chapters are original; and whereas the prescription for a coercive remedial army renders a thoroughly resented programme even tougher, the last four chapters (20–23) have the looks of concessions to the barons. These include assurances that 'this institute' shall in no way derogate from the 'written *usatge*' in respect to the power of castles, that the king will henceforth impose no tax for the *bovatge* (*bouaticum*, another word for the 'peace of beasts') or the 'constituted peace' anywhere in Catalonia, and that he will appoint none but Catalans as vicars.[242] In the form of a great charter, like its analogues, this text refers to consultation *at Girona* (with Archbishop Berenguer and unnamed magnates of the land); and it closes with a protocol located *at Vilafranca del Penedès*, bearing notice of the king's oath to uphold the statutes, and of the king's subscription—his alone, in stark contrast with the charter of 1187. How can this anomaly be explained?

What had happened, quite certainly, is that a diplomatic of celebratory power had broken down under the stress of angry debate. The scene may be reconstructed as follows. Many Catalan barons, and not only the rebellious viscounts, were upset about the new vicarial armies of enforcement. They resisted this innovation as contrary to custom; and it looks as if they also resented recent claims on the power of castles as unjustified by the

---

[241] *CPT* no. 16; and for background Gener Gonzalvo i Bou, 'La pau i treva de l'any 1187 per al comtat d'Urgell i vescomtat d'Àger,' *Ilerda* XLVIII (1990) 157–70.

[242] *CPT* no. 17 as a whole, and cc. 20–23.

Usatges, while objecting to efforts (of which we otherwise know next to nothing) to tax in support of the peace.[243] Their objection to the Aragonese vicar Pedro is all but audible. As for King Alfons, he and the archbishop surely tried to dissuade the barons, and they failed. They argued from justice, equity, and 'common utility,' but in vain.[244] No one was willing to swear to the draft presented at Girona. So it would seem that a revised draft was prepared, including some new chapters meant to address baronial objections, and presented to the king some time later. All that he could do then, with no assembly at hand, was to swear and subscribe himself, and send the parchment on its way. Conceivably, an original received some adhesions; but in light of what happened next it seems more likely that a canon of Girona carried it home where, a century later, it would be copied.[245]

The 'constituted peace,' which as defined in the statutes had become the first territorial government of Catalonia, was in deep crisis, with worse yet to come. King Alfons himself wrote of it sadly in 1192:

> We believe you all know for sure how for a long time the peace and truce had been established by our illustrious predecessor counts of Barcelona before [we established] new peaces . . . by the common assent of our great men and magnates, but [which] owing to their excessive truculence and vehemence, we caused to be abolished in a great court at Barcelona.

Tendentious words, these, about a tumultuous assembly that left no record as such. Yet clear enough to prove that the barons after 1188 had begun to concert their opposition, leaving their lord-king helpless. Retaining little more than self-styled dignity, in November 1192 Alfons once more convoked the men of Catalonia to

---

[243] For a *bovatge* in 1174–75, *FAC* II, no. 27; and for the power of castles, cf. *Usatges de Barcelona* c. 26 (30).

[244] *CPT* no. 17 arenga (94).

[245] Arxiu capitular, Girona, 'Llibre verd,' fols. 206v–208v.

approve what he represented as the gist of the old programme, in a rewritten and reduced charter. It contained protections and prohibitions as well as the controversial provision for the episcopal-vicarial army; but there was nothing belligerent about this late salvo. All this in a charter that for once survives in an original parchment. It betrays no intention to seek sworn adhesions. Yet it holds, after all, two surprises: it was issued in Aragon (Barbastro, well to the west of the Catalan border), and it was addressed to the Catalans in a new way: to the 'good men of the cities and towns' as well as to the 'prelates and magnates' (of Catalonia). Was it that the climate of opinion in Catalonia was too hostile to admit of a meeting there? Deployed not as a weapon but as evidence of something akin to policy, this royal diploma—and this one alone—survived.[246]

A moment of truth had come and gone. In a terrible test of lord-kingship the peace had been politicised. It was no longer possible to secure adhesions to peace like oaths of fidelity. Peace had been reduced, and customary lordship elevated, to the ranks of negotiable causes; both were subject to argument and persuasion. Or at least this was so in the count-king's own lands, for in May 1189, probably well before the obstreperous assembly of Barcelona, Count Ponç Hug III of Empúries imposed his own statute of 'truce and peace' with the support of the bishop of Girona. Patterned like the statutes of Urgell on the programme of 1173, yet quite without the assertive clauses of 1188, this charter affords a welcome hint that the count-king was 'campaigning,' with (now) almost all the Catalan bishops on record as favouring the constituted peace.[247]

What Alfons I had expected of his convocations was consent, not debate. His scribes, having no diplomatic template save that for celebratory approbation, presumably made no record for an historic assembly of which the lord-king lost control. The trouble

[246] *CPT* no. 18. See plate 8A.
[247] ed. Stephen P. Bensch, 'Three peaces of Empúries (1189–1220),' *Anuario de Estudios medievales* XXVI (1996) 592–95.

had surely been foreseen. By virtue of his upbringing Alfons I had taken on the outlook of his archbishops. Ceasing to share the exploitative ethos of his barons as he came of age, he substituted a political conception of territorial order for the traditional dynamic of expansionist aggression. This is what he meant by stipulating that his statutes would have force in his lands from the bounds of Lleida to those of Salses; it was as much as to say that he meant to dominate everywhere in Catalonia without regard to such great public lordships—Urgell, Empùries, and several viscounties—as lay beyond his dominion.[248] As peace began to look like policy, barons came to pine for campaigns such as had enriched their fathers, and bitterly to resent a lord-king bent on suppressing the customs by which they were struggling to render their lordships profitable. And the king, at least, must soon have learned the need to persuade to his cause. The words 'debate and deliberation' in the charters of 1173 and 1188 may not have been quite formulaic.[249] The archbishop if not the king himself would have been obliged to propose the new institutes of peace to assembled men, from whom some response or objection would have been heard. And in about 1177, when Alfons tried to persuade the people of Hix and Perpignan to relocate their houses so as to render their settlements better defensible, his scribes contrived to enlarge the explanatory protocol so as to record the debate itself. These curious charters have the interest of showing how the count-king, fresh from his initiatives of peace, came to rely on the argument of public utility. Moreover, in the debate he provoked at Perpignan, he was willing to have it recorded that the townsfolk prevailed on him to withdraw his scheme to move the settlement. They also won his confirmation of their customs at the price of granting him 6000s. *melg.* And what might have been represented as a convention in Andorra or Italy worked here within

---

[248] See the *arengae* to *CPT* nos. 15 (Fondarella 1173), 17, and 18; and cf. 19 (1198): 'per totam Cathaloniam, videlicet a Salsis usque ad Ilerdam.'

[249] . . . super hoc tractatu et deliberacione cum [apud],' ibid., nos. 14, 15, 17.

the formality of a charter granted by a lord-prince responsive to the 'prayers of his people.'[250]

This last detail matters more than may appear. If Alfons I saw fit to persuade, he was of no mind to overdo it. Having put the barons in the wrong with their manifestly retrograde cause, what more could he do but enlist his townspeople in a new way? It was unthinkable to incite peasants against their masters. Custom had the upper hand, which may be one reason why the *Usatges* dropped out of sight in the later twelfth century. And when Pere I (1196–1213) succeeded his father he renewed the peace and truce in a series of great courts (Barcelona 1198, 1200; Cervera 1202; Puigcerdà 1207) as if nothing had changed. Like all preceding occasions except Barbastro (1192), these courts are known only from late copies, the lost originals keeping an impenetrable silence.[251]

Once again these great charters (as we have them) conceal as much as they reveal. King Pere abandoned the army of enforcement; and having introduced a protection for townspeople in 1198, dropped it in the charter of Barcelona (June 1200), which was modeled on those of 1173.[252] So it seems that baronial dissidence persisted; and indeed it burst forth in 1202 as never before. According to a truncated record of dubious transmission, the lord-king, attended by the archbishops of Tarragona and Narbonne and many other magnates, made two concessions: first, that he will take no man into his protection without the consent of his lord; and second, that 'if lords maltreat their peasants, or seize from them, they are in no way answerable to the king if not themselves commended to the king.'[253]

So there it is: the *ne plus ultra* of bad lordship! Nowhere else in medieval Europe do we find anyone seeking to legislate as rightfully customary a regime conceded to be unjust. This event

[250] *Privilèges et titres relatifs aux franchises . . . de Roussillon*, ed. Bernard Alart (Perpignan 1874) 160; *CPC* I¹, no. 154 (216–17); II, 443–44, 523–24.

[251] *CPT*, nos. 19–22. See also Kosto, 'Limited impact of the *Usatges de Barcelona*.'

[252] *CPT*, nos. 19, 20.   [253] ibid., no. 21.

cannot be explained away. As Paul Freedman has shown, the 'bad customs' of this region (*mals usos*) were just then on the point of securing the legitimacy of tolerated practise; Catalans came to speak of the 'right to abuse' (*jus maltractandi*).[254] And what looks to us like cynical bluster can indeed be explained. The quest for lordship had for generations been a quest for nobility. Everywhere, and not least in Catalonia, this had promoted a disparagement of peasants. Mere tools of lordship, they were unworthy of the protections accorded to free men.[255] This is why the Catalan lord-kings never fully responded to the memorials of rural complaint; it is also why they could not mobilise peasants in the crisis of the peace. Yet as a baronial cause exploitative domination must have been deeply vulnerable, its own adherents shamed into a contagious silence that has obscured its formative role in Catalan political experience.

In fact, by 1202 the conflict over the peace had been overtaken by fiscal issues. The constriction of military opportunity had injured the lord-kings as well as their barons; neither in Aragon nor Catalonia could they tax their patrimonies like northern princes. When Alfons I made the peace of 1173 the occasion for imposing a general tax on Catalonia—and this too must have required some explanation at Fondarella—he surely met with resistance not confined to the upland barons. This was the cow-tax (*bouaticum*, Cat. *bovatge*), a novelty everywhere save in Cerdanya, where a forgotten precedent dated from as early as 1118; and Alfons was compelled to renounce it in 1188.[256] In his time also the increasingly standard coinages of Jaca (in Aragon) and Barcelona, which the king tried at least once to manipulate for profit, came to pose issues of associative interest. Ignoring his father's renunciation, Pere I imposed the

---

[254] Paul H. Freedman, *The origins of peasant servitude in medieval Catalonia* (Cambridge 1991), chs. 3, 4.

[255] This attitude is perfectly visible in the memorials examined in *TV*; perhaps best of all in ACA, Cancelleria, perg. extrainv. 3451 (Gavà, etc.) and perg. R.B. IV extrainv. 2501 (Caldes de Malavella and Llagostera).

[256] *CPT* nos. 15, 17; *FAC* II, no. 27.

bovatge at his accession; and in 1197 he demanded a 'redemption of the coinage' in exchange for confirming the customs of Vic.[257]

Mounting financial need compounded the existing crisis by multiplying the people in resistance. Neither the *bovatge* nor the money-tax were customary, even if both had precedents; and it pointed to new conceptual dexterity that the lord-kings sought to justify them not by custom but by need. Although the logic of selling one's promise to hold the coinage stable so as to meet 'urgent' military 'necessity' may seem less than cogent, Pere I did so not only in 1197 but again in 1212, and probably on other occasions as well.[258] This improvident ruler surely had to explain, more so than his father, in order to collect; and on at least one occasion other than the solemn courts of Barcelona and Cervera that have been mentioned, the people of Catalonia forced the lord-king into retreat.

And this time for once a royal scribe broke free of the celebratory template. By a charter devoid of rhetoric dated March 1205 he recorded the lord-king's confession that he had levied new taxes in Catalonia, and his promise to clergy, barons, knights, and 'good men of all Catalonia' to desist from all such impositions, retaining only customary levies in his own domains and tolls. Vicars, he also promised, were to be Catalan knights, chosen 'by the counsel of great and wise men,' and subject to an oath 'to treat the land lawfully' by preserving right and custom. Finally, the king promised to maintain the coinage of Barcelona stable for his lifetime, and to desist from exacting ransoms of the coinage or the peace.[259]

---

[257] *FAC* II, no. 105; ACA, perg. Pere I, 26, ed. Bisson, 'Sur les origines du *monedatge*: quelques textes inédits,' *Annales du Midi* LXXXV (1973) 99–100 (*MFrPN* 333–34). See also Pere Orti Gost, 'La primera articulación del estado feudal en Cataluña a través de un impuesto: el bovaje (ss. XII–XIII),' *Hispania* LXI (2001) 967–98.

[258] ACA, perg. Pere I, 26 (see preceding note); AHN, Clero, Poblet 2109; *FAC*, no. 136.

[259] Arxiu diocesà, Girona, Cartoral 'Carlesmany,' fol. 65, ed. T. N. Bisson, 'An "Unknown Charter" for Catalonia (1205),' *Album Elemér Mályusz* . . . (Brussels 1976) 75–76 (*MFrPN* 211–12).

These engagements have the looks of a great charter for Catalonia. It was (or was to be?) secured by two of the king's barons under oath. And its substance may be read as the representation of a confrontation between King Pere and his magnates. It suffices to prove how the crises of peace and taxation had merged and how, midway through a tumultuous reign, the barons held the upper hand. Moreover, it hints at temperate bargaining, for if vicars were now to swear oaths of office as well as speak Catalan, the concession of 1188, validated or not, had proved its worth.[260]

Yet there is no sign that this *magna carta* was ever promulgated, let alone observed. Conceivably it entailed a fee not paid, for the lord-king was in need of money upon return from precedent-shattering ventures in southern France and a scheme to conquer Majorca. He not only imposed a money-tax on both his realms in November 1205, but also debased the coinage of Barcelona in 1209. He borrowed massively, having virtually to abandon the new patrimonial accountability in the process. He taxed ecclesiastical domains, thereby creating a clerical opposition with which he was forced to terms in an assembly at Lleida (March 1211), where he separately granted charters of nonprejudice to the churches.[261]

So the compounded crisis was defused, with the king retaining little more than his ceremonial initiative. While giving up the clerical demand to abolish the bad customs, Pere and his successors retained the vicarial jurisdiction of the peace, which became the basis of public order in later medieval Catalonia. After a quarter-century of murky confrontation, both sides had become all sides. Their needs were becoming negotiable issues, sometimes in assemblies that, for the first time, drew attention to themselves.

---

[260] "Unknown Charter,"' 76: 'Promitto etiam quod non instituam in ipsa terra aliquos uicarios nisi milites et de ipsa terra et cum consilio magnatum et sapientum illius terre. Qui uicarii iurent ut legaliter tractent terram et communem iusticiam et ius et consuetudinem terre bene seruent. . . .'

[261] *FAC* I, Introduction, ch. 4.

THE CRISIS OF MAGNA CARTA (1212–15)

Nowhere else in Europe can we find an aristocracy defending a shameless lordship of inhumane exploitation. That it survived in Catalonia can only be explained as the result of unwritten compromise and the moral inertia of prelates and popes preoccupied by heresy and the crusade. Yet it should not be overlooked that *remença* servitude hardened into custom at the same time when in England the masses of dependent peasants, deprived of access to the lord-king's justice, became legally unfree themselves. Different servitudes, yes, but the difference should not be exaggerated. While the Catalans preserved a cruel vestige of once brutal struggles for power, in most lands, and in England, the pretensions of rural lordship mellowed with age.[262]

So it is ironic in the extreme that the most conspicuous crisis of power of this age turned on the bad lordship not of a castellan or baron but of a king, no less. The crisis of Magna Carta, although by no means uncomplicated, would never have happened had it not been for the arbitrary, sometimes brutal behaviour of King John (1199–1216). John wriggled out of one jam after another. In the end the Great Charter of 1215 itself played into his canny strategy. But already by 1210, with the loss of Normandy unavenged and the English church under costly interdict, John's authority had plummeted as his habits of coercive violence became clear. Everyone knew that Matilda of Braose together with her son had been wilfully starved to death in a Windsor dungeon because of her husband's financial default and alleged contumacy. Perhaps not everyone knew, or dared to say, what one (unreliable) chronicler ungallantly said of Matilda: that 'with womanish impudence' she had blabbed to the king's men that she knew what had happened to Arthur of

---

[262] Freedman, *Peasant servitude in Catalonia*; Paul R. Hyams, *King, lords and peasants in medieval England . . .* (Oxford 1980). *Remença* (redemption) refers to the Catalan custom of requiring serfs to pay heavily for their enfranchisement.

Brittany.[263] In this event were linked the two worst atrocities of John's stormy reign.

Yet both were uncharacteristic. John's oppressive way, as with lesser bad lords, was to coerce and to exploit, not to kill. It was abuse in the courts and the manipulative excesses of customary obligation that induced his victims to converse and to compare experiences. In 1205 Nicholas de Stuteville was plunged into hopeless indebtedness when compelled to pay a staggering 10,000 marks for succession to his lands. And when in the following year Roger de Cressi was disseised for marrying without his guardian's leave, he had to fine 1200 marks 'for having [the lord-king's] benevolence.'[264] Countless such events figure in the rolls of court and exchequer. Many of John's sworn barons ceased to trust him. Thanks to the researches of J. E. A. Jolliffe and Sir James Holt we can discern how and when the victims of such treatment became disaffected. But because modern writers so easily conceive of John and his magnates as engaged in 'political' behaviour they beg the question how that behaviour changed over time; whether allusions to alliance, faction, and conspiracy can bear any hermeneutic differentiation; whether something like politicising is visible in the English crisis.[265]

It is the process that remains obscure. In an incomparable wealth of contemporary verbiage to be read in claims, judgments, fiscal accounts, and narratives, there are few hints that disgruntled men, including the king, thought they were doing other than what lordship and fidelity required of them. Yet it was Professor Holt himself who pointed out that when John de Lacy (and

---

[263] 'Roger of Wendover, *Flowers of history* . . . , ed. Henry G. Hewlett, 3 vols. (London 1886–89) II, 48–49, 57. See also 'Barnwell annals,' fol. 61rb (*Mem.* II, 202); and cf. *Histoire des ducs de Normandie* . . . , ed. Francisque Michel (Paris 1840) 114–15.

[264] J. C. Holt, *The northerners. A study in the reign of King John* (Oxford 1961) 27; Jolliffe, *Angevin kingship*, 2d ed., 72–73. See also *King John: new interpretations*, ed. D. S. Church (Woodbridge 1999).

[265] For Holt's normal usage, see *Northerners* 94; *Magna Carta*, 2d ed., 188; but see also next paragraph.

Gilbert fitz Reinfrey) submitted to King John in January 1216 they were obliged not simply to renew their personal fidelity to John but also to renounce their adherence to the 'king's enemies' and to the 'charter of liberties' they had wrung from the king; their fidelity, that is, to a 'cause,' to a 'political programme.'[266] And whereas the king and the pope had rejected their enterprise as conspiracy, there is reason to believe that the rebellious barons had arrived at a new way of conspiring by subordinating their personal rights to a collective interest that was, indeed, subversive of lord-kingship.

How such thinking might have evolved is suggested by the experience of the English church. If Thomas Becket could not extricate his cause from his personal right, the 'liberty of the church' took on new life when beset by the financial exactions of Richard and John. The kings themselves inadvertently abetted this shift. By imposing collectively in convocations they invited questioning or resistance with the force of numbers, or even of principle. A case in point related to King Richard's interminable wars in France. In December 1197 the archbishop-justiciar Hubert Walter urged the king's desperate 'necessities' in a 'general colloquium' of the English magnates at Oxford, winning some assent to the appeal to provide for a force of three hundred knights in France. But Bishop Hugh of Lincoln objected, claiming that service outside England was uncustomary. When this principled resistance was taken up also by Bishop Herbert of Salisbury, Archbishop Hubert dismissed the assembly in fury, provoking the lord-king to order the Salisbury lands to be confiscated.[267]

No record of this assembly as such survived. Quite as at Barcelona in 1190 conflicting positions were voiced but not reconciled, leaving only anger to prevail. But Saint Hugh's biographer enables

---

[266] *Northerners*, 1. That we know of two individuals so pressed suggests that John, fully as obstinate as he was resilient, aimed finally not to dissuade but to impose on his adversaries.

[267] Roger of Howden, *Chronica* IV, 40; *Magna vita sancti Hugonis* iv.5, ed. Decima L. Douie, David Hugh Farmer, 2 vols. (Oxford 1985) II, 98–102.

us to reconstruct the confrontation of 1197 in plausible detail. Enraged by the bishops' response, with only Richard of London timidly acquiescing, Hubert Walter seems to have made no effort beyond his opener to persuade. He had been upstaged by the venerable Hugh, whose ascetic charisma evidently counted for more than his argument about customary service, which was in fact mistaken. Whatever else happened in the assembly, Archbishop Hubert and the king chose to dominate, not to concede, so that neither the pretension to collective customary exemption nor the case for service in light of the lord-king's asserted need was opened to scrutiny. It is possible that the issue of customary right was swamped in a confused emotional response to Bishop Hugh's speech.[268]

Hubert Walter acquitted himself better in 1201 when a similar confrontation came about. King John met some Cistercian abbots at York and asked them to commit their order to contribute to a carucage levied generally to pay for the relief owed to Philip Augustus for accession to the great fiefs in France. When they claimed exemption from such an exaction, deferring consent on behalf of absent abbots, and spoke of seeking 'counsel and consent' from the general chapter of Cîteaux, John flew into a rage and ordered 'his sheriffs' to treat Cistercian monks and tenants with the brutality accorded to outlaws. Whereupon Archbishop Hubert intervened, rebuking the king for his wrath, and offered 'on behalf of the [Cistercian] order' a fine of 1000 marks for the confirmation of their charters. John refused, went to France in high dudgeon, and when he returned in September directed his head forester to require the Cistercians to remove their animals from the royal forests on pain of losing them. So the abbots appealed again to Hubert Walter, who arranged for them to petition the king in a personal meeting at Lincoln; and when John temperamentally declined to address the abbots, the archbishop undertook to mediate. In an emotional reconciliation the lord-king promised his humble reverence, while the abbots fell on their

[268] *Magna vita* v.5 (II, 98–100); and for sources and context I, pp. xlii–xlv.

faces in heartfelt thanks. It cost them, to be sure, the 1000 marks formerly promised.[269]

Such is the usual version of this encounter. Clearly, the dynamic was that of a capricious lord-king more concerned to have his power conceded than to persuade great tenants of their obligation to support him in fidelity. But here again there is more. Whether from memory or eyewitness reports, the chronicler told of how the abbots conversed, and how they argued from the strength of consensus and numbers. First, there was the tactical question where to meet the king: in the city of Lincoln (as they prudently decided) or in a field outside? Then, while some thought they should hold firm against any payment for the king's mercy, others proposed 'to placate' him, producing the further question whether they dared to pay more than the 1000 marks first offered for the confirmation of their charters. The abbots were groping towards a consensus of pragmatic strength without supposing that John would counter them with his reasoned case. As their lord he could do no wrong save to violate what they believed to be their customs. But as they are represented we have a rare glimpse of a cause arguable, and argued.

John was not yet done with the white abbots. In 1210 he summoned them to York and requested their aid in money with which to recover and defend Normandy. 'But they all replied with a single voice,' wrote the continuator of William of Newburgh, that they had no money 'in their own power' to give, nor did they wish to have it, being themselves merely custodians and stewards of alms bestowed by the faithful for pious works. Once again John was infuriated. Prohibiting the monks to attend general chapter, he ordered his sheriffs, justiciars, and foresters to withhold justice and he nullified the Cistercians' charters.[270]

---

[269] *Radulphi de Coggeshall chronicon Anglicanum*, ed. Joseph Stevenson (London 1875) 102–10; Sidney Painter, *The reign of King John* (Baltimore 1949) 155–56; Jolliffe, *Angevin kingship* 100–103.

[270] *Continuatio chronici Willelmi de Novoburgi*, ed. Richard Howlett, *Chronicles* II, 510–11; also 'Barnwell annals,' fols. 60vb–61ra (*Mem.* 201); Coggeshall 163.

The phrase *una voce* suggests that the Cistercians had learned to strengthen their cause(s) by professing unanimity. Anger was inevitably John's response, for he had no political recourse. Although the recovery of dynastic lands was arguably a public cause, John had not cultivated it as such. The abbots, by contrast, were not merely united; they had adopted a well crafted doctrine currently professed in the schools of Paris. It was an unwittingly timely doctrine, for to contend that prelates were the stewards of charitable patrimony was to underscore the functional meaning of office, about which King John, like most princes of his day, was at once informed and negligent. One of the professors was Stephen Langton, whose teaching on clerical property may have been known to the Cistercians.[271]

King John was hardly naïve about causes and consent. His resolve to reconquer Normandy proved as constant as his failure to defend it had been baffling. Within a year of the Capetian triumph he wished to persuade 'to our great and arduous affairs and the common utility of our realm'; but when the massive army of June 1205 disbanded in futility a cleavage formed in elite opinion that would impede consensus for years to come.[272] The campaign of 1214 relied heavily on foreign allies. The unyielding abbots had plenty of sympathy; indeed, the bishops had anticipated them in 1207. Following the disputed election of Stephen Langton to Canterbury, England was awash in causes, of which John's was potentially the best. The summons was his for most of the reign. His convocations were show-cases of the argument from public necessity and utility, the insistence of many on customary exemptions surely tiresome to some. But John's suspicious lordship got in the way of his social prudence. In September 1209, fresh from an expedition to Scotland yet now excommunicated and

---

[271] Robert of Courson, 'Summa' xv.13.16, BnF, MS latin 14524, fol. 66vab; Stephen Langton, 'Questiones,' St John's (Cambridge), MS C7 (old 57) fols. 195rab–196va.

[272] SC 277; A. L. Poole, *From Domesday Book to Magna Carta*, 2d ed. (Oxford 1955) 440–41.

beset with anxieties about the powers abroad, John convoked the free men of England as massively as he could, and in what must have been an uneasy assembly at Marlborough exacted their sworn professions of homage and fidelity. King John lived by oaths—he was already distrustful of some northern barons—and from 1210 increasingly by guarantees of personal fidelity. This was hardly tyrannical; he was never so dependent on hostages as Philip Augustus, nor had he a customary 'power of castles,' such as existed in some Mediterranean lands. But his reliance on sworn followers and allies fed his suspicions of the powerful men he seldom saw. Their growing distrust of John may have been the only abiding cause before the crisis of Magna Carta.[273]

The trouble that forced John to treat with his magnates began in 1212. Hearing of a plot against him, the king aborted his punitive campaign to Wales, dismissed his fighting men, and sent to some magnates he suspected, demanding hostages for his inquiry into their fidelity. In the months that followed, John became aware that the crisis, while contained, remained dangerously unresolved. He acted firmly to secure the northern castles, only to realize that his pursuit of a settlement with the pope coincided with a groundswell of disapproval in England. It was a time of symptomatic events: the prophecy of a Yorkshire hermit about John's impending death, the muster of a huge army to defend against a French invasion encouraged by the pope, and the appearance of a change of heart in John. Even as he seized castles when the plot on his life was exposed, and began to demand written affirmations from prelates that his seizures had been free gifts, 'he began to act more kindly towards his people.' In northern counties he reduced the forest exactions while affecting to respond to complaints that the sheriffs were extorting money that never got to the exchequer. In the summer of 1213, following his

---

[273] Gervase of Canterbury, *Chronicle* II, 104; Wendover II, 51; 'Barnwell annals,' fol. 60v (*Mem.* 200); *Annales monasterii de Waverleia* . . . , ed. Henry Richard Luard, *Annales monastici*, 4 vols. (London 1864–69) II, 262; Holt, *Magna Carta*, 193–95.

submission to papal conditions and the consecration of Archbishop Stephen, this impulse was renewed in a more general promise of reform.[274]

John had accepted the pope's terms for lifting sanctions in May 1213. It was his way out of a dangerous predicament. By conceding papal lordship over his realms John deprived his adversaries of a major grievance and reduced their options.[275] He could safely renew preparations for recovering his French-speaking lands. His concessions of summer 1213 coincided with or soon followed his absolution on 20 July, when he must surely have renewed his coronation oath.[276] One need not believe the unlikely story that Stephen Langton produced the charter of liberties of 1100 on this occasion to see that the dynamic of power was changing. A potential opposition uniting clergy and laity lurked just out of sight. John was making promises even before knowing of concerted complaints,[277] a gamble on which there could be no payoff short of victory in France.

John's cause was not negligible, nor were the disillusioned yet a solidarity. At least twelve future rebels sailed with the king to Poitou in February 1214.[278] But he had tried and failed to secure the northern barons, first by force following their unanimous claim to exemption and exhaustion, then in a meeting at Wallingford (1 November 1213) mediated by the legate Nicholas and Archbishop Stephen. Whatever John agreed to on this occasion was conditioned on a confirmation of the northerners' 'ancient liberties,' a settlement the king failed to observe. Successively confrontation in arms and peace-making (of a familiar sort), these dealings anticipated the wary interchange between larger armies sixteen months later. This may be why, in his very next entry, the

---

[274] *Coggeshall*, 165–68; 'Barnwell annals,' fols. 62rb–65va (*Mem.* 206–15); Holt, *Northerners* 79–89.

[275] 'Barnwell annals,' fols. 63rb–64ra (*Mem.* 209–11).

[276] ibid., fol. 65rb (*Mem.* 213).

[277] Holt, *Northerners* 93; *Magna Carta* 224–25.

[278] Painter, *King John* 213, 280.

Coggeshall chronicler wrote that 'almost all the barons of England joined together to protect the liberty of the church and of the whole realm.'[279]

Whatever the agreement at Wallingford, it collapsed at once. Within days or hours, John decided on a new tack: he would convert a major lay assembly scheduled in Oxford on 15 November into an unprecedented confrontation of armed knights and unarmed barons. How such a threat of force was to go with persuasion is hard to fathom, yet it sounds like John in one of his impetuous postures. Nothing else is heard of an assembly that would have been even more historic than the lonesome extant summons of knights of the shire that tells of an intention; and if some items in the so-called 'Unknown Charter' conceivably date from Wallingford, the parleys in which they became associated with the Henrician charter of liberties seem to have occurred early in 1215.[280]

By that time the king was engulfed in the renewal of crisis brought on by the fiasco of Bouvines, where on 27 July 1214 Philip Augustus routed John's continental allies, decisively overturning the scheme to recover Normandy. Returning to England in October 1214 John faced a metastatic resistance leaving him no choice but negotiation or war. 'The road from Bouvines to Runnymede,' wrote Holt, 'was direct, short, and unavoidable.'[281] It became harder than ever for the king to collect the scutage levied for the Poitevin campaign; the accountants at Michaelmas 1214 left massive blanks; Yorkshire was still in arrears in 1219.[282] John strove to retain his adherents elsewhere, even winning over some in need of his favour; but disaffected men could now be found in southern and eastern counties. The tenets of a collective cause,

[279] *Coggeshall*, 167; *Annales prioratus de Dunstaplia . . .*, ed. Henry Richard Luard, *Annales monastici* III, 40; *SC* 281–82; Holt, *Northerners* 95–96.

[280] *SC* 282; Holt, *Magna Carta* 418–28. The king's activity around Wallingford shows the legate's mitigating influence on John, *Rotuli litterarum patentium . . .*, ed. T. Duffus Hardy (London 1835) 105ab.

[281] *Northerners* 100.   [282] ibid., 101.

ascribed to northern barons by two reliable chroniclers, became known: they were to the effect that required service outside England was uncustomary, an argument that justified resistance to the compensatory tax (scutage); and further, that the church and kingdom were suffering in general from bad customs in need of reform. By this time, moreover, the first Henry's charter of 1100 had become known, to be deployed by the dissidents (anachronistically) as a venerable icon of good lord-kingship.[283]

What happened during the six months preceding the grant of Magna Carta (15–19 June 1215) is well enough recorded. John's grant of free election to the clergy (21 November 1214) looks like an effort to stave off clerical defections;[284] if so, it is the nearest the king came overtly to defining his cause politically. He was momentarily on the defensive when, after Christmas, the barons invited him to meet in London and petitioned him, including, probably, that he confirm the charter of Henry I. When he asked to defer his response until the octaves of Easter (26 April) some men opined that he was prevaricating; and with both sides engaging the pope with their claims John was well positioned to subvert the baronial cause. On 4 March 1215 he took the cross as an avowed crusader, a move calculated to put any show of force by the dissident barons (and clergy) legally in the wrong.[285] A fortnight later Innocent III wrote separately to the barons and the king, making clear to the former that if he was right in believing they had entered into 'conspiracies and conjurations' against their lord-king, they must desist, putting any reasonable petitions before him 'not violently but reverently.' John was advised to treat the barons kindly, but assured that as the pope's sworn man and crusader, he had the law entirely on his side.[286]

---

[283] *Coggeshall* 170; 'Barnwell annals,' fol. 66rb (*Mem.* 217–18).

[284] *SC* 283–84.

[285] 'Barnwell annals,' fol. 66va (*Mem.* 218–19).

[286] *Selected letters of Pope Innocent III concerning England (1198–1216)*, ed. C. R. Cheney, W. H. Semple (London 1953) no. 74.

The appeal for John to confirm the Henrician charter surely prompted the lord-king to insist on the renewal of sworn fidelity. By late spring baronial demands had become articulate in new formed articles presented to the king under the mounting threat of armed resistance. When the barons seized London on 17 May, the dynamic of power shifted in their favour; defections from John's loyalty multiplied and the king was obliged to seek accommodation in order to avoid violent conflict. At this point it looks as if positions of defiance and principled insistence on service and fidelity were coming to resemble political confrontation; that is, virtually arguments for opposed causes. Works of compromise went on in talks at or near Staines around 10–11 June, seeming to prove that the meeting of 15 June at Runnymede was meant to ratify the substance (or detail) of prior agreements.[287] The Barnwell annalist was probably close to the mark in representing the Great Charter as practically extorted from an unwilling lord-king biding his time. Yet John's subscription was not wholly in bad faith; he ate and drank with his adversaries, received their homages and fealties, restored some castles, and ordered that the Charter be despatched to shires and churches.[288] It was a fragile consensus, even so, given the king's expectation. Little more than news of the pope's emphatic rejection of the Charter (24 August 1215) was required to renew the crisis. England fell into a state of desultory civil war that lasted until John's death a year later.[289]

This part of the history need not be pursued in detail. The renewed crisis played out under the constraints of nature (the deaths of Innocent III and John, respectively 16 July and 18–19 October 1216), opportunism (Prince Louis as willing contender), and dynastic succession (the deflationary compromise in John's young son as king). Holt well showed how the imprecisions of Magna Carta

---

[287] Holt, *Magna Carta* 231–49; and for the Articles of the Barons, 429–40.

[288] 'Barnwell annals,' fol. 68 (*Mem.* 221–22); convenient texts of Magna Carta in *SC* 292–302; and (with translation) in Holt, *Magna Carta* 448–72.

[289] *Selected letters*, nos. 82, 83; 'Barnwell annals,' fols. 69–72 (*Mem.* 222–32); *Coggeshall* 173–84.

impeded or disrupted local implementation while fostering new suspicions, how both sides let go of the Charter.[290] Given the formative European experience, including the incipient impulses of associative action, two events of these months stand out. First, as allegiances in the shires became problematic, many of the dissident barons moved to organize something like a government by the Charter 'in that part of the realm which seemed to have fallen to them': Geoffrey de Mandeville in Essex, Robert fitzWalter in Northamptonshire, and so forth. 'Each of them in his assigned province was to serve as justiciar, having to provide for the peace of provincial people.' Here the public connotation of 'peace' (*pax*) is clear: it binds with other pointers towards justice as a social need, such as the recollection of King John's 'so-called sheriffs of the peace' earlier in 1215, or the institution of 'peace-men' (*paciarii*) in towns of southern France towards 1200–1225. In all these cases rights are envisaged collectively as in need of official custody.[291]

Second, as the defiant barons lost hope of the king's compliance, perhaps even before learning that the pope had condemned the Charter, they aimed to secure the 'common consensus of the whole realm' as prerequisite to 'electing' a new 'lord' (-king). The contingency of a vacant lordship requiring baronial initiative was hardly new; it had occurred to the northern barons already in 1212, and the case of 1215 would seem to mark a palpable advance towards an administrative conception of interim baronial power.[292]

THE BARNWELL annalist remembered these events as if they were consecutive, surely not by accident. To modern readers, including the writer of this book, the crisis of Magna Carta looks for all the world like the convergence of an abiding progressive maturation

[290] *Magna Carta* chs. 10, 11.

[291] 'Barnwell annals,' fol. 68va (*Mem.* 224); and for *paciarii* in the Midi, Bisson, 'Organized peace,' 306–7 (*MFrPN*, 231–32).

[292] 'Barnwell annals,' fols. 62va, 68va (*Mem.* 207, 224); *Annales de Dunstaplia* 33.

of societal and jurisdictional experience and a short-term crisis of power. Sir James Holt understandably referred to 'political thought,' the rule of law, and the rights of subjects within lay and clerical hierarchies.[293] Contemporaries thought of it as a crisis of lordship. Pope Innocent III thought so emphatically. In the influential letters of 1215 he repeatedly alluded to the king's domination in England as challenged, threatened, violated.[294] His was, to be sure, a tendentious view, but once harnessed to his well-coached insistence on King John's claim to service as of (non-negotiable) right, it easily sufficed to bring down the quasi-peace of Runnymede. John's failings were not so much those of incompetence as of affectivity; personal failings by which he forfeited the trust of his commended men. It was their homage and fidelity that John sought desperately to recover at several critical junctures; and his leveraging contention that their service or money was his by right of their vassalic submission unless disproved in court was a doctrinaire invocation of a law of fiefs even more substantial than the customary exemptions to which northern barons and abbots laid claim. Countless chapters of the Charter in all its sections—those relating to the church, to abuses of feudal law, to justice, and to the deportment of officials—tell of the design to remodel lord-kingship, not replace it.[295] This was not lost on John, who nevertheless found it tactically inconvenient even before he had the lord-pope's license to ignore it.

As for the dissident barons and clergy, what they negotiated were the lord-king's concessions of grace. By an astonishing clause of security the barons were entitled to empower twenty-five of their number to hold John to his promises, to the point of approving the harsh constraints characteristic of exploitative lordships everywhere in twelfth-century Europe; and if the Twenty-Five

---

[293] *Magna Carta* 188.

[294] *Selected letters*, nos. 74, 78, 80, 82, 83. If it is the papal *dominium* that is explicit, it is the king's lordship (manifest in vassalic fealty owed to him) that has allegedly been violated.

[295] Magna Carta (1215), cc. 1; 2–8, 37, 43; 17–22, 38–40; 9, 24, 28, 31, 38, 44, 50.

themselves felt compelled to take initiatives during the summer of 1215, neither cap. 61 nor any other provision aimed at a baronial government as such.[296] On the contrary, the provincial justiciarships of peace mentioned by one chronicler would have sprung from the great honorial lordships of the magnates who held them. So far from pretending to any revolutionary deconstruct of lordship, the dissidents of Magna Carta could only extol the dominations by which they themselves lived—and seek a better lord-king.

Ironies abound. A bad-lord king is exonerated by the lord-pope who came closer to governing the church than any of his medieval predecessors. Driven by a compulsive vision of crusade that was permitted to override any concrete response to the baronial petitions, Innocent III felt constrained to rescue the king who had virtually looted the English church after 1206. Both king and pope played the parts of great lords in this crisis, cynically manipulating a widely recognized northern custom of fiefs as well as the canon law protective of crusaders' lands. Yet both potentates were more nearly governors in their realms, indeed practically bureaucrats riding herd on their chanceries and skilfully holding to tenets of common utility, than any of John's lay adversaries.

Yet John was less adroit than the barons (or the pope) in promoting his interests. For all the existential regality in which he gathered allies, John failed, save possibly for moments in his last year (late 1215–16), to render kingship a cause such as the barons had woven about the Charter.[297] For the pope to rail against their 'conspiracies' not only betrayed the genetic blindness of lordship to politicised debate but also Innocent's own failure to imagine what moved these distant pests to conspire. In all likelihood the provoked barons together with Stephen Langton and other clergy had wondered how to legitimate their resistance in talks of which we have no record; that they arrived at no conceptual device to

---

[296] ibid., c. 61; Holt, *Magna Carta* 347–77.

[297] 'Barnwell annals,' fols. 69ra–70vb (*Mem.* 226–31); cf. fol. 63rb (*Mem.* 209) *an.* 1213.

this end seems proven by the chroniclers who merely hint at efforts to render demands persuasive: arguments put forward *una voce*, for instance, or the mention of 'liberty of the church and the whole realm' as cause for 'confederation' as distinct from conspiracy.[298] The *partes* of which the Barnwell annalist speaks can only be rendered literally as 'sides,' or 'groups of partisans,' but hardly as 'parties.'[299] Of 'politicking' in our modern sense there must have been plenty, to be sure; but it is the avoidance of that meaning that holds hope for making historical sense of power in the crisis of Magna Carta. John's ultimate success in sundering the adversarial solidarity comes to mind; yet here again the sources resist all inflection of novelty. Circumstances pushed the rebels towards self-defining power that fell short of overt redefinition. Caps. 12 and 14 of the Charter, which by prescribing 'common counsel' might appear to have spelt out a practical definition of collective interest, were silently dropped from the reissues of 1216 and after. Yet as time swiftly showed, the insistent reality of a consultative role for the general interest in English society had overtaken the reticence of custom.

States and Estates of Power

Considered as crises of lordship, the commotions in England and Catalonia must have appeared to many like provincial trifles. The bad lords prevailed in both regions, although hardly for long; indeed, the very events of their momentary successes revealed an adverse groundswell of societal interests that could no longer be suppressed. More shocking to most contemporary Europeans would have been the crisis of lord-kingship in Germany (1197–1212), which incited a renewed violence of castles worse than anything unleashed by Catalan or English barons. 'Discord, the mother and nurse of all evils,' wrote Burchard of Ursberg,

---

[298] *Coggeshall* 167.
[299] 'Barnwell annals,' fol. 66vab (*Mem.* II, 218–20).

'refused to be quieted'; and the chronicler of Cologne told of 'wicked men [instigated] like rapacious wolves to plunder destitute flocks.'[300] Here yet again was the endemic predicament of interregnum, foreseen by Henry VI when he tried with small success to abrogate the princely custom of choosing the king of Germany;[301] and upon his death in August 1197 the claims of his brother Philip of Swabia (d. 1208) and Otto of Brunswick (d. 1218) could not be reconciled.

What marks off this crisis is not so much politicising as the tiresome persistence of the abrasive modes of power so characteristic of the twelfth century. Henry VI and his claimant-successors, while they surely sought to persuade, created followings rather than causes; where confrontations can be glimpsed, as in the court of Würzburg (31 March 1196), the withholding of any record of debate shows that, as in Catalonia, the working out of alternative or conflicting positions still had no recognized place in royal or imperial decision-making.[302] In the empire as almost everywhere else the interests in play were the lord-prince's to impose in his forum of choice. And what the evidence suggests is that the repression of violence was foremost among those concerns. This was hardly the only such interest in the age of the Third and Fourth Crusades, still less one that has appealed to modern historians. Yet it was arguably the most revealing preoccupation of rulers seeking to govern as well as to dominate.

THE STATES OF TROUBLED REALMS

In 1186, meeting with his magnates at Nuremberg after Christmas and acting with their counsel and consent, Frederick Barbarossa

[300] *Cronik des propstes Burchard* 79–80; *Chronica regia Coloniensis* 160, 224. Also Burchard 96.

[301] *Annales Marbacenses*, ed. Franz-Josef Schmale, *Die Chronik Ottos von St. Blasien und die Marbacher Annalen* (Darmstadt 1988) 196; Gervase of Tilbury, *Otia imperialia* ii.19 (462).

[302] *Annales Marbacenses* 196; *Chr. regia Colon.* 159; Barraclough, *Origins of modern Germany*, 2d ed., 200–203.

prohibited the 'outrages of arsonists' in a solemn ordinance aimed at suppressing this scourge in all its guises. Intended to supplement the existing peace, yet plainly responding to fears of armed bands that had lately worsened, these statutes show that the responsibility of lords and castellans for their commended men had become an issue on which the German elite could agree with the emperor.[303]

On a wider view, this was only the beginning. One year later King Alfonso II of Aragon promulgated 'constitutions' in a solemn court at Huesca by which the violators of public and rural order and their protectors were to be stigmatized and prosecuted. This is a more comprehensive protection than the German ordinance, although incompletely transmitted; but here too the violence of procedural distraints is addressed.[304] Then, just six months later (July 1188), come the famous 'decrees' by which the new king Alfonso IX of León not only promised to preserve 'good customs' and to consult his people on issues of war, peace, and justice; but also enjoined strict conformity to royal customs of justice administered by 'justices and mayors.' Here quite explicitly extra-judicial distraint and vengeance are targeted, to the extent of envisaging the pretext that a coercive act was not 'violent.'[305] On the same occasion Alfonso IX addressed complaints from his people (here called 'vassals') against malefactors of all kinds: thieves, pillagers (some pretending to distrain), and those seeking to dominate others.[306] And it was only weeks after this that the same king who had promulgated the constitutions of Huesca for Aragon in January sought to remodel the peace and truce of Catalonia in the jolting way that we have seen.[307]

---

[303] *CAP* I, no. 318, esp. cc. I, 7, II, 14, 16.

[304] Zaragoza, Facultad de Derecho, MS 225, fol. 21rv, ed. José María Ramos y Loscertales, 'Documentos para la historia del derecho español,' *AHDE* I (1924) 398–400; *Cartulario de Santa Cruz de la Serós*, ed. Antonio Ubieto Arteta (Valencia 1966) no. 44.

[305] Ed. José María Fernández Catón, *La curia regia de León de 1188 y sus 'decreta' y constitución* (León 1993) 98–117, cc. 5, 8, 12, 13.

[306] ibid., 138–39.

[307] *CPT*, no. 17; above, pp. 507–9.

Nor is this all. In 1192 King Sancho VI of Navarre (1150–94), acting with the approval of knights and nobles, laid down what he represented as customary sanctions against those who assault or retaliate without observing the rules of public notice.[308] And in 1195, still within a decade of the ordinance of Nuremberg, the justiciar Hubert Walter issued an order, only partly anticipated by the Assize of Clarendon (1166), rendering all free Englishmen responsible—indeed, liable—for the sworn peace in England. They were not to rob or help robbers and to see to it that thieves are captured, including pursuit when the cry is sounded, on pain of being taken for malefactors themselves. They were to swear to these commitments, defined as the 'lord-king's peace,' to knights assigned to hear their oaths.[309]

These measures of prohibition go together not because they were concerted, which is hardly likely, nor because they form a closed series,[310] but because they witness collectively to a distinct stage of European political formation. That the violence of distraint, thievery, and arson persisted in spite of local mechanisms of justice was hardly new, it is true, least of all in England. Moreover, the enactments of 1186 to 1195 were diversely precedented in the statutory peace and truce both in Germany and in Pyrenean lands. For different reasons neither Sicily nor France figure as subject to these injunctions. To judge from the epithets bestowed on him William II of Sicily (1166–89) was too successful and popular to face any such need; but it was otherwise in France. Here the question is why Philip Augustus failed to renew the peace of Soissons (1155) in which his father had assembled clergy and 'baronage to repress the fervour of wicked men and constrain the violence of robbers.'[311] That sworn peace was to hold for ten

---

[308] 'Documentos para la historia de las instituciones navarras,' ed. J. M. Lacarra, *AHDE* XI (1934) 496–97.

[309] *SC* 257–58.

[310] Philip of Swabia (in 1207) and Otto IV (1208) held courts for the peace, *Chr. regia Colon.* 224; Otto of St. Blasien, c. 50 (150).

[311] *Historiae Francorum scriptores*, ed. Duchesne, IV, 583–84.

years, and we know of no attempt to prolong it. Yet there is reason to believe that King Philip was quite as challenged by the endemic violence of 'wicked men' as his counterparts in Spain and Germany, simply choosing to face it differently. The lesson of 1155 may have been that (greater) France was too vast to police by princely oaths. In 1190 Philip directed his provosts and bailiffs to protect the monks and nuns of several houses in the royal domain from the 'incursions of wicked men.'[312] And these privileges immediately preceded the testamentary ordinance of late spring 1190, by which the lord-king, more concerned with management than with violence, nevertheless envisaged remedies for the misdeeds of bailiffs and provosts. And in another respect this famous ordinance points to. the very novelty it shares with the statutes against violence—its allusions to the 'utility' and the 'state of the realm.'[313]

But this is to get ahead of our story. What the statutes of security demonstrate is how the lord-princes and their scribes were coming to enlist their peoples in the (princely) cause of collective law and order. That this was not a popular cause is illustrated by the precedents. In 1155 at Soissons, the peremptory voice of Louis VII is all but audible: 'In full council and before all we said by royal decree that we should hold this peace unbreakably; and if there should be violators of the ordained peace, we should do justice on them as fully as we can.'[314] At Roncaglia in November 1158, one of Emperor Frederick's written impositions was a sworn peace sanctioned by imperial judges.[315] And when the child-king Alfonso II of Aragon was produced in a festal assembly at Zaragoza on 11 November 1164, he was made by his regent-prelates and -barons to denounce 'the perversities of the bad men of my land and to remedy the many transgressions that are perpetrated daily in my land'; he thereupon imposed his 'power' in the baronial castles, reaffirmed his 'peaces and truces,' and prohibited plunder and larceny, all this sanctioned

[312] RAPh2 I, nos. 337, 340; cf. no. 330.
[313] Rigord, Gesta, c. 70 (I, 100–105).   [314] ed. Duchesne IV, 583.
[315] DDFrI II, nos. 229–43; Burchard von Ursberg, Chronik 30–31.

by the oaths of all men present and, by evident design, yet to be enlisted, one sworn adhesion after another.[316]

In these portentous manifestations three major lord-kings had imposed the peace heretofore chiefly ecclesiastical as their own cause by securing the solemnly sworn commitments of their peoples, perhaps more fully assembled (we shall see) than ever before. The oaths were as much consent as fulfillment, sprung from the emotional consensus of open-ended occasions. But violence persisted, everywhere, it seems: the petty violences of multiplied castles not yet fully restored to defensive or delegated status, of distraints, and of under-disciplined banded knights. Towards 1166–76, even as other interests were being sounded collectively, an incessant clerical clamour against seizures and pillage had got through to Henry II; it had won royal backing in Catalonia although not, it seems, after 1164 in Aragon; and by the 1180s it could no longer be resisted in Germany, Aragon, León, and Navarre. One need only review the statutory verbiage more closely to sense the purport of the new campaign.

In his ordinance against arsonists (Nuremberg, 29 December 1186), Barbarossa not only claimed to act 'in the presence of his princes [and] with their counsel and consent,' but also dwelt rhetorically on his imperial obligation 'to provide for the general tranquillity of his provincial peoples.'[317] More problematic are the 'constitutions' of January 1188, said to have been promulgated by King Alfonso II at Huesca 'before barons, knights, and many people of the realm of Aragon, and wise men.' That such measures were indeed imposed need hardly be doubted: King Alfonso is otherwise known to have held a 'solemn court' in Huesca at this time. But these chapters point to a petty jurisprudence of the king's *merinos* while keeping silence about the power of castles. They read as if the programme of 1164 had been ignored or forgotten, which is likely enough. The royal 'power' to recover castles was a Catalan custom otherwise unknown in Aragon. So for all we know the Aragonese barons may have re-

<hr />

[316] *DI* VIII, no. 10.   [317] *CAP* I, no. 318.

sisted their lord-king, as did the Catalonian magnates later that year. The 'constitutions' break off incomplete in our only copy; there is no claim that they received the assent of the assembled people; and one may plausibly imagine that, as in Catalonia, the originals of the constitutions of Huesca were destroyed early. What remains even so is the strong presumption that the elaborated rubric with which these chapters open points to the king's intention to win over the people of Aragon to the observance of an original statute of security.[318] Still more obscure, and therefore exempt from all conjecture, is the situation in Navarre. All we know is that Sancho VI meant to create or confirm a custom when, with the approval of his knights and 'other nobles,' he sought to reduce the violence of anger and retaliation by requiring the formality of renunciation (*diffidatio*). It may be some further indication of engagement with his people that Sancho VI ('the Wise') had previously taken interest in the incipient *fueros* of Navarre.[319]

What all these enactments have in common is best shown by the legislation of León (1188–94). Critically expounded by José María Fernández Catón, these records can now be recognized as a deeply revealing indicator of royal purpose in the waning twelfth century. Here uniquely we have a lord-king's own assessment of his remedial programme and its shortcomings. At the end of 1194 or soon after, Alfonso IX sent copies of his statutes of 1188 and 1194 to the bishop of Orense, enjoining him to see to their observance. His covering mandate reads partly as follows:

> Just as through compliance with our decrees the state of our kingdom began to be reformed, so by their neglect it [i.e., the 'state'] is seen to have declined considerably from its state of

---

[318] Citations in note 304 above.

[319] '. . . cum comuni assensu militum et aliorum nobilium genere qui sunt de meo regno, statuo et confirmo in forum . . . Si quis nobilis . . . non diffidiet illum . . . ,' ed. Lacarra, 'Documentos,' 496–97; *Fueros derivados de Jaca. 1 Estella-San Sebastián*, ed. José Ma. Lacarra (Pamplona 1969) 59–61.

fulfillment. So whereas we have confirmed the statutes by common oath, having first secured the counsel and deliberation of prelates and judges and the consent of all our princes, once again, restoring the due validity formerly strictly in force, by the same rigour we wish and command them all to be inviolably observed.[320]

Three points require notice here: first, the nature of the king's concern; second, his identification of violence and disorder with the 'state of the realm [*status regni*]'; and third, the evident presumption that the troubled state of the realm is not merely the lord-king's problem, but also that of the men he has consulted.

1. It is quite beyond doubt that Alfonso IX had in mind the prevailing violence in León and Galicia that was the subject of the statutes of 1188 and 1194, and that the latter precisely were what the king sent to the bishop. These two statutes deal exclusively with the remedy of violence, and together with the covering mandate they survive only in a near-contemporary copy preserved in the cathedral of Orense. What is more, the first of these statutes, which is recorded in the king's first-person (singular) voice, contains in its preamble an extended recitation of the alleged troubles. 'When I came to León,' said Alfonso, 'I learned there from plaintiffs and my other vassals that my kingdom was greatly troubled by malefactors who had wilfully perverted the state of the realm.' Some seized property out of hatred. Others assaulted persons on pretext of their servility, and their goods. Others just stole, secretly or openly. Others seized property as if it were pledged. Still others thought lightly of helping themselves to the food, water, and fodder of neighbours or their tenants, or of seizing by force from travellers. The easier it seemed to oppress lesser men the harder one tried.[321]

---

[320] Fernández Catón, *Curia regia* 144–48; quotation from 132.

[321] Orense, Archivo de la Catedral, Privilegios I, 51; ed. Fernández Catón, *Curia regia* 133, 138–39, 144–48; facsimile lámina xv.

So that even Spain has its showcase of the iniquities so well documented in other European lands. The violence of greed or temptation, of hasty vengeance, of judicial procedure, and (note well) of pretensions to lordship: it's all here. To the lord-king's generalities his courtiers and jurists brought precision, especially in the longer statute of 1194. To that record (as we have it) were added regulations showing that the king's men had tried to convoke and list pillagers and thieves.[322] It follows, and perhaps needs to be underscored: what first engaged Alfonso IX in 1188 and after was internal violence in all its forms. This was his cause, presented in great courts at León in July (1188) and in September 1194, resulting in highly pertinent statutes. What is not clear from the royal diplomatic is whether the suppression of violence met with dissent in those assemblies.

Yet it would hardly be surprising if the bishops and lay magnates when assembled with the new king had ideas of their own. For in a great court at León, probably if not quite certainly that of July 1188 whence issued his first statute, King Alfonso IX agreed to the renowned *decreta* that survive only in problematic copies from the sixteenth century. At least three of their seventeen chapters are manifestly concessions. First, the lord-king, alluding to a 'court' comprising bishops, magnates, and 'elected citizens from every city,' promised to observe their 'good customs.' He 'promised further,' in his words, that 'I shall not make war or peace or plea [*placitum*] without the counsel of bishops, nobles, and good men, by whose counsel I should be ruled' (c. 4). And he directed that no one be summoned to judgment 'in my court or to the judgment of León except for those causes' mandated by their customs (c. 16). But that is the extent of these clues. Save for the interest in custom, it is impossible to discern a constitutional programme here. The famous c. 4 is as likely to have been the king's idea as that of his magnates. Indeed, the only confrontation over the 'decrees' may have formed about the eight chapters aimed at suppressing the violences of anger and procedure. As we

[322] ibid.,147–48, cc. 14–16.

have it, this great charter has the looks of hasty contrivance, conceivably the response of his scribes in an early session to the need to reconcile two functions or impulses in a great court the newly acceded king claimed for his own.[323]

2. With respect to the 'state of the realm,' not only was the endangered *status regni* mentioned in the royal mandate of 1194–95; that very expression had also figured in the statute of July 1188, where the lord-king contended that malefactors had perverted the 'state of the kingdom.'[324] What matters here is not the novelty of the Latin term, but the context. *Status regni* was hardly new in 1188. It is widely attested in the twelfth century, a constant if feeble pointer to the conceptual continuity of public order. In the usage of clerks, chroniclers, and scribes, *status* referred to condition(s)—as of the church in Burchard of Worms or Diego Gelmírez—such as were vulnerable, in need of defence.[325] At Roncaglia in 1154 and 1158 Frederick I spoke of the 'state of individuals' and that of his 'dignity' as requiring his attention. Close to Romanist sources, his scribes would have known that 'public law is what pertains to the status of the republic.'[326] In Hispanic sources *status regni* is so constantly found in the context of assemblies as to suggest that it echoes a subsistent notion of public order going back to the Visigothic kings.[327]

Yet perhaps never before 1188 had the usage *status regni* been employed with such conceptual fitness to reinforce a timely

[323] ibid., 98–117; and ch. 1 for older editions.

[324] ibid., 138–39. Carlos Estepa Díez has questioned the authenticity of these records as we have them, 'Curia y Cortes en el reino de León,' in *Las Cortes de Castilla y León en la edad media*, 2 vols. (Valladolid 1988) 1, 96; but in light of Fernández Catón's critique, his case seems unpersuasive.

[325] Burchard, *Decreta* i.33 (*PL* CXL, 558); *HC* iii.14 (441); 24 (458). See also *Annales Altahenses*, 53; OV x.19 (v, 314); Gilbert Foliot, *Letters*, no. 143; *Dialogue of the exchequer* 2; i.5, 7 (27, 40); Rigord xi (23). See also Harding, *Law and the foundations of the state*, discussions indexed on p. 389.

[326] *DDFri* I, no. 91; II, no. 242; Rahewin, *Gesta Friderici imperatoris* iv.4 (236); *Brachylogus* i.1 (2).

[327] See e.g., *Regesta de Fernando II*, no. 41, a privilege for the Order of Santiago (1181).

circumstance: a lord-prince engaging his assembled people so as to define the condition of their realm as an arguable cause. This is where politicising, which is my word for a phenomenon then unvoiced, may be perceptible in the circumstantial—and wholly historical—need of powerful lords and prelates to work out their unaccustomed ways of common interest; to begin to see their inheritances in relation to collective advantage by which together they could influence a changing state of the realm.

3. In truth, the whole interest of *status regni* in 1188 lies in its pertinence to the lord-king's attempt to enlist the people of León in his reforming cause. As in Aragon and Catalonia—and in the very same year—it seemed useless to impose stiff prohibitions of violence without seeking to dissuade the violent. But here too, as in England, it is hard to discern the interests of dissidents, let alone 'conspirators,' and harder still to imagine what might have motivated the people habitually excluded from assemblies. That we possess the 'articles' of the English barons (1214–15) looks like an anomaly for which we have Stephen Langton to thank.[328] Returning to the Spanish case, whose idea was it to place Alfonso IX under the obligation to consult in matters of war, peace, and plea? Were not these, too, states of interest such as might be claimed by others than himself? All we can safely infer is that the king was prepared to allow that these causes were customary restraints. That he really acted under this chapter would seem to be borne out by the record of a judgment passed in a 'full court' held at Benavente in 1202; and it is in this assembly, as it happens, that we first hear of an issue in León that could only have been resolved following debate—an interest, that is, which may have originated with knights and townspeople—: namely, the cost to them of the lord-king's promise to hold the coinage stable.[329] In 1204 yet another statute prohibiting violence bears some sign of interest to townspeople; a fragmentary record dated 1207 appears

---

[328] Holt, *Magna Carta* 285–91, 432–40.
[329] *Córtes de los antiguos reinos de León y de Castilla*, 5 vols. (Madrid 1861–1903) I, 43–44.

to show Alfonso VIII (of Castile) responding to the *concejo* of Toledo concretely about prices, possibly the trace of a general court otherwise unknown; and in 1208 the bishops of León secured the king's guarantee of the integral transmission of clerical property in a great court attended by bishops, barons, and deputy city-men.[330]

Yet it looks as if Alfonso IX decided that the cost of urging his cause(s) with massively assembled subjects was too high (whatever that may mean),[331] for after 1208 we know of no further plenary courts for the rest of his long reign. Likewise in Castile, where Alfonso VIII had convoked on a large scale in 1187 and 1188, he too seems to have done without assemblies for the quarter-century he had still to rule.[332] That the interests of barons, clergy, and townspeople were forming on the peripheries of these assemblies seems hard to doubt. What cannot be claimed is that questions of inheritance, taxation and coinage, or clerical rights were yet privileged as such. Even in Catalonia the only visibly politicised interest was the disreputable one of the bad-lord barons, a cause they largely salvaged by giving it up under Jaume I (1213–76).

Tendentious though they inevitably are, the statutes of Benavente (1202), Lugo (1204), and León (1208) make clear that Alfonso IX meant to claim all causes as his own.[333] That both Alfonsos now thought of their towns as integral to the status of their realms can be shown in another way. When Alfonso VIII arranged for the betrothal of his daughter Berenguela to Prince Conrad of Rothenburg in a court at San Esteban de Gormaz in May 1187, he was attended not only by the primate-archbishop of Toledo, three other bishops, and twelve lay magnates, but also by the notables (*maiores*) of some fifty cities and towns; their sworn

---

[330] Gonzalez, *Alfonso IX* II, nos. 192, 221; Francisco Hernández, 'Las Cortes de Toledo de 1207,' *Las Cortes de Castilly y León* I, 219–63.

[331] See below, pp. 553–68.

[332] Evelyn S. Procter, *Curia and Cortes in León and Castile 1072–1295* (Cambridge 1980) chs. 2, 3; Gonzalo Martínez Díez, 'Curia y Cortes en el reino de Castilla,' *Las Cortes* I, 140–42; Gonzalez, *Alfonso VIII* II, no. 471.

[333] *Córtes de León y de Castilla* I, 43–44; Gonzalez, *Alfonso IX*, nos. 192, 221.

adhesions to the treaty were recorded in an agreement passed at Seligenstadt a year later.[334] Because major concessions of lands in Castile and Swabia figured in the stipulations of endowment, this attendance may be likened to that of an interregnal event whereby the status of the kingdom is in its people's hands. The same circumstance a generation later surely explains the attendance of 'the leading men of cities' in a great court at Burgos (November 1219) wherein Fernando III (1217–52) celebrated his knighting and his marriage to Beatrice of Swabia.[335]

THE GREAT LORDSHIP OF CONSENSUS

One lesson from the Hispanic evidence might be that for a period of years extending into the thirteenth century, status—the conditions of people and things, including the kingdom—was slow to be politicised. Who but the few, with suspicious if not tainted motives, could have wished it otherwise? Almost everywhere towards 1200–1225 the customary experience of consecrated power favoured lord-kingship as seldom before. It was for kings to proclaim, not to elicit debate. The great cross-takings in 1188–89 were religious not political events; the Saladin tithe was virtually the Lord's novel exaction.[336] Nor did Innocent III wish for the crusade to become a debatable cause in Christian realms; it was to be preached and promoted, preferably not defended, and it was to be conspicuously his cause—his test of the state of Christendom—in the Fourth Lateran Council.[337] After the Fourth Crusade, diverted to Byzantium by underfinanced barons, many must have wondered who but lord-kings could be entrusted to lead armed expeditions to the Holy Land? Or anywhere else, for that matter?

---

[334] Gonzalez, *Alfonso VIII* II, nos. 471, 499; Peter Rassow, *Der Prinzgemahl. Ein Pactum matrimoniale aus dem Jahre 1188* (Weimar 1950).

[335] Citations in Martínez Díez, 'Curia y Cortes,' 146.

[336] *GrH* II, 30; Rigord c. 56 (83–84).

[337] 'New eyewitness account of the Fourth Lateran Council,' 123–29.

In France Philip Augustus cannot have felt such constraint about security from violence as did the peninsular kings, least of all after Bouvines. Yet he had begun by suppressing magnates of ill repute, and to the end, it seems, nothing pleased him more. For nothing so well extended the boundaries of his secure domination. As late as 1210 complaints of illicit fortification on the Breton border and of assaults on churches by Count Gui of Auvergne provoked resounding royal campaigns. The second of these, completed in 1213 by the king's captain Guy of Dampierre, put an end to the autonomous county of Auvergne; having financed the campaign from the royal fisc, the lord-king meant to retain the county in his domain.[338] But if the problem is viewed in wider perspective to be that of lesser elite pretensions to major lordships whereby to rival the powers of the dynastic aristocracy, then it looks as if Philip Augustus had another means to deploy. No fewer than fourteen acts from 1213 to 1223 show him confirming or imposing settlements by which lesser lords renounced claims on clerical lands or gave up castles. To take but one instance, in 1219 the lord-king ended a long dispute between Ponce de Montlaur and the bishop of Le Puy by judging that the two should share a toll levied where the public road adjoined the bishop's castle of Charbonnier; that only the bishop might fortify that castle (or authorize the building of any other in his domain); and declaring that Ponce had done liege homage to the king and sworn 'faithful service' for six (other) castles.[339] Efficiently served here, the lord-king's aim, as in other such settlements in a widening zone of multiplied fidelities, was chiefly to discourage the encroachments of untitled castellans while affirming their lordships.[340]

---

[338] Guillaume le Breton, *Gesta Philippi Augusti*, cc. 150–51, 156; *Chronica Albrici monachi Trium fontium*, ed. Paul Scheffer-Boichorst, *MGHSS* xxiii (1874) 891. A lesser branch of the dynastic lordship retained rights.

[339] *RAPh2* iv, no. 1612.

[340] See also ibid., no. 1491 (cf. Guy Devailly, *Le Berry du Xe siècle au milieu du XIIIe* [Paris 1973] 433–34); nos. 1415, 1497, 1499, 1534 (cf. 1532), 1566, 1618, 1629, 1638, 1660, 1696 (also 1697), 1733, 1758; vi, no. 79*.

Philip Augustus did little to promote collective interests except those entailed by his own causes, chiefly the (Third) Crusade and the wars against Richard and John. His success in the latter together with his canny exploitation of Normandy to the advantage of Normans and French alike simply undid potential opposition. In 1207 the canons of Reims conceded that they must serve the king 'when summoned as is customary in the kingdom of France through Christianity for the defence of the crown and realm . . . like other chapters of France.'[341] The *status* of this realm was conceptually territorial as well as public, something larger than its manifestation in a baronial consensus grounded north and east of the Loire. King Philip thought that Toulouse was 'one of the greatest baronies of our kingdom' even if its count Raimond VI had never performed his required military service.[342]

The interests in society other than those imposed are quite unevenly visible. That the king's advisers and scribes classified tenants by social status is of little help. Philip Augustus dealt with towns like lordships, the better fortified the more secure for his purposes as well as theirs, their charters so many local determinations of service, taxes, and justice. Of any collective urban initiative no trace survives, save possibly in the mention of a lost 'big charter' whereby the king commuted local obligations known otherwise only for Auxerre.[343] Although he may have addressed the communes collectively, King Philip is not known to have convoked them.[344] As for the barons, their aims figure chiefly in their service and attendance on the lord-king. They were his allies, not always easy to keep in the fold, and they must often, even severally, have received his letters.[345] Baronial interests could be differentiated from clerical ones, as appears in an inquiry into

---

[341] *LTC* I, no. 827*bis*.

[342] *RAPh2* III, no. 1021. See also IV, no. 1440, about a castle 'in marchia Francie et Campanie.'

[343] ibid., II, no. 628; cf. v, 183, no. 13.

[344] ibid., v, 191, no. 23.

[345] ibid., III, no. 1015; VI, nos. 71*, 88*.

rights of patronage over churches in Normandy. In an anomalous charter dated 13 November 1205, twenty-two barons,
headed by Count Renaud of Boulogne and including Norman
notables, recorded their own agreement about past practise, concluding amiably that, in view of the absence of some and their
own lapses of memory, they were willing to work further and
convene again.[346]

The higher clergy were more practised in their interests than
the other estates, experienced in synodal audition and debate. In
1207 the king acted on the petition of Norman bishops to institute a procedure of settlement in cases of disputed patronage.[347]
Yet in both Norman cases just cited some concern for unanimity
catches the eye. And it flares up again in the records of an illustrious court at Melun in July 1216, when the lord-king presided
over a judgment disallowing the appeal of Erard of Brienne for
the succession to Champagne. It was a case in which rights converged with policy, one of the first occasions when the great prelates and barons in attendance are termed 'peers' (*pares*); and when
Bishop Manasses of Orléans had the 'temerity' to speak 'against
the judgment of the peers of France,' he was publicly arraigned
before the king and peers.[348]

So much for opposition in the king's court. But something new
was in the wind, as we learn from a record of altogether singular
interest. In April 1220 Philip Augustus put a written complaint
before a legatine synod at Paris, and then, without waiting for a
response, proclaimed publicly that bailiffs and provosts were to
disallow markets in which oaths had some bearing on transactions. Writing to the bishops of Reims province, Archbishop
Pierre of Sens explained that this was prejudicial to the 'Gallican
church' and that, having consulted with his advisers, he had asked
the king to revoke this statute and await a response from the

---

[346] *LTC* I, no. 785.

[347] ibid., no. 828; *RAPh2* III, no. 992. See also IV, no. 1757, a charter of general protection for Cistercian houses (1221–22).

[348] *RAPh2* IV, nos. 1436, 1488.

prelates with which he might then engage. 'To which he replied to us,' wrote the archbishop, 'that he could not respond further until he had taken counsel with his barons whom he had convoked in a parliament [*parlamentum*].'[349]

Here for the first time the king of France is revealed in something resembling political negotiation. Two arresting points in the archbishop's letter should be underscored. First, it recalls in detail the to-and-fro of divergent arguments with respect to custom and policy. Such debates were hardly new in 1220—they can safely be imagined from narrative accounts of treaties or elections or from preambles to charters[350]—but the experience of them now seemed worth recalling. Second, this record not only contains the earliest known allusion to 'parliament' in a French diplomatic source; it also makes explicit that this assembly was to be concerned with a debatable issue. For that is surely what *parlamentum* meant in the vocabulary of a prelate who had once taught theology to the future Innocent III and who was long known to (and trusted by) Philip Augustus. His letter is framed in canonist legal terminology, referring to the affair as adversely affecting the 'status of the church,' and as 'touching the Gallican church.'[351] It is just such an affair as this that, already in the testamentary ordinance of 1190, had been spoken of as 'affairs of the state of the realm' in France.[352]

Even as new impulses in elite consensus and debate become visible, power remains rooted in law and right (or their absence). No 'theory,' as Gavin Langmuir pointed out, 'allowed a legitimate place for competing interests.'[353] Practise, however, did make allowance for them, and if the interests often boil down (in

---

[349] ibid., v, 192–95, no. 25. The editor (192n) has overlooked Gavin Langmuir's citation of this record, 'Politics and parliaments in the early thirteenth century,' *Etudes sur l'histoire des assemblées d'états* (Paris 1966) 59, from a derivative source.

[350] Langmuir, 'Politics,' 50, 55.

[351] *Register Innocenz' III.*, I, no. 478; Baldwin, *Masters* I, 46; II, 36–37. For the background of two laws, Gaines Post, *Studies in medieval legal thought . . .* (Princeton 1964).

[352] Rigord c. 70 (102).   [353] 'Politics,' 49.

our terms) to matters of right, the experience of arguing and deciding was changing in France, as everywhere else. Yet perhaps in
its own way. For Philip Augustus it was enough to have sway
with his favourite bishops and barons, an affective domination of
veterans (for much of the reign) mostly heedless of bureaucracy.
Once at least he spoke of the 'royal and public authority of all
churchmen and princes of the realm' as if statutory power were
shared; but this was exceptional usage in a 'constitution' of nonprejudice (1189) to the archbishop and people of Reims who had
consented to the recent crusading taxes.[354] Philip's scribes employed no template of injunctive command. Of some thirty-five
plus ordinances, constitutions, or 'establishments' from his reign,
only three survive in originals, only five others in plausible copies. Only four figure in the registers, where (as late as 1220) they
had no rubric to themselves. Philip's ordinance-testament of June
1190 we have perhaps only because Rigord kept a copy (or original?) when the crusading party departed. If Philip expected compliance with his commands about Jews, fortification, and dowry,
he left little to prove it. Of an edict addressed to Norman knights
who had fled with King John nothing survived but diffuse recollections.[355] Even so, the normative texts we do have seem to show
that what mattered for the record were commands in the nature
of conventions and regulations. Some of these came out of inquiries following the conquest of Normandy, such as the *stabilimentum* on rights over the Norman clergy (1205) and a determination
(called *scriptum de foagio*) how the customary Norman money-tax
should be assessed.[356]

A statute in all but name, the latter text was copied in Register
E (1220) together with a ducal constitution of 1185 relating to
successions in baronies and fiefs in Brittany.[357] What needed to be
settled in the royal domain and contiguous baronies was custom

---

[354] *RAPh2* I, no. 252.   [355] ibid., v, 184–85, no. 15.
[356] *LTC* I, no. 785; *Registres de Philippe Auguste* 556–57, no. 9.
[357] *Registres* 555–57, nos. 8, 9.

and customary right, so it is no accident that amongst the preserved royal ordinances are found important conventions—that
is, Philip Augustus acting *with* his barons in their princely
attributes—relative to feudal tenures and the possession of Jews.
Moreover, having virtually become such a prince himself, Philip
took over a Norman exchequer whose practised clerks had already produced a compilation of provincial custom from their
experience, and whose successors about 1220 compiled the
king's first gathering of statutes together with a revised version
of Norman custom drawing on the ducal archives. Custom
would not always be the lord-king's cause, but as it first appears
in the Norman compilations, it was a windfall for the protector-
king.[358]

The consensus of Philip's lordship had another peculiarity. It
had no necessary tie with his assemblies. His chroniclers seldom
refer to his 'court' (still less to 'his court') other than in strictly
procedural contexts, often in the king's absence. What is repeatedly attested is the summons (*convocare*, in whatever form) or the
attendance of magnates on occasions or in 'councils' (and 'great
councils') in which debate is as routinely concealed as adhesion
to the king's purpose is on view.[359] There was no diplomatic of
convocation, such as in Catalonia, save for written summonses
almost all of which have perished.[360] King Philip's scribes were
surely familiar with the scholastic doctrine of equitable social
utility, with what Robert of Courson called the 'whole status of

---

[358] *Le Très ancien Coutumier de Normandie*, ed. Ernest-Joseph Tardif, *Coutumiers de Normandie*, 2 vols. (Rouen 1881–1903) i.15, 16, 31, 48 (I, 15–18, 27, 39), but
many other chapters imply violence. Also Baldwin, *Government* 225–30 (*Ph-
Aug.* 291–98).

[359] See generally Rigord, Guillaume le Breton, and *RAPh2*. For *convocare*
Rigord cc. 41, 43, 70, 108, 131, 140, 144; Guil. le Breton cc. 165; and for *curia*
Rigord cc. 35, 48, 50; *RAPh2* VI, nos. 22*, 68*, 69* (illustrations of *dictamen*).

[360] They were often cited or imitated by those who had read them: e.g.,
Récits d'un ménestrel de Reims au treizième siècle, ed. Natalis de Wailly (Paris 1876)
c. 252; *RAPh2* VI, nos. 25*, 26*, 75*, 131*.

subjects.'[361] Yet it is unlikely that these compilers of their master's written domination thought of such status as embodied in assembled people, nor was it for them to insist on the new ideologies of public necessity and Capetian destiny. Philip himself, like his biographers, was content to let his triumphs speak for themselves[362]

TOWARDS ESTATES OF ASSOCIATIVE POWER

Early in his reign Philip Augustus exploited a dynastic lapse in the county of Nevers to secure the marriage of the heiress Agnès to his cousin Pierre de Courtenay. In 1188 the two of them, acting in the abbey-town of Corbigny 'with the counsel and consent of bishops, abbots, and barons,' announced a new coinage on standards of one-third fine silver weighing 16s. 8d. to the mark of Troyes. They swore to maintain this money 'perpetually' on these standards and to see to it that their successors did the same. They provided for remedies in case of violations, for supervision by money-changers and experts on monetary alloy and weight. And they added this clause: 'for the perpetuity of this coinage and for the journey to Jerusalem, it pleased the ecclesiastical persons and barons of our land that we may collect from every house having its own resident and hearth, in this year only, twelve pennies, through the cities and castles and *bourgs* and villages in which our coinage has rightful currency.' Churches and barons were to receive written assurance that their willing grant of this tax would form no precedent. All these engagements were recorded in a charter bearing the seals of Pierre II and Agnès of Nevers.[363]

---

[361] 'Summa' xv.6, BnF MS latin 14524, fol. 65rb (quoted by Baldwin, *Masters* II, 174 note).

[362] Elizabeth A. R. Brown, 'La notion de la légitimité et la prophétie à la cour de Philippe Auguste,' *La France de Philippe Auguste* . . . (Paris 1982) 82, 96.

[363] AD Nièvre 2G11, no. 1, presently missing; ed. Maurice Prou, 'Recueil de documents relatifs à l'histoire monétaire,' *Revue numismatique* 3d series, XIV (1896) 287–88; reprinted in *CC* 201–2.

It is hard to know which urgency was foremost in this event: Pierre de Courtenay's reputation for violence, including his exploitation of monetary prerogatives, or the royal campaign to raise money for crusade? What is certain is that some short time after the cross-taking and redefinition of the crusading tithe (March 1188) King Philip confirmed the charter of Corbigny in a suitably revised form. That *these* events go together is hard to doubt: the royal confirmation was preserved at Auxerre, whose bishop and canons complained bitterly about the counts of Nevers.[364] Once again the year 1188 rings its bell. The charter of Corbigny, although it has not quite the significance of the peninsular statutes of those months, stands sentinel at the convergence of public taxation and coinage as societal interests, auspicious determinants of a new model of associative power.

The congenital instability of coinages was a worsening problem for lord-princes everywhere after 1150. Mercantile exchange was expanding, customary dues from peasant tenants were normally fixed, and for both scenes the suspicion of circulating coins, typically the blackened pennies of less than one-half alloyed silver, was constant. Nothing better illustrates the preponderance of self-serving lordship even in princely powers—for with few exceptions only they had monetary rights—than the fact that profits of coinage had ceased to be a publicly accountable revenue. The very word 'lordship' (*senioraticum, seigneuriage*) came to refer to the master's cut in the profits of money. In reality, the mint (*moneta*) and the exchange of silver or worn coins that fed it were arbitrary prerogatives of lordship, more or less profitable depending (chiefly) on the proprietor-prince's rapport with his technicians who exchanged, melted, alloyed, and struck on dies. 'When he wishes,' it was proclaimed on behalf of the count of Namur, 'it [the coinage] will be stable; when he wishes it will be changed.' The *fuero* of Jaca attributed the same power

---

[364] *RAPh2* I, nos. 228, 229, 237; cf. no. 184; *Gestes des évêques d'Auxerre* II, 165–69.

to the king of Aragon.[365] And the consequences of manipulated coinages—typically, debasements surreptitiously effected, but also reinforcements in alloy and weight—if not wilfully blatant were hard to conceal for long. The earliest manifestations of sustained collective resistance to arbitrary lordship relate to the coinage.

These took two forms, both of which are illustrated by the charter of Corbigny. The first was a compensatory tax, such as is found in Normandy some time before 1100, when the duke seems to have consented to renounce his right to alter the coinage in return for a periodic levy on his people; in the early twelfth century this became customary as a triennial tax of 12*d*. on hearths. Comparable compensatory taxes appeared in the Ile-de-France under Louis VI and his son, first at Orléans, then at Etampes, and finally at Paris. In the first two cases the lord-king's sworn promise to hold his coinages stable appears explicitly. The sworn confirmation also appears as an uncompensated promise in the counties of Blois, Troyes, Barcelona, and Burgundy (1164 to 1187); and in Germany Frederick I imposed unsworn confirmations of coinage in Basel (1154) and Aachen (1166). So it looks as if the princely promise and the people's commitment were the separable elements of negotiations with variable outcomes; and it is even clearer that the sworn confirmation of coinage was a privilege (among others) responsive to petitions, fully comparable to pleas for the remedy of violence. The stable coinage was assimilated to the Peace of God in Cerdanya as early as 1118; and from at least the time of the First Lateran Council (1123) it seemed that alterations in weight and alloy were thought indistinct from counterfeiting, a species of fraud and, accordingly, of violence as well.[366]

To the extent that the money-tax was commutative, it was ambivalent in nature. Because the coinage was a public and utilitarian instrument, the princely right to the mint and its profits was

---

[365] *Actes des comtes de Namur* 89, c. 4; *El Fuero de Jaca*, ed. Mauricio Molho (Zaragoza 1964) 156. In general, Bisson, *CC*, ch. 1.

[366] *CC*, chs. 2, 3, and 50–64, 126–35; *DDFr1* I, no. 67; II, no. 503.

unassailable; yet arbitrary mutations provoked indignation of exactly the sort elicited by lords imposing bad customs. Hence the uncompromising face of the confirmation: it was typically a vow never, or never again, to alter the coinage, without the least allowance for the economic circumstances that in all historical societies sometimes *require* the adjustment of monetary standards. Nor was this the limit of the anomaly, for by the 1180s, just when the lord-kings of France and England were in need of new taxes for crusade, they encountered the resistance of their tenant-peoples who naturally viewed these 'novel exactions' as violations of custom. By that time the money-taxes in Normandy and the Ile-de-France had long since lost any pretence of public utility; the levies in Orléans and Paris were known as customary tallages. Yet they were substantial revenues for Philip Augustus, as was from 1204 or even before that, the Norman *fouage*, during a reign when the crusading taxes (for disastrous expeditions) set a bad example for public utility and were not repeated.[367]

In these circumstances the charter of Corbigny can be deconstructed, if not fully explained. In its tradition of 'conserving the coinage' it was a laggard. Already in France and England attention was shifting to issues of technical proficiency in the mints and of economic impact. With the need of raising money for crusade urgently in mind in the spring of 1188, coinciding as it did with complaints about the money in Nevers, some prelates must have thought of harnessing a subsidy 'for the trip to Jerusalem' to a deal over the coinage that had sanction in custom. And what lends support to this hypothesis is that the same idea had already occurred to the lord-king. In an astonishing charter of 1183 Philip Augustus had contracted with his tenants at Orléans and neighbouring patrimonial villages to give up his arbitrary tallage in wine and grain in exchange for an annual payment of two pennies per mode of wine and grain. It was explicit that for any two years of collection the assessment would commute the former tallage, while in the

---

[367] *CC* 36–44, 144–65; and on profitability Baldwin, *Government* 158–60 (*Ph.-Aug.* 212–15).

third year it purchased the 'stability of money.' People living outside the privileged zones must continue to pay the triennial money-tax at its accustomed rate of 2*d*. on wine and winter grain, 1*d*. on summer-grain.[368] So in effect the customary money-tax is trebled, as the only imposition with any pretence to utility, in exchange for abandoning the bad custom of tallage. This was to rationalize taxation in still another way, for by providing for a panel of royal servants and elected burghers to collect the 'tallage of grain and wine,' the king anticipated the practise of the Saladin tithe.[369]

The hearth-tax decreed in Nevers was a money-tax in name alone. Like the Saladin tithe and unlike the *fouage* and tallage on bread and wine it was an ad hoc imposition for crusade, and since it came with the reserve of nonprejudice for a single levy, we may conclude that the people of Nevers secured their coinage at a bargain price. Lighting up their old county for a last time, the charter of 1188 was to have no successor in northern lands, where the exploitative coinage ceased to tempt princes whose mints returned acceptable profits in the hands of regulated moneyers. What mattered there were the quasi-public subsidies such charters had portended, and just as in France the money-tax had lost its once utilitarian impulse to be preserved as a virtual (great-) lordly custom, so in England the Old English Danegeld, having survived the Norman Conquest, gave way to imposed 'gifts' and 'aids' under Henry II that came to be labelled 'tallage' under Richard and John. For some of these levies the Angevin kings expected consent (as well as payment), but recurrent impositions created an undercurrent of resentment that led finally to the provision of 1215 fixing a distinction between customary aids (ransom, knighting, and marriage) and all others requiring 'common counsel.'[370] It would be useless today to maintain that Magna

---

[368] *RAPh2* I, no. 84; facsimile of original in *CC*, pl. 6; also 35–36.

[369] *RAPh2* I, no. 84; cf. no. 123.

[370] See generally G. L. Harriss, *King, parliament, and public finance in medieval England to 1369* (Oxford 1975) ch. 1.

Carta thus distinguished between 'feudal' and non-feudal taxes. *All* scutages and aids were the impositions of a *lord*-king. The novelty of cap. 12 (1215) was that *any* of them should require consent. Moreover, in England as in France appeals for money or service could be denatured or relabelled as needed to expedite compliance. In the case of the ransom of King Richard in 1193 the unprecedented demand for £100,000 required regents and collectors to justify payments in excess of custom by resort to arguments from public necessity.[371]

The assemblies of Geddington, Paris, and Corbigny in prospect of the Third Crusade[372] were hardly the only such premonitory events in their day; not even in 1188, as we have seen. But northern lord-kings, surely including John, were already wary of convoking tenants for their consent in the early thirteenth century, and the requirement of Magna Carta that they do so (1215, cap. 14) may have seemed excessive to some. In England it was only under Henry III (1216–72) that something resembling a debate over fiscal ends and means can be discerned in the fragmentary records of the king's entourage.[373] And by that time the phenomenon was a generation old in Mediterranean lands.

THE WORKINGS of power, community, and consent were more precocious in the South, experienced in more complex manifestations of societal change. How causes get politicised becomes a more accessible problem, opening these further questions: how the personnel of attested interests is enlarged so that states of regional affairs find expression in assemblies newly identified with those people and interests; how and why celebration is overtaken by persuasion in new-fashioned instruments of power within princely governments.

---

[371] Howden III, 225; William of Newburgh iv.38 (I, 399).
[372] *GrH* ii, 33; Rigord c. 57; *CC* 202.
[373] See Stacey, *Politics*, ch. 1; Carpenter, *Minority of Henry III*, chs. 3–9.

To begin with, the confirmation of coinage remained current in southern France, Catalonia, and Spain even as it receded into vestigial status elsewhere. Having originated as an element of the regional peace, it persisted with the peace and truce: in Cerdanya from 1118, when the first known payment to secure a southern coinage simply doubled as a purchase of the peace of peasants, their cattle, and their plows; in León from some short time before 1202; and in Quercy from about the same time. In these lands security had become an issue of collective complaint leading to imposed remedy in the twelfth century; and it may be because for Catalans peace was more controversial than the stable coinage that attempts to collect an allegedly uncustomary imposition refer to the 'cow-tax' (*bovaticum*) not 'money-tax' in 1188. But when Pere I came to power in 1196 he tried to exploit the coinage of Barcelona for profit. Having first confirmed his father's debased coinage under oath, he then imposed a 'redemption of this coinage' while seeking papal absolution for his incautious oath.[374] Resistance to the ransom of coinage surely figured among the grievances of Catalonian barons who vindicated their license to abuse peasants in 1202, for their draft-charter of 1205 included the king's promise to hold the coinage of Barcelona unaltered for life while renouncing the 'redemption' of coinage and the peace.[375]

The time had passed for any such bargain to hold. The barons had too little to win, the king too much to lose, by giving up these excuses to tax; and what Pere I seems to have done thereafter was to return to the expedient of 1197—that is, to justify a money-tax by reference to public necessity—and to insist on it as never before. What happened in 1205 remains obscure, even though the records employed by Zurita have lately come to light. Most likely the draft-charter was simply jettisoned, perhaps in a 'general court' at Huesca of which no substantive

[374] ACA, Cancelleria, Butlles, Lligall 3, no. 4 Innocent III, ed. Bisson, *CC* 203–4; also 86–87, and ch. 4.
[375] '"Unknown Charter" for Catalonia,' 75–76 (*MFrPN* 211–12).

record survived. All we know is that the king somehow got the consent of a few to levy the *monetaticum* in both his realms. What is certain is that Pere employed the argument from necessity to levy further taxes: an unprecedented hearth-tax on ecclesiastical tenants for the repayment of debts in 1207, and a (further) *bovaticum* in 1211, justified by the projected campaign against the Almohads and approved by 'all the barons and knights' of Catalonia.[376] These events show how collective customary exemption was coming to interest Catalonian prelates as it did the English Cistercian abbots; how the king was having to negotiate with the clergy (and barons) as distinctive forces in society. Moreover, they show how royal appeals for money to support anti-Muslim campaigns were becoming tiresome even as special pleas to justify customary taxes at uncustomary intervals.

By the turn to the thirteenth century almost any illustration will show how the interests in coinage and peace were being politicised in consequence of rising princely needs for money beyond tenurial revenues. In July 1205 Count Raimond VI of Toulouse swore to maintain his relatively strong (*septena*) coinage unchanged for his lifetime. This looks archaic on first reading: a solemn promise in the cloister of the Daurade to the churches, consuls, and people of Toulouse, with no mention of compensation. Yet it was the elected consuls who ordered it and who had it copied into the cartulary *they* began to keep in that very year. Proof of their interest in a strong currency—were they not lords themselves?—this event was put forward as an initiative of public

---

[376] ACA, Canc., pergamins Pere I, 265–68; AC Vic, calaix 37 (Privilegis i Estatuts iv) no. 68; Arxiu diocesà, Girona, 'Carles Many,' fols. 51–52 (1207); and for 1211, ACA, perg. Pere I, 385, and many other privileges dated 21 March 1211. In his important article, 'La primera articulación del estado feudal en Cataluna,' cited above, p. 513n, Pere Orti Gost has revised my account of taxation under Pere I on the basis of long-lost records of the *bovaticum*. But the *bovaje* of 1211 was not the first general tax justified for a public purpose other than the peace, as he claims (983); this had been tried in 1196, if not already in the 1170s (above, p. 508).

welfare on their part.[377] At Cahors a few years later the stakes were reversed. Here a lord-bishop with a comparatively weak coinage tried to strengthen it, only to arouse a storm of protest from barons of Quercy and burghers of Cahors, who in effect reimposed the old coinage at the price of 10,000s. paid by the people of Cahors. The puzzling economics of this are addressed elsewhere; what matters here is the evidence that the bishop was facing divergent representations of the best monetary interest of his parishioners and tenants.[378]

Towards a Parliamentary Custom of Consent

And in this perspective it remains to revisit the plenary court of Benavente convoked by King Alfonso IX in March 1202. For the record by which we know it is not simply a diplomatic listing of decisions; it is also, for the first time, the virtual notice of an assembly as such. To be sure, the same king had referred to 'celebrating court at León' in 1188 when he decreed the very promise by which the court of 1202 was required; but in 1202 something further becomes clear. Only then does the king make explicit that those present came as 'bishops, my vassals, and many from each town of my realm,' and did so 'in full court'; moreover, he affirms that the statutes and judgments were made 'in this court.' One of those decisions was to 'sell the coinage' to his people for seven years at the substantial rate of one morabetin per household. The king, that is, renounced his right to change the coinage during that term in return for a tax conceptually identical with the Catalonian 'ransom' of coinage.[379] The seven-year interval recurs a generation later in León and Aragon, when a term of stable

---

[377] ed. from cartulary of the *bourg*, fol. 91rv, by Limouzin-Lamothe, *Commune de Toulouse* 403–4.

[378] Guillaume de Lacroix, *Series & acta episcoporum Cadurcensium* . . . (Cahors 1617) 87; BnF, Manuscrits, Doat cxviii, fols. 7–8v; and for the contexts in Toulouse and Cahors, *CC* 104–12.

[379] *Córtes de León y de Castilla* I, 43–44 (Gonzalez, *Alfonso IX* II, no. 167). A rubricator wrote: 'Judicium regis Alfonsi et aliorum regni sui.'

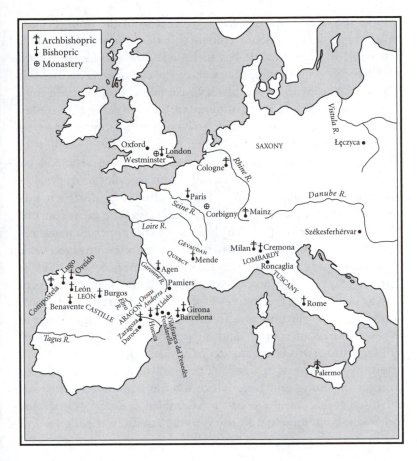

5. TOWARDS A PARLIAMENTARY CUSTOM OF CONSENT (ca. 1150–ca. 1230)

These are the locations of notable assemblies illustrating the enlargement of societal interests in power.

coinage had become a customary norm for public taxation in these lands. And by that time the custom of coinage had been appropriated by the Cortes as a custom of parliamentary consent.[380]

[380] See Procter, *Curia and Cortes* 54–56, 82–84, 186–90, 261–63; with this correction, 261: the decree of Monzón (1236) is *not* explicit about a seven-year term.

How did assemblies as such, as distinct from the doings of assembled people, become instrumental in the exercise of power? It is one last big question. It has to be asked of people who were hardly the inventors of parliamentary government. To answer it requires a detour from the history of interests and taxation long enough to appreciate that contemporaries *could* sense the importance of assemblies even as they were pardonably disengaged from the future. They knew, for example, that the great diets of Roncaglia (1154, 1158) were memorable occasions attended by prelates, barons, and the deputies of towns in order to impose an imperial settlement on Italy.[381] Equally famous in northern Europe, although of quite different character, was the great court of Mainz in 1184, a veritable celebration of the imperial aristocracy.[382] Unlike either of these assemblies, yet no less engaged with its moment, was the 'parliament' held by Simon de Montfort at Pamiers in 1212. This event, with due regard for circumstance, may be classed with the statutes of security of the 1180s and 1190s. Simon's explicit purpose was to suppress heresy and 'to extirpate the wickedness of robbers and all malefactors.' The latter aim, although historians seem not to have noticed, was focal; it targeted the violence of castles.[383] The work of devising acceptable customs of tenure and inheritance for the conquered lands was entrusted to a committee of the assembled prelates and barons; moreover, contemporary allusions to the assembly as *parlemen* and

---

[381] Otto of Freising, *Gesta* ii.12; iv.1–10 (Rahewin); Burchard von Ursberg, *Chronicon* 30–32; *DDFr1* II, nos. 238–43.

[382] Otto of St Blasien, *Chronik* c. 26; Burchard von Ursberg 57; *Chr. regia Colon.* 133; Gislebert of Mons, *Chronique* c. 109 (154–63); etc. Also Josef Fleckenstein, 'Friedrich Barbarossa und das Rittertum. Zur Bedeutung der grossen Mainzer Hoftage von 1184 und 1188,' *Festschrift für Hermann Heimpel . . .*, 3 vols. (Göttingen 1972) II, 1023–41.

[383] *HL* VIII, no. 165, and cc. 2, 8. Among the negligent, Thomas N. Bisson, *Assemblies and representation in Languedoc in the thirteenth century* (Princeton 1964) 43–48. See in general Timothy Reuter, 'Assembly politics in western Europe from the eighth century to the twelfth' (2001) *Medieval politics and modern mentalities*, ch. 11.

colloquium generale point to a current perception that it was a scene of talk or debate. Yet the diploma that passes for its record contains no sign of deliberative autonomy.

What these examples suggest is that even the most exceptional and spectacular convocations were more or less implements of their lords' powers. This was not true of all assemblies down to about 1225. It would be mistaken to overlook the assemblies of autonomous communities or those of incipient urban polities; both sorts have their place in the evolution of associative power. Yet what little we know about European assemblies from the sources is overwhelmingly in the shadow of lordship. That is why the writers of narratives everywhere, and perhaps especially in the German empire and southern Europe, employ the word *curia* (court) far more than any other in reference to celebration and consultation. It was a word of absorptive semantic genius. It could refer to a court of justice; to an entourage of advisers, servants, and family; to the celebration of a feast (Christmas, Pentecost); to a purposive occasion, often on a feast-day, such as when men were knighted or married; and to hearings of 'business' (*negotia*).'[384] These are the sociabilities of lordship, almost exclusively so. It is the lord's justice or entourage or business that the court invariably takes up. There is something obsessively domineering about it. 'In that year [1170] the king held his court in Paschal solemnity at Windsor.'[385] Of a well connected knight Archbishop Henri of Reims wrote to King Louis VII that 'he is prepared to face the judgment of your court [ca. 1170].'[386]

As in any convocation aimed at eliciting consent the lord-prince's power in his *curia* could be arbitrary. Yet it was ritual power, and accordingly an expression of shared elite status as well

[384] e.g., from countless instances: imperial: TrSEm no. 877 (*an.* 1156); *Otoboni annales* 65 (1162); *Annales Marbacenses* 174, 196, 224 (1187, 1196, 1215); knightings: Bernard Itier, *Chronique*, ed. Jean-Loup Lemaitre (Paris 1998), paragraphs 95, 126 (1167, 1205); dynastic marriage: *Chronica latina regum Castellae* c. 40 (83–84, *an.* 1222).
[385] *GrH* I, 4; see also 131.
[386] *HF* XVI, 152, no. 456; see also 160, no. 473.

as of deference. That courts were 'celebrated' (in two senses: *curiam celebravit, curia celebris*) was axiomatic in Latin culture; and the ritual action of this celebration surely lies at the root of parliamentary procedure.[387] It is no better than a reasoned guess that the ritual constraints of curial talk had some bearing on the multiplying allusions to *consilium* or *colloquium* or *parlement*. But from evidence already presented, it is clear that debate could be heard in assemblies of whatever description before 1200; and far less clear to what extent assemblies were coming to be viewed as embodiments of states of interest within society, or even of the state of the realm, as precociously in León.

This is where the fullness of courts and convocations confronts us as an insistent question. What was new about big assemblies?—when and why? Some of the most spectacular occasions of the twelfth century—witness the imperial coronation of Alfonso VII at León in May 1135, or the great 'council' convoked by Duke Kazimierz II of Poland at Łęczyca in 1180[388]—were among the least novel with respect to the elite representations of their realms. Contemporaries had no better criterion than common sense for describing some 'courts' as 'full' or 'general' or 'solemn,' nor do their modifiers necessarily point to some novelty visible only to us.[389] Sometimes the only trace of an assembly is the mention of persons who were there or of counsel and consent. The sources do, however, evoke yet again the persistence of public order within historically defined spaces. Like the assemblies of León (1135) and Łęczyca (1180), those of Corbigny and León in 1188 told of princely lands, conforming respectively to a county and a

---

[387] i.e., the initial mass of the Holy Spirit, the proclamation of purpose, etc. The word *celebrare* in all its forms is found everywhere in sources of every kind: e.g., *GpP* iii.25 (280); Rigord c. 57; *HL* VIII, no. 49; *CAP* I, no. 328; *Annales de Wintonia* 74; *Chronica latina regum Castellae* cc. 33, 40, 44 (76, 84, 87). See generally Gerd Althoff, *Family, friends and followers. Political and social bonds in medieval Europe*, tr. Christopher Carroll (Cambridge 2004) 142–44.

[388] *Chronica Adefonsi imperatoris* i.69–72 (181–84); Vincent Kadłubek, *Chronica Polonorum* iv.9 (148–50); Alexander III to Duke Kazimierz, *PL* CC, no. 1512.

[389] e.g., *Cart. Dax*, no. 12 (1167–77); Jocelin of Brakelond, *Chronicle* 44.

kingdom. As matters of record both were lord-princely events. Yet the second was attended by men 'chosen' (*electi*) from several cities.[390] What did this mean?

It surely meant continuity. There were precedents for the summons of townspeople even in Spain, but also quite remarkably in the Pyrenean realms. These precedents not only matter in their own right; they draw our attention to the rarely attested experience of communities faced with lord-princely needs. In a precariously confined world of shepherds, peasants, and poor merchants, the 'powers' of society were close to their peoples. Whereas the count of Nevers could only engage with his castled barons and knights, the bishop and count of Urgell rubbed shoulders with masses of unfortified free men. In 1162 they settled a dispute with the people of Andorra by having their lordship—or the form thereof—acknowledged via the ritualistic enactment of homage and fidelity. Thirty-six named men performed the submission, acting, six for each of six villages, 'for all others of our parish and of the whole valley of Andorra.' For a deliberate scheme of representation, there is nothing to match this testimony in the twelfth century. And what is equally extraordinary, the written agreement, which includes the itemized concessions by the lord-bishop and -count, is cast in the voice of the valley—'we all people of the valley of Andorra'—, rendering their record a harbinger of self-referential parliamentary behaviour.[391] That was a pregnant time in mountain-shadowed societies. Less than three years later, when courtiers of the boy-king Alfons—including Bishop Guillem of Barcelona, who had attended the settlement of Andorra—organized an assembly of Aragon to promulgate a royal programme of peace and security, the barons were joined by the named notables of six cities and towns in professing their fidelity under oath.[392]

[390] Fernández Catón, *Curia regia* 98.

[391] *Privilegis i ordinacions de les valls pirinenques*, ed. Ferran Valls Taberner, 3 vols. (Barcelona 1915–20) III, no. 3. See also Viader, *L'Andorre* 338–43, who argues that the homage and fealty were not those of vassalic submission.

[392] *DI* VIII, no. 10.

Yet it would be mistaken to read this experience of power as progressive. Inventive it may have been, but it is hard to catch people in the twelfth century devising solutions to perceived problems. What they were trying to do in Andorra and Aragon was to engage all their people, the more of them the better, and to do so, indeed, preferably as sworn tenants. When the bishop and canons of Urgell came to a further settlement with the Andorrans in 1176, the men of villages were listed in extenso, not identified as deputies.[393] Yet here again, even as tenants, the people of Andorra speak and act for themselves, as if for these solemn moments their associative identity is foremost. People in the uplands of Europe routinely acted collectively, often no doubt in resistance to encroaching lordship, although this is seldom visible in writing before the thirteenth century. In 1187 the 'neighbours' (besiaus) of Ossau and Aspe, valleys in the central Pyrenees, drew up a peace (patz) that is wholly comparable in substance to the great charters of security in adjacent realms.[394] Their sort of associative identity—a status that is moral as well as objectively defensible—is precisely what princely lords were seeking to harness in their courts of these very years. Yet to summon the villagers and townspeople was not to charter them as such. They were not so much 'interested' men as possessors of local powers whom the bishop, or count, or king wanted as allies. Carlos Estepa has shown that the 'chosen' townsmen who attended the courts of León (1188) and Benavente (1202) were probably of lesser military standing, hardly to be reckoned urban by any juridical test.[395] To have the towns with him was for the ruler to subject their 'leaders,' to use the terms of 1164; and it is no accident that all across this west Mediterranean world the notables of towns and villages,

---

[393] *Privilegis* III, no. 4.

[394] *Cartulaires de la vallée d'Ossau*, ed. Pierre Tucoo-Chala (Zaragoza 1970) A, no. 1.

[395] Estepa Díez, 'Curia y Cortes,' 78–87. This interpretation, although it may not prove definitive, supersedes previous arguments about the origins of urban representation in Spain.

their names and affiliations now marked off in the lists, as in Urgell in 1188 (yet again), were convoked with barons and knights simply to profess their submission in homage and fidelity.[396] Was there any more urgent purpose than this in the summons of Lombard and Tuscan towns to Roncaglia in 1158?

And in southern France for about two generations starting in the 1170s this inchoate mode of representation opened a byway in the history of power visible nowhere else in Europe. Here was a heartland of bad castles, extending from the Bordelais far into the Massif Central, where the territorial princes were weak, weakened, or distant; where bishops and counts carried on the struggles formerly waged by Bishop Aldebert and the poor carpenter of Le Puy.[397] Requiring money and fighting men, this exertion now became a campaign, imposing the princely cause of peace on the peasants and townsfolk who craved it. Their occasional assemblies became a veritable custom in the Agenais: a princely custom in form, to be sure, for it obliged the consuls of villages to attend at local expense when summoned, or even to fight upon demonstrated need, yet in effect a privilege of associated villages and the city of Agen; for the assembly once instituted, possibly in the time of Duke Richard (1169–89), assumed autonomous power as the 'general court of the Agenais' in the thirteenth century.[398]

There was nothing quite like this elsewhere. The lower Garonne valley was accessible and prosperous, provoking a singular

---

[396] ACA, perg. Alfons I, 470, 472; Pere I, 238–40, 356; T. N. Bisson, 'Poder escrit i successió al comtat d'Urgell (1188–1210),' *Acta historica et archaeologica mediaevalia* xx–xxi (1999–2000) 187–201. See also ACA, perg. R. B. IV, 268; Alfons I, 81 (ed. Pierre Tucoo Chala, *La vicomté de Béarn* . . . [Bordeaux 1961] 147–50).

[397] Above, pp. 312–14, 475–78.

[398] *Les coutumes de l'Agenais*, ed. Paul Ourliac, Monique Gilles, 2 vols. (Montpellier-Paris 1976–81) I, 140, cc. 70, 71; also Introduction, 3–7. Full citations in T. N. Bisson, 'An early provincial assembly: the general court of Agenais in the thirteenth century,' *Speculum* xxxvi (1961) 254–81 (*MFrPN* ch. 1); see also Nicholas Vincent, 'The Plantagenets and the Agenais 1154–1216,' forthcoming.

intervention in regional custom by the count of Toulouse. Yet even in Agenais the bishops (of Agen) claimed to keep the peace with the support of fighting men and compensatory taxation; and there as everywhere else they had to share or defend (or both) this privilege with or against lay princes. Moreover, in no fewer than four dioceses, possibly five, the institution or mobilisation of men or money occurred in assemblies that seem invariably to have deliberated on causes represented *and accepted* as the associative responsibility of the assembled people, not simply the bishop's self-serving cause. This means that the notables who gathered at Rodez towards 1168 and at Albi in 1191 were no less virtually 'representative' of their counties than the assembly of the Agenais with its deputations. But of the former dioceses little more than this can be said. In the Rouergue, the Albigeois, and the Vivarais the associative pursuit of peace may have ended early. All we know is that a tax to uphold the peace (*compensum*) soon became customary, long outliving any pretence of social need.[399]

It was otherwise in Quercy and the Gévaudan, where the bishops, hard pressed by successive counts of Toulouse and in the Gévaudan (from 1229) by the king's seneschal, carried on the peace-keeping so conspicuously undertaken by Bishop Aldebert in the 1160s. Thanks to royal inquiries dating from about 1250 and after into the rights of summons and imposition, it is possible to reconstruct the peace as it was recalled by participants; even to view it in action as a quasi-governmental agency. In both regions people were taxed 'for the peace'; in Quercy this was explicitly 'by the bishop's authority with the consent of barons and great towns and then amends were made and wages paid to those doing military service.'[400] In both regions 'peace-men' (*paciarii*) were appointed, apparently in assemblies. In the Gévaudan they were said

---

[399] *HF* xv, 886–87; *GXa* I, inst. 6; Bisson, *Assemblies in Languedoc* 106–11, 132–33.

[400] AN J.896, 33, *t.* I, confirmed thereafter (printed by Edmond Albe, *Cahors: Inventaire raisonné & analytique des archives municipales . . . [XIIIᵉ–XVIᵉ s.]*, 3 vols. [Cahors 1915–26] I [*Première partie . . .*] 46–47, 49).

to receive complaints, warn violators, and mobilise force if necessary.[401] In Quercy, priests collected money that was brought to
treasuries at Cahors and Figeac. And because in that diocese each
proclaimed peace required a separate negotiation, the barons *and*
towns in Quercy retained control of their taxation for the peace.[402]
Whereas in the Gévaudan the main issue in dispute was by what
right the bishop could convoke and tax, so that we find there the
neatly anomalous claim that a baron did homage and fealty to a
bishop in recognition of his *regalia*,[403] in Quercy what mattered
most was the associative cause of peace. At least one of their assemblies of 'great towns' with barons took place before 1200, according to testimony that amounts to the earliest explicit evidence
of multiple representative deputations in southern France.[404]

All this notwithstanding, it is the general court of the Agenais
that best illustrates a tendency for assemblies to assume the identity
of right. When Bishop Géraud of Agen confirmed his coinage for
life in 1232 in return for a twelve-penny hearth-tax, he needed
approval not only from the lord-count of Toulouse but also from
'the barons and the knights and the burghers [*borzes*] and the *cort
general d'Agenes*.'[405] Nor was this the limit, for even as this interest
in the coinage became customary the barons of the Agenais tried
in 1270 to encroach on the count's justice by instituting four
courts general each year to convene without summons.[406]

That assemblies might have, or claim to have, or some people
say they have, power or autonomy should come as no surprise.

[401] AN J.894, 9, *t.* 4, plus *Mémoire relatif au paréage de 1307 conclu entre l'évêque
Guillaume Durand II et le roi Philippe-le-Bel* (Mende 1896) 223–24; also *tt.* 6, 42,
49. Also J.896, 33, *tt.* 4, 6, 9.

[402] AN J.896, 33, *t.* 11 (*Cahors* 47–49).

[403] 'Documents linguistiques du Gévaudan,' ed. Clovis Brunel, *BEC* LXXVII
(1916), 23: 'eu, W. de Castelnou sobredigs, per la reconoisensa de la sobredicha
regalia, faz homenesc e jure fedeltat. . . .'

[404] AN J.896, 33, *t.* 1 (*Cahors* 46).

[405] AD Lot-et-Garonne, new G.2, 1, quoted in *Speculum* XXXVI (1961) 275–76
n. 129 (*MFrPN* 24–25).

[406] AN J.1031, 11, quoted in *Speculum* XXXVI, 269 n. 97 (*MFrPN* 18).

When Walter Map likened the court to hell or Gerald of Wales punned on courtly cares (*curia curarum genetrix*) they implied that even lord-kings might lose hold of their offspring.[407] But the courts they *convoked* worked differently, harbouring experiences of submission, deference, and alliance that are seldom vouchsafed to posterity. In every land of Europe the scribes who wrote charters and diplomas took more interest in the glittering finality of decisions or intentions than in decision-making, still less in debate, which as a rule must have seemed suspect. In every land of Europe except one the chroniclers likewise shrank from the stenography of sessions, perhaps in fear of being taken for story tellers.[408] England is the exception, and this is the place to wonder why. Is it the comparative opulence of English narrative sources that enables us to hear about talk in and around assemblies? Or to reverse the question, could it be that an exceptional subsistence of English consultative experience, perhaps even unbroken from pre-Conquest times, is itself what explains a burst of historical writing in Plantagenet domains without equal elsewhere? In the chronicles of Battle abbey and Bury St Edmunds one can all but hear the spoken give and take of petition and conflict.[409] With Roger of Howden the reader is made to feel close to the king's intentions concerning justice and management; only Rigord in France, who wrote much less about consultation, is comparable in this respect.[410] Richard of Devizes tells of a series of baronial

[407] Walter Map, *De nugis* i.1–2 (2–8); Gerald of Wales, first preface *In librum de principis instructione*, ed. G. F. Warner, *Giraldi Cambrensis opera* VIII (1891), lvii–lviii.

[408] Accounts of debate in literary texts, as problematic as they are enticing, are a huge yet arguably different subject. See for but two exemplary texts: Chrétien de Troyes, *Erec et Enide*, ed. Mario Roques (Paris 1978) ll. 311–41, 1171–1237, 5493–5620, 6411–6510; cf 6799ff.; *Raoul de Cambrai*, ed. Sarah Kay (Oxford 1992) cc. 9, 29–34.

[409] e.g., *Chronicle of Battle Abbey* 186–88; Jocelin of Brakelond 3–4, 21–23, 28.

[410] See generally *GrH*, which I accept to be the work of Howden; *Chronica Rogeri de Houedene* II–IV; Rigord, *Gesta Philippi Augusti*.

assemblies in which the dowager queen Eleanor tried to restrain Count John in 1191; and then, with dripping sarcasm, of Archbishop Walter's futile convocation—'everyone ventilating his words'—in the discredited chancellor's interest.[411]

In England, according to the records, assemblies happen thick and fast: festival courts of the lord-king year by year, many of them scenes of pronouncement and baronial consent; convocations labelled 'council' (*concilium*) or, increasingly *colloquium*, or not labelled at all. While it is unsafe to guess from the labels, it does appear that councils and colloquia often dealt with debatable matters, such as will describe 'parliaments' from the 1230s. In England as everywhere else courts and assemblies were 'celebrated'; there more than elsewhere responsive debate can sometimes be discerned in them.[412]

Yet there is no sign before 1215 of assemblies other than ad hoc convocations on the king's summons or, infrequently, on clerical or baronial initiatives. (The courts of shire or husting are another matter, as are ecclesiastical synods, provided for in canon law.) What seems to be the first claim for the customary status of a lay assembly, having been made by or for the barons in revolt, was registered in caps. 12 and 14 of Magna Carta (1215).[413] That the stipulation was dropped from the reissues is a reminder that it must have seemed to some an infringement of kingly lordship; that it came to be observed even so suggests that consent to extraordinary taxation in a decently convoked assembly of the realm was a precedented convenience that had become hard to oppose. Many years were to pass before the assembly assumed customary attributes. When it did so a baronial identification with the kingdom

---

[411] *Chronicle* 61–63.

[412] e.g., festal: Gervase of Canterbury I, 160; *GrH* I, 131, 133; Robert de Torigni, II, 117, 125; Wendover I, 242; *concilium*: *GrH* I, 92–3; Richard of Devizes 52; Howden III, 240; *Annales de Waverleia* 258; *consilium*: *GrH* I, 302, 311, 336; II, 6; Howden III, 236, 240–42; *colloquium*: Howden III, 242; William of Newburgh, *Historia* v.17 (II, 461); *tractatus*: *Annales de Wintonia* 74; none of these: *GrH* I, 167, 286; Devizes 61.

[413] *SC* 294–95; or Holt, *Magna Carta* 454.

had long since rendered the king's status a distinct and special interest; the 'business of the king *and* kingdom' would have to be managed politically. And from the early years of Henry III, when the irrepressible ambitions of castellans became associated with a newly contagious resentment of foreigners, a potential for political resistance was revealed that would find expression in great councils and parliaments.[414]

Nothing like this is visible in the empire. As he came of age Frederick II convoked great courts of which the records were insistently his own, even as they displayed a characteristic affinity with feudal law, office, and regalian authority. In the *Constitutions of Melfi* (1231) the emperor prescribed a 'general court' for the hearing and disposition of complaints, to meet twice yearly in designated Sicilian towns. Comprising representative townsmen as well as clergy and nobles, this body superficially anticipated the reformed court later proposed in the Agenais; but Frederick's was an imposed court designed to empower the imperial justices.[415] Neither in Sicily nor in Germany, although for different reasons, had the princes much influence over a ruler who managed to do without them; nowhere did princely autonomy so flourish around 1250 as in Germany.[416] In Italy communal 'parliaments,' a residuum of customary popular powers, were losing their autonomy around 1200.[417] In Hungary the Golden Bull (1222) of King Andrew II (1205–35) gave renewed life to a festival court to be held by the lord-king annually in Székesfehérvár on Saint Stephen's day (20 August). As with the English Magna Carta, this marked a settlement between king and barons; but the resemblance is rather with imperial Sicily, for the customary assembly it sanctioned was

---

[414] *SC* 321–22; J. E. A. Jolliffe, *The constitutional history of medieval England . . .* , 3d ed. (London 1954) 263–76; David Carpenter, *The struggle for mastery. Britain 1066–1284* (London 2003) ch. 10.

[415] *Die Konstitutionen Friedrichs II. für das Königreich Sizilien*, ed. Wolfgang Stürner (Hanover 1996) E 2 (458–60).

[416] David Abulafia, *Frederick II: a medieval emperor* (London 1988), part 3.

[417] Jones, *Italian city-state* 406–7.

to be more like a great court open to petitioners than a political body.[418]

The potential for plenary consultation in the early thirteenth century was nowhere so evident as in Aragon and Catalonia. Their child-king came to power with an inherited cause (peace) and a problematic asset (coinage) for his regency to exploit; these together with increasing wealth in the hands of barons, churches, and towns rendered an enlarged summons imperative and recurrent. Cities and towns were henceforth routinely represented together with prelates and barons: from both realms at Lérida in 1214 and 1218; from Aragon in 1221, 1223, 1228, and 1236; and from Catalonia in 1217, 1218, 1225, and 1228.[419] The first of these (Lérida 1214) Jaume the Conqueror recalled as a *Cort* convoked in 'our name' by the regent Templars and others and comprising bishops, abbots, nobles (*rics hòmens*) from each realm, and empowered men from each city. He also remembered that his uncles Ferran and Sanç, in or out of sight, were lobbying 'each' to be 'king' himself; and that at the end all assembled swore fidelity to the child-king in the archbishop's arms.[420] Royalist celebration and sworn solidarity: the bi-regnal court of 1214 in its bi-regnal place (Lérida, Lleida) perpetuated traditions of collective security that would persist in the Crown of Aragon.

[418] *The laws of the medieval kingdom of Hungary*, ed. János M. Bak *et al.* (Idyllwild 1999) 32–35, 95–101; see also c. 11 (33), a provision thereafter renewed.

[419] Both realms: *CPT*, no. 23, and citations in next note; *Colección diplomática del concejo de Zaragoza*, ed. Angel Canellas Lopez (Zaragoza 1972) no. 48; Aragon: *Colección de Zaragoza*, nos. 49, 52; 'A general court of Aragon (Daroca, February 1228),' ed. T. N. Bisson, *EHR* XCII (1977) 117–22 (*MFrPN* 41–6); Catalonia: *Documentos de Jaime I de Aragón*, ed. Ambrosio Huici Miranda, Maria Desamparados Cabanes Pecourt, 5 vols. to date (Valencia 1976–88) I, no. 5; *CPT*, nos. 24–26.

[420] (*CPT*, no. 23); ACA, perg. extrainventari 3131 (see below); and (Jaume I) *Llibre dels feits* c. 11, ed. Ferran Soldevila, *Les quatre grans cròniques* (Barcelona 1971) 7. The uninventoried *pergamí* 3131 is a contemporary list of those who 'have sworn fidelity to lord-king Jaume' and corresponds to previous lists of jurors to the peace or count or king (above, pp. 502–11). The statutes survive only in late copies.

The very repetition of the royal summons in both realms created an increasingly experienced personnel, together with a customary procedure that virtually empowered the assembled men. Some of the notables from Aragonese towns in the 'general court celebrated' at Daroca in February 1228 can be traced in prior courts of Aragon.[421] By December 1228, when King Jaume triumphantly swayed a great court of Barcelona to share the risks and profits of conquering Majorca, a foral procedure had evolved that would become a fixture in parliamentary practise: the hortatory proposition; responses by *ad hoc* delegates of clergy, barons, and towns; discussion within these orders; and public agreements.[422]

Much of this we know, for once, from a king's own words. Assembled in 'general court' at Barcelona with men from the three orders, Jaume recalled, across a long experience with dissent in his convocations, how on this early occasion (1228) the responses to his stirring and devout proposition—made for the clergy by the same archbishop who had held him as a child at Lérida, for the nobles by Guillem de Montcada, and for the towns by Berenguer Girart of Barcelona—had been warmly favourable.[423] Yet even on this auspicious occasion he knew little of the debates preceding the offers of service, and we know less. The record of such massive assemblies continues to be the lord-king's celebratory diploma setting forth the confirmation of coinage with its associated tax (or ransom) in Aragon, or the sworn statutes of peace and truce in Catalonia. One can only infer that while the Catalans resisted the money-tax as contrary to custom (probably at Vilafranca del Penedès in 1218), the Aragonese rejected the peace (probably at Lérida in 1218, or even in 1214). What is new is that the solemnity of these occasions now derives from the court itself. The impersonally worded diploma of February 1228 virtually identified the sworn fidelity to the infant Alfonso with the

[421] Bisson, 'General court of Aragon,' 112 notes (*MFrPN* 36).
[422] *CPT*, no. 26; *Documentos de Jaime I* i, no. 112; *Llibre dels feits*, cc. 47–54.
[423] *Llibre dels feits*, cc. 47–54.

'general court' in which it occurred.[424] On the eve of the Balearic campaign ten months later royal decrees 'with the approval of the general court' were explicitly engaged with the 'state of the realm.'[425] It was as if the king might no longer impose or tax or campaign without the assembly's consent. Jaume sometimes tried to do so. But by 1228–36 almost all the attributes of the Cort(e)s in Aragon and Catalonia were in place.

IN ONE of his moralising tales Jacques de Vitry ridiculed the 'foolish people who rejoice when sons are born to their lords. For there are too many lords already to make this a cause for joy.' It was like the sun-god Phoebus, he went on, who took another sun to wife, only to have Earth refrain from merriment with the lament that the drought caused by a single sun would only be worsened under the heat of two.[426]

Lordship cannot have been quite the scourge affected by this opinionated preacher. Only a systematic study of justice in the new princely governments could show whether the incidence of uncustomarily exploitative lordship was reduced in the thirteenth century. But to the 'manyness' (*pluralitas*) of lords Vitry would have been as good a witness as any, if only from his experience in France. And to their ambitions. The Catalan barons, knights, and townsmen who crowded into the Conqueror's boats in 1229 hungered for first patrimonies as well as new ones in Majorca. In Hungary, León, and England lesser knightly classes (of lords) were coming to princely notice. In Germany and France, if not everywhere else as well, divided patrimonial inheritances were

---

[424] 'General court of Aragon,' 117 (*MFrPN* 41).

[425] *Documentos de Jaime I* i, no. 112: 'cognoscentes veraciter quod status regni nostri provisione sollicita semper debet in melius reformari, ut per statuta salubria . . . prout necessitas postulat, utilitatis senciant incrementa, in generali curia Barchinone . . . statuimus ea, que inferius. . . .'

[426] *Die Exempla des Jacob von Vitry . . .* , ed. Goswin Frenken (Munich 1914) 64, no. 142.

supporting younger sons whose lordships left few traces other than those of management and right.

If persuasion made headway in this world of towers and armed men, the experience of power remained uneasy. For us, so to speak, as well as for contemporaries, although for us the discomfort is conceptual. How hard it is to free ourselves of preconceptions about public taxation, relations of class, and politics and law when trying to make sense of the generation of 1200! If these are not the subheadings introduced above, it is because they would have baffled people beset by issues of fidelity, custom, violence, peace, coinage, and rights. If it is for us to discern precedents in the raw evidence of states, estates, consent, and self-conscious associative identities, this is no license to overlook their un-parliamentary contexts. In the end Jacques de Vitry had a point. What bailiff or sheriff or consul in pursuit of status or patrimony was much troubled by temporal days of reckoning? In Catalonia the new fiscal accountancy collapsed beneath the debts run up by Pere I. The Emperor Frederick II, by seeking to dominate in Italy, would enable the German magnates and bishops to consolidate their lordships. So the narrative of power towards 1200 is not simply that of peace, office, and politics in flickering states of cities, kingdoms, and discontent. Symptoms of a revitalized public order, these things were too cozy with the prevalent culture of power to threaten it. Few would have disputed Master Vincent of Kraków when he opined that 'public administrations' and 'protections of the republic' were best served from the preëminence of primogeniture.[427] Yet causes, once tried, proved tenacious; competence, once discerned, insidious. And if nothing else the misshapen fears of those 'conspiracies' were, in a sense, borne out. They were (indeed) about power. Government ceased to be intrusive.

---

[427] *Chronica* ii.28.6 (74).

·VII·

Epilogue

CONCERNING the little castle of Montlhéry overlooking the road from Paris to Etampes, two famous remarks span the period of this book. King Philip I was said to have deplored the 'treacherous wickedness' of its knights ever disruptive of his 'peace and quiet.' And it was recalled of Louis IX (1226–70) that in an elaborate moral simile contrasting the dangers of the Poitevin frontier with the tranquillity of the Ile-de-France, he had observed that it would be no great feat of prowess to defend Montlhéry, 'which is in the heart of France and in a land of peace.'[1]

From the Montlhéry of about 1100 to that of Saint-Louis runs a familiar history of power. The lord-kings of France progressively imposed a public domination on lordships and principalities ever more distant from Paris. It is a narrative of continuity that might seem to have little to do with crisis. Much the same narrative could be written of Sicily, the Iberian peninsular realms, Normandy and England, while (in the long twelfth century) the distinctiveness of German and west Slavic experience, driven by baronial dynastic ambitions, hardly subverts the paradigm. Everywhere the greater princely powers worked to subordinate men with the weapons and the will—and the castles—to coerce people.

This history of power, for all its abiding value, holds much less than the whole truth. The problem lies not with continuity, for all history is continuous. Nor is it simply a matter of the popular 'experience' of power, for the dominated masses of the twelfth

---

[1] Suger, *Vita* c. 8; Jean de Joinville, *Vie de Saint Louis*, ed. Jacques Monfrin (Paris 1995) c. 48.

century largely survived and seldom rebelled. Nevertheless, the suffering of peasants and townsfolk, well documented in some places and highly suspect in much of Europe, is not only a major element of the continuous history of power; it is the key to understanding *which* continuities of the twelfth century were most characteristically disrupted. Without continuity there would have been no crisis in this age.

What then *was* the 'crisis' of the twelfth century? In response to this question two normal continuities of power have been explored: the conceptual persistence of public order and the tenacious implantation of customary coercive lordships. It was the violation of the first of these norms in the tenth and eleventh centuries—*not* for the first time, but perhaps with newly disruptive force—that created the second one. Not only was lordship on a massive scale a new phenomenon almost everywhere, it speedily became customary. What is more, by about 1100 it was becoming customary even in its coercive or violent forms. If a perceptive biographer of King Henry IV and a great abbot of Cluny were among the few to see *and say* this clearly and explicitly, their testimony is borne out by incessant hints, insinuations, and complaints from almost every corner of Europe. And this is evidence, let us not forget, of a mode of coercive lordship that had no outlet of literate expression of its own. Even so, its tongue-tied norm must have been virtually as ubiquitous as customary vengeance, yet another continuity reeking of violence and one quite as ancient and tenacious as public order. Far more expressive than new lordship, vengeance was often a factor in crises of power, and not only in that of Flanders; yet it was hardly a debatable determinant in itself.

What moved the crises of the twelfth century were not simply the designs and dynastic accidents of the powerful amidst growing populations and wealth, but chiefly the new customs of coercive lordship: the craving for status tied to banal powers and the possession of castles. How better to justify one's superiority than by imposing on people? This dynamic explains—not alone, but substantially—the violence and violations of which monks in England (and elsewhere) and peasants in Catalonia (and elsewhere) complained. The violences and societal 'mutation'[2] of the (long) millennium had by 1050–1100 settled into a pervasively 'normal' dislocation marked by harshly imposing lordships, whether of knights around castles or of managers or advocates on patrimonial domains. And it is this customarily coercive lordship, a novel continuity seemingly in conflict with that of public order, that invites us to think of the recurrent crises of power that have been sampled as the symptoms of an unstable confrontation of forces that may justly be thought of as one protracted crisis of the twelfth century.

That our subject was indeed a structural crisis is suggested by a singularly precious witness. Master Vincent of Kraków, having attended the schools in France, returned to his homeland around 1175–78, when he became associated with Duke Kazimierz II (d. 1194). He attended a ducal-episcopal council held at Łęczyca in 1180 and recorded its enactments. By his account the Polish bishops prohibited three kinds of violence under ecclesiastical sanction: (1) the seizure of grain from the 'poor' by force or wile; (2) the imposition of labour services (*angaria*) or obligations of transport, save in case of hostile threats; and (as we have seen, 3) the spoliation of deceased prelates by princes or other magnates and their agents. These prohibitions require little (further) commentary. They suggest that, as in many other lands, the exploitative lordship of peasants was normal in Poland. But Vincent's testimony goes deeper. His record makes clear that Łęczyca was the scene of angry baronial dissent, and that brakes on lay lordship were by no means the only issue. The council had virtually confirmed the princely succession to Duke Kazimierz who, by virtue of his father's decree, was an illegitimate pretender in the eyes of his elder brother Mieszko and many others. 'So arose the voices and swelled the tumult of sedition amongst the magnates,' wrote Vincent. 'For as they said, behold just what we feared has happened.' And what they

---

[2] As argued by Poly and Bournazel, *Mutation féodale* (1st ed., 1980) and others, and much debated.

meant, he explained, was that brother against brother was like the crow that refuses to put another crow's eyes out: (so) 'this is our most evident danger . . . our crisis [*discrimen*].' [3] Here the very word for crisis figures in Vincent's classical vocabulary in precisely the context where the modern concept of crisis best fits: the Polish predicament over the princely succession.

Does it follow that Vincent got his crises mixed up? Surely not. From his sparely intense text we cannot be sure that he meant to distinguish between the troubles of bad lordship and those of succession. If nothing more he is simply telling us which of two liabilities of power mattered most in the twelfth century. What he labeled 'crisis' was a genetic affliction of great lordship, to judge from the instances of Navarre, Barcelona, Maine, and Flanders.[4] Gervase of Tilbury would write of it as deplorable that the customs of princely succession virtually invited the lordship (*dominatio*) of incompetents or fools.[5]

What Vincent could not see, or did not say, was that the conflict between customary seigneurial violence and new forces mobilising against it had also reached a critical stage. Yet in some measure this prelate, familiar with French academic talk about power and in touch with Alexander III just when that pope was abandoning the peace to regional initiatives, must have known. Vincent's witness to the prohibitions of Łęczyca rivals that of Alfonso IX a decade later as irrefutable evidence of a widely typical exercise of exploitative lordship. The Polish council of 1180 may be viewed as precursor to the great series of assemblies in which, from 1185 to 1195, European lord-kings first seriously addressed the violences of lordship and unmobilised knights. This was to recognize a deeper and more prolonged crisis (in the modern sense), a crisis, almost everywhere, of multiplied castles in the hands of people in quest of status and power. Not all such were defiant of princely authority, but quite enough of them were so to defeat the purposes of high justice in almost every European

---

[3] *Chronica Polonorum* iv.8–9 (147–50); and see above, p. 474.
[4] As mentioned above, pp. 188–91.   [5] *Otia* i.20 (126).

realm. Few castellans or advocates anywhere were popular. To most historians their impulse has seemed so futile as to be negligible; yet the case-history of Catalonia surely suggests otherwise.[6] The kings of France and Germany were having to campaign against bad castles well past 1200.

Even so, the crisis of the castellans would hardly merit study were it not for the wider sociology of lordship it exemplified. Service could hardly be pried loose from aspirations to power. This is why the spectacle of vicars abusing Italian townsfolk or sheriffs trafficking in commended or escheated lands may not be written off as corruption; it further explains why the improving mechanisms of accountancy were not enough to turn provosts and bailiffs into officials. Corruption is an abuse of government, such as hardly yet existed in the twelfth century. Not even learned courtiers, let alone their masters, commonly spoke of power deliberately exercised in the common interest. Few princes or prelates would have disclaimed such a purpose, yet one senses that the Parisian masters had it right when they belaboured the old distinction between serving and dominating.

Lordship remained the normative expression of human power in the later twelfth century. The deployment of patrimonial wealth to reward warriors and servants reached it apogee, amounting in some regions to a 'feudalism' (that is, an 'ism' of fiefs) in all but name: in troubadour lands at once a regime of fiefs and a culture of fidelity (-betrayal); in Normandy, Flanders, England, and Germany the variable matter of codified custom. So far from subverting lordship and dependence, the fitful intrusions of expertise and accountability became its timid prop. Collective privileges and offices were awash in the imperatives of affective service and fidelity, to the ironic extent of requiring external 'powers' to rescue civic purposes in Italian communes.

---

[6] This crisis found its resolution in a revival of aggressive and lucrative lord-kingship under Jaume the Conqueror, a subject beyond the scope of this book.

ONE MORE turn of the lens is required. To speak of the crisis of the twelfth century is not simply to magnify the dilemma of castellans and the misfortunes of dynastic families. Nor is it that the truth of this history must somehow displace those of renaissance, reformation, and societal-economic growth. Those well-rehearsed events justly define their age. Yet the concept of crisis, however flabby in modern (non-medical) usage,[7] has the metaphorical resonance to awaken the human meaning of an experience of power no less historic than changes of mind, belief, and wealth; a problematic experience in which justice for the masses was elusive at best, the violence of castles habitual, and the suffering of peasants and working people massively normal. For one tiny moment an eccentric count of Flanders governed his people, fatefully offending his killers—and he was remembered as the 'good Charles.' A generation later a conqueror-prince of Barcelona tried to hear the complaints of his peasants, whose troubled voices somehow survived to inform a near-unique archive of suffering. In Catalonia, government—the imposition of peace as cause and policy—provoked a violent crisis of power in which the triumph of government was far from assured as late as 1213.

If government arose as a reaction against exploitative lordship and violence in Catalonia, much the same may be said of other lands. The critical confrontation between lord-princely justice and the privilege of barons and castellans has been exemplified almost everywhere in Europe. But nowhere else was it quite the same. Only in Catalonia did exploitative lordship outlast the twelfth century, although the violence of castles persisted in parts of southern France if no longer in the Ile-de-France. The peace of Soissons

[7] See generally Fr. Graus, 'The crisis of the Middle Ages and the Hussites' (1969), tr. James Heaney, *The reformation in medieval perspective*, ed. Steven Ozment (Chicago 1971) 77–103; and Randolph Starn, 'Historians and "crisis,"' *Past & Present* no. 52 (1971) 5–22.

(1155) was the last of its kind in France. In England the Inquest of Sheriffs (1170) coincided with new efforts to secure the reputation and revenues of the king's court. Yet in both lands it was just in this third quarter of the twelfth century that incessant allegations of dispossession and seizure goaded their lord-kings to take new notice, even new measures. In England the 'assizes' of 1166 and 1176 are veritable manifestos of pacification aimed at reducing petty violence and securing lawful order. The 'common law' incomparably displayed in *Glanvill* was not all new; yet its witness to expertise in procedure virtually coincides with new evidence of official work for the king and of its recognition by chroniclers.

Likewise responsive to violence was the incipient recognition of associative interests. In Catalonia and the Hispanic realms, peace itself was the first perceptible cause, the work of lord-kings presuming to impose it. Taxation for crusade was another new cause, characteristically contaminated with that of the confirmed coinage in north and south alike. That such impositions served public purposes, such as the peace-taxes in Catalonia and Quercy, could not be sustained; that they were seen to violate custom pushed lordly right in the direction of debate. In France and the empire the quasi-professionalizing of justice and finance was delayed for another generation. In León, King Alfonso IX sought to identify monetary stability and the suppression of violence with the 'state of the realm,' a precocious hint that the responsible exercise of power is what might already be viewed as the power of state, or government. Such an understanding of consent, while inexplicit in other lands, was widespread towards 1200–1225. Except in southern France and Lombardy, it owed next to nothing to Roman-canonical legal teachings. For in fact what is most striking about the records of power is how consistently the diplomatic and conversation of princely courts remain those of ill-tutored lordship. Offices, officers, even accountancy there might be; but fidelity remains the key to vocational success. Brother Guérin, William Marshall, and Cencius (by now Pope Honorius III) were competent, experienced men; yet hardly more than the accomplished personnel of governments bounded by courtly fidelity. Perhaps more original than they, Ramon de Caldes was spared the sight of his contrivance of administrative service wrecked by the demands of a spendthrift lord-king.

So the narrative of progressive change is offset by those of responsive shifts of direction, setbacks, and complacency. Which, upon reflection, is quite what might have been expected of this famous one of the 'Middle Ages.' The societies of 1100, continuous with their early medieval pasts, had been nonetheless disrupted, even deformed, by growing populations dominated by a newly stratified elite, of which the larger and militantly ambitious element was an incorrigible challenge to old public order. The world of 1225 was still a world of horses and castles, of peasants and knights, as it had been in the eleventh century. Now there were far more people, doubtless most noticeably in towns; in Germany, France, and England the rebuilding of cathedral churches pointed to new wealth and enterprise as well as to the 'shadowed peace.' Government distinct from lordship, even in most towns perhaps, was hardly to be found. At most we may suspect that the insistence on patrimonial rights was giving grudging way to the recognition of collective interest. The bad-lord castellans of Old Catalonia had shown the way; the barons of Magna Carta had a better cause. People were talking in assemblies, even talking back, and learning how to argue. A new sort of convocation lurked, one less easy for rulers to exploit. Its novelty lay not so much in who or how as in what it did, for it was not so much the representation as the elite expression of incipient societal status—of the state.

To speak of the 'origins of European government' in such reserved ways may seem overly fastidious in the end. But the beginnings of great things in history are seldom other than problematic. And what we have found in the present case is that the very expression quoted above would have been as meaningless to contemporaries as it is alluring to us. Of 'government' they had neither a definition nor a vision. What they knew about was power. And it is by insisting on power, as they did, that it becomes clear that if ever government was the solution, not the problem, it was so for

European peoples in the twelfth century. Hence the interest to their history of not only justice and law but also: office, accountability, competence, social utility, and persuasion to tenets of collective interest; that is, of pregnant stirrings in a distant time that were to have a famous modern destiny. To reflect on their (original) historical meaning may be still today, as it was in the course that nurtured this book, a resonant exercise. Cultures explain power, help us to understand it. Few perhaps are like our own.

WITH ALL its scars and regrets the south of France was a busy scene at the end of our story. The Roman church was poised to impose its orthodoxy even as King Louis VIII (1223–26) virtually imposed a colonial administration. An old elite clung to compromised powers as favoured knights and ministerial people from the north trickled in. The people clung, too, and hoped, living their habitual forgotten lives. Until, years later in his remorse, Louis IX set about to rescue *their* voices: he sent friars and knights to ask about their experience. In what they learned, not everything seemed hopeless, nor entirely unchanged. Something like government hovered. When a knight complained of arbitrary seizures by a royal bailiff, the seneschal ordered an inventory, to be followed by restitution. More typical was the case of a poor villager named Durand, who told investigators that a bailiff of his place (Langlade, not far from Nîmes) had bullied him so badly that he had felt compelled to flee; and that as he tried to go away, the bailiff intimidated him by forcing excrement into his mouth. To which, said Durand, he responded to the bailiff, first when threatened, then, having suffered the brutal 'oppression,' a second time in the same words, this time 'on bended knees' before the bailiff in sight of the villagers. These were his words: 'You can do it, as lord and bailiff of the village'![8]

---

[8] AN, J.1033 no. 13, fol. 24a; J.899 fol. 141a, ed. Auguste Molinier, *HL* VII *Enquêteurs royaux* 88 (no. 81), 148–49.

Lord and bailiff? Was that conceptual confusion still normal in Durand's society? Was it not, indeed, the abiding crisis of the twelfth century? The inability of agents to exercise power on accountable terms, to behave as servants not masters, was to be its conspicuous legacy in later medieval Europe. Justice, law, accountability, office and election, the perception and debate of causes: all these, of which only the first two or three were yet functions of record, were waiting in the wings. How little we know about the human experience of power! Yet the evidence is there, however problematic it may seem. In the end it is the image of Durand that prevails: the haunting image of an ignorant peasant in the Languedoc—'poor, simple, on bended knees,' these were the scribe's words—who could imagine no better world than his old one of arbitrary lordship, the only world he had ever known; a shared culture not so much of rights as of power: the pitiless, disdainful power into which his tormentor had so easily lapsed. 'You can do it,' for you have the power. It is for us to imagine in his place.

· GLOSSARY ·

adiit presentiam	'he came [into] the presence [of]'
advocacy, *advocatura*	lay protectorate of church lands
affective	personally, humanly engaged
alberga	obligation to lodge men and beasts
almud(s)	dry measure(s)
arenga(-ae)	introductory verbal flourish(es)
assart	clearing of land
assisa	customary court in Normandy
banal lordship	coercive power of command, rights deriving therefrom
basileus	imperial epithet
bovaticum (bovatge, bovaje)	cow-tax, peace-tax
burgeses	townsmen, people of *burg*
caballarius	horseman
cafis(ses)	measure(s) of capacity
cancellarius	chancellor, chief of scribes
carucage	tax on carrucates, units of arable land
chanson de geste	'song of deeds'
concejo (concilium)	town, local community in Spain
coniuratio	sworn band, conspiracy
consilium	counsel
consuetudines	customs
consul(-es)	officers, often elected, in towns; Romanist term for princely powers
contado	region surrounding a town
coterelli, coterels	mercenary fighting men, brigands
creditio	demand for loan of money
curia	court, assembly
dīwān	administrative bureau (Sicily)
dominium	lordship, property
échevins, see *scabini*	
façedores	servants

Facit malum	'he does wrong'
faneca(-ques)	dry measure(s)
feodale ministerium	'feudal function'
feudal	of or pertaining to conditional tenures (chiefly fiefs, *feuda*)
feudalism	regime of fiefs together with the lordships and dependencies they entail
fidelis(-es)	faithful person(s), one sworn in homage and/or fidelity
fief (*feudum, fevum, feodum*)	conditional tenure, the holding from a lord
fouage (*foagium*)	Norman money tax. See also *monetagium*
fuero(s)	custom(s) in Spanish realms
germanitas, see *hermandad*	
gistum	*gîte*, hospitality
gravamina	grievances
hermandad (*germanitas*)	brotherhood
imperium	power of an emperor
inbreviator	one who writes down, who records
infa(n)zones	men of lesser elite in Spain, knights
investiture	ritual act of commendation, as of churches or fiefs
jarā'id	register (Sicily)
judicium	judgment
Landrecht	law of the land
libertas ecclesiae	'liberty of the church'
legis doctor	doctor of law
maior domus	chief of the house (palace)
marchio	marquis, princely lord of march (borderland)
mark	in this book chiefly a unit of monetary account, often reckoned at 13*s.* 4*d.*, or 2/3 of a pound
merino	king's agent (Spain)
mezquinos	wretched people, dominated peasants (Spain)
miles	knight (as a rule); classical meaning: fighting man

ministeriales	servants; of privileged status in German-speaking lands
misericordia	mercy
mode (*modius*)	dry measure
monetagium, monetaticum	tax to compensate stability of coinage. See also *fouage*
morabetin	Almoravid gold coin, often accounted at 7s.
ordines	written or liturgical ritual procedures
patrimonial	of or pertaining to the social and economic power or inheritance of lordship
placitum(-a)	plea(s), court(s)
población	settlement (Spain)
podestà (*potestas*)	in communal Italy, lord from elsewhere invited to assume power in a town
potestas(-tes)	power, powerful person(s). Especially in Mediterranean lands, the lord's right to recover a castle on request. See also *podestà*
poyes	penny (*denarius*) of Le Puy (en Velay)
praeesse / prodesse	to dominate / to serve
prévôté (*prepositura*)	delegated power or district of a provost (*prévôt*)
prince (*princeps*)	public authority: viscount or count or duke or king
provost (*praepositus*)	patrimonial agent, 'one set over [another]'
Redeninge	reckoning
regalia	royal powers, typically those in hands of Christian prelates; also some of those claimed by Italian towns
remença servitude	'servility of redemption' in Catalonia, entailing the purchase of freedom
res publica	'public thing,' public order; 'republic' only in neo-classical usage
routiers	armed men on roads
sacramentum(-a), sagrementals	written oaths in Catalonia, southern France
saio, sayo(nes)	local agent(s) in Spanish realms

scabini, scabiones (Fr.: *échevins*)	local judges, magistrates (Flanders, northern France)
septena	coinage of Toulouse (7/12 fine silver)
sirventes	satirical poem about power
soc, soke	jurisdiction
stabilimentum	*établissement*, ruling
tallage (*tallia*, etc.)	*taille*, arbitrary (unconsented) tax
thegn	retainer of honorable status, especially of Old English kings
Traditionsbücher	collections of patrimonial records
trouvères	singers of lyrics in Old French
valvassor, vavasour	lesser commended man (*vassus vassorum*) in Italy, N. France
voluntas	will
voyer	lesser patrimonial functionary

· BIBLIOGRAPHY ·

Works fully listed in Abbreviations (pp. xxi–xxviii) are omitted here. Places of publication are in native forms, except when familiar English equivalents seem preferable (e.g., Brussels, Milan, Munich, Rome). Dates in square brackets refer to first editions.

Manuscript Sources

AGEN. AD Lot-et-Garonne, new G.2, 1.

ANGERS. AD Maine-et-Loire, H 1840, no. 5.

BARCELONA. ACA, *Cancelleria reial*: Butlles, Lligall 3, 4; pergamins R.B. III 20, 39, 104*dupl.*; R.B. IV 258, 268, sense data 12, extrainventari 2501; Alfons I 81, 86, 144, 146, 249, 278, 470, 472; Pere I 26, 238–40, 265–8, 356, 385; extrainventari 3131, 3141, 3145, 3217, 3275, 3288, 3409, 3433, 3451; Registre 1 (*liber domini regis*); Monacals: Sant Llorenç de Munt 353.

CAMBRIDGE. St John's College Library, MS C7 (old 57), fols. 171–345 (Stephen Langton, *quaestiones,*).

EXETER. Library of the Dean and Chapter, MS 3500 ('Exon Domesday').

GIRONA. Arxiu capitular, 'Llibre verd' (s. xiii); Arxiu diocesà, Cartoral 'Carles Many' (s. xiii).

LONDON. BL, MS Cotton Tiberius A xiii; Cotton Vespasian B xxiv; College of Arms, MS Arundel 10 (Barnwell annals).

MADRID. AHN, *Clero* Poblet 2109.

MONTPELLIER. Société archéologique de Montpellier, MS 10 (cartulaire des Trencavel)

NEVERS. AD Nièvre, 2 G 11, 1.

PARIS. AN, Trésor des Chartes: J.894, 9 (*enquête* in Gévaudan); J.896, 33 (*enquête* in Quercy); J.899; J.1031, 11; J.1033, 13; BnF, *Collections*: Doat 118; Moreau 68; MSS latin 10936, latin 14524 (Robert of Courson, *summa de sacramentis*).

TOULOUSE. Archives municipales, AA. 1 (cartulaire du Bourg).
VATICAN CITY. Vatican Library, MS Ottoboni 2796 (first register of Philip Augustus); MS Reg. lat 179.
VIC. Arxiu capitular, Calaix 37 (Privilegis i Estatuts iv).
ZARAGOZA. Archivo historico provincial, Fondos Hijar II.52.1.; Biblioteca de la Facultad de Derecho, MS 225.

Printed Sources

Abbo of Fleury, *Collectio canonum*, PL cxxxix, 473–508.
Abbot Suger on the abbey-church of St.-Denis and its art treasures, ed. and tr. Erwin Panofsky (Princeton 1979 [1946]).
The acta *of King Henry II, 1154–1189*, ed. Nicholas Vincent, J. C. Holt, and J. Everard (Oxford, forthcoming).
Acta *of Henry II and Richard I. Hand-list of documents surviving in the original in repositories in the United kingdom*, ed. J. C. Holt, Richard Mortimer (1986).
Actes des comtes de Namur de la première race, 946–1196, ed. Félix Rousseau. Académie royale des Sciences, des Lettres et des Beaux-Arts de Belgique (etc.) Recueil des Actes des Princes belges 1 (Brussels 1936).
Actus pontificum Cenomannis in urbe degentium, ed. G. Busson, A. Ledru. Archives historiques du Maine 2 (Le Mans 1901).
[Adam of Bremen] *Magistri Adam Bremensis gesta Hammaburgensis ecclesiae pontificum*, ed. Bernhard Schmeidler, 3d ed. *MGHSSRG* (Hanover-Leipzig 1917 [1846]).
Adam de Perseigne, *Lettres* 1, ed. and tr. Jean Bouvet. Sources chrétiennes 66 (Paris 1960).
Ademari Cabannensis chronicon, ed. Pascale Bourgain *et al*. *CCCM* 129:1 (Turnhout 1999).
[Adso] *Miracula SS. Waldeberti et Eustasii abbatum*, PL cxxxvii, 687–700.
Alanus de Insulis, *Liber poenitentialis*, ed. Jean Longère, 2 vols. Analecta mediaevalia Namurcensia 17–18 (Louvain 1965).
Alan of Lille, *Summa de arte praedicatoria*, PL ccx, 109–98.
Alain de Lille. Textes inédits . . . , ed. Marie-Thérèse d'Alverny. Etudes de Philosophie médiévale 52 (Paris 1965).
Alexandri III pontificis Romani epistolae et privilegia, PL cc, 69–1318.

Alexandri Telesini abbatis ystoria Rogerii regis Sicilie Calabrie atque Apulie, ed. Ludovica De Nava. FSI 112 (Rome 1991).

Alfonso II rey de Aragón, conde de Barcelona y marqués de Provenza. Documentos (1162–1196), ed. Ana Isabel Sánchez Casabón. Fuentes históricas Aragonesas 23 (Zaragoza 1995).

Andrea Cappellano, de amore, ed. Graziano Ruffini. Testi de Documenti della Fenice (Milan 1980).

Anglo-Saxon charters, ed. and tr. A. J. Robertson, 2d ed. Cambridge Studies in English Legal History (Cambridge 1956 [1939]).

[Anglo-Saxon Chronicle] *Two of the Saxon chronicles parallel with supplementary extracts from the others,* ed. John Earle, rev. Charles Plummer, 2 vols. (Oxford 1892–99).

Annales Altahenses maiores, ed. Wilhelm von Giesebrecht, Edm. L. B. von Oefele. MGHSSRG 4 (Hanover 1979 [1891]).

[*Annales Blandinienses*] *Les annales de Saint-Pierre de Gand et de Saint-Amand . . . ,* ed. Philip Grierson. Commission royale d'Histoire. Recueil de Textes pour servir à l'Histoire de Belgique (Brussels 1937).

Annales Marbacenses, see Otto of St Blasien.

Annales monasterii de Waverleia (A.D. 1–1291.), ed. Henry Richards Luard. *Annales monastici,* 4 vols. RS 36 (London 1864–69) II, 127–411.

Annales prioratus de Dunstaplia. 1–1297, ed. Luard. *Annales monastici* III, 1–420.

Annales de Saint-Bertin, ed. Félix Grat *et al.* SHF (Paris 1964).

Annales sancti Disibodi, ed. Georg Waitz. MGHSS XVII (Hanover 1861) 4–30.

Annales Weissenburgenses, ed. Oswaldus Holder-Egger, see *Lamperti annales.*

[Anonymous of Laon] *Chronicon universale Anonymi Laudunensis. Von 1154 bis zum Schluss (1219) für akademische Übungen,* ed. Alexander Cartellieri, Wolf Stechele (Leipzig 1909).

[Anselm] *Historia dedicationis ecclesiae S. Remigii apud Remos auctore Anselmo ejusdem loci monacho et aequali,* PL CXLII, 1415–40.

[Assizes of Roger II] Monti, Gennaro Maria, 'Il testo e la storia esterna delle assise normanne,' *Studi di storia e di diretto in onore di Carlo Calisse,* 3 vols. (Milan 1940) I, 295–348 (309–48).

Auctarium Laudunense, continuation of Sigibert of Gembloux, ed. L. C. Bethmann. MGHSS VI (1844) 445–7.

The Bayeux Tapestry, new ed. Lucien Musset, tr. Richard Rex (Wood-bridge 2005 [2002]).

[Beaumont-en-Argonne] Charter by Archbishop Guillaume of Reims, 1182, ed. A. Teulet. *LTC* I (1863) no. 314.

[Bernard of Clairvaux] *De consideratione ad Eugenium papam* in *Sancti Bernardi opera*, ed. Jean Leclercq *et al.*, 9 vols. (Rome 1957–77) III, 393–493; tr. John D. Anderson, Elizabeth T. Kennan. Cistercian Fathers 37 (Kalamazoo 1976).

Bernard Itier. *Chronique*, ed. Jean-Loup Lemaitre. CHFMA 39 (Paris 1988).

[Bernold of Saint-Blasien] *Bernoldi chronicon*, ed. G. H. Pertz. *MGHSS* v (Hanover 1844) 385–467.

[Bertran de Born] *The poems of the troubadour Bertran de Born*, ed. William D. Paden Jr. *et al.* (Berkeley-Los Angeles 1986).

Biographies des troubadours: Textes provençaux des XIIIᵉ et XIVᵉ siècles, ed. Jean Boutière, I.-M. Cluzel. Les Classiques d'Oc (Paris 1964 [1950]).

[*Brachylogus*]. *Corpus legum sive Brachylogus iuris civilis . . .*, ed. Eduardus Böcking (Berlin 1826).

Brève histoire des premiers comtes de Nevers, ed. R. B. C. Huygens, *MV* 235–41.

I brevi dei consoli del comune di Pisa degli anni 1162 e 1164 . . ., ed. Ottavio Banti. FSI Antiquitates 7 (Rome 1997).

Die Briefe Heinrichs IV., ed. Carl Erdmann. *MGH. Deutsches Mittelalter. Kritische Studientexte* I (Stuttgart 1978 [1937; original series title revised]).

Die Briefe des Bischofs Rather von Verona, ed. Fritz Weigle. *MGH. Briefe* I (Weimar 1949).

Die Briefsammlung Gerberts von Reims, ed. Fritz Weigle. *MGH. Briefe* 2 (Weimar 1966).

Briefsammlungen der Zeit Heinrichs IV., ed. Carl Erdmann, Norbert Fickermann. *MGH. Briefe* 5 (Munich 1977 [1950]).

[Bruno] *Brunos Buch vom Sachsenkrieg [Saxonicum bellum]*, ed. Hans-Eberhard Lohmann. *MGH. Deutsches Mittelalter. Kritische Studientexte* 2 (Stuttgart 1980 [1937]).

[Burchard of Ursberg] *Die Cronik des propstes Burchard von Ursberg*, ed. Oswald Holder-Egger, Bernhard von Simson, 2d ed. *MGHSSRG* (Hanover-Leipzig 1916 [1874]).

Burchardi Wormaciensis ecclesiae episcopi decretorum libri viginti, PL CXL, 538–1058.

Caesarii Heisterbacensis monachi ordinis Cisterciensis Dialogus miraculorum . . . , ed. Josephus Strange, 2 vols. (Cologne-Bonn-Brussels 1851).

[Caffaro] *Annali genovesi di Caffaro e de' suoi continuatori, dal MXCIX al MCCXCII*, ed. L. T. Belgrano, Cesare Imperiale di Sant'Angelo, 5 vols. FSI . . . Scrittori secoli XII e XIII, 11–14*bis* (Rome-Genoa 1890–1901).

Cahors: Inventaire raisonné & analytique des archives municipales (XIIIe–XVI ^e s.), ed. Edmond Albe, 3 vols. (Cahors 1915–26). *Première partie, XIIIe siècle (1200–1300)*.

Capitularia regum Francorum, ed. Alfredus Boretius, Victor Krause, 2 vols. MGH Legum sectio II (Hanover 1883–97).

Carmen de bello saxonico, ed. Oswald Holder-Egger MGHSSRG 17 (Hanover 1978 [1889]).

[Carmina Houghtoniensia] *A garland of satire, wisdom, and history: latin verse from twelfth-centruy France*, ed. Jan M. Ziolkowski, Bridget K. Balint, et al. (Cambridge, M., 2007).

Le carte degli archivi reggiani (1051–1060), ed. Pietro Torelli, F. S. Gatta. Biblioteca della R. Deputazione di Storia patria dell'Emilia e della Romagna . . . (Reggio-Emilia 1938).

Cartulaire de l'abbaye de Lézat, ed. Paul Ourliac, Anne-Marie Magnou, 2 vols. CDIHF. Série in 8° 17 (Paris 1984–87).

Cartulaire de l'abbaye de Saint Jean de Sorde, ed. Paul Raymond (Paris 1873).

Cartulaire de l'abbaye de Saint-Vaast d'Arras rédigé au XIIe siècle par Guimann, ed. Eugène van Drival (Arras 1875).

Cartulaire de Béziers (Livre noir), ed. J. Rouquette (Paris 1918).

Cartulaire de la cathédrale de Dax: Liber rubeus (XIe–XIIe siècles), ed. and tr. Georges Pon, Jean Cabanot (Dax 2004).

Cartulaire de la commune de Couvin, ed. Stanislas Bormans. Documents inédits relatifs à l'Histoire de la Province de Namur (Namur 1875).

Cartulaire de l'église collégiale Saint-Seurin de Bordeaux, ed. J. A. Brutails (Bordeaux 1897).

Cartulaire de Notre-Dame de Chartres d'après les cartulaires et les titres originaux, ed. E. de Lépinois, L. Merlet, 3 vols. Société archéologique d'Eure-et-Loir (Chartres 1862–65).

'Le cartulaire de Saint-Maur sur Loire,' ed. Paul Marchegay, *Archives d'Anjou. Recueil de documents et mémoires inédits sur cette province* . . . , 3 vols. (Angers 1843–54) I.

'Cartulaire du prieuré de Saint-Pierre de la Réole,' ed. Ch. Grellet-Balguerie, *Archives historiques du Départment de la Gironde* v (1864) 99–186.

Cartulaire de Sauxillanges, ed. Henry Doniol (Clermont 1864).

Cartulaire de Trinquetaille, ed. P.-A. Amargier. Centre d'Etudes des Sociétés méditerranéennes (Aix-en-Provence 1972).

Cartulaires des Templiers de Douzens, ed. Pierre Gérard, Elisabeth Magnou. CDIHF. Série in 8° 3 (Paris 1965).

Cartulaires de la vallée d'Ossau, ed. Pierre Tucoo-Chala. Fuentes para la Historia del Pirineo 7 (Zaragoza 1970).

Cartulario de Santa Cruz de la Seros, ed. Antonio Ubieto Arteta. TM 19 (Valencia 1966).

Cartularium saxonicum . . . , ed. Walter de Gray Birch, 3 vols. (London 1885–93).

Catalogne romane, ed. Eduard Junyent, 2 vols. La Nuit des Temps (Zodiaque 1960–61).

Catalogue des actes de Philippe-Auguste, ed. Léopold Delisle (Paris 1856).

Catalogus baronum, ed. Evelyn Jameson. FSI 101 (Rome 1972).

La Chanson de Roland, ed. F. Whitehead, 2d ed. Blackwell's French Texts (Oxford 1946 [1942]).

Les chansons de Guilhem de Cabestanh, ed. Arthur Långfors. CFMA 42 (Paris 1924).

'Chartes angevines des onzième et douzième siècles,' ed. Paul Marchegay, *BEC* xxxvi (1875) 381–441.

Chartes de coutume en Picardie: XIIᵉ–XIIIᵉ siècle, ed. Robert Fossier. CDIHF. Série in 8° 10 (Paris 1974).

[Chrétien de Troyes] *Erec et Enide*, ed. Mario Roques. CFMA 80. *Les romans de Chrétien de Troyes . . .* (Paris 1978).

Chronica Adefonsi imperatoris, ed. Antonio Maya Sánchez. *Chronica hispana saeculi XII*, ed. Emma Falque Rey et al. CCCM 71 (Turnhout 1990) 147–248.

Chronica Albrici monachi Trium fontium a monacho novi monasterii Hoiensis interpolata, ed. Paul Scheffer-Boichorst. *MGHSS* xxiii (1874) 631–950.

Chronica de gestis consulum Andegavorum, ed. Louis Halphen, René Poupardin, *Chroniques des comtes d'Anjou et des seigneurs d'Amboise*. CTEEH (Paris 1913) 25–73.

Chronica latina regum Castellae, ed. L. Charlo Brea. *Chronica hispana sae-culi XIII*, ed. Brea *et al. CCCM* 73 (Turnhout 1997) 7–118.

Chronica monasterii Casinensis. Die Chronik von Montecassino, ed. Hartmut Hoffmann. *MGHSS* xxxiv (Hanover 1980).

Chronica regia Coloniensis (Annales maximi Colonienses) cum continuationi-bus . . . , ed. Georg Waitz *MGHSSRG* 18 (Hanover 1880).

Chronica vel sermo de rapinis, injusticiis et malis consuetudinibus a Giraudo de Mosteriolo exactis, et de eversione castri ejus a Gaufrido comite, ed. Paul Marchegay, Emile Mabille. *Chroniques des églises d'Anjou*. SHF (Paris 1869) 83–90.

The chronicle of Battle Abbey, ed. and tr. Eleanor Searle. OMT (Oxford 1980).

The chronicle of the election of Hugh abbot of Bury St. Edmunds and later bishop of Ely, ed. and tr. R. M. Thomson. OMT (Oxford 1974).

The chronicle of Jocelin of Brakelond concerning the acts of Samson abbot of the monastery, ed. and tr. H. E. Butler. Medieval Classics (London 1949); also tr. Diana Greenway, Jane Sayers. The World's Classics (Oxford 1989).

Chronicon abbatiae Rameseiensis a saec. X. usque ad an. circiter 1200, ed. W. Dunn Macray. RS (London 1886)

Chronicon breve de gestis Aldeberti, ed. Clovis Brunel, *Les Miracles de saint Privat* . . . (cited fully below) 126–32.

Chronicon Casauriense, auctore Johanne Berardi ejusdem coenobii monacho ab ejus origine usque ad annum MCLXXXII. quo scriptor forebat, deductum. RIS ii:2 (1726) 775–916.

Chronicon Compostellanum, ed. Henrique Flórez, *ES* xx (Madrid 1765) 608–13.

Chronique et chartes de l'abbaye de Saint-Mihiel, ed. André Lesort. *Mettensia* vi (Paris 1909–12).

Chronique ou livre de fondation du monastère de Mouzon . . . , ed. and tr. Michel Bur. Sources d'Histoire Médiévale. IRHT (Paris 1989).

La chronique de Morigny (1095–1152), ed. Léon Mirot, 2d ed. CTEEH 41 (Paris 1912).

La chronique de Nantes (570 environ–1049), ed. René Merlet. CTEEH 19 (Paris 1896).

La chronique de Saint-Hubert dite Cantatorium, ed. Karl Hanquet. Com-mission Royale d'Histoire. Recueil de Textes pour servir a l'Etude de l'Histoire de Belgique (Brussels 1906).

Chronique de Silvanès, ed. P.-A. Verlaguet. *Cartulaire de l'abbaye de Silvanès*. Archives historiques du Rouergue 1 (Rodez 1910), no. 470.

[El Cid] *The world of El Cid. Chronicles of the Spanish reconquest*, ed. Simon Barton, Richard Fletcher. Manchester Medieval Sources (Manchester 2000).

Colección diplomática del concejo de Zaragoza, ed. Angel Canellas Lopez, with Album (Zaragoza 1972).

Colección de fueros municipales y cartas pueblas de las reinos de Castilla, Leon, Corona de Aragon y Navarra, ed. Tomás Muñoz y Romero. Tomo I (Madrid 1847).

Compilatio antiqua, ed. Karl Lehmann, *Consuetudines feudorum* (*Libri feudorum, jus feudale Langobardorum*) 1 (Göttingen 1892); repr. Karl August Eckhardt, *Consuetudines feudorum*. Bibliotheca rerum historicarum (Aalen 1971).

Le compte général de 1187, connu sous le nom de 'Gros Brief,' et les institutions financières du comté de Flandre au XIIe siècle, ed. Adriaan Verhulst, Maurits Gysseling. Commission Royale d'Histoire (Brussels 1962).

'Concilio nacional de Burgos (18 febrero 1117),' ed. Fidel Fita, *BRAH* XLVIII (1906) 387–407.

[Conon de Béthune] *Les chansons de Conon de Béthune*, ed. Alex Wallensköld. CFMA 24 (Paris 1968).

Consuetudines et iusticie, ed. C. H. Haskins. *Norman institutions* (fully cited below) 277–84.

'Conventum inter Guillelmum Aquitanorum comes [*sic*] et Hugonem Chiliarchum,' ed. Jane Martindale, *EHR* LXXXIV (1969) 528–48.

Le conventum (vers 1030): Un précurseur aquitain des premières épopées, ed. George Beech *et al.* Publications romanes et françaises 212 (Geneva 1995).

Córtes de los antiguos reinos de León y de Castilla, 5 vols. (Madrid 1861–1903).

[Cosmas of Prague] *Die Chronik der Böhmen des Cosmas von Prag*, ed. Bertold Bretholz. *MGHSSRG* nova series 2 (Berlin 1923).

The councils of Urban II. 1 Decreta Claromontensia, ed. Robert Somerville. Annuarium Historiae Conciliorum. Supplementum 1 (Amsterdam 1972).

Le couronnement de Louis. Chanson de geste du XIIe siècle, ed. Ernest Langlois, 2d ed. CFMA 22 (Paris 1966 [1920]); tr. Joan M. Ferrante, *Guillaume d'Orange: four twelfth-century epics*. Records of Civilization, Sources and Studies 92 (NY 1974).

'La coutume originale de Saint-Antonin [Tarn-et-Garonne] (1140–1144),' ed. Robert Latouche, *Bulletin philologique et historique (jusqu'à 1715) du Comité des Travaux historiques et scientifiques. Année 1920* (1922) 257–62.

Les coutumes de l'Agenais, ed. Paul Ourliac, Monique Gilles, 2 vols. Publications de la Société d'Histoire du Droit et des Institutions des Anciens Pays de Droit écrit 2 (Montpellier-Paris 1981).

Curia regis rolls of the reigns of Richard I and John, ed. C. T. Flower, 7 vols. (London 1922–35).

Decretales ineditae saeculi XII, ed. Walther Holtzmann, Stanley Chodorow, Charles Duggan. MIC. Series B. Corpus collectionum 4 (Vatican City 1982).

Dialogue (of the exchequer; Dialogus . . .), see Richard fitz Nigel.

Diego Garcia, natural de Campos, *Planeta (obra ascética del siglo XIII)*, ed. P. Manuel Alonso. CSIC. Patronato Raimundo Lulio. Instituto Francisco Suárez, Serie D. 1 (Madrid 1943).

Diplomata belgica ante annum millesimum centesimum scripta, ed. Maurits Gysseling, A. C. F. Koch, 2 parts (Brussels 1950).

Diplomatari de la catedral de Vic. Segles IX–X, ed. Eduard Junyent i Subirà. Publicacions del Patronat d'Estudis osonencs. Publicacions de l'Arxiu, Biblioteca i Museu episcopals de Vic (Vic 1980–96).

Diplomatario de la reina Urraca de Castilla y León, 1109–1126, ed. Cristina Monterde Albiac. TM 91 (Zaragoza 1996).

Documentación medieval de Leire (siglos IX a XII), ed. Angel J. Martín Duque. Diputación foral de Navarra (Pamplona 1983).

'Documentos para la historia del derecho español,' ed. José María Ramos y Loscertales, *AHDE* I (1924) 398–400.

Documentos para la historia de las instituciones de León y de Castilla (siglos X–XIII), ed. Eduardo de Hinojosa (Madrid 1919).

'Documentos para la historia de las instituciones navarras,' ed. J. M. Lacarra, *AHDE* XI (1934) 487–503.

Documentos de Jaime I de Aragón, ed. Ambrosio Huici Miranda, Maria Desamparados Cabanes Pecourt, 5 vols. to date. TM 49–51, 55, 77 (Valencia 1976, Zaragoza 1988 [1916]).

Los documentos del Pilar, siglo XII, ed. Luis Rubio. Archivo de Filologia aragonesa. Anejo 11 (Zaragoza 1971).

Documentos reales Navarro-Aragoneses hasta el año 1004, ed. Antonio Ubieto Arteta. TM 72 (Zaragoza 1986).

'Documents linguistiques du Gévaudan,' ed. Clovis Brunel, *BEC* LXXVII (1916) 5–57, 241–85.

596 BIBLIOGRAPHY

Documents relatifs au comté de Champagne et de Brie, 1172–1361, ed. Auguste Longnon. CDIHF (Paris 1901–14).

[Donizo] *Vita Mathildis celeberrimae principis Italiae carmine scripta a Donizone prebytero qui in arce Canusina vixit*, ed. Luigi Simeoni. *RIS*² v:2 (Bologna 1940).

[Eadmer] *The life of St Anselm archbishop of Canterbury by Eadmer*, ed. R. W. Southern. (Nelson) Medieval Texts (London 1962).

Eadmeri historia novorum in Anglia . . . , ed. Martin Rule. RS 81 (London 1884).

'The early surveys of Evesham abbey . . . ,' ed. H. B. Clarke. PhD thesis, Birmingham, 246–70 (not seen).

Ekkehard, *see* Frutolf.

English lawsuits from William I to Richard I, ed. R. C. Van Caenegem, 2 vols. Selden Society 106–7 (London 1990).

The Epistolae vagantes *of Pope Gregory VII*, ed. and tr. H. E. J. Cowdrey. OMT (Oxford 1972).

[Etienne de Bourbon] *Anecdotes historiques, légendes et apologues, tirés du recueil inédit d'Etienne de Bourbon, dominicain du XIIIᵉ siècle*, ed. Albert Lecoy de la Marche. SHF 185 (Paris 1877).

Eudes de Saint-Maur, *Vie de Bouchard le Vénérable comte de Vendôme, de Corbeil, de Melun et de Paris (Xᵉ et XIᵉ siècles)*, ed. Charles Bourel de la Roncière. CTEEH 13 (Paris 1892).

Exceptiones Petri, ed. Carlo Guido Mor, 2 vols. *Scritti giuridici preirneriani* 3, 10 (Milan 1935–38) II.

Feet of fines of the reign of Henry II. and of the first seven years of the reign of Richard I. A.D. 1182 to A.D. 1196. PRS 17 (London 1894).

[Flodoard] *Les annales de Flodoard*, ed. Philippe Lauer. CTEEH (Paris 1905).

[Folquet de Marseille] *Le troubadour Folquet de Marseille . . .* , ed. Stanisław Stroński (Crakow 1910).

Formularium tabellionum di Irnerio, ed. G. B. Palmieri, *Appunti e documenti per la storia dei glossatori* I (Bologna 1892).

Fors de Bigorre, ed. Xavier Ravier, Benoît Cursente, *Le cartulaire de Bigorre (XIᵉ–XIIIᵉ siècle)*. CDIHF. Section d'Histoire . . . Série in 8° 36 (Paris 2005), no. 61.

'Het Fragment van een grafelijke Rekening van Vlaanderen uit 1140,' ed. Egied I. Strubbe, *Mededelingen van de koninklijke Vlaamse Academie voor Wetenschappen, Klasse der Letteren en schone Kunsten van Belgie* XII:9 (Brussels 1950) 28 pp., 5 plates.

[Frutolf and Ekkehard] *Frutolfi et Ekkehardi chronica necnon anonymi chronica imperatorum*, ed. Franz-Josef Schmale, Irene Schmale-Ott. Ausgewählte Quellen zur deutschen Geschichte des Mittelalters 15 (Darmstadt 1972)

El fuero de Jaca, ed. Mauricio Molho. CSIC. Fuentes para la Historia del Pirineo 1 (Zaragoza 1964).

Fueros derivados de Jaca. 1 Estella–San Sebastián, ed. José Ma. Lacarra. Fueros de Navarra 1 (Pamplona 1969).

[Fulbert] *The letters and poems of Fulbert of Chartres*, ed. Frederick Behrends. OMT (Oxford 1976).

[Fulk Richin] *Fragmentum historiae Andegavensis*, ed. Louis Halphen, René Poupardin. *Chroniques des comtes d'Anjou et des seigneurs d'Amboise*. CTEEH (Paris 1913) 231–38.

Galbert of Bruges, *De multro, traditione et occisione gloriosi Karoli comitis Flandriarum*, ed. Henri Pirenne, *Histoire du meurtre de Charles le Bon comte de Flandre (1127–1128) par Galbert de Bruges suivie de poésies latines contemporaines*. CTEEH 10 (Paris 1891); ed. Jeff Rider. *CCCM* 131 (Turnhout 1994); tr. James Bruce Ross, *The murder of Charles the Good*, rev. ed. Harper Torchbooks (NY 1967 [1959]).

Genealogiae comitum Flandriae, ed. L. C. Bethmann. *MGHSS* IX (1851) 302–36.

[Geoffroi de Vigeois] *Chronica Gaufredi coenobitae monasterii S. Martialis Lemovicensis ac prioris Vosciencis coenobii*, ed. Ph. Labbe, *Novae bibliothecae manuscriptorum librorum tomus [secundus]* . . . , 2 vols. (Paris 1657) II, 279–342.

Gaufredi prioris Vosiensis pars altera chronici Lemovicensis, ed. Michel-Jean-Joseph Brial, *HF* XVIII (Paris 1822) 211–23.

'A general court of Aragon (Daroca, February 1228),' ed. T. N. Bisson, *EHR* XCII (1977) 107–24 (reprinted in *MFrPN* ch. 2).

Gerald of Wales, *De principis instructione*, ed. George F. Warner, *Giraldi Cambrensis opera*, ed. J. S. Brewer *et al.*, 8 vols. RS 21 (London 1861–91) VIII.

——— *Libri III de rebus a se gestis*, ed. J. S. Brewer, *Opera* I, 3–122; tr. H. E. Butler, *The autobiography of Gerald of Wales*, new ed. (Rochester, NY, 2005).

Giraldi Cambrensis gemma ecclesiastica, ed. J. S. Brewer, *Opera* II.

'Gerichtsurkunden aus Italien bis zum Jahre 1150,' ed. Rudolf Hübner, *ZRG. Romanische Abtheilung* XIV:2 (1893) Anhang.

[Gervase of Canterbury] *The chronicle of the reigns of Stephen, Henry II, and Richard I. by Gervase, the monk of Canterbury*, ed. William Stubbs, *The historical works of Gervase of Canterbury*, 2 vols. RS 73 (London 1879–80) I.

Gervase of Tilbury:Otia imperialia. Recreation for an emperor, ed. and tr. S. E. Banks, J. W. Binns. OMT (Oxford 2002).

Die Gesetze der Angelsachsen, ed. Felix Liebermann, 3 vols. (Halle 1903–16).

[*Gesta Francorum*] *The deeds of the Franks and the other pilgrims to Jerusalem*, ed. Rosalind Hill. OMT (Oxford 1972 [1962]).

The Gesta Normannorum ducum of William of Jumièges, Orderic Vitalis, and Robert of Torigni, ed. Elisabeth M. C. Van Houts, 2 vols. OMT (Oxford 1992–95).

Gesta pontificum Cameracensium, ed. L. C. Bethmann. *MGHSS* VII (1846) 393–489; *Continuatio*, 489–525,

Les gestes des évêques d'Auxerre, ed. Guy Lobrichon *et al.*, 2 vols. CHFMA 42–43 (Paris 2002–06)

[Gilbert Foliot] *The letters and charters of Gilbert Foliot, abbot of Gloucester (1139–48), bishop of Hereford (1148–63), and London (1163–87)*, ed. Z. N. Brooke, Adrian Morey, C. N. L. Brooke (Cambridge 1967).

[Gislebert] *La chronique [Chronicon Hanoniense] de Gislebert de Mons*, ed. Léon Vanderkindere. Commission royale d'Histoire. Recueil de Textes pour servir à l'Etude de l'Histoire de Belgique (Brussels 1904).

[Glanvill] *Tractatus de legibus et consuetudinibus regni Anglie qui Glanvilla vocatur*, ed. and tr. G. D. H. Hall, rev. OMT (Oxford 1993 [1965]).

The great roll of the pipe for the twelfth year of the reign of King Henry the Second . . . PRS 9 (London 1891).

The great roll of the pipe for the first year of the reign of King John. Michaelmas 1199 (Pipe Roll 45), ed. Doris M. Stenton. PRS 48 (London 1933).

Gregory [I, the Great], *Regula pastoralis*, PL LXXVII (1896) 13–128.

Guibert de Nogent, *Autobiographie [De vita sua, sive monodiae]*, ed. Edmond-René Labande. CHFMA 34 (Paris 1981); tr. Paul J. Archambault, *A monk's confession: the memoirs of Guibert of Nogent* (University Park 1996).

Le Guide du pèlerin de Saint-Jacques de Compostelle, ed. Jeanne Vielliard, 5th ed. (Paris 1984 [1938]).

Guillaume le Breton, *Gesta Philippi Augusti*, ed. H.-Fr. Delaborde, *Oeuvres de Rigord et de Guillaume le Breton* . . . , 2 vols. SHF (Paris 1882–85) I, 168–333.

——— *Philippide*, ed. Delaborde, *Oeuvres* II, 1–385.

Guillelmi I. regis diplomata, ed. Horst Enzensberger. Codex diplomaticus regni Siciliae. Series prima. Diplomata regum et principum e gente Normannorum 3 (Cologne 1996).

[Guilhem IX] *Les chansons de Guillaume IX duc d'Aquitaine (1071–1127)*, ed. Alfred Jeanroy, 2d ed. CFMA 9 (Paris 1927 [1913]).

[Guillem de Berguedà] *Les poesies del trobador Guillem de Berguedà*, ed. Martí de Riquer. Sèrie gran 18 (Barcelona 1996).

Guiot de Provins, *La Bible*, in *Les oeuvres de Guiot de Provins, poète lyrique et satirique*, ed. John Orr. Publications de l'Université de Manchester. Série française 1 (Manchester 1915).

Guiraut de Cabrera, *Ensenhamen*, ed. Martin de Riquer, *Les chansons de geste françaises*, tr. Irénée Cluzel, 2d ed. (Paris n.d. [1957]) 342–51.

[Hariulf] *Vita sancti Arnulfi episcopi Suessionensis auctore Hariulfo coaequali*, PL CLXXIV, 1367–1438.

Hemingi chartularium ecclesie Wigorniensis, ed. Thomas Hearne, 2 vols. (Oxford 1723).

[Herbert of Bosham] *Vita sancti Thomae, archiepiscopi et martyris, auctore Herberto de Boseham, Materials* III (1877) 155–534.

Herefordshire Domesday, circa 1160–1170, reproduced by collotype from facsimile photographs of Balliol College manuscript 350, ed. V. H. Galbraith, James Tait. PRS 63 (new series 25) (London 1950).

[Heriman of Tournai] *Herimanni liber de restauratione monasterii Sancti Martini Tornacensis*, ed. Georg Waitz. MGHSS XIV (1883) 274–317.

[Herman of Laon] *Hermanni monachi de miraculis S. Mariae Laudunensis de gestis venerabilis Bartholomaei episcopi et S. Nortberti libri tres*, PL CLVI, 961–1018.

[Hildebert] *Ven[erabilis] Hildeberti epistolae*, PL CLXXI, 141–312.

——— *Moralis philosophia de honesto et utili*, PL CLXXI, 1007–56.

——— *[Venerabilis Hildeberti Cenomanensis episcopi] sermones de tempore*, PL CLXXI, 343–606.

Hincmar of Reims, *Ad episcopos regni admonitio altera*, PL CXXV, 1007–18.

Histoire des ducs de Normandie et des rois d'Angleterre . . . , ed. Fr. Michel. SHF (Paris 1840).

Historia ecclesie Abbendonensis. The history of the church of Abingdon, ed. John Hudson, 2 vols. OMT (Oxford 2002–07)

Historia monasterii Selebiensis, in *The Coucher Book of Selby*, ed. J. T. Fowler, 2 vols. Yorkshire Archaeological and Topographical Association. Record Series 10, 13 (York 1891–93) I, 1–54.

Historia Roderici, ed. Emma Falque Rey *et al.*, *Chronica hispana saeculi XII*. CCCM 71 (Turnhout 1990) 47–98.

Historia Welforum, ed. and tr. Erich König, 2d ed. Schwäbische Chroniken der Stauferzeit 1 (Sigmaringen 1978 [1938]).

Historiae Francorum scriptores, ab Hugone et Roberto regg. usque ad Philippi Augusti tempora . . ., ed. [André] Franciscus Duchesne, 5 vols. (Paris 1636–49).

Homilies d'Organyà, ed. D'Amadeu-J. Soberanas, Andreu Rossinyol. Els Nostres Clàssics. Colecció B 20 (Barcelona 2001).

Hugh the Chanter, *The history of the church of York, 1066–1127*, ed. Charles Johnson, rev. Martin Brett *et al.* OMT (Oxford 1990).

[Hugo Falcandus] *La historia o Liber de regno Sicilie di Ugo Falcando e la epistola ad Petrum Panormitane ecclesie thesaurarium . . .*, ed. Giovanni Battista Siragusa. FSI 22 (Rome 1897); tr. Graham A. Loud, Thomas Wiedemann, *The history of the tyrants of Sicily by 'Hugo Falcandus,' 1154–69*. Manchester Medieval Sources (Manchester 1998).

Hugues le Poitevin, *Chronique de l'abbaye de Vézelay*, ed. R. B. C. Huygens, *MV* 395–607.

Humberti cardinalis libri III adversus simoniacos, ed. Frederick Thaner, *Ldl*, I, 95–253.

De iniusta vexacione Willelmi episcopi primi per Willelmum regem filium Willelmi magni regis, ed. H. S. Offler, *Chronology, conquest and conflict in medieval England*. Camden Miscellany 34, Camden 5th series 10 (Cambridge 1997) 49–104.

Inventari altomedievali di terre, coloni e redditi, ed. Andrea Castagnetti *et al.* FSI 104 (Rome 1979).

[Jacques de Vitry] *Die Exempla des Jacob von Vitry: ein Beitrag zur Geschichte der Erzählungsliteratur des Mittelalters*, ed. Goswin Frenken. Quellen und Untersuchungen zur lateinischen Philologie des Mittelalters 5:1 (Munich 1914).

——— *Die Exempla aus den* Sermones feriales et communes *des Jakob von Vitry*, ed. Joseph Greven. Sammlung mittellateinischer Texte 9 (Heidelberg 1914).

———— The Historia occidentalis of Jacques de Vitry, ed. John Frederick Hinnebusch. Spicilegium Friburgense 17 (Fribourg 1972).

———— Lettres de Jacques de Vitry, 1160/1170–1240, évêque de Saint-Jean d'Acre, ed. R. B. C. Huygens (Leiden 1960).

[Jaufré Rudel] The songs of Jaufré Rudel, ed. Rupert T. Pickens. PIMS Studies and Texts 41 (Toronto 1978).

[Jaume Ier] Llibre dels feits, ed. Ferran Soldevila, Les quatre grans cròniques. Biblioteca Perenne 26 (Barcelona 1971) 3–402.

Jean Bodel, trouvère artésien du XIIIᵉ siècle. Le jeu de Saint Nicolas, ed. Alfred Jeanroy. CFMA 48 (Paris 1925).

Jean de Marmoutier, Historia Gaufredi ducis Normannorum et comitis Andegavorum, ed. Louis Halphen, René Poupardin, Chroniques des comtes d'Anjou. . . . CTEEH (Paris 1913) 172–231.

Jean Renart, Le Roman de la Rose ou de Guillaume de Dol, ed. Félix Lecoy. CFMA 91 (Paris 1979).

Johannes Berardi, see Chronicon Casauriense.

Ioannis Saresberiensis historia pontificalis, ed. and tr. Marjorie Chibnall. Medieval Texts (London 1956).

[John of Salisbury] The letters of John of Salisbury, ed. and tr. W. J. Millor, H. E. Butler, rev. C.N.L. Brooke, 2 vols. OMT (Oxford 1979–86 [I first published 1955]).

———— Ioannis Saresberiensis episcopi Carnotensis policratici sive de nugis curialium et vestigiis philosophorum libri VIII, ed. C. C. J. Webb, 2 vols. (Oxford 1909).

Joinville, Jean de, Vie de Saint Louis, ed. Jacques Monfrin. Classiques Garnier (Paris 1995).

Die Kaiserurkunden des X., XI. und XII. Jahrhunderts chronologisch verzeichnet als Beitrag zu den Regesten und zur Kritik derselben, ed. Karl Friedrich Stumpf-Brentano (Innsbruck 1865).

Die Konstitutionen Friedrichs II. für das Königreich Sizilien, ed. Wolfgang Stürner. MGH, CAP II Supplementum (Hanover 1996).

[Lambert] Le registre de Lambert évêque d'Arras (1093–1105), ed. Claire Giordanengo. Sources d'Histoire médiévale 34 (Paris 2007).

Lamberti Ardensis historia comitum Ghisnensium, ed. Johann Heller, MGHSS XXIV (1879) 550–642; tr. Leah Shopkow, Lambert of Ardres, the history of the counts of Guines and lords of Ardres. The Middle Ages (Philadelphia 2001).

Lamberti S. Audomari canonici Liber floridus, ed. Albert Derolez (Ghent 1968).

[Lampert of Hersfeld] *Lamperti annales,* in *Lamperti monachi Hersfeldensis opera,* ed. Oswald Holder-Egger. *MGHSSRG* 38 (1984 [1894]) 58–304. Includes *Annales Weissenburgenses,* 9–57.

[Landulf Senior] *Landulphi Senioris Mediolanensis historiae libri quatuor,* ed. Alessandro Cutolo. *RIS*² iv:2 (Bologna 1942).

The laws of the medieval kingdom of Hungary [*Decreta regni mediaevalis Hungariae*], tr. and ed. János M. Bak, György Bónis, James Ross Sweeney. The Laws of Hungary 1:1 (Idyllwild 1999).

Das Lebenzeugnis Walthers von der Vogelweide. Die Reiserechnungen des Passauer Bischofs Wolfger von Erla, ed. Hedwig Heger (Vienna 1970) 77–146.

Leges Henrici primi, ed. and tr. L. J. Downer (Oxford 1972).

Leges Visigothorum, ed. Karl Zeumer. *MGH, Leges 1* (Hanover-Leipzig 1902).

The letters of Arnulf of Lisieux, ed. Frank Barlow. Camden Third Series 61 (London 1939).

Lex Baiwariorum, ed. Ernst von Schwind. *MGH. Leges nationum Germanicarum* 5, 2 (Hanover 1926).

Libellus de diversis ordinibus et professionibus qui sunt in aecclesia, ed. and tr. Giles Constable, Bernard Smith. OMT (Oxford 1972).

Liber Eliensis, ed. E. O. Blake. Camden Third Series 92 (London 1962).

Liber instrumentorum memorialium. Cartulaire des Guillems de Montpellier . . . , ed. Alexandre Germain (Montpellier 1884–86).

Liber miraculorum sancte Fidis, ed. Luca Robertini. Biblioteca di Medioevo latino 10 (Spoleto 1994).

Liber testamentorum sancti Martini de Campis: reproduction annotée du manuscrit de la Bibliothèque nationale. Mémoires et Documents de la Société historique & archéologique de Corbeil, d'Etampes et du Hurepoix 5 (Paris 1904).

The Lincolnshire Domesday and the Lindsey survey, tr. and ed. C. W. Fowler, Thomas Longley. The Publications of the Lincoln Record Society 19 (Horncastle 1924).

[Lorris] Prou, Maurice, 'Les coutumes de Lorris et leur propagation aux XIIᵉ et XIIIᵉ siècles,' *NRHDFE* viii (1884) 139–209, 267–320, 441–57, 523–56.

Loup de Ferrières, *Correspondance,* ed. and tr. Léon Levillain, 2 vols. CHFMA 10, 16 (Paris 1927).

Magna vita sancti Hugonis . . . , ed. Decima L. Douie, rev. David Hugh Farmer, 2 vols. OMT (Oxford 1985 [1961]).

Magnus rotulus scaccarii, 31 Henry I, ed. Joseph Hunter. Record Commission (London 1833).

Mainzer Urkundenbuch. Arbeiten der historischen Kommission für den Volkstaat Hessen (Darmstadt 1932).

Un manuscrit chartrain du XIe siècle . . . , ed. René Merlet, l'Abbé Clerval. Société archéologique d'Eure-et-Loir (Chartres 1893).

Marbodus discipulo suo de ornamentis verborum, PL CLXXI, 1687–92.

Mémoire relatif au paréage de 1307 conclu entre l'évêque Guillaume Durand II et le roi Philippe-le-Bel. Société d'Agriculture, Sciences & Arts de la Lozère (Mende 1896).

The memoranda roll for the Michaelmas term of the first year of . . . *King John (1199–1200),* ed. H. G. Richardson. PRS 59 (London 1943).

'The miracles of St Bega,' *The Register of the priory of St Bees,* ed. James Wilson. Surtees Society 126 (London 1915) 509–20.

Les Miracles de Saint Privat suivis des opuscules d'Aldebert II, évêque de Mende, ed. Clovis Brunel. CTEEH (Paris 1912).

Miracula sanctae Virginis Mariae, ed. Elise F. Dexter. University of Wisconsin Studies in the Social Sciences and History 12 (Madison 1927).

Monuments de l'histoire des abbayes de Saint-Philibert (Noirmoutier, Grandlieu, Tournus), ed. René Poupardin. CTEEH 38 (Paris 1905).

'A new eyewitness account of the Fourth Lateran Council,' ed. Stephan Kuttner, Antonio García y García, *Traditio* XX (1964) 115–78.

Nigellus de Longchamp, dit Wireker. Tractatus contra curiales et officiales clericos, ed. A. Boutemy. Université libre de Bruxelles. Faculté de Philosophie et Lettres 16 (Paris 1959).

'Notae de Mathilda comitissa,' ed. Percy Ernst Schramm, *MGHSS* XXX² (1929) 973–75.

Oberti cancellarii annales ann. MCLXIV–MCLXXIII, ed. L. T. Belgrano, *Annali genovesi di Caffaro* [*see* Caffaro] I (1890) 153–261.

Odo (of Cluny) *Vita Geraldi comitis Auriliacensis, PL* CXXXIII, 639–704; tr. Gerard Sitwell, *St. Odo of Cluny* . . . The Makers of Christendom (London 1958) 89–180.

Ogerii panis annales ann. MCLXXXXVII–MCCXIX, Annali genovesi di Caffaro [*see* Caffaro] II (1901) 67–154.

De oorkonden der graven van Vlaanderen (*juli 1128–september 1191*), ed. Thérèse de Hemptinne *et al.* Verzameling van de akten der belgische vorsten 6 (Brussels 1988).

De ordinando pontifice auctor Gallicus, ed. Ernest Dümmler, *Ldl* 1, 14.

Ordines coronationis Franciae. Texts and ordines for the coronation of Frankish and French kings and queens in the Middle Ages, ed. Richard A. Jackson, 2 vols. Middle Ages Series (Philadelphia 1995–2000).

Otoboni scribae annales ann. MCLXXIV–MCLXXXXVI, ed. L. T. Belgrano, Cesare Imperiale de Sant'Angelo, *Annali genovesi de Caffaro* [*see* Caffaro] II, 3–66.

[Otto of Freising] *Ottonis et Rahewini gesta Friderici I. imperatoris*, ed. Georg Waitz, B. de Simson, 3d ed. *MGHSSRG* 46 (Hanover 1912 [1868]); tr. C. C. Mierow, *The deeds of Frederick Barbarossa . . .* , Records of Civilization (NY 1966 [1953]).

[Otto of St Blasien] *Die Chronik Ottos von St. Blasien und die Marbacher Annalen*, ed. and tr. Franz-Josef Schmale. Ausgewählte Quellen zur deutschen Geschichte des Mittelalters Freiherr vom Stein-Gedächtnisausgabe 18a (Darmstadt 1998).

Papal decretals relating to the diocese of Lincoln in the twelfth century, ed. Walther Holtzmann, tr. Eric Waldram Kemp. The Publications of the Lincoln Record Society 47 (Hereford 1954).

Papsturkunden für Templer und Johanniter: Archivberichte und Texte, ed. Rudolf Hiestand. Abhandlungen der Akademie der Wissenschaften in Göttingen, Philologische-Historische Klasse Dritte Folge 77 (Göttingen 1972).

Parodistische Texte. Beispiele zur lateinischen Parodie im Mittelalter, ed. Paul Lehmann (Munich 1923).

Peire Vidal, poesie, ed. D'Arco Silvio Avalle, 2 vols. Documenti di Filologia 4 (Milan 1960).

Peter Abelard, *Dialectica*, ed. L. M. Rijk, 2d ed. Wijsgerige Teksten en Studies 1 (Assen 1970 [1956]).

Petri Abaelardi sermones, PL CLXXVIII, 379–610.

[Peter of Blois, ca. 1135–ca. 1212] *The later letters of Peter of Blois*, ed. Elizabeth Revell. Auctores Britannici medii aevi 13 (Oxford 1993).

Petri Blesensis epistolae, PL CCVII, 1–560.

[Peter the Chanter] *De oratione et speciebus illius*, ed. Richard C. Trexler, *The Christian at prayer: an illustrated prayer manual attributed to Peter the*

Chanter (d. 1197). Medieval & Renaissance Texts & Studies 44 (Binghamton 1987) 171–234.

———— Petrus Cantor, *Summa de sacramentis et animae consiliis*, ed. Jean-Albert Dugauquier. Analecta mediaevalia Namurcensia 4, 7, 11, 16, 21 (Louvain 1954–67),

———— *Petri Cantoris Parisiensis verbum adbreviatum. Textus conflatus*, ed. Monique Boutry. *CCCM* 196 (Turnhout 2004). Short version: *PL* CCV, 21–370.

The Peterborough chronicle 1070–1154, ed. Cecily Clark, 2d ed. (Oxford 1970 [1957]).

Petrus Damiani, *Liber gratissimus*, ed. Kurt Reindel, *BrPD* 1 (1983) no. 40.

Petrus de Ebulo, *Liber ad honorem Augusti sive de rebus Siculis. Codex 120 II der Burgerbibliotek Bern. Ein Bilderchronik der Stauferzeit*, ed. Theo Kölzer, Marlis Stähli, rev. and tr. (German) Gereon Becht-Jördens (Sigmaringen 1994).

Pilii, Tancredi, Gratiae libri de iudiciorum ordine, ed. Fridericus Bergmann (Göttingen 1842).

Pipe rolls of the exchequer of Normandy for the reign of Henry II, 1180 and 1184, ed. Vincent Moss. PRS 91, new series 53 (London 2004).

Placentini summa 'Cum essem Mantue' siue de accionum uarietatibus, ed. Gustav Pescatore. Beiträge zur mittelalterlichen Rechtsgeschichte 5 (Greifswald 1897).

I placiti del 'Regnum Italiae,' ed. Cesare Manaresi, 5 vols. FSI 92, 96 (1, 2), 97 (1, 2) (Rome 1953–60).

Les plus anciennes chartes en langue provençale. Recueil des pièces originales antérieures au XIIIe siècle . . ., ed. Clovis Brunel (Paris 1926).

Le premier budget de la monarchie française. Le compte général de 1202–1203, ed. Ferdinand Lot, Robert Fawtier. BEHE 256 (Paris 1932).

Le premier registre de Philippe-Auguste. Reproduction héliotypique du manuscrit du Vatican, ed. Léopold Delisle (Paris 1883).

[Prisches] 'La fameuse charte-loi de Prisches,' ed. Léo Verriest, *RBPH* 11 (1923) 327–49.

Privilèges et titres relatifs aux franchises, institutions et propriétés communales de Roussillon et de Cerdagne depuis le XIe siècle jusqu'à l'an 1660. Ire partie, ed. Bernard Alart (Perpignan 1874).

Privilegis i ordinacions de les valls pirinenques, ed. Ferran Valls Taberner, 3 vols. Textes de Dret català 2 (Barcelona 1915–20).

Quellensammlung zur Frühgeschichte der deutschen Stadt (bis 1250), ed. Bernhard Diestelkamp. EFHU 1 (Leiden 1967) 1–277.

Quinque compilationes antiquae nec non Collectio canonum Lipsiensis . . . , ed. Aemilius Friedberg (Leipzig 1882).

Radulfus Niger, *De re militari et triplici via peregrinationis Ierosolimitane (1187–88)*, ed. Ludwig Schmugge. Beiträge zur Geschichte und Quellenkunde des Mittelalters 6 (Berlin 1977).

Radulphi de Coggeshall chronicon Anglicanum [etc.] . . . , ed. Josephus Stevenson. RS 66 (London 1875) 1–208.

Rahewin, *see* Otto of Freising.

[Raimon Vidal] *The* Razos de trobar *of Ramon Vidal and associated texts*, ed. J. H. Marshall. University of Durham Publications (London 1972).

Ralph of Diceto, *Ymagines historiarum*, ed. William Stubbs, *The historical works of Master Ralph de Diceto, dean of London*, 2 vols. RS 68 (London 1876) 1, 3–263, 267–440; 11, 3–174.

Raoul de Cambrai, ed. Sarah Kay (Oxford 1992).

Ratherii Veronensis praeloquiorum libri VI . . . , ed. P. L. D. Reid. CCCM 46A (Turnhout 1984).

Récits d'un ménestrel de Reims au treizième siècle, ed. Natalis de Wailly. SHF (Paris 1876)

Recueil des actes de Charles II le Chauve, roi de France . . . , ed. Georges Tessier, 3 vols. CDHF 8 (Paris 1943–55).

Recueil des actes des ducs de Normandie de 911 à 1066, ed. Marie Fauroux. Mémoires de la Société des Antiquaires de Normandie 36, 4ᵉ série, 6 (Caen 1961).

Recueil des chartes de l'abbaye de Cluny, ed. Auguste Bernard, Alexandre Bruel, 6 vols. CDIHF (Paris 1876–1903).

Recueil des chartes de l'abbaye de la Grasse, ed. Elisabeth Magnou-Nortier et al., 2 vols. CDIHF Série in 8° 24, 26 (Paris 1996).

'Recueil de documents relatifs à l'histoire monétaire,' ed. Maurice Prou, *Revue numismatique* 3d series XIV (1896) 283–305.

Recueil de textes d'histoire urbaine française des origines au milieu du XIIIᵉ siècle, ed. A.-M. Lemasson, Philippe Wolff, B.-M. Tock. EFHU 2:1 (Arras 1996) 1–297.

Recueil de textes d'histoire urbaine néerlandaise des origines au milieu du XIIIᵉ siècle, ed. C. Van de Kieft. EFHU 1 (Leiden 1967) 405–504.

The Red Book of the Exchequer, ed. Hubert Hall, 3 vols. RS 99 (London 1896).

Regesta de Fernando II, ed. Julio González. CSIC. Instituto Jerónimo Zurita (Madrid 1943).

Regesta regum Anglo-Normannorum. The acta of William I (1066–1087), ed. David Bates (Oxford 1998).

Regesto di Camaldoli, ed. Luigi Schiaparelli *et al.*, 4 vols. (Rome 1907–22).

Regesto della chiesa di Tivoli, ed. Luigi Bruzza (Bologna 1983 [Rome 1880]).

[Reginald of Durham] *Reginaldi monachi Dunelmensis libellus de admirandis beati Cuthberti virtutibus quae novellis patratae sunt temporibus*, ed. James Raine. Surtees Society 1 (London 1835).

Das Register Gregors VII., ed. Erich Caspar, 2 vols. *MGH Epistolae selectae* 2 (Berlin 1920–23).

Die Register Innocenz' III., ed. Othmar Hageneder, Anton Haidacher, 10 (?) vols. to date. Publikationen der Abteilung für historische Studien des österreichischen Kulturinstituts in Rom (Graz-Cologne 1964–).

Les registres de Philippe Auguste. Volume I: Texte, ed. John W. Baldwin. Recueil des Historiens de la France. Documents financiers et administratifs 7 (Paris 1992).

[Richard of Devizes] *The chronicle of Richard of Devizes of the time of King Richard the First*, ed. John T. Appleby. Medieval Texts (London 1963).

Richard, fitz Nigel, *Dialogus de scaccario . . .* [together with *Constitutio domus Regis . . .*], ed. and tr. Charles Johnson, corrected ed. F. E. L. Carter, D. E. Greenway. OMT (Oxford 1983 [1950]).

Richer, *Histoire de France (888–995)*, ed. Robert Latouche, 2 vols. CHFMA 12, 17 (Paris 1930–37).

[Rigord] *Gesta Philippi Augusti*, in *Oeuvres de Rigord et de Guillaume le Breton, historiens de Philippe-Auguste*, ed. H. François Delaborde, 2 vols. SHF (Paris 1882–85).

[Robert of Auxerre] *Roberti canonici S. Mariani Autissiodorensis chronicon*, partly ed. Oswald Holder-Egger, *MGHSS* XXVI (1882) 226–87.

Robert de Clari, *La conquête de Constantinople*, ed. Philippe Lauer. CFMA 40 (Paris 1927).

Robert of Courson, 'Summa de sacramentis,' partly ed. Georges Lefèvre, *Le traité 'de usura' de Robert de Courçon*. Travaux et Mémoires de l'Université de Lille 10, Mémoire 30 (Lille 1902); and Vincent L. Kennedy, 'Robert Courson on penance.' *Mediaeval Studies* VII (1945) 291–336.

Robert of Flamborough, *Liber poenitentialis* . . . , ed. J. J. Francis Firth. PIMS. Studies and Texts 18 (Toronto 1971).

[Robert de Torigni] *Chronique de Robert de Torigni, abbé du Mont-Saint-Michel, suivie de divers opuscules historiques*, ed. Léopold Delisle, 2 vols. Société de l'Histoire de Normandie (Rouen 1872–73).

Roderici Ximenii de Rada historia de rebus Hispanie, sive historia gothica, ed. Juan Fernández Valverde. *CCCM* 72 (Turnhout 1987).

Rogerii quaestiones super Institutis, ed. Hermann Kantorowicz, *Studies in the glossators of the Roman law* . . . (Cambridge 1938) 271–81.

[Roger of Howden] *Chronica magistri Rogeri de Houedene*, ed. William Stubbs, 4 vols. RS 51 (London 1868–71)

[Roger of Wendover] *The flowers of history by Roger de Wendover: from the year of our Lord 1154* . . . , ed. Henry G. Hewlett, 3 vols. RS 84 (London 1886–89).

Rotuli litterarum patentium in turri Londinensi asservati, ed. Thomas Duffus Hardy. Vol. I. *Pars I. ab anno MCCI. ad annum MCCXI* (London 1835).

Rouergue roman, ed. Jean-Claude Fau, 3d ed. La Nuit des Temps (Zodiaque 1990).

[Rufinus] *Die Summa decretorum des Magister Rufinus*, ed. Heinrich Singer (Paderborn 1902).

The Rule of Saint Benedict, ed. and tr. Justin McCann. The Orchard Books (London 1952).

Ruodlieb. Faksimile-Ausgabe des Codex latinus Monacensis 19486 der Bayerischen Staatsbibliothek München und der Fragmente von St. Florian, ed. Benedikt Vollmann, 2 vols. (Wiesbaden 1974–85).

Ryccardi de Sancto Germano notarii chronica, ed. Carlo Alberto Garufi. *RIS²* VII:2 (Bologna 1938).

Sacrosancta concilia ad regiam editionem exacta . . . , ed. Ph. Labbe, Gabriel Cossart, 17 vols. (Paris 1671–72).

Sampiro. Su cronica y la monarquia leonesa en el siglo X, ed. Justo Perez de Urbel. CSIC. Escuela de Estudios medievales. Estudios 26 (Madrid 1952).

Selected letters of Pope Innocent III concerning England (1198–1216), ed. C. R. Cheney, W. H. Semple. Medieval Texts (London 1953).

Sigibert of Gembloux, *Chronica*, ed. L. C. Bethmann, *MGHSS* VI (1844) 268–374.

[Sigiberti Gemblacensis] *Continuatio praemonstratensis*, ed. L. C. Bethmann, *MGHSS* VI (1844) 447–56.

[Simon of Tournai] *Les disputationes de Simon de Tournai. Texte inédit*, ed. Joseph Warichez. Spicilegium sacrum Lovaniense (Louvain 1932).

Songs of the troubadours and trouvères. An anthology of poems and melodies, ed. Samuel N. Rosenberg, Margaret Switten, Gérard Le Vot. Garland Reference Library of the Humanities 1740 (NY 1998).

Statuta consulatus Ianuensis anni MCXLIII. Leggi del consolato di Genova del MCXLIII, ed. G. B. F. Raggio. Monumenta Historiae Patriae edita iussu regis Caroli Alberti ii:1 (Turin 1838) 233–52 (text 242–52).

[Stephen of Grandmont] *Liber de doctrina*, ed. Jean Becquet, *Scriptores ordinis Grandimontensis. CCCM* 8 (Turnhout 1968) 1–62.

Stephen Langton, *Commentary on the Book of Chronicles*, ed. Avrom Saltman (Ramat-Gan, 1978).

———— *Selected sermons of Stephen Langton*, ed. Phyllis B. Roberts. Toronto Medieval Latin Texts 10 (Toronto 1980).

[Suger] *Gesta Suggerii abbatis*, ed. Françoise Gasparri, *Suger. Oeuvres* (listed below) 1, 54–154.

———— *De glorioso rege Ludovico, Ludovici filio*, ed. August Molinier, *Vie de Louis le Gros par Suger suivie de l'histoire du roi Louis VII*. CTEEH (Paris 1887) 147–78.

———— *Oeuvres*, ed. Françoise Gasparri, 2 vols. CHFMA 37, 41 (Paris 1996–2001)

———— *Vie de Louis VI le Gros* [*Vita Ludovici grossi regis*], ed. and tr. Henri Waquet. CHFMA 11 (Paris 1929); tr. Richard Cusimano, John Moorhead, *The deeds of Louis the Fat* (Washington 1992).

La Summa Institutionum 'Justiniani est in hoc opere,' ed. Pierre Legendre. Ius Commune. Sonderheft 2 (Frankfurt 1973).

[*Summa Trecensis*] *Summa Codicis des Irnerius*, ed. Hermann Fitting (Berlin 1894).

Surveys of the estates of Glastonbury abbey c. 1135–1201, ed. N. E. Stacy. British Academy. Records of Social and Economic History. New Series 33 (Oxford-NY 2001).

Das Tafelgüterverzeichnis des römischen Königs (MS. Bonn S. 1559), ed. Carlrichard Brühl, Theo Kölzer (Cologne-Vienna 1979).

Die Tegernseer Briefsammlung (Froumund), ed. Karl Strecker. MGH Epistolae selectae 3 (Munich 1978 [1925]).

[Thietmar] *Die Chronik des Bischofs Thietmar von Merseburg*, ed. Robert Holtzmann. *MGHSSRG* nova series 9 (Berlin 1935; tr. David A.

Warner, *Ottonian Germany: the chronicon of Thietmar of Merseburg*. Manchester Medieval Sources [Manchester 2001]).

[Thomas Becket] *The correspondence of Thomas Becket, archbishop of Canterbury (1162–1170)*, ed. Anne J. Duggan, 2 vols. OMT (Oxford 2000).

Thomas de Chobham, *Summa confessorum*, ed. F. Broomfield. Analecta mediaevalia Namurcensia 25 (Louvain 1968).

[Thomas of Monmouth] *The life and miracles of St William of Norwich by Thomas of Monmouth*, ed. Augustus Jessopp, Montague Rhodes James (Cambridge 1896).

'Three peaces of Empúries (1189–1220),' ed. Stephen P. Bensch, *Anuario de Estudios medievales* XXVI (1996) 583–603.

Three rolls of the king's court in the reign of King Richard the First, A.D. 1194–1195, ed. Frederick William Maitland. PRS 14 (London 1891).

Le Très ancien Coutumier de Normandie, Coutumiers de Normandie. Textes critiques, ed. Ernest-Joseph Tardif, 2 vols. (Rouen 1881–1903), première partie.

Tumbo A de la catedral de Santiago. Estudio y edición, ed. Manuel Lucas Alvarez. Cabildo de la S.A.M.I Catedral. Seminario de Estudos Galegos (Santiago 1998).

'An "Unknown Charter" for Catalonia (1205),' ed. T. N. Bisson, *Album Elemér Mályusz*. SPICHRPI 56 (Brussels 1976) 61–76 (reprinted in *MFrPN* 199–212).

'Die Urkunden Kaiser Alfons VII. von Spanien,' ed. Peter Rassow, *Archiv für Urkundenforschung* X (1928) 327–468.

Urkundenbuch der Stadt Hildesheim, ed. Richard Doebner, 9 vols. (Aalen 1980 [1881–1901])

Usatges de Barcelona. El codi a mitjan segle XII, ed. Joan Bastardas. Fundació Noguera. Textos i Documents 6 (Barcelona 1984).

Vetus collectio, ed. Gustav Haenel, *Dissensiones dominorum* . . . (Leipzig 1834) 1–70.

Villehardouin [Geoffroi de], *La conquête de Constantinople*, ed. Edmond Faral, 2d ed., 2 vols. CHFMA 18–19 (Paris 1961 [1938]).

[Vincent Kadłubek] *Magistri Vincentii dicti Kadłubek chronica Polonorum*, ed. Marian Plezia. Monumenta Poloniae historica. Nova series 11 (Kraków 1994).

Vita Heinrici IV. imperatoris, ed. Wilhelm Eberhard. MGHSSRG 58 (Hanover 1990 [1899]); tr. T. E. Mommsen, Karl Morrison, *Imperial lives and letters of the eleventh century.* Records of Civilization, Sources and Studies 67 (NY 1962; new ed. 2000) 101–37.

'Vita, Inventio et Miracula Sanctae Enimiae,' ed. Clovis Brunel, *Analecta Bollandiana* LVII (1939) 237–98.

Walter Map, *De nugis curialium. Courtiers' trifles,* ed. and tr. M. R. James, rev. C. N. L. Brooke, R.A.B. Mynors. OMT (Oxford 1983 [1914]).

[Walter of Thérouanne] *Vita Karoli comitis auctore Waltero archidiaconi Tervanensi,* ed. Rudolf Köpke. *MGHSS* XII (1856) 531–61.

William IX, *see* Guilhem.

[William FitzStephen] *Vita sancti Thomae, Cantuariensis archiepiscopi et martyris, auctore Willemo filio Stephani,* Materials III (1877) 1–154.

[William Ketell] *Alia miracula [S. Johannis episcopi] auctore ut plurimum teste oculato,* ed. James Raine, *The historians of the church of York and its archbishops,* 3 vols. RS 71 (London 1879–94) I, 293–320.

Willelmi Malmesbiriensis monachi de gestis pontificum Anglorum libri quinque, ed. N. E. S. A. Hamilton. RS 52 (London 1870).

William of Malmesbury, *Gesta regum Anglorum. The history of the English kings,* ed. R. A. B. Mynors, R. M. Thomson, Michael Winterbottom, 2 vols. OMT (Oxford 1998–99).

[William of Newburgh] *Historia rerum Anglicarum,* ed. Richard Howlett. *Chronicles of the reigns of Stephen, Henry II, and Richard I,* 4 vols. RS 82 (London 1884–89) I, 3–408; II, 411–500. *Continuatio chronici Willelmi de Novoburgo ad annum 1298,* ibid., II, 503–83.

[Wipo] *Gesta Chuonradi II. imperatoris,* ed. Harry Bresslau, *Die Werke Wipos,* 3d ed. *MGHSSRG* (Leipzig 1915 [1878]).

Secondary Works

Abbot Suger and Saint Denis. A symposium, ed. Paula Lieber Gerson (NY 1986).

Abulafia, David, 'The crown and the economy under Roger II and his successors.' *Dumbarton Oaks Papers* XXXVII (1983) 1–14.

——— *Frederick II: A medieval emperor* (London 1988).

Allen, D. F., *A catalogue of English coins in the British Museum: the cross and crosslet type of Henry II* (London 1951).

Althoff, Gerd, *Family, friends and followers. Political and social bonds in medieval Europe*, tr. Christopher Carroll (Cambridge 2004 [1990]).

⸻ *Heinrich IV.*, ed. Peter Herde (Darmstadt 2006).

⸻ 'Ira regis: prolegomena to a history of royal anger,' *Anger's past: the social uses of an emotion in the Middle Ages*, ed. Barbara H. Rosenwein (Ithaca, NY, 1998) 59–74.

⸻ *Die Macht der Rituale. Symbolik und Herrschaft im Mittelalter* (Darmstadt 2003).

The anarchy of King Stephen's reign, ed. Edmund King (Oxford 1994).

Andreolli, Bruno, and Massimo Montanari, *L'azienda curtense in Italia: proprietà della terra e lavoro contadino nei secoli VIII–XI* (Bologna 1983).

Arendt, Hannah, *Crises of the republic: lying in politics, civil disobedience, on violence, thoughts on politics and revolution* (NY 1972).

Arnold, Benjamin, *Princes and territories in medieval Germany* (Cambridge 1991).

Arnoux, Mathieu, 'Classe agricole, pouvoir seigneurial et autorité ducale. L'évolution de la Normandie féodale d'après le témoignage des chroniqueurs (X^e–XIIe siècles),' *Le Moyen Âge* xcviii (1992) 35–60.

Audouin, Eduard, *Essai sur l'armée royale au temps de Philippe Auguste* (Paris 1913).

Aurell, Martin, *L'empire des Plantagenêt 1154–1224* (Perrin 2003).

Bachrach, Bernard S., *Fulk Nerra, the neo-Roman consul, 987–1040: a political biography of the Angevin count* (Berkeley 1993).

Baldwin, John W., *The government of Philip Augustus. Foundations of French royal power in the Middle Ages* (Berkeley-Los Angeles 1986; tr. Béatrice Bonne, *Philippe Auguste et son gouvernement. Les fondations du pouvoir royal en France au Moyen Age* [Paris 1991]).

⸻ *The language of sex. Five voices from northern France around 1200* (Chicago 1994).

⸻ *Masters, princes and merchants. The social views of Peter the Chanter & his circle*, 2 vols. (Princeton 1970).

⸻ 'Philippe Auguste, Pierre le Chantre et Etienne de Gallardon: la conjoncture de *regnum*, *studium* et *cancellaria*,' *CRAIBL* (Paris 2000) 437–57.

Baluze, [Etienne], *Histoire généalogique de la maison d'Auvergne justifiée par chartes, titres, histoires anciennes, & autres preuves authentiques*, 2 vols. (Paris 1708).

BIBLIOGRAPHY 613

Barlow, Frank, *Thomas Becket* (Berkeley–Los Angeles 1986).
—— *William Rufus.* English Monarchs (London 1983).
Barraclough, Geoffrey, *The origins of modern Germany*, 2d ed. (Oxford 1947 [1946]).
Barrero, Ana Maria, 'Los fueros de Sahagún,' *AHDE* XLII (1972) 385–597.
Barthélemy, Dominique, *L'an mil et la paix de Dieu. La France chrétienne et féodale, 980–1060* (Paris 1999).
—— *Chevaliers et miracles. La violence et le sacré dans la société féodale.* Les Enjeux de l'Histoire (Paris 2004)
—— 'Debate: The "feudal revolution",' *Past & Present* no. 152 (1996) 196–205.
—— *Les deux âges de la seigneurie banale. Pouvoir et société dans la terre des sires de Coucy (milieu XIe–milieu XIIIe siècle).* Université de Paris IV. Série Histoire ancienne et médiévale 12 (Paris 1984).
—— 'La mutation féodale a-t-elle eu lieu? (Note critique),' *Annales: E.S.C.* (1992) 767–77.
—— 'Quelques réflexions sur Louis VI, Suger et la chevalerie.' *Liber largitorius. Etudes d'histoire médiévale offertes à Pierre Toubert par ses élèves*, ed. D. Barthélemy, Jean-Marie Martin. EPHE. Sciences historiques et philologiques. Hautes Etudes médiévales et modernes 84 (Geneva 2003) 435–53.
—— *La société dans le comté de Vendôme de l'an mil au XIVe siècle* (Paris 1993).
Bartlett, Robert, *England under the Norman and Angevin kings, 1075–1225.* The New Oxford History of England (Oxford 2000).
—— *The making of Europe. Conquest, colonization and cultural change, 950–1350* (Princeton 1993).
Bass, Allen, 'Early Germanic experience and the origins of representation,' *Parliaments, Estates and Representation* XV (1995) 1–11.
Bates, David, *Normandy before 1066* (London 1982).
Baudon de Mony, Ch(arles), *Relations politiques des comtes de Foix avec la Catalogne jusqu'au commencement du XIVe siècle*, 2 vols. (Paris 1896).
Bautier, Robert-Henri, 'Paris au temps d'Abélard.' *Abélard en son temps.* Actes du Colloque international organisé à l'occasion du 9e centenaire de la naissance de Pierre Abélard (Paris 1979) (Paris 1981) 40–71.

Becker, Alfons, *Studien zum Investiturproblem in Frankreich: Papsttum, Königtum und Episkopat im Zeitalter der gregorianischen Kirchenreform (1049–1119)*. Schriften der Universität des Saarlandes (Saarbrücken 1955).

Bedos, Brigitte, *La châtellenie de Montmorency des origines à 1368: aspects féodaux, sociaux et économiques.* Société historique et archéologique de Pontoise, du Val d'Oise et du Vexin (Pontoise 1981).

Benson, Robert L., 'Political *renovatio*: two models from Roman antiquity,' *Renaissance and renewal in the twelfth century* (fully cited below) 339–86.

Berkhofer, Robert F. (III), *Day of reckoning. Power and accountability in medieval France.* The Middle Ages Series (Philadelphia 2004).

Biggs, Anselm Gordon, *Diego Gelmirez, first archbishop of Compostela.* The Catholic University of America. Studies in Mediaeval History, new series 12 (Washington 1949).

Bisson, Thomas N., *Assemblies and representation in Languedoc in the thirteenth century* (Princeton 1964).

———— 'Les comptes des domaines au temps de Philippe-Auguste,' *La France de Philippe Auguste. Le temps des mutations . . .* , ed. R.-H. Bautier. Colloques internationaux du CNRS 602 (Paris 1982) 521–38 (reprinted in *MFrPN*, ch. 14).

———— 'An early provincial assembly: the general court of Agenais in the thirteenth century,' *Speculum* XXXVI (1961) 254–81 (reprinted in *MFrPN*, ch. 1).

———— 'L'expérience du pouvoir chez Pierre Abélard (c. 1100–1142),' *Pierre Abélard. Colloque international de Nantes*, ed. Jean Jolivet, Henri Habrias. Histoire (Rennes 2003) 91–108.

———— 'The "feudal revolution",' *Past & Present* no. 142 (1994) 6–42; no. 155 (1997) 208–25.

———— 'The finances of the young James I (1213–1228),' *MFrPN*, ch. 19 (1980).

———— 'A general court of Aragon (Daroca, February 1228),' *EHR* XCII (1977) 107–24 (reprinted in *MFrPN*, ch. 2).

———— 'The lure of Stephen's England: *tenserie*, Flemings, and a crisis of circumstance,' *King Stephen's reign . . .* (2008, fully cited below) 171–81.

———— 'The organized peace in southern France and Catalonia (c. 1140–1233),' *AHR* LXXXII (1977) 290–311 (*MFrPN*, ch. 11).

———— 'Poder escrit i successió al comtat d'Urgell (1188–1210),' *Acta historica et archaeologica mediaevalia* xx–xxi (*Homenatge al Dr. Manuel Riu i Riu*) (Barcelona 1999–2000) 187–201.

———— 'Pouvoir et consuls à Toulouse (1150–1205),' *Les sociétés méridionales à l'âge féodal (Espagne, Italie et sud de la France, X^e–XIIIe s.). Hommage à Pierre Bonnassie*, ed. Hélène Débax. Méridiennes. CNRS. Université de Toulouse-Le Mirail (Toulouse 1999) 197–202.

———— 'Princely nobility in an age of ambition,' *Nobles and nobility in medieval Europe: concepts, origins, transformations*, ed. Anne J. Duggan (Woodbridge 2000) 101–13.

———— 'The problem of feudal monarchy: Aragon, Catalonia and France,' *Speculum* LIII (1978) 460–78 (reprinted in *MFrPN*, ch. 12).

———— 'Ramon de Caldes (c. 1135–1199): dean of Barcelona and king's minister,' *Law, church and society. Essays in honor of Stephan Kuttner*, ed. Kenneth Pennington, Robert Somerville. Middle Ages (Philadelphia 1977) 281–92 (*MFrPN*, ch. 9).

———— 'Sur les origines du *monedatge*: quelques textes inédits,' *Annales du Midi* LXXXV (1973) 91–104 (*MFrPN*, ch. 17).

———— 'An "Unknown Charter" for Catalonia (1205),' *Album Elemér Mályusz* . . . SPICHRPI 56 (Brussels 1976) 61–76 (*MFrPN*, ch. 10).

———— 'The war of the two Arnaus: a memorial of the broken peace in Cerdanya (1188),' *Miscel.lània en homenatge al P. Agustí Altisent* (Tarragona 1991) 95–107.

Bloch, Marc, *Les caractères originaux de l'histoire rurale française*, new ed., 2 vols. Librairie Armand Colin 'Economies-Sociétés-Civilisations' (Paris 1955–60 [1931]; tr. Janet Sondheimer, *French rural history* . . . [Berkeley 1966]).

———— *La société féodale*, 2 vols. L'Evolution de l'Humanité 34, 34*bis* (Paris 1939–40; tr. L. A. Manyon, *Feudal society* [Chicago 1961]).

Blumenthal, Uta-Renata, *The Investiture Conflict. Church and monarchy from the ninth to the twelfth century*. Middle Ages (Philadelphia 1988 [1982]).

Bonnassie, Pierre, *La Catalogne du milieu du Xe à la fin du XIe siècle: croissance et mutations d'une société*, 2 vols. PUT-LeM Série A 23, 29 (Toulouse 1975–76).

———— 'Sur la genèse de la féodalité catalane: nouvelles approaches,' *Il feudalesimo nell'alto medioevo, 8–12 aprile 1999*, 2 vols. Settimane di

Studio del Centro italiano di Studi sull'alto medioevo 47 (Spoleto 2000) II, 569–606.

——— 'Les *sagreres* catalanes: la concentration de l'habitat dans le "cercle de paix" des églises (XIe s.),' *L'environnement des églises et la topographie religieuse des campagnes médiévales,* ed. Michel Fixot, Elis. Zadora-Rio. Documents d'Archéologie française 46 (Paris 1994) 68–94.

——— *From slavery to feudalism in south-western Europe,* tr. Jean Birrell. Past & Present Publications (Cambridge 1991).

Bonne, Jean-Claude, 'Depicted gesture, named gesture; postures of the Christ on the Autun tympanum,' *History and Anthropology* 1 (1984) 77–93.

Boorman, Julia, 'The sheriffs of Henry II and the significance of 1170,' *Law and government in medieval England and Normandy. Essays in honour of Sir James Holt,* ed. George Garnett, John Hudson (Cambridge 1994) 255–75.

Boquillet, A., 'Les prévôts laïques de Saint-Amand du XIe au XIVe siècle,' *Bulletin de la Société des Etudes de la Province de Cambrai* XXVI (1926) 161–87.

Bosl, Karl, *Frühformen der Gesellschaft im mittelalterlichen Europa. Ausgewählte Beiträge zu einer Strukturanalyse der mittelalterlichen Welt* (Munich 1964).

Bouchard, Constance, *'Strong of body, brave and noble': chivalry and society in medieval France* (Ithaca, NY, 1998).

Bourdieu, Pierre, *Outline of a theory of practice,* tr. Richard Nice. Cambridge Studies in Social Anthropology (Cambridge 1977 [1972]).

Bourin-Derruau, Monique, *Village médiévaux en bas-Languedoc: genèse d'une sociabilité (X^e–XIVe siècle),* 2 vols. Chemins de la Mémoire (Paris 1987).

Bournazel, Eric, *Le gouvernement capétien au XIIe siècle, 1108–1180. Structures sociales et mutations institutionnelles.* Publications de la Faculté de Droit et des Sciences économiques de Limoges (Paris 1975).

Boussard, Jacques, *Le comté d'Anjou sous Henri Plantagenêt et ses fils (1151–1204)* (Paris 1938).

——— *Le gouvernement d'Henri II Plantagenêt.* Bibliothèque Elzévirienne. Nouv. série. Etudes et Documents (Paris 1956).

Brooke, Christopher, 'John of Salisbury and his world,' in *The world of John of Salisbury,* ed. Michael Wilks. Studies in Church History Subsidia 3 (Oxford 1984) 1–20.

Brown, Elizabeth A. R., 'Franks, Burgundians, and Aquitanians' and the royal coronation ceremony in France. Transactions of the American Philosophical Society 82:7 (Philadelphia 1992).

—————— 'La notion de la légitimité et la prophétie à la cour de Philippe Auguste,' La France de Philippe Auguste . . . (1982, cited above, Bisson, 'Comptes de domaine') 77–110.

Brühl, Carlrichard, Fodrum, gistum, servitium regis. Studien zu den wirtschaftlichen Grundlagen des Königtums im Frankreich und in den fränkischen Nachfolgestaaten Deutschland, Frankreich und Italien vom 6. bis zur Mitte des 14. Jahrhunderts, 2 vols. Kölmer historische Abhandlungen 14:1–2 (Cologne 1968).

Brundage, James A., Medieval canon law and the crusader (Madison 1969).

Brunel, Clovis, 'Les juges de la paix en Gévaudan au milieu du XIᵉ siècle,' BEC cix (1951) 32–41.

Buc, Philippe, L'ambiguïté du livre: prince, pouvoir, et peuple dans les commentaires de la Bible au moyen âge. Théologie historique 95 (Paris 1994).

—————— 'Principes gentium dominantur eorum: princely power between legitimacy and illegitimacy in twelfth-century exegesis,' in Cultures of power . . . (1994, fully cited below) 310–28.

Caille, Jacqueline, 'Origine et développement de la seigneurie temporelle de l'archevêque dans la ville et le terroir de Narbonne (IXᵉ–XIIᵉ siècles),' Narbonne. Archéologie et histoire, 3 vols. Fédération historique du Languedoc méditerranéen et du Roussillon (Montpellier 1973) II, 22–30.

Campbell, James, The Anglo-Saxon state (London 2000).

—————— 'The significance of the Anglo-Norman state in the administrative history of western Europe' (1980), Essays in Anglo-Saxon history (London 1986) ch. 11.

Cantarella, Glauco Maria, Pasquale II e il suo tempo. Nuovo Medioevo 54 (Naples 1997).

Carpenter, David, The minority of Henry III (London 1990).

—————— The struggle for mastery. Britain 1066–1284 (London 2003).

Caruana, Jaime, 'Itinerario de Alfonso II de Aragón.' Estudios de Edad media de la Corona de Aragón VII (1962) 73–298.

Castignoli, Piero, Storia di Piacenza, 6 vols. (Piacenza 1984–2003).

La charte de Beaumont et les franchises municipales entre Loire et Rhin. Actes du colloque organisé par l'Institut de recherche régionale de l'Université de Nancy II (Nancy, 22–25 septembre 1982) (Nancy 1988).

Chartrou, Josèphe, *L'Anjou de 1109 à 1151. Foulque de Jérusalem et Geoffroi Plantagenet*. Université de Paris-Faculté des Lettres (Paris 1928).

Chédeville, André, *Chartres et ses campagnes (XIᵉ–XIIIᵉ s.)* (Paris 1973).

Cheney, C. R., *Hubert Walter*. Leaders of Religion (London 1967).

Cheney, Mary G., *Roger, bishop of Worcester, 1164–1179*. OHM (Oxford 1980).

Cheyette, Fredric L., *Ermengard of Narbonne and the world of the troubadours*. Conjunctions of Religion and Power in the Medieval Past (Ithaca, NY, 2001).

——— 'The invention of the state,' *Essays on medieval civilization*, ed. Bede K. Lackner, Kenneth Roy Philp. The Walter Prescott Webb Memorial Lectures 12 (Austin 1980) 143–78.

——— 'The "sale" of Carcassonne to the counts of Barcelona and the rise of the Trencavels,' *Speculum* LXIII (1988) 826–64.

Chodorow, S. A., 'Ecclesiastical politics and the ending of the Investiture Conflict,' *Speculum* XLVI (1971) 613–40.

Clanchy, M. T., *From memory to written record: England 1066–1307*, 2d ed. (Oxford 1993 [1979]).

Clark, Cecily, ' "This ecclesiastical adventurer": Henry of Saint-Jean d'Angély,' *EHR* LXXXIV (1969) 548–60.

Clarke, H. B., 'The Domesday satellites,' *Domesday Book. A reassessment*, ed. Peter Sawyer (London 1985), ch. 4.

——— 'The early surveys of Evesham Abbey: an investigation into the problem of continuity in Anglo-Norman England' (PhD thesis, University of Birmingham 1977).

Classen, Peter, 'Richterstand und Rechtswissenschaft in italienischen Kommunen des 12. Jahrhunderts,' reprinted in *Studium und Gesellschaft im Mittelalter*. MGH, *Schriften* 29 (Stuttgart 1983 [1980]).

Coll i Alentorn, Miquel, *La llegenda de Guillem Ramon de Montcada* (Barcelona 1958).

Conflict in medieval Europe. Changing perspectives on society and culture, ed. Warren C. Brown, Piotr Górecki (Aldershot 2003).

Constable, Giles, *The reformation of the twelfth century*. The Trevelyan lectures given at the University of Cambridge, 1985 (Cambridge 1996).

Cooper, Alan, 'Extraordinary privilege: the trial of Penenden Heath and the Domesday Inquest,' *EHR* CXVI (2001) 1167–92.

Coronations: medieval and early modern monarchic ritual, ed. János M. Bak (Berkeley 1990).

Las Cortes de Castilla y León en la edad media, 2 vols. Actas de la primera etapa del Congreso científico sobre la historia de las Cortes de Castilla y León, Burgos, 30 de Septiembre a 3 de Octubre de 1986 (Valladolid 1988).

Coulson, Charles, 'The castles of the anarchy,' in *The anarchy of Stephen's reign* (1994), cited above, ch. 2.

——— *Castles in medieval society: fortresses in England, France, and Ireland in the central Middle Ages* (Oxford 2003).

Cowdrey, H. E. J., 'The Gregorian reform in the Anglo-Norman lands and in Scandinavia,' *Studi Gregoriani* XIII (1989) 321–52.

——— *Pope Gregory VII, 1073–1085* (Oxford 1998).

Cronne, H. A., *The reign of Stephen, 1135–54. Anarchy in England* (London 1970).

Crouch, David, *The Beaumont twins. The roots and branches of power in the twelfth century*. CSMLT 4th series (Cambridge 1986).

——— *The birth of nobility. Constructing aristocracy in England and France 900–1300* (Harlow 2005).

——— *The reign of King Stephen, 1135–1154* (Harlow 2000).

Cultures of power. Lordship, status, and process in twelfth-century Europe, ed. Thomas N. Bisson. Middle Ages (Philadelphia 1995).

D'Amico, Ruggiero, 'Note su alcuni rapporti tra città e campagna nel contado di Pisa tra XI e XII secolo.' *Bollettino storico Pisano* XXXIX (1970) 15–29.

Davis, R. H. C., *King Stephen 1135–1154*, 3d ed. (London 1990 [1967]).

Débax, Hélène, 'Le cartulaire des Trencavel (*Liber instrumentorum vicecomitalium*),' *Les cartulaires*. Actes de la Table ronde organisée par l'Ecole nationale des Chartes et le G.D.R. 121 du CNRS (Paris, 5–7 décembre 1991), ed. Olivier Guyotjeannin, Laurent Morelle, Michel Parisse. Mémoires et Documents de l'Ecole des Chartes 39 (Paris 1993) 291–99.

——— *La féodalité languedocienne, XIe–XIIe siècles. Serments, hommages et fiefs dans le Languedoc des Trencavel*. Tempus (Toulouse 2003).

Delisle, Léopold, 'Etienne de Gallardon clerc de la chancellerie de Philippe-Auguste, chanoine de Bourges,' *BEC* LX (1899) 5–44.

Delumeau, Jean-Pierre, *Arezzo, espace et sociétés, 715–1230: recherches sur Arezzo et son contado du VIIIe au début du XIIIe siècle*, 2 vols. Collection de l'Ecole française de Rome 219 (Rome 1996).

Devailly, Guy, *Le Berry du Xe siècle au milieu du XIIIe. Etude politique, religieuse, sociale et économique.* EPHE-Sorbonne VIe Section . . . Civilisations et Sociétés 19 (Paris-La Haye 1973).

Dhondt, Jan, ' "Ordres" ou "puissances." L'exemple des états de Flandre,' *Annales: E.S.C.* v (1950) 289–305.

———— 'Les "solidarités" médiévales. Une société en transition: la Flandre en 1127–28,' *Annales: E.S.C.* xii (1957) 529–60.

Dollinger, Philippe, *L'évolution des classes rurales en Bavière depuis la fin de l'époque carolingienne jusqu'au milieu du XIIIe siècle.* Publications de la Faculté des Lettres de l'Université de Strasbourg 112 (Paris 1949).

Domesday studies. Papers read at the Novocentenary Conference of the Royal Historical Society and the Institute of British Geographers, Winchester 1986 (Woodbridge 1987).

Doubleday, Simon R., *The Lara family: crown and nobility in medieval Spain.* Harvard Historical Studies 141 (Cambridge, M., 2001).

Douglas, David C., *William the Conqueror. The Norman impact upon England.* English Monarchs (London 1964).

Duby, Georges, 'Le budget de l'abbaye de Cluny entre 1080 et 1155. Economie domaniale et économie monétaire,' *Annales: E.S.C.* vii (1952) 155–71 (reprinted in *Hommes et structures du moyen âge. Recueil d'articles.* EPHE-Sorbonne VIe Section. Le Savoir historique 1 [Paris 1973] 61–82).

———— *L'économie rurale et la vie des campagnes dans l'Occident médiéval (France, Angleterre, Empire, IXe–XVe siècles). Essai de synthèse et perspectives de recherches,* 2 vols. Collection historique (Paris 1962; tr. Cynthia Postan, *Rural economy and country life in the medieval West* [London 1968]).

———— *Le moyen âge de Hugues Capet à Jeanne d'Arc 987–1460.* Histoire de France Hachette (Paris 1987).

———— *La société aux XIe et XIIe siècles dans la région mâconnaise.* Bibliothèque générale de l'EPHE VIe Section (Paris 1953 [reset and reprinted 1971]).

———— *Les trois ordres ou l'imaginaire du féodalisme.* Bibliothèque des Histoires (Paris 1978; tr. Arthur Goldhammer, *The three orders: feudal society imagined* [Chicago 1980; corrected ed. 1982]).

Duggan, Charles, *Twelfth-century decretal collections and their importance in English history.* University of London Historical Studies 12 (London 1963).

Duhamel-Amado, Claudie, *L'aristocratie languedocienne du Xe au XIIe siècle*, 2 vols. (Toulouse 2001–07).

Dunbabin, Jean, *France in the making 843–1180*, 2d ed. (Oxford 2000 [1985]).

Elze, Reinhard, 'The ordo for the coronation of King Roger II of Sicily: an example of dating from internal evidence,' in *Coronations* . . . (fully cited above) 165–78.

Engels, Odilo, 'Papsttum, Reconquista und spanisches Landeskonzil im Hochmittelalter,' *Annuarium historiae conciliorum* I (1969) 37–49, 241–87.

Ertman, Thomas, *Birth of the Leviathan: building states and regimes in medieval and early modern Europe* (Cambridge 1997).

Escalona, Romualdo, *Historia de la Real Monasterio de Sahagún* (reprint León 1982 [1782]).

Estepa Díez, Carlos. 'Curia y cortes en el reino de León,' *Las Cortes de Castilla y León* (1988; fully cited above) I, 23–103.

———— *Estructura social de la ciudad de León (siglos XI–XIII)*. Fuentes y Estudios de Historia leonesa 19 (León 1977).

———— 'Sobre las revueltas burguesas en el siglo XII en el reino de León,' *Archivos Leoneses* XXVIII (1974) 291–307.

Evergates, Theodore, *Feudal society in the bailliage of Troyes under the counts of Champagne, 1152–1284* (Baltimore 1975).

Fabre, Paul, *Etude sur le Liber censuum de l'église romaine*. BEFAR 62 (Paris 1892).

Fasoli, Gina, 'Note sulla feudalità canossiana,' *Studi Matildici*. Atti e memorie del convegno di studi Matildici. Deputazione di Storia patria per le antiche provincie modenesi. Biblioteca-N. 2 (Modena 1964) 69–81.

Fernández Catón, José María, *La curia regia de León de 1188 y sus 'decreta' y constitución*. Centro de Estudios e Investigación 'San Isidoro' Archivo Histórico Diocesano (León 1993).

Fiorentini, Francesco Maria, *Memorie della gran contessa Matilda*, 2d ed. Gian Domenico Mansi (Lucca 1756).

Flach, Jacques, *Les origines de l'ancienne France*, 4 vols. (Paris 1886–1917).

Fleckenstein, Josef, 'Friedrich Barbarossa und das Rittertum. Zur Bedeutung der grossen Mainzer Hoftage von 1184 und 1188,' *Festschrift für Hermann Heimpel zum 70. Geburtstag am 19. September 1971*, 3 vols. Veröffentlichungen des Max-Planck-Instituts für Geschichte 36 (Göttingen 1971–72) II, 1023–41.

Fletcher, R. A., *The episcopate in the kingdom of León in the twelfth century.* OHM (Oxford 1978).

——— *Saint James's catapult. The life and times of Diego Gelmírez of Santiago de Compostela.* (Oxford 1984).

Fliche, Augustin, *Le règne de Philippe Ier, roi de France (1060–1108)* (Paris 1912).

Flori, Jean, *L'essor de la chevalerie XIe–XIIe siècles.* Travaux d'Histoire Ethico-Politique 46 (Geneva 1986).

Fluvià, Armand de, *Els primitius comtats i vescomtats de Catalunya. Cronologia de comtes i vescomtes.* Enciclopèdia Catalana. Biblioteca Universitària 11 (Barcelona 1989).

Fossier, Robert, *Enfance de l'Europe X^e–XIIe siècles: aspects économiques et sociaux,* 2 vols. Nouvelle Clio 17, 17bis (Paris 1982).

——— *Polyptyques et censiers.* TSMA 28 (Turnhout 1978).

——— 'Rural economy and country life,' *NCMH* III (1999), ch. 2.

Foucault, Michel, *Power,* ed. James D. Faubion, tr. Robert Hurley *et al.* Essential works of Foucault 1954–84, 3 vols. (London 2002) III.

Fowler-Magerl, Linda, Ordines iudiciarii *and* Libelli de ordine iudiciorum *from the middle of the twelfth to the end of the fifteenth century.* TSMA 63 (Turnhout 1994).

Frank, István, 'Pons de la Guardia, troubadour catalan du XIIe siècle,' *BRABLB* XXII (1949) 229–327.

Freedman, Paul H., *The origins of peasant servitude in medieval Catalonia.* CILAS (Cambridge 1991).

Fried, Johannes, *Die Entstehung des Juristenstandes im 12. Jahrhundert . . .* Forschungen zur neuren Privatrechtsgeschichte 21 (Cologne-Vienna 1974).

Fuhrmann, Horst, *Germany in the high middle ages c. 1050–1200,* tr. Timothy Reuter. Cambridge Medieval Textbooks (Cambridge 1986 [1978]).

Fumagalli, Vita, 'Mantua al tempo di Matilda di Canossa,' *Sant'Anselmo, Mantova e la lotta per le investiture.* Atti del convegno internazionale di studi (Mantova 23–24–25 maggio 1986), ed. Paolo Golinelli. Il Mondo medievale (Bologna 1987) 159–67.

Ganshof, F. L., *Feudalism,* tr. Philip Grierson, 3d English ed. (NY 1964 [1944]).

Ganz, David, 'The ideology of sharing: apostolic community and ecclesiastical property in the early middle ages,' *Property and power in the early Middle Ages*, ed. Wendy Davies, Paul Fouracre (Cambridge 1995) ch. 1.

García de Cortázar y Ruiz de Aguirre, José Angel, *La sociedad rural en la España medieval* (Madrid 1988).

García Gallo, Alfonso, 'El concilio de Coyanza. Contribución al estudio del derecho canónico español en la Alta Edad media,' *AHDE* xx (1950) 275–633.

Gasparri, Françoise, *L'écriture des actes de Louis VI, Louis VII et Philippe Auguste*. Centre de Recherches d'Histoire et de Philologie de la IVᵉ Section de l'EPHE. Hautes Etudes Médiévales et Modernes 20 (Geneva-Paris 1973).

——— 'Manuscrit monastique ou registre de chancellerie? A propos d'un recueil épistolaire de l'abbaye de Saint-Victor,' *Journal des Savants* (1976) 131–40.

——— 'Note sur le *Registrum veterius*: le plus ancien registre de la chancellerie de Philippe-Auguste,' *Mélanges de l'Ecole française de Rome* LXXXIII (1971) 363–88.

Gibson, Margaret T., *Lanfranc of Bec* (Oxford 1978).

Gilissen, John, *La coutume*. TSMA 41 (Turnhout 1982).

Gillingham, John, *Richard I*. Yale English Monarchs (New Haven 1999).

Giry, Arthur, *Etude sur les origines de la commune de Saint-Quentin* (Saint-Quentin 1887).

Gluckman, Max, 'The peace in the feud,' *Past & Present* no. 8 (1955) 1–14.

González, Julio, *Alfonso IX*, 2 vols. CSIC. Instituto Jerónimo Zurita (Madrid 1944).

——— *El reino de Castilla en la época de Alfonso VIII*, 3 vols. CSIC. Textos 25–27 (Madrid 1960).

Gonzalvo i Bou, Gener, 'La pau i treva de l'any 1187 per al comtat d'Urgell i vescomtat d'Ager,' *Ilerda* XLVIII (1990) 157–70.

Gouron, André, 'Diffusion des consulats méridionaux et expansion du droit romain aux XIIᵉ et XIIIᵉ siècles,' *BEC* CXXI (1963) 26–76 (reprinted in *La science du droit* . . . , cited below, ch. 1).

——— 'Une école ou des écoles? Sur les canonistes français (vers 1150–vers 1210),' *Proceedings of the sixth international congress of medieval canon law, Berkeley, California, 28 July–2 August 1980*, ed. Stephan Kuttner, Kenneth Pennington. MIC. Series C: Subsidia 7 (Vatican City 1985) 223–40.

———— L'entourage de Louis VII face aux droits savants: Giraud de Bourges et son *ordo*,' *BEC* CXLVI (1988) 5–29.

———— 'L'inaliénabilité du domaine public: à l'origine du principe,' *CRAIBL* (Paris 2001) 817–25.

———— 'Petrus "démasqué",' *Revue d'Histoire de Droit* LXXXII (2004) 577–88.

———— *La science du droit dans le Midi de la France au Moyen Age.* Variorum CS 196 (London 1984).

———— 'Sur les plus anciennes rédactions coutumières du Midi: les "chartes" consulaires d'Arles et d'Avignon,' *Annales du Midi* CIX (1997) 189–200.

Gransden, Antonia, *Historical writing in England c. 550–c. 1307* (London 1996 [1974]).

Grassotti, Hilda, 'El estado,' *Los reinos cristianos en los siglos XI y XII. Historia de España Menéndez Pidal* x, ed. Reyna Pastor *et al.*, 2 vols. (Madrid 1992) II, 13–186.

Graus, Frantisek, 'The crisis of the Middle Ages and the Hussites,' tr. James Heaney, *The reformation in medieval perspective*, ed. Steven Ozment. Modern Scholarship on European History (Chicago 1971) 76–103 [1969].

Gravier, Henri, *Essai sur les prévôts royaux du XIe au XIVe siècle* (Paris 1904).

Green, Judith A., *English sheriffs to 1154.* Public Record Office Handbooks 24 (London 1996).

———— *The government of England under Henry I.* CSMLT 4th series 3 (Cambridge 1986).

———— *Henry I. King of England and duke of Normandy* (Cambridge 2006).

Greenaway, George William, *Arnold of Brescia* (Cambridge 1931).

Grivot, Denis, and George Zarnecki, *Gislebertus, sculptor of Autun* (London 1961).

Grosdidier de Matons, Marcel, *Le comté de Bar des origines au traité de Bruges (vers 950–1301)* (Paris 1922).

Guillot, Olivier, 'Administration et gouvernement dans les états du comte d'Anjou au milieu du XIe siècle,' *Histoire comparée de l'administration (IVe–XVIIIe siècles).* Actes du XIVe colloque historique franco-allemand, Tours, 27 mars–1er avril 1977 . . . , ed. Werner Paravicini, Karl Ferdinand Werner. Beiheft der *Francia* 9 (Munich 1980) 311–32.

——— *Le comte d'Anjou et son entourage au XIe siècle*, 2 vols. (Paris 1972).

——— 'La participation au duel judiciaire de témoins de condition serve dans l'Ile-de-France du XIe siècle: autour d'un faux diplôme de Henri Ier,' *Droit privé et institutions régionales. Etudes historiques offertes à Jean Yver*. Publications de l'Université de Rouen (Paris 1976) 345–60.

Güterbock, Ferdinando, 'Alla vigilia della Lega Lombarda. Il dispotismo dei vicari imperiali a Piacenza,' *Archivio storico italiano* xcv:1 (1937) 188–217; 'Documenti,' xcv:2 (1937) 64–77.

Habermas, Jürgen, *The structural transformation of the public sphere. An inquiry into a category of bourgeois society*, tr. Thomas Burger (Cambridge, M., 1991 [1962]).

Hagger, Mark, 'A pipe roll for 25 Henry I,' *EHR* cxxii (2007) 133–40.

Halphen, Louis, *Le comté d'Anjou au XIe siècle* (Paris 1906).

——— 'La place de la royauté dans le système féodal,' reprinted in *A travers l'histoire du moyen âge* (Paris 1950 [1932]) 266–74.

——— 'Prévôts et voyers du XIe siècle. Région angevine,' reprinted in *A travers l'histoire du moyen âge* (1950 [1902]) 203–25.

Hamilton, Bernard, 'The Albigensian crusade and heresy,' *NCMH* v (1999), ch. 6.

Harding, Alan, *Medieval law and the foundations of the state* (Oxford 2002).

Harriss, G. L., *King, parliament, and public finance in medieval England to 1369* (Oxford 1975).

Harvey, P. D. A., *Manorial records*, rev. ed. Archives and the User 5 (London 1999 [1984]).

Haskins, Charles Homer, 'The abacus and the exchequer,' *Studies in the history of mediaeval science*. Harvard Historical Studies 27 (Cambridge, M., 1924) 327–35.

——— *Norman institutions*. Harvard Historical Studies 24 (Cambridge, M., 1918).

——— *The Normans in European history* (Boston 1915).

——— *The renaissance of the twelfth century* (Cambridge, M., 1928).

Hefele, Charles Joseph, *Histoire des conciles d'après les documents originaux*, tr. Henri Leclercq, 11 vols. (Paris 1907–52).

Hernández, Francisco, 'Las Cortes de Toledo de 1207,' *Las Cortes de Castilla y León* (1988; cited above) 1, 219–63.

Hilton, Rodney, *Bond men made free. Medieval peasant movements and the English rising of 1381* (NY 1973).

Hoffmann, Hartmut, *Gottesfriede und Treuga Dei. MGH, Schriften* 20 (Stuttgart 1964).

Hollister, C. W., *Henry I*, ed. Amanda Clark Frost. Yale English Monarchs (New Haven 2001).

———— *Monarchy, magnates and institutions in the Anglo-Norman world* (London 1986).

Holt, J. C., 'The assizes of Henry II: the texts,' *The study of medieval records. Essays in honour of Kathleen Major*, ed. D. A. Bullough, R. L. Storey (Oxford 1971) 85–106.

———— *Magna Carta*, 2d ed. (Cambridge 1992 [1965]).

———— *The northerners. A study in the reign of King John* (Oxford 1961).

———— 'Politics and property in early medieval England,' *Past & Present* no. 57 (1972) 3–52.

[Holtzmann, Walther] *Studies in the collections of twelfth-century decretals from the papers of the late Walther Holtzmann*, ed. C. R. Cheney, Mary G. Cheney. MIC i Series B: Corpus collectionum 3 (Vatican City 1979).

Houben, Hubert, *Roger II of Sicily: a ruler between east and west*, tr. Graham A. Loud. Cambridge Medieval Textbooks (Cambridge 2002 [1997]).

Hudson, John, *Land, law, and lordship in Anglo-Norman England*. OHM (Oxford 1994).

Hyams, Paul R., *King, lords and peasants in medieval England: the common law of villeinage in the twelfth and thirteenth centuries*. OHM (Oxford 1980).

———— 'Trial by ordeal: the key to proof in the early common law,' *On the laws and customs of England. Essays in honor of Samuel E. Thorne*, ed. Morris S. Arnold *et al.* (Chapel Hill 1981) 90–126.

Jaeger, C. Stephen, 'Courtliness and social change,' *Cultures of power . . .* (1995, cited above) 287–309.

———— *The origins of courtliness: civilizing trends and the formation of courtly ideals, 939–1210*. The Middle Ages (Philadelphia 1985).

Johns, Jeremy, *Arabic administration in Norman Sicily: the royal dīwān*. Cambridge Studies in Islamic Civilization (Cambridge 2002).

Jolliffe, J. E. A., *Angevin kingship*, 2d ed. (London 1963 [1955]).

———— *The constitutional history of medieval England from the English settlement to 1485*, 3d ed. (London 1954 [1937]).

Jones, Philip, *The Italian city-state. From commune to signoria* (Oxford 1997).

Jordan, Karl, 'Das Eindringen des Lehnswesen in das Rechtsleben der römischen Kurie,' *Archiv für Urkundenforschung* XII (1931) 13–110.

―――― *Henry the Lion: a biography*, tr. P. S. Falla (Oxford 1986 [1979]).

Kealey, Edward J., *Roger of Salisbury, viceroy of England* (Berkeley-Los Angeles 1972).

Keller, Hagen, *Adelsherrschaft und stätische Gesellschaft in Oberitalien (9.–12. Jahrhundert)*. Bibliothek des Deutschen Historischen Instituts in Rom 52 (Tübingen 1979).

Kempf, Friedrich *et al.*, *The church in the age of feudalism*, tr. Anselm Biggs, *History of the church*, ed. Hubert Jedin, John Tolan, III (London 1980).

King, Edmund, 'The anarchy of King Stephen's reign,' *TRHS* 5th series XXXIV (1984) 133–53.

King John: new interpretations, ed. S. D. Church (Woodbridge 1999).

King Stephen's reign (1135–1154), ed. Paul Dalton, Graeme J. White (Woodbridge 2008).

Knowles, David, 'Archbishop Thomas Becket: a character study,' *PBA* XXXV (1949) 177–205 (reprinted in *The historian and character . . .* [Cambridge 1963] ch. 6).

―――― *The monastic order in England. A history of its development from the times of St Dunstan to the Fourth Lateran Council 943–1216*, corrected reprint (Cambridge 1950 [1940]).

Kosto, Adam, 'The *Liber feudorum maior* of the counts of Barcelona: the cartulary as an expression of power,' *Journal of Medieval History* XXVII (2001) 1–22.

―――― 'The limited impact of the *Usatges of Barcelona* in twelfth-century Catalonia,' *Traditio* LVI (2001) 53–88.

―――― *Making agreements in medieval Catalonia. Power, order, and the written word, 1000–1200*. CSMLT, 4th series (Cambridge 2001).

Koziol, Geoffrey, *Begging pardon and favor: ritual and political order in early medieval France* (Ithaca, NY, 1992).

Kuttner, Stephan, 'The revival of jurisprudence,' *Renaissance and renewal in the twelfth century* (1982, fully cited below) 299–323.

Lacroix, Guillaume de, *Series et acta episcoporum Cadurcensium . . .* (Cahors 1617).

Landau, Peter, 'Die Entstehung der systematischen Dekretalsammlungen und die europaïsche Kanonistik des 12. Jahrhunderts,' *ZRG
Kan. Abt.* 96 (1979) 120–48.

Lange, Hermann, *Römisches Recht im Mittelalter* I (Munich 1997).

Langmuir, Gavin I., ' "Judei nostri" and the beginning of Capetian legislation,' *Traditio* XVI (1960) 203–39.

———— 'Politics and parliaments in the early thirteenth century,' *Études
sur l'histoire des assemblées d'états.* SPICHRPI 29 (Paris 1966) 47–62.

Larrea, Juan José, *La Navarre du IVe au XIIe siècle: peuplement et société.*
Bibliothèque du Moyen Age 14 (Paris-Brussels 1998).

Lauranson-Rosaz, Christian, *L'Auvergne et ses marges (Velay, Gévaudan)
du VIIIe au XIe siècle. La fin du monde antique?* (Le Puy-en-Velay
1987).

Le Bras, Gabriel, *et al., L'âge classique 1140–1378. Sources et théories du droit.*
Histoire du droit et des institutions de l'Eglise en Occident 7 (Paris
1965).

Lemarignier, J.-Fr., 'La dislocation du "pagus" et le problème des "consuetudines" (X^e–XIe siècles),' *Mélanges d'histoire du moyen âge dédiés à la
mémoire de Louis Halphen* (Paris 1951) 401–10.

———— *Le gouvernement royal aux premiers temps capétiens (987–1108).*
CNRS (Paris 1965).

———— 'Les institutions ecclésiastiques en France de la fin du Xe au
milieu du XIIe siècle,' in (Ferdinand Lot, Robert Fawtier) *Histoire des
institutions françaises au moyen âge,* 3 vols. (Paris 1957–62) III, Livre
premier.

———— *Recherches sur l'hommage en marche et les frontières féodales.* Travaux
et Mémoires de l'Université de Lille. Nouv. série Droit et Lettres 24
(Lille 1945).

Le Patourel, John, *The Norman empire* (Oxford 1976).

Lewis, Andrew W., *Royal succession in Capetian France: studies on familial
order and the state.* Harvard Historical Studies 100 (Cambridge, M.,
1981).

Leyser, Karl, *Communications and power in medieval Europe. The Gregorian
revolution and beyond,* ed. Timothy Reuter (London 1994).

———— 'The crisis of medieval Germany,' *PBA* LXIX (1983) 409–43 (reprinted in *Communications and power,* 21–49).

———— 'Frederick Barbarossa and the Hohenstaufen polity,' *Viator* XIX
(1988) 153–76 (*Communications and power,* ch. 7).

Limouzin-Lamothe, Roger, *La commune de Toulouse et les sources de son histoire (1120–1249). Etude historique et critique suivie de l'édition du cartulaire du consulat.* Bibliothèque méridionale 2d ser. 26 (Toulouse 1932).

López Alsina, Fernando, *La ciudad de Santiago de Compostela en la alta edad media* (Santiago de Compostela 1988).

López Ferreiro, Antonio, *Historia de la santa iglesia de Santiago de Compostela*, 11 vols. (Santiago 1898–1911).

Lot, Ferdinand, *Etudes sur le règne de Hugues Capet et la fin du Xe siècle.* BEHE 147 (Paris 1903).

Loud, G. A., *Church and society in the Norman principality of Capua, 1058–1197.* OHM (Oxford 1985).

Luchaire, Achille, *Etudes sur les actes de Louis VII* (Paris 1885).

——— *Louis VI le Gros. Annales de sa vie et de son règne (1081–1137)* (Paris 1890).

——— *La société française au temps de Philippe-Auguste* (Paris 1909).

Macé, Laurent, *Les comtes de Toulouse et leur entourage XIIe–XIIIe siècles. Rivalités, alliances et jeux de pouvoir.* Bibliothèque historique Privat (Toulouse 2000).

Magnou-Nortier, Elisabeth, 'Note sur le sens du mot *fevum* en Septimanie et dans la Marche d'Espagne à la fin du Xe et au début du XIe siècle,' *Annales du Midi* LXXVI (1964) 141–52.

——— *La société laïque et l'église dans la province ecclésiastique de Narbonne (zone cispyrénéenne) de la fin du VIIIe à la fin du XIe siècle.* PUT-LeM Série A 20 (Toulouse 1974).

Maitland, F. W., *Domesday Book and beyond. Three essays in the early history of England*, new ed. (Cambridge 1987 [1897]).

Marca, Petrus de, *Marca hispanica sive limes hispanicus, hoc est, geographica & historica descriptio Cataloniae, Ruscinonis, & circumjacentium populorum . . .* , ed. Etienne Baluze (Paris 1688).

Mariotte-Löber, Ruth, *Ville et seigneurie. Les chartes de franchises des comtes de Savoie, fin XIIe siècle—1343.* Mémoires et Documents publiés par l'Académie Florimontane 4 (Annecy-Geneva 1973).

Martin, Jean-Marie, *La Pouille du VIe au XIIe siècle.* Collection de l'Ecole française de Rome 179 (Rome 1993).

Martín Rodríguez, José-Luis, 'Un vasallo de Alfonso el Casto en el reino de León: Armengol VII, conde de Urgel,' *VII Congreso de Historia de la Corona de Aragón* [1962], 3 vols. (Barcelona 1964) II, 223–33.

Martínez Díez, Gonzalo, 'Curia y Cortes en el reino de Castilla,' *Las Cortes de Castilla y León* I, 105–51.

Martínez Sopena, Pascual, *La Tierra de Campos occidental: poblamiento, poder y comunidad del siglo X al XIII* (Valladolid 1985).

Matthew, Donald, *King Stephen* (London 2002).

Mayer, Theodor, 'The state of the dukes of Zähringen' (1935), tr. Geoffrey Barraclough, *Mediaeval Germany, 911–1250. Essays by German historians*, 2 vols. Studies in Mediaeval History (Oxford 1938) II, 175–202.

Menant, François, *Campagnes lombardes du moyen âge. L'économie et la société rurales dans la région de Bergame, de Crémone et de Brescia du Xe au XIIIe siècle*. BEFAR 281 (Rome 1993).

Menéndez Pidal, Ramon, *La España del Cid*, 7th ed., 2 vols. (Madrid 1969 [1929]; tr. Harold Sunderland, *The Cid and his Spain* [London 1971]).

Meyer von Knonau, Gerold, *Jahrbücher des deutschen Reiches unter Heinrich IV. und Heinrich V.*, 7 vols. (Leipzig 1890–1909).

Miller, Edward, *The abbey & bishopric of Ely. The social history of an ecclesiastical estate from the tenth century to the early fourteenth century*. CSMLT (Cambridge 1951).

Miller, William Ian, *Humiliation and other essays on honor, social discomfort, and violence* (Ithaca, NY, 1993).

Milsom, S. F. C., *The legal framework of English feudalism*. The Maitland Lectures given in 1972. Cambridge Studies in English Legal History (Cambridge 1976).

Mitteis, Heinrich, *Der Staat des hohen Mittelalters. Grundlinien einer vergleichenden Verfassungsgeschichte des Lehnszeitalters*, 9th ed. (Weimar 1974 [1940]).

Monier, Raymond, *Les institutions centrales du comté de Flandre de la fin du IXe siècle à 1384*. Bibliothèque de la Société d'Histoire du Droit des Pays flamands, picards et wallons 13 (Paris 1943).

Montecchi Palazzi, Thérèse, 'Cencius camerarius et la formation du "Liber censuum" de 1192,' *Mélanges de l'Ecole française de Rome. Moyen âge et Temps modernes* XCVI (1984) 49–93.

Moore, R. I., *The formation of a persecuting society. Authority [power] and deviance in western Europe, 950–1250*, 2d ed. (changed title, Malden 2007 [1987]).

Morera y Llaurado, Emilio, *Tarragona cristiana. Historia del arzobispado de Tarragona y del territorio de su provincia (Cataluña la Nueva)*, 2 vols. (Tarragona 1897–99).

Morey, Adrian, *Bartholomew of Exeter, bishop and canonist. A study in the twelfth century* (Cambridge 1937).

Morris, Colin, *The discovery of the individual 1050–1200.* Church History Outlines 5 (London 1972).

―――― *The papal monarchy. The western church from 1050 to 1250.* Oxford History of the Christian Church (Oxford 1989).

Morris, William Alfred, *The medieval English sheriff to 1300.* Publications of the University of Manchester 176. Historical Series 46 (Manchester 1927).

Mundó, Anscari M., 'El pacte de Cazola del 1179 i el "Liber feudorum maior." Notes paleogràfiques i diplomàtiques,' *Jaime I y su época,* 3 vols. X Congreso de Historia de la Corona de Aragón (Zaragoza 1979–82) II (Comunicaciones I) 119–29 (plates).

Mundy, John Hine, *Liberty and political power in Toulouse, 1050–1230* (NY 1954).

Munz, Peter, *Frederick Barbarossa: a study in medieval politics* (London 1969).

Murray, Alexander, *Reason and society in the Middle Ages* (Oxford 1978).

Nelson, Janet L., *Politics and ritual in early medieval Europe* (London 1986).

Newman, William Mendel, *Le domaine royal sous les premiers capétiens (987–1180)* (Paris 1937).

Norgate, Kate, *England under the Angevin kings,* 2 vols. (London 1887).

North, William, 'The fragmentation and redemption of a medieval cathedral: property, conflict, and public piety in eleventh-century Arezzo,' *Conflict in medieval Europe* . . . (2003, listed above) 109–30.

Oppermann, O., 'Die unechte Urkunde des Grafen Robert II von Flandern fuer S. Donatien zu Bruegge von 1089 und Verlindens Kritik der Fontes Egmundenses,' *RBPH* XVI (1937) 178–82.

Orti Gost, Pere, 'La primera articulación del estado feudal en Cataluña a través de un impuesto: el bovaje (ss. XII–XIII),' *Hispania* LXI (2001) 967–98.

Ourliac, Paul, 'Les fors de Bigorre' (1992), *Les pays de Garonne vers l'an mil. La société et le droit.* Le Midi et son Histoire (Toulouse 1993) 213–35.

―――― 'L'hommage servile dans la région toulousaine,' *Mélanges* . . . *Louis Halphen* (1951) 551–56

―――― 'La réforme grégorienne à Toulouse: le concile de 1079' (1979), *Les pays de Garonne* . . . (cited above) 51–64.

―――― 'Les sauvetés du Comminges: Etudes et documents sur les villages fondés par les Hospitaliers dans la région des côteaux Commingeois,' *Recueil de l'Académie de Législation* XVIII (Toulouse 1947) 23–147.

Pacaut, Marcel, *Louis VII et son royaume*. Bibliothèque générale de l'EPHE VIᵉ Section (Paris 1964).

Painter, Sidney, *The reign of King John* (Baltimore 1949).

Pascua Echegaray, Esther, *Guerra y pacto en el siglo XII. La consolidación de un sistema de reinos en Europa occidental*. CSIC. Biblioteca de Historia 31 (Madrid 1996).

Pastor de Togneri, Reyna, *Conflictos sociales y estancamiento económico en la España medieval* (Barcelona 1973 [1964]).

———— *Resistencias y luchas campesinas en la época del crecimiento y consolidación de la formación feudal. Castilla y León, siglos X–XIII*, 3d ed. Historia de los Movimientos sociales (Madrid 1993 [1980]).

Paxton, Jennifer Ann, 'Chronicle and community in twelfth-century England' (forthcoming).

The Peace of God. Social violence and religious response in France around the year 1000, ed. Thomas Head, Richard Landes (Ithaca, NY, 1992).

Perrin, Ch.-E., 'Chartes de franchise et rapports de droits en Lorraine,' *Le Moyen Age* XL (1946) 11–42.

Peters, Wolfgang, '*Coniuratio facta est pro libertate.* Zu den *coniurationes* in Mainz, Köln und Lüttich in den Jahren 1105/06,' *Rheinische Vierteljahrsblätter* LI (1987) 303–12.

Petit-Dutaillis, Charles, *Les communes françaises. Caractères et évolution des origines au XVIIIᵉ siècle*. L'Evolution de l'Humanité 44 (Paris 1947; tr. Joan Vickers, *The French commune in the Middle Ages*. Europe in the Middle Ages 6 [Amsterdam 1978]).

Pfaff, V., 'Papst Coelestin III.,' *ZRG Kan. Abt.* XLVII (1961) 109–28.

Pfister, Christian, *Etudes sur le règne de Robert le Pieux (996–1031)* (Paris 1885).

Pirenne, Henri, *Medieval cities. Their origins and the revival of trade*, tr. Frank D. Halsey (Princeton 1925).

Platelle, Henri, *La justice seigneuriale de l'abbaye de Saint Amand. Son organisation judiciaire, sa procédure et sa compétence du XIᵉ au XVIᵉ siècle*. Bibliothèque de la Revue d'Histoire ecclésiastique 41 (Louvain-Paris 1965).

———— 'La violence et ses remèdes en Flandre au XIᵉ siècle,' *Sacris Erudiri* XX (1971) 101–73.

Poly, Jean-Pierre, *La Provence et la société féodale (879–1166). Contribution à l'étude des structures dites féodales dans le Midi*. Collection "Etudes" (Paris 1976).

Poly, Jean-Pierre, and Eric Bournazel, *La mutation féodale X^e–XIIe siècle,* 3d ed. Nouvelle Clio (Paris 2004 [1980]; tr. Caroline Higgitt, *The feudal transformation, 900–1200* [NY 1990]).

Poole, Austin Lane, *From Domesday Book to Magna Carta, 1087–1216,* 2d ed. Oxford History of England (Oxford 1955 [1951]).

Poole, Reginald L., *The exchequer in the twelfth century. The Ford Lectures delivered in the University of Oxford in Michaelmas Term, 1911* (Oxford 1912).

Portela, Ermelindo, and Mª Carmen Pallares, 'Revueltas feudales en el camino de Santiago. Compostela y Sahagún,' *Las peregrinaciones a Santiago de Compostela y San Salvador de Oviedo en la Edad Media.* Actas del Congreso internacional celebrado en Oviedo del 3 al 7 de diciembre de 1990, ed. Juan Ignacio Ruiz de la Piña Solar (Oviedo 1993) 313–33.

Post, Gaines, *Studies in medieval legal thought. Public law and the state, 1100–1322* (Princeton 1964).

I poteri dei Canossa, da Reggio Emilia all'Europa. Atti del convegno internazionale di studi (Reggio Emilia-Carpineti, 29–31 ottobre 1992), ed. Paolo Golinelli. Il Mondo medievale (Bologna 1994).

Powicke, F. M., 'Gerald of Wales' (1928), *The Christian life in the Middle Ages and other essays* (Oxford 1935) 107–29.

——— *Stephen Langton, being the Ford Lectures delivered in the University of Oxford in Hilary Term 1927* (Oxford 1928).

Prestwich, J. O., 'The career of Ranulf Flambard,' *Anglo-Norman Durham 1093–1193,* ed. David Rollason *et al.* (Woodbridge 1994) 299–310.

Prochnow, Fritz, *Das Spolienrecht und die Testierfähigkeit der Geistlichen im Abendland bis zum 13. Jahrhundert.* Historische Studien 136 (Berlin 1919).

Procter, Evelyn S., *Curia and Cortes in León and Castile 1072–1295.* CILAS (Cambridge 1980).

Radding, Charles M., *The origins of medieval jurisprudence: Pavia and Bologna 851–1150* (New Haven 1988).

Rassow, Peter, *Der Prinzgemahl. Ein Pactum matrimoniale aus dem Jahre 1188.* Quellen und Studien zur Verfassungsgeschichte des Deutschen Reiches in Mittelalter und Neuzeit 8:1 (Weimar 1950).

Reilly, Bernard F., 'The *Historia Compostelana*: the genesis and composition of a twelfth-century Spanish *Gesta*,' *Speculum* XLIV (1969) 78–85.

——— *The kingdom of León-Castilla under King Alfonso VI, 1065–1109* (Princeton 1988).

——— *The kingdom of León-Castilla under King Alfonso VII, 1126–1157. The Middle Ages* (Philadelphia 1998).

——— *The kingdom of León-Castilla under Queen Urraca, 1109–1126* (Princeton 1982).

Los reinos cristianos en los siglos XI y XII. Economías, sociedades, instituciones, 2 vols., ed. María del Carmen Carlé, Reyna Pastor *et al.*, *Historia de España Menéndez Pidal* x (Madrid 1992).

Remensnyder, Amy G., 'Pollution, purity, and peace: an aspect of social reform between the late tenth century and 1076.' *The Peace of God* . . . , ed. Head and Landes (cited above) ch. 12.

Renaissance and renewal in the twelfth century, ed. Robert L. Benson, Giles Constable (Cambridge, M., 1982).

Reuter, Timothy, 'Assembly politics in western Europe from the eighth century to the twelfth' (2001), reprinted in *Medieval politics* . . . , cited just below, ch. 11.

——— 'Debate: the "feudal revolution",' *Past & Present* no. 155 (1997) 177–95 (reprinted in *Medieval politics* . . . , cited below, ch. 4).

——— *Germany in the early Middle Ages, 800–1056.* Longman History of Germany (London 1991).

——— 'The "imperial church system" of the Ottonian and Salian rulers: a reconsideration,' *Journal of Ecclesiastical History* xxxiii (1982) 347–74 (reprinted in next work below, ch. 18).

——— *Medieval politics and modern mentalities*, ed. Janet L. Nelson (Cambridge 2006).

Reynolds, Susan, *Fiefs and vassals. The medieval evidence reinterpreted* (Oxford 1994).

——— 'Government and community,' *NCMH* vi:1 (2004) 86–112.

——— *Kingdoms and communities in western Europe, 900–1300* (Oxford 1984).

Richardson, H. G., and G. O. Sayles, *The governance of mediaeval England from the Conquest to Magna Carta.* Edinburgh University Publications: History, Philosophy and Economics 16 (Edinburgh 1963).

Riley-Smith, Jonathan, 'The crusades, 1095–1198,' *NCMH* iv:1, 534–63.

Riquer, Martin de, *Les chansons de geste françaises*, tr. Irénée Cluzel, 2d ed. (Paris 1957 [1952]).

———'La littérature provençale à la cour d'Alphonse II d'Aragon,' *Cahiers de Civilisation médiévale* II (1959) 177–201.

Robinson, I. S., *Authority and resistance in the Investiture Contest. The polemical literature of the late eleventh century* (Manchester 1978).

——— *Henry IV of Germany 1056–1106* (Cambridge 1999).

——— 'The institutions of the church, 1073–1216,' *NCMH* IV:1, 368–460.

——— 'The papacy, 1122–1198,' *NCMH* IV:2, ch. 13.

——— 'Reform and the church, 1073–1122,' *NCMH* IV:1, 263–334.

Roffe, David R., 'The *descriptio terrarum* of Peterborough Abbey,' *Bulletin of the Institute of Historical Research* LXV (1992) 1–16.

——— *Domesday. The inquest and the book* (Oxford 2000).

Le roi de France et son royaume autour de l'an mil. Actes du Colloque Hugues Capet 987–1987. La France de l'An Mil, Paris–Senlis 22–25 juin 1987, ed. Michel Parisse, Xavier Barral i Altet (Paris 1992).

Round, J. H., *Geoffrey de Mandeville. A study of the anarchy* (London 1892).

Rouse, Richard and Mary, 'John of Salisbury and the doctrine of tyrannicide,' *Speculum* XLII (1967) 693–709.

Rubenstein, Jay, *Guibert of Nogent: portrait of a medieval mind* (NY 2002).

Salvador Martínez, H., *La rebelión de los burgos. Crisis de estado y coyuntura social.* Historia (Madrid 1992).

Sánchez-Albornoz, Claudio, *España: un enigma histórico*, 3d ed., 2 vols. (Buenos Aires 1971 [1956]; tr. Colette Joly Dees, David Sven Reher, *Spain, a historical enigma* [Madrid 1975]).

Sayers, Jane E., *Papal judges delegate in the province of Canterbury 1198–1254. A study in ecclesiastical jurisdiction and administration.* OHM (Oxford 1971).

Schlesinger, Walter, 'Herrschaft und Gefolgschaft in der germanisch-deutschen Verfassungsgeschichte,' *Historische Zeitschrift* CLXXVI (1953) 225–75 (tr. Fredric Cheyette, *Lordship and community in medieval Europe* [NY 1968] 64–99).

Schmitt, Jean-Claude, *Les revenants. Les vivants et les morts dans la société médiévale.* Bibliothèque des Histoires (Paris 1992; tr. Teresa Lavender Fagan, *Ghosts in the Middle Ages: the living and the dead in medieval society* [Chicago 1998]).

Schramm, Percy Ernst, *A history of the English coronation*, tr. Leopold G. Wickham Legg (Oxford 1937).

Schulze, Hans K., *Adelsherrschaft und Landesherrschaft.* Mitteldeutsche Forschungen 29 (Cologne-Graz 1963).

Scott, James C., *The moral economy of the peasant. Rebellion and subsistence in southeast Asia* (New Haven 1976).

Settia, Aldo A., *Castelli e vilaggi nell'Italia padana: popolamento, potere e sicurezza fra IX e XIII secolo.* Nuovo Medioevo 23 (Naples 1984).

Shideler, John C., *A medieval Catalan noble family: the Montcadas, 1000–1230.* Publications of the UCLA Center for Medieval and Renaissance Studies 20 (Berkeley 1983).

Smith, Lucy M., *The early history of the monastery of Cluny* (London 1920).

Sobrequés i Vidal, Santiago, *Els grans comtes de Barcelona.* Biografies Catalanes 2 (Barcelona 1961).

Soldevila, Ferran, *Història de Catalunya,* 2d ed. (Barcelona 1963 [1955]).

Somerville, Robert, 'The council of Beauvais, 1114,' *Traditio* XXIV (1968) 493–503.

Southern, R. W., 'King Henry I' (1962), *Medieval humanism and other studies* (Oxford 1970) 206–33.

———— *The making of the Middle Ages.* Hutchinson's University Library (London 1953).

———— 'Peter of Blois: a twelfth-century humanist?' (1963), *Medieval humanism . . .* (cited above) 105–32.

———— 'Ranulf Flambard,' *Medieval humanism . . .* , ch. 10 (revised from first printing, 1933).

Spiegel, Gabrielle M., *Romancing the past. The rise of vernacular prose historiography in thirteenth-century France* (Berkeley 1993).

'Spolienrecht,' *Lexikon des Mittelalters* VII (1995) 2131–32.

Spufford, Peter, 'Coinage and currency,' *The Cambridge economic history of Europe,* ed. J. H. Clapham *et al.,* 8 vols. (Cambridge 1941–89) III (ed. M. M. Postan *et al.,* 1965) 576–602.

Stacey, Robert C., *Politics, policy, and finance under Henry III 1216–1245* (Oxford 1987).

Stack, Gilbert, 'A lost law of Henry II: the Assize of Oxford and monetary reform,' *The Haskins Society Journal* XVI (2005) 95–103.

Stacy, N. E., 'Henry of Blois and the lordship of Glastonbury,' *EHR* CXIV (1999) 1–33.

Starn, Randolph, 'Historians and "crisis",' *Past & Present* no. 52 (1971) 5–22.

Steinmetz, Wolf-Dieter, *Geschichte und Archäologie der Harzburg unter Saliern, Staufern und Welfen 1065–1254* (Bad Harzburg 2001).

Stenton, Doris May, 'England: Henry II,' *Cambridge medieval history*, 8 vols. (Cambridge 1911–36) v, ch. 17.

Stenton, F. M., *The first century of English feudalism 1066–1166, being the Ford Lectures delivered in the University of Oxford in Hilary Term 1929*, 2d ed. (Oxford 1961 [1932]).

——— *The Latin charters of the Anglo-Saxon period* (Oxford 1955).

Stephenson, Carl, 'The origin and nature of the *taille*' (1926), reprinted in *Mediaeval institutions: selected essays*, ed. Bryce Lyon (Ithaca, NY, 1954) 41–103.

Störmer, Wilhelm, 'Bayern und der bayerische Herzog im 11. Jahrhundert. Fragen der Herzogsgewalt und der königlichen Interessenpolitik,' *Die Salier und das Reich*, ed. Stefan Weinfurter, 4 vols. (Sigmaringen 1991) I, 503–47.

Strayer, Joseph Reese, *The administration of Normandy under Saint Louis*. Monographs of the Mediaeval Academy of America 6 (Cambridge, M., 1932).

——— *Feudalism*. Anvil Books (Princeton 1965).

——— *Medieval statecraft and the perspectives of history. Essays by Joseph R. Strayer*, ed. John F. Benton, Thomas N. Bisson (Princeton 1971).

——— *On the medieval origins of the modern state* (Princeton 1970; new ed. 2007).

Strickland, Matthew, *War and chivalry. The conduct and perception of war in England and Normandy, 1066–1217* (Cambridge 1996).

Tabacco, Giovanni, *The struggle for power in medieval Italy. Structures of political rule*, tr. Rosalind Brown Jensen. Cambridge Medieval Textbooks (Cambridge 1989 [1973]).

Tellenbach, Gerd, *Church, state and Christian society at the time of the Investiture Contest*, tr. R. F. Bennett. Studies in Mediaeval History (Oxford 1940 [1936]).

Teunis, Henk, *The appeal to the original status. Social justice in Anjou in the eleventh century*. Middeleeuwse Studies en Bronnen xic (Hilversum 2006).

Tierney, Brian, *The crisis of church & state, 1050–1300, with selected documents*. Spectrum (Englewood Cliffs 1964).

——— *Foundations of the conciliar theory. The contribution of the medieval canonists from Gratian to the Great Schism*, new ed. Studies in the History of Christian Thought 81 (Leiden-NY 1998 [1955]).

Toubert, Pierre, *Les structures du Latium médiéval: le Latium méridional et la Sabine du IXe siècle à la fin du XIIe siècle*, 2 vols. BEFAR 221 (Rome 1973).

De Toulouse à Tripoli. La puissance toulousaine au XIIe siècle. Musée des Augustins, 6 janvier 1989–20 mars 1989 (Toulouse 1989).

Tout, T. F., *Chapters in the administrative history of mediaeval England: the wardrobe, the chamber and the small seals*, 6 vols. Publications of the University of Manchester. Historical Series 34–35, 48–49, 57, 64 (Manchester 1920–33).

The troubadours. An introduction, ed. Simon Gaunt, Sarah Kay (Cambridge 1999).

Tucoo-Chala, Pierre, *La vicomté de Béarn et le problème de sa souveraineté des origines à 1620* (Bordeaux 1961).

Türk, Egbert, Nugae curialium. *Le règne d'Henri II Plantagenêt (1145–1189) et l'éthique politique.* IVe Section de l'EPHE. V. Hautes Etudes médiévales et modernes 28 (Geneva 1977).

Turner, Ralph V., *Men raised from the dust. Administrative service and upward mobility in Angevin England.* Middle Ages (Philadelphia 1988).

Tyerman, Christopher, *God's war. A new history of the crusades* (Cambridge, M., 2006).

Ullmann, Walter, *The growth of papal government in the Middle Ages. A study of the ideological relation of clerical to lay power*, 3d ed. (London 1970 [1955]).

Urban and rural communities in medieval France: Provence and Languedoc, 1000–1500, ed. Kathryn Reyerson, John Drendel (Leiden-Boston 1998).

Valdeavellano, Luis G. de, *Curso de historia de las instituciones españolas de los orígenes al final de la Edad Media*, 3d ed. (Madrid 1973 [1968]).

Van Caenegem, R. C., *Royal writs in England from the Conquest to Glanvill: studies in the early history of the common law.* Selden Society 77 (London 1959).

Van Engen, John, 'Sacred sanctions for lordship,' *Cultures of power . . .* (1995, fully cited above) ch. 9.

Van Laarhoven, Jan, 'Thou shalt *not* slay a tyrant! The so-called theory of John of Salisbury,' *The world of John of Salisbury*, ed. Wilks (1984) 319–41.

Vázquez de Parga, Luis, 'La revolución comunal de Compostela en los años 1116 y 1117,' *AHDE* xvi (1945) 685–703.

Verlinden, Charles, *Robert Ier le Frison, comte de Flandre. Etude d'histoire politique* (Antwerp-Paris 1935).

Viader, Roland, *L'Andorre du IXe au XIVe siècle. Montagne, féodalité et communautés.* Tempus (Toulouse 2003).

Vicaire, M.-H., ' "L'affaire de paix et de foi" du Midi de la France,' *Paix de Dieu et guerre sainte en Languedoc au XIIIe siècle. Cahiers de Fanjeaux* 4 (Toulouse 1969) 102–27.

Vincent, Nicholas, 'The Plantagenets and the Agenais, 1154–1216,' forthcoming.

—— 'Why 1199? Bureaucracy and enrolment under John and his contemporaries,' *English government in the thirteenth century,* ed. Adrian Jobson (Woodbridge 2004) 17–48.

Wadle, Elmar, 'Heinrich IV. und die deutsche Friedensbewegung,' *Investitur und Reichsverfassung,* ed. Josef Fleckenstein. Vorträge und Forschungen 17 (Sigmaringen 1973) 141–73.

Warlop, Ernest, *The Flemish nobility before 1300,* tr. J. B. Ross, 4 vols. (The Hague 1974).

Warren, W. L., *The governance of Norman and Angevin England 1086–1272.* The Government of England (Stanford 1987).

—— *Henry II* (Berkeley-Los Angeles 1973).

Weber, Max, *Economy and society: an outline of interpretive sociology,* tr. Ephraim Fischoff *et al.,* ed. Guenther Roth, Claus Wittich, 2 vols. (Berkeley-Los Angeles 1978).

Weinfurter, Stefan, *Herrschaft und Reich der Salier. Grundlinien einer Umbruchzeit* (Sigmaringen 1991; tr. Barbara M. Bowlus, *The Salian century. Main currents in an age of transition.* Middle Ages [Philadelphia 1999]).

Werner, Karl Ferdinand, *Les origines (avant l'an mil).* Histoire de France (Fayard) 1 (Paris 1984).

Werner, Matthias, 'Der Herzog von Lothringen in salischer Zeit,' *Die Salier und das Reich* 1 (1991) 367–473.

White, G(raeme) J., *Restoration and reform, 1153–1165: recovery from civil war in England.* CSMLT, 4th series 46 (Cambridge 2000).

White, Stephen D., 'The discourse of inheritance in twelfth-century France: alternative models of the fief in "Raoul de Cambrai",' *Law and government in medieval England and Normandy. Essays . . . Holt,* ed. Garnett, Hudson (1994), ch. 6.

—— 'Debate: the "feudal revolution",' *Past & Present* no. 152 (1996) 205–23.

———— 'Repenser la violence: de 2000 à 1000,' *Médiévales* XXXVII (1999) 99–113.

Wickham, Chris, *Community and clientele in twelfth-century Tuscany: the origins of the rural commune in the plain of Lucca* (Oxford 1998 [1995]).

———— *Courts and conflict in twelfth-century Tuscany* (Oxford 2003).

———— 'Debate: the "feudal revolution",' *Past & Present* no. 155 (1997) 196–208.

———— 'Justice in the kingdom of Italy in the eleventh century,' *La giustizia nell'alto medioevo (secoli IX–X)*, 2 vols. Settimane di Studio del Centro italiano di Studi sull'alto medioevo 44 (11–17 aprile 1996) (Spoleto 1997) I, 179–250.

———— *The mountains and the city. The Tuscan Appennines in the early Middle Ages* (Oxford 1988).

———— 'La signoria rurale in Toscana,' *Strutture e trasformazioni della signoria rurale nei secoli X–XIII*, ed. Gerhard Dilcher, Cinzio Violante. Annali dell'Istituto storico italo-germanico 44 (Bologna 1996) 343–409.

Winroth, Anders, *The making of Gratian's* Decretum. CSMLT 4th series 49 (Cambridge 2000).

Wolfram, Herwig, *Conrad II, 990–1039: emperor of three kingdoms*, tr. Denise A. Kaiser (University Park 2006 [2000]).

Wormald, Patrick, *The making of English law: King Alfred to the twelfth century*, Volume I, *Legislation and its limits* (Oxford 1999).

Zerbi, Piero, 'Il termine "fidelitas" nelle lettere di Gregorio VII,' *Studi Gregoriani* III (1948) 129–48.

Zimmermann, Harald, *Der Canossagang von 1077: Wirkungen und Wirklichkeit*. Abhandlungen der Geistes- und Sozialwissenschaftlichen Klasse, Akademie der Wissenschaften und der Literatur, Jahrg. 1975, Nr 5 (Mainz 1975).

· INDEX ·

The following abbreviations are used: abp = archbishop, abss = abbess, abt = abbot, bp = bishop, c = castle, ct = count, ctss = countess, cty = county, d. = died, emp = emperor, fl = *floruit*, k(gs) = king(s), kt(s) = knight(s), q = queen, vct = viscount. Parenthetical terms following toponyms refer to regions, *départements*, or *provincias(es)*